TRANSLATORS AND EDITORS:
Rabbi David Strauss
Rabbi Yehezkel Anis

MANAGING EDITOR:
Baruch Goldberg

EDITOR:
Dr. Edward L. Tepper

ASSOCIATE EDITORS:
Dr. Jeffrey M. Green
Rabbi Ḥayyim Ya'akov Bulka

COPY EDITOR:
Alec Israel

BOOK DESIGNER:
Ben Gasner

GRAPHIC ARTIST:
Michael Etkin

TECHNICAL STAFF:
Muriel Stein
Rona Katz

Random House Staff

PRODUCTION MANAGER:
Richard Elman

ART DIRECTOR:
Bernard Klein

The Talmud
The Steinsaltz Edition

Volume XVI
Tractate Sanhedrin
Part II

Volume XVI
Tractate Sanhedrin
Part II

Random House
New York

THE TALMUD

תלמוד בבלי

THE STEINSALTZ EDITION

Commentary by Rabbi Adin Steinsaltz (Even Yisrael)

Published in the United States by Random House, Inc., New York, and simultaneously in Canada by Random House of Canada Limited, Toronto.

This is an English translation of a work originally published in Hebrew by The Israel Institute for Talmudic Publications, Jerusalem, Israel.

Library of Congress Cataloging-in-Publication Data
(Revised for volume XVI)
The Talmud
English, Hebrew, Aramaic.
Includes bibliograpical references.
Contents: v. 1. Tractate Bava metzia-
v. 16. Tractate Sanhedrin, pt. 2.
Accompanied by a reference guide.
I. Title.
BM499.5.E4 1989 89-842911
ISBN 0-394-57665-9 (guide)
ISBN 0-394-57666-7 (v. 1)
ISBN 0-375-50063-4 (v. 16)

Random House website address: http://www.randomhouse.com/

Printed in the United States of America on acid-free paper

2 4 6 8 9 7 5 3

First Edition

In loving memory of
Illean K. Goldberg
חיה מרים בת חנוך ושרה
נפטרה ט׳ בניסן תשנ״ו
whose life was dedicated to imbuing in
her children
the love of Torah and mitzvot
and
in honor of her granddaughter
Sarah Caroline
שרה
בת אהרון אברהם ומינדל רבקה
whom she so deeply loved,
on the occasion of
her Bat Mitzvah

״עֲטֶרֶת זְקֵנִים בְּנֵי בָנִים
וְתִפְאֶרֶת בָּנִים אֲבוֹתָם״
(משלי יז, ו)

"The crown of the elders are children's children
and the glory of children are their parents"
(Proverbs XVII, 6)

***

Miriam and Alan E. Goldberg
י״ח באייר תשנ״ז

The Steinsaltz Talmud in English

The English edition of the Steinsaltz Talmud is a translation and adaptation of the Hebrew edition. It includes most of the additions and improvements that characterize the Hebrew version, but it has been adapted and expanded especially for the English reader. This edition has been designed to meet the needs of advanced students capable of studying from standard Talmud editions, as well as of beginners, who know little or no Hebrew and have had no prior training in studying the Talmud.

The overall structure of the page is similar to that of the traditional pages in the standard printed editions. The text is placed in the center of the page, and alongside it are the main auxiliary commentaries. At the bottom of the page and in the margins are additions and supplements.

The original Hebrew-Aramaic text, which is framed in the center of each page, is exactly the same as that in the traditional Talmud (although material that was removed by non-Jewish censors has been restored on the basis of manuscripts and old printed editions). The main innovation is that this Hebrew-Aramaic text has been completely vocalized and punctuated, and all the terms usually abbreviated have been fully spelled out. In order to retain the connection with the page numbers of the standard editions, these are indicated at the head of every page.

We have placed a *Literal Translation* on the right-hand side of the page, and its punctuation has been introduced into the Talmud text, further helping the student to orientate himself. The *Literal Translation* is intended to help the student to learn the meaning of specific Hebrew and Aramaic words. By comparing the original text with this translation, the reader develops an understanding of the Talmudic text and can follow the words and sentences in the original. Occasionally, however, it has not been possible to present an exact literal translation of the original text, because it is so different in structure from English. Therefore we have added certain auxiliary words, which are indicated in square brackets. In other cases it would make no sense to offer a literal translation of a Talmudic idiom, so we have provided a close English equivalent of the original meaning, while a note, marked "lit.," explaining the literal meaning of the words, appears in parentheses. Our purpose in presenting this literal translation was to give the student an appreciation of the terse and enigmatic nature of the Talmud itself, before the arguments are opened up by interpretation.

Nevertheless, no one can study the Talmud without the assistance of commentaries. The main aid to understanding the Talmud provided by this edition is the *Translation and Commentary,* appearing on the left side of the page. This is Rabbi Adin Steinsaltz's highly regarded Hebrew interpretation of the Talmud, translated into English, adapted and expanded.

This commentary is not merely an explanation of difficult passages. It is an integrated exposition of the entire text. It includes a full translation of the Talmud text, combined with explanatory remarks. Where the translation in the commentary reflects the literal translation, it has been set off in bold type. It has also been given the same reference numbers that are found both in the original text and in the literal translation. Moreover, each section of the commentary begins with a few words of the Hebrew-Aramaic text. These reference numbers and paragraph headings allow the reader to move from one part of the page to another with ease.

There are some slight variations between the literal translation and the words in bold face appearing in the *Translation and Commentary.* These variations are meant to enhance understanding, for a juxtaposition of the literal translation and the sometimes freer translation in the commentary will give the reader a firmer grasp of the meaning.

The expanded *Translation and Commentary* in the left-hand column is intended to provide a conceptual understanding of the arguments of the Talmud, their form, content, context, and significance. The commentary also brings out the logic of the questions asked by the Sages and the assumptions they made.

Rashi's traditional commentary has been included in the right-hand column, under the *Literal Translation.* We have left this commentary in the traditional "Rashi script," but all quotations of the Talmud text appear in standard square type, the abbreviated expressions have all been printed in full, and Rashi's commentary is fully punctuated.

Since the *Translation and Commentary* cannot remain cogent and still encompass all the complex issues that arise in the Talmudic discussion, we have included a number of other features, which are also found in Rabbi Steinsaltz's Hebrew edition.

At the bottom of the page, under the *Translation and Commentary*, is the *Notes* section, containing additional material on issues raised in the text. These notes deepen understanding of the Talmud in various ways. Some provide a deeper and more profound analysis of the issues discussed in the text, with regard to individual points and to the development of the entire discussion. Others explain Halakhic concepts and the terms of Talmudic discourse.

The *Notes* contain brief summaries of the opinions of many of the major commentators on the Talmud, from the period after the completion of the Talmud to the present. Frequently the *Notes* offer interpretations different from that presented in the commentary, illustrating the richness and depth of Rabbinic thought.

The *Halakhah* section appears below the *Notes.* This provides references to the authoritative legal decisions reached over the centuries by the Rabbis in their discussions of the matters dealt with in the Talmud. It explains what reasons led to these Halakhic decisions and the close connection between the Halakhah today and the Talmud and its various interpreters. It should be noted that the summary of the Halakhah presented here is not meant to serve as a reference source for actual religious practice but to introduce the reader to Halakhic conclusions drawn from the Talmudic text.

English commentary and expanded translation of the text, making it readable and comprehensible

Hebrew/Aramaic text of the Talmud, fully vocalized, and punctuated

Literal translation of the Talmud text into English

Marginal notes provide essential background information

Hebrew commentary of Rashi, the classic explanation that accompanies all editions of the Talmud

Numbers link the three main sections of the page and allow readers to refer rapidly from one to the other

Notes highlight points of interest in the text and expand the discussion by quoting other classical commentaries

REALIA

קַלְתָּהּ **Her basket.** The source of this word is the Greek κάλαθος, kalathos, and it means a basket with a narrow base.

Illustration from a Greek drawing depicting such a basket of fruit.

CONCEPTS

פֵּאָה ***Pe'ah.* One of the presents left for the poor** (מַתְּנוֹת עֲנִיִּים). The Torah forbids harvesting "the corners of your field," so that the produce left standing may be harvested and kept by the poor (Leviticus 19:9).

The Torah did not specify a minimum amount of produce to be left as *pe'ah*. But the Sages stipulated that it must be at least one-sixtieth of the crop.

Pe'ah is set aside only from crops that ripen at one time and are harvested at one time. The poor are allowed to use their own initiative to reap the *pe'ah* left in the fields. But the owner of an orchard must see to it that each of the poor gets a fixed share of the *pe'ah* from places that are difficult to reach. The poor come to collect *pe'ah* three times a day. The laws of *pe'ah* are discussed in detail in tractate *Pe'ah*.

TRANSLATION AND COMMENTARY

[1]**and her husband threw her a bill of divorce into her lap or into her basket**, which she was carrying on her head, [2]would you say **here, too,** that **she would not be divorced**? Surely we know that the law is that she *is* divorced in such a case, as the Mishnah (*Gittin* 77a) states explicitly!

אֲמַר לֵיהּ [3]Rav Ashi **said** in reply **to** Ravina: The woman's **basket is** considered to be **at rest, and it is she who walks beneath it.** Thus the basket is considered to be a "stationary courtyard," and the woman acquires whatever is thrown into it.

MISHNAH הָיָה רוֹכֵב [4]**If a person was riding on an animal and he saw an ownerless object** lying on the ground, **and he said to another person** standing nearby, **"Give that object to me,"** [5]if **the other person took** the ownerless object **and said, "I have acquired it for myself,"** [6]he has **acquired it** by lifting it up, even though he was not the first to see it, and the rider has no claim to it. [7]But **if, after he gave** the object **to** the rider, the person who picked it up **said, "I acquired** the object **first,"** [8]**he** in fact **said nothing**. His words are of no effect, and the rider may keep it. Since the person walking showed no intention of acquiring the object when he originally picked it up, he is not now believed when he claims that he acquired it first. Indeed, even if we maintain that when a person picks up an ownerless object on behalf of someone else, the latter does *not* acquire it automatically, here, by *giving* the object to the rider, he makes a gift of it to the rider.

GEMARA תְּנַן הָתָם [9]**We have learned elsewhere** in a Mishnah in tractate *Pe'ah* (4:9): **"Someone who gathered *pe'ah*** — produce which by Torah law [Leviticus 23:22] is left unharvested in the corner of a field by the owner of the field, to be gleaned by the poor — **and said, 'Behold, this *pe'ah*** which I have gleaned **is** intended **for so-and-so the poor man,'** [10]**Rabbi Eliezer says:** The person who gathered the *pe'ah* **has acquired it**

בִּרְשׁוּת הָרַבִּים [1]וְזָרַק לָהּ גֵּט לְתוֹךְ חֵיקָהּ אוֹ לְתוֹךְ קַלְתָּהּ — [2]הָכָא נַמִּי דְּלָא מִגָּרְשָׁה? [3]אֲמַר לֵיהּ: קַלְתָּהּ מֵינָח נַיְיחָא, וְאִיהִי דְּקָא מְסַגְּיָא מִתּוּתָהּ.

מִשְׁנָה [4]הָיָה רוֹכֵב עַל גַּבֵּי בְהֵמָה וְרָאָה אֶת הַמְּצִיאָה, וְאָמַר לַחֲבֵירוֹ "תְּנָה לִי", [5]נְטָלָהּ וְאָמַר, "אֲנִי זָכִיתִי בָּהּ", [6]זָכָה בָּהּ. [7]אִם, מִשֶּׁנְּתָנָהּ לוֹ, אָמַר, "אֲנִי זָכִיתִי בָּהּ תְּחִלָּה", [8]לֹא אָמַר כְּלוּם.

גְּמָרָא [9]תְּנַן הָתָם: "מִי שֶׁלִּיקֵּט אֶת הַפֵּאָה וְאָמַר, 'הֲרֵי זוֹ לִפְלוֹנִי עָנִי', [10]רַבִּי אֱלִיעֶזֶר

LITERAL TRANSLATION

in a public thoroughfare [1]and [her husband] threw her a bill of divorce into her lap or into her basket, [2]here, too, would she not be divorced?

[3]He said to him: Her basket is at rest, and it is she who walks beneath it.

MISHNAH [4][If a person] was riding on an animal and he saw a found object, and he said to another person, "Give it to me," [5][and the other person] took it and said, "I have acquired it," [6]he has acquired it. [7]If, after he gave it to him, he said, "I acquired it first," [8]he said nothing.

GEMARA [9]We have learned there: "Someone who gathered *pe'ah* and said, 'Behold this is for so-and-so the poor man,' [10]Rabbi Eliezer says:

RASHI

קלתה – סל שעל ראשה, שנותנת בה כלי מלאכתה וטווי שלה. הכי נמי דלא הוי גיטא – והאנן תנן במסכת גיטין (עז,א): זרק לה גיטה לתוך חיקה או לתוך קלתה – הרי זו מגורשת!

משנה לא אמר כלום – דאפילו אמרינן המגביה מציאה לחבירו לא קנה חבירו, כיון דיהבה ליה – קנייה ממה נפשך. אי קנייה קמא דלא מתכוין להקנות לחבירו – הא יהבה ניהליה במתנה. ואי לא קנייה קמא משום דלא היה מתכוין לקנות – הויא ליה הפקר עד דמטא לידיה דהאי, וקנייה האי במאי דעקרה מידיה דקמא לשם קנייה.

גמרא מי שליקט את הפאה – אדם בעלמא שאינו בעל שדה. דאי בבעל שדה – לא אמר רבי אליעזר זכה. דליכא למימר "מגו דזכי לנפשיה", דאפילו הוא עני מוזהר הוא שלא ללקט פאה משדה שלו, כדאמר בשחיטת חולין (קלא,ב): "לא תלקט לעני" – להזהיר עני על שלו.

NOTES

מִי שֶׁלִּיקֵּט אֶת הַפֵּאָה **If a person gathered *pe'ah*.** According to *Rashi*, the Mishnah must be referring to someone other than the owner of the field. By Torah law the owner of a field is required to separate part of his field as *pe'ah*, even if he himself is poor, and he may not take the *pe'ah* for himself. Therefore the "since" (מגו) argument

HALAKHAH

קַלְתָּהּ **A woman's basket.** "If a man throws a bill of divorce into a container that his wife is holding, she thereby acquires the bill of divorce and the divorce takes effect." (*Shulḥan Arukh, Even HaEzer* 139:10.)

הַמְּלַקֵּט פֵּאָה עֲבוּר אַחֵר **A person who gathered *pe'ah* for someone else.** "If a poor person, who is himself entitled to collect *pe'ah*, gathered *pe'ah* for another poor person, and said, 'This *pe'ah* is for X, the poor person,' he acquires the *pe'ah* on behalf of that other poor person. But if the person who collected the *peah* was wealthy, he does not acquire the *pe'ah* on behalf of the poor person. He must give it instead to the first poor person who appears in the field," following the opinion of the Sages, as explained by Rabbi Yehoshua ben Levi. (*Rambam, Sefer Zeraim, Hilkhot Mattenot Aniyyim* 2:19.)

On the outer margin of the page, factual information clarifying the meaning of the Talmudic discussion is presented. Entries under the heading *Language* explain unusual terms, often borrowed from Greek, Latin, or Persian. *Sages* gives brief biographies of the major figures whose opinions are presented in the Talmud. *Terminology* explains the terms used in the Talmudic discussion. *Concepts* gives information about fundamental Halakhic principles. *Background* provides historical, geographical, and other information needed to understand the text. *Realia* explains the artifacts mentioned in the text. These notes are sometimes accompanied by illustrations.

The best way of studying the Talmud is the way in which the Talmud itself evolved - a combination of frontal teaching and continuous interaction between teacher and pupil, and between pupils themselves.

This edition is meant for a broad spectrum of users, from those who have considerable prior background and who know how to study the Talmud from any standard edition to those who have never studied the Talmud and do not even know Hebrew.

The division of the page into various sections is designed to enable students of every kind to derive the greatest possible benefit from it.

For those who know how to study the Talmud, the book is intended to be a written Gemara lesson, so that, either alone, with partners, or in groups, they can have the sense of studying with a teacher who explains the difficult passages and deepens their understanding both of the development of the dialectic and also of the various approaches that have been taken by the Rabbis over the centuries in interpreting the material. A student of this kind can start with the Hebrew-Aramaic text, examine Rashi's commentary, and pass on from there to the expanded commentary. Afterwards the student can turn to the Notes section. Study of the *Halakhah* section will clarify the conclusions reached in the course of establishing the Halakhah, and the other items in the margins will be helpful whenever the need arises to clarify a concept or a word or to understand the background of the discussion.

For those who do not possess sufficient knowledge to be able to use a standard edition of the Talmud, but who know how to read Hebrew, a different method is proposed. Such students can begin by reading the Hebrew-Aramaic text and comparing it immediately to the *Literal Translation*. They can then move over to the *Translation and Commentary*, which refers both to the original text and to the *Literal Translation*. Such students would also do well to read through the *Notes* and choose those that explain matters at greater length. They will benefit, too, from the terms explained in the side margins.

The beginner who does not know Hebrew well enough to grapple with the original can start with the *Translation and Commentary*. The inclusion of a translation within the commentary permits the student to ignore the *Literal Translation*, since the commentary includes both the Talmudic text and an interpretation of it. The beginner can also benefit from the *Notes*, and it is important for him to go over the marginal notes on the concepts to improve his awareness of the juridical background and the methods of study characteristic of this text.

Apart from its use as study material, this book can also be useful to those well versed in the Talmud, as a source of additional knowledge in various areas, both for understanding the historical and archeological background and also for an explanation of words and concepts. The general reader, too, who might not plan to study the book from beginning to end, can find a great deal of interesting material in it regarding both the spiritual world of Judaism, practical Jewish law, and the life and customs of the Jewish people during the thousand years (500 B.C.E.–500 C.E.) of the Talmudic period.

Contents

THE STEINSALTZ TALMUD IN ENGLISH	IX
INTRODUCTION TO CHAPTER TWO	1
CHAPTER TWO	3
CONCLUSION TO CHAPTER TWO	73
INTRODUCTION TO CHAPTER THREE	75
CHAPTER THREE	77
CONCLUSION TO CHAPTER THREE	205
LIST OF SOURCES	207

The Talmud

The Steinsaltz Edition

Volume XVI

Tractate Sanhedrin

Part II

Introduction to Chapter Two

כֹּהֵן גָּדוֹל

The basic principle that every Jew has equal status before the law is written several times in the Torah, and it is expressed in the warning to the judge: "Do not favor the poor or show deference to the rich; judge your kinsman fairly" (Leviticus. 19:15). While the Torah does recognize various strata within the people — priests, Levites, Israelites, residents and citizens of the country, Torah scholars and ignorant people — these groups have significance with respect to particular laws that apply to them, to the structure of privileges and obligations of each one toward the other, or to special obligations that are imposed upon them. However, with regard to general obligations, responsibility, and legal rights, everyone is equal.

Within this egalitarian system, we find only two salient individuals, who have special status because of their function: The king and the High Priest. The High Priest expresses the sanctity of the people. From the moment he is appointed as High Priest, special sanctity applies to him, above that applying to any other Jew. Only he is entitled to enter the Holy of Holies to perform the sacred ritual; only he is entitled to perform the special rites of the Day of Atonement. For his part, the king expresses the sovereignty and political authority of the Jewish people. The king is the head and source of authority of the executive arm of the Jewish people. His person expresses and symbolizes the power of the nation in creating a poltical body. In addition to their special status deriving from their functions, the Torah also applied special positive and negative commandments to them alone. They were also obligated to offer certain atonement sacrifices different from those of other Jews. These two personages are appointed to office with a special sanctification ceremony, annointment with the annointing oil ("the annointed priest," and "the annointed of the Lord" = the king), which gives them a certain personal sanctity which is not connected only to their function.

We have already seen in the first chapter that matters touching upon eminent people are judged in a court of seventy-one, the great tribunal. However, aside from this difference, nothing was said about their other duties and rights. Do the king and High Priest stand above ordinary law, or are they merely special instances that fit into the general legal system of the nation?

The relation of the king and the High Priest to the general system of law has another aspect: the king stands at the head of the state and has far-reaching authority to act within the state (even special judiciary and administrative authority deriving from his position). The High Priest also stands at the head of a great judicial and social structure: the Temple. Rule over the Temple and its internal arrangements (including the "Court of Priests") lies in the hands of the High Priest. Therefore it is worthwhile to examine the relations between the judicial and political structure of the Sanhedrin and the various structures of government controlled by the king and the High Priest.

The following chapter investigates these issues.

כֹּהֵן

[1]גָּדוֹל דָּן וְדָנִין אוֹתוֹ. [2]מֵעִיד וּמְעִידִין אוֹתוֹ.
[3]חוֹלֵץ וְחוֹלְצִין לְאִשְׁתּוֹ, [4]וּמְיַיבְּמִין אֶת אִשְׁתּוֹ. [5]אֲבָל הוּא אֵינוֹ מְיַיבֵּם, [6]מִפְּנֵי שֶׁהוּא אָסוּר בְּאַלְמָנָה.
[7]מֵת לוֹ מֵת — אֵינוֹ יוֹצֵא אַחַר הַמִּטָּה, [8]אֶלָּא הֵן נִכְסִין וְהוּא נִגְלֶה, [9]הֵן נִגְלִין וְהוּא נִכְסֶה,

LITERAL TRANSLATION

MISHNAH [1]The High Priest may judge and be judged. [2]He may testify and be testified against. [3]He may perform *ḥalitzah*, and *ḥalitzah* may be performed with his wife. [4]And they [his brothers] enter into levirate marriage with his wife, [5]but he does not enter into levirate marriage, [6]because he is forbidden to [marry] a widow.

[7]If someone [related] to him dies, he may not go out after the bier; [8]rather they become hidden [from sight] and he [may then] appear; [9]they appear and he [must remain] hidden [from sight].

TRANSLATION AND COMMENTARY

MISHNAH כֹּהֵן גָּדוֹל [1]If properly qualified, **a High Priest** may sit on a court and **judge** others. A High Priest **may be judged** by a court. [2]**He may testify** against others **and be testified against**.

חוֹלֵץ [3]A man whose brother died childless is obliged by Torah law to marry his deceased brother's widow or to perform the *ḥalitzah* ceremony and thereby release her from the levirate tie so that she may remarry (Deuteronomy 25:7-10). If a High Priest's brother dies childless, the High Priest may **participate in** the *ḥalitzah* ceremony, even though his brother's widow must spit at him and declare, "So shall it be done unto the man who does not build up his brother's house." If the High Priest himself died childless, one of his brothers may **perform** *ḥalitzah* **with his widow.** [4]If the brother prefers, **he may enter into levirate marriage with** the High Priest's **widow,** for he is allowed to marry a widow. [5]**However,** the High Priest **may not enter into levirate marriage** with his brother's widow, [6]**for he is forbidden** by Torah law (Leviticus 21:14) **to** marry **a widow.**

מֵת לוֹ מֵת [7]The High Priest is forbidden by Torah law to defile himself through contact with a dead body, even that of a close relative (Leviticus 21:11). Thus, if **someone** related **to him dies,** the High Priest **may not go out** to join the funeral procession and follow immediately **after the bier,** lest he forget himself in his grief and make contact with the corpse. [8]**Rather,** he must attend the funeral from a distance. Once those accompanying the bier turn a corner and **become hidden** from sight, the High Priest **may appear** on the street where they have just passed, [9]**but when they** again **appear** in his sight, **he** must stay back and remain **out**

RASHI

משנה כהן גדול אינו יוצא אחר המטה — דילמא אתא למינגע, והיינו דאזהר קרא "ומן המקדש לא יצא" — מקדושתו לא יצא, כלומר יתרחק מן הכיעור שלא יבא לידי טומאה. והאי קרא בכהן גדול אונן כתיב, דכתיב לעיל מיניה "לאביו ולאמו לא יטמא". הן נכסין והוא נגלה — כשהן יוצאין ממבוי זה ונכנסין למבוי אחר, ונכסין ממבוי הראשון — שאינו רואה אותן, הוא נגלה ונכנס למבוי הראשון, והן נכסין ממבוי השני והוא נגלה ונכנס לתוכו.

NOTES

כֹּהֵן גָּדוֹל **The High Priest.** Toward the end of the previous chapter we learned that a High Priest charged with a capital offense can only be tried by a court of seventy-one judges. Our Mishnah continues to discuss other procedural issues related to the High Priest. (*Tosafot, Rabbenu Yonah, Ran.*)

הֵן נִכְסִין וְהוּא נִגְלֶה **They become hidden from sight, and he appears.** It has been suggested that this measure is necessary in order to prevent the High Priest from contracting ritual impurity by coming into contact with other mourners, for according to Rabbinic decree impurity can be transmitted to an unlimited number of people through secondary physical contact. At a crowded funeral where people are huddled together, all are considered ritually impure even when only one of them is in actual contact with the corpse. Thus the Mishnah teaches that when individual mourners become hidden from sight by crowding together around the bier, the High Priest must make himself visible by standing apart from them. But if the individual mourners are themselves visible by virtue of keeping sufficient distance between the bier and each other, then the High Priest may become less visible by joining them. (*Rabbi A.M. Horowitz.*)

HALAKHAH

כֹּהֵן גָּדוֹל **The High Priest.** "The High Priest may judge and be judged. He is not required to testify in court on behalf of anyone other than the king. The High Priest may be testified against." (*Rambam, Sefer Avodah, Hilkhot Kelei HaMikdash* 5:8-9.)

חוֹלֵץ וְחוֹלְצִין לְאִשְׁתּוֹ **He may perform *ḥalitzah,* and *ḥalitzah* may be performed with his wife.** "The High Priest may perform *ḥalitzah* with his late brother's wife, and the brother may perform *ḥalitzah* with the High Priest's widow. The brother may enter into levirate marriage with the High Priest's widow, but the High Priest may not enter into levirate marriage with his brother's widow." (*Rambam, Sefer Avodah, Hilkhot Kelei HaMikdash* 5:10.)

מֵת לוֹ מֵת **If someone related to him dies.** "If a relative of the High Priest dies, the High Priest may not leave the Temple or his house to join the funeral," following the view

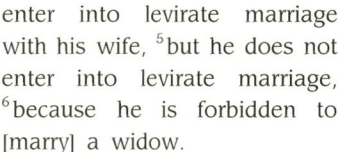

TRANSLATION AND COMMENTARY

of sight. [1]The High Priest may **follow** the bier from a distance **until** he arrives at **the door of the city gate,** where he must stop, for outside the city there is no place to conceal himself. [2]These are **the words of Rabbi Meir.** [3]**Rabbi Yehudah** disagrees and **says:** The High Priest **may not leave the Temple** at all to attend his relative's funeral, [4]**for it is stated** in the verse (Leviticus 21:12): **"And from the sanctuary he shall not go out,** nor shall he profane the sanctuary of his God; for the crown of his God's anointing oil is upon him."

וּכְשֶׁהוּא מְנַחֵם [5]After the funeral party returns from the burial, the mourners stand in line and the people who here come to pay their condolences pass by and comfort them. **When** the High Priest is among those who come to **comfort** the mourners, [6]**it is customary that all the people pass** by in a row **one after the other** to comfort them, [7]**while the one appointed** as the Deputy High Priest **positions himself between** the High Priest **and** the rest of **the people.** [8]**When** the High Priest is in mourning, **and people** come to **comfort** him, [9]**all the people say to him: "We are your atonement,** ready to accept any punishment or affliction intended for you." [10]**And he says to them** in reply: **"May you be blessed from Heaven."** [11]**When** the High Priest **is given the mourner's meal** (the customary meal given to the bereaved upon returning from burying his dead), [12]**all the people sit on the ground** as a gesture of participation in his grief, **and** the High Priest **sits on a bench** in a dignified manner.

הַמֶּלֶךְ לֹא דָּן [13]Having concluded its presentation of some of the laws regarding a High Priest, the Mishnah now considers the laws regarding a king. Even if **the king** has the appropriate qualifications, he **may not** sit on a court and **judge** others, **and** in the event that a claim is brought against him, **he may not** appear before a court to **be judged.** [14]The king **may not** appear before a court and **testify** against others, **and** he **may not be testified against,** since cases against him never reach a court for judgment.

[1]וְיוֹצֵא עִמָּהֶן עַד פֶּתַח שַׁעַר הָעִיר, [2]דִּבְרֵי רַבִּי מֵאִיר. [3]רַבִּי יְהוּדָה אוֹמֵר: אֵינוֹ יוֹצֵא מִן הַמִּקְדָּשׁ, [4]מִשּׁוּם שֶׁנֶּאֱמַר "וּמִן הַמִּקְדָּשׁ לֹא יֵצֵא".

[5]וּכְשֶׁהוּא מְנַחֵם אֲחֵרִים, [6]דֶּרֶךְ כָּל הָעָם עוֹבְרִין בְּזֶה אַחַר זֶה. [7]וְהַמְּמוּנֶּה מְמַצְּעוֹ בֵּינוֹ לְבֵין הָעָם. [8]וּכְשֶׁהוּא מִתְנַחֵם מֵאֲחֵרִים, [9]כָּל הָעָם אוֹמְרִים לוֹ: "אָנוּ כַּפָּרָתְךָ", [10]וְהוּא אוֹמֵר לָהֶן: "תִּתְבָּרְכוּ מִן הַשָּׁמַיִם". [11]וּכְשֶׁמַּבְרִין אוֹתוֹ, [12]כָּל הָעָם מְסוּבִּין עַל הָאָרֶץ וְהוּא מֵיסֵב עַל הַסַּפְסָל.

[13]הַמֶּלֶךְ לֹא דָּן וְלֹא דָּנִין אוֹתוֹ. [14]לֹא מֵעִיד וְלֹא מְעִידִין אוֹתוֹ.

LITERAL TRANSLATION

[1]And he goes with them until the door of the city gate. [2][These are] the words of Rabbi Meir. [3]Rabbi Yehudah says: He does not leave the Temple, [4]since it is said: "And from the sanctuary he shall not go out."

[5]And when he comforts others, [6]it is customary (lit., "the way") that all the people pass [by], one after the other. [7]And the deputy (lit., "the appointed one") positions him between himself and the people. [8]And when he is comforted by others, [9]all the people say to him: "We are your atonement." [10]And he says to them: "May you be blessed from Heaven." [11]And when they give him the mourner's meal, [12]all the people sit on the ground and he sits on a bench.

[13]The king may not judge nor be judged. [14]He may not testify nor be testified against.

RASHI

רבי יהודה — דריש "מן המקדש" דווקא. וכשהוא מנחם — בשורה כשחוזרין מקבור את המת שאין שלו, דרך כל העם עוברין זה אחר זה ומנחמין את האבל שעומד במעמדו. והממונה — סגן הכהנים ממצעו לכהן גדול בינו לבין העם, שהממונה בימינו וכל העם בשמאלו, והוא באמצע. אנו כפרתך — בנו תתכפר אתה, ואנחנו תחתיך לכל הראוי לבא עליך. וכשמברין אותו — כדקיימא לן (במועד קטן כז,ב) אבל — סעודה ראשונה אסור לאכול משלו. מסובין על הארץ — הן מצירין ומתאבלין על צערו, והוא מיסב בכבוד על הספסל.

SAGES

רַבִּי מֵאִיר **Rabbi Meir.** See *Sanhedrin*, Part I, pp. 54-55.

רַבִּי יְהוּדָה **Rabbi Yehudah (bar Il'ai).** See *Sanhedrin*, Part I, p. 12.

BACKGROUND

הַמְּמוּנֶּה **Deputy High Priest.** *Rashi* explains that this refers to the Deputy High Priest, whose main function was to be prepared so that if anything should happen to the High Priest that would prevent him from serving, the deputy would be able to replace him immediately. However, throughout most of the year, the Deputy High Priest was responsible for managing the affairs of the Temple. Since the High Priest was not expected to deal with the details of the service, the assistant oversaw the implementation of arrangements and the appointment of priests for various tasks.

אָנוּ כַּפָּרָתְךָ **We are your atonement.** That is to say, we take upon ourselves mourning over this disaster, so that it might not afflict you. For the High Priest atones for the entire Jewish people, particularly on Yom Kippur, but also through the special priestly garments that he wore. The Torah prevents him from observing the customs of mourning because of his sanctity, and therefore the people, as it were, took his mourning upon themselves. Similarly, it was said of Aaron the Priest that he was forbidden to mourn because of his priestly office, and Moses said to him: "And your brothers, the whole house of Israel, shall bewail the fire that the Lord has burned" (Leviticus 10:7).

HALAKHAH

of Rabbi Yehudah. (*Rambam, Sefer Avodah, Hilkhot Kelei HaMikdash* 5:5.)

כְּשֶׁהוּא מְנַחֵם אֲחֵרִים **When he comforts others.** "The High Priest may go to a house of mourning in order to comfort the mourners. When he goes, the other priests surround him as a sign of honor. The Deputy High Priest arranges that the High Priest be in the middle, between him and the people." (*Rambam, Sefer Avodah, Hilkhot Kelei HaMikdash* 5:4.)

כְּשֶׁהוּא מִתְנַחֵם מֵאֲחֵרִים **When he is comforted by others.** "When the people come to comfort the High Priest, he stands in line with his deputy to his right and the head of that week's priestly watch and the rest of the people to his left. The people say to him: 'We are your atonement,' and he replies: 'May you be blessed from Heaven.' When the High Priest is offered the mourner's meal the people sit on the ground and he sits on a bench." (*Rambam, Sefer Avodah, Hilkhot Kelei HaMikdash* 5:5-6; *Sefer Shofetim, Hilkhot Evel* 7:6.)

הַמֶּלֶךְ לֹא דָּן **The king may not judge.** "The king may not judge others, nor may he be judged. He may not testify against others, nor may he be testified against. These laws

TRANSLATION AND COMMENTARY

לֹא חוֹלֵץ [1]If the king's brother died childless, the king **may not perform** the *ḥalitzah* ceremony with brother's widow. If the king died childless, his brother **may not perform** ***ḥalitzah* with** the king's **widow.** Since she is forbidden to remarry, there is no reason to release her from the levirate tie. [2]Should the king's brother die childless, the king **may not enter into levirate marriage** with his brother's widow, so as not to appear as a substitute for his brother; **nor** may a king's brother **enter into levirate marriage with** the king's **widow,** since she is forbidden to remarry.

רַבִּי יְהוּדָה אוֹמֵר [3]**Rabbi Yehudah** disagrees and **says: If** the king's brother died childless, and the king **wishes to** forgo his honor and **perform *ḥalitzah*** with his sister-in-law **or enter into levirate marriage** with her, he may do so, and **he is remembered for good.** [4]The Sages **said to** Rabbi Yehudah: **We do not listen to him,** for the honor due to a king is not a personal privilege of his to waive.

וְאֵין נוֹשְׂאִין אַלְמְנָתוֹ [5]If the king dies, **nobody may marry his widow.** [6]**Rabbi Yehudah** disagrees and **says: A king may marry the widow of** another **king,** if the marriage is not otherwise prohibited, [7]**for we find that** King **David married the widow of** King **Saul,** [8]**as it is said** (II Samuel 12:8): **"And I gave unto you your master's house, and your master's wives into your bosom."**

GEMARA כֹּהֵן גָּדוֹל דָּן [9]We learned in the Mishnah: **"The High Priest** may sit on a court and **judge** others." The Gemara raises a question: [10]**This is** indeed **obvious!** Why should the High Priest be disqualified from sitting on a court?

וְדָנִין אוֹתוֹ [11]The Gemara answers: **It was necessary** for the Tanna to teach the second clause, "the High Priest **may be judged,"** otherwise one might have thought that it was beneath the dignity of the High Priest to appear before a court. He therefore also taught "he may judge" for stylistic consideration.

הָא נַמִּי פְּשִׁיטָא [12]The Gemara rejects this answer: This second clause **is also obvious!** [13]For **if he cannot be judged, how can he judge?** [14]**Surely it is written** (Zephaniah 2:1): **"Gather yourselves together and** then

[1]לֹא חוֹלֵץ וְלֹא חוֹלְצִין לְאִשְׁתּוֹ. [2]לֹא מְיַיבֵּם וְלֹא מְיַיבְּמִין לְאִשְׁתּוֹ.

[3]רַבִּי יְהוּדָה אוֹמֵר: אִם רָצָה לַחֲלוֹץ אוֹ לְיַיבֵּם, זָכוּר לְטוֹב. [4]אָמְרוּ לוֹ: אֵין שׁוֹמְעִין לוֹ. [5]וְאֵין נוֹשְׂאִין אַלְמְנָתוֹ. [6]רַבִּי יְהוּדָה אוֹמֵר: נוֹשֵׂא הַמֶּלֶךְ אַלְמְנָתוֹ שֶׁל מֶלֶךְ, [7]שֶׁכֵּן מָצִינוּ בְּדָוִד שֶׁנָּשָׂא אַלְמְנָתוֹ שֶׁל שָׁאוּל, [8]שֶׁנֶּאֱמַר ״וָאֶתְּנָה לְךָ אֶת בֵּית אֲדֹנֶיךָ וְאֶת נְשֵׁי אֲדֹנֶיךָ בְּחֵיקֶךָ״.

גמרא [9]״כֹּהֵן גָּדוֹל דָּן״. [10]פְּשִׁיטָא! [11]״וְדָנִין אוֹתוֹ״ אִיצְטְרִיכָא לֵיהּ. [12]הָא נַמִּי פְּשִׁיטָא! [13]אִי לָא דַּיְינִינַן לֵיהּ, אֵיהוּ הֵיכִי דָּיֵין? [14]וְהָכְתִיב ״הִתְקוֹשְׁשׁוּ וָקוֹשּׁוּ״,

LITERAL TRANSLATION

[1]He may not perform *ḥalitzah*, and *ḥalitzah* is not performed with his wife. [2]He does not enter into levirate marriage, and they do not enter into levirate marriage with his wife.

[3]Rabbi Yehudah says: If he wishes to perform *ḥalitzah* or enter into levirate marriage, [he will] be remembered for good. [4]They said to him: We do not listen to him.

[5]And one may not marry his [the king's] widow. [6]Rabbi Yehudah says: A king may marry the widow of a [another] king, [7]for we find that David married the widow of Saul, [8]as it is said: "And I gave unto you your master's house, and your master's wives into your bosom."

GEMARA [9]"The High Priest may judge." [10]It is obvious!

[11]"And be judged" was necessary for him [to say].

[12]That too is obvious! [13]If we may not judge him, how may he judge others? [14]For surely it is written: "Gather yourselves together and gather together [others]."

RASHI

גמרא דנין אותו איצטריכא ליה – סלקא דעתך אמינא לא ליזלזל למיתי קמי בי דינא.

NOTES

וְהָכְתִיב ״הִתְקוֹשְׁשׁוּ וָקוֹשּׁוּ״ **For surely it is written: "Gather yourselves together, and gather together [others]."** *Rashbam* (*Bava Batra* 60b) explains the relationship between the literal meaning of the verse and its homiletic interpretation as being based upon the use of the root קשש, from which the Hebrew word for "straw" (קַשׁ) is also derived. According

HALAKHAH

apply only to those who ruled over the Kingdom of Israel, as they often ignored the laws of the Torah. Kings of the Davidic line, who ruled over the Kingdom of Judea, may be judged and be testified against." (*Rambam, Sefer Shofetim, Hilkhot Sanhedrin* 2:4-5; *Hilkhot Melakhim* 3:7.)

לֹא חוֹלֵץ וְלֹא חוֹלְצִין לְאִשְׁתּוֹ **He may not perform *ḥalitzah*, and *ḥalitzah* is not performed with his wife.** "The king may not perform *ḥalitzah* with his brother's widow, nor may he take her in levirate marriage. If the king dies, his wife is not subject to *ḥalitzah* or levirate marriage. No one may marry a woman who was once married to the king, not even another king," following the view of the Sages. (*Rambam, Sefer Shofetim, Hilkhot Melakhim* 2:2-3.)

BACKGROUND

קַשֵּׁט עַצְמְךָ, וכו׳ Adorn yourself, etc. This saying of Resh Lakish is normally taken as moral counsel: A person may not instruct or guide others if he himself does not do what he demands of them. Here, however, the saying has legal meaning: Anyone who is not subject to a certain law cannot be active in enforcing it. Therefore, someone who cannot be judged is not permitted to serve as a judge.

וַהֲרֵי הוּא כְּהֶדְיוֹט, וכו׳ And he is like an ordinary man, etc. Even though there are laws set out in the Torah with specific application to the High Priest, these laws give him certain unusual privileges, as well as many special obligations. But the laws do not give him a different personal status. Therefore, he has no privileges or exemptions from all the obligations that apply to any Jew.

TRANSLATION AND COMMENTARY

gather together others [הִתְקוֹשְׁשׁוּ וָקוֹשׁוּ]," which, [1]as **Resh Lakish said**, implies the following: **Adorn** (קַשֵּׁט) **yourself** first, by behaving properly, **and** only **afterwards adorn others,** by demanding the same standard. It follows from this principle that one who does not submit himself to judgment cannot judge others. And since it is obvious that the High Priest can judge others, it must be that he himself can be judged!

אֶלָּא [2]The Gemara now suggests a different answer: **Rather,** the first two clauses of the Mishnah are indeed superfluous, but they were included in order to maintain stylistic uniformity. **Since** the Tanna **wanted to teach that "a king may not judge** nor **be judged,"** [3]**he also taught** in the beginning of the Mishnah **that "a High Priest may judge and be judged."**

וְאִי בָּעֵית [4]**And if you wish,** you can **say** that the clause stating that the High Priest may be judged **teaches us** the following law, [5]**as it was taught** in the Baraita: **"A High Priest who killed someone intentionally,** having been duly warned of the consequences, **is** himself **executed.** [6]If he killed someone **unintentionally, he is exiled** to a city of refuge [see Numbers 35]. [7]**And he transgresses a positive commandment and a negative commandment,** [8]**for he is like an ordinary man in all respects."**

בְּמֵזִיד נֶהֱרָג [9]The Gemara now proceeds to analyze the first clause of the Baraita: "A High Priest who killed someone **intentionally is executed."** The Gemara comments: Surely, [10]**this is obvious!**

בְּשׁוֹגֵג גּוֹלֶה [11]The Gemara elaborates: Indeed this clause was not needed, but it was required because of the law mentioned directly afterwards, that "if the High Priest killed someone **unintentionally, he is exiled** to a city of refuge," which **was necessary for** the Tanna to teach.

הָא נַמִי פְּשִׁיטָא [12]The Gemara objects: But **this, too, is obvious!** Since exile is the punishment prescribed by the Torah for the unintentional killing of another person, why should the High Priest be treated differently from any other person?

אִיצְטְרִיךְ [13]The Gemara answers: **It was** indeed **necessary** for the Baraita to state that the High Priest is sent into exile for the unintentional killing of another person, for **otherwise it might have entered your mind to say** that he is exempt from the punishment of exile. [14]**Since it is written** about the exiled person (Numbers 35:25): **"And he shall dwell in it until the death of the High Priest,"** [15]you might have thought that only someone **who has a remedy** for his exile **in** the right to **return** home after the High Priest's death **is exiled;**

[1]וְאָמַר רֵישׁ לָקִישׁ: קַשֵּׁט עַצְמְךָ, וְאַחַר כָּךְ קַשֵּׁט אֲחֵרִים! [2]אֶלָּא, אַיְּידֵי דְּקָא בָּעֵי לְמִיתְנֵי ״מֶלֶךְ לֹא דָן וְלֹא דָּנִין אוֹתוֹ״, [3]תְּנָא נַמִי ״כֹּהֵן גָּדוֹל דָּן וְדָנִין״.
[4]וְאִי בָּעֵית אֵימָא: הָא קָא מַשְׁמַע לָן, [5]כִּדְתַנְיָא: ״כֹּהֵן גָּדוֹל שֶׁהָרַג אֶת הַנֶּפֶשׁ בְּמֵזִיד, נֶהֱרָג. [6]בְּשׁוֹגֵג, גּוֹלֶה. [7]וְעוֹבֵר עַל עֲשֵׂה וְעַל לֹא תַעֲשֶׂה, [8]וַהֲרֵי הוּא כְּהֶדְיוֹט לְכָל דְּבָרָיו״.
[9]״בְּמֵזִיד נֶהֱרָג״. [10]פְּשִׁיטָא!
[11]״בְּשׁוֹגֵג גּוֹלֶה״ אִיצְטְרִיכָא לֵיהּ.
[12]הָא נַמִי פְּשִׁיטָא!
[13]אִיצְטְרִיךְ. סָלְקָא דַּעְתָּךְ אָמִינָא: [14]הוֹאִיל וּכְתִיב ״וְיָשַׁב בָּהּ עַד מוֹת הַכֹּהֵן הַגָּדֹל״, [15]אֵימָא: כָּל דְּאִית לֵיהּ תַּקַּנְתָּא

LITERAL TRANSLATION

[1]And Resh Lakish said: Adorn yourself, and afterwards adorn others.

[2]Rather, since he wanted to teach [that] "a king may not judge or be judged," [3]he also taught "a High Priest may judge and be judged."

[4]And if you wish, say: It teaches us this, [5]as it was taught: "A High Priest who killed someone intentionally, he is executed. [6]Unintentionally, he is exiled. [7]And he transgresses a positive commandment and a negative commandment, [8]and he is like an ordinary man in all respects."

[9]"Intentionally, he is executed." [10]It is obvious!

[11]"Unintentionally, he is exiled" was necessary for him [to say].

[12]This too is obvious!

[13]It was necessary. [Otherwise] you might have thought of saying: [14]Since it is written: "And he shall dwell in it until the death of the High Priest," [15]say: Whoever has a remedy

RASHI

ועובר על עשה — לקמן פריך: לא סגי דלא עביד? **והרי הוא כהדיוט** — לקמיה מיתוקמא שפיר.

NOTES

to Resh Lakish, the implication is that one should first remove the straw adhering to oneself before demanding the same from others.

Ran asks: Why does the Gemara not state that in teaching us that the High Priest can be judged like anyone else, the Mishnah seeks to convey the principle that Resh Lakish first introduced later on, that only he who subjects himself to judgment can judge others? He answers: Had the Mishnah wished to convey Resh Lakish's principle, it would have stated it explicitly, rather than allude to it obliquely in the context of certain regulations affecting the High Priest.

TRANSLATION AND COMMENTARY

[1]but someone who **does not have a remedy** for his exile and cannot **return** home upon the High Priest's death, **is not** subject **to exile.** Indeed, the High Priest himself has no remedy for his exile, [2]**for we have learned** elsewhere in the Mishnah (*Makkot* 11b): [18B] [3]**"If someone** unintentionally **kills a High Priest, or if a High Priest** unintentionally **killed** another **person,** and the killer is sentenced to exile before another High Priest is appointed, [4]the killer is exiled to a city of refuge and **may never leave there."** [5]Thus you might **say** that **he should not be exiled** at all! Therefore, [6]**it** was necessary for the Baraita to **teach us** that even the High Priest is subject to exile.

וְאֵימָא הָכִי נַמִי [7]The Gemara seeks clarification: **But say that this is indeed so,** that the High Priest is not subject to exile!

אָמַר קְרָא [8]The Gemara comments: This cannot be, for **the verse** dealing with cities of refuge **states** (Deuteronomy 19:3): **"That every killer may flee thither."** [9]The word "every" means that **even a High Priest is included** within the meaning of the verse.

עוֹבֵר עַל עֲשֵׂה [10]The Gemara now analyzes the next clause of the Baraita: "The High Priest **transgresses a positive commandment and a negative commandment."** The Gemara, astonished by this formulation, asks: Does the Baraita imply that the High Priest is required to violate commandments of the Torah! [11]**Is there no way that he does not transgress** any commandments?!

הָכִי קָאָמַר [12]The Gemara answers: Rather, understand the Tanna of the Baraita as if **he is saying the following: If** the High Priest **transgressed a positive commandment or a negative commandment** punishable by lashes, [13]**he is like an ordinary man in all respects** and is judged by a court of three.

LITERAL TRANSLATION

of return is exiled; [1][whoever] does not have a remedy of return is not exiled. [2]For we have learned: [18B] [3]"Someone who kills a High Priest, or a High Priest who killed a person, [4]may never leave there." [5]Say he should not be exiled! [6][Therefore], it teaches us [otherwise].

[7]But say that this is indeed so!

[8]The verse states: "That every killer flee thither," [9]even a High Priest is included.

[10]"He transgresses a positive commandment and a negative commandment." [11]Is there no way that he does not transgress?!

[12]He is saying the following: If he transgressed a positive commandment or a negative commandment, [13]he is like an ordinary person in all respects.

בַּחֲזָרָה לִיגְלֵי, [1]דְּלֵית לֵיהּ תַּקַּנְתָּא בַּחֲזָרָה לָא לִיגְלֵי. [2]דִּתְנַן: [18B] [3]הַהוֹרֵג כֹּהֵן גָּדוֹל, אוֹ כֹּהֵן גָּדוֹל שֶׁהָרַג אֶת הַנֶּפֶשׁ, [4]אֵינוֹ יוֹצֵא מִשָּׁם לְעוֹלָם. [5]אֵימָא לָא לִיגְלֵי! [6]קָא מַשְׁמַע לָן.

[7]וְאֵימָא הָכִי נַמִי!

[8]אָמַר קְרָא: ״לָנוּס שָׁמָּה כָּל רֹצֵחַ״, [9]אֲפִילּוּ כֹּהֵן גָּדוֹל בְּמַשְׁמַע.

[10]״עוֹבֵר עַל עֲשֵׂה וְעַל לֹא תַעֲשֶׂה״. [11]לָא סַגִּי דְּלֹא עָבַר?!

[12]הָכִי קָאָמַר: אִם עָבַר עַל עֲשֵׂה וְעַל לֹא תַעֲשֶׂה, [13]הֲרֵי הוּא כְּהֶדְיוֹט לְכָל דְּבָרָיו.

RASHI

ההורג כהן גדול — בשוגג גולה לעיר מקלט, ואינו יוצא משם לעולם, דכיון דאין כהן גדול במקדש כשהוא גולה, במיתת מי ישוב? וכן כהן גדול שהרג את הנפש בשוגג, במיתת מי ישוב? הא ליכא כהן גדול. הרי הוא כהדיוט — לידון בשלשה.

BACKGROUND

הַהוֹרֵג כֹּהֵן גָּדוֹל **Someone who kills a High Priest.** The general law is that a person who has accidentally killed someone may leave the city of sanctuary after the death of the High Priest who was serving when the killer was sentenced to exile. In the two cases under discussion, no remedy is available to the killer until his death. When the High Priest was killed, there was no incumbent High Priest, so that even after a new High Priest was appointed, the killer of the former High Priest could not return from exile after the death of the new one. When the High Priest killed someone, even though a replacement was certainly appointed, the High Priest who killed could not return from exile after the death of his replacement.

NOTES

דְּלֵית לֵיהּ תַּקַּנְתָּא בַּחֲזָרָה לָא לִיגְלֵי **Whoever does not have the remedy of returning is not exiled.** The Rishonim ask: How can the Gemara suggest that the High Priest may not be subject to exile, when the Baraita which informs us that the High Priest can never return from the city of refuge implies that he is in fact subject to exile? It has been suggested that the Baraita refers to a High Priest who fled to a city of refuge on his own, and thus it does not necessarily imply that the court may exile him. (*Ran.*) Alternatively, the Baraita might be referring to a High Priest who unintentionally killed someone while in a city of refuge, but it does not necessarily imply that he is exiled if he killed someone while outside such a city. (*Talmidei Rabbenu Peretz.*)

עוֹבֵר עַל עֲשֵׂה **He transgresses a positive commandment.** The Torah does not prescribe any punishment for the violation of a positive commandment. What, then, does the Baraita mean when it says that a High Priest who transgresses a positive commandment is treated like any other person? It has been suggested that it is referring to the administration of lashes by a three-man court, as is prescribed by Rabbinic decree for anyone who refuses to fulfill a positive Torah commandment. (*Rabbi Yosef Rafael, Tzafnat Pa'ane'aḥ.*)

HALAKHAH

הַהוֹרֵג כֹּהֵן גָּדוֹל **Someone who kills a High Priest.** "If the High Priest unintentionally killed someone, or if someone unintentionally killed a High Priest, and another High Priest has not yet been appointed, the killer is exiled to a city of refuge and never leaves." (*Rambam, Sefer Nezikin, Hilkhot Rotze'aḥ* 7:10.)

הֲרֵי הוּא כְּהֶדְיוֹט לְכָל דָּבָר **He is like an ordinary person in all respects.** "If the High Priest violated a prohibition punishable by lashes, he is judged by a court of three, like any other person." (*Rambam, Sefer Avodah, Hilkhot Kelei HaMikdash* 4:22.)

TRANSLATION AND COMMENTARY

פְּשִׁיטָא [1]The Gemara seeks clarification: But surely **it is obvious!**

סָלְקָא דַּעְתָּךְ [2]The Gemara elaborates: It is not all that obvious, for **you might have thought of saying** that **since we learned** in the Mishnah in the previous chapter (2a): [3]**"A tribe** of Israel, **or a false prophet, or a High Priest may not be tried except by a court of seventy-one** judges," implying that a High Priest must be judged in all cases by a court of seventy-one. [4]**And Rav Adda bar Ahavah said:** The source regarding how to judge a High Priest is the verse in which Moses, acting in the capacity of a court of seventy-one, is told: **"Every great matter they shall bring to you"** (Exodus 18:22). [5]The phrase "every great matter" refers to **matters** involving **a great man,** such as the High Priest. [6]Thus you might have thought **of saying** that **all matters** involving **a great man,** like the High Priest, must be tried by a court of seventy-one. [7]Therefore, **it** was necessary for the Baraita to **teach us** that the High Priest is tried for noncapital offenses by a court of three, just like anybody else.

וְאֵימָא הָכִי נַמִי [8]The Gemara continues: **But say that indeed it is so**, that all matters affecting the High Priest must be adjudicated by a court of seventy-one judges!

מִי כְּתִיב [9]The Gemara asks: **Is it written** in the verse: **"The matters of a great man** they shall bring to you"? This would imply that all cases involving a High Priest must be brought before a court of seventy-one! [10]In fact, "every **great matter** they shall bring to you" is what **is written**, [11]implying that only a case that can **literally** be considered **a "great matter,"** a capital offense, must be brought before a court of seventy-one.

מֵעִיד [12]The Gemara now discusses the next clause of our Mishnah: "A High Priest **may testify and be testified against."** [13]The Gemara raises an objection: Is it really so, that "a High Priest may **testify"** against others? [14]**But surely it was taught** otherwise in a Baraita: "The Torah states [Deuteronomy 22:1]: 'You shall not see your brother's ox or his lamb go astray, and hide yourself from (ignore) them. You shall surely bring them back to your brother.' The wording of the verse permits the expression וְהִתְעַלַּמְתָּ — 'and hide yourself' — to be interpreted as descriptive, as in the simple meaning of the verse given above, or as a positive injunction — **'and you shall hide yourself** from them,' [15]implying that **sometimes you** are permitted to **hide yourself** and ignore a lost object, while **sometimes you cannot hide yourself.** [16]**How is this so?** People

[1]פְּשִׁיטָא!

[2]סָלְקָא דַּעְתָּךְ אָמִינָא: הוֹאִיל וּתְנַן: [3]"אֵין דָּנִין לֹא אֶת הַשֵּׁבֶט וְלֹא אֶת נְבִיא הַשֶּׁקֶר, וְלֹא אֶת כֹּהֵן גָּדוֹל אֶלָּא עַל פִּי בֵּית דִּין שֶׁל שִׁבְעִים וְאֶחָד", [4]וְאָמַר רַב אַדָּא בַּר אַהֲבָה: "כָּל הַדָּבָר הַגָּדֹל יָבִיאוּ אֵלֶיךָ" — [5]דְּבָרָיו שֶׁל גָּדוֹל; [6]אֵימָא כָּל דְּבָרָיו שֶׁל גָּדוֹל! [7]קָא מַשְׁמַע לָן.

[8]וְאֵימָא הָכִי נַמִי!

[9]מִי כְּתִיב "דִּבְרֵי גָדוֹל"? [10]"הַדָּבָר הַגָּדֹל" כְּתִיב! [11]"דָּבָר גָּדוֹל" מַמָּשׁ.

[12]"מֵעִיד וּמְעִידִין אוֹתוֹ".

[13]מֵעִיד? [14]וְהָתַנְיָא: "'וְהִתְעַלַּמְתָּ' — [15]פְּעָמִים שֶׁאַתָּה מִתְעַלֵּם, וּפְעָמִים שֶׁאִי אַתָּה מִתְעַלֵּם. [16]הָא כֵּיצַד?

LITERAL TRANSLATION

[1]It is obvious!

[2]It might have entered your mind to say: Since we learned: [3]"A tribe, or a false prophet, or a High Priest may not be tried except by a court of seventy-one," [4]and Rav Adda bar Ahavah said: "Every great matter they shall bring to you" — [5]the matters of a great man. [6][You might then] say: all matters of a great man! [7][Therefore,] it teaches us [otherwise].

[8]But say that it is indeed so!

[9]Is it written: "The matters of a great man"? [10]"Great matter" is written! [11]A "great matter," literally.

[12]"He may testify and be testified against." [13]He may testify? [14]But surely it was taught: "'And you shall hide yourself' — [15]sometimes you hide yourself, and sometimes you do not hide yourself. [16]How is this so?

RASHI

דבר גדול ממש — אם עבר עבירה שיש בה מיתת בית דין הוא דבעי סנהדרי גדולה, אבל במלקות לא. הרי שהיה מוצא אבידה — כהן, והיה האבידה בבית הקברות, או שהיה זה זקן ואינה לפי כבודו, שאם היתה שלו לא היה מחזירה.

SAGES

רַב אַדָּא בַּר אַהֲבָה **Rav Adda bar Ahavah.** A famous Babylonian Amora of the first and second generations. He was born (or was circumcised) on the day Rabbi Yehudah HaNasi died. Rav Adda was a disciple of Rav, and transmitted several teachings in his name. Among his colleagues were Rav Huna, Rav Ḥisda, and Rav Naḥman. Many teachings are transmitted in his name in the Talmud. He was renowned for his piety, righteousness, and modesty, and lived to an advanced age.

NOTES

"דָּבָר גָּדוֹל" מַמָּשׁ **A "great matter," literally.** The Jerusalem Talmud explains that the Torah does not require the High Priest to appear before the Great Sanhedrin every time he is charged with a noncapital offense, in order to protect his dignity. Minor offenses may be dealt with by a court of three to avoid the humiliation of repeated appearances before the Great Sanhedrin, which would reduce his stature rather than enhance it.

LITERAL TRANSLATION

[1]A priest and it is in a graveyard, [2][or] an elder and it is not in accordance with his honor, [3]or if his own work is more than his fellow's. [4]For this it was said: 'And you shall hide yourself.'"

[5]Rav Yosef said: He may testify for the king.

[6]But surely we have learned: "He may not judge nor be judged. [7]He may not testify nor be testified against!"

[8]Rather, Rabbi Zera said: He testifies for the king's son.

[9]The king's son is a commoner!

[10]Rather, he may testify in the presence of the king.

[1]כֹּהֵן וְהוּא בְּבֵית הַקְּבָרוֹת, [2]זָקֵן וְאֵינָהּ לְפִי כְבוֹדוֹ, [3]אוֹ שֶׁהָיְתָה מְלָאכָה שֶׁלּוֹ מְרוּבָּה מִשֶּׁל חֲבֵירוֹ. [4]לְכָךְ נֶאֱמַר 'וְהִתְעַלַּמְתָּ'"!

[5]אֲמַר רַב יוֹסֵף: מֵעִיד לַמֶּלֶךְ.

[6]וְהָתְנַן: "לֹא דָּן וְלֹא דָּנִין אוֹתוֹ, [7]לֹא מֵעִיד וְלֹא מְעִידִין אוֹתוֹ"!

[8]אֶלָּא אֲמַר רַבִּי זֵירָא: מֵעִיד לְבֶן מֶלֶךְ.

[9]בֶּן מֶלֶךְ הֶדְיוֹט הוּא!

[10]אֶלָּא: מֵעִיד בִּפְנֵי הַמֶּלֶךְ.

TRANSLATION AND COMMENTARY

in the following situations may ignore a lost object: (1) [1]**A priest,** who is forbidden by Torah law to come into contact with or go near a dead body (Leviticus 21:1), **if** the lost object **is in a graveyard**; (2) [2]**an elder, if it is beneath his dignity** to trouble himself with a lost object; [3]**or** (3) **if** the loss incurred by the finder, should he neglect **his own work** in his search for the lost object, **would be greater than his friend's** loss should he forfeit the object. [4]Regarding such situations, **it was said** in the Torah: **'And you shall hide yourself from** them.'" Now, if an elder can ignore a Biblical obligation because it is beneath his dignity, then certainly we can exempt a High Priest from testifying in court for the same reason.

אֲמַר רַב יוֹסֵף [5]**Rav Yosef said:** When the Mishnah says that the High Priest may testify, it is referring to a case where **he** comes to **testify on behalf of the king,** which is not beneath his dignity.

וְהָתְנַן [6]The Gemara objects: **But surely we learned** in our Mishnah: "The king **may not judge nor be judged,** [7]**he may not testify nor be testified against."** When could a High Priest ever testify in a king's favor?

אֶלָּא [8]The Gemara answers: **Rather, Rabbi Zera said:** The Mishnah is referring to a case where the High Priest comes to **testify on behalf** of the **king's son,** which would also not be beneath his dignity.

בֶּן מֶלֶךְ הֶדְיוֹט הוּא [9]The Gemara objects: But **the king's son is a commoner,** and so it should be beneath the High Priest's dignity to appear as a witness on his behalf!

אֶלָּא [10]The Gemara replies: **Rather,** the Mishnah is referring to a case where the High Priest **testifies in the presence of the king,** who himself participates in that particular session of the court but is not on trial.

RASHI

או שהיתה מלאכה שלו מרובה משל חבירו – כגון נוקב מרגליות שאם ילך ויחזירנה, יפסיד בבטלותו יותר מדמיה. **לכך נאמר והתעלמת** – אלמא כבוד הבריות דוחה לאו ד"לא תוכל להתעלם", והכי נמי זילותא הוא לגבי כהן גדול ליתי לאסהודי לבעל דין. **אמר רב יוסף** – הא דקתני **מעיד** – למלך קאמר, שהיה מלך בעל דין וכהן גדול יודע לו עדות. **והא לא דנין אותו** – מאי סהדותא בעי? **בן מלך הדיוט הוא** – והדר קושיין לדוכתא דאיכא זילותא לכהן גדול. **בפני המלך** –

SAGES

רַב יוֹסֵף **Rav Yosef.** A Babylonian Amora of the third generation. See *Sanhedrin*, Part I, p.88.

BACKGROUND

בֶּן מֶלֶךְ הֶדְיוֹט הוּא **The king's son is a commoner.** In fact, a king's son had an important position, especially the son who was expected to inherit his father's throne. However, with respect to his Halakhic status, until he had been crowned, the king's son was no different from any other Jew, and in the view of the Halakhah, he was a layman in every respect.

NOTES

מֵעִיד לַמֶּלֶךְ **He may testify on behalf of the king.** *Rosh* suggests that Rav Yosef was referring to a case involving a king of the House of David, who in his own opinion (see 19a) may in fact be judged. The Gemara rejects this explanation because it assumes our Mishnah to be dealing only with Kings of Israel and not those of Davidic descent.

HALAKHAH

כֹּהֵן וְהוּא בְּבֵית הַקְּבָרוֹת **A priest and it is in a graveyard.** "A priest who sees a lost object or a beast in need of assistance on the grounds of a cemetery is not allowed to contract ritual impurity by retrieving the object or helping the beast." (*Shulḥan Arukh, Ḥoshen Mishpat* 272:2.)

זָקֵן וְאֵינָהּ לְפִי כְבוֹדוֹ **An elder and it is not in accordance with his honor.** "If a lost object is found by a scholar or an elder, who would not ordinarily bother himself with such an object, even if it were his own, he is not required to retrieve it and return it to its owner. One who wishes to act righteously, beyond the strict requirements of the law, can return lost property even if it is beneath his dignity. *Rema* notes that, according to some authorities (*Tur* in the name of *Rosh*), one may never compromise honor, even willingly. Thus, should a venerable individual see a lost object and wish to return it, he may compensate the owner for the loss out of his own pocket, but he cannot concern himself with retrieving the object itself." (*Shulḥan Arukh, Ḥoshen Mishpat* 263:1,3.)

הָיְתָה מְלָאכָה שֶׁלּוֹ מְרוּבָּה מִשֶּׁל חֲבֵירוֹ **If his own work is greater than his fellow's.** "Protecting oneself from financial loss takes precedence over returning lost property. Nevertheless, it is considered proper for a person to act beyond the strict requirements of the law and return lost property even if one will suffer a loss." (*Shulḥan Arukh, Ḥoshen Mishpat* 264:1.)

מֵעִיד **He testifies.** "The High Priest is not allowed to testify about civil matters, even in a court of seventy-one, for doing so would be undignified. Nevertheless, he may appear before the Great Sanhedrin in order to offer testimony on behalf of the king," following Rav Yosef, who maintains that a king of Davidic descent may stand trial. (*Rambam, Sefer Avodah, Hilkhot Kelei HaMikdash* 5:9.)

BACKGROUND

לֹא תַעֲנֶה עַל רִב **You shall not respond to a dispute.** Since the Torah commands us to behave with respect and awe toward a king, judges are also similarly commanded. In other instances, one also makes certain that judges should not be reluctant to differ with the opinion of a distinguished Torah authority. However, a session of the Sanhedrin has an additional aspect, for the Sages are supposed to debate against each other, but because of their respect for the king, the judges will not wish to contradict him.

TRANSLATION AND COMMENTARY

וְהָא [1]The Gemara seeks clarification: **But surely** it has been stated in a Baraita that **we do not seat a king on a Sanhedrin!** How, then, can the High Priest testify before the king?

מִשּׁוּם [2]The Gemara explains: In the case in question, **because of the High Priest's honor,** the king **comes and sits** with the judges to hear his testimony. [3]Once the judges **receive his testimony,** [4]the king **rises and leaves** before the deliberations commence so as not to intimidate the members of the Sanhedrin. [5]**And** at that point, the judges **examine** the **case.**

גּוּפָא [6]The Gemara now turns its attention to the Baraita, a part of **which was quoted** in the previous discussion. [7]**"We do not seat a king on a Sanhedrin, nor** do we appoint **a king or a High Priest** to the court that determines whether to **intercalate the year."** [8]The Gemara explains: We do not seat **a king on a Sanhedrin, for it is written** in regard to judicial procedure (Exodus 23:2): **"You shall not respond to a dispute** [רִב] by inclining toward the majority to distort justice." The word רִב (*riv*) is interpreted as if it read רַב, *rav* ("master" or "superior"), [9]thus implying that **you shall not rebut a superior.** Hence a king may not sit on a court since any opinion offered by him would cause other members of the court to suppress their opinions in deference to him.

[1]וְהָא אֵין מוֹשִׁיבִין מֶלֶךְ בַּסַּנְהֶדְרִין!
[2]מִשּׁוּם יְקָרָא דְּכֹהֵן גָּדוֹל, אָתָא וְיָתֵיב. [3]מְקַבְּלֵי נִיהֲלֵיהּ לְסָהֲדוּתֵיהּ, [4]קָאֵי הוּא, [5]וְאָזֵיל וּמְעַיְּינִינָא לֵיהּ אֲנַן בְּדִינֵיהּ.
[6]גּוּפָא: [7]"אֵין מוֹשִׁיבִין מֶלֶךְ בַּסַּנְהֶדְרִין, וְלֹא מֶלֶךְ וְכֹהֵן גָּדוֹל בְּעִיבּוּר שָׁנָה". [8]מֶלֶךְ בַּסַּנְהֶדְרִין — דִּכְתִיב "לֹא תַעֲנֶה עַל רִב" — [9]לֹא תַעֲנֶה עַל רַב.

LITERAL TRANSLATION

[1]But surely we do not seat a king on the Sanhedrin! [2]For the sake of the High Priest's honor, he comes and sits. [3]They receive his testimony, [4]he rises and leaves, [5]and we examine his case.

[6]Returning to the statement quoted above (lit., "the thing itself"): [7]"We do not seat a king on the Sanhedrin, nor a king nor a High Priest for the intercalation of the year." [8]A king on the Sanhedrin — because it is written: "You shall not respond to a dispute" — [9]you shall not rebut a superior.

RASHI

שהמלך יושב ודן בסנהדרין. אין מושיבין מלך בסנהדרין — לקמן מפרש טעמא. משום יקרא דכהן גדול — דידע בסהדותא לבריה. אתי — מלך יתיב עד דמיקבל סהדותא, וקאי מלך ואזיל ומעיינין אנן בדינא. לא תענה על רב — אינך רשאי לסתור את דברי מופלא שבדיינין, ואי אמר מלך חובה, תו לא מצי איניך למחזי ליה זכותא.

NOTES

מֶלֶךְ בַּסַּנְהֶדְרִין **The king on a Sanhedrin.** The Rishonim ask: Why may the king not be seated on the Sanhedrin? If the problem is that the other judges would be reluctant to contest his opinion, let them speak first and only then let the king announce how he has decided. *Ramah* and *Meiri* explain that it would be disrespectful for the other judges to speak before the king himself voices his opinion. How then does Rav Yosef later maintain that a Davidic king may be allowed to act as a judge (see 19a)? *Tosafot* explains that a Davidic king is in fact only permitted to adjudicate civil matters, where there is no prohibition against contesting one's superior. Although King David himself sat on a court which judged a capital case, that was an exception, for the trial concerned Nabal's rebellion against the throne, in which case it was deemed more dignified to have the other judges express their position before the king himself. *Ran* argues that a Davidic king may serve as a judge even in capital cases. Having him reserve his opinion so that the other judges could first voice their own would not be considered disrespectful, since it indicates our concern for the king's honor. Our Baraita, however, is dealing with a non-Davidic king who is not permitted to serve as a judge, and it comes to add that such a king may not even be present in the courtroom during deliberations, lest he express his opinion while the court is still considering the matter, and the other judges will then be forbidden to rule against him.

מֶלֶךְ...בְּעִיבּוּר שָׁנָה **The king...at the intercalation of the year.** The Jerusalem Talmud explains this restriction differently: The king may not sit on a special court to consider intercalation of the year, for it is beneath his dignity to serve on a court that consists of only seven members.

The question has been raised: If the king may not be a member of the Sanhedrin, how could he possibly have been appointed to a court that decides on intercalation, since the members of such a court are chosen from the Sanhedrin? *Meiri* answers that the Sanhedrin may ask somebody who is not a member of the High Court to sit on the court that

HALAKHAH

אֵין מוֹשִׁיבִין מֶלֶךְ בַּסַּנְהֶדְרִין **We do not seat the king on a Sanhedrin.** "The king may not be appointed to a Sanhedrin, for the other judges would be reluctant to disagree with him or reject his opinion. The High Priest, however, may receive such an appointment, provided he is otherwise qualified for the position." (*Rambam, Sefer Shofetim, Hilkhot Sanhedrin* 2:4.)

וְלֹא מֶלֶךְ וְכֹהֵן גָּדוֹל בְּעִיבּוּר שָׁנָה **Nor the king nor the High Priest for the intercalation of the year.** "Neither the king nor the High Priest may be appointed to sit on the court that considers intercalating the year, for there is concern that they might favor or oppose intercalation on the basis of personal considerations." (*Rambam, Sefer Zemanim, Hilkhot Kiddhush HaḤodesh* 4:11.)

TRANSLATION AND COMMENTARY

לֹא מֶלֶךְ [1]**Nor** do we appoint **a king or a High Priest** to the court that determines whether to **intercalate the year,** for they may have personal reasons for favoring or opposing the insertion of an additional month into the year. [2]**A king** might favor intercalation **because of the** savings it would afford him when supplying his soldiers with their fixed annual **provisions;** [3]whereas **a High Priest** might oppose intercalation **because of the cold** weather that can be expected in the month of Tishri when the year is extended. He must immerse himself five times in the course of performing his duties on the Day of Atonement (which occurs in the month of Tishri) and walk barefoot on the stone floors of the Temple.

אָמַר רַב פַּפָּא [4]**Rav Pappa said: Understand from** the previous discussion that when **the year** is intercalated, the changes in season **proceed after the month** ordinarily associated with them, making Tishri and Ḥeshvan colder than usual.

אִינִי [5]The Gemara challenges this conclusion: But **is it** really **so?** [6]What about **those three cowherds who were standing** and talking during the month of Adar, [7]**within earshot of the Rabbis?** [8]**One** cowherd **said: If the early and the late sowing sprout together** at the same time, [9]it is a sign that **this is** indeed the month of **Adar,** when the earth is generally warm enough to make such a thing possible. [10]**But if** the crops do **not sprout together** at the same time, **it is not Adar,** but rather the colder month of Shevat. [11]**And the second** cowherd **said: If** the day starts out so cold that **an ox can die in the morning from the cold,** [12]but **in the afternoon** that same animal is so hot that you find it **sleeping in the shade of a fig tree,** [13]rubbing up against the bark as if **to strip** itself of **its** own **hide,** it is a sign that **this is** indeed the month of **Adar,** when such extremes in temperature are not unusual. [14]**But if** such extremes do **not** occur, **it is not Adar,** but rather Shevat. [15]**And the third** cowherd **said: If** the weather has become so mild so that even when **a strong east wind** (which is at that time of year a cold wind) **blows towards one,** [16]and the breath you blow from your **mouth** can **go out towards it** and

LITERAL TRANSLATION

[1]Nor a king or a High Priest for the intercalation of the year — [2]a king, because of the provisions; [3]a High Priest, because of the cold.

[4]Rav Pappa said: Understand from this that the [weather during the] year follows the month[s].

[5]But is it so? [6]Behold those three cowherds who were standing, [7]and the Rabbis heard them talking. [8]One said: If the early sowing and the late sowing sprout together, [9]it is Adar, [10]but if not, it is not Adar. [11]And one said: If an ox can die in the morning as a result of the cold, [12]and at noon it sleeps in the shade of a fig tree, [13][rubbing against it] to strip off its hide, this is Adar, [14]and if not, this is not Adar. [15]And one said: If a strong east wind [blows] towards one, [16][and] a blowing [of air] from your mouth goes out to meet it,

[1]לֹא מֶלֶךְ וְכֹהֵן גָּדוֹל בְּעִיבּוּר שָׁנָה — [2]מֶלֶךְ, מִשּׁוּם אַפְסַנְיָא; [3]כֹּהֵן גָּדוֹל, מִשּׁוּם צִינָּה.
[4]אָמַר רַב פַּפָּא: שְׁמַע מִינָּהּ שַׁתָּא בָּתַר יַרְחָא אָזֵיל.
[5]אִינִי? [6]וְהָא הָנָךְ שְׁלֹשָׁה רוֹעֵי בָקָר דַּהֲווּ קַיְימִי, [7]וּשְׁמָעִינְהוּ רַבָּנַן דְּקָאָמְרִי; [8]חַד אֲמַר: אִם בַּכִּיר וְלָקִישׁ כַּחֲדָא יֵינֵץ, [9]דֵּין הוּא אֲדָר, [10]וְאִם לָאו, לֵית דֵּין אֲדָר. [11]וְחַד אֲמַר: אִם תּוֹר בְּצַפְרָא בְּתַלְגָּא יְמוּת, [12]וּבְטִיהֲרָא בְּטוּל תְּאֵינָה יִדְמוֹךְ, [13]יַשְׁלַח מַשְׁכֵּיהּ, דֵּין הוּא אֲדָר, [14]וְאִם לָאו, לֵית דֵּין אֲדָר. [15]וְחַד אֲמַר: אִם קִידּוּם תַּקִּיף לַחֲדָא יְהֵא, [16]יִפַּח בְּלוּעָךְ נָפֵיק לְקִיבְלֵיהּ,

RASHI

משום אפסניא — מחלק ממון לחיילותיו כך וכך לשנה, ונוח לו שיהו כל השנים מעוברות. **כהן גדול** — אינו רוצה שתתעבר שנה מפני הצינה, שצריך לטבול ולקדש ביום הכפורים חמש טבילות ועשרה קידושין, ואם תתעבר שנה הרי תשרי במרחשון, וצינת מרחשון תהיה בתשרי. **אמר רב פפא שמע מינה** — מהא דקתני ולא כהן גדול בעיבור שנה. **שתא בתר ירחי אזלא** — אחר ירחים הראוים להיות אם לא נתעברה הולך קור וחום של שנה, וצינה הראויה במרחשון הויא בתשרי כשמתעברת. **אם בכיר ולקיש כחדא יינץ דין הוא אדר** — אם יהא חום בקרקע ויצמח זרע הבכיר והאפילה יחד, חיטין שנזרעו בראש החודש והשעורין שנזרעו עכשיו — דין הוא אדר, ואם לאו — לית דין אדר אלא שבט. **אם תור בצפר בתלג ימות** — אם בבקר יהא קור חזק עד שיהא השור קרוב למות מחמת הצינה. **ובטיהרא בטול תאינתא ידמוך** — ובצהרים יגדל כח החום עד שיהא השור מיצל בצל התאנה מחמת החום. **וישלח משכיה** — ויפשיט עורו, כלומר יתחכך בתאינה מחמת החום. **אם קידום תקיף לחדא יהא יפח בלועך נפיק לקבליה** — אם כבר תשש כח החורף כל כך שכשיהא רוח מזרחית חזקה מאד והיא מביאה צינה, ואתה מנשב בפיך ויוצא לקראתה ונפיתחך קשה מן הרוח ומחממתה — דין הוא אדר.

SAGES

רַב פַּפָּא **Rav Pappa.** One of the leading Babylonian Amoraim of the fifth generation, Rav Pappa was a student of Abaye and Rava, and was a colleague of Rav Huna the son of Rav Yehoshua. After Rava's death Rava's yeshivah was divided: Some of the students went to Pumbedita with Rav Naḥman bar Yitzḥak, and the others went to Neresh with Rav Pappa. Rav Pappa's yeshivah was famous and had many students; among his disciples were Rav Ashi and Ravina. He served as head of his yeshivah for nineteen years.

BACKGROUND

שַׁתָּא בָּתַר יַרְחָא אָזֵיל **The year follows the month[s].** The Rishonim (see *Tosafot*) already expressed astonishment about the discussion of this question, since the whole purpose of intercalation is to coordinate the lunar months with the solar calendar. Therefore, they explain that, because intercalation depends not only on coordinating the solar and lunar calendars, but also on the state of the ripening produce and the weather, it is necessary to discuss how to weigh these two sets of factors, or whether one of them alone is sufficient to justify intercalation.

וְהָא הָנָךְ שְׁלֹשָׁה רוֹעֵי **The conversation of the three cowherds.** From their remarks, it appears that the three cowherds were discussing weather conditions in mountainous regions of Eretz Israel. At high altitudes, because the atmosphere is thin, the rays of the sun are particularly strong. As a result, it can be very cold in the morning and very hot at noon. In Eretz Israel, the east wind is cold throughout the winter, and at the end of the winter it is very cold and strong. Nevertheless, in the month of Adar, one can see how the vapor of one's breath can be blown into the wind and, as it were, overcome it.

NOTES

considers intercalating the year, provided he is known to be a great Torah scholar.

אִם תּוֹר **If the ox.** Our commentary follows most Rishonim who understand the word *tor* in its Aramaic sense, as an "ox." Some Geonim understand the word in its Hebrew sense, as a "dove." The implication would then be that, during the month of Adar, a dove can be deathly cold in the morning, but by afternoon be picking at its feathers to cool itself.

[1] דֵּין הוּא אֲדָר, [2] וְאִם לָאו, לֵית דֵּין אֲדָר. [3] וְעִבְּרוּהָ רַבָּנַן לְהַהִיא שַׁתָּא!

[4] וְתִסְבְּרָא, רַבָּנַן אַרַעֲוָותָא סַמוּךְ? [5] אֶלָּא, רַבָּנַן אַחוּשְׁבְּנַיְיהוּ סַמוּךְ, [6] וְרוֹעֵי בָקָר אִיסְתַּיּוּעֵי הוּא דְּאִיסְתַּיְּיעָא מִילְּתַיְיהוּ.

[7] ״חוֹלֵץ וְחוֹלְצִין כו׳״. [8] קָא פָּסֵיק וְתָנֵי, [9] לָא שְׁנָא מִן הָאֵירוּסִין, וְלָא שְׁנָא מִן הַנִּישּׂוּאִין. [10] בִּשְׁלָמָא מִן הַנִּישּׂוּאִין — [11] הֲוֵי עֲשֵׂה וְלֹא תַעֲשֶׂה, [19A] [12] וְאֵין עֲשֵׂה דוֹחֶה לֹא תַעֲשֶׂה וַעֲשֵׂה. [13] אֶלָּא מִן

LITERAL TRANSLATION

[1] this is Adar, [2] and if not, this is not Adar. [3] And the Rabbis intercalated the year!

[4] Do you think the Rabbis relied on the cowherds? [5] Rather, the Rabbis relied on their [own] calculations, [6] and the words of the cowherds [merely] corroborated their decision.

[7] "He may perform *ḥalitzah,* and *ḥalitzah* may be performed with his wife, etc." [8] It states categorically (lit., "it decides and teaches") [9] [that there is] no difference [if she is widowed] after (lit., "from") betrothal or after marriage. [10] Granted [where she is widowed] after marriage — [11] there is a positive commandment and a negative commandment, [19A] [12] and a positive commandment does not supersede a negative commandment and a positive commandment. [13] But [when

TRANSLATION AND COMMENTARY

warms it up, [1] then **this is** indeed the month of **Adar.** [2] **But if** one's breath is **not** yet warmer than the east wind, **this is not Adar,** but rather Shevat. [3] **And** it is related that when **the Rabbis** saw that the signs designated by the three cowherds for identifying the month of Adar had not presented themselves, they **intercalated the year!** Thus, we see that the newly designated months of an intercalated year do retain the kind of weather that is typical of these months in a normal year!

וְתִסְבְּרָא [4] The Gemara rebuts this objection: **Do you** really **think** that **the Rabbis relied on** what **the cowherds** had to say when determining whether the year should be intercalated? [5] **Rather the Rabbis relied on their** own **calculations.** [6] It just happened that what **the cowherds said corroborated** the other factors impelling the Rabbis to act as they did. Generally, though, the months that follow the intercalation of a particular year experience weather typical of that normally found one month later in a nonintercalated year.

חוֹלֵץ [7] The Gemara now discusses the next clause of our Mishnah: "If the High Priest's brother dies childless, the High Priest **may perform** the *ḥalitzah* ceremony. If the High Priest dies childless, one of his brothers may **perform *ḥalitzah* with his** widowed **wife.** [8] The Gemara notes that the Mishnah appears to decide the law and **to teach categorically** that the High Priest may never enter into levirate marriage with his brother's widow, [9] as it does **not differentiate** between her being widowed **after betrothal or after marriage.** [10] **Granted** that the High Priest is not allowed to marry his late brother's wife, for she is forbidden to him on two counts — [11] because of **the positive commandment** (Leviticus 21:13): "And he shall take a woman in her virginity," **and** because of **the negative commandment** (Leviticus 21:14): "A widow he shall not take." [19A] [12] And there is a general rule that **a positive commandment,** such as that which requires a man to take his late brother's widow in levirate marriage (Deuteronomy 25:5: "Her husband's brother shall come upon her, and take her to him for a wife"), **does not supersede** both **a negative commandment and a positive commandment,** such as those dictating that the High Priest marry a virgin and not a widow. [13] **But** if the woman was widowed

RASHI

ואם לאו — שעדיין יש צינה חזקה — לית דין אדר אלא שבט. **ועברוה רבנן** — ועשאוהו כשבט, שקבעו אדר השני אחריו. אלמא שתא בתר עיבורא אזיל, ולא נהגא חום דניסן באדר, אלא מנהג אדר באדר השני. **רבנן אחושבנייהו סמוך** — ובלאו הכי מעברינן ליה, והכא איסתייועי מיסתייעא מילתייהו, כלומר איתרמי להו מזל חשיבות דאיקלע עיבור כמלתייהו, ומיהו ברוב העבורים שתא בתר ירחא אזלא. **קא פסיק ותני** — הוא אינו מייבם, לא שנא נפלה לו יבמתו בין מן הנשואין בין מן האירוסין, בשלמא מן הנשואין איכא עשה ולא תעשה באיסורא ״בתולה יקח״ (ויקרא כא) — ולא בעולה, דהיינו עשה ״אלמנה לא יקח״ (שם) — הרי לאו. **ואין עשה** — יבמה יבא עליה (דברים כה).

TERMINOLOGY

קָא פָּסֵיק וְתָנֵי It states categorically, i.e., the Tannaitic source under discussion speaks in general terms, without distinguishing between specific cases where one might have expected the law to be different. These words introduce criticism of a seemingly over-general Mishnaic ruling and are commonly followed by לָא שְׁנָא...וְלָא שְׁנָא...בִּשְׁלָמָא...אֶלָּא...אַמַּאי. The Mishnah does not distinguish between X and Y; as far as X is concerned, all is well, but as far as Y is concerned, why does it state...?

HALAKHAH

חוֹלֵץ **He performs *ḥalitzah.*** "If the High Priest's brother died childless, the High Priest may not enter into levirate marriage with his widow (even if she had only been betrothed to him), but rather he must perform *ḥalitzah* with her." (*Rambam, Sefer Kedushah, Hilkhot Issurei Bi'ah* 17:12.)

וְאֵין עֲשֵׂה דוֹחֶה לֹא תַעֲשֶׂה וַעֲשֵׂה **A positive commandment does not supersede a negative commandment and a positive commandment.** "A positive commandment does not supersede both a negative commandment and a positive commandment, and therefore the High Priest may not enter into levirate marriage with his sister-in-law, but rather must perform *ḥalitzah* with her." (*Rambam, Sefer Nashim, Hilkhot Yibbum* 6:11.)

TRANSLATION AND COMMENTARY

on the death of the High Priest's brother, while still only **betrothed** to him — i.e., prior to the consummation of their marriage — [1]**why** is the High Priest forbidden from entering with her into levirate marriage? Since she is only forbidden to him on one count — the negative commandment prohibiting him from marrying a widow — [2]**the positive commandment** obligating him to enter into levirate marriage **should come and supersede the negative commandment!**

גְּזֵירָה [3]The Gemara answers: Indeed, by Torah law the High Priest should be allowed to enter into the levirate bond with his brother's betrothed widow. But the Rabbis enacted **a decree** forbidding **the first act of intercourse** between them **on account of** their **second act of intercourse,** which is forbidden. Their first union constitutes the fulfillment of the positive commandment and thus supersedes the prohibition forbidding a High Priest to marry a widow. However, subsequent acts of intercourse between them do not fulfill any special commandment, and thus they do not supersede the prohibition. The Rabbis decreed that even the initial levirate union be forbidden, lest they continue having relations.

תַּנְיָא נַמִי הָכִי [4]**It was also taught thus** in a Baraita: "**If** one (such as the High Priest), whose widowed sister-in-law is forbidden to him under penalty of lashes by a negative commandment, **proceeded and engaged** with the woman **in his first act of intercourse**, **he acquired** her as his wife. [5]Nevertheless, **he is forbidden to keep her** as his wife and engage in **a second act of intercourse with** her."

מֵת לוֹ מֵת [6]We learned in the next clause of the Mishnah: "If **someone** related **to him dies,** the High Priest may not go out to join the funeral procession and follow the bier, lest he forget himself in his grief and touch the corpse, thereby contracting ritual impurity. Rather, he may only attend the funeral from a distance." [7]**Our Rabbis taught** a related Baraita: "The verse states in regard to a High Priest whose relatives have died (Leviticus 21:12): **'And from the sanctuary he shall not go out,'** teaching that the High Priest **may not go out with** the rest of the funeral party, [8]**but he may go out after them** and follow from a distance. [9]**How so?** [10]When those who are escorting the deceased turn down a path and **become hidden** from sight, the High Priest **may appear** on the street where they have just passed, and **when they** once **again appear, he must remain out of sight.**"

[1]הָאֵירוּסִין, אַמַּאי? [2]יָבֹא עֲשֵׂה וְיִדְחֶה לֹא תַּעֲשֶׂה!
[3]גְּזֵירָה בִּיאָה רִאשׁוֹנָה אַטּוּ בִּיאָה שְׁנִיָּה.
[4]תַּנְיָא נַמִי הָכִי: "אִם קָדְמוּ וּבָעֲלוּ בִּיאָה רִאשׁוֹנָה, קָנוּ, [5]וְאָסוּר לְקַיְּימָן בְּבִיאָה שְׁנִיָּה."
[6]"מֵת לוֹ מֵת כו'". [7]תָּנוּ רַבָּנַן: "'וּמִן הַמִּקְדָּשׁ לֹא יֵצֵא' — לֹא יֵצֵא עִמָּהֶן, [8]אֲבָל יוֹצֵא הוּא אַחֲרֵיהֶן, [9]כֵּיצַד? [10]הֵן נִכְסִין וְהוּא נִגְלֶה, הֵן נִיגְלִין וְהוּא נִכְסֶה."

LITERAL TRANSLATION

widowed] after betrothal, [1]why? [2]The positive commandment should come and supersede the negative commandment!

[3][The Rabbis issued] a decree [forbidding] the first [act of] intercourse on account of a second [act of] intercourse.

[4]It was also taught thus: "If they proceeded and engaged in the first [act of] intercourse, they acquired [them], [5]but they are forbidden to keep them for a second [act of] intercourse."

[6]"If someone [related] to him dies, etc." [7]Our Rabbis taught: "'And from the sanctuary he shall not go out' — he shall not go out with them, [8]but he may go out after them. [9]How so? [10]They become hidden [from sight] and he [then] appears; they appear and he becomes hidden [from sight]."

RASHI

ביאה ראשונה — דייבום, מקיימא מלות עשה, ביאה שניה לאו מלות יבום הוא. **ומן המקדש לא יצא** — בכהן גדול אונן כתיב (ויקרא כא), דהא כתיב לעיל מיניה "לאביו ולאמו לא יטמא".

NOTES

מִן הַמִּקְדָּשׁ לֹא יֵצֵא And from the Sanctuary he shall not go out. According to *Rambam* (*Sefer HaMitzvot*, Negative Commandment, no. 165), this verse teaches us that the Torah forbids a High Priest to leave the Temple area in order to participate in the funeral of even a close family member. But *Ramban* (in his commentary to Leviticus 21:12 and his critique to *Rambam's Sefer HaMitzvot,* principle 5) and *Ran* (and perhaps even *Rambam* himself in his *Mishneh*

HALAKHAH

בִּיאָה רִאשׁוֹנָה אַטּוּ בִּיאָה שְׁנִיָּה First and second acts of intercourse. "If a woman was forbidden to a man either by Biblical mandate or Rabbinic decree, her late husband's brother must release her from the levirate tie by performing *ḥalitzah*, and he may not take her as his levirate wife. Even when Torah law allows a man to exercise his levirate duty in spite of an opposing stricture, the Rabbis decreed that he may not do so since it is only the first act of intercourse

BACKGROUND

יָבֹא עֲשֵׂה וְיִדְחֶה The positive commandment should come and supersede. Occasional conflict may arise between two commandments in a particular matter — a positive commandment to do something and a negative injunction against doing it. For example, a person is circumcised even if he has a leprous lesion on the outside tip of his penis. This despite the prohibition against destroying leprous lesions (Deuteronomy 24:8; Tosefta, *Nega'im* 3:1-2.) As a general rule in the Talmud, in such cases the positive commandment supersedes the negative one. The first pages of tractate *Yevamot* contain a long proof of this general rule, as well as a discussion of its limitations. Does it matter, for example, whether the negative commandment is severe or not? Does a single positive commandment supersede several negative ones? The discussion there also establishes that a positive commandment does not supersede a negative one which entails both a contrary positive commandment and a prohibition.

קָנוּ, וְאָסוּר לְקַיְּימָן They acquired them but they are forbidden to keep them. The Halakhah distinguishes between marriages that are forbidden to be contracted but which are valid if contracted, and marriages that cannot be valid under any circumstances. If a man marries a woman such as his sister, who is forbidden to him because of the laws of incest, that marriage has neither legal validity nor Halakhic status. However, if he marries a woman forbidden to him solely because of a negative commandment, such as a priest who marries a divorced woman, the marriage is valid. The woman is regarded as married, and she is sexually forbidden to men other than her husband. She cannot marry again unless she receives a bill of divorce. Nevertheless, the marriage is forbidden, and the court forces the husband to divorce his wife.

TERMINOLOGY

שַׁפִּיר קָאָמַר ר׳ פְּלוֹנִי Rabbi X said well. Sometimes, when there is a controversy between Tannaim, one of the scholars gives an explanation of his viewpoint to the other scholar or scholars, and the latter are silent. The Gemara may then probe the position of the latter scholars: "Rabbi A, the first scholar, explained his point of view well. What is the reply of Rabbi B [or the Sages]?"

BACKGROUND

סְגָן וּמָשׁוּחַ שֶׁעָבַר The deputy and the anointed one who left the High Priesthood. When the High Priest became ritually impure or fell ill, the Deputy High Priest would take his place on Yom Kippur. He would wear the eight garments and perform all the duties of the High Priest. However, after the High Priest became fit again, the formerly anointed assistant no longer had any duties. He was no longer permitted to serve as an ordinary priest, because that which has been raised in sanctity may not be lowered, and all the prohibitions applying to the High Priest also apply to him. Moreover, he could never serve as High Priest while the current High Priest was alive. For that reason the restored High Priest might have thought that the formerly anointed priest was pleased at his misfortune, since he caused him to leave his high position.

TRANSLATION AND COMMENTARY

וְיוֹצֵא עַד פֶּתַח [1]The Mishnah continues: "**And** so **he goes out** with them **until** he reaches **the door** of the city **gate**. He may not follow the cortege outside the city into open territory, where it would be harder for him to maintain his distance. These are the words of Rabbi Meir. Rabbi Yehudah disagrees and says: The High Priest may not depart from the area of the Sanctuary on the Temple Mount to participate in his relative's funeral, for it is stated in the verse: "And from the sanctuary he shall not go out, nor shall he profane the sanctuary of his God; for the crown of his God's anointing oil is upon him." [2]**Rabbi Yehudah stated** his position **well,** for a simple reading of the verse seems to imply that the High Priest may not leave the Temple area at all! How does Rabbi Meir rebut this interpretation of the verse?

אָמַר לָךְ [3]The Gemara explains: **Rabbi Meir can say to you: If** it is **so,** that the verse is to be understood literally, then the High Priest should **also not** be permitted to retire **to his house,** since doing so involves leaving the Temple! [4]**Rather,** the verse meant to **say: "From the sanctuary he shall not go out"** — [5]the High Priest **shall not remove himself from** the state of **sanctity** associated with his position on account of his deceased relative. Thus he may attend the funeral from a distance, following after the bier, but remaining off the street down which it is proceeding. [6]**Since he has** this **distinguishing sign,** that he waits for the cortege to turn a corner before he himself follows behind it, [7]we are not concerned that **he will come to touch** the corpse and contract ritual impurity.

וְרַבִּי יְהוּדָה [8]The Gemara asks: **And** how does **Rabbi Yehudah** counter this argument? [9]The Gemara answers: He maintains that, **as a result of his bitterness** and distress, **it might happen that he will come to** rush forward and **touch** the corpse, thereby defiling himself.

כְּשֶׁהוּא מְנַחֵם [10]The next clause of our Mishnah, **"When** the High Priest **is** the one **comforting** others," teaches us how he and the mourners position themselves. [11]**Our Rabbis taught** a related Baraita: **"When** the High Priest **passes in the row to comfort other** mourners, [12]**the Deputy** High Priest **and** the priest who had for a time served as **the High Priest** and subsequently **left the High Priesthood, are on his right,** [13]**and the head of**

[1]״וְיוֹצֵא עַד פֶּתַח כו׳״. [2]שַׁפִּיר קָאָמַר רַבִּי יְהוּדָה!
[3]אָמַר לָךְ רַבִּי מֵאִיר: אִי הָכִי לְבֵיתוֹ נַמִי לֹא! [4]אֶלָּא הָכִי קָאָמַר: ״מִן הַמִּקְדָּשׁ לֹא יֵצֵא״ — [5]מִקְּדוּשָּׁתוֹ לֹא יֵצֵא. [6]וְכֵיוָן דְּאִית לֵיהּ הֶכֵּירָא, [7]לָא אָתֵי לְמִינְגַּע.
[8]וְרַבִּי יְהוּדָה? [9]אַגַּב מְרָרֵיהּ דִּילְמָא מִקְרֵי וְאָתֵי וְנָגַע.
[10]״כְּשֶׁהוּא מְנַחֵם״. [11]תָּנוּ רַבָּנַן: ״כְּשֶׁהוּא עוֹבֵר בְּשׁוּרָה לְנַחֵם אֶת אֲחֵרִים, [12]סְגָן וּמָשׁוּחַ שֶׁעָבַר בִּימִינוֹ, [13]וְרֹאשׁ בֵּית אָב

LITERAL TRANSLATION

[1]"And he goes out until the gate, etc." [2]Rabbi Yehudah said well!

[3]Rabbi Meir can say to you: If so, to his house also not! [4]Rather, this is what it said: "From the sanctuary he shall not go out" — [5]from his [state of] sanctity he shall not go out. [6]And since he has a distinguishing sign [to remind him], [7]he will not come to touch.

[8]And Rabbi Yehudah? [9]Because of his bitterness it might happen that he will come and touch.

[10]"When he comforts." [11]Our Rabbis taught: "When he passes in the row to comfort others, [12]the deputy and the anointed one who left (lit., 'passed from' [the High Priesthood]) are on his right, [13]and the head of [the] *bet av*

RASHI

מקדושתו לא יצא — כלומר יעשה חיזוק לדבריו שלא יגרוס לצאת מקדושה וליטמא. **מרריה** — מרירות לבו. **משוח שעבר** — כגון שאירע בו פסול בכהן גדול ומינו אחר תחתיו, וכשעבר פסולו של ראשון חוזר לעבודתו, ושני קרא ליה משוח שעבר.

NOTES

Torah, Hilkhot Kelei HaMikdash 5:5) maintain that the verse cited here serves merely as textual support for what is essentially a Rabbinic decree forbidding the High Priest's participation in a funeral. The true intent of the verse is to obligate the High Priest, even at the moment when a loved one dies, to continue with the Temple duties in which he is engaged, as well as to permit him to assume new ones; for, unlike an ordinary priest, the High Priest is allowed to serve in the Temple even while in a state of mourning.

וְרֹאשׁ בֵּית אָב And the head of the *bet av*. The priests who served in the Temple were divided into twenty-four shifts, or "duty-guards," each of which served for one week at a

HALAKHAH

that is permitted in such a case, and we are afraid that once relations are initiated, the couple will continue to cohabit together." (*Rambam, Sefer Nashim, Hilkhot Yibbum* 6:10.)

כְּשֶׁהוּא מְנַחֵם When he is comforting. "When the High Priest prepares to console a group of mourners, the Deputy High Priest, as well as the High Priest's temporary replacement, stand to his right; while the head of the *bet av*

TRANSLATION AND COMMENTARY

the ***bet av*** (priestly family) whose day it was to serve in the Temple, as well as **the mourners and all the** rest of the **people, are to his left.** [1]**And when** it is the High Priest who **stands in the row** of mourners **and is comforted by others,** [2]**the deputy** High Priest **is on his right, while the head of the** ***bet av*** **and all the** rest of the **people are on his left."** [3]The Gemara notes that the priest who had for a time served as **the High Priest** but subsequently **left the High Priesthood does not come to comfort him,** and asks: [4]**What is the reason** for this? [5]The reply: We are afraid that such a gesture from one who held his position **will cause** the High Priest **to be distressed,** [6]bringing him to **think**: **"He is** certainly **rejoicing at my** misfortune."

אָמַר רַב פַּפָּא [7]**Rav Pappa said:** It is possible to **infer three** things **from this Baraita**: [8]**Infer from it** that **the** one designated as the **deputy** (*segan*) in the Baraita **is the same as** the one designated as **the appointed one** (*memuneh*) in the Mishnah, since both these terms are used to describe the appointee standing to the right of the High Priest. [9]**And infer from it** as well that, during the ceremony of consolation, **the mourners stand** in their place while **all the people pass** before them offering condolences. [10]**And** finally, **infer from it** that the custom is for **the mourners** to **stand to the left of the consolers** when they pass before them.

תָּנוּ רַבָּנַן [11]**Our Rabbis taught** a related Baraita: **"At first, the mourners would stand** in a row **and all the people would pass** before them to offer condolences. [12]It once happened that **there were two families in**

וַאֲבֵלִים וְכָל הָעָם מִשְּׂמֹאלוֹ.
1 וּכְשֶׁהוּא עוֹמֵד בְּשׁוּרָה
וּמִתְנַחֵם מֵאֲחֵרִים, 2 סְגַן
מִימִינוֹ, וְרֹאשׁ בֵּית אָב וְכָל
הָעָם מִשְּׂמֹאלוֹ״. 3 אֲבָל מָשׁוּחַ
שֶׁעָבַר לָא אָתֵי גַּבֵּיהּ? 4 מַאי
טַעֲמָא? — 5 חָלְשָׁא דַּעְתֵּיהּ.
6 סָבַר: קָא חָדֵי בִּי.
7 אָמַר רַב פַּפָּא: שְׁמַע מִינָּהּ,
מֵהָא מַתְנִיתָא, תְּלָת: 8 שְׁמַע
מִינָּהּ: הַיְינוּ סְגָן הַיְינוּ מְמוּנֶּה.
9 וּשְׁמַע מִינָּהּ: אֲבֵלִים עוֹמְדִין
וְכָל הָעָם עוֹבְרִין. 10 וּשְׁמַע
מִינָּהּ: אֲבֵלִים לִשְׂמֹאל
הַמְנַחֲמִין הֵן עוֹמְדִין.
11 תָּנוּ רַבָּנַן: ״בָּרִאשׁוֹנָה הָיוּ
אֲבֵלִים עוֹמְדִין, וְכָל הָעָם
עוֹבְרִין 12 וְהָיוּ שְׁתֵּי מִשְׁפָּחוֹת

LITERAL TRANSLATION

and the mourners and all the people are on his left. [1]And when he stands in the row and is comforted by others, [2]the deputy is on his right, and the head of [the] *bet av* and all the people are on his left." [3]However, the anointed one who left [the High Priesthood] does not come before him. [4]What is the reason? [5]He will be distressed (lit., "his mind will weaken"). [6]He thinks: He is rejoicing at my [misfortune] (lit., "me").

[7]Rav Pappa said: Infer from it, from this Baraita, three [things]: [8]Infer from it: The *segan* (deputy) is the same as the *memuneh* (appointed one). [9]And infer from it: The mourners stand and all the people pass. [10]And infer from it: The mourners stand to the left of the comforters.

[11]Our Rabbis taught: "At first the mourners would stand [in place], and all the people would pass, [12]and there were two families

RASHI

חלשה דעתיה — דכהן גדול. **חדי בי** — שמח באבלי. **שמע מינה** — מדקתני סגן מיכן והעם מיכן וכהן באמצע, היינו סגן היינו ממונה, דמתניתין דקתני הממונה ממצעו לכהן ונותנו בינו לבין העם. **אבלים לשמאל המנחמים** — מדקתני ואבל וכל העם משמאלו, והרי הוא היה מן המנחמין, וקתני אבלים לשמאלו. **ושמע מינה** — כן מנהג תנחומין, שורה, שיהו אבלים עומדין במקומן וכל העם עוברין איש איש, כשמגיע אצל האבל מנחמו ועובר, מדקתני כשהוא עובר לנחם, וגבי מתנחם קתני כשהוא עומד בשורה להתנחם.

NOTES

time. Each of these duty-guards comprised several priestly families (*batei av*), presided over by a "head," and each family would serve one day of the week.

HALAKHAH

whose day it is to serve in the Temple, the mourners, and the rest of the people stand to his left." (*Rambam, Sefer Avodah, Hilkhot Kelei HaMikdash* 5:4.)

כְּשֶׁהוּא עוֹמֵד בְּשׁוּרָה When he stands in the row. "When others come to console the High Priest, he stands in the mourner's row with the Deputy High Priest to his right and the head of the *bet av* and the rest of the people to his left." (*Rambam, Sefer Avodah, Hilkhot Kelei HaMikdash* 5:5.)

סְגָן וּמְמוּנֶּה The ***segan*** **and the** ***memuneh.*** "The priest appointed to serve as deputy to the High Priest is at times referred to as the *segan* and at times as the *memuneh*. The title *memuneh* (appointed one) stems from his appointment as supervisor over the other priests in the Temple. As a sign of honor, the *segan* accompanies the High Priest at all times, standing to his right." (*Rambam, Sefer Avodah, Hilkhot Kelei HaMikdash* 4:16.)

אֲבֵלִים עוֹמְדִין The mourners stand. "The mourners stand to the left of the consolers, who pass by them one by one and say: 'May you be consoled from Heaven,'" in accordance with the Mishnah and the enactment instituted by Rabbi Yose. (*Rambam, Sefer Shofetim, Hilkhot Evel* 13:2.)

SAGES

רָמִי בַּר אַבָּא Rami bar Abba. He is also called by his full name, Rav Ammi bar Abba. He was an Amora of the third generation in Babylonia. He was a student of Rav Huna's and quotes his teachings. We find him in discussion with Rav Yosef regarding the Halakhah. Rav Yosef and others cite teachings in his name.

רַבִּי יוֹסֵי Rabbi Yose. This is Rabbi Yose ben Ḥalafta, one of the greatest Tannaim. See *Sanhedrin*, Part I, pp. 84-5.

רַב מְנַשְׁיָא בַּר עוּת Rav Menshaya bar 'Ut. Some commentators have the reading "בַּר עוּת" and others have "בַּר אִילַת". This Sage is mentioned only here, and he appears to have been one of the last of the Tannaim.

רַבִּי יֹאשִׁיָּה רַבָּה Rabbi Yoshiyah the Great. Also known as Rabbi Yoshiyah. See *Sanhedrin*, Part I, p. 22.

TRANSLATION AND COMMENTARY

Jerusalem who were quarreling with one another. [1]One family **would say: 'We will pass first,** for ours is the more distinguished family,' [2]**and** the other family **would say:** 'No, **we will pass first.'** [3]Consequently, the Rabbis **enacted that the people** coming to comfort the mourners **should** be the ones to **stand** in place **while the mourners pass** by them in order to receive their condolences."

חָזַר וְהָלַךְ וְסִיפֵּר [4]The Gemara now records three decrees instituted by Rabbi Yose in Sepphoris, the first of which relates to the way mourners are to be consoled. The sequence of verbs, **"he returned, and walked, and conversed,"** can be used as **a mnemonic** device for remembering these enactments.

אָמַר רָמִי בַּר אַבָּא [5]**Rami bar Abba said: Rabbi Yose returned the matter to its original state in** his city of **Sepphoris** — [6]**that the mourners should stand** in a row while **all the people** who come to comfort them **pass** by to offer their condolences.

וְאָמַר רָמִי בַּר אַבָּא [7]**And** Rami bar Abba further **stated: Rabbi Yose enacted in Sepphoris that a woman should not walk in the market with her** young **son behind her,** but rather in front of her so that she can see him at all times. [8]This was decreed **because of an incident that occurred** when a woman was walking in the market ahead of her son, and bandits abducted the boy. Later, one of the abductors offered to lead her to her son. She followed him and the bandits raped her.

וְאָמַר רָמִי בַּר אַבָּא [9]**And Rami bar Abba said: Rabbi Yose** also **decreed in Sepphoris that women should converse** loudly while **in an outhouse** in order to prevent a man from entering, [10]**on account** of the prohibition forbidding a man to be in **seclusion** with one or two women.

אָמַר רַב מְנַשְׁיָא בַּר עוּת [11]**Rav Menashya bar 'Ut said:** I once **asked Rabbi Yoshiyah the Great,** while we were standing together **in the cemetery of Hotzel,** about the consolation of mourners, [12]**and he said to me** the

בִּירוּשָׁלַיִם מִתְגָּרוֹת זוֹ בְּזוֹ. [1]זֹאת אוֹמֶרֶת: 'אֲנִי עוֹבֶרֶת תְּחִלָּה', [2]וְזֹאת אוֹמֶרֶת: 'אֲנִי עוֹבֶרֶת תְּחִלָּה'. [3]הִתְקִינוּ שֶׁיְּהֵא הָעָם עוֹמְדִין וַאֲבֵלִים עוֹבְרִין".

[4]חָזַר וְהָלַךְ וְסִיפֵּר, סִימָן.

[5]אָמַר רָמִי בַּר אַבָּא: הֶחֱזִיר רַבִּי יוֹסֵי אֶת הַדָּבָר לְיוֹשְׁנוֹ בְּצִיפּוֹרִי, [6]שֶׁיִּהְיוּ אֲבֵלִים עוֹמְדִין וְכָל הָעָם עוֹבְרִין.

[7]וְאָמַר רָמִי בַּר אַבָּא: הִתְקִין רַבִּי יוֹסֵי בְּצִיפּוֹרִי שֶׁלֹּא תְּהֵא אִשָּׁה מְהַלֶּכֶת בַּשּׁוּק וּבְנָהּ אַחֲרֶיהָ, [8]מִשּׁוּם מַעֲשֶׂה שֶׁהָיָה.

[9]וְאָמַר רָמִי בַּר אַבָּא: הִתְקִין רַבִּי יוֹסֵי בְּצִיפּוֹרִי שֶׁיִּהְיוּ נָשִׁים מְסַפְּרוֹת בְּבֵית הַכִּסֵּא, [10]מִשּׁוּם יִיחוּד.

[11]אָמַר רַב מְנַשְׁיָא בַּר עוּת: שְׁאִילִית אֶת רַבִּי יֹאשִׁיָּה רַבָּה בְּבֵית עָלְמִין דְּהוֹצֵל, [12]וַאֲמַר

LITERAL TRANSLATION

in Jerusalem who were quarreling with one another. [1]This [one] would say: 'I will pass first,' [2]and this [one] would say: 'I will pass first.' [3]They enacted that the people stand [in place] and the mourners pass."

[4]"He returned, and walked and conversed," a mnemonic.

[5]Rami bar Abba said: Rabbi Yose returned the matter to its original state in Sepphoris, [6]that the mourners stand and all the people pass.

[7]And Rami bar Abba stated: Rabbi Yose enacted in Sepphoris that a woman should not walk in the market with her son behind her, [8]because of an incident that occurred.

[9]And Rami bar Abba said: Rabbi Yose enacted in Sepphoris that women should converse in the outhouse, [10]because of seclusion.

[11]Rav Menashya bar 'Ut said: I asked Rabbi Yoshiyah the Great in the cemetery of Hotzel, [12]and he said

RASHI

ובנה אחריה — בנה הקטן לא יהלך אחריה אלא לפניה. **משום מעשה שהיה** — שגנבוהו פריצים מאחריה ונתנוהו בביתו, וכשחזרה ולא ראתהו, התחילה צועקת ובוכה, בא אחד מהם ואמר: בואי ואראנו לך, ונכנסה אחריו ועינו אותה. **מספרות** — זו עם זו. **משום ייחוד** — שמא ילך אדם שם ואם לא ישמע קול אדם יכנס ויתייחד שם, ותנן (קידושין פ,ב): לא יתייחד אדם עם שתי נשים. ובבית הכסא שבשדות קמיירי, שהיה בית הכסא שלהם בשדה חוץ לעיר והכל נפנים שם.

HALAKHAH

שֶׁלֹּא תְּהֵא אִשָּׁה מְהַלֶּכֶת בַּשּׁוּק וּבְנָהּ אַחֲרֶיהָ That a woman should not walk in the marketplace with her son following behind her. "A woman should not walk in the marketplace with her young son behind her, for there is concern that the child might be abducted and the mother raped should she attempt to retrieve him from his abductors." (*Shulḥan Arukh, Even HaEzer* 22:14.)

שֶׁיִּהְיוּ נָשִׁים מְסַפְּרוֹת בְּבֵית הַכִּסֵּא That women should converse in the outhouse. "The Sages decreed that women should converse with each other loudly while in an outhouse, so that no man will enter and violate the prohibition against secluding himself with a woman. *Rema* writes that, according to some authorities (*Haggahot Maimoniyot*), this enactment applied only when outhouses were in open and secluded fields; today, when public facilities are erected in populated areas, the issue of seclusion in them is no longer relevant." (*Shulḥan Arukh, Even HaEzer* 22:13.)

לִי: אֵין שׁוּרָה פְּחוּתָה מֵעֲשָׂרָה בְּנֵי אָדָם, [1]וְאֵין אֲבֵלִים מִן הַמִּנְיָן, [2]בֵּין שֶׁאֲבֵלִים עוֹמְדִין וְכָל הָעָם עוֹבְרִין, [3]בֵּין שֶׁאֲבֵלִים עוֹבְרִין וְכָל הָעָם עוֹמְדִין.

[4]״כְּשֶׁהוּא מִתְנַחֵם כו׳״. [5]אִיבַּעְיָא לְהוּ: כִּי מְנַחֵם הוּא אַחֲרִינֵי, הֵיכִי אָמַר לְהוּ? [6]תָּא שְׁמַע: ״וְהוּא אוֹמֵר ׳תִּתְנַחֲמוּ׳״. [7]הֵיכִי דָּמֵי? [8]אִילֵימָא כִּי מְנַחֲמֵי אַחֲרִינֵי לְדִידֵיהּ, אָמַר לְהוּ אִיהוּ: ״תִּתְנַחֲמוּ״, [9]נַחֲשָׁא קָא רָמֵי לְהוּ? [10]אֶלָּא, כִּי מְנַחֵם לְאַחֲרִינֵי, אֲמַר לְהוּ: ״תִּתְנַחֲמוּ״. [11]שְׁמַע מִינָּהּ.

[12]״מֶלֶךְ לֹא דָּן כו׳״. [13]אָמַר רַב יוֹסֵף: לֹא שָׁנוּ אֶלָּא מַלְכֵי

LITERAL TRANSLATION

to me: A row is not less than ten people, [1]and the mourners are not of the quorum, [2]whether the mourners stand and all the people pass, [3]or the mourners pass and all the people stand.

[4]"When he is being comforted, etc." [5]It was asked of them: When he is comforting others, what does he say to them? [6]Come [and] hear: "And he says: 'May you be comforted.'" [7]How is it like? [8]If you should say when others comfort him, he says to them: "May you be comforted," [9]would he cast an evil omen upon them? [10]Rather, when he comforts others, he says to them: "May you be comforted." [11]Conclude from here.

[12]"A king may not judge, etc." [13]Rav Yosef said: They did not teach [this] except [with regard to] the Kings

TRANSLATION AND COMMENTARY

following two rulings: (1) **A row** of consolers **should not be** composed of **fewer than ten people**, [1]**and the mourners** themselves **are not** counted as valid constituents **of that quorum.** (2) [2]It is irrelevant **whether the mourners stand and all the people pass** before them to offer consolation, [3]**or the mourners pass** by while **all the people** comforting them **stand** in place, as both practices are acceptable.

כְּשֶׁהוּא מִתְנַחֵם [4]Our Mishnah continues: **"When** the High Priest is in mourning and **comforted** by others, all the people say to him: 'We are your atonement, ready to accept the suffering you are going through.' And he says to them in reply: 'May you be blessed from Heaven.'" [5]The following question **was asked of** the Sages: **When** the High Priest is the one **comforting others**, **what does he say to them?**

תָּא שְׁמַע [6]**Come and hear** a possible answer to this question. It is taught in a Baraita: **"And** the High Priest **says** to the others: **'May you be comforted.'"** [7]The Gemara asks: **How is it like?** What is the case discussed in the Baraita? [8]**If you should say** that the High Priest is in mourning and **others** come to **comfort him,** and that it comes to inform us that **he says to** the consolers in turn: **"May you be comforted,"** this is unreasonable — [9]for **would he cast an evil omen upon** those who come to comfort him by wishing that they also find themselves in need of consolation?! [10]**Rather,** the Baraita must be referring to a High Priest who is **comforting others,** informing us that **he says to them: "May you be comforted."** [11]The Gemara summarizes that we should indeed **infer from here** that this is the case.

מֶלֶךְ לֹא דָּן [12]We learned in the next clause of our Mishnah: **"The king may not** sit on a court and **judge** others. If a claim is brought against him, he may not be judged." [13]**Rav Yosef said: They did not teach** this ruling **except** with regard to **the Kings of Israel,** who ruled outside of Judea, and the Hasmonean kings.

RASHI

בין שאבלים עומדין שם כו׳ — וכך הורה לי שאין שינוי מנהג בדבר, בין שהיו אבלים עומדין בין אבלים עוברין אין כאן קלקול. **והוא אומר תתנחמו** — ברייתא היא. **נחשא קא רמי?** — סימן הוא מטיל להם להרע, שיצטרכו לנחומים? בתמיה.

SAGES

רַב יוֹסֵף **Rav Yosef.** The son of Rav Ḥiyya, and one of the greatest of the Babylonian Amoraim of the third generation. See *Sanhedrin,* Part I, p. 88.

NOTES

אָמַר לְהוּ אִיהוּ ״תִּתְנַחֲמוּ״ **He says to them: May you be comforted.** How could the Gemara have entertained the possibility that, when the High Priest is in mourning and others come to console him, he says to them: "May you be consoled"? *Ohel Yitzḥak* suggests that the Gemara may have been responding to the custom referred to in the Mishnah, that those who come to console a High Priest assume certain mourning practices that would be undignified for the High Priest to assume himself, such as sitting on the ground. Thus, one might have thought that the High Priest may be consoling those who have taken his own mourning upon themselves. The Gemara, however, rejects this premise, for no matter who displays the grief, it is still the High Priest who is in mourning and not others.

לֹא שָׁנוּ אֶלָּא מַלְכֵי יִשְׂרָאֵל **They did not teach this except with regard to the Kings of Israel.** It has been asked:

HALAKHAH

שׁוּרָה **A row.** "When a row of comforters forms in order to pass by a mourner and offer condolences, it should not be composed of less than ten people. The mourners themselves are not counted among the ten." (*Rambam, Sefer Shofetim, Hilkhot Evel* 13:1.)

לֹא שָׁנוּ אֶלָּא מַלְכֵי יִשְׂרָאֵל **They teach this except with regard to the Kings of Israel.** "Kings of Davidic descent may serve as judges, as well as be judged by others; they

יִשְׂרָאֵל, [1]אֲבָל מַלְכֵי בֵּית דָּוִד דָּן וְדָנִין אוֹתָן, [2]דִּכְתִיב "בֵּית דָּוִד כֹּה אָמַר ה׳ דִּינוּ לַבֹּקֶר מִשְׁפָּט". [3]וְאִי לָא דָּיְינִינַן לֵיהּ — אִינְהוּ הֵיכִי דָּיְינֵי? [4]וְהָכְתִיב "הִתְקוֹשְׁשׁוּ וָקוֹשׁוּ", [5]וְאָמַר רֵישׁ לָקִישׁ: קַשֵּׁט עַצְמְךָ וְאַחַר כָּךְ קַשֵּׁט אֲחֵרִים.

[6]אֶלָּא מַלְכֵי יִשְׂרָאֵל, מַאי טַעְמָא לֹא? [7]מִשּׁוּם מַעֲשֶׂה שֶׁהָיָה. [8]דְּעַבְדֵּיהּ דְּיַנַּאי מַלְכָּא קְטַל נַפְשָׁא, [9]אֲמַר לְהוּ שִׁמְעוֹן בֶּן שָׁטַח לַחֲכָמִים: "תְּנוּ עֵינֵיכֶם בּוֹ, וּנְדוּנֶנּוּ". [10]שָׁלְחוּ לֵיהּ: "עַבְדְּךָ קְטַל נַפְשָׁא". [11]שַׁדְרֵיהּ לְהוּ. [12]שָׁלְחוּ לֵיהּ: תָּא אַנְתְּ נַמִי לְהָכָא, [13]׳וְהוּעַד בִּבְעָלָיו׳, אָמְרָה תּוֹרָה — [14]יָבֹא בַּעַל הַשּׁוֹר וְיַעֲמוֹד עַל שׁוֹרוֹ". [15]אֲתָא וִיתֵיב. [16]אָמַר לֵיהּ שִׁמְעוֹן בֶּן שָׁטַח:

LITERAL TRANSLATION

of Israel. [1]But the Kings of the House of David may judge and be judged, [2]for it is written: "O House of David, thus says the Lord: Execute judgment in the morning." [3]And if we may not judge him, how may they judge? [4]Behold it is written: "Gather yourselves together, and gather together." [5]And Resh Lakish said: Adorn yourself, and then adorn others. [6]But the Kings of Israel, what is the reason [that they may] not? [7]Because of an incident that occurred. [8]For a slave of King Yannai killed someone. [9]Shimon ben Shataḥ said to the Sages: "Set your eyes upon him, and we shall judge him." [10]They sent [a message] to him: "Your slave killed someone." [11]He sent him to them. [12]They sent [another message] to him: "You too must come here. [13]The Torah said: 'And its owner had been warned' — [14]let the owner of the ox come and stand by his ox." [15]He came and sat. [16]Shimon ben Shataḥ said to him:

TRANSLATION AND COMMENTARY

[1]**But the kings of the House of David** may sit on a court and **judge** others **and they may be judged,** [2]**for it is written** (Jeremiah 21:12): **"O House of David, thus says the Lord: Execute judgment in the morning."** Since Scripture explicitly calls for these kings to judge others, they may be judged as well, [3]for **if we may not judge** a king of Davidic descent, then **how may they judge others?** [4]For **behold it is written** (Zephaniah 2:1): **"Gather yourselves together, and gather together** others [הִתְקוֹשְׁשׁוּ וָקוֹשׁוּ]," which, as we saw earlier in the chapter (18a), [5]**Resh Lakish explained** as following: First **adorn** (קַשֵּׁט) **yourself** with a virtuous character, **and then** you may seek to **adorn others** by demanding the same of them. So, too, we assume that a king of Davidic descent must be capable of being judged if the Torah deems him worthy of judging others.

אֶלָּא [6]The Gemara asks: **But what,** then, **is the reason** that, unlike kings descended from David, **the Kings of Israel** may **not** serve as judges or be judged? [7]The Gemara answers: This is **because of an incident that occurred.** [8]For once **King Yannai's slave killed someone.** [9]**Shimon ben Shataḥ,** who at the time was the Nasi of the Sanhedrin, **said to the Sages: "Set your eyes on** that slave **and let us judge him** with no regard for his status as the king's slave." [10]**They** immediately **sent** a message **to** the king, saying: **"Your slave killed someone.** Hand him over for judgment." [11]The king acceded to the request and **sent the** slave **to** the Sages. [12]The Sages then **sent** the king a second message, saying: **"You, too, must come here** and stand before the court, [13]for **the Torah said** (Exodus 21:29): 'If the ox was a goring kind from days gone by, **and its owner had been warned,** yet he did not watch it, and it killed a man or a woman.' [14]From this verse we learn that, during the trial, **the owner of the ox should come and stand by his ox,** since it is his property. So, too, in the case of your slave, who if convicted will be killed, we require you to be present at the time of testimony." [15]Acceding to this request as well, Yannai **came** to court **and sat** down. [16]**Shimon ben Shataḥ**

RASHI

תנו עיניכם — לדונו כדין ולא תחניפו ולא תשאו פניו.

SAGES

שִׁמְעוֹן בֶּן שָׁטַח Shimon ben Shataḥ. Nasi of the Sanhedrin during the reign of Alexander Yannai.

Shimon ben Shataḥ was one of the most important Jewish leaders of his time and one of the greatest teachers of the Oral Law. He was a demanding leader who insisted upon the precise observance of the Torah, and he acted effectively against any effort to challenge the authority of the accepted Halakhah, whether in response to outside pressure or to sectarians of any kind from within the camp.

He extirpated sorcery from the land through special ordinances, and he also settled the laws for taking testimony. Similarly, he accorded greater authority to a wife's marriage contract. Because of his insistence upon the authority of the Sanhedrin, he even summoned the king to judgment and commanded him to act like an ordinary citizen in giving respect to the court. For this reason and many others, he found himself in conflict with King Yannai, and on several occasions was forced to hide for fear of the king's revenge. However, he did not succumb to threats, nor was he swayed by honors and flattery. When people conspired and testified falsely against his son, he and his son accepted punishment in order to avoid overthrowing the standard laws.

Although his sister was Queen Shlomzion, the wife of Yannai, Shimon ben Shataḥ nevertheless worked for a living at something to do with the treatment of leather. After Yannai's death, his widow Shlomzion continued to rule the country. During her reign, domestic rule was in Shimon ben Shataḥ's hands, and this period is regarded as a fortunate one in Jewish history.

NOTES

Since it is apparent from the Gemara that initially all kings could judge or be judged, why would we not assume that the Rabbinic decree taught in our Mishnah does not apply to all kings? *Rosh* answers that since the verse in Jeremiah states explicitly that Kings of the House of David may judge others, the Rabbis would not have declared them unfit to do so.

תְּנוּ עֵינֵיכֶם בּוֹ, וּנְדוּנֶנּוּ Set your eyes on him, and let us judge him. The question has been raised: Shimon ben Shataḥ was King Yannai's brother-in-law. How, then, could he have served on a court which was to determine Yannai's liability for the actions of his slave? *Ḥamra Veḥaye* answers that Shimon ben Shataḥ participated only in the capacity of an observer, while it was his colleagues who actually heard the case.

HALAKHAH

may also testify against others and be testified against. But kings who are not of Davidic descent may neither serve as judges nor be judged by others; nor may they testify against others or be testified against, for there is concern that they will not submit to the court's decision." (*Rambam, Sefer Shofetim, Hilkhot Sanhedrin* 2:5; *Hilkhot Melakhim* 3:7.)

”יַנַּאי הַמֶּלֶךְ! [1]עֲמוֹד עַל רַגְלֶיךָ וְיָעִידוּ בְּךָ. וְלֹא לְפָנֵינוּ אַתָּה עוֹמֵד, [2]אֶלָּא לִפְנֵי מִי שֶׁאָמַר וְהָיָה הָעוֹלָם אַתָּה עוֹמֵד, [3]שֶׁנֶּאֱמַר ׳וְעָמְדוּ שְׁנֵי הָאֲנָשִׁים אֲשֶׁר לָהֶם הָרִיב וגו׳״. [4]אָמַר לוֹ: ׳לֹא כְּשֶׁתֹּאמַר אַתָּה, אֶלָּא כְּמָה שֶׁיֹּאמְרוּ חֲבֵרֶיךָ׳. [19B] [5]נִפְנָה לִימִינוֹ, כָּבְשׁוּ פְּנֵיהֶם בַּקַּרְקַע. [6]נִפְנָה לִשְׂמֹאלוֹ, וְכָבְשׁוּ פְּנֵיהֶם בַּקַּרְקַע. [7]אָמַר לָהֶן שִׁמְעוֹן בֶּן שָׁטַח: ׳בַּעֲלֵי מַחֲשָׁבוֹת אַתֶּם. יָבֹא בַּעַל מַחֲשָׁבוֹת וְיִפָּרַע מִכֶּם׳! [8]מִיָּד בָּא גַּבְרִיאֵל וַחֲבָטָן בַּקַּרְקַע, וָמֵתוּ. [9]בְּאוֹתָהּ שָׁעָה אָמְרוּ: ”מֶלֶךְ לֹא דָּן וְלֹא דָּנִין אוֹתוֹ, לֹא מֵעִיד וְלֹא מְעִידִין אוֹתוֹ״. [10]”לֹא חוֹלֵץ וְלֹא חוֹלְצִין וכו׳״.

LITERAL TRANSLATION

"King Yannai! [1]Stand on your feet and they will testify against you. [2]And it is not before us whom you are standing, but rather it is before He Who spoke and brought the world into being that you stand, [3]as it is said: 'And the two men unto whom is the dispute etc.'" [4]He said to him: "Not as you say, but rather as your colleagues say." [19B] [5]He turned to his right, [and] they cast their faces toward the ground. [6]He turned to his left, and they cast their faces toward the ground. [7]Shimon ben Shataḥ said to them: "You are masters of [deep] thought. Let the Master of thoughts come and exact [payment] from you!" [8]Immediately, Gabriel came and struck them to the ground, and they died. [9]At that time, they said: "The king may not judge nor be judged. He may not testify nor be testified against."

[10]"He may not perform *ḥalitzah*, and *ḥalitzah* is not performed [with his wife], etc."

TRANSLATION AND COMMENTARY

said to him: "King Yannai! [1]**Stand on your feet** so that the witnesses may **testify against you.** [2]And know **it is** ultimately **not before us that you are standing, but rather it is before He Who spoke and brought the world into being that you stand,** [3]**as is it said** (Deuteronomy 19:17): **'And the two men unto whom is the dispute** shall stand before the Lord, before the priests and the judges who shall be in those days.'" [4]The king **said to him:** "I shall **not** act **as you say, but rather as your colleagues say.** If they agree that I must stand, then I will do so." [19B] [5]Shimon ben Shataḥ **turned to** the judges sitting on **his right**, expecting them to express their support, but **they cast their faces toward the ground** in fear of the king. [6]He then **turned to** the judges sitting on **his left, but they** too **cast their faces toward the ground.** [7]**Shimon ben Shataḥ said to** the judges: "Since **you are** such **masters of** deep, calculating **thought,** who on account of fear hesitate to carry out justice, **let the** ultimate **Master of thoughts come and exact** payment **from you** all!" [8]**Immediately,** the angel **Gabriel came and struck** those judges **to the ground, and they died.** [9]**At that time**, to avoid similar occurrences, the Sages **said: "The king may not** sit on a court and **judge** others, **nor may he be judged.** The king **may** also **not** appear before a court and **testify** against others, **nor may he be testified against."**

לֹא חוֹלֵץ [10]Our Mishnah continues: "If the king's brother died childless, the king **may not perform *ḥalitzah*** with his widow because of the indignity involved, and if the king died childless, his brother **may not perform *ḥalitzah*** with his widowed wife. Since she is forbidden to remarry, there is no reason to release her from the levirate tie. Rabbi Yehudah disagrees and says: If the king wishes to forgo his honor

RASHI

ויעידו בך — שעבדך הרג את הנפש דעבדו כחמורו, והפסד ממון הוא לו, לפיכך צריך לדונו בפניו. **נפנה** — שמעון לימינו לידע אם יאמרו כמותו. — **כבשו פניהם** — שהיו יראין ממנו. **בעל מחשבות** — הקדוש ברוך הוא. **ולא חולצין לאשתו** — מפני שאסורה לינשא. **חליצה** — גנאי היא לו לצאת לבית דין ותהא רוקקת לפניו, וייבום גנאי הוא לו לקום על שם אחיו.

NOTES

עֲמוֹד עַל רַגְלֶיךָ Stand on your feet. The Rishonim raise an objection: We learn elsewhere that the court may allow litigants to sit during litigation proceedings as long as both parties do so. Why, then, did Shimon ben Shataḥ insist that King Yannai stand rather than order the other party to sit with him? Moreover, a Torah scholar may be seated even if his opposing litigant stands. All the more so, then, should the king have been allowed to sit! Some suggest that Shimon ben Shataḥ insisted because Yannai sat down without being directed to do so, whereas even a Torah scholar must wait for the court's permission before seating himself. (*Ran, Rashba* in *Shevuot* 30a). Others argue that Shimon ben Shataḥ insisted that Yannai stand only while the verdict was being delivered, at which time all are required to stand — even a Torah scholar. (*Ran, Tosafot* in *Shevuot*). Others maintain that we do indeed distinguish between the requirement to honor a Torah scholar, which necessitates allowing him to sit even when his opponent is standing, and the Biblical duty to fear a king, which does not obligate the court at all, since judges are enjoined by the Torah to fear no one. (*Rabbi David,* cited by *Ran.*) It has also been suggested that Shimon ben Shetaḥ erred when he demanded that Yannai stand before the court, for the court could indeed have forgone its own honor and allowed the king to sit down (*Ran*).

לֹא חוֹלֵץ וכו׳ He may not perform *ḥalitzah*, etc. *Rambam* (*Hilkhot Melakhim* 2:3) explains that whoever cannot perform levirate marriage can also not perform *ḥalitzah*, and

SAGES

רַב אַשִׁי Rav Ashi. Born in the year that Rava died, he became one of the greatest Amoraim of Babylonia during the sixth generation. He edited the Babylonian Talmud and headed the yeshivah of Mata Meḥasya for sixty years. His main teacher was Rav Kahana. Rav Ashi's father-in-law was Rami bar Abba, and his son, Mar bar Rav Ashi, succeeded him. Another of his sons, Rav Sama, was also a Sage.

TRANSLATION AND COMMENTARY

and perform either *ḥalitzah* or levirate marriage, he may do so and he will be remembered for good." The Gemara raises an objection against Rabbi Yehudah: [1]**Is it** really **so,** that the king may perform *ḥalitzah* in spite of the indignity involved? [2]**But surely Rav Ashi said: Even according to the** Sage **who said** (*Kiddushin* 32b) that in the case of **a Nasi** of the Sanhedrin **who waived the honor** due him, **his honor is waived,** but in the case of [3]**a king who waived his honor, his honor is not waived.** [4]**For it is said** in reference to appointing a king (Deuteronomy 17:15): **"You shall surely set a king over you,"** implying through the emphatic double verb (שׂוֹם תָּשִׂים — "you shall surely set") [5]**that his fear shall be upon you** at all times. So why is he allowed to waive his dignity when it comes to performing *ḥalitzah*?

מִצְוָה שָׁאנֵי [6]The Gemara answers: When a king forgoes his honor in order to perform **a mitzvah,** this **is different** from other situations, since upholding the honor of the Torah can never be construed as an indignity.

וְאֵין נוֹשְׂאִין [7]We learn in the next portion of the Mishnah: "If the king died, **no one** — not even another king — **may marry** his widow. Rabbi Yehudah disagrees and says: A king may marry the widow of another king, for we find in the case of King David that he married the widow of King Saul, as the verse states (II Samuel 12:8): 'And I gave unto you your master's house, and your master's wives into your bosom.'" [8]**It was taught** in a Baraita: "The Sages **said to Rabbi Yehudah:** There is no support for your position from the verse that you bring, for the expression נְשֵׁי אֲדֹנֶיךָ need not be understood as 'your master's wives.' Rather, it can be understood as 'your master's women,' [9]and as referring to **women who were fit for** David to take **from the House of the King**, unlike Saul's widows who were forbidden to him. [10]**And who were** these women? **Merab and Michal,** the daughters of Saul."

שָׁאֲלוּ תַּלְמִידָיו [11]It was taught in another Baraita: **"The disciples of Rabbi Yose asked him** the following question: [12]**How did David marry two sisters** — Merab and Michal — **in their lifetimes?** Surely the Torah forbids a man to marry his wife's sister while she is still alive and married to him! [13]Rabbi Yose **said to**

LITERAL TRANSLATION

[1]Is it so? [2]But surely Rav Ashi said: Even according to the one who said: A Nasi who waived his honor, his honor is waived; [3]a king who waived his honor, his honor is not waived, [4]for it is said: "You shall surely set a king over you" — [5]that his fear shall be upon you.

[6]A mitzvah is different.

[7]"And one may not marry, etc." [8]It was taught: "They said to Rabbi Yehudah: [9]Women who are fit for him from the House of the King. [10]And who are they? Merab and Michal."

[11]"The disciples of Rabbi Yose asked him: [12]How did David marry two sisters in their lifetimes? [13]He said to them: He married Michal

[1]אִינִי? [2]וְהָאָמַר רַב אַשִׁי: אֲפִילּוּ לְמַאן דְּאָמַר נָשִׂיא שֶׁמָּחַל עַל כְּבוֹדוֹ כְּבוֹדוֹ מָחוּל; [3]מֶלֶךְ שֶׁמָּחַל עַל כְּבוֹדוֹ אֵין כְּבוֹדוֹ מָחוּל, [4]שֶׁנֶּאֱמַר "שׂוֹם תָּשִׂים עָלֶיךָ מֶלֶךְ" — [5]שֶׁתְּהֵא אֵימָתוֹ עָלֶיךָ!

[6]מִצְוָה שָׁאנֵי.

[7]"וְאֵין נוֹשְׂאִין כו'". [8]תַּנְיָא: "אָמְרוּ לוֹ לְרַבִּי יְהוּדָה: [9]נָשִׁים הָרְאוּיוֹת לוֹ מִבֵּית הַמֶּלֶךְ. [10]וּמַאי נִינְהוּ? מֵירַב וּמִיכַל".

[11]שָׁאֲלוּ תַּלְמִידָיו אֶת רַבִּי יוֹסֵי: [12]הֵיאַךְ נָשָׂא דָּוִד שְׁתֵּי אֲחָיוֹת בְּחַיֵּיהֶן? [13]אָמַר לָהֶן: מִיכַל

RASHI

הא דרב אשי — בפרק קמא דקידושין (לב,ב). **הראויות לו** — המותרות לו, אבל נשיו של שאול לא.

NOTES

vice versa. Thus, since the king cannot perform *ḥalitzah* with his sister-in-law, it being undignified for him to do so, he can also not take her in levirate marriage. And since the king's brother cannot take the king's widow as his levirate wife, since she is forbidden to remarry, he can also not perform the *ḥalitzah* ceremony with her.

מִצְוָה שָׁאנֵי A mitzvah is different. The Sages who disagree with Rabbi Yehudah concede that, generally speaking, the king may waive the honors due him in order to perform a mitzvah. In this case, however, the indignity involved in proceeding with either *ḥalitzah* or levirate marriage is considered too great, even though it would enable a commandment to be performed (*Ran*). Others (*Rabbi David*, cited by *Ran*) suggest that, according to the Sages, the king

HALAKHAH

נָשִׂיא שֶׁמָּחַל עַל כְּבוֹדוֹ A Nasi who waived his honor. "If a Torah scholar, even a Nasi, waives the honors due him, one may act according to his desire. Nevertheless, it is commendable to preserve some outward sign of respect in relation to him," following the Gemara in tractate *Kiddushin*. (*Shulḥan Arukh, Yoreh De'ah* 244:14.)

מֶלֶךְ שֶׁמָּחַל עַל כְּבוֹדוֹ A king who waived his honor. The king may not perform *ḥalitzah* with his late brother's widow, for even if he is willing to waive the respect due him as a king, his wishes are not recognized," in accordance with the Sages of our Mishnah and against Rabbi Yehudah. (*Rambam, Sefer Shofetim, Hilkhot Melakhim* 2:3.)

TRANSLATION AND COMMENTARY

them: David only **married Michal after the death of Merab.** [1]But **Rabbi Yehoshua ben Korḥah says:** This was not the case. [2]Rather, David **had had a faulty betrothal with Merab** and thus was never legitimately married to her, leaving him free to marry Michal even while Merab was still alive. [3]**For it is said** (II Samuel 3:14) in David's appeal to Ish Bosheth, the son of Saul: **'Deliver my wife, Michal, whom I betrothed to me for a hundred foreskins of the Philistines.'"**

מַאי תַּלְמוּדָא [4]The Gemara asks: **What** exactly **is the proof** implicit in this verse that informs us of David's faulty betrothal to Merab? [5]**Rav Pappa said:** By his referring in the verse to **Michal** as **"my wife,"** [6]David seems to be implying that **Merab is not** and never was his **"wife,"** for their betrothal was executed in error.

מַאי קִידּוּשֵׁי טָעוּת [7]The Gemara now explains **what** was **faulty** about Merab's **betrothal:** When King Saul summoned forth warriors to combat Goliath, [8]**as it is written** (I Samuel 17:25): **"And the man who kills him, the king will enrich him with great riches,** and will give him his daughter, and make his father's house free in Israel," [9]David **went out and killed** Goliath. When he came to claim his reward, [10]Saul **said to him: "You have** something akin to **a loan with me,** for the riches in my possession that I promised Goliath's killer rightfully belong to you. Let us, therefore, consider a portion of those riches as payment due me for my daughter Merab's betrothal." Consequently, David, in lieu of betrothal money, waived his claim to part of the debt owed him by Saul. [11]The law states, however, that if **one betroths** a woman **with a debt** that she (or her father) owes him, **the betrothal is not valid.** Thus, David never properly executed his marriage to Merab. [12]Rather, Saul **went and gave her** in marriage **to Adriel** of Meholat, **for it is written** (I Samuel 18:19): **"And it came to pass at the time when Merab, Saul's daughter, should have been given to David,** that she was given to Adriel the Meholathite as a wife." [13]Subsequently, Saul went to David and **said to him: "If you wish that I should give you** my other daughter, **Michal,** in marriage, [14]you must first **go** and **bring me one hundred**

אַחַר מִיתַת מֵירַב נְשָׂאָהּ. [1]רַבִּי יְהוֹשֻׁעַ בֶּן קׇרְחָה אוֹמֵר: [2]קִידּוּשֵׁי טָעוּת הָיוּ לוֹ בְּמֵירַב, [3]שֶׁנֶּאֱמַר "תְּנָה אֶת אִשְׁתִּי אֶת מִיכַל אֲשֶׁר אֵרַשְׂתִּי לִי בְּמֵאָה עָרְלוֹת פְּלִשְׁתִּים". [4]מַאי תַּלְמוּדָא? [5]אָמַר רַב פַּפָּא: מִיכַל "אִשְׁתִּי", [6]וְלֹא מֵירַב "אִשְׁתִּי". [7]מַאי קִידּוּשֵׁי טָעוּת? [8]דִּכְתִיב: "וְהָיָה הָאִישׁ אֲשֶׁר יַכֶּנּוּ יַעְשְׁרֶנּוּ הַמֶּלֶךְ עֹשֶׁר גָּדוֹל" וגו'. [9]אֲזַל קַטְלֵיהּ. [10]אָמַר לוֹ: מִלְוָה אִית לָךְ גַּבַּאי, [11]וְהַמְקַדֵּשׁ בְּמִלְוָה, אֵינָהּ מְקוּדֶּשֶׁת. [12]אֲזַל יְהָבָהּ לְעַדְרִיאֵל, דִּכְתִיב, "וַיְהִי בְּעֵת תֵּת אֶת מֵירַב בַּת שָׁאוּל לְדָוִד" וגו'. [13]אָמַר לֵיהּ: "אִי בָּעֵית דְּאֶתֵּן לָךְ מִיכַל, [14]זִיל אַיְיתֵי לִי

LITERAL TRANSLATION

after the death of Merab. [1]Rabbi Yehoshua ben Korḥah says: [2]He had had a faulty (lit., 'mistaken') betrothal with Merab, [3]for it is said: 'Deliver my wife, Michal, whom I betrothed to me for a hundred foreskins of the Philistines.'"

[4]What is the proof (lit., "teaching")? [5]Rav Pappa said: Michal is "my wife," [6]but Merab is not "my wife."

[7]What faulty betrothal? [8]For it is written: "And the man who strikes him, the king will enrich him with great riches, etc." [9]He went [and] killed him. [10]He said to him: "You have a loan with me," [11]and [if] one betroths with a loan, she is not betrothed. [12]He went [and] gave her to Adriel, for it is written: "And it came to pass at the time when Merab, Saul's daughter, should have been given to David, [that she was given to Adriel the Meholathite to wife.]" [13]He said to him: "If you wish that I should give you Michal, [14]go bring me

RASHI

מלוה אית לך גבאי — עושר גדול, וקידושין אחרים לא קיבלתי.
בעת תת — כשהגיע עת לתתה לדוד נתנה לעדריאל.

SAGES

רַבִּי יְהוֹשֻׁעַ בֶּן קׇרְחָה Rabbi Yehoshua ben Korḥah. See *Sanhedrin,* Part I, p. 54.

NOTES

cannot participate in either of these two mitzvot, not because of his honor, for they would agree that he is allowed to forgo his honor in the pursuit of a mitzvah, but rather because others (in this case, his late brother's wife) are forbidden to demean him.

הַמְקַדֵּשׁ בְּמִלְוָה One who betroths with a loan. One of the ways that a man can betroth a woman is by giving her either money or an article worth money, such as a ring. The betrothal is valid even if what is given is worth only a perutah. Nevertheless, a man cannot betroth a woman by exempting her from repaying him a loan that he extended her, even if it amounts to a large sum of money. He must actually give her money (or an article worth money) to betroth her.

HALAKHAH

הַמְקַדֵּשׁ בְּמִלְוָה One who betroths with a loan. "If someone betroths a woman by forgoing a debt that she owes him, the betrothal is not valid," in accordance with the Gemara's ruling in tractate *Kiddushin.* (*Shulḥan Arukh, Even HaEzer* 28:7.)

מֵאָה עָרְלוֹת פְּלִשְׁתִּים״. [1]אֲזַל אַיְיתֵי לֵיהּ. [2]אֲמַר לֵיהּ: ״מִלְוֶה וּפְרוּטָה אִית לָךְ גַּבַּאי״. [3]שָׁאוּל סְבַר: מִלְוֶה וּפְרוּטָה — דַּעְתֵּיהּ אַמִּלְוֶה, [4]וְדָוִד סְבַר: מִלְוֶה וּפְרוּטָה — דַּעְתֵּיהּ אַפְּרוּטָה.

[5]וְאִיבָּעֵית אֵימָא: דְּכוּלֵּי עָלְמָא מִלְוֶה וּפְרוּטָה [6]דַּעְתֵּיהּ אַפְּרוּטָה, [7]שָׁאוּל סָבַר: לָא חֲזוּ וְלָא מִידֵּי, [8]וְדָוִד סָבַר: חֲזוּ לְכַלְבֵּי וְשׁוּנְרֵי.

[9]וְרַבִּי יוֹסֵי, הַאי, ״תְּנָה אֶת אִשְׁתִּי אֶת מִיכַל״, [10]מַאי דָּרֵישׁ בֵּיהּ?

[11]רַבִּי יוֹסֵי לְטַעֲמֵיהּ, [12]דְּתַנְיָא: ״רַבִּי יוֹסֵי הָיָה דּוֹרֵשׁ מִקְרָאוֹת מְעוּרָבִין. [13]כְּתִיב: ׳וַיִּקַּח הַמֶּלֶךְ אֶת שְׁנֵי בְּנֵי רִצְפָּה בַת אַיָּה אֲשֶׁר יָלְדָה לְשָׁאוּל אֶת אַרְמֹנִי

LITERAL TRANSLATION

one hundred foreskins of Philistine men." [1]He went [and] brought [them] to him. [2]He said to him: "You have a loan and a perutah with me." [3]Saul thought: A loan and a perutah — his mind is on the loan. [4]And David thought: A loan and a perutah — his mind is on the perutah.

[5]And if you wish, say that all (lit., "the whole world") agree that [in the case of] a loan and a perutah, [6]his mind is on the perutah. [7]Saul thought: They are not fit for anything. [8]And David thought: They are fit for dogs and cats.

[9]And Rabbi Yose, that "deliver my wife, Michal," [10]how does he expound it?

[11]Rabbi Yose [is consistent according] to his reasoning, [12]for it was taught: "Rabbi Yose would expound [these] confused passages [lit., 'mixed verses']. [13]It is written: 'And the king took the two sons of Ritzpah, the daughter of Aiah, whom she bore to Saul: Armoni

TRANSLATION AND COMMENTARY

foreskins of Philistine men." [1]David **went** out **and brought** Saul two hundred foreskins, and then asked for Michal. [2]Saul **said to him**: "Now **you have** both **a loan and a perutah** held **by me.** The loan consists of those riches that I still owe you for having killed Goliath, while the perutah represents the value of the foreskins that you have just given me. Let us consider a portion of the loan, together with the perutah that you actually gave me, as payment for my daughter Michal's betrothal to you." [3]**Saul thought** that when a man betroths a woman on the basis of **a** large **loan** and **an** additional **perutah, his mind is** inclined to attach importance **to the loan,** which is worth much more. Thus, he assumed Michal's betrothal to be no more valid than Merab's and did not refrain from later giving her in marriage to Palti, the son of Laish (I Samuel 25:44). [4]**David,** however, **thought** that when a man betroths a woman on the basis of **a loan and a perutah, his mind is** inclined to attach importance **to the perutah,** which was given substantively. Thus, David considered his marriage to Michal valid.

וְאִיבָּעֵית אֵימָא [5]The argument between David and Shmuel can also be understood differently: **If you wish,** you can **say that** both Saul and David are of the opinion **that** when a man betroths a woman on the basis of **a loan** owed him **and a perutah,** [6]**his mind is** more inclined to attach importance **to the perutah.** [7]Nevertheless, **Saul thought** that the foreskins that David brought him **were not fit for anything,** and thus were not even worth a perutah. Saul meant to mislead David. [8]However, **David thought** that since the foreskins **were fit** as food **for dogs and cats,** they were worth a perutah and were acceptable as payment for Michal's betrothal.

וְרַבִּי יוֹסֵי [9]The Gemara now raises a question according to **Rabbi Yose,** who said that David was legitimately married to Merab, but only married her sister Michal after she had died. Regarding **that** verse, in which David states, **"Deliver my wife, Michal,"** [10]implying that Michal was his wife while Merab was not, **how does** Rabbi Yose **expound its** meaning?

רַבִּי יוֹסֵי [11]The Gemara anwers: **Rabbi Yose** is actually loyal **to his** own **reasoning,** as stated elsewhere. [12]**For it was taught** in a Baraita: **"Rabbi Yose would expound** these **confusing passages** as follows: From the Book of Samuel it appears that Michal was married to two other men, aside from David: [13]**It is written** (II Samuel 21:8): **'And the king took the two sons of Ritzpah, the daughter of Aiah, whom she bore to Saul: Armoni**

RASHI

מלוה ופרוטה — מלוה עושר גדול שנתחייבתי לך בשביל גלית, ופרוטה שוה כסף שקבלתי ממך בהללו ערלות פלשתים. **שאול סבר דעתיה** — דמקדש למקדש במלוה דחשיבא, הלכך לאו קידושי נינהו, ואזל ויהבה לפלטי בן ליש. **ודוד סבר** — דעתיה אפרוטה, משום הכי קרי לה אשתי. **האי תנה את אשתי את מיכל** — דמשמע זו אשתי ולא מירב אשתי. **מאי דריש ביה** — רבי יוסי דלא דריש ולא מירב אשתי. **לטעמיה** — דדריש ממקרא מעורבב כדלקמן, מה מיכל אשתי אף מירב אשתי.

HALAKHAH

מִלְוֶה וּפְרוּטָה A loan and a perutah. "If a man who was owed money by a woman gave her an additional perutah and said that he wished to betroth her with both the outstanding debt owed him and the perutah, the betrothal is valid," in accordance with the Gemara's ruling in tractate *Kiddushin*. (*Shulhan Arukh, Even HaEzer* 28:14.)

TRANSLATION AND COMMENTARY

and Mephibosheth; and the five sons of Michal, the daughter of Saul, **whom she bore to Adriel** the son of Barzillai **the Meholathite.'** ¹But did Saul really give Michal to Adriel? ²**Is it not the case that he gave her to Palti the son of Laish,** ³**for it is written** (I Samuel 25:44): **'And Saul had given Michal his daughter, David's wife, to Palti the son of Laish,** who was from Gallim'? Why, then, does the verse say that she was given to Adriel? ⁴**Rather,** the verse means to **equate Merab's betrothal to Adriel with Michal's betrothal to Palti.** ⁵**Just as Michal's betrothal to Palti** was carried out **in sin,** since Michal was certainly married to David at the time, ⁶**so too** was **Merab's betrothal to Adriel** carried out **in sin,** as she, too, was married to David at the time."

וְרַבִּי יְהוֹשֻׁעַ בֶּן קָרְחָה ⁷The Gemara now raises a question according to **Rabbi Yehoshua ben Korḥah,** who disagrees with Rabbi Yose and maintains that David was never legitimately married to Merab, must surely **also** explain the anomaly in the verse, ⁸for **it is surely written: "And the five sons of Michal the daughter of Saul,** whom she bore to Adriel the son of Barzillai the Meholathite," and we know that it was Merab who married Adriel!

אָמַר לָךְ ⁹The Gemara answers: **Rabbi Yehoshua would say to you: Did Michal** indeed **bear** children to Adriel? ¹⁰**But surely Merab bore** those children! ¹¹Indeed, **Merab bore** them to Adriel, but after she died **Michal raised** them. ¹²**Therefore the children were called by** Michal's **name.** ¹³This is in order **to teach you that whoever raises an orphan in his home,** Scripture ascribes **to him** the same status **as if he had begotten him.**

חֲנִינָא קְרָא ¹⁴The Gemara now quotes several other Scriptual sources to support the idea that whoever raises another's child is valued as if he were the natural parent. The following is **a mnemonic** device for remembering the sequence of these sources: **"Ḥanina called, Yoḥanan and his wife, Elazar and redemption, and Shmuel in my studies."**

LITERAL TRANSLATION

and Mephibosheth; and the five sons of Michal, the daughter of Saul, whom she bore to Adriel [the son of Barzillai] the Meholathite.' ¹But did he give her to Adriel? ²Is it not the case that he gave her to Palti the son of Laish, ³for it is written: 'And Saul had given Michal his daughter, David's wife, to Palti the son of Laish, etc.'? ⁴Rather, it equates Merab's betrothal to Adriel with Michal's betrothal to Palti. ⁵Just as Michal's betrothal to Palti [was] in sin, ⁶so too [was] Merab's betrothal to Adriel in sin."

⁷And Rabbi Yehoshua ben Korḥah also, ⁸it is surely written: "And the five sons of Michal the daughter of Saul."

⁹Rabbi Yehoshua would say to you: Did Michal bear [them]? ¹⁰But surely Merab bore [them]! ¹¹Merab bore [them] and Michal raised [them]. ¹²Therefore, they were called by her name, ¹³to teach you that whoever raises an orphan in his home, Scripture ascribes to him as if he had begotten him.

¹⁴"Ḥanina called, Yoḥanan and his wife, Elazar and redemption, and Shmuel in my studies" — a mnemonic.

וְאֶת מְפִיבֹשֶׁת וְאֶת חֲמֵשֶׁת בְּנֵי מִיכַל אֲשֶׁר יָלְדָה לְעַדְרִיאֵל הַמְּחֹלָתִי' וְגו'. ¹וְכִי לְעַדְרִיאֵל נְתָנָהּ? ²וַהֲלֹא לְפַלְטִי בֶּן לַיִשׁ נְתָנָהּ! ³דִּכְתִיב: 'וְשָׁאוּל נָתַן אֶת מִיכַל בִּתּוֹ אֵשֶׁת דָּוִד לְפַלְטִי בֶן לַיִשׁ' וְגו'! ⁴אֶלָּא, מַקִּישׁ קִידּוּשֵׁי מֵירַב לְעַדְרִיאֵל לְקִידּוּשֵׁי מִיכַל לְפַלְטִי. ⁵מַה קִּידּוּשֵׁי מִיכַל לְפַלְטִי בַּעֲבֵירָה, ⁶אַף קִידּוּשֵׁי מֵירַב לְעַדְרִיאֵל בַּעֲבֵירָה".

⁷וְרַבִּי יְהוֹשֻׁעַ בֶּן קָרְחָה נַמִי, ⁸הָכְתִיב: "אֶת חֲמֵשֶׁת בְּנֵי מִיכַל בַּת שָׁאוּל".

⁹אָמַר לָךְ רַבִּי יְהוֹשֻׁעַ: וְכִי מִיכַל יָלְדָה? ¹⁰וַהֲלֹא מֵירַב יָלְדָה! ¹¹מֵירַב יָלְדָה וּמִיכַל גִּידְּלָה. ¹²לְפִיכָךְ נִקְרְאוּ עַל שְׁמָהּ. ¹³לְלַמֶּדְךָ שֶׁכָּל הַמְגַדֵּל יָתוֹם בְּתוֹךְ בֵּיתוֹ, מַעֲלֶה עָלָיו הַכָּתוּב כְּאִילּוּ יְלָדוֹ.

¹⁴חֲנִינָא קְרָא, יוֹחָנָן וְאִשְׁתּוֹ, אֶלְעָזָר וּגְאוּלָה, וּשְׁמוּאֵל בְּלִימּוּדַי, סִימָן.

RASHI

קדושי מיכל לפלטי — פשיטא לן דבעבירה, דהא כתיב: "אשתי מיכל", וקיימא לן (קידושין מז,א): דעתיה אפרוטה, דנת קידושין היא.

NOTES

כָּל הַמְגַדֵּל יָתוֹם בְּתוֹךְ בֵּיתוֹ **Whoever raises an orphan in his home.** It has been suggested that the Scriptural quotations that are recorded here in support of this position add some new element to the discussion: The first example is Michal, who raised her late sister's children. However, since raising a motherless child confers qualties of natural parenthood in any event, this example is rather ordinary. Rabbi Ḥanina therefore mentions Naomi, who helped Ruth raise her newborn son, who was orphaned before birth (according to Midrashic tradition) on the death of his father Boaz. Rabbi Yoḥanan goes even further and shows that even one who raises a child who is merely separated from his parents, such as Bithiah, who raised Moses after he was deposited on the Nile, is still viewed by Scripture as meriting the status of a natural parent. Rabbi Elazar then shows how this status is extended by Scripture to even one

SAGES

רַבִּי חֲנִינָא Rabbi Ḥanina. A first-generation Palestinian Amora. See *Sanhedrin*, Part I, p. 16.

רַבִּי יוֹחָנָן Rabbi Yoḥanan. See *Sanhedrin*, Part I, p. 46.

רַבִּי אֶלְעָזָר Rabbi Elazar. In the Talmud, citations of Rabbi Elazar with no patronymic refer to Rabbi Elazar ben Pedat, an Amora of the second generation. He was born in Eretz Israel, where he eventually succeeded to Rabbi Yoḥanan's position as head of the Tiberias Yeshivah. In Babylonia, he was a student of both Rav and Shmuel. His teacher in Eretz Israel was Rabbi Ḥanina bar Ḥama. He also studied with Rabbi Oshaya, but his main teacher was Rabbi Yoḥanan, and in time he came to be considered his colleague. He was given the honorific title of מָרָא — master — of Eretz Israel. Many Sages transmit teachings in his name, especially Rabbi Abbahu. He did not live long after Rabbi Yoḥanan died. We know that he had sons who died during his lifetime. His only son to survive was Rabbi Pedat, who was the Amora (translator) in Rabbi Assi's yeshivah.

TRANSLATION AND COMMENTARY

רַבִּי חֲנִינָא [1] **Rabbi Ḥanina says:** The value attached to raising someone else's child is learned **from here** (Ruth 4:17): [2] **"And the neighbors called him a name, saying:** [3] **There is a son born to Naomi."** [4] Now, **did Naomi indeed bear** this child? [5] **But surely it was Ruth who bore him!** [6] **Rather, Ruth bore the child and Naomi raised him.** [7] **Therefore, the child was called by** Naomi's **name,** as "a son born to Naomi."

רַבִּי יוֹחָנָן [8] **Rabbi Yoḥanan said:** Learn the idea **from here** (I Chronicles 4:18): **"And his wife Ha-Jehudijah bore Jered the father of Gedor,** and Ḥever the father of Sokho, and Jekuthiel the father of Zanoaḥ. [9] **And these are the sons of Bithiah the daughter of Pharaoh whom Mered took."** [10] Now **Mered is** actually **Caleb** the son of Jephunneh. [11] So **why is his name** here given as **Mered?** [12] He was given that name **because** along with Joshua **he rebelled** (מָרַד) **against the counsel of the spies** who dissuaded Israelites from conquering Eretz Israel. His wife Bithiah, the daughter of Pharaoh, is referred to at the beginning of the verse as Ha-Jehudijah (meaning "the Jewess") as a way of honoring her decision to renounce idolatry and embrace the faith of Israel. [13] Nevertheless, **did Bithiah** the daughter of Pharaoh really **bear** those children? As explained elsewhere (*Megillah* 13a), the names Jered, Gedor, Ḥever, Sokho, Jekuthiel and Zanoaḥ are all allusions to Moses! [14] **But surely Jochebed,** the mother of Moses, **bore him!** [15] **Rather, Jochebed bore** the child **and Bithiah** the daughter of Pharaoh **raised him.** [16] **Therefore, the child was called by** Bithiah's **name,** as if she had actually given birth to him.

רַבִּי אֶלְעָזָר [17] **Rabbi Elazar said:** It is **from here** (Psalms 77:16) that we learn this idea: [18] **"You have with Your arm redeemed Your people, the sons of Jacob and Joseph."** Why does the verse refer to the people of Israel who were redeemed from Egypt as the sons of both Jacob and Joseph? [19] **Did Joseph** really **sire** the twelve tribes? [20] **But surely it was Jacob who sired them!** [21] **Rather, Jacob sired** them **and Joseph provided** for them during their sojourn in Egypt. [22] **Therefore, they were** all **called by** Joseph's **name,** as if they were his actual sons.

LITERAL TRANSLATION

[1] Rabbi Ḥanina says: From here: [2] "And the neighbors called him a name, saying: [3] There is a son born to Naomi." [4] Did Naomi bear [him]? [5] But surely Ruth bore [him]! [6] Rather, Ruth bore [him] and Naomi raised [him]. [7] Therefore, he was called by her name.

[8] Rabbi Yoḥanan said: From here: "And his wife Ha-Jehudijah bore Jered the father of Gedor, etc. [9] And these are the sons of Bithiah the daughter of Pharaoh whom Mered took." [10] Mered is Caleb. [11] And why is his name called Mered (rebel)? [12] Because he rebelled against the counsel of the spies. [13] Did Bithiah bear [him]? [14] But surely Jochebed bore [him]! [15] Rather, Jochebed bore [him] and Bithiah raised [him]. [16] Therefore, he is called by her name.

[17] Rabbi Elazar said: From here: [18] "You have with [Your] arm redeemed Your people, the sons of Jacob and Joseph." [19] Did Joseph sire [them]? [20] But surely Jacob sired [them]! [21] Rather, Jacob sired [them] and Joseph provided [for them]. [22] Therefore they were called by his name.

---

[1] רַבִּי חֲנִינָא אוֹמֵר: מֵהָכָא: [2] "וַתִּקְרֶאנָה לוֹ הַשְּׁכֵנוֹת שֵׁם, לֵאמֹר: [3] יֻלַּד בֵּן לְנָעֳמִי". [4] וְכִי נָעֳמִי יָלְדָה? [5] וַהֲלֹא רוּת יָלְדָה! [6] אֶלָּא, רוּת יָלְדָה וְנָעֳמִי גִּידְּלָה. [7] לְפִיכָךְ נִקְרָא עַל שְׁמָהּ.

[8] רַבִּי יוֹחָנָן אָמַר: מֵהָכָא: "וְאִשְׁתּוֹ הַיְהֻדִיָּה יָלְדָה אֶת יֶרֶד אֲבִי גְדוֹר וְגוֹ'. [9] וְאֵלֶּה בְּנֵי בִתְיָה בַת פַּרְעֹה אֲשֶׁר לָקַח (לוֹ) מָרֶד". [10] מֶרֶד זֶה כָּלֵב. [11] וְלָמָּה נִקְרָא שְׁמוֹ מֶרֶד? [12] שֶׁמָּרַד בַּעֲצַת מְרַגְּלִים. [13] וְכִי בִתְיָה יָלְדָה? [14] וַהֲלֹא יוֹכֶבֶד יָלְדָה! [15] אֶלָּא, יוֹכֶבֶד יָלְדָה וּבִתְיָה גִּידְּלָה, [16] לְפִיכָךְ נִקְרָא עַל שְׁמָהּ.

[17] רַבִּי אֶלְעָזָר אָמַר: מֵהָכָא: [18] "גָּאַלְתָּ בִּזְרוֹעַ עַמֶּךָ בְּנֵי יַעֲקֹב וְיוֹסֵף סֶלָה". [19] וְכִי יוֹסֵף יָלַד? [20] וַהֲלֹא יַעֲקֹב יָלַד. [21] אֶלָּא, יַעֲקֹב יָלַד וְיוֹסֵף כִּילְכֵּל. [22] לְפִיכָךְ נִקְרְאוּ עַל שְׁמוֹ.

RASHI

ואשתו היהודית — בכלב בן יפונה משתעי קרא, "יהודית" — על שם שכפרה בעבודה זרה ומתגיירת — שכל הכופר בעבודה זרה נקרא "יהודי", דכתיב (דניאל ג): איתי גוברין יהודאין וגו'. ירד אביגדור — כולן שמותן של משה הן. מרד — כלב שמרד בעצת מרגלים.

NOTES

who merely provides financial support for a child whose parent is still living, as in the case of Joseph, who maintained his family in Egypt and thereby merited that they be called the "children of Joseph." Rabbi Shmuel bar Naḥmani concludes the discussion with support for the idea that teaching another's child Torah qualifies one as well for the status of fatherhood, even though spiritual sustenance does not satisfy a child's physical needs (*Rabbi Ḥayyim Vital*).

TRANSLATION AND COMMENTARY

אָמַר [1] **Rabbi Shmuel bar Naḥmani said in the name of Rabbi Yonatan: Whoever teaches his friend's son Torah,** [2] **Scripture ascribes to him** the same status **as if he had begotten him,** [3] **for it is stated** (Numbers 3:1): **"And these are the generations of Aaron and Moses."** [4] Immediately after this it **is written: "And these are the names of the sons of Aaron:** Nadab the firstborn, and Abihu, Eleazar, and Ithamar." The fact that in the previous verse the generations of Aaron are associated with Moses comes [5] **to say to you** that **Aaron sired** them **but Moses taught** them Torah. [6] **Therefore they were called by** Moses' **name** as well, as if he had sired them.

לָכֵן [7] The Gemara brings a related Midrash: The verse states (Isaiah 29:22): **"Therefore thus says the Lord to the house of Jacob, who redeemed Abraham."** [8] It may be asked: **Where do we find regarding Jacob that he redeemed Abraham?** [9] **Rav Yehudah said:** We find **that he redeemed him from the anguish of child rearing,** for Jacob accepted upon himself the burden and responsibility of raising the twelve tribes out of which came the innumerable seed promised by God to Abraham. [10] **And this is** the meaning of **what is written** in the continuation of the verse cited above: **"Jacob shall not now be ashamed;** neither shall his face now grow pale." [11] **"Jacob shall not now be ashamed" — because of his father.** [12] **"Neither shall his face now grow pale" — because of his father's father,** for he proudly fulfilled the duty that they passed on to him.

כְּתִיב ״פַּלְטִי״ [13] The Gemara now turns its attention to Palti the son of Laish, who took David's wife, Michal, at the urging of her father, King Saul. In one place his name **is written** as **"Palti** the son of Laish" (I Samuel 25:44), [14] whereas in another place **it is written** as **"Paltiel** the son of Laish" (II Samuel 3:15). [15] **Rabbi Yoḥanan**

[1] אָמַר רַבִּי שְׁמוּאֵל בַּר נַחְמָנִי אָמַר רַבִּי יוֹנָתָן: כָּל הַמְלַמֵּד בֶּן חֲבֵירוֹ תּוֹרָה, [2] מַעֲלֶה עָלָיו הַכָּתוּב כְּאִילּוּ יְלָדוֹ, [3] שֶׁנֶּאֱמַר ״וְאֵלֶּה תּוֹלְדֹת אַהֲרֹן וּמֹשֶׁה״. [4] וּכְתִיב ״וְאֵלֶּה שְׁמוֹת בְּנֵי אַהֲרֹן״. [5] לוֹמַר לְךָ: אַהֲרֹן יָלַד וּמֹשֶׁה לִימֵּד. [6] לְפִיכָךְ נִקְרְאוּ עַל שְׁמוֹ.

[7] ״לָכֵן כֹּה אָמַר ה׳ אֶל בֵּית יַעֲקֹב אֲשֶׁר פָּדָה אֶת אַבְרָהָם״. [8] וְכִי הֵיכָן מָצִינוּ בְּיַעֲקֹב שֶׁפְּדָאוֹ לְאַבְרָהָם? [9] אָמַר רַב יְהוּדָה: שֶׁפְּדָאוֹ מִצַּעַר גִּידּוּל בָּנִים. [10] וְהַיְינוּ דִּכְתִיב ״עַתָּה יֵבוֹשׁ יַעֲקֹב וגו׳״. [11] ״לֹא עַתָּה יֵבוֹשׁ יַעֲקֹב״ — מֵאָבִיו, [12] ״וְלֹא עַתָּה פָּנָיו יֶחֱוָרוּ״ — מֵאֲבִי אָבִיו.

[13] כְּתִיב ״פַּלְטִי״. [14] וּכְתִיב ״פַּלְטִיאֵל״. [15] אָמַר רַבִּי יוֹחָנָן:

LITERAL TRANSLATION

[1] Rabbi Shmuel bar Naḥmani said in the name of Rabbi Yonatan: Whoever teaches his friend's son Torah, [2] Scripture ascribes it to him as if he had begotten him, [3] for it is stated: "And these are the generations of Aaron and Moses." [4] And it is written: "And these are the names of the sons of Aaron." [5] [This is] to say to you [that] Aaron sired [them] and Moses taught [them]. [6] Therefore, they were called by his name.

[7] "Therefore thus says the Lord to the house of Jacob, who redeemed Abraham." [8] Where do we find regarding Jacob that he redeemed Abraham? [9] Rav Yehudah said: [We find] that He redeemed him from the anguish of child rearing. [10] And this is what is written: "Jacob shall not now be ashamed, etc." [11] "Jacob shall not now be ashamed" — because of his father. [12] "Neither shall his face now grow pale" — because of his father's father.

[13] It is written: "Palti." [14] And it is written: "Paltiel." [15] Rabbi Yoḥanan said:

RASHI

תולדות אהרן ומשה – ומפרש בתריה בני אהרן, ולא הוזכרו בני משה שם. **שפדאו מצער גידול בנים** – שהוטל עליו טורח השבטים, שעל אברהם היה מוטל אותו טורח דכתיב (בראשית כו) "והרביתי את זרעך" והוא פדאו.

SAGES

רַבִּי שְׁמוּאֵל בַּר נַחְמָנִי **Rabbi Shmuel bar Naḥmani.** A Palestinian Amora of the second and third generations. See *Sanhedrin*, Part I, p. 65.

רַבִּי יוֹנָתָן **Rabbi Yonatan.** A Tanna who was a member of the generation that lived prior to the completion of the Mishnah. See *Sanhedrin*, Part I, p. 22.

NOTES

שֶׁפְּדָאוֹ מִצַּעַר גִּידּוּל בָּנִים **He redeemed him from the anguish of child rearing.** Our commentary follows *Rashi* who understands the "anguish of child rearing" as referring to the day-to-day hardships involved in raising a large family. *Tosafot* argues that raising the twelve tribes of Israel did not cause Jacob anguish at all, but rather great happiness. The anguish referred to here should instead be understood as the pain that Jacob endured in the misfortunes that befell his children, such as the sale of Joseph and the rape of Dinah. *Ramah* suggests that the anguish Jacob spared his father and grandfather refers not only to the hardship involved in raising his own children, but also in raising him. By spending many of his younger years away from home, Jacob spared Isaac and Abraham the hardships of parenthood.

לֹא יֵבוֹשׁ יַעֲקֹב מֵאָבִיו **Jacob shall not be ashamed because of his father.** *Maharsha* suggests that the shame Jacob may have experienced because of his father and grandfather may be associated with the role that they played in Jacob's own misfortunes — Isaac, by favoring Esau and thus forcing Jacob to flee his home; and Abraham, by forming family ties with Laban, Jacob's devious father-in-law, as well as by burdening him with the responsibility of siring a nation.

פַּלְטִי שְׁמוֹ. [1] וְלָמָּה נִקְרָא שְׁמוֹ פַּלְטִיאֵל? [2] שֶׁפְּלָטוֹ אֵל מִן הָעֲבֵירָה. [3] מֶה עָשָׂה? [4] נָעַץ חֶרֶב בֵּינוֹ לְבֵינָהּ, [5] אָמַר: ״כָּל הָעוֹסֵק בְּדָבָר זֶה — יִדָּקֵר בְּחֶרֶב זֶה״. [6] וְהָכְתִיב ״וַיֵּלֶךְ אִתָּהּ אִישָׁהּ״! [7] שֶׁנַּעֲשָׂה לָהּ כְּאִישָׁהּ. [8] וְהָכְתִיב: ״הָלוֹךְ וּבָכֹה״! [9] עַל הַמִּצְוָה דְּאָזֵיל מִינֵּיהּ. [10] ״עַד בַּחֻרִים״ — שֶׁנַּעֲשׂוּ שְׁנֵיהֶם כְּבַחוּרִים, [11] שֶׁלֹּא טָעֲמוּ טַעַם בִּיאָה.

[12] אָמַר רַבִּי יוֹחָנָן: תּוֹקְפּוֹ שֶׁל יוֹסֵף — עַנְוְותָנוּתוֹ שֶׁל בּוֹעַז. [13] תּוֹקְפּוֹ שֶׁל בּוֹעַז — עַנְוְותָנוּתוֹ שֶׁל פַּלְטִי בֶּן לַיִשׁ. [14] תּוֹקְפּוֹ שֶׁל יוֹסֵף עַנְוְותָנוּתוֹ שֶׁל בּוֹעַז, [15] דִּכְתִיב ״וַיְהִי בַּחֲצִי הַלַּיְלָה וַיֶּחֱרַד הָאִישׁ וַיִּלָּפֵת״. [16] מַאי ״וַיִּלָּפֵת״? [17] אָמַר רַב שֶׁנַּעֲשָׂה

LITERAL TRANSLATION

Palti was his name. [1] And why was his name called Paltiel? [2] Because God spared him from sin. [3] What did He do? [4] He stuck a sword between him and her, [5] [and] said: "Whoever engages in this thing will be stabbed by this sword."

[6] But it is surely written: "And her husband went along with her"!

[7] That he acted toward her like her husband.

[8] But it is surely written: "Walking and weeping"!

[9] Over the mitzvah that he lost (lit., "went away").

[10] "To Bahurim" — that the two of them became like unmarried youths, [11] who never tasted the taste of intercourse.

[12] Rabbi Yoḥanan said: The strength of Joseph [is] the modesty of Boaz. [13] The strength of Boaz [is] the modesty of Palti the son of Laish. [14] The strength of Joseph [is] the modesty of Boaz, [15] for it is written: "And it came to pass at midnight that the man was startled and turned over." [16] What is [meant by] "and he turned over" (וַיִּלָּפֵת)? [17] Rav said: That his flesh became [as hard]

TRANSLATION AND COMMENTARY

said: Palti was his name. [1] **Why,** then, **was his name** elsewhere **called Paltiel** (פַּלְטִיאֵל)? [2] **Because God spared him** (פְּלָטוֹ אֵל) **from** the **sin** of adultery. [3] **What did He do?** [4] When Palti was about to engage in sexual relations with David's wife, Michal, **He stuck a sword between him and her,** [5] **and said: "Whoever engages in this thing will be pierced by this sword."**

וְהָכְתִיב [6] The Gemara raises a difficulty: But **surely** he consummated the marriage, for **it is written** regarding David's command to take Michal away from Paltiel and bring her to him (II Samuel 3:16): **"And her husband went along with her,** walking and weeping behind her to Baḥurim." The word אִישָׁהּ ("her husband") implies that Palti did have marital relations with her.

שֶׁנַּעֲשָׂה לָהּ [7] The Gemara answers: The intent of this word is to demonstrate **that** despite the absence of marital relations **he** nevertheless **acted toward her as her husband,** expressing affection and concern.

וְהָכְתִיב [8] If Palti understood that Michal was really David's wife, why, then, did he weep when she was taken from him? For **behold it is written** that he was **"walking and weeping** behind her to Baḥurim"!

עַל הַמִּצְוָה [9] In truth, Palti was crying **about** his loss of the opportunity to engage in **meritorious behavior**, for he would no longer be in the position of successfully restraining his evil impulse as he was while living chastely with Michal.

עַד בַּחֻרִים [10] Moreover, the verse itself, referring to Palti's having tearfully accompanied Michal **"to Baḥurim,"** alludes to the fact that **the two of them** — Palti and Michal — **conducted themselves like "young unmarried youths"** (in Hebrew, *baḥurim*), [11] **who never experienced sexual intercourse.**

אָמַר [12] The Gemara continues with a discussion of the self-control displayed by other Biblical figures. **Rabbi Yoḥanan said:** The restraint that was an act of great **strength** on the part **of Joseph** would have been considered simple **modesty** when compared to the self-control exercised by **Boaz,** for Boaz's achievement was far greater than that of Joseph. [13] And the act of great **strength** achieved **by Boaz** would be simple **modesty** when compared to the self-control exercised by **Palti the son of Laish,** for Palti's achievement was even greater than that of Boaz. [14] How do we see that the act of great **strength** on the part **of Joseph** was mere **modesty** when compared to the act **of Boaz?** [15] **For it is written** with respect to Boaz (Ruth 3:8): **"And it came to pass at midnight, that the man was startled and turned over;** and, behold, a woman lay at his feet." [16] **What is** the meaning of the word וַיִּלָּפֵת, translated here as "and he turned over"? [17] **Rav said: His flesh** (his member) **became** as hard **as turnip heads** (a לֶפֶת being a "turnip") upon finding Ruth lying at his feet. Nevertheless, he did not give in to lust. This was a display of self-control far greater than Joseph's in resisting the advances of Potiphar's wife (Genesis 39:12), for Ruth was an unmarried woman lying beside him, while Potiphar's wife was forbidden

RASHI

והא כתיב אישה — אלמא בא עליה. **שנעשה לה כאישה** — שהיה מגדלה ומחבבה. **הלך ובכה אחריה** — בקושיא קא נסיב לה. **עד בחורים** — קרא קא דריש ואזיל. **תוקפו של יוסף ענוותנותו של בועז** — דבר גדול של יוסף כדבר קל וקטן שבבועז, תוקף = דבר גדול וחמור ויש לו שם, ענוה = דבר שאין לו שם, שאדם עושה לפי תומו. **שנעשה בשרו** — אבר.

בְּשָׂרוֹ כְּרָאשֵׁי לְפָתוֹת. [20A] [1]תּוֹקְפּוֹ שֶׁל בּוֹעַז עַנְוְותָנוּתוֹ שֶׁל פַּלְטִי בֶּן לַיִשׁ, [2]כְּדַאֲמָרַן.
[3]אָמַר רַבִּי יוֹחָנָן: מַאי דִּכְתִיב: [4]״רַבּוֹת בָּנוֹת עָשׂוּ חָיִל וְאַתְּ עָלִית עַל כֻּלָּנָה״. [5]״רַבּוֹת בָּנוֹת עָשׂוּ חָיִל״ — זֶה יוֹסֵף וּבוֹעַז. [6]״וְאַתְּ עָלִית עַל כֻּלָּנָה״ — זֶה פַּלְטִי בֶּן לַיִשׁ.
[7]אָמַר רַבִּי שְׁמוּאֵל בַּר נַחְמָן אָמַר רַבִּי יוֹנָתָן: מַאי דִּכְתִיב: [8]״שֶׁקֶר הַחֵן, וְהֶבֶל הַיֹּפִי״. [9]״שֶׁקֶר הַחֵן״ — זֶה יוֹסֵף. [10]״וְהֶבֶל הַיֹּפִי״ — זֶה בּוֹעַז. [11]״יִרְאַת ה׳ הִיא תִתְהַלָּל״ — זֶה פַּלְטִי בֶּן לַיִשׁ.
[12]דָּבָר אַחֵר: ״שֶׁקֶר הַחֵן״ — זֶה דּוֹרוֹ שֶׁל מֹשֶׁה. [13]״וְהֶבֶל הַיֹּפִי״ — זֶה דּוֹרוֹ שֶׁל יְהוֹשֻׁעַ. [14]״יִרְאַת ה׳ הִיא תִתְהַלָּל״ — זֶה דּוֹרוֹ שֶׁל חִזְקִיָּה.
[15]דָּבָר אַחֵר: ״שֶׁקֶר הַחֵן״ — זֶה דּוֹרוֹ שֶׁל מֹשֶׁה וִיהוֹשֻׁעַ. [16]״וְהֶבֶל הַיֹּפִי״ — זֶה דּוֹרוֹ שֶׁל חִזְקִיָּה.

TRANSLATION AND COMMENTARY

to him and not touching him. [20A] [1]The act of great **strength** achieved **by Boaz** would be mere **modesty** when compared to the self-control **of Palti the son of Laish.** For Boaz resisted temptation for one night, when Ruth lay down beside him, [2]but **as we said above,** Palti the son of Laish avoided sexual intercourse with Michal for years.

אָמַר רַבִּי יוֹחָנָן [3]**Rabbi Yoḥanan said: What is** the meaning of the verse **that states** (Proverbs 31:29): [4]**"Many daughters have done virtuously, but you excel them all"?** [5]**"Many daughters have done virtuously" — this refers to Joseph and Boaz,** who overcame their sexual desire. [6]**"But you excel them all" — this refers to Palti the son of Laish.**

אָמַר [7]**Rabbi Shmuel bar Naḥman said in the name of Rabbi Yonatan: What is the** meaning of **that which is written** (Proverbs 31:30): [8]**"Grace is deceitful, and beauty is vain;** but a woman who fears the Lord, she shall be praised"? [9]**"Grace is deceitful" — this refers to Joseph.** [10]**"And beauty is vain" — this refers to Boaz.** [11]**"But a woman who fears the Lord, she shall be praised" — this refers to Palti the son of Laish.**

דָּבָר אַחֵר [12]The Gemara now offers **another explanation** of this verse: **"Grace is deceitful" — this refers to the generation of Moses** that God miraculously redeemed from bondage in Egypt. [13]**"And beauty is vain" — this refers to the generation of Joshua** that God brought into Eretz Israel. Neither of these generations deserves special praise for its devotion, seeing that it was so favored. [14]**"But a woman who fears the Lord, she shall be praised" — this refers to the generation of Ḥezekiah** that lived through war and foreign conquest, and yet devoted itself to Torah study more than any previous generation, and thus earned for itself the highest praise.

דָּבָר אַחֵר [15]The Gemara adds yet **another** slightly different **explanation** of this verse: **"Grace is deceitful" — this refers to the generation of Moses and Joshua.** [16]**"And beauty is vain" — this refers to the generation of Ḥezekiah,** during whose days the Kingdom of Judah

LITERAL TRANSLATION

as turnip-heads. [20A] [1]The strength of Boaz [is] the modesty of Palti the son of Laish, [2]as we have said.

[3]Rabbi Yoḥanan said: What is that which is written: [4]"Many daughters have acted virtuously, but you rise above them all"? [5]"Many daughters have acted virtuously" — this [refers to] Joseph and Boaz. [6]"But you rise above them all" — this [refers to] Palti the son of Laish.

[7]Rabbi Shmuel bar Naḥman said in the name of Rabbi Yonatan: What is that which is written: [8]"Grace is deceitful, and beauty is vain"? [9]"Grace is deceitful" — this [refers to] Joseph. [10]"And beauty is vain" — this [refers to] Boaz. [11]"A woman who fears the Lord, she shall be praised" — this [refers to] Palti the son of Laish.

[12]Another interpretation: "Grace is deceitful" — this [refers to] the generation of Moses. [13]"And beauty is vain" — this [refers to] the generation of Joshua. [14]"A woman who fears the Lord, she shall be praised" — this [refers to] the generation of Ḥezekiah.

[15]Another interpretation: "Grace is deceitful" — this [refers to] the generation of Moses and Joshua. [16]"And beauty is vain" — this [refers to] the generation of Ḥezekiah.

RASHI

בראשי לפתות — נתקשה, ואף על פי כן כבש יצרו, ואף על פי שפנויה היתה, ועמו במיטה. אבל יוסף — אשת איש היתה, ואינה עמו במיטה. **תוקפו של בועז ענוותנותו של פלטי** — דאילו בועז חדא לילה, ופלטי שנים רבות. **דורו של משה ויהושע** — עסקו בתורה הרבה, ודורו של חזקיהו יותר מהם, כדכתיב (ישעיה י): ״וחובל עול מפני שמן״, ואמרינן ב״חלק״ (סנהדרין צד,ב): חובל עול של סנחריב מפני שמנו של חזקיה, שהיה דולק בבתי מדרשות, עד שבדקו מדן ועד באר שבע ולא מצאו עם הארץ.

BACKGROUND

שֶׁקֶר הַחֵן וכו׳ **"Grace is deceitful."** Both of these Midrashim refer to the same idea, that there are beautiful and good things well-known to all, but that true glory is reserved for things which are not so well-known, but represent a greater accomplishment as understood from within.

NOTES

תּוֹקְפּוֹ שֶׁל בּוֹעַז **The strength of Boaz.** *Ramah* explains that Boaz had to muster all his strength to resist temptation, but Palti the son of Laish overcame sin with ease, for he had no erotic desire for Michal.

TRANSLATION AND COMMENTARY

was miraculously saved from the hands of Sennacherib. [1] **"But a woman who fears the Lord, she shall be praised" — this refers to the generation of Rabbi Yehudah, the son of Rabbi Il'ai,** which lived through the Hadrianic persecutions and yet continued to study and practice Torah. The Gemara illustrates the piety of that generation with the following observation: [2] **They said about Rabbi Yehudah, the son of Rabbi Il'ai, that six** of his **disciples would cover themselves with one cloak** because they were so poor, **and** nevertheless they **engaged in the study of Torah.**

MISHNAH מֵת לוֹ מֵת [3] If a relative of the king **dies, he may not go out of the door of his palace** to participate in the funeral, for it is beneath his dignity to display his grief in public. [4] **Rabbi Yehudah** disagrees and **says: If the** king **wishes to** join the funeral procession and **follow the bier, he may do so, for we** indeed **find that** King **David followed Abner's bier** along with the rest of the funeral party, [5] **as it is said** (II Samuel 3:31): "And David said to Joab, and to all the people that were with him, 'Rend your clothes, and gird yourselves with sackcloth, and mourn before Abner.' **And King David walked behind the bier."** [6] The Sages **said to** Rabbi Yehudah: The incident involving David does not prove that a king is permitted to join a funeral procession. For David **only** followed Abner's bier in order **to appease the people,** as it was vitally necessary for the stability of his reign to show that he was not responsible for Abner's death. But under ordinary circumstances the king may not participate in his relative's funeral.

וּכְשֶׁמַּבְרִין אוֹתוֹ [7] If a relative of the king dies, and the king **is offered the mourner's meal, all the people** who come to console him **sit on the ground** to show they are participating in his grief, [8] **and** the king himself **sits on a *dargash*** (the meaning of this term will be explained in the Gemara).

GEMARA תָּנוּ רַבָּנַן [9] **Our Rabbis taught** a related Baraita, which stated: **"In a place where it is customary for the women to follow the bier, they follow** the bier, and the men precede it. [10] And in a place where it is

[1] ״יִרְאַת ה׳ הִיא תִתְהַלָּל״ — זֶה דּוֹרוֹ שֶׁל רַבִּי יְהוּדָה בְּרַבִּי אֶילְעַאי. [2] אָמְרוּ עָלָיו עַל רַבִּי יְהוּדָה בְּרַבִּי אֶילְעַאי שֶׁהָיוּ שִׁשָּׁה תַּלְמִידִים מִתְכַּסִּין בְּטַלִּית אַחַת וְעוֹסְקִין בַּתּוֹרָה.

מִשְׁנָה [3] מֵת לוֹ מֵת, אֵינוֹ יוֹצֵא מִפֶּתַח פַּלְטֵרִין שֶׁלּוֹ. [4] רַבִּי יְהוּדָה אוֹמֵר: אִם רוֹצֶה לָצֵאת אַחַר הַמִּיטָּה, יוֹצֵא, שֶׁכֵּן מָצִינוּ בְּדָוִד שֶׁיָּצָא אַחַר מִיטָּתוֹ שֶׁל אַבְנֵר, [5] שֶׁנֶּאֱמַר: ״וְהַמֶּלֶךְ דָּוִד הֹלֵךְ אַחֲרֵי הַמִּטָּה״. [6] אָמְרוּ לוֹ: לֹא הָיָה הַדָּבָר אֶלָּא לְפַיֵּיס אֶת הָעָם.

[7] וּכְשֶׁמַּבְרִין אוֹתוֹ, כָּל הָעָם מְסוּבִּין עַל הָאָרֶץ, [8] וְהוּא מֵיסֵב עַל הַדַּרְגָּשׁ.

גְּמָרָא [9] תָּנוּ רַבָּנַן: ״מָקוֹם שֶׁנָּהֲגוּ נָשִׁים לָצֵאת אַחַר הַמִּיטָּה, יוֹצְאוֹת. [10] לִפְנֵי הַמִּיטָּה,

LITERAL TRANSLATION

[1] "A woman who fears the Lord, she shall be praised" — this [refers to] the generation of Rabbi Yehudah the son of Rabbi Il'ai. [2] They said about Rabbi Yehudah, the son of Rabbi Il'ai, that six disciples would cover themselves with one cloak and engage in [the study of] Torah.

MISHNAH [3] [If] someone [related] to him dies, [the king] may not exit the portal of his palace. [4] Rabbi Yehudah says: If he wishes to follow after the bier, he may exit, for we find that David followed Abner's bier, [5] as it is said: "And King David walked behind the bier." [6] They said to him: That matter was only to appease the people.

[7] And when they feed him the mourner's meal, all the people sit on the ground, [8] and he sits on the *dargash.*

GEMARA [9] Our Rabbis taught: "[In] a place where women are accustomed to follow the bier, they follow [the bier]. [10] To precede the bier,

RASHI

מתכסין בטלית אחת — עניים היו.

SAGES

רַבִּי יְהוּדָה בְּרַבִּי אֶילְעַאי Rabbi Yehudah, the son of Rabbi Il'ai. One of the greatest Tannaim of the fourth generation. See *Sanhedrin,* Part I, p. 12.

BACKGROUND

אֵינוֹ יוֹצֵא מִפֶּתַח פַּלְטֵרִין He may not exit the portal of his palace. This ruling has no support in Scripture, but it derives from the emphasis given to the king's honor. It does no honor to the king to see him in a time of humiliation. Therefore, it is not proper for him to accompany the deceased and display signs of mourning in public.

לְפַיֵּיס אֶת הָעָם To appease the people. Therefore the Halakhah is not to be derived from this, since the king did not do so because of a Halakhic leniency, but solely out of political necessity. Otherwise, everyone would have believed that Abner was killed by an act of betrayal by King David.

LANGUAGE

פַּלְטֵרִין Palace. This word derives from the Latin *palatium,* meaning palace. It might have entered the Hebrew language through the borrowed Greek form, *παλάτιον, palation.*

HALAKHAH

מֵת לוֹ מֵת If a relative of his dies. "The king is bound by all of the laws applying to mourners, except that he may not go beyond the entrance of his palace in order to follow the bier, not even if the deceased was a close relative whom he must mourn, and certainly not if the deceased was not related to him. Nor does he go out to console the mourners," following the anonymous first Tanna of the Mishnah. (*Rambam, Sefer Shofetim, Hilkhot Avelut* 7:7; *Hilkhot Melakhim* 2:4.)

וּכְשֶׁמַּבְרִין אוֹתוֹ And when they feed him. "When the meal of comfort is offered to the king, all the people who came to console him recline on the ground, and the king himself reclines on a couch. Nobody may go in to console the grieving king except his servants or people with permission to enter. No one is permitted to offer condolences to the king without his permission." (*Rambam, Sefer Shofetim, Hilkhot Avelut* 7:8; *Hilkhot Melakhim* 2:4.)

מָקוֹם שֶׁנָּהֲגוּ נָשִׁים לָצֵאת אַחַר הַמִּיטָּה In a place where the women are accustomed to follow the bier. "In a place where it is customary for the women to go out in front of the bier, they do so, and in a place where it is customary for them to go out after the bier, they do that. Now it is the accepted custom that women only follow the bier." (*Shulḥan Arukh, Yoreh De'ah* 359:1.)

יוֹצְאוֹת. [1]רַבִּי יְהוּדָה אוֹמֵר: לְעוֹלָם נָשִׁים לִפְנֵי הַמִּיטָּה יוֹצְאוֹת, שֶׁכֵּן מָצִינוּ בְּדָוִד שֶׁיָּצָא אַחַר מִיטָּתוֹ שֶׁל אַבְנֵר, [2]שֶׁנֶּאֱמַר: ׳וְהַמֶּלֶךְ דָּוִד הֹלֵךְ אַחַר הַמִּטָּה׳. [3]אָמְרוּ לוֹ: לֹא הָיָה הַדָּבָר אֶלָּא לְפַיֵּיס אֶת הָעָם, וְנִתְפַּיְּיסוּ. [4]שֶׁהָיָה דָּוִד יוֹצֵא מִבֵּין הָאֲנָשִׁים וְנִכְנַס לְבֵין הַנָּשִׁים, [5]וְיָצָא מִבֵּין הַנָּשִׁים וְנִכְנַס לְבֵין הָאֲנָשִׁים, [6]שֶׁנֶּאֱמַר: ׳וַיֵּדְעוּ כָל הָעָם וְכָל יִשְׂרָאֵל כִּי לֹא הָיְתָה מֵהַמֶּלֶךְ לְהָמִית אֶת אַבְנֵר״.

[7]דָּרַשׁ רָבָא: מַאי דִּכְתִיב: ״וַיָּבֹא כָל הָעָם לְהַבְרוֹת אֶת דָּוִד״. [8]כְּתִיב ״לְהַכְרוֹת״ וְקָרֵינַן ״לְהַבְרוֹת״. [9]בַּתְּחִלָּה — לְהַכְרוֹתוֹ, וּלְבַסּוֹף — לְהַבְרוֹתוֹ.

[10]אָמַר רַב יְהוּדָה אָמַר רַב: מִפְּנֵי מָה נֶעֱנַשׁ אַבְנֵר? [11]מִפְּנֵי שֶׁהָיָה לוֹ לִמְחוֹת בְּשָׁאוּל, וְלֹא מִיחָה. [12]רַבִּי יִצְחָק אָמַר: מִיחָה, וְלֹא נַעֲנָה. [13]וּשְׁנֵיהֶן

LITERAL TRANSLATION

they precede. [1]Rabbi Yehudah says: Women always precede the bier, for we find that David followed Abner's bier, [2]as it is said: 'And King David walked behind the bier.' [3]They said to him: The matter was only to appease the people, and they were appeased. [4]For David went out from among the men and entered among the women, [5]and he went out from among the women and entered among the men, [6]as it is said: 'And all the people and all Israel understood [that day] that the slaying of Abner [the son of Ner] did not come from the king.'"

[7]Rava expounded: What is that which is written: "And all the people came to feed David"? [8]It is written "to destroy," and we read "to feed." [9]At first — to destroy him, but in the end — to feed him [the mourner's meal].

[10]Rav Yehudah said in the name of Rav: Why was Abner punished? [11]Because he should have protested before Saul, but did not protest. [12]Rabbi Yitzḥak said: He protested, but was not answered. [13]And both of them

TRANSLATION AND COMMENTARY

customary for the women **to precede the bier, they precede** it, and the men follow it. [1]**Rabbi Yehudah says: Women** must **always precede the bier, for we find that David followed Abner's bier,** [2]**as** the verse **states** (II Samuel 3:31): **'And King David followed the bier.'** Now, if David followed the bier, the women must have preceded the bier, for it is certainly reasonable to assume that David did not walk among the women. And since there is a Biblical precedent for women walking ahead of the bier, women should not follow the bier, even if that is the local custom. [3]The Sages **said to** Rabbi Yehudah: David's actions at the funeral of Abner prove nothing about normal procedures. For David **only** participated in Abner's funeral in order **to appease the people** and convince them that he did not have a hand in Abner's death, **and** indeed the people **were appeased.** [4]How did **David** appease them? He **went out from among the men and entered among the women,** [5]**and** then **he went out from among the women and entered among the men, demonstrating** to all that he mourned the loss of Abner. David succeeded, [6]**as it is said** (II Samuel 3:37): **'For all the people and all Israel understood that day that the slaying of Abner** (the son of Ner) **did not come from the king.'"**

דָּרַשׁ רָבָא [7]**Rava expounded: What is** the meaning **of the verse that states** (II Samuel 3:35): **"And all the people came to feed David"?** [8]In the Biblical text, the word **is written** לְהַכְרוֹת, **"to destroy," but** according to the traditional Masoretic reading, **we read** the word as if it were spelled לְהַבְרוֹת, **"to feed."** [9]**At first** the people came **to destroy** King David, for they thought that he had ordered Joab to kill Abner, **but in the end** they came **to offer him the meal of comfort.**

אָמַר רַב יְהוּדָה [10]**Rav Yehudah said in the name of Rav: Why was Abner punished?** [11]**Because he should have protested** and prevented **Saul** from executing the priests at Nov (see I Samuel 22:18-19), but **he did not protest.** [12]**Rabbi Yitzḥak said:** Abner **protested but** Saul **did not listen** to him. [13]The Gemara notes: **Both** Rav Yehudah and Rabbi Yitzḥak **expounded the same verse,** but arrived at opposite conclusions. The verse

RASHI

רבי יהודה אומר לעולם — לפני המטה יוצאות, שכן מצינו בדוד שיצא אחר מטתו של אבנר. ואי סלקא דעתך נשים אחר המטה, אורחיה דדוד להלך עם הנשים? **בתחילה להכרותו** — שהיו סבורין שמאתו היתה הריגת אבנר. **ולבסוף להברותו** — שידעו הבירור שלא מאת דוד נהרג אבנר. **למחות בשאול** — בהריגת נוב עיר הכהנים.

BACKGROUND

מִפְּנֵי מָה נֶעֱנַשׁ אַבְנֵר? Why was Abner punished? This question does not seek the reason why Abner was killed, for the Bible states explicitly that Joab killed him in revenge for his brother, who had been killed by Abner. Rather the question refers to the ultimate causes for events in the world. What sin did Abner commit for which he was punished with death? Elsewhere it is suggested that he was punished because he proposed holding a battle that was not for a serious purpose but merely a kind of war game (II Samuel 2), which caused several men to be killed in vain.

NOTES

לְהַכְרוֹת — לְהַבְרוֹת To destroy — to feed. A number of commentators note that in the Biblical texts before them, the word is written just as it is pronounced, לְהַבְרוֹת. But some of the early grammarians did indeed have the reading לְהַכְרוֹת (see *Radak*, II Samuel 3:35).

שֶׁהָיָה לוֹ לִמְחוֹת Because he should have protested. Our commentary follows *Rashi*, who explains that Abner should have intervened and prevented Saul from executing the priests at Nov.

Rosh suggests that Abner was punished because he should have objected to Saul's attempts to kill David, but he failed to do so.

מִקְרָא אֶחָד דָּרְשׁוּ: [1]"וַיְקֹנֵן הַמֶּלֶךְ אֶל אַבְנֵר וַיֹּאמַר הַכְּמוֹת נָבָל יָמוּת אַבְנֵר יָדֶיךָ לֹא אֲסֻרוֹת וְרַגְלֶיךָ לֹא לִנְחֻשְׁתַּיִם הֻגָּשׁוּ". [2]מַאן דְּאָמַר לֹא מִיחָה — הָכִי קָאָמַר: "יָדֶיךָ לֹא אֲסֻרוֹת, וְרַגְלֶיךָ לֹא לִנְחֻשְׁתַּיִם הוּגָּשׁוּ". [3]מַאי טַעְמָא לֹא מָחִיתָ? [4]"כִּנְפוֹל לִפְנֵי בְנֵי עַוְלָה נָפָלְתָּ". [5]וּמַאן דְּאָמַר מִיחָה, וְלֹא נַעֲנָה — [6]אִיתְמַהוּיֵי מִתַּמַּהּ: "הַכְּמוֹת נָבָל יָמוּת? [7]יָדֶיךָ לֹא אֲסוּרוֹת, וְרַגְלֶיךָ לֹא לִנְחֻשְׁתַּיִם". [8]מִכְּדִי מַחוֹיֵי מָחִית. [9]מַאי טַעְמָא "כִּנְפוֹל לִפְנֵי בְנֵי עַוְלָה נָפָלְתָּ"? [10]לְמַאן דְּאָמַר מִיחָה, [11]מַאי טַעְמָא אִיעֲנַשׁ?

[12]אָמַר רַב נַחְמָן בְּרַבִּי יִצְחָק: שֶׁשִּׁהָא מַלְכוּת בֵּית דָּוִד שְׁתֵּי שָׁנִים וּמֶחֱצָה.

[13]"וּכְשֶׁמַּבְרִין אוֹתוֹ כו'". [14]מַאי דַּרְגָּשׁ?

[15]אָמַר עוּלָּא: עַרְסָא דְּגַדָּא.

LITERAL TRANSLATION

expounded the same verse: [1]"And the king lamented over Abner, and said: Should Abner die as a villain dies? Your hands were not bound, nor were your feet put into fetters." [2][According to] the one who said [that] he did not protest — he said as follows: "Your hands were not bound, nor were your feet put into fetters." [3]What is the reason that you did not protest? [4]"You fell as a man falls before the wicked." [5]And [according to] the one who said [that] he protested, but was not answered — [6]he asked in astonishment: "Should [Abner] die as a villain dies? [7]Your hands were not bound, nor were your feet [put] into fetters." [8]Now, surely you protested. [9]What is the reason [that] "you fell as a man falls before the wicked"? [10]According to the one who said he protested, [11]what is the reason that he was punished? [12]Rav Naḥman, the son of Rabbi Yitzḥak, said: Because he delayed the reign of the House of David for two-and- a-half years. [13]"And when they feed him, etc." [14]What is a *dargash*? [15]Ulla said: A bed of good fortune.

TRANSLATION AND COMMENTARY

states (II Samuel 3:33-34): [1]**"And the king lamented over Abner, and said: Should Abner die as a villain dies? Your hands were not bound, nor were your feet put into fetters;** you fell as a man falls before the wicked." [2]**According to the** opinion of Rav Yehudah, **who said that** Abner **did not protest** to prevent Saul from killing the priests at Nov, David **said as follows: "Your hands were not bound, nor were your feet put into fetters."** [3]**What is the reason,** then, **that you did not protest?** [4]Since you did intervene, **"you fell as a man falls before the wicked."** [5]**And according to the** opinion of Rabbi Yitzḥak, **who said that** indeed Abner **protested, but** Saul **did not listen** to him, [6]David **asked in astonishment: "Should he die as a villain dies?** [7]**Your hands were not bound, nor were your feet put into fetters."** [8]**Surely you protested.** [9]**What, then, is the reason that "you fell as a man falls before the wicked"?**

לְמַאן דְּאָמַר [10]The Gemara asks: **According to the** opinion of Rabbi Yitzḥak, **who said** that Abner **protested,** but Saul did not listen to him, [11]**what is the reason that** Abner **was punished** with a violent death?

אָמַר [12]**Rav Naḥman the son of Rabbi Yitzḥak said:** Abner was punished **because,** after Saul died, he made his son Ish-Bosheth king over Israel (see II Samuel 2:9), and thus **delayed the reign** of the kingdom **of the House of David for** another **two-and-a-half years.**

וּכְשֶׁמַּבְרִין אוֹתוֹ [13]The next clause of our Mishnah states: "**When** the king **is offered the meal of comfort,** everyone who comes to console him sits on the ground, and the king sits on a *dargash*." [14]The Gemara asks: **What is a** ***dargash*****?**

אָמַר עוּלָּא [15]**Ulla said:** This refers to **a bed** that was not ordinarily used, but was set aside **for** good **luck.**

RASHI

ידיך לא אסורות — אדם חשוב היית לשאול והיה לך למחות, ולפי שלא מחית — "כנפול לפני בני עולה נפלת". מכדי מחויי מחית — והכי קאמר: "ידיך לא אסורות" היו — לא ניהגת בעצמך כאדם חשוב, אלא בכל כוחך גילית בדעתך ומחית בשאול. **ששהה מלכות בית דוד** — שהעמיד את איש בושת למלך. ואם לא המליכו אבנר, היו ממליכין את דוד. ומשמלך איש בושת עד יום שמלך דוד על כל ישראל היו שתי שנים ומחצה: שתי שנים לאיש בושת, וחצי שנה בין מיתתו למלכות דוד, שמשמת שאול מלך דוד בחברון, וכתיב "בחברון מלך שבע שנים וששה חדשים", לא מהן חמש שנים שבין מיתת שאול למלכות איש בושת, דתניא בסדר עולם (וסנהדרין קז,א): "והימים אשר מלך דוד על" וגו', נמצאת מלכות ישראל בטילה חמש שנים. אלמא חמש שנים היו בלא מלך, נשתיירו שתי שנים ומחצה ממלכות איש בושת למלכות בית דוד. **דרגש ערסא דגדא** — נוהגין היו לערוך מטה ושלחן בבית, ולא היו משתמשין בהן

LANGUAGE

דַּרְגָּשׁ *Dargash.* It appears that the Sages of the Talmud were not entirely sure what a *dargash* was. Moreover, the source of the word is unclear. Some authorities relate it to the Armenian *dargue*, meaning a stretcher or litter. But it is not known whether the source of the word is Persian or comes from some other language.

SAGES

עוּלָּא Ulla. A Palestinian Amora of the second and third generations. See *Sanhedrin,* Part I, p.79.

NOTES

עַרְסָא דְּגַדָּא A bed for luck. Our commentary follows *Rashi* and others who explain that this refers to a bed which is set

HALAKHAH

מַבְרִין They feed him. "When a mourner returns from the funeral, he is forbidden to eat his first meal from his own food. (But he may eat his own food during his second meal, even if he eats it on the day of the funeral.) His friends or

TRANSLATION AND COMMENTARY

אָמְרוּ לֵיהּ [1]**The Rabbis said to Ulla:** Is it reasonable to say that **until now he did not sit** on this bed, [2]**and now we** require **him to sit** on it?

מַתְקִיף לָהּ [3]**Rava strongly objected** to this criticism: **What is the difficulty** with Ulla's teaching? [4]**Perhaps** the law regarding the mourner's bed **is like** that regarding his **eating and drinking,** all of which cause the mourner to engage in unusual behavior. [5]For **before** his relative died, the mourner **would not have been fed or given to drink** from foods and beverages that are not his own, [6]**and now** that he is mourning, **he is fed and given to drink** from foods and beverages that are not his own: The mourner's meal. Similarly, it should not surprise us that during that meal the grieving king is made to sit on a bed that had not previously been used for seating.

אֶלָּא [7]**Rather, if there is a difficulty** with Ulla's explanation, **this is the difficulty.** During the first seven days of mourning, people turn over their beds. But, as we learn from a Baraita: [8]**"The** ***dargash*** **is not required to be turned over, but rather the mourner should set it on its side."** [9]**Now if you think that** the ***dargash*** **is an** ornamental **bed** set aside **for** good **fortune,** [10]**why is** the mourner **not required to turn it over?** [11]**But surely it was taught** in a Baraita: "The mourner **who** is required to **turn over his bed** must **turn over not only his own bed,** [12]**but he must turn over all of the beds in his house."**

מַאי קוּשְׁיָא [13]The Gemara asks: **What is difficult** about this? [14]**Perhaps a** ***dargash*** **is like a bed that is set aside for utensils,** [15]**about which we have learned** in a Baraita: **"If a bed was set aside for utensils,** the mourner **is not required to turn it over."** Like a bed set aside for utensils, a bed set aside for good fortune should also not require overturning!

[1]אָמְרוּ לֵיהּ רַבָּנַן לְעוּלָּא: מִי אִיכָּא מִידֵּי דְּעַד הָאִידָּנָא לָא אוֹתְבִינֵיהּ, [2]וְהָשְׁתָּא מוֹתְבִינַן לֵיהּ?

[3]מַתְקִיף לָהּ רָבָא: מַאי קוּשְׁיָא? [4]דִּילְמָא מִידֵּי דַּהֲוָה אַאֲכִילָה וּשְׁתִיָּה, [5]דְּעַד הָאִידָּנָא לָא אָכִילְנֵיהּ וְלָא אַשְׁקִינֵיהּ, [6]הָשְׁתָּא קָא מוֹכְלִינַן לֵיהּ וְקָא מַשְׁקִינַן לֵיהּ!

[7]אֶלָּא, אִי קַשְׁיָא, הָא קַשְׁיָא: [8]"דַּרְגָּשׁ אֵינוֹ צָרִיךְ לִכְפּוֹתוֹ, אֶלָּא זוֹקְפוֹ". [9]וְאִי סָלְקָא דַּעְתָּךְ עַרְסָא דְּגַדָּא, [10]אַמַּאי אֵינוֹ צָרִיךְ לִכְפּוֹתוֹ? [11]וְהָתַנְיָא: הַכּוֹפֶה אֶת מִטָּתוֹ לֹא מִטָּתוֹ בִּלְבַד הוּא כּוֹפֶה, [12]אֶלָּא כָּל מִטּוֹת שֶׁיֵּשׁ לוֹ בְּתוֹךְ בֵּיתוֹ הוּא כּוֹפֶה".

[13]מַאי קוּשְׁיָא? [14]דִּילְמָא מִידֵּי דַּהֲוָה אַמִּטָּה מְיוּחֶדֶת לְכֵלִים, [15]דְּקָתָנֵי: "אִם הָיְתָה מְיוּחֶדֶת לְכֵלִים, אֵינוֹ צָרִיךְ לִכְפּוֹתָהּ".

LITERAL TRANSLATION

[1]The Rabbis said to Ulla: Is there anything that until now he did not sit on it, [2]and we now have him sit [on it]?

[3]Rava objected: What is the difficulty? [4]Perhaps it is something like eating and drinking, [5]for until now we did not feed him nor did we give him to drink, [6][and] now we feed him and we give him to drink!

[7]Rather, if there is a difficulty, this is the difficulty: [8]"He is not required to overturn the *dargash,* but rather he sets it upright." [9]And if it enters your mind [that it is] a bed of good fortune, [10]why is he not required to turn it over? [11]But surely it was taught: "One who turns over his bed not only turns over his own bed, [12]but he turns over all of the beds in his house."

[13]What is the difficulty? [14]Perhaps it is like a bed that is set aside for utensils, [15]for we have learned: "If it was set aside for utensils, he is not required to turn it over."

RASHI

כלל, אלא למזל הבית מונחת משום ניחוש, גדא = מזל, ודומה: גד גדי וסנוק לא (שבת סז,ב). עד השתא לאו אותביניה — עד הנה לא ישב על אותה מיטה, שהרי מונחת היא לנוי הבית. והשתא — דאבל הוא, בעינן לאותביה עלה, מהיכא תיפוק לן? השתא מוכלינן ליה — משל אחרים.

NOTES

aside to bring good luck to the house. *Ramah* notes that this practice is similar to that described in Isaiah 65:11: "You that set out a table for fortune." There, however, the table was set out as part of an idolatrous rite. *Ran* argues that the custom should be forbidden, for it is a superstitious rite practiced by non-Jews, which could lead to idol-worship. Rather, with the expression, "a bed of good fortune," the Gemara refers here to a bed that is used to display its owner's wealth.

HALAKHAH

neighbors should prepare the mourner a meal from food that does not belong to him." (*Shulḥan Arukh, Yoreh De'ah* 378:1.)

הַכּוֹפֶה אֶת מִטָּתוֹ One who inverts his bed. "According to Talmudic law, a mourner is obligated to turn over his bed. He sleeps and eats on the inverted bed, and the rest of the day he sits on the ground. Today it is customary for the mourner not to invert his bed, because his non-Jewish

LANGUAGE

קַרְבִיטִין Straps. This word apparently derives from the Greek χραββατος, *karabbatos*, which means a mattress, a mat, or a bed covering.

TERMINOLOGY

כִּי אֲתָא ר׳ פְּלוֹנִי When Rabbi X came.... This expression introduces a tradition or a new legal ruling quoted by a particular Sage when he came to the Academy, usually when he came to Babylonia from Eretz Israel.

BACKGROUND

עַרְסָא דְּגַדָּא A bed of good fortune. It was customary to have a decorated bed in one's home that was not slept in but kept for good luck and as a good augury for the home. Some Sages maintained that this custom was tinged with idol worship.

עַרְסָא דְּצַלָּא A bed of leather. This is a bed of which the mattress support is not made of a rope mesh, unlike most beds at that time, but rather from a piece of leather.

סֵירוּגוֹ מִתּוֹכוֹ Its strapping passes through the frame.

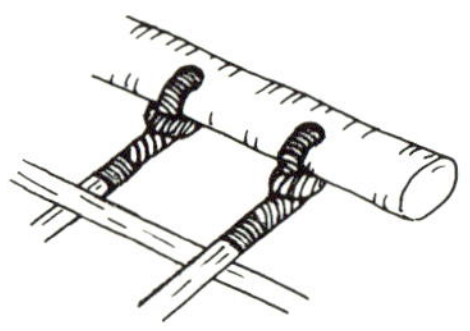

A bed to which the webbing is attached by holes through the bed frame itself.

TRANSLATION AND COMMENTARY

אֶלָּא [1]**Rather, if there is a difficulty** with Ulla's understanding of *dargash*, **this is the difficulty,** for the Baraita cited above continues: [2]**"Rabban Shimon ben Gamliel says:** As for **a *dargash*,** there is no need for the mourner to overturn it, but rather **he should untie the straps supporting** the mattress, **and it will fall** to the ground **by itself."** This Baraita implies that a *dargash* is the type of bed that has removable straps. [3]**But if you think that** a ***dargash*** **is an** ornamental **bed** set aside **for good fortune, would it have** such **straps?** That bed was not made to be taken apart, but to be displayed in the home.

אֶלָּא [4]**Rather, when Ravin came** to Babylonia from Eretz Israel **he said: One of the Rabbis** in Eretz Israel, **named Rav Taḥlifa, told me that he frequented the leather-workers' market,** [5]**and said to me: What is a *dargash*?** A bed made of **leather** that is attached to a bedframe with straps. The posts on such a bed did not extend above the mattress; so the Rabbis did not require the mourner to invert it, lest the leather become damaged through contact with the damp ground. According to the first Tanna of the Baraita, the mourner should set the bed on its side, allowing the leather surface to stand upright. Rabban Shimon ben Gamliel says that the mourner should untie the straps supporting the leather mattress, and it will fall to the ground by itself, without causing any damage to the upper leather surface.

אָמַר רַבִּי יִרְמְיָה [6]**Rabbi Yirmeyah said in the name of Rabbi Yoḥanan:** Like an ordinary bed, the mattress of a *dargash* is supported by straps attached to the bed frame. But in the case of **a *dargash*** [20B] the bars of the bed frame have holes and the **straps** supporting the mattress are laced **through them,**

LITERAL TRANSLATION

[1]Rather, if there is a difficulty, this is the difficulty: [2]"Rabban Shimon ben Gamliel says: [Regarding] a *dargash* he unties its straps and it falls by itself." [3]But if it enters your mind [that it is] a bed of good fortune, does it have straps? [4]Rather, when Ravin came he said: One of the Rabbis — and Rav Taḥlifa is his name — told me that he frequented the leather-workers' market, [5]and he said to me (lit., "him"): What is a *dargash*? A bed of leather. [6]Rabbi Yirmeyah said in the name of Rabbi Yoḥanan: A *dargash* [20B] — its strapping [passes] through [the frame];

[1]אֶלָּא, אִי קַשְׁיָא, הָא קַשְׁיָא: [2]"רַבָּן שִׁמְעוֹן בֶּן גַּמְלִיאֵל אוֹמֵר: דַּרְגָּשׁ, מַתִּיר קַרְבִיטִין וְהוּא נוֹפֵל מֵאֵילָיו". [3]וְאִי סָלְקָא דַּעֲתָךְ עַרְסָא דְּגַדָּא, קַרְבִיטִין מִי אִית לֵיהּ? [4]אֶלָּא, כִּי אֲתָא רָבִין אָמַר: אָמַר לִי הַהוּא מֵרַבָּנַן — וְרַב תַּחֲלִיפָא שְׁמֵיהּ — דַּהֲוָה שְׁכִיחַ בְּשׁוּקָא דְּגִילְדָּאֵי, [5]וַאֲמַר לֵיהּ: מַאי דַּרְגָּשׁ — עַרְסָא דְּצַלָּא. [6]אָמַר רַבִּי יִרְמְיָה אָמַר רַבִּי יוֹחָנָן: דַּרְגָּשׁ [20B] סֵירוּגוֹ מִתּוֹכוֹ;

RASHI

אלא אי קשיא — אדעולא, הא קשיא עלה דתניא בעלמא (מועד קטן כז,א): דרגש אין צריך האבל לכפותו. **מתיר קרביטין** — בימי אבלו, קרביטין = לולאות. **קרביטין מי אית ליה** — הלא כשאר מטות עושין אותה מטה. **גילדאי** — רצענין. **ערסא דצלא** — מטה של עור, ותולין רצועות בשפת העור סביב. וכשרוצין לנטותו עונבין הרצועות בארוכות המטה, וכשמתירין אותה הוא נופל, והן הן קרביטין. וחס הוא עליו לכפותו, שלא יתקלקל העור בלחלוח הקרקע, שלא היו ראשי כרעיו גבוהין מסירוגו למעלה. וקאמר תנא קמא: זוקפו על דופן הכרעים וארוכותיו למעלה, ואמר ליה רבן שמעון: מתיר קרביטין והוא נופל. **סירוגו** — קשירתו. **מתוכו** — שיש נקבים בארכבותיו, ותוחבין בהן ראשי רצועות התלויות בעור, ועונבים, ואין מרכיבין הרצועה על גבי ארוכות המטה.

NOTES

עַרְסָא דְּגַדָּא, קַרְבִיטִין מִי אִית לֵיהּ? A bed of good fortune, does it have straps? The Geonim explain that since this bed was not used for sleeping or sitting, but only to bring good luck to the house, it was not constructed with straps, but rather a wooden plank was laid across the frame, and ornamental bedding was then placed on it. *Ran* understands the Gemara's argument differently: A bed set aside for good fortune was not constructed in a particular way, for any bed could be set aside for that purpose. Such a bed, therefore, would not necessarily have had straps which could be untied. How, then, can Rabban Shimon ben Gamliel have stated categorically that in the case of a *dargash* the mourner should untie the straps and allow the mattress to fall to the ground?

HALAKHAH

neighbors might regard the practice as an act of sorcery, and the mourner would find himself in danger. Furthermore, beds are no longer made as they were during the Talmudic period, so that today inverting the bed does not have the same effect as it once had (following *Tosafot*). Moreover, a lodger is not required to turn his bed upside down, and Jews living in the Diaspora are regarded as lodgers (*Tur* in the name of *Rosh*). The mourner must, however, sit and sleep on the ground (today, even that is not done, perhaps because people are in a weaker physical condition than in previous generations). Today, those who come to console mourners may sit on benches, for it is assumed that the mourners waive the respect that is due them (*Shakh*). It is customary, for Kabbalistic reasons, not to sit on the ground itself, but that there be some separation — three handbreadths or less — between the mourner and the ground." (*Shulḥan Arukh, Yoreh De'ah* 387:1-2.)

TRANSLATION AND COMMENTARY

[1] whereas the frame of **a bed** is solid and the **straps** are looped **around the bars.**

מֵיתִיבִי [2] **An objection was raised** against this explanation from a Mishnah (*Kelim* 16:1), which teaches: "An object does not become susceptible to ritual impurity until it is a finished product. **When are wooden utensils** considered finished so that they may **contract ritual impurity? A bed and a cradle** are considered finished **when** the craftsman **smooths** their wooden frames **with the skin of a fish."** [3] **Now, if** the **straps** of [4] **a bed are** looped **around the bars** of the frame, [5] **what is the purpose of smoothing** the bed frame **with fish skin?** Why smooth a surface that is not exposed?

אֶלָּא [6] **Rather,** with both a bed and a *dargash,* the straps supporting the mattress are laced **through** the frame, instead of around it. [7] But the straps of **a bed go in and out through slits** made in the bars themselves, [8] whereas the straps of **a *dargash* go in and out through loops** attached to the bars of the bed frame.

אָמַר רַבִּי יַעֲקֹב [9] **Rabbi Ya'akov said in the name of Rabbi Yehoshua ben Levi: The law is in accordance with** the position of **Rabban Shimon ben Gamliel,** who maintains that a mourner should untie the straps supporting the mattress of a *dargash* and allow it to fall to the ground by itself.

אָמַר [10] Regarding a related matter, **Rabbi Ya'akov bar Ammi said: A bed whose poles protrude** to form a frame for a curtain cannot be inverted properly. [11] The mourner **should set** a bed of that kind **on its side,** and then sit on some overturned bed or on the ground, **and that is enough.**

MISHNAH וּמוֹצִיא לְמִלְחֶמֶת הָרְשׁוּת [12] The king **may send the people out to** fight **an optional war** to enlarge the boundaries of Israel or to subjugate the neighboring nations only **with the** prior **permission of the** High

מִטָּה — [1] סֵירוּגָהּ מֵעַל גַּבָּהּ. [2] מֵיתִיבִי: "כְּלֵי עֵץ מֵאֵימָתַי מְקַבְּלִין טוּמְאָה? [3] הַמִּטָּה וְהָעֲרִיסָה מִשֶּׁיְּשׁוּפֵם בְּעוֹר הַדָּג". [4] וְאִי מִטָּה מְסוֹרֶגֶת הִיא מֵעַל גַּבָּהּ, [5] לָמָּה לִי שִׁיפַת עוֹר הַדָּג? [6] אֶלָּא, הָא וְהָא מִתּוֹכוֹ. [7] מִטָּה, אַעוּלֵי וְאַפּוּקֵי בְּבִזְיוֹנֵי. [8] דַּרְגָּשׁ, אַעוּלֵי וְאַפּוּקֵי בְּאִבְקָתָא. [9] אָמַר רַבִּי יַעֲקֹב אָמַר רַבִּי יְהוֹשֻׁעַ בֶּן לֵוִי: הֲלָכָה כְּרַבָּן שִׁמְעוֹן בֶּן גַּמְלִיאֵל. [10] אָמַר רַבִּי יַעֲקֹב בַּר אַמִּי: מִטָּה שֶׁנַּקְלִיטֶיהָ יוֹצְאִין, [11] זוֹקְפָהּ, וְדַיּוֹ.

מִשְׁנָה [12] וּמוֹצִיא לְמִלְחֶמֶת הָרְשׁוּת עַל פִּי בֵּית דִּין

LITERAL TRANSLATION

[1] a bed — its strapping [loops] around it.

[2] They raised an objection: "From when do wooden utensils contract ritual impurity? [3] A bed and a cradle from when he smooths them with the skin of a fish." [4] And if [the strapping of] a bed is wrapped around it, [5] why do I need smoothing with the skin of a fish?

[6] Rather, this and that [are looped] through it. [7] A bed — they go in and out through slits. [8] A *dargash* — they go in and out through loops.

[9] Rabbi Ya'akov said in the name of Rabbi Yehoshua ben Levi: The law is in accordance with Rabban Shimon ben Gamliel.

[10] Rabbi Ya'akov bar Ammi said: A bed whose posts protrude, [11] he sets it up [on its side], and it is sufficient.

MISHNAH [12] And [the king] sends [the people] out to an optional war with the permission of a court

RASHI

סירוגה מעל גבה — החבלים מרכיבין על ארוכות המטה מיכן ומיכן, ואורג, והוא סירוג. **העריסה** — עריסת תינוקות, *ברייץ. **משישופם בעור הדג** — משפשפם בעור הדג כדי להחליק הארוכות, ליפותם. **למה לי שיפת עור הדג** — הלא אין יופיה ניכר, שהרי מכוסות הן תמיד בראשי החבלים המסורגין על גבן. **מטה אעולי ואפוקי בבזיוניה** — בזועים ונקבים של ארוכות מכניס ומוציא ראש החבל ומסרג. **באבקתא** — לולאות התלויות בנקבי ארכובותיו, ובהן מכניסין ראשי רצועות התלויות בשפת העור. **שנקליטיה יוצאין** — נקליטין = שני עצים ארוכים, ומעמידין אותן באמצע דופני המטה, אחד מראשותיה ואחד מרגלותיה, ומפוצלין הן בראשותיהן, ומניחין קנה מזה לזה ועליו פורסין הכילה. ויש שמחברין אותן נקליטין למטה, והיינו "יוצאין", שמחוברין ויוצאין מן המטה, ואין יכול לכפותה מפני נקליטיה. **זוקפה** — על מראשותיה או על מרגלותיה וארכובותיה למעלה, ודיו.

NOTES

מֵאֵימָתַי מְקַבְּלִין טוּמְאָה? From when do they contract ritual impurity? According to the Halakhah, raw materials are not susceptible to ritual impurity until they are fashioned into finished utensils. A utensil is not considered finished until all the work necessary for its formation has been completed. Elsewhere (in tractate *Kelim*), the Rabbis determine which tasks are considered absolutely necessary for finishing various utensils.

וּמוֹצִיא לְמִלְחֶמֶת הָרְשׁוּת עַל פִּי בֵּית דִּין שֶׁל שִׁבְעִים וְאֶחָד And he sends the people out to an optional war with the permission of a court of seventy-one. The Mishnah does not mention that the Urim and Tumim (the oracular

HALAKHAH

מֵאֵימָתַי מְקַבְּלִין טוּמְאָה? From when do wooden utensils contract ritual impurity? "Utensils do not become susceptible to ritual impurity until they are considered finished products. A bed and a cradle become susceptible to ritual impurity when their wooden frames are smoothed with the skin of a fish." (*Rambam, Sefer Taharah, Hilkhot Kelim* 5:1.)

וּמוֹצִיא לְמִלְחֶמֶת הָרְשׁוּת He sends the people out to an optional war. "The king may not send the people out to

LANGUAGE (RASHI)

ברייץ* From the Old French *brez,* meaning "cradle".

BACKGROUND

סֵירוּגָהּ מֵעַל גַּבָּהּ Its strapping loops around it.

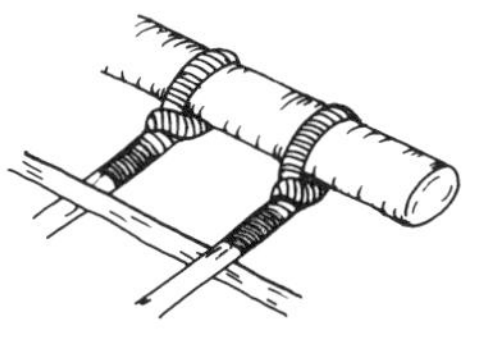

A bed to which the webbing is attached by being tied around the bed frame.

עוֹר הַדָּג The skin of a fish.

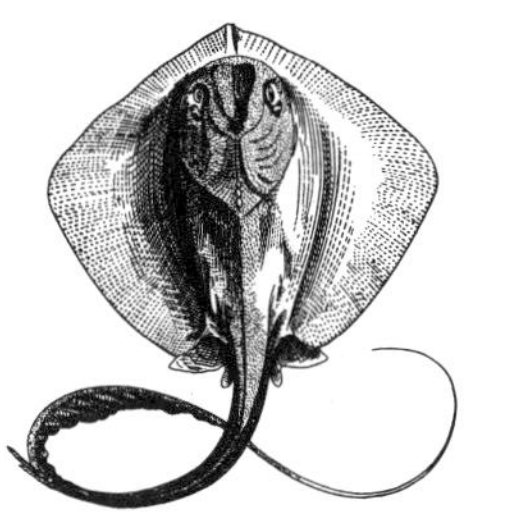

Skate

This ray, from the genera of cartilaginous fishes of the family of Rajidae, has a horizontally flat body, both eyes on the upper surface, widely expanded fins at each side, and a long, slender, whiplike tail. In ancient times the skin of skates was used to scrape wood and other materials, much as sandpaper is used today.

מִטָּה וְנַקְלִיטִין Bed and poles.

Roman bed from the Mishnaic period.

This bed has high supports at the head and foot, to which the word נַקְלִיטִין might refer. Turning a bed like this upside down is not considered as turning it over.

LANGUAGE

נַקְלִיטִין Poles. This word apparently derives from the Greek ἀνάκλιτα, *anaklita,* or ἀνάκλιτον, *anakliton,* meaning the armrest of a bed or chair.

SAGES

רַבִּי יַעֲקֹב Rabbi Ya'akov. A third-generation Amora, Rabbi Ya'akov immigrated to Eretz

TRANSLATION AND COMMENTARY

Court of seventy-one judges, the Great Sanhedrin.

וּפוֹרֵץ [1]The king **may breach** other people's walls and **fences** in order **to make a road** to serve his needs, **and nobody may raise** any **objections.** [2]**The king's road has no** maximum **dimensions,** and thus nobody may object that the road is wider or longer than necessary.

וְכָל הָעָם [3]**The people may plunder** the enemy during war, but then they must **give** all the booty to the king, **and he chooses his portion** of the spoils **first.**

GEMARA תָּנֵינָא [4]The Gemara seeks clarification: The first clause of the Mishnah appears to be superfluous, for **we** already **learned** it **once** before in a Mishnah in the first chapter (2a): [5]"A Jewish king **may not send** the nation **out to** fight **an optional war** unless he receives the permission of **the** High **Court of seventy-one** judges."

אַיְּידֵי [6]The Gemara explains: Indeed, it was unnecessary to state this law in both places. But **since** the Mishnah in this chapter **teaches all the matters relating to a king,** [7]**it also teaches** that he may only **send** the people **out to an optional war** with permission of the Sanhedrin.

אָמַר רַב יְהוּדָה [8]The Sages disagreed about the privileges accorded to the king. **Rav Yehudah said in the name of Shmuel: Whatever was stated in the passage concerning the king** written in I Samuel (8:11-18) **is**

LITERAL TRANSLATION

of seventy-one.

[1]And he breaches [fences] to construct for himself a road, and no one may object. [2]The king's road has no measure.

[3]All the people plunder and give him, and he takes a portion first.

GEMARA [4]We learned [this] once: [5]"[The people] may not be sent (lit., 'brought out') to an optional war except by permission of a court of seventy-one"!

[6]Since it taught all matters relating to a king, [7]it also taught [that] they send [the nation] out to an optional war.

[8]Rav Yehudah said in the name of Shmuel: Whatever is stated in the passage concerning the king

שֶׁל שִׁבְעִים וְאֶחָד.
[1]וּפוֹרֵץ לַעֲשׂוֹת לוֹ דֶּרֶךְ, וְאֵין מְמַחֶה בְּיָדוֹ. [2]דֶּרֶךְ הַמֶּלֶךְ אֵין לוֹ שִׁיעוּר.
[3]וְכָל הָעָם בּוֹזְזִין וְנוֹתְנִין לוֹ, וְהוּא נוֹטֵל חֵלֶק בְּרֹאשׁ.
גמרא [4]תָּנֵינָא חֲדָא זִימְנָא: [5]"אֵין מוֹצִיאִין לְמִלְחֶמֶת הָרְשׁוּת אֶלָּא עַל פִּי בֵית דִּין שֶׁל שִׁבְעִים וְאֶחָד"!
[6]אַיְּידֵי דְּתָנָא כָּל מִילֵּי דְּמֶלֶךְ, [7]תָּנָא נַמִי מוֹצִיאִין לְמִלְחֶמֶת הָרְשׁוּת.
[8]אָמַר רַב יְהוּדָה אָמַר שְׁמוּאֵל: כָּל הָאָמוּר בְּפָרָשַׁת מֶלֶךְ

RASHI

משנה ופורץ – גדרות אחרים. לעשות לו דרך – לשדהו ולכרמו. חלק בראש – חלק היפה בורר ראשון ונוטל תחלה.

גמרא בפרשת מלך – בספר שמואל (א׳ ח): "בניכם ובנותיכם יקח" וכיוצא בהם.

NOTES

פּוֹרֵץ לַעֲשׂוֹת לוֹ דֶּרֶךְ He breaches fences to construct for himself a road. According to *Ramah,* this prerogative only applies during times of war. The king is not required to lead his troops around another person's wall, nor is he required to have his troops pass through single file. Rather, he may make the road as wide as he sees fit. The road does not, however, enter permanently into the king's possession but must be returned to its owner after the war.

stones in the High Priest's breastplate) must also be consulted before the king goes out to an optional war (see above, 16a), because it only deals with requirements that applied during the Second Temple period, when the Urim and Tumim had been lost (*Rabbenu Yonah*).

Rabbenu Yonatan understands the Mishnah differently — that the king must inform the Sanhedrin that he is taking the people out to an optional war, so that its members will pray for his success in battle.

HALAKHAH

an optional war without receiving the prior permission of the Great Sanhedrin." (*Rambam, Sefer Shofetim, Hilkhot Sanhedrin* 5:1; *Hilkhot Melakhim* 8:2.)

פּוֹרֵץ לַעֲשׂוֹת לוֹ דֶּרֶךְ He breaches fences to construct for himself a road. "The king may breach other people's fences in order to make a road, and nobody may raise any objections. He need not alter his route in order to avoid somebody's vineyard or field. The king's road has no maximum dimensions, so he may make it as wide or as long as he needs it to be." (*Rambam, Sefer Shofetim, Hilkhot Melakhim* 5:3.)

כָּל הָאָמוּר בְּפָרָשַׁת מֶלֶךְ Whatever was stated in the passage regarding a king. "Whatever was stated in the passage regarding a king in the First Book of Samuel is permitted to the king. He may levy taxes, and force people into military or domestic service. Whoever fails to obey him may have all of his property confiscated or may even be put to death (for the law is in accordance with Shmuel in civil matters, and in accordance with Rabbi Yose when he disagrees with a colleague; *Kesef Mishneh*)." (*Rambam, Sefer Shofetim, Hilkhot Melakhim* 4:1-7.)

Israel from Babylonia, studied under Rabbi Yoḥanan, and later returned to Babylonia. In his youth, in Babylonia, he was a disciple of Rav Yehudah and Rav Ḥisda. His closest colleague was Rabbi Yirmeyah, and his most distinguished disciple was Rabbi Yirmeyah bar Taḥlifa.

רַבִּי יְהוֹשֻׁעַ בֶּן לֵוִי Rabbi Yehoshua ben Levi. One of the greatest Amoraim of the first generation in Eretz Israel. Rabbi Yehoshua ben Levi was, according to some opinions, the son of Levi ben Sisi, one of the outstanding students of Rabbi Yehudah HaNasi, and it seems that Rabbi Yehoshua ben Levi was himself one of Rabbi Yehudah HaNasi's younger students. Many Halakhic disputes are recorded between him and Rabbi Yoḥanan, who was apparently younger than he was and a student and colleague of his. In general, the Halakhah follows Rabbi Yehoshua ben Levi, even against Rabbi Yoḥanan, whose authority was broadly recognized.

Rabbi Yehoshua ben Levi was also a renowned teacher of Aggadah. Because of the great respect in which he was held, Aggadic statements in his name are presented at the end of the six orders of the Mishnah.

A great deal is told of his piety and sanctity, and he is regarded as one of the most righteous men who ever lived. Among other things, it is told that he would sit with the most dangerously infected lepers and study Torah. He was famous as a worker of miracles, to whom Elijah the Prophet appeared. Moreover, his prayers were always answered. According to tradition he is one of those over whom the Angel of Death had no dominion, and he entered the Garden of Eden alive.

He taught many students. All the Sages of the succeeding generation were his students to some degree, and quote Torah teachings in his name. His son, Rabbi Yosef, was also a Sage, and married into the Nasi's family.

CONCEPTS

מִלְחֶמֶת הָרְשׁוּת Optional war. A war waged by a Jewish King to enlarge the boundaries of Eretz Israel, or

— מֶלֶךְ מוּתָּר בּוֹ. [1]רַב אָמַר: לֹא נֶאֶמְרָה פָּרָשָׁה זוֹ אֶלָּא לְאַיֵּים עֲלֵיהֶם, [2]שֶׁנֶּאֱמַר: ״שׂוֹם תָּשִׂים עָלֶיךָ מֶלֶךְ״ — שֶׁתְּהֵא אֵימָתוֹ עָלֶיךָ.

[3]כְּתַנָּאֵי: [4]״רַבִּי יוֹסֵי אוֹמֵר: כָּל הָאָמוּר בְּפָרָשַׁת מֶלֶךְ — מֶלֶךְ מוּתָּר בּוֹ. [5]רַבִּי יְהוּדָה אוֹמֵר: לֹא נֶאֶמְרָה פָּרָשָׁה זוֹ אֶלָּא כְּדֵי לְאַיֵּים עֲלֵיהֶם, [6]שֶׁנֶּאֱמַר: ׳שׂוֹם תָּשִׂים עָלֶיךָ מֶלֶךְ׳ — שֶׁתְּהֵא אֵימָתוֹ עָלֶיךָ. [7]וְכֵן הָיָה רַבִּי יְהוּדָה אוֹמֵר: שָׁלֹשׁ מִצְוֹת נִצְטַוּוּ יִשְׂרָאֵל בִּכְנִיסָתָן לָאָרֶץ: [8]לְהַעֲמִיד לָהֶם מֶלֶךְ, [9]וּלְהַכְרִית זַרְעוֹ שֶׁל עֲמָלֵק, [10]וְלִבְנוֹת לָהֶם

LITERAL TRANSLATION

— a king is permitted [to engage] in. [1]Rav said: This passage was only stated to intimidate them, [2]for it is said: "You shall surely set a king over you" — that his fear should be upon you.

[3][This is] like [a dispute between] Tannaim: [4]"Rabbi Yose says: Whatever is stated in the passage of the king — a king is permitted. [5]Rabbi Yehudah says: This passage was only stated to intimidate them, [6]for it is said: 'You shall surely set a king over you' — that his fear should be upon you. [7]And thus would Rabbi Yehudah say: Three commandments were commanded [to the people of] Israel upon their entry into the land: [8]To appoint for themselves a king, [9]and to destroy the seed of Amalek, [10]and to build for

TRANSLATION AND COMMENTARY

permitted to the king: "He will take your sons, and appoint them for himself for his chariot, and to be his horsemen; and some shall run before his chariot. And he will appoint for himself captains over thousands, and captains over fifties; and will set them to plow his ground, and to reap his harvest, and to make his instruments of war, and the instruments of his chariots. And he will take your daughters for perfumers, and cooks, and bakers. And he will take your fields, and your vineyards, and your best oliveyards, and give them to his servants. And he will take the tenth of your seed, and of your vineyards, and give to his officers, and to his servants. And he will take your menservants, and your maidservants, and your goodliest young men, and your asses, and put them to his work. He will take the tenth of your sheep: and you shall be his servants." [1]**Rav** disagreed and **said:** These things are not actually permitted to a king, since **this passage was only stated to threaten** the people, [2]**for the verse states** (Deuteronomy 17:15): **"You shall surely set a king over you,"** using the emphatic double verb mode (שׂוֹם תָּשִׂים — "you shall surely set") to indicate **that** the king's **fear should be upon** the nation.

כְּתַנָּאֵי [3]The Gemara now notes that the question of whether a king is entitled to all the privileges listed in the Book of Samuel is the subject of **a dispute between the Tannaim,** for we learned in a Baraita: [4]**"Rabbi Yose says: Whatever was stated in the passage regarding a king** in the Book of Samuel **is permitted to the king.** [5]**Rabbi Yehudah** disagrees and **says:** The king is not actually permitted to assume those privileges, for **this passage was only stated to threaten** the people, [6]**for the verse states** (Deuteronomy 17:15): **'You shall surely set a king over you,' so that his fear will be upon** the nation. [7]**And so too Rabbi Yehudah says: Three commandments were given to** the people of **Israel upon their entry into Eretz Israel.** These commandments did not apply while they were still wandering in the desert, and they had to be fulfilled in a certain order: (1) [8]**To appoint for themselves a king,** as the verse states (Deuteronomy 17:14-15): 'When you come to the land which the Lord your God gives you, and shall possess it, and shall dwell in it...from among your brethren you shall surely set a king over you'; (2) [9]**to** wage war and **destroy the seed of Amalek,** as the verse states (Deuteronomy 25:19): 'Therefore it shall be, when the Lord you God has given you rest from all your enemies round about, in the land which the Lord your God gives you for an inheritance to possess it, that you shall blot out the remembrance of Amalek from under heaven; you shall not forget'; **and** (3) [10]**to build the** permanent **Temple** in Jerusalem, as the verse states

RASHI

רב אמר לא נאמרה פרשה — דשמואל אלא לאיים עליהם שתהא אימת מלכם עליהם, אבל אינו מותר לעשות. הכי גרסינן: **רבי יהודה אומר לא נאמרה פרשה זו אלא לאיים עליהם** — ולא גרס ליראם ולבהלם, דהא לרבי יהודה יפה כיוונו, שהרי נצטוו ישראל על כך, והכי גרס לה בתוספתא. **שלש מצות** — להכי נקט שלש הללו, שהן תלויות זו בזו לעשותן כסדרן, כדמפרש לקמן: בתחלה מלך, ואחריה עמלק, ואחריה בית הבחירה. **בכניסתם לארץ** — דבכולהו כתיב ירושה וישיבה, "וירשת וישבת בה" "ואמרת אשימה עלי מלך" (דברים יז), בעמלק כתיב (שם כה): "והיה בהניח ה' וגו'", ובבנין בית הבחירה כתיב (שם יב): "ועברתם את הירדן וישבתם בארץ וגו'", והדר כתיב: "והיה המקום וגו'".

for some other reason that does not come under the category of mandatory war. Such a war may only be undertaken with the permission of the Sanhedrin.

NOTES

מֶלֶךְ מוּתָּר **A king is permitted.** The Rishonim ask: According to the opinion that the king is indeed permitted to assume all the prerogatives listed in the passage in I Samuel, why was Ahab punished for the incident involving the vineyard of Naboth the Jezreelite (see I Kings 21)? *Rabbenu Yonah* suggests that the king is permitted to confiscate property if necessary for waging war, but he may not arbitrarily seize property for his own personal aggrandizement. (See also *Tosafot.*)

בֵּית הַבְּחִירָה. [1]רַבִּי נְהוֹרַאי אוֹמֵר: לֹא נֶאֶמְרָה פָּרָשָׁה זוֹ אֶלָּא כְּנֶגֶד תַּרְעוּמְתָּן, [2]שֶׁנֶּאֱמַר: 'וְאָמַרְתָּ אָשִׂימָה עָלַי מֶלֶךְ וגו'". [3]תַּנְיָא: "רַבִּי אֱלִיעֶזֶר אוֹמֵר: [4]זְקֵנִים שֶׁבַּדּוֹר כַּהוֹגֶן שָׁאֲלוּ, [5]שֶׁנֶּאֱמַר: 'תְּנָה לָנוּ מֶלֶךְ לְשָׁפְטֵנוּ'. [6]אֲבָל עַמֵּי הָאָרֶץ שֶׁבָּהֶן קִלְקְלוּ, [7]שֶׁנֶּאֱמַר: 'וְהָיִינוּ גַם אֲנַחְנוּ כְּכָל הַגּוֹיִם; וּשְׁפָטָנוּ מַלְכֵּנוּ וְיָצָא לְפָנֵינוּ'". [8]תַּנְיָא: "רַבִּי יוֹסֵי אוֹמֵר: [9]שָׁלֹשׁ מִצְוֹת נִצְטַוּוּ יִשְׂרָאֵל בִּכְנִיסָתָן לָאָרֶץ: [10]לְהַעֲמִיד לָהֶם מֶלֶךְ, [11]וּלְהַכְרִית זַרְעוֹ שֶׁל עֲמָלֵק, [12]וְלִבְנוֹת לָהֶם בֵּית הַבְּחִירָה. [13]וְאֵינִי יוֹדֵעַ אֵיזֶה מֵהֶן תְּחִילָּה. [14]כְּשֶׁהוּא אוֹמֵר: 'כִּי יָד עַל כֵּס יָהּ, מִלְחָמָה לַה' בַּעֲמָלֵק', [15]הֱוֵי אוֹמֵר לְהַעֲמִיד לָהֶם מֶלֶךְ תְּחִילָּה; וְאֵין "כִּסֵּא" אֶלָּא מֶלֶךְ,

LITERAL TRANSLATION

themselves a Temple (lit., 'the house of choice'). [1]Rabbi Nehorai says: This passage [to appoint a king] was only stated in response to their complaint, [2]for it is stated: 'And you shall say: I will set a king over me.'"

[3]It was taught: "Rabbi Eliezer says: [4]The elders who were in that generation asked fittingly, [5]for it is stated: 'Give us a king to judge us.' [6]But the common people among them sinned, [7]as it is said: 'And we shall also be like all the nations; and that our king may judge us, and go out before us.'"

[8]It was taught: "Rabbi Yose says: [9]Three commandments were given to [the people of] Israel upon their entry into the land: [10]To appoint for themselves a king, [11]and to destroy the seed of Amalek, [12]and to build for themselves a Temple. [13]And I do not know which of them is first. [14]When it states: 'For a hand is upon the throne of the Lord, a war for God against Amalek,' [15]one can say [that] to establish for themselves a king is first; [as] there is no throne but [that of] a king,

TRANSLATION AND COMMENTARY

(Deuteronomy 12:10-11): 'But when you traverse the Jordan, and dwell in the land which the Lord your God gives you to inherit, and when He gives you rest from all your enemies round about, so that you dwell in safety. Then there shall be a place which the Lord your God shall choose to cause His name to dwell there.' [1]**Rabbi Nehorai** disagrees with regard to the command to appoint a king and **says: The passage** in Deuteronomy 17 relating to the king **was only stated as a response to future complaints**. God instructed the people of Israel that they may appoint a king, only because He knew that one day the nation would demand a king so that they could be like all the nations (see I Samuel 8:20). [2]We see this even in **the verse** which **states** (Deuteronomy 17:14): **'And you shall say: I will set a king over me,** like all the nations that are about me.' Appointing a king is not a positive commandment, and it is in fact preferable for the people not to ask to have a king appointed."

תַּנְיָא [3]**It was taught** in another Baraita: **"Rabbi Eliezer says:** [4]**The elders of** Samuel's **generation asked** for a king **in a fitting manner,** [5]**as the verse states** (I Samuel 8:6): **'Give us a king to judge us.'** [6]**But the common people among them sinned** when they asked for a king. They sought a leader who would bring them victory in battle, whereas they should have placed their trust in God, [7]**as the verse states** (v. 20): **'And we shall also be like all the nations; and that our king may judge us, and go out before us,** and fight our battles.'"

תַּנְיָא [8]A similar Baraita **taught: "Rabbi Yose says:** [9]**Three commandments were given to** the people of **Israel upon their entry into Eretz Israel:** (1) [10]**To appoint for themselves a king;** (2) [11]**to** wage war and **destroy the seed of Amalek; and** (3) [12]**to build the** permanent **Temple** in Jerusalem. [13]**But I** still **do not know which of these** commandments **is** to be fulfilled **first.** [14]**Since** the verse **says** (Exodus 17:16): **'Because the Lord has sworn by His throne that the Lord will have war with Amalek** from generation to generation,' [15]**I may conclude** that the commandment to **appoint a king is** to be fulfilled **first, for the throne** of the Lord mentioned here

RASHI

לא נאמרה פרשה זו — ד"שום תשים עליך מלך" משום מלוה, אלא כנגד תרעומתם, שגלוי לפניו שעתידים להתרעם על כך ולומר "והיינו גם אנחנו ככל הגוים", שנאמר "ואמרת אשימה" — עתידין אתם לומר כן. רבי נהוראי אמר כו' לא גרסינן ליה בתוספתא, ותדע דשיבוש הוא, דהא קיימא לן בעירובין (יג,ב) דהוא רבי נחמיה הוא רבי נהוראי. עמי הארץ קלקלו — דאילו זקנים שאלוהו לשופטם ולרדות הסרבנים שבהם, אבל עמי הארץ תלו עליו מלחמותיהם שאמרו "ויצא בראשינו ונלחם את מלחמתנו".

NOTES

וּשְׁפָטָנוּ מַלְכֵּנוּ **That our king may judge us.** *Ran* (in his *Derashot*) explains that the people erred when they asked that a king be anointed so that he may judge them, for, according to Jewish law, the judicial tasks fall upon the judges and not the king.

HALAKHAH

שָׁלֹשׁ מִצְוֹת נִצְטַוּוּ יִשְׂרָאֵל בִּכְנִיסָתָן לָאָרֶץ **Three commandments were given to Israel upon their entry into the land.** "Three commandments were given to the people of Israel upon their entry into Eretz Israel: To appoint a king,

[1] שֶׁנֶּאֱמַר: ׳וַיֵּשֶׁב שְׁלֹמֹה עַל כִּסֵּא ה׳ לְמֶלֶךְ׳״. [2] וַעֲדַיִין אֵינִי יוֹדֵעַ אִם לִבְנוֹת לָהֶם בֵּית הַבְּחִירָה תְּחִלָּה, [3] אוֹ לְהַכְרִית זַרְעוֹ שֶׁל עֲמָלֵק תְּחִלָּה. [4] כְּשֶׁהוּא אוֹמֵר: ׳וְהֵנִיחַ לָכֶם מִכָּל אוֹיְבֵיכֶם וגו׳....וְהָיָה הַמָּקוֹם אֲשֶׁר יִבְחַר ה׳ וגו׳׳, [5] הֱוֵי אוֹמֵר לְהַכְרִית זַרְעוֹ שֶׁל עֲמָלֵק תְּחִלָּה. [6] וְכֵן בְּדָוִד הוּא אוֹמֵר: ׳וַיְהִי כִּי יָשַׁב הַמֶּלֶךְ דָּוִד בְּבֵיתוֹ וַה׳ הֵנִיחַ לוֹ מִסָּבִיב׳, [7] וּכְתִיב: ׳וַיֹּאמֶר הַמֶּלֶךְ אֶל נָתָן הַנָּבִיא, רְאֵה נָא, אָנֹכִי יוֹשֵׁב בְּבֵית אֲרָזִים, וגו׳׳״.

[8] אָמַר רֵישׁ לָקִישׁ: בַּתְּחִילָּה מָלַךְ שְׁלֹמֹה עַל הָעֶלְיוֹנִים, [9] שֶׁנֶּאֱמַר: ״וַיֵּשֶׁב שְׁלֹמֹה עַל כִּסֵּא ה׳״. [10] וּלְבַסּוֹף מָלַךְ עַל הַתַּחְתּוֹנִים, [11] שֶׁנֶּאֱמַר: ״כִּי הוּא רֹדֶה בְּכָל עֵבֶר הַנָּהָר מִתִּפְסַח וְעַד עַזָּה״.

[12] רַב וּשְׁמוּאֵל. [13] חַד אָמַר: תִּפְסַח בְּסוֹף הָעוֹלָם, וְעַזָּה בְּסוֹף הָעוֹלָם. [14] וְחַד אָמַר: תִּפְסַח וְעַזָּה בַּהֲדֵי הֲדָדֵי הָווּ יָתְבוּ, [15] וּכְשֵׁם שֶׁמָּלַךְ עַל תִּפְסַח

LITERAL TRANSLATION

[1] for it is said: 'And Solomon sat on the throne of the Lord as king.' [2] But I still do not know whether [they were] to build for themselves the Temple first, [3] or to destroy the seed of Amalek first. [4] Since it states: 'And when He gives you rest from all your enemies.... Then there shall be a place which the Lord your God shall choose, etc.,' [5] [you have to] say [that] to destroy the seed of Amalek is first. [6] And so does it state concerning David: 'And it came to pass, when David the king sat in his house, and the Lord had given him rest round about'; [7] and it is written: 'And the king said to Nathan the prophet, See now, I dwell in a house of cedar, etc.'"

[8] Resh Lakish said: At first Solomon [also] ruled over the heavenly realms, [9] for it is said: "And Solomon sat on the throne of the Lord." [10] But eventually he ruled over the lower realms, [11] for it is said: "For he had dominion over all [the region] on this side of the river, from Tiphsaḥ to Azza."

[12] Rav and Shmuel [disagreed]. [13] One said: Tiphsaḥ was at [one] end of the world, and Azza was at [the other] end of the world. [14] And one said: Tiphsaḥ and Azza sat next to each other, [15] and just as he ruled over Tiphsaḥ

TRANSLATION AND COMMENTARY

is nothing but the throne of the **King** of the people of Israel, [1] **as the verse states** (I Chronicles 29:23): **'And Solomon sat on the throne of the Lord as king.'** [2] **But I still do not know whether** the obligation **to build the Temple** comes **first,** [3] **or** the obligation **to destroy the seed of Amalek** comes **first.** [4] **Since** the verse **says** (Deuteronomy 12:10-11): **'And when He gives you rest from all your enemies** round about, so that you dwell in safety. **Then there shall be a place which the Lord your God shall choose** to cause His name to dwell there,' [5] **I may conclude** that the obligation **to destroy the seed of Amalek** comes **first,** and only then must the Temple be built, for the obligation to build the Temple does not begin until Israel has rest from all of its enemies. [6] **And so, too, with respect to David** the verse **says** (II Samuel 7:1): **'And it came to pass, when the king sat in his house, and the Lord had given him rest round about** from all his enemies,' [7] **and it** then **says** (v. 2): **'And the king said to Nathan the prophet, See now, I dwell in a house of cedar,** but the ark of God dwells within curtains.' Only after David had subdued his enemies did he begin to consider constructing the Temple."

אָמַר רֵישׁ לָקִישׁ [8] Having mentioned the verse relating to Solomon's throne, the Gemara relates Solomon's greatness and decline: **Resh Lakish said: At first,** Solomon **ruled** not only on earth, but also **over the heavenly creatures,** [9] **as the verse states** (I Chronicles 29:23): **"And Solomon sat on the throne of the Lord** as king." [10] **But finally,** after he had taken foreign wives, **he ruled** only **over the earthly creatures,** [11] **as the verse states** (I Kings 5:4): **"For he had dominion over all the region on this side of the river, from Tiphsaḥ to Azza."**

רַב וּשְׁמוּאֵל [12] The Gemara notes that **Rav and Shmuel disagreed** about how this verse implies that Solomon ruled over the entire world. [13] **One** of these Sages **said: Tiphsaḥ was at one end of the world, and Azza was at the other end of the world,** so that Solomon's dominion extended across the entire world. [14] **And the other one said: Tiphsaḥ and Azza were** located right **next to each other,** [15] **and** the verse means to say that, **just as**

RASHI

בתחילה — קודם שנשא שלמה נשים נכריות, מלך אף על עליונים.

SAGES

רֵישׁ לָקִישׁ Resh Lakish. See *Sanhedrin*, Part I, pp. 56-7.

רַב Rav. See *Sanhedrin*, Part I, pp. 39-40.

שְׁמוּאֵל Shmuel. See *Sanhedrin*, Part I, p. 19.

BACKGROUND

תִּפְסַח Tiphsaḥ. This name was apparently applied to two places. One was the city of תִּפְסָכִים (Ḥirbet Dafsi), in Syria, 115 kilometers north of Tadmor. However, תִּפְסַח also refers to a city in Eretz Israel (perhaps Ḥirbet Tiphseh), twenty-four kilometers northeast of Gaza. These two opinions are based on different identifications of the name תִּפְסַח in the Bible.

HALAKHAH

to destroy the seed of Amalek, and to build a permanent Temple." (*Rambam, Sefer Shofetim, Hilkhot Melakhim* 1:1-2.)

וְעַל עַזָּה, [1]כָּךְ מָלַךְ עַל כָּל הָעוֹלָם כּוּלּוֹ.
[2]וּלְבַסּוֹף לֹא מָלַךְ אֶלָּא עַל יִשְׂרָאֵל, [3]שֶׁנֶּאֱמַר: ״אֲנִי, קֹהֶלֶת, הָיִיתִי מֶלֶךְ עַל יִשְׂרָאֵל וגו׳״. [4]וּלְבַסּוֹף לֹא מָלַךְ אֶלָּא עַל יְרוּשָׁלַיִם, [5]שֶׁנֶּאֱמַר: ״דִּבְרֵי קֹהֶלֶת, בֶּן דָּוִד מֶלֶךְ בִּירוּשָׁלַיִם״. [6]וּלְבַסּוֹף לֹא מָלַךְ אֶלָּא עַל מִטָּתוֹ, [7]שֶׁנֶּאֱמַר: ״הִנֵּה מִטָּתוֹ שֶׁלִּשְׁלֹמֹה וגו׳״. [8]וּלְבַסּוֹף לֹא מָלַךְ אֶלָּא עַל מַקְלוֹ, [9]שֶׁנֶּאֱמַר: ״זֶה הָיָה חֶלְקִי מִכָּל עֲמָלִי״.
[10]רַב וּשְׁמוּאֵל. חַד אָמַר: מַקְלוֹ. [11]וְחַד אָמַר: גּוּנְדּוֹ.
[12]הֲדַר אוֹ לָא הֲדַר? [13]רַב וּשְׁמוּאֵל. [14]חַד אָמַר: הֲדַר. [15]וְחַד אָמַר: לָא הֲדַר. [16]מַאן דְּאָמַר לָא הֲדַר, מֶלֶךְ וְהֶדְיוֹט. [17]וּמַאן דְּאָמַר: הֲדַר, מֶלֶךְ, וְהֶדְיוֹט וּמֶלֶךְ.
[18]״פּוֹרֵץ לַעֲשׂוֹת לוֹ דֶּרֶךְ״.

LITERAL TRANSLATION

and over Azza, [1]so did he rule over the entire world.

[2]And eventually he ruled only over Israel, [3]for it is said: "I, Kohelet, was king over Israel, etc." [4]And eventually he ruled only over Jerusalem, [5]for it is said: "The words of Kohelet, the son of David, king [in Jerusalem]." [6]And eventually he ruled only over his bed, [7]for it is said: "Behold, it is his bed, that of Solomon." [8]And eventually he ruled only over his staff, [9]for it is said: "This was my portion from all my labor."

[10]Rav and Shmuel [disagreed]. One said: His staff. [11]And one said: His cloak.

[12]Did he return [to his former greatness] or did he not return? [13]Rav and Shmuel [disagreed]. [14]One said: He returned. [15]And one said: He did not return. [16][According to] the one who said he did not return, [he was] a king and an ordinary person. [17]And [according to] the one who said: He returned, [he was] a king, and an ordinary person, and a king.

[18]"And he breaches [fences] to construct for himself a road."

TRANSLATION AND COMMENTARY

Solomon **ruled over Tiphsah and over Azza,** [1]**so** too did **he rule over the entire world.**

וּלְבַסּוֹף [2]However, Solomon's dominion steadily declined. **And finally,** when he continued to maintain those foreign wives, **he ruled only over Israel,** [3]**as the verse states** (Ecclesiastes 1:12): **"I Kohelet was king over Israel** in Jerusalem." [4]**And finally** his reign declined even further, so that **he ruled only over Jerusalem,** [5]**as the verse states** (Ecclesiastes 1:1): **"The words of Kohelet, the son of David, king in Jerusalem."** [6]**And finally he ruled only over his** own **bed,** [7]**as the verse states** (Song of Songs 3:7): **"Behold, it is his bed, that of Solomon!"** [8]**And finally** his reign declined even further, so that in the end **he ruled only over his** own **staff,** [9]**as the verse states** (Ecclesiastes 2:10): **"This was my portion of all my labor."** Solomon taught us here that all his labor was reduced to nothing, and, as the Gemara explains, he was impoverished like Jacob, who crossed the river with his staff alone (Genesis 32:11).

רַב וּשְׁמוּאֵל [10]Rav and Shmuel also disagreed about the meaning of this verse: **One said** that Solomon was referring to **his staff.** [11]And the other **said** that he was referring to **his** royal **cloak** which still remained in his possession.

הֲדַר [12]The Gemara asks: **Did** Solomon ever **return** to his former glory **or did he not?** [13]**Rav and Shmuel** also **disagreed** about the matter: [14]**One said** that, in the end, Solomon **returned** to his former glory. [15]**And** the other **said** that **he did not.** [16]**According to** the opinion of **the one who said** that **he did not return** to rule over the entire world, Solomon **was** first **a king, and** then **an ordinary person.** [17]**And according to** the opinion of **the one who said** that **he did return,** Solomon **was** first **a king, and** then **an ordinary person, and** then a **king** again.

פּוֹרֵץ לַעֲשׂוֹת לוֹ [18]We learn in the next clause of our Mishnah: "The king **may breach** other people's **fences** in order **to make a road** to serve his needs, and nobody may raise any objections. The people may plunder the enemy during war, but then they must hand the booty over to the king, and he takes his portion of the spoils first, and then the people divide the remainder among themselves."

RASHI

וכשם שמלך על תפסח ועזה כך מלך על כל העולם כולו — והכי קאמר קרא: ״כי הוא רודה בכל עבר הנהר״ — כמתפסח ועד עזה. **על מקלו** — שהשליכו אשמדאי מכסאו, כדאמרינן במסכת גיטין (סח,ב). **גונדו** = טליתו, ובסדר טהרות (כלים פרק טז) פירש רב האיי: מקידה = הוא מקידה של חרש, ודומה לו, חד אמר: קודו, וחד אמר: מקלו (ויקרא רבה פרשה אחרי), והוא מקידה ששותה בה מים. **מלך והדיוט** — ושוב לא חזר למלכותו.

NOTES

מַקְלוֹ, גּוּנְדּוֹ **His staff, his cloak.** All agree that both of these terms allude to the ultimate decline of Solomon's authority. *Iyyun Ya'akov* understands the word גּוּנְדּוֹ to mean "his intimate circle," for a small circle of associates remained loyal to Solomon until the end. The Geonim had the reading: קוּדוֹ — an earthenware or wooden utensil used as a drinking bowl.

LANGUAGE

גּוּנְדּוֹ **Cloak.** *Gundo* is the name of an outer garment that was worn during the Talmudic period. It derives from the Persian verb, *gund*, meaning, "to wear."

הֶדְיוֹט **Ordinary person.** This word derives from the Greek ἰδιώτης *hidiot*, meaning a simple citizen who has no official position.

[1]תָּנוּ רַבָּנַן: ״אוֹצְרוֹת מְלָכִים לַמֶּלֶךְ. [2]וּשְׁאָר בִּיזָּה שֶׁבּוֹזְזִין, [3]מֶחֱצָה לַמֶּלֶךְ וּמֶחֱצָה לָעָם״. [4]אָמַר לֵיהּ אַבַּיֵי לְרַב דִּימִי, וְאָמְרִי לָהּ לְרַב אַחָא: [5]בִּשְׁלָמָא אוֹצְרוֹת מְלָכִים לַמֶּלֶךְ — [6]אוֹרְחָא דְּמִלְּתָא. [7]אֶלָּא שְׁאָר בִּיזָּה שֶׁבּוֹזְזִין, מֶחֱצָה לַמֶּלֶךְ וּמֶחֱצָה לָעָם מְנָלַן? [8]דִּכְתִיב: [21A] [9]״וַיִּמְשְׁחוּ לַה׳ לְנָגִיד וּלְצָדוֹק״. [10]מַקִּישׁ נָגִיד לְצָדוֹק. [11]מַה צָדוֹק — מֶחֱצָה לוֹ וּמֶחֱצָה לְאֶחָיו, [12]אַף נָגִיד — מֶחֱצָה לוֹ וּמֶחֱצָה לְאֶחָיו. [13]וְצָדוֹק גּוּפֵיהּ, מְנָלַן? [14]דְּתַנְיָא: ״רַבִּי אוֹמֵר: [15]׳וְהָיְתָה לְאַהֲרֹן וּלְבָנָיו׳ — [16]מֶחֱצָה לְאַהֲרֹן וּמֶחֱצָה לְבָנָיו״.

מִשְׁנָה [17]״לֹא יַרְבֶּה לוֹ נָשִׁים״ — אֶלָּא שְׁמוֹנֶה עֶשְׂרֵה. [18]רַבִּי יְהוּדָה אוֹמֵר: מַרְבֶּה הוּא לוֹ, [19]וּבִלְבַד שֶׁלֹּא יְהוּ מְסִירוֹת

LITERAL TRANSLATION

[1]Our Rabbis taught: "Royal treasures to the king. [2]And the rest of the spoils that they plunder, [3]half to the king and half to the people." [4]Abaye said to Rav Dimi, and some say to Rav Aḥa: [5]Granted that royal treasures [go] to the king — [6]for [that is] the way of things. [7]But from where do we know [that] the rest of the spoils that they plunder, half [goes] to the king and half to the people? [8]For it is written: [21A] [9]"And they annointed him to the Lord to be the chief governor, and Zadok [to be priest]." [10]It compares the chief governor to Zadok. [11]Just as [with] Zadok — half to him and half to his brethren, [12]so too [with] the chief governor — half to him and half to his brethren.

[13]And [regarding] Zadok himself, from where do we [derive this rule]? [14]As it was taught: "Rabbi says: [15]'And it shall be for Aaron and his sons' — [16]half to Aaron and half to his sons."

MISHNAH [17]"He shall not multiply wives for himself" — but [only] eighteen. [18]Rabbi Yehudah says: He may multiply [wives], [19]but only if they do not turn

TRANSLATION AND COMMENTARY

[1]**Our Rabbis taught** a related Baraita: **"Royal treasures** that are taken in a war belong **to the king.** [2]As for **the rest of the plunder that the people take** during war, [3]**half** must be given **to the king, and** the remaining **half** is then divided **among the people."**

אָמַר לֵיהּ [4]**Abaye said to Rav Dimi, and some say** that he said this **to Rav Aḥa:** [5]**Granted that the royal treasures** taken during war **belong to the king,** [6]for that is **the usual way** of things. [7]**But from where do we know** that regarding **the rest of the plunder that is taken** during war, **half** must be given to the king, **and** the remaining **half** is then divided **among the people?** What is the Biblical source of this ruling? Rav Dimi (or Rav Aḥa) answered: [8]**For the verse states** (I Chronicles 29:22): [21A] [9]"And they made Solomon the son of David king the second time, **and annointed him to the Lord to be the chief governor, and Zadok to be priest."** [10]Scripture **compares the chief governor** (the king) **to Zadok** (the High Priest). [11]**Just as** with **Zadok** — **half** of the Temple shewbreads were given **to him and** the other **half** were given **to** the rest of **his** priestly **brethren,** [12]**so too** with **the chief governor** — **half** of the booty must be given **to him and** the other **half** is then divided up among **his brethren,** the people of Israel.

וְצָדוֹק גּוּפֵיהּ [13]The Gemara asks: **And** regarding **Zadok himself, from where do we** know that he is entitled to receive half of the shewbreads each week? [14]The Gemara answers: **As it was taught in** a Baraita: **"Rabbi** Yehudah HaNasi **says:** The verse dealing with the shewbreads states (Leviticus 24:9): [15]**'And it shall be for Aaron and his sons,** and they shall eat it in the holy place.' [16]From here we learn that **half** of the shewbreads must be given **to Aaron,** the High Priest, **and** the other **half** must be divided up **among his sons,** the rest of the priests."

MISHNAH לֹא יַרְבֶּה לוֹ נָשִׁים [17]The king's right to marry is limited by the verse in the Torah that states (Deuteronomy 17:17): **"He shall not multiply wives for himself."** The king may take up to **eighteen** wives. [18]**Rabbi Yehudah says:** The king **is** indeed **permitted to marry many wives,** even more than eighteen, [19]**but only if** he marries women who **will not turn his heart away** and cause him to sin, for the very same

RASHI

וימשחו אותו — בשלמה כתיב. **והיתה לאהרן ולבניו** — בלחם הפנים כתיב.

משנה שמנה עשרה — לקמן נפקא לן.

SAGES

אַבַּיֵי Abaye. One of the greatest Sages of the Talmud, Abaye was a member of the fourth generation of Babylonian Amoraim. He was left an orphan and was raised in the home of his uncle, Rabbah. Although Rabbah was a priest and the head of a yeshivah, he and Abaye lived in poverty. Abaye was also the student of Rav Yosef, and after Rav Yosef's death Abaye became head of the Pumbedita Yeshivah.

Apart from his eminence as a Torah scholar, Abaye was considered outstanding in his piety and acts of charity.

Halakhic discussions between him and Rabbah, and even more so between him and Rav Yosef, are found throughout the Talmud. But his most important discussions are with his colleague, Rava. These are considered examples of the most profound and creative Halakhic dialectic, and form an important element in the structure of the Babylonian Talmud. Though the intellectual approaches of these two Sages are similar, Abaye's approach is generally more formalistic. In Halakhic decision-making the general principle is that in disputes between Abaye and Rava, the opinion of Rava is accepted, except in a small number of cases.

Abaye's son, Bivei bar Abaye, was also a well-known Sage.

רַב דִּימִי Rav Dimi. An Amora of the third and fourth generations. See *Sanhedrin,* Part I, p.67.

BACKGROUND

מֶחֱצָה לוֹ וּמֶחֱצָה לְאֶחָיו Half to him and half to his brethren. Twelve shewbreads were placed on the sacred table in the Sanctuary each Sabbath. The previous week's breads were divided among the priests, who ate them. Just as the High Priest is entitled to take half of the loaves for himself, so too is the king permitted to take for himself half of the plunder acquired in battle.

HALAKHAH

אוֹצְרוֹת מְלָכִים לַמֶּלֶךְ Royal treasures to the king. "The royal treasures that are captured during a war belong to the king. As for the rest of the plunder, half belongs to the king, and he takes his portion first; and the other half is divided between the troops who waged the war and the rest of the people who stayed behind guarding the camp." (*Rambam, Sefer Shofetim, Hilkhot Melakhim* 4:9.)

לֹא יַרְבֶּה לוֹ נָשִׁים He shall not multiply wives for himself. "The king is not permitted to marry more than eighteen women," following the anonymous first Tanna of the

SAGES

רַבִּי שִׁמְעוֹן **Rabbi Shimon.** See *Sanhedrin*, Part I, p. 23.

TRANSLATION AND COMMENTARY

verse continues: "And his heart shall not turn away." [1]**Rabbi Shimon says:** The king is not permitted to take **even one** wife, **if she** is a woman who will **turn his heart away.** [2]But you might ask: **If** it is **true** that the prohibition applies even if the king takes only one such wife, **why does** the verse **say: "And he shall not multiply wives for himself"?** What Halakhic rule is being taught here? The verse teaches that the king is not permitted to take more than eighteen wives, [3]**even** if he marries women **like Abigail,** the righteous wife of King David who, according to David's own testimony (see I Samuel 25:33), prevented him from sinning.

GEMARA לְמֵימְרָא [4]The Gemara now discusses the difference of opinion between Rabbi Yehudah and Rabbi Shimon in our Mishnah. The Gemara asks: **Is this to say that** in general **Rabbi Yehudah interprets the rationale behind a Biblical verse** as a basis for drawing Halakhic conclusions, and limits the law accordingly? In the present case, the Torah seeks to keep the king from going astray. Is this the reason that Rabbi Yehudah permits the king to marry as many women as he desires, provided they are righteous? [5]The Gemara also asks **whether** it is because **Rabbi Shimon,** in general, **ignores the rationale behind the verse** and applies the Scriptural law literally, that he forbids more than eighteen wives, even if they are all righteous? [6]**But surely we have heard** elsewhere that **their positions** on the matter are just **the opposite,** [7]**for it was taught** in the following Baraita: **"It is not permitted to take a pledge from a widow, whether she is rich or poor,** [8]**for the verse states** (Deuteronomy 24:17): **'And you shall not take a widow's garment as a pledge.'** If a widow is unable to repay a loan, her creditor may not take a pledge from her, not even through the courts. [9]**This is the opinion of Rabbi Yehudah,** who argues that, since the Torah does not specify otherwise, the prohibition applies to all widows. [10]But **Rabbi Shimon** disagrees with Rabbi Yehudah **and says:** If the widow is **a rich woman, a pledge may be taken from her.** [11]But if she is **a poor woman, it is forbidden to take a pledge from her.** [12]Rabbi Shimon explains that the creditor **is obliged to return** a pledge of property frequently used **to** a poor widow daily (Deuteronomy 24:12-13), [13]**and** their being seen together frequently for purposes of exchanging the pledge, he **will give her a bad reputation among her neighbors.**

אֶת לִבּוֹ. [1]רַבִּי שִׁמְעוֹן אוֹמֵר: אֲפִילּוּ אַחַת, וּמְסִירָה אֶת לִבּוֹ, הֲרֵי זֶה לֹא יִשָּׂאֶנָּה. [2]אִם כֵּן, לָמָּה נֶאֱמַר: ״לֹא יַרְבֶּה לּוֹ נָשִׁים״? [3]דַּאֲפִילּוּ כַּאֲבִיגַיִל.

גמרא [4]לְמֵימְרָא דְּרַבִּי יְהוּדָה דָּרֵישׁ טַעְמָא דִּקְרָא, [5]וְרַבִּי שִׁמְעוֹן לָא דָּרֵישׁ טַעֲמָא דִּקְרָא? [6]וְהָא אִיפְּכָא שָׁמְעִינַן לְהוּ, [7]דְּתַנְיָא: ״אַלְמָנָה, בֵּין שֶׁהִיא עֲנִיָּה בֵּין שֶׁהִיא עֲשִׁירָה, אֵין מְמַשְׁכְּנִין אוֹתָהּ; [8]שֶׁנֶּאֱמַר: ׳לֹא תַחֲבֹל בֶּגֶד אַלְמָנָה׳. [9]דִּבְרֵי רַבִּי יְהוּדָה. [10]רַבִּי שִׁמְעוֹן אוֹמֵר: עֲשִׁירָה, מְמַשְׁכְּנִין אוֹתָהּ. [11]עֲנִיָּיה, אֵין מְמַשְׁכְּנִין אוֹתָהּ. [12]וְאַתָּה חַיָּיב לְהַחֲזִיר לָהּ, [13]וְאַתָּה מַשִּׂיאָהּ שֵׁם רַע

LITERAL TRANSLATION

his heart away. [1]Rabbi Shimon says: Even one, if she turns his heart away, he may not marry her. [2]If so, why does it say: "And he shall not multiply wives for himself"? [3]Even like Abigail.

GEMARA [4]Is this to say that Rabbi Yehudah expounds the rationale of Scripture, [5]and Rabbi Shimon does not expound the rationale of Scripture? [6]But surely we have heard them [say] the opposite, [7]for it was taught: "A widow, whether she is poor or she is rich, we do not take a pledge from her; [8]for it is said: 'You shall not take the garment of a widow.' [9][These are] the words of Rabbi Yehudah. [10]Rabbi Shimon says: A rich [widow], we take a pledge from her. [11]A poor [widow], we do not take a pledge from her. [12]And you are obliged to return [it] to her, [13]and you give her a bad name

RASHI

גמרא עשירה ממשכנין אותה — לפי שאינה צריכה לאותו כסות להחזירו לה בלילה. משיאה שם רע — שתכנס לביתך שחרית וערבית.

NOTES

רַבִּי יְהוּדָה וְרַבִּי שִׁמְעוֹן **Rabbi Yehudah and Rabbi Shimon.** According to *Tosafot* (*Pesaḥim* 83a and elsewhere), there are only two conflicting opinions in the Mishnah, the positions of Rabbi Yehudah and Rabbi Shimon, who both explain the somewhat ambiguous position of the anonymous first Tanna. *Ramah* disagrees and says that there is a three-way dispute in the Mishnah. According to the anonymous first Tanna, the king may take up to eighteen

HALAKHAH

Mishnah. This includes both his wives and his concubines. (According to *Ra'avad,* the king may have eighteen wives in addition to his concubines.) If the king takes an additional wife and engaged in sexual intercourse with her, he is punishable by lashes. (*Rambam, Sefer Shofetim, Hilkhot Melakhim* 3:2.)

אַלְמָנָה אֵין מְמַשְׁכְּנִין אוֹתָהּ **A widow, we do not take a pledge from her.** "A pledge must not be taken from a widow — whether she is rich or poor — unless it is taken at the time of the loan. Even an officer of the court is not permitted to take a pledge from a widow," following the anonymous Mishnah and Rabbi Yehudah against Rabbi Shimon. (*Shulḥan Arukh, Ḥoshen Mishpat* 97:14.)

TRANSLATION AND COMMENTARY

[1] **And we said** about this: **What did** Rabbi Shimon mean to **say** here? [2] **He** meant to **say as follows:** The creditor may not take a pledge from a poor widow, for **if he took a pledge from** her, he would be **obliged to return it to her** every day, [3] **and** by meeting her so frequently to take and return the pledge, he **would give her a bad reputation among her neighbors.** However, if the widow is wealthy, she will not need the pledge, and so it will not have to be returned until the loan is repaid. Hence, there is no concern that her good name will be tarnished." [4] **Thus,** it would seem from this Baraita that **Rabbi Yehudah does not interpret the rationale behind a Biblical verse,** but instead applies the law in all cases, [5] **whereas Rabbi Shimon interprets the rationale behind a Biblical verse** as a basis for drawing Halakhic conclusions, and limits the law to those cases where that reason applies. And this is just the opposite of what emerges from our Mishnah!

בְּעָלְמָא [6] The Gemara resolves the apparent contradiction: In fact, **Rabbi Yehudah does not usually expound the rationale behind the verse.** [7] **Here, however,** the situation **is different, because the rationale behind the verse is stated explicitly:** "And he shall not multiply wives for himself, and his heart shall not turn away." [8] **What is the reason that "he shall not not multiply wives for himself"?** [9] **So that "his heart shall not turn away."** Because the Torah itself states the rationale of the law, the prohibition must be restricted accordingly. Thus, Rabbi Yehudah rules that a king may take as many wives as he wishes, provided that none of them will turn his heart away.

וְרַבִּי שִׁמְעוֹן [10] The Gemara continues: **And** in general **Rabbi Shimon considers** the reason underlying a law when determining its scope, which is why he maintains that the prohibition against taking a pledge from a widow applies only to a poor widow. However, he disregards the reason stated explicitly in the verse limiting the number of a king's wives because he **can say to you** as follows: [11] **Since, in general, we expound the rationale behind the verse** as the basis for drawing Halakhic conclusions, [12] **the verse could** simply **have written: "He shall not multiply wives for himself,"** [13] **and** then it could have **remained silent.** We would not have needed the rest of the verse that explains the prohibition, "and his heart shall not turn away." For even if this had not been stated, [14] **we would have said: What is the reason that "he shall not multiply wives for himself"?** [15] **So that "his heart not turn away."** [16] **Why, then, was it necessary** for the Torah to write explicitly: **"And his heart shall not turn away"?** Because the Torah is seeking to add another prohibition: [17] That the king **must not marry even one** wife, **if she** is a woman **who will turn his heart away.**

בִּשְׁכֵנוֹתֶיהָ״. [1] וְאָמְרִינַן: מַאי קָאָמַר? [2] הָכִי קָאָמַר: מִתּוֹךְ שֶׁאַתָּה מְמַשְׁכְּנָהּ אַתָּה חַיָּיב לְהַחֲזִיר לָהּ, [3] וְאַתָּה מַשִּׂיאָהּ שֵׁם רַע בִּשְׁכֵנוֹתֶיהָ״. [4] אַלְמָא, רַבִּי יְהוּדָה לָא דָּרֵישׁ טַעְמָא דִּקְרָא, [5] וְרַבִּי שִׁמְעוֹן דָּרֵישׁ טַעְמָא דִּקְרָא!
[6] בְּעָלְמָא, רַבִּי יְהוּדָה לָא דָּרֵישׁ טַעְמָא דִּקְרָא, [7] וְשָׁאנֵי הָכָא, דִּמְפָרֵשׁ טַעְמָא דִּקְרָא: [8] מַה טַּעַם ״לֹא יַרְבֶּה לּוֹ נָשִׁים״? [9] מִשּׁוּם דְּ״לֹא יָסוּר לְבָבוֹ״.
[10] וְרַבִּי שִׁמְעוֹן אָמַר לָךְ: [11] מִכְּדִי בְּעָלְמָא דָּרְשִׁינַן טַעְמָא דִּקְרָא, [12] אִם כֵּן לִכְתּוֹב: קְרָא ״לֹא יַרְבֶּה לּוֹ נָשִׁים״, [13] וְלִישְׁתּוֹק. [14] וַאֲנָא אָמֵינָא: מַה טַּעַם ״לֹא יַרְבֶּה״? [15] מִשּׁוּם דְּ״לֹא יָסוּר״. [16] ״לֹא יָסוּר״ לָמָּה לִי? [17] אֲפִילּוּ אַחַת, וּמְסִירָה אֶת לִבּוֹ, הֲרֵי זוֹ

LITERAL TRANSLATION

among her neighbors." [1] And we said: What did he say? [2] He said as follows: Since you take a pledge from her, you are obligated to return [it] to her, [3] and you give her a bad name among her neighbors." [4] Hence, Rabbi Yehudah does not expound the rationale of Scripture, [5] and Rabbi Shimon expounds the rationale of Scripture!

[6] In general, Rabbi Yehudah does not expound the rationale of Scripture, [7] but it is different here, for the rationale of Scripture is explained: [8] What is the reason [that] "he shall not multiply wives for himself"? [9] So that "his heart shall not turn away."

[10] And Rabbi Shimon says to you: [11] Now since, in general, we expound the rationale of Scripture, [12] if so let the verse write: "He shall not multiply wives for himself," [13] and be silent. [14] And I would say: What is the reason [that] "he shall not multiply [wives for himself]"? [15] So that "[his heart] not turn away." [16] Why then do I need "[his heart] shall not turn away"? [17] Even one, if she turns his heart away, he may

BACKGROUND

לֹא יָסוּר לָמָּה לִי? Why do I need "his heart shall not turn away"? To sum up his position, Rabbi Yehudah believes that the words "לֹא יָסוּר" are merely an explanation and a limitation of the previous verse, meaning that "he shall not take many wives" so that "his heart will not stray." Hence, if wives do not cause his heart to stray, he may take as many as he wishes. However, in the opinion of Rabbi Shimon, "לֹא יָסוּר" is a separate prohibition, unconnected to the previous one, meaning that the king, more than others, because he is the leader of the nation, is forbidden to marry any woman who will cause his heart to stray.

NOTES

wives, but no more, whether they are known to be as righteous as Abigail or not. Rabbi Yehudah maintains that the king may indeed take more than eighteen wives, provided that they are known to be righteous women who will not lead him astray. Rabbi Shimon maintains that a king may not take even a single wife unless she is known to be righteous. And he certainly may not take more than eighteen wives, even if they are all known to be as righteous as Abigail.

TRANSLATION AND COMMENTARY

[1]And **how,** then, **should we interpret** the first part of the verse: **"He shall not multiply wives for himself"?** The verse teaches that the king is not permitted to multiply wives, [2]**even** if he marries women **like Abigail.**

הָנֵי שְׁמוֹנָה עֶשְׂרֵה [3]The Gemara now analyzes the position of the anonymous first Tanna of the Mishnah: **From where do we know this** rule, that the king is limited to **eighteen** wives? [4]The Gemara answers: **For the verses state** (II Samuel 3:2-5): **"And to David sons were born in Hebron: And his firstborn was Amnon, of Ahinoam the Jezreelitess; and his second, Chileab, of Abigail the wife of Nabal the Carmelite; and the third, Absalom the son of Maachah the daughter of Talmai king of Geshur; and the fourth, Adonijah the son of Haggith; and the fifth, Shephatiah the son of Abital; and the sixth, Ithream [son] of Eglah, David's wife. These were born to David in Hebron."** Scripture refers here to the children of six of David's wives. [5]And when Nathan **the Prophet** later rebuked David about the incident involving Uriah the Hittite, he **said to him** (II Samuel 12:8): "And I gave you your master's house, and your master's wives into your bosom; **and if that had been too little, I would moreover have given you like these and like these."** [6]**"Like these"** — another **six** wives. [7]**"And like these"** — yet another **six** wives. [8]And, in that case, David **would have had eighteen** wives in all.

מַתְקִיף לָהּ [9]**Ravina strongly objected** to this explanation: [10]But you can just as well **say** that the verse should be understood as follows: **"Like these"** — implies another six wives, bringing the subtotal to **twelve.** [11]**"And like these"** — implies yet another twelve wives — bringing the grand total to **twenty-four!**

תַּנְיָא נַמִי הָכִי [12]The Gemara notes: Indeed, the same thing **was also taught** in a Baraita, which stated: [13]"The verse, **'He shall not multiply wives for himself,'** teaches that the king may not take for himself **more than twenty-four** wives."

לֹא יִשָּׂאֶנָּה. [1]אֶלָּא מָה אֲנִי מְקַיֵּים "לֹא יַרְבֶּה"? [2]דַּאֲפִילּוּ כַּאֲבִיגַיִל.

[3]הָנֵי שְׁמוֹנֶה עֶשְׂרֵה, מְנָלַן? [4]דִּכְתִיב: "וַיִּוָּלְדוּ לְדָוִד בָּנִים בְּחֶבְרוֹן: וַיְהִי בְכוֹרוֹ אַמְנוֹן, לַאֲחִינֹעַם הַיִּזְרְעֵאלִית; וּמִשְׁנֵהוּ, כִלְאָב, לַאֲבִיגַיִל אֵשֶׁת נָבָל הַכַּרְמְלִי; וְהַשְּׁלִשִׁי, אַבְשָׁלוֹם בֶּן מַעֲכָה; וְהָרְבִיעִי, אֲדֹנִיָּה בֶן חַגִּית; וְהַחֲמִישִׁי, שְׁפַטְיָה בֶן אֲבִיטָל; וְהַשִּׁשִּׁי, יִתְרְעָם לְעֶגְלָה, אֵשֶׁת דָּוִד. אֵלֶּה יֻלְּדוּ לְדָוִד בְּחֶבְרוֹן". [5]וְקָאָמַר לֵיהּ נָבִיא: "אִם מְעָט וְאֹסִפָה לְּךָ כָּהֵנָּה וְכָהֵנָּה". [6]"כָּהֵנָּה" — שִׁית. [7]"וְכָהֵנָּה" — שִׁית. [8]דְּהָווּ לְהוּ תְּמָנֵי סְרֵי. [9]מַתְקִיף לָהּ רָבִינָא: [10]אֵימָא: "כָּהֵנָּה" — תַּרְתֵּי סְרֵי. [11]"וְכָהֵנָּה" עֶשְׂרִין וְאַרְבַּע! [12]תַּנְיָא נַמִי הָכִי: [13]"לֹא יַרְבֶּה לוֹ נָשִׁים" — יוֹתֵר מֵעֶשְׂרִים וְאַרְבַּע.

LITERAL TRANSLATION

not marry her. [1]So how do I interpret "he shall not multiply [wives for himself]"? [2]Even like Abigail.

[3]These eighteen, from where [do we know this]? [4]For it is written: "And to David sons were born in Hebron: And his firstborn was Amnon, of Ahinoam the Jezreelitess; and his second, Chileab, of Abigail the wife of Nabal the Carmelite; and the third, Absalom the son of Maacah [the daughter of Talmai king of Geshur]; and the fourth, Adonijah the son of Haggith; and the fifth, Shefatiah the son of Abital; and the sixth, Ithream of Eglah, David's wife. These were born to David in Hebron." [5]And the Prophet said to him: "And if that had been too little, I would moreover have given you like these and like these." [6]"Like these" — six. [7]"And like these" — six. [8]So that they are eighteen.

[9]Ravina strongly objected: [10]Say: "Like these" — twelve. [11]"And like these" — twenty-four!

[12]It was also taught thus: [13]"'He shall not multiply wives for himself' — more than twenty-four."

NOTES

שְׁמוֹנָה עֶשְׂרֵה **Eighteen.** *Rabbi Ya'akov Emden* notes that there is additional Scriptural proof regarding how many wives a king may take, for we find that King Rehoboam took only eighteen wives, even though he had many more concubines.

וְאֹסִפָה לְּךָ כָּהֵנָּה וְכָהֵנָּה **I would moreover have given you like these and like these.** Even though David had taken at least seven wives by this time, for he had already married Bath-Sheba, Bath-Sheba is surely not included in this count, because Nathan the Prophet rebuked David regarding that marriage (*Arukh LeNer*).

[1] לְמַאן דְּדָרֵישׁ וי״ו, [2] אַרְבָּעִים וּשְׁמֹנֶה" הֲווּ!
[3] תַּנְיָא נַמִי הָכִי: [4] "'לֹא יַרְבֶּה לּוֹ נָשִׁים' — יוֹתֵר מֵאַרְבָּעִים וּשְׁמֹנֶה".
[5] וְתַנָּא דִּידָן, מַאי טַעְמֵיהּ?
[6] אָמַר רַב כָּהֲנָא: מַקִּישׁ "כָּהֵנָּה" בַּתְרָא לְ"כָהֵנָּה" קַמָּא. [7] מַה "כָּהֵנָּה" קַמָּא שִׁית, [8] אַף "כָּהֵנָּה" בַּתְרָא שִׁית.
[9] וְהָא הֲוַאי מִיכַל!
[10] אָמַר רַב: עֶגְלָה זוֹ מִיכַל. [11] וְלָמָּה נִקְרָא שְׁמָהּ עֶגְלָה? [12] שֶׁחֲבִיבָה עָלָיו כְּעֶגְלָה. [13] וְכֵן הוּא אוֹמֵר: "לוּלֵי חֲרַשְׁתֶּם בְּעֶגְלָתִי, וגו׳".
[14] וּמִי הֲווּ לְמִיכַל בְּנֵי? [15] וְהָכְתִיב: "וּלְמִיכַל בַּת שָׁאוּל לֹא הָיָה לָהּ וָלָד עַד יוֹם מוֹתָהּ"!
[16] אָמַר רַב חִסְדָּא: [17] עַד יוֹם מוֹתָהּ לֹא הָיָה לָהּ; [18] בְּיוֹם מוֹתָהּ הָיָה לָהּ.

TRANSLATION AND COMMENTARY

לְמַאן דְּדָרֵישׁ וי״ו [1] The Gemara now suggests that, **according to the** opinion of the Sage **who** as a rule **interprets** the word "and" expressed by **the** letter **vav** attached to the beginning of a word as amplifying the meaning of a verse, we should say as follows: The first "like these" implies another six wives, and the second "like these" implies an additional twelve wives, bringing the subtotal to twenty-four, and the letter vav doubles that sum, [2] bringing the grand total to **forty-eight!**

תַּנְיָא נַמִי הָכִי [3] The Gemara notes: Indeed, **the same** thing **was also taught** in the following Baraita: which stated: "The verse, **'He shall not multiply wives for himself,'** [4] teaches that the king may not take for himself **more than forty-eight** wives."

וְתַנָּא דִּידָן [5] The Gemara asks: **What is the reason** that **the Tanna of our** Mishnah says that the king is permitted only eighteen wives? Why does he not interpret the verse as implying twenty-four, or even forty-eight, wives?

אָמַר רַב כָּהֲנָא [6] **Rav Kahana said:** The Tanna of our Mishnah interprets the verse to be **comparing the second "like these" to the first "like these."** [7] **Just as the first "like these"** should be interpreted to imply another **six** wives, bringing the intermediate total to twelve, [8] **so too the second "like these" implies** another **six** wives and no more, bringing the grand total to eighteen.

וְהָא הֲוַאי מִיכַל [9] The Gemara now seeks clarification: **But surely** in addition to the six wives who gave birth to David's children in Hebron, **there was also Michal,** the daughter of Saul, to whom David was married! Thus, when Nathan the Prophet rebuked David, he had at least seven wives, and so the phrase "like these and like these" should be interpreted to imply that a king is permitted to take at least twenty-one wives!

אָמַר רַב [10] **Rav said: Eglah,** mentioned among the women who bore David children in Hebron, **is** in fact **Michal.** [11] **Why,** then, **was she called Eglah,** literally "heifer"? [12] **Because she was as dear to him as a heifer.** [13] **And similarly** we see that Samson used the word "heifer" to describe his wife Delilah, for **he said** (Judges 14:18): **"If you had not ploughed with my heifer,** you would not have found out my riddle."

וּמִי הֲווּ [14] The Gemara raises a difficulty regarding its identification of Eglah as Michal: The verse states (II Samuel 3:5): "And the sixth, Ithream son of Eglah, David's wife." But if Eglah is Michal, there is a problem: **Did Michal have** any **children?** [15] **For surely** another **verse states** (II Samuel 6:23): **"And Michal the daughter of Saul had no child to the day of her death"!**

אָמַר רַב חִסְדָּא [16] **Rav Ḥisda said:** There is really no difficulty here, for the verse means to say [17] that, **until the day of her death,** Michal **did not have any** children, [18] but **on the day of her death she had** a child. And

LITERAL TRANSLATION

[1] According to the one who interprets the vav, [2] they are forty-eight!

[3] It was also taught thus: [4] "'He shall not multiply wives for himself' — more than forty-eight."

[5] And our Tanna, what is his reason?

[6] Rav Kahana said: It compares the last "like these" to the first "like these." [7] Just as the first "like these" is six, [8] so too the last "like these" is six.

[9] But surely there was Michal!

[10] Rav said: Eglah is Michal. [11] And why was her name called Eglah? [12] Because she was as dear to him as a heifer (Heb., *"eglah"*). [13] And similarly it says: "If you had not ploughed with my heifer, etc."

[14] But did Michal have children? [15] But surely it is written: "And Michal the daughter of Saul had no child to the day of her death"!

[16] Rav Ḥisda said: [17] To the day of her death she had no [child]; [18] on the day of her death she had [a child].

RASHI

למאן דדריש וי״ו – רבי עקיבא בארבע מיתות בית דין (סנהדרין נא,ב): ישמעאל אחי, בת ובת אני דורש.

חרשתם בעגלתי – שמשון קרי לה לאשתו, כשהגידה להם חידתו.

NOTES

עֶגְלָה זוֹ מִיכַל **Eglah is Michal.** Elsewhere (*Midrash Shoḥar Tov*), the Midrash explains that Michal was called Eglah, because she behaved just like a heifer who was not yet trained to accept a yoke from its master. She refused to submit to any authority, even that of her father.

BACKGROUND

פִּלֶגֶשׁ Concubine. Halakhic authorities have disagreed about the definition of פִּלֶגֶשׁ. Even those who maintain that she is not married and has no ketubah do agree that she is reserved to one man alone, and that she is like a wife to him in other respects. But a woman who has relations with more than one man is forbidden as a courtesan.

TRANSLATION AND COMMENTARY

that is the son, Ithream, who, according to Scripture, was born to David's wife Eglah.

מִכְּדִי [1]The Gemara asks: **But where does** Scripture **count the children** born to David? And it answers: **In Hebron.** [2]**Yet the incident involving Michal was in Jerusalem,** [3]**as the verse states** (II Samuel 6:16): **"Michal, Saul's daughter, looked through a window, and saw King David dancing and leaping before the Lord, and she despised him in her heart."** [4]**And Rav Yehudah said, and some say** that **it was Rav Yosef** who said: [5]**Michal immediately received the punishment** that was due her, as Scripture states several verses later (II Samuel 6:23): "And Michal the daughter of Saul had no child to the day of her death." Now, if Michal died on the day that she gave birth to her first and only child, that must have occurred in Jerusalem. Michal then could not be indentical with Eglah, who gave birth in Hebron. The original difficulty now returns: David seemingly had seven wives, not six!

אֶלָּא [6]**Rather,** you can **say** that the matter should be understood as follows: Michal and Eglah are indeed one and the same person, and **before that incident** in Jersualem Michal **did** in fact **have a child** — the child that Scripture says was born to Eglah in Hebron. [7]**But from then on** and until the day of her death **she had no** more children.

וְהָכְתִיב [8]The Gemara now questions its assumption that David had only eighteen wives: **But surely the verse states** (II Samuel 5:13): **"And David took more concubines and wives of Jerusalem,** after he had come from Hebron; and more sons and daughters were born to David."

לְמַלּוּיֵי [9]The Gemara concludes: With these women David **completed the** count of **eighteen** wives which were permitted to him.

מַאי נָשִׁים [10]This last verse raises a basic question: **What are wives, and what are concubines?** [11]**Rav Yehudah said in the name of Rav:** A **wife** cohabits with her husband **with a ketubah** (marriage contract) **and** with **betrothal,** [12]**whereas** a **concubine** gives herself to one particular man, but **without a ketubah and without betrothal.**

[1]מִכְּדִי. בָּנִים הֵיכָא קָא חָשֵׁיב לְהוּ — בְּחֶבְרוֹן. [2]וְאִילּוּ מַעֲשֶׂה דְּמִיכַל, בִּירוּשָׁלַיִם הֲוָה, [3]דִּכְתִיב: ״וּמִיכַל בַּת שָׁאוּל נִשְׁקְפָה בְּעַד הַחַלּוֹן וַתֵּרֶא אֶת הַמֶּלֶךְ דָּוִד מְפַזֵּז וּמְכַרְכֵּר לִפְנֵי ה׳ וַתִּבֶז״! [4]וְאָמַר רַב יְהוּדָה וְאִיתֵּימָא רַב יוֹסֵף: [5]שְׁקַלְתָּה מִיכַל לְמִיטַרְפְּסָה.

[6]אֶלָּא, אֵימָא: עַד אוֹתוֹ מַעֲשֶׂה הָיָה לָהּ, [7]מִכָּאן וְאֵילָךְ לֹא הָיָה לָהּ.

[8]וְהָכְתִיב: ״וַיִּקַּח דָּוִד עוֹד פִּלַגְשִׁים וְנָשִׁים בִּירוּשָׁלַיִם״. [9]לְמַלּוּיֵי שְׁמוֹנָה עָשָׂר.

[10]מַאי נָשִׁים וּמַאי פִּלַגְשִׁים? [11]אָמַר רַב יְהוּדָה אָמַר רַב: נָשִׁים בִּכְתוּבָּה וּבְקִידּוּשִׁין. [12]פִּלַגְשִׁים בְּלֹא כְּתוּבָּה וּבְלֹא קִידּוּשִׁין.

LITERAL TRANSLATION

[1]But children where does it count them? In Hebron. [2]Yet the incident involving Michal was in Jerusalem, [3]as it is written: "Michal, Saul's daughter, looked through a window and saw King David dancing and leaping before the Lord, and she despised [him in her heart]." [4]And Rav Yehudah said, and some say [it was] Rav Yosef: [5]Michal received her punishment.

[6]Rather, say: Until that incident she had [a child]; [7]from then on she had no [child].

[8]But surely it is written: "And David took more concubines and wives in Jerusalem."

[9]To complete the eighteen.

[10]What are wives, and what are concubines? [11]Rav Yehudah said in the name of Rav: Wives with a ketubah and betrothal. [12]Concubines without a ketubah and without betrothal.

RASHI

ואמר רב שקלה מיכל למטרפסה — זה היה פרעון חטאתה, מה שנכתב בילדו: ״לא היה לה ולד״, אלמא: מההוא מעשה ואילך לא הוה לה, אבל מקמי הכי — איכא למימר דהוה לה. **והא כתיב ויקח דוד עוד** — אלמא: טובא הוו ליה נשים.

NOTES

מִכָּאן וְאֵילָךְ לֹא הָיָה לָהּ From then on she had no child. *Rashash* suggests that not only did Michal not bear another child, but she even lost the children she had previously had.

HALAKHAH

נָשִׁים וּפִלַגְשִׁים Wives and concubines. "The king is permitted to have wives and concubines. The wives he takes with a ketubah and with betrothal; the concubines he takes without a ketubah and without betrothal. The king may keep concubines, but an ordinary person may not." According to some, a concubine is taken without a ketubah, but with betrothal (*Rambam,* according to *Maggid Mishneh's* reading; *Ra'avad, Rashi* on the Torah). Some authorities maintain that a concubine who gives herself to one particular man is permitted not only to the king, but also to commoners (*Ra'avad, Ramban*). (*Rambam, Sefer Shofetim, Hilkhot Melakhim* 4:4; *Sefer Nashim, Hilkhot Ishut* 1:4.)

LITERAL TRANSLATION

[1]Rav Yehudah said in the name of Rav: David had four hundred children, and all of them were children of beautiful captive women (lit., "women beautiful in appearance"), [2]and they grew long locks, [3]and all sat in carriages of gold, and went at the head of the troops, [4]and they were the men of strength (lit., "fist") in the House of David.

[5]And Rav Yehudah said in the name of Rav: Tamar was the daughter of a beautiful captive woman, [6]as it is said: "Now, therefore, I pray, speak to the king; for he will not withhold me from you." [7]But if it should enter your mind that she was the product of marriage, would his sister be permitted to him? [8]Rather, infer from here that she was the daughter of a beautiful captive woman.

[9]"But Amnon had a friend, whose name was Jonadab, the son of Shimeah, David's brother; and Jonadab was a [very] wise man."

[1]אָמַר רַב יְהוּדָה אָמַר רַב: אַרְבַּע מֵאוֹת יְלָדִים הָיוּ לוֹ לְדָוִד, וְכוּלָּן בְּנֵי יְפַת תּוֹאַר הָיוּ, [2]וּמְגַדְּלֵי בְלוֹרִיּוֹת הָיוּ, [3]וְכוּלָּן יוֹשְׁבִין בִּקְרוֹנוֹת שֶׁל זָהָב, וּמְהַלְּכִין בְּרָאשֵׁי גְיָיסוֹת הָיוּ, [4]וְהֵם הָיוּ בַּעֲלֵי אֶגְרוֹפִין שֶׁל בֵּית דָּוִד.

[5]וְאָמַר רַב יְהוּדָה אָמַר רַב: תָּמָר בַּת יְפַת תּוֹאַר הָיְתָה, [6]שֶׁנֶּאֱמַר: "וְעַתָּה דַּבֶּר נָא (עַל) [אֶל] הַמֶּלֶךְ; כִּי לֹא יִמְנָעֵנִי מִמֶּךָּ". [7]וְאִי סָלְקָא דַּעֲתָךְ בַּת נִישּׂוּאִין הֲוַאי, אֲחָתֵיהּ מִי הֲוָה שַׁרְיָא לֵיהּ? [8]אֶלָּא, שְׁמַע מִינָּהּ בַּת יְפַת תּוֹאַר הָיְתָה.

[9]"וּלְאַמְנוֹן רֵעַ, וּשְׁמוֹ יוֹנָדָב בֶּן שִׁמְעָה, אֲחִי דָוִד; (וְהָיָה) אִישׁ

TRANSLATION AND COMMENTARY

אָמַר רַב יְהוּדָה [1]In addition to David's concubines, he had what are known as "beautiful captive women." During a war, a Jewish soldier was allowed to have sexual relations just once with a non-Jewish captive woman (see Deuteronomy 21: 10-14). Afterwards, sexual relations with her was forbidden, unless she converted to Judaism, and he took her as his legal wife. **Rav Yehudah said in the name of Rav: David had four hundred sons, all of whom were children** conceived **by** such **non-Jewish female prisoners of war** the first time he engaged in sexual relations with them. [2]All of these sons **grew** their hair **long**, as was customary among the non-Jews. [3]**All rode in carriages of gold, and went at the head of the troops.** [4]**These were the strong men** upon whom the stability **of the House of David** rested.

וְאָמַר רַב יְהוּדָה [5]**Rav Yehudah said in the name of Rav: Tamar was** conceived **by** Maacah while she was King David's captive **prisoner of war**, before she converted to Judaism and became his wife. Her full-brother, Absalom, was born to David and Maacah, after Maacah had converted and David took her in marriage. When Tamar's half-brother, Amnon, developed a passion for her, he tricked her into coming into his room. As he was about to force himself upon her, Tamar pleaded with him that he speak with the king and ask for her hand in marriage. [6]**For the verse states** (II Samuel 13:13): **"Now, therefore, I pray, speak to the king; for he will not withhold me from you."** [7]Now, **if you** should **think that** Tamar **was a product of marriage, would** Amnon **have been permitted to** marry **his sister?** Amnon was David's son by Aḥinoam the Jezreelitess. Had Tamar been the product of David's marriage to Maacah, she would have been Amnon's legal half-sister and therefore forbidden to him in marriage. [8]**Rather, infer from here that** Tamar **was conceived by** Maacah while she was David's **prisoner of war.** Being the product of that union, Tamar was born as a non-Jew, so that she too required conversion. According to Jewish law, a convert is like a newborn child, and is therefore considered to have no legal ties to his biological parents or relatives. Thus, there would have been nothing barring Amnon from taking Tamar as his wife, for the relationship between the two would not have been legally incestuous.

וּלְאַמְנוֹן רֵעַ [9]The Gemara continues its discussion of the incident involving Tamar and Amnon: The verse states (II Samuel 13:3): **"But Amnon had a friend, whose name was Jonadab, the son of Shimeah, David's**

RASHI

יפת תואר – הנשבית במלחמה, כדכתיב (דברים כא): "וראית בשביה". **תמר** – אחות אבשלום בת יפת תואר היתה, קודם שנתגיירה בלב שלם, מעכה אמו ילדה לו לדוד את תמר, והיתה אצלו בתורת יפת תואר. **ועתה דבר נא וגו'** – תמר מנסיב ליה עצה לאמנון. **מי הוה שרייה ליה אלא שמע מינה** – עדיין לא נתגיירה אמו כשילדתה, ותנן: ולד שפחה וכותית מישראל – אין לו קורבת אב, במסכת יבמות (כב,א): מי שיש לו בן מכל מקום וכו'.

NOTES

אַרְבַּע מֵאוֹת יְלָדִים Four hundred children. Elsewhere (*Kiddushin* 66b), *Rashi* explains that these four hundred young men were not actually King David's children, but were soldiers who had been raised in his house. All of them had been conceived by non-Jewish female prisoners who had been captured in earlier battles, and with whom his troops had engaged in sexual relations.

BACKGROUND

בְּלוֹרִית Long locks.

Statue of a Greek soldier. According to descriptions given by the Sages, the *belorit* (בְּלוֹרִית) was especially long hair behind the head, a ponytail. It was ornamental and also had certain ritual meaning. For that reason Jews generally did not grow a *belorit*, with the exception of military men or those who had to live among gentiles.

קְרוֹנִית Carriage.

A Roman relief of a carriage laden with soldiers.

תָּמָר בַּת יְפַת תּוֹאַר Tamar was the daughter of a beautiful captive woman. This is implied by the language of the verse, and every time Tamar is mentioned, she is referred to as the sister of Absalom and not as the daughter of David, meaning that she was the daughter of Absalom's mother by a previous marriage but not related in any way to David. (See *Tosafot.*)

LANGUAGE (RASHI)

פרייי"ט* This apparently should be פרי"ט, from the Old French *frit*, meaning "fried."

TRANSLATION AND COMMENTARY

brother; and Jonadab was a very wise man." [1]**Rav Yehudah said in the name of Rav:** Jonadab was **a man wise in evil** deeds, for it was he who counseled Amnon how to get Tamar into his room, so that he could force himself upon her.

וַיֹּאמֶר [2]The story continues (II Samuel 13:4-8): **"And he said to him, Why are you, being the king's son, so wasted,** from day to day? Will you not tell me? And Amnon said to him, I love Tamar, my brother Absalom's sister. **And Jonadab said to him, Lie down on your bed, and feign to be sick,** and when your father comes to see you, say to him, I pray you, let my sister Tamar come, and give me bread, **and prepare the food in my sight,** that I may see it, and eat it at her hand.... **And she took a pan and poured** them **out before him;** but he refused to eat." [3]**Rav Yehudah said in the name of Rav:** This means that **she made him fried cakes,** which are best prepared before the diner.

וַיִּשְׂנָאֶהָ [4]Later, Amnon's feelings toward Tamar changed, as the verse states (II Samuel 13:15): **"And Amnon hated her exceedingly,** so that the hatred with which he hated her was greater than the love with which he had loved her." [5]**What is the reason** that Amnon suddenly hated her? [6]**Rabbi Yitzḥak said:** While they were having sexual intercourse her pubic **hair became entangled around his penis, and it became mutilated** as a result.

וְכִי [7]The Gemara asks: Even **if** Tamar's pubic hair **got wound around** Amnon's penis, and he suffered an injury as a result, **what did she do** to deserve his hatred?

אֶלָּא [8]The Gemara answers: **Rather say** that the matter should be understood as follows: Amnon hated Tamar because she purposely **tied** her pubic **hair around** his penis, [9]**and it became mutilated** as a result.

אִינִי [10]The Gemara asks: But **is this so?** [11]**But surely Rava expounded** as follows: **What is** the meaning of **the verse that states** (Ezekiel 16:14): **"And your renown went forth among the nations for your beauty"?** [12]**It means that the daughters of Israel do not have** long **hair in their armpits or in their pubic regions.** How, then, could Tamar have caused Amnon such an injury?

חָכָם, וגו׳". [1]אָמַר רַב יְהוּדָה אָמַר רַב: אִישׁ חָכָם לְרִשְׁעָה. [2]"וַיֹּאמֶר, מַדּוּעַ אַתָּה כָּכָה דַּל בֶּן הַמֶּלֶךְ....וַיֹּאמֶר לוֹ יוֹנָדָב, שְׁכַב עַל מִשְׁכָּבְךָ וְהִתְחָל וגו׳" עַד "וְעָשְׂתָה לְעֵינַי אֶת הַבִּרְיָה....וַתִּקַּח הַמַּשְׂרֵת וַתִּצֹּק לְפָנָיו". [3]אָמַר רַב יְהוּדָה אָמַר רַב: שֶׁעָשְׂתָה לוֹ מִינֵי טִיגּוּן. [4]"וַיִּשְׂנָאֶהָ אַמְנוֹן שִׂנְאָה גְּדוֹלָה מְאֹד". [5]מַאי טַעְמָא? [6]אָמַר רַבִּי יִצְחָק: נִימָא נִקְשְׁרָה לוֹ, וַעֲשָׂאַתּוּ כְּרוּת שָׁפְכָה. [7]וְכִי נִקְשְׁרָה לוֹ, אִיהִי מַאי עָבְדָה? [8]אֶלָּא אֵימָא: קָשְׁרָה לוֹ נִימָא, [9]וַעֲשָׂאַתּוּ כְּרוּת שָׁפְכָה. [10]אִינִי? [11]וְהָא דָּרַשׁ רָבָא: מַאי דִּכְתִיב "וַיֵּצֵא לָךְ שֵׁם בַּגּוֹיִם בְּיָפְיֵךְ" — [12]שֶׁאֵין לָהֶן לִבְנוֹת יִשְׂרָאֵל לֹא שֵׂעָר בֵּית הַשֶּׁחִי וְלֹא בֵּית הָעֶרְוָה.

LITERAL TRANSLATION

[1]Rav Yehudah said in the name of Rav: A man wise in evil [ways].

[2]"And he said [to him], Why are you, being the king's son, so wasted...? And Jonadab said to him, Lie down on your bed, and feign to be sick, etc. And prepare the food in my sight.... And she took a pan and poured [them] out before him." [3]Rav Yehudah said in the name of Rav: She made him fried [cakes].

[4]"And Amnon hated her exceedingly." [5]What is the reason? [6]Rabbi Yitzḥak said: A hair became entangled on him, and his penis was mutilated. [7]And if it became entangled, what did she do?

[8]Rather say: She tied a hair around him, [9]and his penis was mutilated.

[10]Is it so? [11]But surely Rava expounded: What is that which is written: "And your renown went forth among the nations for your beauty"? — [12][It means that] the daughters of Israel do not have hair in their armpits or on their pubic regions.

RASHI

והתחל — עשה עצמך כחולה. **הבריה** = מאכל טיגון, *פריי"ט. **שלא היה להם לבנות ישראל** — קודם שחטאו וגבהו בנות ציון (ישעיה ג). **לא שער בית השחי** — תחת אצילי זרועותיהן.

NOTES

קָשְׁרָה לוֹ נִימָא **She tied a hair.** It has been suggested that Tamar was concerned that Amnon's professed love was mere sexual lust, and he had no real desire to marry a woman born as a non-Jew. She, therefore, desired to mutilate Amnon's genitals, to prevent him from marrying a Jewish-born woman (for a man with mutilated genitals is forbidden to marry a woman who was born Jewish; see Deuteronomy 23:2). He then would have had reason to marry Tamar, for as a convert, she would be permitted a man with mutilated genitals. (*Arukh LeNer*).

שֶׁאֵין לָהֶן לִבְנוֹת יִשְׂרָאֵל **That the daughters of Israel do not have.** *Maharsha* explains that this does not mean that Jewish women are naturally endowed with less hair under their arms or in the pubic region than other women. However, the Gemara teaches that they shave those areas more regularly than do women of other nations.

[1]שָׁאנֵי תָּמָר, דְּבַת יְפַת תּוֹאַר הֲוַאי.
[2]"וַתִּקַּח תָּמָר אֵפֶר עַל רֹאשָׁהּ וְאֵת כְּתֹנֶת הַפַּסִּים אֲשֶׁר עָלֶיהָ קָרָעָה". [3]תָּנָא מִשְּׁמֵיהּ דְּרַבִּי יְהוֹשֻׁעַ בֶּן קָרְחָה: "גָּדֵר גָּדוֹל גָּדְרָה תָּמָר בְּאוֹתָהּ שָׁעָה. [4]אָמְרוּ: לִבְנוֹת מְלָכִים כָּךְ, לִבְנוֹת הֶדְיוֹטוֹת עַל אַחַת כַּמָּה וְכַמָּה. [5]אִם לִצְנוּעוֹת כָּךְ, לִפְרוּצוֹת עַל אַחַת כַּמָּה וְכַמָּה".
[6]אָמַר רַב יְהוּדָה אָמַר רַב: בְּאוֹתָהּ שָׁעָה גָּזְרוּ [21B] עַל הַיִּיחוּד, וְעַל הַפְּנוּיָה.
[7]יִחוּד, דְּאוֹרָיְיתָא הוּא, [8]דְּאָמַר רַבִּי יוֹחָנָן מִשּׁוּם רַבִּי שִׁמְעוֹן בֶּן יְהוֹצָדָק: רֶמֶז לְיִיחוּד מִן הַתּוֹרָה מִנַּיִין? [9]שֶׁנֶּאֱמַר "כִּי יְסִיתְךָ אָחִיךָ בֶן אִמֶּךָ". [10]וְכִי בֶּן אֵם מֵסִית, בֶּן אָב אֵינוֹ מֵסִית? [11]אֶלָּא לוֹמַר לְךָ: בֵּן מִתְיַיחֵד עִם אִמּוֹ, [12]וְאֵין אַחֵר מִתְיַיחֵד עִם כָּל עֲרָיוֹת שֶׁבַּתּוֹרָה.

LITERAL TRANSLATION

[1]Tamar was different, for she was the daughter of a beautiful captive woman.
[2]"And Tamar put ashes on her head, and tore her long-sleeved garment that was on her." [3][A Sage] taught in the name of Rabbi Yehoshua ben Korḥah: "Tamar erected a great fence at that time.
[4]They said: If [it is] thus with the daughters of kings, all the more so with the daughters of ordinary people. [5]If so with modest women, all the more so with licentious ones."
[6]Rav Yehudah said in the name of Rav: At that time, [the Elders] decreed [21B] about seclusion, and about an unmarried woman.
[7]Seclusion? It is by Torah law, [8]for Rabbi Yoḥanan said in the name of Rabbi Shimon ben Yehotzadak: From where is there a hint in the Torah regarding [the prohibition of] seclusion? [9]For it is stated: "If your brother, the son of your mother... entice you." [10]But does the son of a mother entice [others to idolatry and] the son of a father not entice? [11]Rather to teach you: A son may seclude himself with his mother, [12]but nobody else may seclude himself with a woman forbidden to him by Torah law.

TRANSLATION AND COMMENTARY

שָׁאנֵי תָּמָר [1]The Gemara answers: **Tamar was different, for she was conceived by a** non-Jewish **woman** who had been captured as a **prisoner of war.** She therefore had the physical attributes of a non-Jewish woman.

וַתִּקַּח [2]The incident involving Tamar and Amnon continues (II Samuel 13:19): **"And Tamar put ashes on her head, and tore her long-sleeved garment that was on her,** and laid her hand on her head, crying aloud as she went." [3]**A Sage taught** a Baraita **in the name of Rabbi Yehoshua ben Korḥah: "At that time,** when **Tamar** cried out and made a public display of the grief and shame of her rape, she **erected a great fence** around the Torah for the protection of female chastity, [4]for everyone **said: If** this can happen **to the daughter of a king,** then **all the more so** can it happen **to the daughters of ordinary people.** [5]**If** this can happen **to a modest woman** like Tamar, then **all the more so** can it happen **to licentious women."**

אָמַר רַב יְהוּדָה [6]**Rav Yehudah said in the name of Rav: At that time,** and as a result of Tamar's rape and public grief, the Elders enacted **decrees** [21B] **about** a man **being alone** behind closed doors with a woman forbidden to him, **and about an unmarried woman.**

יִחוּד [7]At this point the Gemara understands that in David's day, the Elders enacted two decrees: First, that a man may not seclude himself in a room with a married woman or some other woman who is forbidden to him. And second, that a man may not engage in sexual relations with an unmarried woman. The Gemara therefore asks: Since **being alone** with a woman with whom sexual relations are prohibited **is** forbidden **by Torah law,** why did the Elders of David's time enjoin it? [8]**For Rabbi Yoḥanan said in the name of Rabbi Shimon ben Yehotzadak: From where do we** derive **a hint that** the prohibition of **seclusion is in the Torah?** [9]From **the verse that states** (Deuteronomy 13:7): **"If your brother, the son of your mother**...**entice you** secretly, saying, Let us go and serve other gods." A question may be raised here: [10]**Can** only a brother who is **the son of** one's **mother entice** one to commit idolatry, while a brother who is **the son of** one's **father cannot entice** one to do so? Why is the maternal brother mentioned as the inciter and not the paternal one? [11]**Rather** understand that the verse was formulated in this manner **to teach you that a son may seclude himself** in a room **with his mother,** [12]but **nobody else may seclude himself with a woman who is forbidden to him by Torah law,** lest they come to engage in sexual intercourse. It is for this reason that the Torah warns about being enticed to commit idolatry by one's

RASHI

גדרה תמר — בדמעתה וזעקתה, ונהגה עצמה בבזיון, נשאו שאר נשים קל וחומר בעצמן: מה בנות מלכים אירע קלקול זה — בהדיוטות על אחת כמה וכמה. על הייחוד — דאשת איש ועל הפנויה.

BACKGROUND

גָּדֵר גָּדוֹל גָּדְרָה תָּמָר **Tamar erected a great fence.** As explained later, it was forbidden to be alone with an unmarried woman, in order to avoid the possibility of illicit sexual relations, whether consensual or forced.

SAGES

רַבִּי שִׁמְעוֹן בֶּן יְהוֹצָדָק **Rabbi Shimon ben Yehotzadak.** A Palestinian Sage who lived in the transition period between the Tannaim and the Amoraim, he taught the famous Amora Rabbi Yoḥanan, who transmits many teachings in Rabbi Shimon's name.

Little is known of his life, other than that he was a priest and probably lived in the southern part of the country. The Jerusalem Talmud recounts that he died in the city of Lydda, and that the Sages of the generation, his companions in study, attended his funeral.

HALAKHAH

יִחוּד **Seclusion.** "A man and a woman between whom sexual relations are forbidden may not be alone together behind closed doors. Exceptions to this rule include a father and his daughter, a mother and her son, and a husband

[1]אֶלָּא אֵימָא: [2]גָּזְרוּ עַל יִיחוּד דִּפְנוּיָה.

[3]״וַאֲדֹנִיָּה בֶן חַגִּית מִתְנַשֵּׂא לֵאמֹר אֲנִי אֶמְלֹךְ״. [4]אָמַר רַב יְהוּדָה אָמַר רַב: מְלַמֵּד שֶׁבִּיקֵּשׁ לְהוֹלְמוֹ, וְלֹא הוֹלַמְתּוֹ.

[5]״וַיַּעַשׂ לוֹ רֶכֶב וּפָרָשִׁים וַחֲמִשִּׁים אִישׁ רָצִים לְפָנָיו״. [6]מַאי רְבוּתָא? [7]אָמַר רַב יְהוּדָה אָמַר רַב: כּוּלָּן נְטוּלֵי טְחוֹל, וַחֲקוּקֵי כַּפּוֹת רַגְלַיִם הָיוּ.

מִשְׁנָה [8]״לֹא יַרְבֶּה לּוֹ סוּסִים״ — [9]אֶלָּא כְּדֵי מֶרְכַּבְתּוֹ. [10]״וְכֶסֶף וְזָהָב לֹא יַרְבֶּה לּוֹ מְאֹד״ — [11]אֶלָּא כְּדֵי לִיתֵּן אַסְפַּנְיָא.

LITERAL TRANSLATION

[1]Rather, say: [2]They decreed about seclusion with an unmarried woman.

[3]"And Adonijah the son of Ḥaggith exalted himself, saying, I will be king." [4]Rav Yehudah said in the name of Rav: This teaches that he tried to make it fit, but it didn't fit.

[5]"And he set up chariots and horsemen for himself, and fifty men to run before him." [6]What is special [about this]? [7]Rav Yehudah said in the name of Rav: All of them had their spleens removed, and the soles of their feet hollowed out.

MISHNAH [8]"He shall not multiply horses to himself" — [9]rather as much as is required for his chariots. [10]"Neither shall he greatly multiply to himself silver and gold" — [11]rather as much as is required to supply wages [for his soldiers].

TRANSLATION AND COMMENTARY

maternal brother, and not by one's paternal brother. Because of the particular closeness between a son and his mother, and the fact that they may be alone together, maternal brothers — i.e., half-brothers having the same mother — are likely to develop a close relationship with one another. Hence there is particular concern that the one might entice the other to engage in idolatry. But a person is forbidden to seclude himself with the mother of his paternal half-brother, for she is his father's wife who is forbidden to him. Therefore, paternal half-brothers are less likely than maternal half-brothers to develop a close relationship with one another, and so there is less concern that one will entice the other to commit idolatry. Since seclusion with a woman with whom one is forbidden to engage in sexual relations is forbidden by Torah law, how could Rav Yehudah say in the name of Rav that the prohibition is a decree enacted at the time of King David?

אֶלָּא אֵימָא [1]The Gemara answers: **Rather,** you must **say** that Rav Yehudah meant to say as follows: [2]After Tamar's rape, the Elders **decreed** that **being alone with an unmarried woman** is also forbidden.

וַאֲדֹנִיָּה בֶן חַגִּית [3]Having related to the incident involving Amnon and Tamar, Rav Yehudah now cites a verse dealing with another one of King David's sons (I Kings 1:5): **"And Adonijah the son of Ḥaggith exalted himself, saying, I will be king."** [4]**Rav Yehudah said in the name of Rav:** The expression "exalted himself" **teaches that Adonijah tried** on the royal crown **to** see whether it would **fit** his head, **but** to his dismay **it did not fit.** He, nevertheless, desired the kingdom, for which he was not fit.

וַיַּעַשׂ לוֹ רֶכֶב [5]The verse describing Adonijah's royal aspirations continues (I Kings 1:5): **"And he set up chariots and horsemen for himself, and fifty men to run before him."** [6]**What was the novelty** of this act? Surely many other wealthy people did the same! [7]**Rav Yehudah said in the name of Rav: All** of the fifty runners **had their spleens removed and the soles of their feet hollowed out,** so they would be able to run faster.

MISHNAH לֹא יַרְבֶּה [8]The Torah states (Deuteronomy 17:16): **"[The King] shall not multiply horses to himself,** nor send the people back to Egypt, to add to his horses." [9]**Rather** he may only keep **as many** horses **as is required for his chariots** and horsemen in time of war. The king's right to fill his coffers with gold and silver is also limited, for the next verse states (Deuteronomy, 17:17): [10]**"Neither shall he [the king] greatly multiply to himself silver and gold."** [11]**Rather,** he may only keep **as much gold** and silver **as is required to supply** ample **wages** and provisions for his soldiers.

RASHI

שבקש להולמו ולא הולמתו — שתשב בראשו כתר מלכות, ולא הולמתו, לפי שהיה טרביע של זהב בתוך חללה מדופן לדופן ואינה מתיישב בראשו אלא למי שיש לו חריץ בראשו, והיא עדות לבית דוד. שכל הראוי למלכות — הולמתו, ומי שאינו ראוי למלכות — אינו הולמתו. **מאי רבותיה** — דחמשים איש לבן מלך. **נטולי טחול וחקוקי כפות הרגלים** — נטולי טחול על ידי סם, שהטחול מכבידו לאדם, וחקוקי כפות הרגלים — אין בשר בפרסותיהם ורצים על הקוצים ועל הברקנין ואינן ניזוקין.

משנה **אספניא** — שכר חיילות מדי שנה בשנה הנכנסין והיוצאין עמו כל השנה.

NOTES

שֶׁבִּיקֵּשׁ לְהוֹלְמוֹ **That he tried to have it fit.** *Arukh* explains that the crown worn by the kings of the House of David fit perfectly on top of the head of each of the kings. Any candidate for the throne whose head did not fully fill that crown was regarded as unfit to serve as king. (See also *Rashi.*)

HALAKHAH

יִיחוּד דִּפְנוּיָה **Seclusion with an unmarried woman.** "King David and his court decreed that a man may not be alone

and his wife who is temporarily forbidden to him because she is menstruating." (*Shulḥan Arukh, Even HaEzer* 22:1.)

BACKGROUND

נְטוּלֵי טְחוֹל **Had their spleens removed.** In antiquity, it was noticed that the spleen, especially when enlarged, interferes with running. An enlarged spleen is the aftereffect of malaria. Operations for the removal of the spleen are described in ancient medical literature. If the patient survived the operation itself without bleeding to death or contracting an infection, he could live a normal life; and not having a spleen would make it easier for him to run.

חֲקוּקֵי כַּפּוֹת רַגְלַיִם **Soles of their feet hollowed out.** This might refer to an orthopedic operation to correct the arch of the foot, if it was too low.

LANGUAGE

אַסְפַּנְיָא **Wages.** This is the correct reading. The word derives from the Greek, ὀψώνιον, *ospsonion*, which sometimes appears in the form ὀψωία, *ospsonia*, meaning wages, a payment.

[1]וְכוֹתֵב לוֹ סֵפֶר תּוֹרָה לִשְׁמוֹ. [2]יוֹצֵא לַמִּלְחָמָה, מוֹצִיאָהּ עִמָּהּ. [3]נִכְנָס, הוּא מַכְנִיסָהּ עִמּוֹ. [4]יוֹשֵׁב בַּדִּין, הִיא עִמּוֹ. [5]מֵיסֵב, הִיא כְּנֶגְדּוֹ, [6]שֶׁנֶּאֱמַר: "וְהָיְתָה עִמּוֹ וְקָרָא בוֹ כָּל יְמֵי חַיָּיו".

גמרא [7]תָּנוּ רַבָּנַן: "'לֹא יַרְבֶּה לוֹ סוּסִים', [8]יָכוֹל אֲפִילּוּ כְּדֵי מֶרְכַּבְתּוֹ וּפָרָשָׁיו. [9]תַּלְמוּד לוֹמַר: 'לוֹ' — [10]לוֹ אֵינוֹ מַרְבֶּה, אֲבָל מַרְבֶּה הוּא כְּדֵי רִכְבּוֹ וּפָרָשָׁיו. [11]הָא מָה אֲנִי מְקַיֵּים 'סוּסִים'? [12]סוּסִים הַבַּטְלָנִין. [13]מִנַּיִין שֶׁאֲפִילּוּ סוּס אֶחָד וְהוּא בָּטֵל שֶׁהוּא בְּ'לֹא יַרְבֶּה'? [14]תַּלְמוּד לוֹמַר: 'לְמַעַן הַרְבּוֹת סוּס'. [15]וְכִי מֵאַחַר דַּאֲפִילּוּ סוּס אֶחָד וְהוּא בָּטֵל, קָאֵי בְּ'לֹא יַרְבֶּה', [16]'סוּסִים' לָמָּה לִי?

LITERAL TRANSLATION

[1]And he writes a Torah scroll for himself. [2][When] he goes out to war, he takes it out with him. [3][When] he goes in, he brings it in with him. [4][When] he sits in judgment, it is with him. [5][When] he reclines, it is opposite him, [6]as it is stated: "And it shall be with him, and he shall read in it all the days of his life."

GEMARA [7]Our Rabbis taught: "'He shall not multiply horses to himself.' [8]I might have thought [not] even as many as are required for his chariots and horsemen. [9]The Torah states: 'To himself' — [10]for himself he does not multiply [horses], but he multiplies [horses] as many as are required for his chariots and horsemen. [11]Then how do I interpret 'horses'? [12]Horses that are idle. [13]From where [do we know] that even one horse if it is idle is included under 'He shall not multiply'? [14]The Torah states: 'To the end that he should multiply [the] horse.' [15]Now since even one horse, if it is idle, is included under 'He shall not multiply,' [16]why do I need 'horses'?

TRANSLATION AND COMMENTARY

וְכוֹתֵב לוֹ [1]The king must **write himself a Torah scroll** which must remain with him at all times. [2]**When** the king **goes out to war, he must take** the Torah scroll **with him,** [3]and **when he returns from** battle, **he must bring** the Torah scroll home **with him.** [4]**When** the king **sits in judgment,** the Torah scroll **must be with him** in the courtroom, [5]and **when he reclines** to eat, the scroll **must be** placed **opposite him,** [6]**for the verse states** (Deuteronomy 17:19): **"And it shall be with him, and he shall read in it all the days of his life."**

GEMARA תָּנוּ רַבָּנַן [7]A Baraita explores the limitation upon the number of horses a king is permitted to maintain: "The verse states (Deuteronomy 17:16): **'He shall not multiply horses to himself.'** Without the words 'to himself,' [8]**I might have thought that** the king is **not even** permitted to keep **as many** horses **as are required for his chariots and horsemen** in times of war and peace. [9]Therefore, **the Torah states: 'To himself,'** for his personal pleasures. [10]It is only **for his personal** pleasure and aggrandizement that the king **may not multiply horses, but he** is permitted to **multiply horses as many as are required for his chariots and horsemen** for waging war and for other needs of state. The Gemara now asks: [11]**How, then, do I interpret** the prohibition against multiplying **'horses'?** [12]The king may not multiply **horses that stand idle** and are kept only to demonstrate his wealth. [13]**From where do we know that even one horse, if it is idle, is included under** the prohibition that stipulates: **'He shall not multiply** horses'? This is derived from the end of the verse, [14]for **the Torah states: 'To the end that he should multiply the horse.'** The use of the singular form 'horse' (סוס) teaches that the king may not maintain even a single horse for his personal pleasures. [15]But **now that even one horse, if it is idle, is included under** the prohibition that stipulates: **'He shall not multiply,'** [16]**why,** then, **does** the first part of the verse use the plural form

RASHI

גמרא לו — משמע להרחיב דעתו ולהגדיל ברבוי סוסים. הסוסים באים ממצרים לארץ ישראל, וצריך לשלוח שלוחים לקנות לו סוסים, ועוברים ב"לא תוסיפו לראותם עוד עד עולם" (שמות יד).

NOTES

יוֹשֵׁב בַּדִּין הִיא עִמּוֹ When he sits in judgment, it is with him. The Rishonim seek clarification: We learned above (18a) that the king may not sit on a court and judge others. What, then, does the Mishnah mean when it says that when the king sits in judgment, his Torah scroll must be with him? *Ran* answers that the Mishnah refers to civil cases, which the king may indeed adjudicate. Alternatively, the Mishnah refers to kings of the House of David who may judge capital cases as well. *Meiri* suggests that the Mishnah is dealing with matters which the king may judge on his own as part of his royal prerogative.

HALAKHAH

behind closed doors with an unmarried woman." (*Shulḥan Arukh, Even HaEzer* 22:2.)

לֹא יַרְבֶּה לוֹ סוּסִים He shall not multiply horses. "A king is not permitted to multiply horses for himself. He may only keep as many horses as he needs for his chariots and horsemen. He may not keep even a single horse just to run before him, as do other kings," following our Gemara. (*Rambam, Sefer Shofetim, Hilkhot Melakhim* 3:3.)

[1]לַעֲבוֹר בְּלֹא תַעֲשֶׂה עַל כָּל סוּס וְסוּס״. [2]טַעְמָא דִּכְתַב רַחֲמָנָא ״לוֹ״. [3]הָא לָאו הָכִי, הֲוָה אָמִינָא אֲפִילּוּ כְּדֵי רִכְבּוֹ וּפָרָשָׁיו נַמִי לָא!

[4]לָא, צְרִיכָא לְאַפּוּשֵׁי.

[5]״׳וְכֶסֶף וְזָהָב לֹא יַרְבֶּה לּוֹ׳ — [6]אֶלָּא כְּדֵי לִיתֵּן אַסְפַּנְיָא״. [7]תָּנוּ רַבָּנַן: ״׳וְכֶסֶף וְזָהָב לֹא יַרְבֶּה לּוֹ׳. [8]יָכוֹל אֲפִילּוּ כְּדֵי לִיתֵּן אַסְפַּנְיָא. [9]תַּלְמוּד לוֹמַר: ׳לוֹ׳ — [10]לוֹ אֵינוֹ מַרְבֶּה, [11]אֲבָל מַרְבֶּה הוּא כְּדֵי לִיתֵּן אַסְפַּנְיָא״.

LITERAL TRANSLATION

[1]So that he transgress a negative commandment with every single [idle] horse." [2]The reason is that the Torah (lit., "the Merciful") wrote "to himself." [3]But without this, would I have said [he may] not [have] even as many as are required for his chariots and horsemen!

[4]No, it was necessary for adding.

[5]"'Neither shall he greatly multiply to himself silver and gold' — [6]rather as much as is required to supply wages." [7]Our Rabbis taught: "'Neither shall he greatly multiply to himself silver and gold.' [8]I might have thought [not] even as much as is required to supply wages. [9]The Torah states: 'To himself' — [10]for himself he does not multiply [silver and gold], [11]but he multiplies [silver and gold] as much as is required to supply wages."

RASHI

בעשה ולא תעשה לא גרסינן. **הוה אמינא אפילו כדי רכבו לא?** — בתמיה, מלכות בלא רכב ופרשים מי איכא? **לאפושי** — רכב ופרשים וסוסים, לרכוב בהרווחה ולא בצמצום. לישנא אחרינא: לאפוחי גרסינן, כשרוכב סוס אחד ומושך סוס אחד אצלו ביד, ורוכב פעם על זה ופעם על זה להרגיע את חבירו.

TRANSLATION AND COMMENTARY

'horses' (סוּסִים)? [1]The plural form is used **in order** to teach **that** the king **transgresses** a **negative commandment with each** additional idle **horse** that he acquires." The Gemara raises a question about the Baraita's interpretation of the verse limiting the number of horses that a king may keep. [2]The Baraita implies that **the reason** that the king is permitted to have as many horses as required for his chariots and horsemen **is that the Torah wrote "to himself,"** teaching that only when it is for his personal pleasure and aggrandizement is the king not allowed to multiply the number of horses he owns. [3]**But without** those extra words **would I have said** that he may **not even** keep in his possession **as many** horses **as are required for his chariots and horsemen!**

לָא [4]The Gemara answers: **No,** even without the words "to himself" we would have known that the king is permitted to have as many horses as he requires for his chariots and horsemen. The words "to himself" **were** only **necessary** in order to teach us that the king is permitted **to add** as many horsemen, chariots, and horses as necessary. But he is forbidden to increase the number of his horses if he does so solely for his personal pleasure.

וְכֶסֶף וְזָהָב [5]We learn in the next clause of our Mishnah: "The verse states (Deuteronomy 17:17): **'Neither shall he greatly multiply to himself silver and gold.'** [6]**Rather,** the king may only keep **as much** gold and silver **as is required to supply his** soldiers with ample **salaries** and provisions." [7]**Our Rabbis taught** a Baraita that examines this prohibition: "The verse states: **'Neither shall he greatly multiply to himself silver and gold.'** Had the Torah not appended to this prohibition the words 'to himself,' [8]**I might have thought** that the king is **not even** permitted to keep **as much** gold and silver **as is required to supply** his soldiers with ample **salaries.** [9]Therefore, **the Torah states 'to himself,'** meaning, for his personal pleasures. [10]It is only **for his** personal pleasures that the king **may not multiply silver and gold,** [11]**but he is** permitted to **multiply silver and gold as much as is required to supply** his soldiers with their **salaries."** The Gemara points out a

NOTES

לְאַפּוּשֵׁי **For adding.** A number of Rishonim had the reading לְאַפּוּחֵי. *Ri Migash* (cited by *Ramah*) understands this word as being derived from the root נפח — "to blow up, to swell." The words "to himself" were necessary in order to teach that the king is permitted to "swell" the number of horses and chariots in his army and place them in his camp, to make his army appear larger than it actually is. *Meiri* understands the word in the sense of "to rest." The words "to himself" teach that the king is permitted to add to the number of horses in his possession, so that he and his soldiers can always have a spare horse, which would allow them to rest the one that was just ridden. *Meiri* notes that this explanation also fits the reading לְאַפּוּשֵׁי, for that, too, may be understood in the sense of "rest."

וְכֶסֶף וְזָהָב לֹא יַרְבֶּה **Neither shall he greatly multiply silver and gold.** *Ramah* explains that this prohibition forbids the king to place an excessive burden on his people, but there are no restrictions regarding the amount of gold or silver that the king may amass through gifts or conquest.

HALAKHAH

וְכֶסֶף לֹא יַרְבֶּה **He shall not multiply silver.** "A king is not permitted to multiply silver and gold for himself and keep it as his personal treasure in order to add to his glory. He may only keep as much silver and gold as he needs to maintain his soldiers, servants, and attendants. It is, however, commendable for the king to amass great wealth and deposit it in the Temple treasury, so that it be available for communal needs and in times of war (as we find with David and other righteous kings; *Kesef Mishneh, Radbaz*)." (*Rambam, Sefer Shofetim, Hilkhot Melakhim* 3:4.)

[1]טַעְמָא דִּכְתַב רַחֲמָנָא "לוֹ". [2]הָא לָאו הָכִי הֲוָה אָמִינָא אֲפִילּוּ כְּדֵי לִיתֵּן אַסְפַּנְיָא נַמִי לֹא!

[3]לָא, צְרִיכָא לְהַרְוָוחָה.

[4]הַשְׁתָּא, דְּאָמְרַתְּ "לוֹ" לִדְרָשָׁה, [5]"לֹא יַרְבֶּה לוֹ נָשִׁים", מַאי דָּרְשַׁתְּ בֵּיהּ?

[6]לְמַעוּטֵי הֶדְיוֹטוֹת.

[7]רַב יְהוּדָה רָמֵי: [8]כְּתִיב: "וַיְהִי לִשְׁלֹמֹה אַרְבָּעִים אֶלֶף אֻרְוֹת סוּסִים לְמֶרְכַּבְתּוֹ". [9]וּכְתִיב: "וַיְהִי לִשְׁלֹמֹה אַרְבַּעַת אֲלָפִים אֻרְוֹת סוּסִים".

[10]הָא כֵּיצַד? [11]אִם אַרְבָּעִים אֶלֶף אִיצְטַבְלָאוֹת הָיוּ — כָּל אֶחָד וְאֶחָד הָיוּ בּוֹ אַרְבַּעַת אֲלָפִים אֻרְוֹת סוּסִים. [12]וְאִם אַרְבַּעַת אֲלָפִים אִיצְטַבְלָאוֹת הָיוּ — כָּל אֶחָד וְאֶחָד הָיוּ בּוֹ אַרְבָּעִים אֶלֶף אֻרְוֹת סוּסִים.

[13]רַבִּי יִצְחָק רָמֵי: [14]כְּתִיב: "אֵין כֶּסֶף נֶחְשָׁב בִּימֵי שְׁלֹמֹה לִמְאוּמָה". [15]וּכְתִיב: "וַיִּתֵּן

LITERAL TRANSLATION

[1]The reason is that the Torah wrote "to himself." [2]But without this, would I have said [he may] not [have] even as much as is required to provide wages?

[3]No, it was necessary for being liberal.

[4]Now, that you say that "to himself" is for exposition, how do you interpret: [5]"Neither shall he multiply wives to himself"?

[6]To exclude commoners.

[7]Rav Yehudah raised a contradiction (lit., "threw"): [8]It is written: "And Solomon had forty thousand stalls of horses for his chariots." [9]And it is written: "And Solomon had four thousand stalls for horses."

[10]How so? [11]If there were forty thousand stables — each one had four thousand stalls of horses. [12]And if there were four thousand stables — each one had forty thousand stalls of horses.

[13]Rabbi Yitzḥak raised a contradiction: [14]It is written: "Silver counted for nothing in Solomon's days." And it is written: [15]"And the

TRANSLATION AND COMMENTARY

difficulty similar to the one raised above: [1]It follows from the Baraita that **the reason** the king is permitted to have as much gold and silver as he needs to feed his soldiers **is that the Torah wrote "to himself,"** teaching that it is only for his personal pleasures that the king may not amass gold and silver. [2]**But without** those extra words **would I have said** that he may **not even** have in his possession **as much** gold and silver **as is required to supply** his soldiers with ample **salaries** and provisions?

לָא [3]The Gemara answers: **No,** the words "to himself" **were necessary** to teach us that the king is permitted **to be liberal** with his troops and provide them with more than the minimum wages and supplies, and he may even keep money in reserve to hire additional soldiers should the need arise.

הַשְׁתָּא [4]The Gemara asks: **Now, since you say that** the phrase **"to himself"** as used regarding the king's horses and money is a restrictive expression **from which legal inferences may be drawn,** [5]**how do you interpret** that expression as used in the verse (Deuteronomy 17:17): **"Neither shall he multiply wives to himself"?**

לְמַעוּטֵי הֶדְיוֹטוֹת [6]The Gemara answers: The words "to himself" come **to exclude commoners** from the prohibition. One who is not a king may take as many wives as he wishes.

רַב יְהוּדָה [7]**Rav Yehudah pointed out the contradiction** between the following two verses: [8]One **verse states** (I Kings 5:6): **"And Solomon had forty thousand stalls of horses for his chariots."** [9]**And** another **verse states** (II Chronicles 9:25): **"And Solomon had four thousand stalls for horses** and chariots."

הָא כֵּיצַד [10]**How** can these two verses be reconciled? One verse refers to the number of stables and the other relates to the number of horses in each stable, i.e., the number of individual stalls. [11]**If there were forty thousand stables,** then **each stable had four thousand** individual **stalls for horses.** [12]**And if there were four thousand stables,** then **each** stable **had forty thousand** individual **stalls for horses.** This implies that Solomon owned one hundred sixty million horses!

רַבִּי יִצְחָק [13]**Rabbi Yitzḥak pointed out the contradiction** between another set of verses relating to Solomon's kingdom: [14]One **verse states** (II Chronicles 9:20): **"Silver counted for nothing in Solomon's days."** It had no value due to its unimaginable abundance. [15]**And another verse states** (I Kings 10:27): **"And the**

RASHI

להרווחה — שלא לצמצם, ואם יצטרך לשכור עוד חיילות שיהיה מצוי בידו. למעוטי הדיוטות — דמותרין להרבות נשים. אצטבלאות — בית גדול למדור הסוסים. ארוות — הבדלה בין שורה לשורה על פני הבית.

LANGUAGE

אִיצְטַבְלָאוֹת Stables This word derives from the Greek στάβλον, *stablion*, or the Latin *stablum*, meaning "stable."

NOTES

לְמַעוּטֵי הֶדְיוֹטוֹת To exclude commoners. The Rishonim ask: Why not say that the phrase "to himself," written with respect to the number of horses and the amount of gold and silver which the king may amass, should also be interpreted to exclude commoners from those prohibitions? *Ran* answers that it is obvious that those prohibitions do not apply to ordinary people, but one might have thought that even a commoner is forbidden to multiply the number of his wives, because he too faces the danger of having his heart turned away. So it was necessary for the Torah to teach us that an ordinary person is excluded from the prohibition. An entirely different interpretation has also been suggested. The Gemara

LANGUAGE

שִׁירְטוֹן Bank. This word derives from the Greek συρτόν, *syrton*, meaning a "sandbank," mud or sand piled up at the side of river.

BACKGROUND

כְּרַךְ גָּדוֹל שֶׁבְּרוֹמִי City of Rome. It appears that the establishment of the Latins in Italy took place coterminously with the kingdom of Solomon. This is to be viewed as the origin of Rome.

TRANSLATION AND COMMENTARY

king made silver to be in Jerusalem like stones," implying that silver did indeed have value in Solomon's day!

לָא קַשְׁיָא [1]The Gemara explains: **There is** in fact **no difficulty.** [2]**Here,** the verse that says silver had no value refers to the period **before King Solomon** sinned and **married the daughter of Pharaoh.** [3]And **there,** the verse that implies that silver was indeed valued refers to the period **after Solomon** sinned and **married the daughter of Pharaoh.**

אָמַר רַבִּי יִצְחָק [4]**Rabbi Yitzḥak said: When Solomon married the daughter of Pharaoh,** the angel **Gabriel descended** from Heaven **and stuck a reed into the sea, and** over time **a bank rose around it,** forming a land mass [5]**upon which the great city of Rome was built.** King Solomon's marriage to Pharaoh's daughter led to the destruction of the Second Temple by the Romans.

וְאָמַר רַבִּי יִצְחָק [6]**Rabbi Yitzḥak asked: Why were the reasons for the Torah's** commandments **not revealed?** [7]**Because in the case of two verses the reasons were indeed revealed, and** none less than **the greatest man in the world,** King Solomon, **was led to sin** as a result. [8]**The verse states** (Deuteronomy 17:17): **"Neither shall he multiply wives to himself,** that his heart not turn away." [9]**Solomon said** to himself: I am not governed by that prohibition, for even if **I multiply** the number of my **wives,** my heart **will not be turned away** from God. But Solomon was led astray by his wives, [10]as **the verse states** (I Kings 11:4): **"It came to pass, when Solomon was old, that his wives turned away his heart after other gods,** and his heart was not perfect with the Lord his God, as was the heart of David his father." [11]**And** similarly **the verse states** (Deuteronomy 17:16): **"He shall not multiply horses to himself,** nor cause the people to return to Egypt, to add to his horses." [12]**Solomon said** to himself: **"I can multiply horses, and** still **I will not return** the people to Egypt." Thus, Solomon disregarded the prohibition and in the end he sent people to buy horses for him in Egypt, [13]as **the verse states** (I Kings 10:29): **"And a chariot going out of Egypt would cost six hundred shekels**

שְׁלֹמֹה אֶת הַכֶּסֶף בִּירוּשָׁלַיִם כָּאֲבָנִים״!
[1]לָא קַשְׁיָא. [2]כָּאן, קוֹדֶם שֶׁנָּשָׂא שְׁלֹמֹה אֶת בַּת פַּרְעֹה. [3]כָּאן, לְאַחַר שֶׁנָּשָׂא שְׁלֹמֹה אֶת בַּת פַּרְעֹה.
[4]אָמַר רַבִּי יִצְחָק: בְּשָׁעָה שֶׁנָּשָׂא שְׁלֹמֹה אֶת בַּת פַּרְעֹה, יָרַד גַּבְרִיאֵל וְנָעַץ קָנֶה בַּיָּם, וְהֶעֱלָה שִׂירְטוֹן, [5]וְעָלָיו נִבְנָה כְּרַךְ גָּדוֹל שֶׁבְּרוֹמִי.
[6]וְאָמַר רַבִּי יִצְחָק: מִפְּנֵי מָה לֹא נִתְגַּלּוּ טַעֲמֵי תוֹרָה? [7]שֶׁהֲרֵי שְׁתֵּי מִקְרָאוֹת נִתְגַּלּוּ טַעְמָן, נִכְשַׁל בָּהֶן גְּדוֹל הָעוֹלָם. [8]כְּתִיב: ״לֹא יַרְבֶּה לּוֹ נָשִׁים״. [9]אָמַר שְׁלֹמֹה: אֲנִי אַרְבֶּה וְלֹא אָסוּר. [10]וּכְתִיב: ״וַיְהִי לְעֵת זִקְנַת שְׁלֹמֹה נָשָׁיו הִטּוּ אֶת לְבָבוֹ״. [11]וּכְתִיב: ״לֹא יַרְבֶּה לּוֹ סוּסִים״. [12]וְאָמַר שְׁלֹמֹה: ״אֲנִי אַרְבֶּה וְלֹא אָשִׁיב״. [13]וּכְתִיב: ״וַתֵּצֵא מֶרְכָּבָה מִמִּצְרַיִם בְּשֵׁשׁ וגו׳״.

LITERAL TRANSLATION

king made silver in Jerusalem like stones"!
[1]It is not difficult. [2]Here, before Solomon married the daughter of Pharaoh. [3]Here, after Solomon married the daughter of Pharaoh.
[4]Rabbi Yitzḥak said: When Solomon married the daughter of Pharaoh, Gabriel descended and stuck a reed into the sea, and a bank rose [around it], [5]and upon it was built the great city of Rome.
[6]And Rabbi Yitzḥak said: Why were the reasons of the Torah not revealed? [7]Because [in the case of] two verses their reasons were revealed, [and] the greatest man in the world stumbled on them. [8]It is written: "Neither shall he multiply wives to himself." [9]Solomon said: I will multiply [wives] and I will not turn away. [10]And it is written: "It came to pass, when Solomon was old, that his wives turned away his heart [after other gods]." [11]And it is written: "He shall not multiply horses to himself." [12]And Solomon said: "I will multiply [horses] and I will not return." [13]And it is written: "And a chariot going out of Egypt would cost six [hundred shekels]."

RASHI

כאבנים — חשיב מיהא פורתא. **לא נתגלו טעמי תורה** — כגון למה נאסרה לבישת שעטנז, ואכילת חזיר, וכיוצא בהן.

NOTES

means to say here that the words "to himself" come to exclude common women from the prohibition. The king is forbidden to take more than eighteen wives, but there is no restriction on the number of concubines he may have (*Rabbi A. M. Horowitz*).

אֶת הַכֶּסֶף בִּירוּשָׁלַיִם כָּאֲבָנִים Silver to be in Jerusalem like stones. The Jerusalem Talmud asks: If King Solomon's silver was strewn about like stones, how is it that it was not stolen? Rabbi Yose bar Ḥaninah answers that the silver was cast into huge blocks eight or ten cubits long, which could not be lifted.

לֹא נִתְגַּלּוּ טַעֲמֵי תוֹרָה The reasons of the Torah were not revealed. *Meiri* notes that the Torah does in fact reveal the reasons for some of the commandments. For example,

[1]״וְכוֹתֵב סֵפֶר תּוֹרָה לִשְׁמוֹ״. [2]תָּנָא: ״וּבִלְבַד שֶׁלֹּא יִתְנָאֶה בְּשֶׁל אֲבוֹתָיו״.

[3]אָמַר רָבָא: אַף עַל פִּי שֶׁהִנִּיחוּ לוֹ אֲבוֹתָיו לְאָדָם סֵפֶר תּוֹרָה, מִצְוָה לִכְתּוֹב מִשֶּׁלּוֹ, [4]שֶׁנֶּאֱמַר: ״וְעַתָּה כִּתְבוּ לָכֶם אֶת הַשִּׁירָה״.

[5]אֵיתִיבֵיהּ אַבָּיֵי: ״וְכוֹתֵב לוֹ סֵפֶר תּוֹרָה לִשְׁמוֹ, שֶׁלֹּא יִתְנָאֶה בְּשֶׁל אֲחֵרִים״. [6]מֶלֶךְ — אִין, הֶדְיוֹט — לָא!

[7]לָא, צְרִיכָא לִשְׁתֵּי תּוֹרוֹת, [8]וְכִדְתַנְיָא: ״׳וְכָתַב לוֹ אֶת מִשְׁנֵה וגו׳׳ — [9]כּוֹתֵב לִשְׁמוֹ שְׁתֵּי תּוֹרוֹת, [10]אַחַת שֶׁהִיא יוֹצְאָה וְנִכְנֶסֶת עִמּוֹ, וְאַחַת שֶׁמּוּנַּחַת לוֹ בְּבֵית גְּנָזָיו.

LITERAL TRANSLATION

[1]"And he writes a Torah scroll for himself." [2][A Sage] taught: "Provided that he not adorn himself with that of his forefathers."

[3]Rava said: Even if a person's ancestors left him a Torah scroll, he is commanded to write his own, [4]as it is stated: "Now write this song for yourselves."

[5]Abaye raised an objection: "And he writes a Torah scroll for himself, so that he not adorn himself with that of others." [6]A king — yes, an ordinary man — no!

[7]No, it is necessary for two Torah scrolls, [8]and as it was taught: "'And he shall write for himself a duplicate, etc.' — [9]he writes for himself two Torah scrolls, [10]one that goes out and comes in with him, and one that is laid by for him in his treasure house.

TRANSLATION AND COMMENTARY

of silver." Revealing the reason for the commandments tempted the wisest of all men to defy them. The reasons for the other commandments were not revealed so as to avoid this pitfall.

וְכוֹתֵב [1]We learn in the next clause of the Mishnah: "The king must **write himself a Torah scroll.**" [2]**A Sage taught** a related Baraita: **"He may not make use** of a scroll written by one **of his ancestors."**

אָמַר רָבָא [3]The Gemara now raises a parallel case, for **Rava said: Even if a person's ancestors left him a Torah scroll, he is commanded to write** a Torah scroll of **his own,** [4]**as the verse states** (Deuteronomy 31:19): **"Now write this song for yourselves,** and teach it to the children of Israel," from which we learn that it is the duty of every Jew to write a Torah scroll or have one written for him.

אֵיתִיבֵיהּ [5]**Abaye raised an objection** against Rava from a Baraita which stated: "A king must **write a Torah scroll for himself, so that he does not make use of** a copy that was written for **someone else."** [6]The Baraita's singling out of **the king** implies that only he **must write** his own Torah scroll, but **an ordinary Jew** is **not obligated** to do so, and may use a Torah scroll written for others. This contradicts Rava's opinion!

לָא [7]The Gemara answers: **No, it was necessary for** the Baraita to single out the king, for unlike an ordinary Jew, who is only obligated to write a single Torah scroll, the king is obligated to write **two Torah scrolls,** and this second scroll must also be written specifically by (or for) him. [8]**This was taught** in the following Baraita: "The verse states (Deuteronomy 17:18): 'And it shall be when he sits upon the throne of his kingdom, **that he shall write for himself a duplicate** of the law.' [9]This teaches that the king must **write for himself two Torah scrolls,** [10]**one that goes out and comes in with him** wherever he goes,

RASHI

לשתי תורות – הא דשאני מלך מהדיוטות – דאילו היה הדיוט סגי ליה בחדא, ומלך בעי תרתי. **משנה** – שתים במשמע.

NOTES

certain commandments were given so that we should remember that God created the world in six days, or that He delivered the people of Israel from bondage in Egypt. *Meiri* explains that revealing the reason for a commandment does not pose any danger if the commandment commemorates a past event. Only when the commandment was given in order to effect some desired result in the present is there concern that knowing the reason for it will lead a person to think that he can disregard the commandment and still achieve its goal.

HALAKHAH

אַף עַל פִּי שֶׁהִנִּיחוּ לוֹ אֲבוֹתָיו **Even if a person's ancestors left him.** "Each and every Jew is obligated to write a Torah scroll. Even if he had inherited a Torah scroll from his parent, he is still required to write another one for himself. *Rema* adds that a Jew fulfills his obligation if he hires a scribe to write a Torah for him, or if he purchases a Torah scroll that has errors and then corrects them, but not if he purchases a scroll that is not in need of correction. Rishonim say there is an obligation to write other sacred works, such as the Prophets, the Mishnah, the Talmud, and their commentaries (following *Tur* in the name of *Rosh*). Some Aḥaronim understand that this duty is in addition to the obligation to write a Torah scroll (*Bet Yosef, Taz*). Others maintain that this duty stands in place of the original obligation to write a Torah scroll (*Derishah*)." (*Shulḥan Arukh, Yoreh De'ah* 270:1.)

כּוֹתֵב לִשְׁמוֹ שְׁתֵּי תּוֹרוֹת **He writes for himself two Torah scrolls.** "The king is required to write a special Torah scroll for himself in addition to the Torah scroll that he was obligated to write even before he ascended to the throne (or the scroll that he inherited from his ancestors). He deposits the scroll he wrote before he became king in his treasure house, and the scroll that he must write once he becomes king remains with him at all times. (*Rambam*

TRANSLATION AND COMMENTARY

and one that is kept for him permanently **in his treasure house.** [1]Regarding **the copy that goes out and comes in with him** wherever he goes, **he makes it** very small like **a kind of amulet, and** he **hangs it on his arm,** [2]**as the verse states** (Psalms 16:8): **'I have set the Lord always before me; surely He is at my right hand, I shall not be moved.'** [3]**But he does not enter with it into the bathhouse or the outhouse,** [4]**for the verse states** (Deuteronomy 17:19): **'And it shall be with him, and he shall read in it** all the days of his life,' teaching that the king's obligation to have a Torah scroll at his side applies only **in a place where it is fit to read** from the Torah."

אָמַר מָר זוּטְרָא [5]**Mar Zutra said, and some say** that it was **Mar Ukva** who made this statement: [6]**At first the Torah was given to Israel in the** ancient **Hebrew script and in the sacred Hebrew language.** [7]**It was** later **given to them a second time in the days of Ezra in the Assyrian script** — the script still used in Torah scrolls — **and the Aramaic language.** [8]The people of **Israel selected for themselves the Assyrian script and the sacred Hebrew language,** [9]**and left the** ancient **Hebrew script and the Aramaic language for the common people.**

מַאן הֶדְיוֹטוֹת [10]The Gemara asks: **Who are** these **ordinary people** who adopted the ancient Hebrew script and the Aramaic language?

אָמַר רַב חִסְדָּא [11]**Rav Ḥisda said: The Samaritans;** II Kings 17 tells that non-Jews settled in Samaria and the surrounding territory after the exile of the ten tribes. These people converted to Judaism but had ulterior motives for doing so and were not scrupulous about observing the commandments. Accordingly, it was a matter of debate among the Sages whether or not they were Jewish. In any event, these people adopted the ancient Hebrew script and the Aramaic language.

מַאי כְּתָב עִבְרִית [12]The Gemara asks: **What is the** ancient **Hebrew script?**

[1]אוֹתָהּ שֶׁיּוֹצְאָה וְנִכְנֶסֶת עִמּוֹ — עוֹשֶׂה אוֹתָהּ כְּמִין קָמֵיעַ, וְתוֹלֶה בִּזְרוֹעוֹ, [2]שֶׁנֶּאֱמַר: 'שִׁוִּיתִי ה' לְנֶגְדִּי תָמִיד כִּי מִימִינִי בַּל אֶמּוֹט'. [3]אֵינוֹ נִכְנָס בָּהּ לֹא לְבֵית הַמֶּרְחָץ וְלֹא לְבֵית הַכִּסֵּא, [4]שֶׁנֶּאֱמַר: 'וְהָיְתָה עִמּוֹ וְקָרָא בוֹ' — מָקוֹם הָרָאוּי לִקְרֹאת בּוֹ".

[5]אָמַר מָר זוּטְרָא וְאִיתֵּימָא מָר עוּקְבָא: [6]בַּתְּחִלָּה נִיתְּנָה תּוֹרָה לְיִשְׂרָאֵל בִּכְתָב עִבְרִי וּלְשׁוֹן הַקּוֹדֶשׁ. [7]חָזְרָה וְנִיתְּנָה לָהֶם בִּימֵי עֶזְרָא בִּכְתָב אַשּׁוּרִית וּלְשׁוֹן אֲרַמִּי. [8]בֵּירְרוּ לָהֶן לְיִשְׂרָאֵל כְּתָב אַשּׁוּרִית וּלְשׁוֹן הַקּוֹדֶשׁ, [9]וְהִנִּיחוּ לַהֶדְיוֹטוֹת כְּתָב עִבְרִית וּלְשׁוֹן אֲרַמִּי.

[10]מַאן הֶדְיוֹטוֹת?

[11]אָמַר רַב חִסְדָּא: כּוּתָאֵי.

[12]מַאי כְּתָב עִבְרִית?

LITERAL TRANSLATION

[1]The one that goes out and comes in with him — he makes it like a kind of amulet, and hangs it on his arm, [2]as it is stated: 'I have set the Lord always before me; surely He is at my right hand, I shall not be moved.' [3]He does not enter with it into the bathhouse or the outhouse, [4]as it is stated: 'And it shall be with him, and he shall read in it' — [in a] place where it is fit to read in it."

[5]Mar Zutra said, and some say [it was] Mar Ukva: [6]At first the Torah was given to Israel in the Hebrew script and in the sacred [Hebrew] language. [7]It was given to them again in the days of Ezra in the Assyrian script and the Aramaic tongue. [8]Israel selected for themselves the Assyrian script and the sacred [Hebrew] language, [9]and they left for common people the Hebrew script and the Aramaic tongue.

[10]Who are the common people?

[11]Rav Ḥisda said: The Samaritans.

[12]What is the Hebrew script?

RASHI

כתב עברי — של בני עבר הנהר.

SAGES

מָר זוּטְרָא Mar Zutra. A colleague of Rav Ashi, Mar Zutra was one of the leading Sages of his generation, and his teachers, Rav Pappa and Rav Naḥman bar Yitzḥak, accepted him as their equal.

Apart from his greatness in Halakhah and Aggadah, Mar Zutra was noted as a preacher, and his sermons are cited throughout the Talmud. He apparently held an official position as a scholar-in-residence and preacher in the House of the Exilarch. In his old age, he was appointed head of the Pumbedita Yeshivah.

Mar Zutra's meetings with Amemar and Rav Ashi are frequently mentioned in the Talmud, and some of these meetings may well have been formal conferences of the leaders of Babylonian Jewry of that generation.

מָר עוּקְבָא Mar Ukva. He was the Exilarch during the first and second generations of Amoraim in Babylonia. He was famous not only for occupying this elevated position but also for his learning and piety. Mar Ukva was very close to the circles of the Amora Shmuel, who respected him greatly. Mar Ukva was also famous for his philanthropy and great modesty. According to various traditions, Mar Ukva was called Natan Dezuzita, and he was a famous penitent in his generation. He seems to have had two sons who were also Sages.

NOTES

וְתוֹלֶה בִּזְרוֹעוֹ And hangs it on his arm. Some suggest that the scroll that the king hung from his arm like an amulet did not actually contain the entire Torah, for surely it would be difficult for the king to carry a full Torah scroll in that manner. Furthermore, it would be disrespectful to the Torah to have it hang from the king's arm in that way. Rather, the scroll that the king kept with him at all times contained the Ten Commandments, which contains 613 letters corresponding to the 613 Biblical commandments (*Rav Naḥshon Gaon, Tosafot* to the Torah). Alternatively, the scroll the king always kept at his side contained a concise list of the Torah's commandments (*Rashash*).

HALAKHAH

apparently did not have the reading: 'He makes it into a sort of amulet, and hangs it on his arm,' or else he did not understand it literally, but rather took it to mean that the king's special Torah scroll must be with him at all times; *Radbaz, Leḥem Mishneh*). The king must take that scroll wherever he goes, provided that it is a place where reading from the Torah is permitted." (*Rambam, Sefer Mada, Hilkhot Sefer Torah,* 7:2,3; *Sefer Shofetim, Hilkhot Melakhim* 3:1.)

TRANSLATION AND COMMENTARY

אָמַר [1]**Rav Ḥisda said:** This refers to the **Libonaah script,** which was later used by the Samaritans.

תַּנְיָא [2]The Gemara now records various opinions regarding the script in which the Torah was originally given and the changes that took place during the days of Ezra. **It was taught** in a Baraita: **"Rabbi Yose says: Ezra was worthy enough for the Torah to have been given to Israel through him, had Moses not preceded him.** [3]**Regarding Moses, the verse states** (Exodus 19:3): **'And Moses went up to God,'** [4]**and regarding Ezra, the verse states** (Ezra 7:6): **'This Ezra went up from Babylon,** and he was a ready scribe in the Torah of Moses, which the Lord God of Israel had given.' [5]**Just as the ascent mentioned here** with respect to Moses refers to an ascent made for receiving the **Torah, so too the ascent mentioned below** with respect to Ezra refers to an ascent made for **Torah,** for Ezra went up from Babylon in order to teach the Torah to the people of Israel, and he would have been fit to teach it to them for the first time had Moses not preceded him. [6]And furthermore, **regarding Moses, the verse states** (Deuteronomy 4:14): **'And the Lord commanded me at that time to teach you statutes and judgments,'** [7]and **regarding Ezra the verse states** (Ezra 7:10): **'For Ezra had prepared his heart to seek the Torah of the Lord, and to do it, and to teach in Israel statutes and judgments.'** The similarity between the two verses shows that Ezra's contribution was comparable to that of Moses. [8]**But even though the Torah was not** actually **given** to Israel **through** Ezra, **the script** in which the Torah is written **was** indeed **changed through him,** [9]**as the verse states** (Ezra 4:7): [22A] **'And the writing of the letter** (הַנִּשְׁתְּוָן) **was written in the Aramaic script, and translated into the Aramaic tongue.'** Rabbi Yose interprets the word הַנִּשְׁתְּוָן, translated here as 'the letter,' as if it were written הַנִּשְׁתַּנָּה, 'which was changed,' and so the verse speaks here of writing which was changed in the days of Ezra. This script had already appeared on the wall of King Belshazzar's palace in the days of Daniel, [10]as **the verse states** (Daniel 5:8): **'But they could not read the writing, nor make known to the king its meaning.'** During a feast given by King Belshazzar of Babylonia, the fingers of a man's hand appeared and wrote on the wall of the king's palace. But nobody except Daniel could decipher the inscription. Rabbi Yose claims that this was because it was written in a new script. An allusion to the change of scripts in the time of Ezra is found already in the Torah, [11]for **the verse states** (Deuteronomy

[1]אָמַר רַב חִסְדָּא: כְּתָב לִיבּוֹנָאָה.

[2]תַּנְיָא: ״רַבִּי יוֹסֵי אוֹמֵר: רָאוּי הָיָה עֶזְרָא שֶׁתִּינָּתֵן תּוֹרָה עַל יָדוֹ לְיִשְׂרָאֵל, אִילְמָלֵא לֹא קְדָמוֹ מֹשֶׁה. [3]בְּמֹשֶׁה הוּא אוֹמֵר: ׳וּמֹשֶׁה עָלָה אֶל הָאֱלֹהִים׳. [4]בְּעֶזְרָא הוּא אוֹמֵר: ׳הוּא עֶזְרָא עָלָה מִבָּבֶל׳. [5]מָה עֲלִיָּיה הָאָמוּר כָּאן תּוֹרָה, אַף עֲלִיָּיה הָאָמוּר לְהַלָּן תּוֹרָה. [6]בְּמֹשֶׁה הוּא אוֹמֵר: ׳וְאֹתִי צִוָּה ה׳ בָּעֵת הַהִיא לְלַמֵּד אֶתְכֶם חֻקִּים וּמִשְׁפָּטִים׳. [7]בְּעֶזְרָא הוּא אוֹמֵר: ׳כִּי עֶזְרָא הֵכִין לְבָבוֹ לִדְרֹשׁ אֶת תּוֹרַת ה׳ אֱלֹהָיו וְלַעֲשֹׂת וּלְלַמֵּד בְּיִשְׂרָאֵל חֹק וּמִשְׁפָּט׳. [8]וְאַף עַל פִּי שֶׁלֹּא נִיתְּנָה תּוֹרָה עַל יָדוֹ, נִשְׁתַּנָּה עַל יָדוֹ הַכְּתָב, [9]שֶׁנֶּאֱמַר: [22A] ׳וּכְתָב הַנִּשְׁתְּוָן כָּתוּב אֲרָמִית וּמְתֻרְגָּם אֲרָמִית׳. [10]וּכְתִיב: ׳לָא כָהֲלִין כְּתָבָא לְמִקְרֵא וּפִשְׁרֵא לְהוֹדָעָה לְמַלְכָּא׳. [11]וּכְתִיב: ׳וְכָתַב אֶת

LITERAL TRANSLATION

[1]Rav Ḥisda said: Libonaah script.

[2]It was taught: "Rabbi Yose says: Ezra was [sufficiently] worthy for the Torah to have been given to Israel through him, had Moses not preceded him. [3]Regarding Moses, it says: 'And Moses went up to God.' [4]Regarding Ezra, it says: 'This Ezra went up from Babylon.' [5]Just as the ascent mentioned here [refers to] Torah, so the ascent mentioned below [refers to] Torah. [6]Regarding Moses, it says: 'And the Lord commanded me at that time to teach you statutes and judgments.' [7]Regarding Ezra, he says: 'For Ezra had prepared his heart to seek the Torah of the Lord, his God, and to do it, and to teach in Israel statutes and judgments.' [8]But even though the Torah was not given through him, the script was changed through him, [9]as it is stated: [22A] 'And the writing of the letter was written in the Aramaic script, and translated into the Aramaic tongue.' [10]And it is written: 'But they could not read the writing, nor make known to the king its meaning.' [11]And it is written: 'He shall write [for himself]

RASHI

ליבונאה — אותיות גדולות, כעין אותן שכותבין בקמיעות ומזוזות. **וכתב הנשתוון** — כתב שנשתנה, והאי קרא בעזרא כתיב, שהיו כותבין בימיו כתב משונה שנשתנה על ידי מלאך שכתב "מנא מנא תקל ופרסין" בימי דניאל, כתב דארמי ולשון ארמי. ואומר "לא כהלין כתבא למיקרא", (דכיון שחטאו) לא היו יכולין לקרות כתב שכתב המלאך בימי בלשצר. והיו שם יהודים הרבה, שמע מינה נשתנה להם אותו כתב באותו היום. **את משנה התורה** — רמז לנו משה רבינו שכתב שבימיו עתיד להשתנות מן עברי לאשורית שנתן להם בימי דניאל, ובא עזרא וכתב בו את התורה בכתב אשורית.

BACKGROUND

כְּתָב לִיבּוֹנָאָה Libonaah script.

This refers to the ancient Hebrew alphabet, which is still used by the Samaritans. However, it is not clear why the Talmud calls it Libonaah.

SAGES

רַבִּי Rabbi. This is the epithet of Rabbi Yehudah HaNasi. See *Sanhedrin*, Part I, pp. 27-8.

BACKGROUND

בַּתְּחִלָּה בִּכְתָב זֶה At first in this script. The Sages here refer to the relation between the ancient Hebrew script, which is still used, with slight changes, by the Samaritans, and the "Assyrian" script, which is the one used to write Hebrew today. This discussion presents all the possibilities — that the ancient script was the original one and altered at the time of Ezra; that the original Jewish script was, in fact, the Assyrian script, but that the ancient Hebrew script was used concurrently for the writing of secular matters; or that the original script was Assyrian, and that the Hebrew script was introduced later, and Ezra restored the original script for use in Scripture. Archeologists have uncovered various inscriptions in ancient Hebrew script and in the alphabetic Ugaritic script (which is a kind of cuneiform), as well as the remains of writings using other alphabets.

TRANSLATION AND COMMENTARY

17:18): **'He shall write for himself a copy of this Torah.'** The word מִשְׁנֵה, translated here as 'copy,' is understood by Rabbi Yose as also meaning 'change.' [1]Thus, the **script** in which the Torah was originally given **would be changed** at some future point. [2]**Why** then **is** the script in current use **called Assyrian script?** [3]It has this name **because** this script **came** to Eretz Israel **with** the Jewish people when they returned **from** their exile in **Assyria."**

תַּנְיָא [4]**It was taught** in another Baraita: **"Rabbi** Yehudah HaNasi **says:** [5]**At first the Torah was given to Israel in** what is referred to as the Assyrian **script.** [6]But **when** the people of Israel **sinned** during the First Temple period, the script **was changed to Ro'etz,** the script that was later associated with the Samaritans. [7]**And when they repented** in the days of Ezra, the Assyrian script **was restored to them,** [8]**as the verse states** (Zechariah 9:12): **'Return to the stronghold you prisoners of hope; even today will I restore to you a double promise.'** There was a double restoration: Return from the exile to the stronghold of Jerusalem and the restoration of the Assyrian script which had been changed (מִשְׁנֶה). But if the Torah was originally given to the people of Israel in this script, [9]**why is it called the Assyrian script?** Surely it predates the Jewish people's stay in Assyria! [10]It is called the Assyrian (אַשּׁוּרִית) script **because it is the happiest** (i.e., most beautiful and well structured) **of scripts."**

רַבִּי שִׁמְעוֹן בֶּן אֶלְעָזָר [11]The Baraita continues: **"Rabbi Shimon ben Elazar said in the name of Rabbi Eliezer ben Perata that Rabbi Elazar HaModa'i said:** [12]**The script** in which the Torah had been given **was never changed,** for the Torah had originally been given in the Assyrian script, and that script remained with the Jewish people through all subsequent generations. [13]This is alluded to in **the verse** that **states** (Exodus 27:10): **'The hooks...of the pillars.'** The curtains of the court of the Tabernacle were connected to hooks attached to the court's pillars. Those hooks were called *vavim* because their shape was similar to the letter *vav* in the Assyrian script. Thus, it follows that the Assyrian script was already in use during Moses' day. The expression 'the hooks of the pillars' teaches that the script in which the Torah was written never changed, [14]for **just as the pillars did not change** throughout the First Temple period, **so too the *vavs*** and all the other letters **did not change** during that time.

מִשְׁנֵה הַתּוֹרָה הַזֹּאת׳ — [1]כְּתָב הָרָאוּי לְהִשְׁתַּנּוֹת. [2]לָמָּה נִקְרָא אַשּׁוּרִית? [3]שֶׁעָלָה עִמָּהֶם מֵאַשּׁוּר״.

[4]תַּנְיָא: ״רַבִּי אוֹמֵר: [5]בַּתְּחִלָּה בִּכְתָב זֶה נִיתְּנָה תּוֹרָה לְיִשְׂרָאֵל. [6]כֵּיוָן שֶׁחָטְאוּ, נֶהְפַּךְ לָהֶן לְרוֹעַץ.

[7]כֵּיוָן שֶׁחָזְרוּ בָּהֶן, הֶחֱזִירוּ לָהֶם, [8]שֶׁנֶּאֱמַר: ׳שׁוּבוּ לְבִצָּרוֹן אֲסִירֵי הַתִּקְוָה; גַּם הַיּוֹם מַגִּיד מִשְׁנֶה אָשִׁיב לָךְ׳. [9]לָמָּה נִקְרָא שְׁמָהּ אַשּׁוּרִית? [10]שֶׁמְּאוּשֶּׁרֶת בִּכְתָב.

[11]רַבִּי שִׁמְעוֹן בֶּן אֶלְעָזָר אוֹמֵר מִשּׁוּם רַבִּי אֱלִיעֶזֶר בֶּן פְּרָטָא שֶׁאָמַר מִשּׁוּם רַבִּי אֶלְעָזָר הַמּוֹדָעִי: [12]כְּתָב זֶה לֹא נִשְׁתַּנָּה כָּל עִיקָּר, [13]שֶׁנֶּאֱמַר: ׳וָוֵי הָעַמּוּדִים׳. [14]מָה עַמּוּדִים לֹא נִשְׁתַּנּוּ, אַף וָוִים לֹא נִשְׁתַּנּוּ.

LITERAL TRANSLATION

a copy of this Torah' — [1][in a] script that is liable to be changed. [2]Why is it called Assyrian [script]? [3]Because it came up with them from Assyria."

[4]It was taught: "Rabbi says: [5]At first the Torah was given to Israel in this script. [6]When they sinned, it was changed into Ro'etz [script]. [7]When they repented, He returned [the Assyrian script] to them, [8]as it is said: 'Return to the stronghold you prisoners of hope; even today will I restore to you a double promise.' [9]Why is its name called Assyrian [script]? [10]Because it is the happiest of scripts.

[11]Rabbi Shimon ben Elazar says in the name of Rabbi Eliezer ben Perata, who said in the name of Rabbi Elazar HaModa'i: [12]This script was not changed at all, [13]as it is said: 'The hooks (*vavim*) of the pillars.' [14]Just as the pillars were not changed, so too the [letters] *vav* were not changed.

RASHI

בכתב זה נתנה תורה לישראל — בימי משה, ולמה ״לא כהלין כתבא למקרא״ — דכיון שחטאו בבית ראשון ובזו את התורה נהפך להם לרועץ לשון ״תרעץ אויב״ (שמות טו) — ששכחוהו. **שובו לביצרון** — לעיר מבצר שלכם — לירושלים, ואבית שני קא מתנבא. **גם היום מגיד משנה** — מה ששכחת את משנה התורה הזאת. **אשיב לך** — אחזיר לך מה ששכחת את משנה התורה הזאת. **ווי העמודים** — יתדות כסף העשוין כמין אונקלות, וקבעום בעמודים שבהם תוחבין לולאות קלעי החצר והמסך, וכל אונקלאות דומין לווין. אלמא בימי משה עשויין הווין כגון שלנו, והעמודים לא נשתנו לא גרסינן לה בתוספתא. הכי גרסינן בתוספתא: מה לשונם לא נשתנה — דהא דברי הכל בלשון הקודש נאמרה ועדיין בלשון הקודש היא.

NOTES

רוֹעַץ Ro'etz. Our commentary follows the Geonim who understand that Ro'etz, or Ra'atz, is the name given to the ancient Hebrew script, which was later adopted by the Samaritans. The word itself is derived from the root רעצ — "break, shatter" — and it is an inverted form of the word צער — "pain, distress." According to some, the word should read דעץ, meaning "press" or "squeeze into."

[1] וְאוֹמֵר: 'וְאֶל הַיְּהוּדִים כִּכְתָבָם, וְכִלְשׁוֹנָם'. [2] מַה לְּשׁוֹנָם לֹא נִשְׁתַּנָּה, אַף כְּתָבָם לֹא נִשְׁתַּנָּה. [3] אֶלָּא מָה אֲנִי מְקַיֵּים: 'אֶת מִשְׁנֵה הַתּוֹרָה הַזֹּאת'? [4] לִשְׁתֵּי תוֹרוֹת, אַחַת שֶׁיּוֹצְאָה וְנִכְנֶסֶת עִמּוֹ, [5] וְאַחַת שֶׁמּוּנַּחַת לוֹ בְּבֵית גְּנָזָיו. [6] אוֹתָהּ שֶׁיּוֹצְאָה וְנִכְנֶסֶת עִמּוֹ — עוֹשֶׂה אוֹתָהּ כְּמִין קָמֵיעַ, וְתוֹלֶה בִּזְרוֹעוֹ, [7] שֶׁנֶּאֱמַר: 'שִׁוִּיתִי ה' לְנֶגְדִּי תָמִיד'". [8] וְאִידָךְ — הַאי "שִׁוִּיתִי", מַאי דָּרֵישׁ בֵּיהּ? [9] הַהוּא מִיבָּעֵי לֵיהּ כִּדְרַב חָנָה בַּר בִּיזְנָא, דְּאָמַר רַב חָנָה בַּר בִּיזְנָא אָמַר רַבִּי שִׁמְעוֹן חֲסִידָא: [10] הַמִּתְפַּלֵּל צָרִיךְ שֶׁיִּרְאֶה עַצְמוֹ כְּאִילּוּ שְׁכִינָה כְּנֶגְדּוֹ, [11] שֶׁנֶּאֱמַר: "שִׁוִּיתִי ה' לְנֶגְדִּי תָמִיד". [12] לְרַבִּי שִׁמְעוֹן, דְּאָמַר כְּתָב זֶה לֹא נִשְׁתַּנָּה, [13] מַאי: "לָא כָהֲלִין כְּתָבָא לְמִקְרֵא"?

LITERAL TRANSLATION

[1] And it says: 'And to the Jews according to their writing, and according to their language.' [2] Just as their language did not change, so too their script did not change. [3] So how do I interpret: 'A duplicate of this Torah'? [4] [To teach] that [he writes] two Torah scrolls, one that goes out and comes in with him, [5] and one that is laid by for him in his treasure house. [6] The one that goes out and comes in with him — he make it like a kind of amulet, and hangs it on his arm, [7] as it is stated: 'I have set the Lord always before me.'"

[8] And the other one — this "I have set," how does he interpret it?

[9] That he needs [it] for [the words of] Rav Ḥanah bar Bizna, for Rav Ḥanah bar Bizna said in the name of Rabbi Shimon Ḥasida: [10] One who prays must see himself as if the Divine Presence were opposite him, [11] as it is stated: "I have set the Lord always before me."

[12] According to Rabbi Shimon, who said that this script was not changed, [13] what is [the meaning of]: "But they could not read the writing"?

RASHI

כמו קמיע — קטנה בכתב דק, שהיא קלה לשאת. שויתי ה' לנגדי — סיפיה דקרא: "כי מימיני בל אמוט", דוד המלך על שם ספר תורה שבזרועו אמר. לא נשתנה כל עיקר — משמע לא נשתנה מהם כלל, דהא עליה דרבי אתי לאיפלוגי ומאי "לא כהלין כתבא למיקרי".

TRANSLATION AND COMMENTARY

[1] This also follows from **the verse** that **states** (Esther 8:9): **'And to the Jews according to their writing, and according to their language.'** [2] **Just as** the Jews' **language did not change,** for the Jews spoke Hebrew throughout the First Temple period, **so too their script did not change.** [3] **So how,** then, **do I interpret** the verse (Deuteronomy 17:18): 'And he shall write for himself **a duplicate of this Torah,'** which Rabbi Yose interpreted as alluding to a change of script at some future date? [4] I maintain that this verse teaches the obligation of the king to write **two Torah scrolls, one that goes out and comes in with him** wherever he goes, [5] **and one that is kept for him** permanently **in his treasure house.** [6] Regarding **the copy that goes out and comes in with him** wherever he goes, **he makes it** very small, **like a kind of amulet,** and he **hangs it on his arm,** [7] **as the verse states** (Psalms 16:8): **'I have set the Lord always before me;** surely He is at my right hand.'"

וְאִידָךְ [8] The Gemara asks: **And the other** Tanna, who does not interpret the phrase "a duplicate of this Torah" as implying that the king must write two Torah scrolls, one of which must remain at his side at all times — **how does he interpret the** verse, "I **have set** the Lord always before me"?

הַהוּא מִיבָּעֵי לֵיהּ [9] The Gemara answers: **That** verse **is needed for** what **Rav Ḥanah bar Bizna** said, **for Rav Ḥanah bar Bizna said in the name of Rabbi Shimon Ḥasida:** [10] **One who prays must** focus his thoughts and **see himself as standing before the Divine Presence,** [11] **as the verse states: "I have set the Lord always before me."**

לְרַבִּי שִׁמְעוֹן [12] The Gemara asks: **According to Rabbi Shimon** ben Elazar, **who said that the script** in which the Torah had been given to the Jewish people **was never changed,** [13] **what is the meaning of the** verse cited above (Daniel 5:8): **"But they could not read the writing,** nor make known to the king its meaning"? If the script had not changed, why, then, could nobody read the inscription on the wall?

SAGES

רַב חָנָה בַּר בִּיזְנָא **Rav Ḥanah bar Bizna.** A Babylonian Amora of the second and third generations, Rav Ḥanah bar Bizna, who was a Rabbinical judge in Pumbedita, often transmitted the teachings of Rabbi Shimon Ḥasida. He was renowned among the scholars of this time both as an expert on Aggadah and as a Halakhic authority.

רַבִּי שִׁמְעוֹן חֲסִידָא **Rabbi Shimon Ḥasida.** A Palestinian Amora of the first and second generations, Rabbi Shimon Ḥasida must be distinguished from Rabbi Shimon HeḤasid, who was a Tanna and appears in Baraitot.

NOTES

וְאוֹמֵר: וְאֶל הַיְּהוּדִים **And he says: And to the Jews.** This second proof text teaches that not only did the Jews' script not change, but even the names of the letters remained the same (*Arukh Lener*).

HALAKHAH

שִׁוִּיתִי ה' לְנֶגְדִּי תָמִיד **I have set the Lord always before me.** "When a person prays, he should bear in mind that the Divine Presence stands before him." (*Shulḥan Arukh, Oraḥ Ḥayyim* 98:1.)

TRANSLATION AND COMMENTARY

אָמַר רַב [1]**Rav said:** The inscription could not be read, because **it was written in *gematria*,** a cipher. Daniel interpreted the inscription to read: מנא מנא תקל ופרסין (Daniel 5:25), [2]but the words that actually appeared on the wall were יטת יטת אידך פוגחמט. The words were written in the *atbash* code, where the last letter of the alphabet, ת, is substituted for the first letter, א, the penultimate letter, ש, is substituted for the second, ב, etc.

מַאי פָּרֵישׁ [3]The Gemara asks: **How did** Daniel **interpret** the inscription **for** King Belshazzar and his men? The deciphered message read: מנא מנא תקל ופרסין, *"Mene Mene Tekel Ufarsin"* and Daniel interpreted the cryptic message as follows (Daniel 5:26-28): [4]***"Mene"*** ("count") — **God has numbered** the days of **your kingdom, and brought it to an end.** [5]***"Tekel"*** ("weigh") — **You have been weighed in the balances, and have been found wanting.** [6]***"Farsin"*** ("broken up, divided") — **Your kingdom has been divided up, and given to Media and Persia.**

וּשְׁמוּאֵל אָמַר [7]**Shmuel said:** The inscription was indeed written in a cipher, but not the *atbash* code. The message on the wall read ממתוס ננקפי אאלרן. Daniel decoded the message, placing the second word under the first, and the third under the second, and then reading down, so that the inscription could be interpreted to read מנא מנא תקל ופרסין.

וְרַבִּי יוֹחָנָן אָמַר [8]**And Rabbi Yoḥanan said:** The words on the wall read אנם אנם לקת ניסרפו. Rearranging the letters of each word in reverse order, Daniel interpreted the message as saying: מנא מנא תקל ופרסין.

רַב אַשִׁי אָמַר [9]**Rav Ashi said:** The inscription appearing on Belshazzar's wall read נמא נמא קתל פורסין, the first two letters of each word having been transposed. Rearranged in the proper order, the inscription read מנא מנא תקל ופרסין.

MISHNAH אֵין רוֹכְבִין [10]The closing Mishnah of this chapter completes the special laws pertaining to the king: **One may neither ride on** the king's **horse, nor sit on his throne, nor use his scepter** or any other item

---

[1]אָמַר רַב: בְּגִימַטְרִיָּא אִיכְתִּיב לְהוֹן: [2]יטת יטת אידך פוגחמט.

[3]מַאי פָּרֵישׁ לְהוּ: ״מְנֵא מְנֵא תְּקֵל וּפַרְסִין״? [4]״מְנֵא״ — מְנָא אֱלָהָא מַלְכוּתָךְ, וְהַשְׁלְמָהּ לָךְ. [5]״תְּקֵל״ — תְּקִלְתָּא בְּמֹאזַנְיָא, וְהִשְׁתְּכַחַתְּ חַסִּיר. [6]״פַּרְסִין״ — פְּרִיסַת מַלְכוּתָךְ, וִיהִיבַת לְמָדַי וּפָרָס.

[7]וּשְׁמוּאֵל אָמַר: ממתוס ננקפי אאלרן.

[8]וְרַבִּי יוֹחָנָן אָמַר: אנם אנם לקת ניסרפו.

[9]רַב אַשִׁי אָמַר: נמא נמא קתל פורסין.

משנה [10]אֵין רוֹכְבִין עַל סוּסוֹ, וְאֵין יוֹשְׁבִין עַל כִּסְאוֹ, וְאֵין מִשְׁתַּמְּשִׁין בְּשַׁרְבִיטוֹ,

---

LITERAL TRANSLATION

[1]Rav said: [The inscription] was written for them in *gematria*: [2]יטת יטת אידך פוגחמט.

[3]How did he interpret for them: *"Mene mene tekel ufarsin"*? [4]*"Mene"* — God has numbered your kingdom, and brought it to an end. [5]*"Tekel"* — You are weighed in the balances, and are found wanting. [6]*"Farsin"* — Your kingdom is divided, and given to Media and Persia.

[7]And Shmuel said: [The words read:] ממתוס ננקפי אאלרן.

[8]And Rabbi Yoḥanan said: [The words read:] אנם אנם לקת ניסרפו.

[9]Rav Ashi said: [The words read:] נמא נמא קתל פורסין.

MISHNAH [10]One may neither ride on his horse, nor sit on his throne, nor use his scepter,

RASHI

יטת — בא״ת ב״ש ״מנא״, מניח את זו וכתב מה שבצדו: במקום מ״ם כותב יו״ד הסמוכה לה, ובמקום נו״ן כותב טי״ת, ובמקום אל״ף כותב תי״ו. **ופרסין** — שתי פריסות משמע, וזו היא פריסת מלכותו — ויהיבת למדי ופרס. **ממתוס ננקפי אאלרן** — עשאן שלש תיבות של חמשה אותיות, צירף אותיות הראשונות של כל תיבה ועשאן תיבה אחת, ואחר כך צירף השניות ושלישיות.

LANGUAGE

גִּימַטְרִיָּא Gematria. This word derives from the Greek γεωμετρία, *geometria*, the narrow meaning of which is the science of surveying. It was extended to mean any measurement and applied to the mathematical field of geometry. In Rabbinical Hebrew it refers to numerology, the attribution of meaning to words and phrases based on the numerical values of the letters they comprise.

BACKGROUND

א״ת ב״ש. This simple cipher, which appears to be found in the Bible (Jeremiah 25:26, 51:1, 51:41), involves replacing the first letter in the alphabet with the last, in the following order, each letter being substituted for its counterpart:

א — ת
ב — ש
ג — ר
ד — ק
ה — צ
ו — פ
ז — ע
ח — ס
ט — נ
י — מ
כ — ל

ממתוס ננקפי אאלרן This is the order of the letters:

מ מ ת ו ס
נ נ ק פ י
א א ל ר ן

Read the text from top to bottom, from right to left.

NOTES

אֵין רוֹכְבִין עַל סוּסוֹ They may not ride on his horse. The Jerusalem Talmud notes that when the king dies, his horse, his throne, his crown, and his scepter are all burned as a sign of mourning for the deceased. These items were taken because nobody may use them even after his death. This practice is already alluded to in Scripture, for the verse states (Jeremiah 34:5): "But you shall die in peace: and with the burnings of your fathers, the former kings which were before you, so shall they make a burning for you."

HALAKHAH

אֵין רוֹכְבִין עַל סוּסוֹ They may not ride on his horse. "A commoner is forbidden to ride on the king's horse, or to sit in his seat, or to use his scepter, crown, or any other personal item. He is also forbidden to use the king's menservants, maidservants or attendants. Only another king is allowed to make use of what had once been set aside for the former king." (*Rambam, Sefer Shofetim, Hilkhot Melakhim* 2:1.)

TRANSLATION AND COMMENTARY

designated specially for the king. [1]**Nor** may one **observe** the king **while his hair is being cut, or when he is naked, or when he is in the bathhouse.** The king's subjects are bound by all these restrictions, [2]because of **the verse that states** (Deuteronomy 17:15): **"You shall surely set a king over you."** The emphatic double verb mode (שׂוֹם תָּשִׂים — "you shall surely set") teaches that the people must set the king high above them, [3]**so that his fear shall be upon them.**

GEMARA אָמַר רַב יַעֲקֹב [4]**Rav Ya'akov said in the name of Rabbi Yoḥanan: Abishag** the Shunammite, the girl who slept alongside King David to keep him warm in his old age (see I Kings 1:1-4), **was permitted** by law **to Solomon, but** she was **forbidden to his** half-brother **Adonijah.** [5]**She was permitted to Solomon, because he** became **king** after David's death, [6]**and a king is allowed to make use of the** former **king's scepter** — as well as his servant, or anything else which had been set aside for the former king's personal use. [7]**But she was forbidden to** Solomon's half-brother **Adonijah, because he was a commoner.** Thus, Solomon was justified when he had Adonijah executed after he asked for Abishag in marriage. Adonijah's request was nothing but a veiled bid for the throne.

אֲבִישַׁג [8]The Gemara now elaborates. **What is** the story involving **Abishag?** [9]**As the verses state** (I Kings 1:1-2): **"And King David was old,** advanced in years; and they covered him with clothes, but he could not become warm. **So his servants said to him, Let there be sought** for my lord the king a young virgin; and let her stand before the king, and be his attendant; and let her lie in your bosom, that my lord the king may become warm." [10]**And the** next **verse states** (v. 3): **"So they sought for a fair maiden** throughout all the territory of Israel, and found Abishag the Shunammite, and brought her to the king." [11]**And the** next **verse states** (v. 4): **"And the maiden was very fair, and she attended the king, and ministered to him,** but the king did not know her." [12]When Abishag **said** to David: **"Let us marry!"** [13]he **explained to her** that he already had eighteen wives, and so **"you are forbidden to me!"** Suspecting that David was merely making an excuse,

[1]וְאֵין רוֹאִין אוֹתוֹ כְּשֶׁהוּא מִסְתַּפֵּר, וְלֹא כְּשֶׁהוּא עָרוֹם, וְלֹא כְּשֶׁהוּא בְּבֵית הַמֶּרְחָץ, [2]שֶׁנֶּאֱמַר: ״שׂוֹם תָּשִׂים עָלֶיךָ מֶלֶךְ״ — [3]שֶׁתְּהֵא אֵימָתוֹ עָלֶיךָ.

גמרא [4]אָמַר רַב יַעֲקֹב אָמַר רַבִּי יוֹחָנָן: אֲבִישַׁג מוּתֶּרֶת לִשְׁלֹמֹה, וַאֲסוּרָה לַאֲדֹנִיָּה. [5]מוּתֶּרֶת לִשְׁלֹמֹה, דְּמֶלֶךְ הָיָה, [6]וּמֶלֶךְ מִשְׁתַּמֵּשׁ בְּשַׁרְבִיטוֹ שֶׁל מֶלֶךְ. [7]וַאֲסוּרָה לַאֲדֹנִיָּה, דְּהֶדְיוֹט הוּא.

[8]אֲבִישַׁג, מַאי הִיא? [9]דִּכְתִיב: ״וְהַמֶּלֶךְ דָּוִד זָקֵן בָּא בַּיָּמִים וגו׳. וַיֹּאמְרוּ לוֹ עֲבָדָיו יְבַקְשׁוּ וגו׳״. [10]וּכְתִיב: ״וַיְבַקְשׁוּ נַעֲרָה יָפָה וגו׳״. [11]וּכְתִיב: ״וְהַנַּעֲרָה יָפָה עַד מְאֹד וַתְּהִי לַמֶּלֶךְ סֹכֶנֶת וַתְּשָׁרְתֵהוּ.״ [12]אָמְרָה: ״נִינְסַבַן!״ [13]אָמַר לָהּ: ״אֲסִירַת לִי״.

LITERAL TRANSLATION

[1]nor look at him while his hair is being cut, or when he is naked, or when he is in the bathhouse, [2]as it is said: "You shall surely set a king over you" — [3]that his fear shall be upon you.

GEMARA [4]Rav Ya'akov said in the name of Rabbi Yoḥanan: Abishag was permitted to Solomon, but forbidden to Adonijah. [5]She was permitted to Solomon, [6]because he was the king, and a king may use the scepter of a king. [7]And she was forbidden to Adonijah, for he was a commoner.

[8]Abishag, what is her [story]? [9]As it is written: "And King David was old, advanced in years, etc. So his servants said to him, Let there be sought, etc." [10]And it is written: "So they sought for a fair maiden, etc." [11]And it is written: "And the maiden was very fair, and she attended the king, and ministered to him." [12]She said: "Let us marry!" [13]He said to her: "You are forbidden to me."

RASHI

גמרא אסירת לי — שכבר נשאתי שמונה עשרה.

BACKGROUND

אֲבִישַׁג מוּתֶּרֶת לִשְׁלֹמֹה **Abishag was permitted to Solomon.** Abishag was not David's wife, for had she been, she would have been forbidden both to Adonijah and to Solomon, as their father's wife. However, she was physically intimate with David. Because the king made use of her, as it were, she had the status of his "scepter," which only another king was entitled to use. For that reason Solomon regarded Adonijah's request to marry Abishag as a rebellious act, for he was demanding the privileges of a king.

NOTES

אֲבִישַׁג מוּתֶּרֶת לִשְׁלֹמֹה **Abishag was permitted to Solomon.** *Maharsha* explains that the Gemara here explains why Adonijah was sentenced to death after asking for Abishag in marriage. Abishag had been King David's bedfellow in his old age, and therefore she was forbidden to ordinary people. By asking for Abishag, Adonijah demonstrated that he considered himself king, and as such is permitted to use the former king's personal articles. Thus, Solomon was right when he ordered Adonijah to be executed, for his request for Abishag was a direct challenge to Solomon's reign.

נִינְסַבַן **Let us marry.** Granted that David could not marry

HALAKHAH

אֵין רוֹאִין אוֹתוֹ כְּשֶׁהוּא מִסְתַּפֵּר **They may not look at him while his hair is being cut.** "An ordinary person may not look at the king while his hair is being cut, or when he is naked, or when he is in the bathhouse." (*Rambam, Sefer Shofetim, Hilkhot Melakhim* 2:3.)

[1] אֲמַרָה לֵיהּ: ״חַסְרֵיהּ לְגַנָּבָא, נַפְשֵׁיהּ לְשְׁלָמָא נָקֵיט״. [2] אֲמַר לְהוּ: ״קִרְאוּ לִי לְבַת שֶׁבַע״. [3] וּכְתִיב: ״וַתָּבֹא בַת שֶׁבַע אֶל הַמֶּלֶךְ הַחַדְרָה״.

[4] אָמַר רַב יְהוּדָה אָמַר רַב: בְּאוֹתָהּ שָׁעָה קִינְּחָה בַּת שֶׁבַע בִּשְׁלֹשׁ עֶשְׂרֵה מַפּוֹת.

[5] אָמַר רַב שֶׁמֶן בַּר אַבָּא: בֹּא וּרְאֵה כַּמָּה קָשִׁין גֵּירוּשִׁין, שֶׁהֲרֵי דָּוִד הַמֶּלֶךְ הִתִּירוּ לוֹ לְיַיחֵד, [6] וְלֹא הִתִּירוּ לוֹ לְגָרֵשׁ.

[7] אָמַר רַבִּי אֱלִיעֶזֶר: כָּל הַמְגָרֵשׁ אֶת אִשְׁתּוֹ רִאשׁוֹנָה — אֲפִילּוּ מִזְבֵּחַ מוֹרִיד עָלָיו דְּמָעוֹת,

LITERAL TRANSLATION

[1] She said to him: "When a thief has nothing [to steal], he holds himself out [to be] a man of peace." [2] He said to them: "Call Bath-Sheba to me." [3] And it is written: "And Bath-Sheba went in to the king into the chamber." [4] Rav Yehudah said in the name of Rav: At that time Bath-Sheba wiped herself with thirteen cloths.

[5] Rav Shemen bar Abba said: Come and see how difficult divorce is, for they allowed King David to seclude himself [with a woman], [6] but they did not permit him to divorce [his wife].

[7] Rabbi Eliezer said: Whoever divorces his first wife — even the altar sheds tears over him,

TRANSLATION AND COMMENTARY

[1] Abishag **said to him:** "As the adage goes: **'When a thief has nothing** to steal, **he makes himself** out to be **a man of peace.'** She implied that David pronounced himself to be forbidden to her because he had become impotent in his old age and feared that he would be unable to consummate the marriage! [2] David immediately **said to** his attendants: **"Call Bath-Sheba** that she should come **to me."** [3] David's instructions were carried out, as **the verse states** (v. 15): **"And Bath-Sheba went in to the king into the chamber."** David then demonstrated that he had the sexual prowess of a young man, as [4] **Rav Yehudah said in the name of Rav: At that time Bath-Sheba wiped herself with thirteen cloths.** David demonstrated his potency by engaging in thirteen consecutive acts of sexual intercourse with his wife Bath-Sheba (as is alluded to by the thirteen words found in this verse).

אָמַר [5] **Rav Shemen bar Abba said: Come and see how difficult** and undesirable **divorce is, for** the Sages **allowed King David to seclude himself with an** unmarried **woman,** Abishag the Shunammite, even though they had already decreed that a man may not be alone together behind closed doors with an unmarried woman, [6] **but they did not permit him to divorce** one of his eighteen wives so that he could marry Abishag.

אָמַר רַבִּי אֱלִיעֶזֶר [7] The Gemara continues with a series of statements regarding the special relationship that exists between a man and his first wife. **Rabbi Eliezer said: Whoever divorces his first wife, even the**

RASHI

חסריה לגנבא נפשיה לשלמא נקט — כשהגנב חסר, שאינו מוצא מקום לגנוב, מחזיק עצמו בענוה כאיש שלום. כלומר, מפני שזקנת ותשש כחך אתה אומר שאני אסורה לך. **קנחה בת שבע** — שבא עליה שלש עשרה ביאות ומקנחת בין תשמיש לתשמיש. ובמקרא זה כתובים שלש עשרה תיבות: "ותבא בת שבע אל המלך החדרה והמלך זקן מאד ואבישג השונמית משרת את המלך". **התירו לו ליחד** — עם אבישג, ואף על פי שנאסר ייחוד של פנויה. **ולא התירו לו לגרש** — אחת משמונה עשרה וישאנה.

NOTES

Abishag because he already had eighteen wives. But why could he not at least take her as a concubine? According to *Rambam* and others, there is no difficulty, for they maintain that the king may not marry more than eighteen women, including his concubines. *Ran* suggests that David could indeed have taken Abishag as his concubine, but Abishag was unwilling to live with him in that capacity.

חַסְרֵיהּ לְגַנָּבָא When a thief has nothing to steal. The Geonim offer a slightly different explanation: When a thief is lazy or tired and does not steal, he makes himself out to be a man of peace. *Ramah* had the reading: חַסְדֵיהּ לְגַנָּבָא — How do you, David, in comparison to whom a thief appears to be a pious man (חָסִיד), make yourself out to be a man of peace?

כָּל הַמְגָרֵשׁ אֶת אִשְׁתּוֹ רִאשׁוֹנָה Whoever divorces his first wife. *Rabbi David* (cited by *Ran*) had the reading דְּאָמַר רַבִּי אֱלִיעֶזֶר — "For Rabbi Eliezer said," according to which Rabbi Eliezer explains what was said immediately before this. David did not divorce any of his wives, because one is not permitted to divorce his first wife. Even though David had many wives, all of whom could not have been his first wife, here "first wife" means a woman who had married for the first time. And even though Abigail and Bath-Sheba had both been married previously, David never considered divorcing either of them. Alternatively, the Gemara is arguing that, since we see that the altar sheds tears whenever someone divorces his first wife, we may infer how terrible divorce is, even with respect to subsequent wives. We then understand why the Sages did not allow David to divorce any of his wives.

אֲפִילּוּ מִזְבֵּחַ מוֹרִיד דְּמָעוֹת Even the altar sheds tears. *Meiri* explains that if someone divorces his wife without a valid reason, the altar, which would ordinarily act as his advocate, assisting him in attaining atonement, becomes his prosecutor. Other explanations have also been offered: Even though the altar is accustomed to suffering, for it receives the blood of the sacrifices, it sheds tears over divorce because of the agony caused to the woman. Alternatively, since Adam and Eve were formed from the earth on which the altar was later built (as is explained in the Midrash), someone who divorces his wife is treated as if he has caused damage to the altar itself (*Torat Ḥayyim*).

SAGES

רַב שֶׁמֶן בַּר אַבָּא Rav Shemen bar Abba. This is Rav Shemen bar Abba the priest (Shemen is a nickname for Shimon), who belonged to the second generation of Amoraim of Eretz Israel. Rav Shemen bar Abba was born in Babylonia and was a student of Shmuel. He immigrated to Eretz Israel while he was still a young man and was privileged to be a student of Rabbi Ḥanina. However, he was mainly the close disciple of Rabbi Yoḥanan, whom he served with particular affection. Much has been said in praise of his great righteousness and wisdom. He had a particularly difficult life, and the Biblical saying was applied to him, "To the wise there is no bread." He was not only poor, but as a result of all his vicissitudes, Rabbi Yoḥanan did not manage to ordain him, though he was certainly one of the greatest scholars of his generation.

It is mentioned that Rav Shemen bar Abba married the daughters (one after the other) of his first teacher, Shmuel, after they were captured and redeemed in Eretz Israel. All of Rabbi Yoḥanan's students were colleagues of Rav Shemen, and members of the succeeding generation transmit teachings in his name. He had a son, Rav Amram, who was also a Sage, and who transmitted teachings in his father's name.

[1]שֶׁנֶּאֱמַר: "וְזֹאת שֵׁנִית תַּעֲשׂוּ כַּסּוֹת דִּמְעָה אֶת מִזְבַּח ה׳ בְּכִי וַאֲנָקָה מֵאֵין עוֹד פְּנוֹת אֶל הַמִּנְחָה וְלָקַחַת רָצוֹן מִיֶּדְכֶם". [2]וּכְתִיב: "וַאֲמַרְתֶּם, עַל מָה? עַל כִּי ה׳ הֵעִיד בֵּינְךָ וּבֵין אֵשֶׁת נְעוּרֶיךָ אֲשֶׁר אַתָּה בָּגַדְתָּה בָּהּ וְהִיא חֲבֶרְתְּךָ וְאֵשֶׁת בְּרִיתֶךָ". [3]אָמַר רַבִּי יוֹחָנָן וְאִיתֵּימָא רַבִּי אֶלְעָזָר: אֵין אִשְׁתּוֹ שֶׁל אָדָם מֵתָה אֶלָּא אִם כֵּן מְבַקְשִׁין מִמֶּנּוּ מָמוֹן וְאֵין לוֹ, [4]שֶׁנֶּאֱמַר: "וְאִם אֵין לְךָ לְשַׁלֵּם לָמָּה יִקַּח מִשְׁכָּבְךָ מִתַּחְתֶּיךָ"? [5]וְאָמַר רַבִּי יוֹחָנָן: כָּל אָדָם שֶׁמֵּתָה אִשְׁתּוֹ רִאשׁוֹנָה — כְּאִילּוּ חָרַב בֵּית הַמִּקְדָּשׁ בְּיָמָיו, [6]שֶׁנֶּאֱמַר: "בֶּן אָדָם הִנְנִי לֹקֵחַ מִמְּךָ אֶת מַחְמַד עֵינֶיךָ בְּמַגֵּפָה לֹא תִסְפֹּד וְלֹא תִבְכֶּה וְלֹא תָבוֹא דִּמְעָתֶךָ". [7]וּכְתִיב: "וָאֲדַבֵּר אֶל הָעָם בַּבֹּקֶר וַתָּמָת אִשְׁתִּי בָּעָרֶב". [8]וּכְתִיב: "הִנְנִי מְחַלֵּל אֶת מִקְדָּשִׁי גְּאוֹן עֻזְּכֶם מַחְמַד עֵינֵיכֶם". [9]אָמַר רַבִּי אֲלֶכְּסַנְדְּרִי: כָּל אָדָם שֶׁמֵּתָה אִשְׁתּוֹ בְּיָמָיו — עוֹלָם חָשֵׁךְ בַּעֲדוֹ, שֶׁנֶּאֱמַר: "אוֹר

LITERAL TRANSLATION

[1]as it is said: "And this second thing you will do, covering the altar of the Lord with tears, with weeping, and with sighing, because he will not regard the offering any more, or receive it with good will at your hand." [2]And it is written: "And you say, Why is this? It is because the Lord has been witness between you and the wife of your youth, whom you have betrayed: yet she is your companion, and the wife of your covenant."

[3]Rabbi Yoḥanan said, and some say [it was] Rabbi Elazar: A man's wife does not die unless [creditors] demanded money of him and he [claimed] he had none, [4]as it is stated: "If you have nothing with which to pay, why should he take away your bed from beneath you?"

[5]And Rabbi Yoḥanan said: Any man whose first wife died — it is as if the Temple was destroyed in his day, [6]as it is said: "Son of man, behold, I am about to take away from you the delight of your eyes at a stroke: yet you shall neither mourn nor weep, nor shall your tears run down." [7]And it is written: "So I spoke to the people in the morning: and at evening my wife died." [8]And it is written: "Behold, I will profane my sanctuary, the pride of your strength, the delight of your eyes."

[9]Rabbi Alexandri said: Any man whose wife dies during his lifetime — the world darkens around him, as it is stated: "The light

TRANSLATION AND COMMENTARY

altar sheds tears over him, [1]**as the verse states** (Malachi 2:13): **"And this second thing you will do, covering the altar of the Lord with tears, with weeping, and with sighing, because he will not regard the offering any more, or receive it with good will at your hand."** [2]**And the** next verse states (v. 14): **"And you say, Why is this? It is because the Lord has been witness between you and the wife of your youth, against whom you have dealt treacherously: yet she is your companion, and the wife of your covenant."**

אָמַר [3]**Rabbi Yoḥanan said, and some say that it was Rabbi Elazar who said: A man's wife does not die unless** he has become obligated to pay out a certain sum, and then when **the money is demanded of him, he claims he has nothing** with which to pay off his debt — he and his wife asserting that all his property is mortgaged to the wife's ketubah settlement. [4]This is derived from **the verse** that **states** (Proverbs 22:27): **"If you have nothing with which to pay, why should he take away your bed** (your wife) **from beneath you?"** But if you indeed had money or property with which to pay, you may have your wife taken away from you as a punishment.

וְאָמַר רַבִּי יוֹחָנָן [5]**Rabbi Yoḥanan said: For any man whose first wife died, it is as if the Temple was destroyed in his** own **day,** [6]**as the verse states** (Ezekiel 24:16): **"Son of man, behold, I am about to take away from you the delight of your eyes at a stroke: yet you shall neither mourn nor weep, nor shall your tears run down."** [7]**And** two verses later **it is written** (v. 18): **"So I spoke to the people in the morning: and in the evening my wife died."** [8]**And** later in the same chapter **it is written** (v. 21): **"Behold, I will profane my sanctuary, the pride of your strength, the delight of your eyes."** Thus, we see that the loss of the delight of a man's eyes, his wife, is likened to the loss of the delight of all of Israel's eyes, the Sanctuary.

אָמַר רַבִּי אֲלֶכְּסַנְדְּרִי [9]**Rabbi Alexandri said:** When **a man's wife dies during his lifetime, the world darkens**

NOTES

כְּאִילּוּ חָרַב בֵּית הַמִּקְדָּשׁ בְּיָמָיו It is as if the Temple was destroyed in his day. The Jerusalem Talmud notes that while the Temple was being constructed, the workers labored for a month, and then spent the next two months at home, which teaches that procreation and family life are even more important than building the Temple. Thus, the tragedy that a man suffers upon the death of his wife is no less than that of the Temple's destruction. Furthermore, a man only finds satisfaction with his first wife (see Gemara below). Thus, a man who loses his first wife suffers grief which has no consolation, grief the likes of which the people of Israel suffered at the destruction of the Temple (*Maharsha*).

חָשַׁךְ בְּאָהֳלוֹ וְנֵרוֹ עָלָיו יִדְעָךְ".
[1]רַבִּי יוֹסֵי בַּר חֲנִינָא אָמַר:
פְּסִיעוֹתָיו מִתְקַצְּרוֹת, [2]שֶׁנֶּאֱמַר:
"יֵצְרוּ צַעֲדֵי אוֹנוֹ". [3]רַבִּי אַבָּהוּ
אָמַר: עֲצָתוֹ נוֹפֶלֶת, [4]שֶׁנֶּאֱמַר:
"וְתַשְׁלִיכֵהוּ עֲצָתוֹ".
[5]אָמַר רַבָּה בַּר בַּר חָנָה אָמַר
רַבִּי יוֹחָנָן: קָשֶׁה לְזַוְּוגָם,
כִּקְרִיעַת יַם סוּף, [6]שֶׁנֶּאֱמַר:
"אֱלֹהִים מוֹשִׁיב יְחִידִים בַּיְתָה
מוֹצִיא אֲסִירִים בַּכּוֹשָׁרוֹת". [7]אַל
תִּיקְרֵי: "מוֹצִיא אֲסִירִים",
[8]אֶלָּא: "כְּמוֹצִיא אֲסִירִים". [9]אַל
תִּיקְרֵי: "בַּכּוֹשָׁרוֹת", [10]אֶלָּא:
"בְּכִי וְשִׁירוֹת".
[11]אִינִי? [12]וְהָאָמַר רַב יְהוּדָה
אָמַר רַב: אַרְבָּעִים יוֹם קוֹדֶם
יְצִירַת הַוָּלָד בַּת קוֹל יוֹצֵאת
וְאוֹמֶרֶת: [13]"בַּת פְּלוֹנִי לִפְלוֹנִי"!
[14]לָא קַשְׁיָא. [15]הָא — בְּזִוּוּג
רִאשׁוֹן. [16]הָא — בְּזִוּוּג שֵׁנִי.
[17]אָמַר רַבִּי שְׁמוּאֵל בַּר נַחְמָן:
לַכֹּל יֵשׁ תְּמוּרָה, חוּץ מֵאֵשֶׁת

LITERAL TRANSLATION

shall be dark in his tent, and his candle over him shall be put out." [1]Rabbi Yose bar Ḥanina said: His steps are shortened, [2]as it is stated: "The steps of his strength shall be straitened." [3]Rabbi Abbahu said: His counsel fails, [4]as it is stated: "And his own counsel shall cast him down."

[5]Rabbah bar Bar Ḥanah said in the name of Rabbi Yoḥanan: It is as difficult to join them [in marriage] as to split the Red Sea, [6]as it is stated: "God makes the solitary ones dwell in a house; he brings out prisoners into prosperity." [7]Do not read: "He brings out prisoners," [8]but rather: "As He brings out prisoners." [9]Do not read: "Into prosperity," [10]but rather: "[with] crying and [with] songs."

[11]Is it so? [12]But surely Rav Yehudah said in the name of Rav: Forty days before a child is formed, a heavenly voice issues forth and says: [13]"The daughter of so-and-so to so-and-so"!

[14]It is not difficult. [15]Here — regarding the first marriage. [16]There — regarding the second marriage.

[17]Rabbi Shmuel bar Naḥman said: Everything has a substitute, except for the wife

RASHI

אור חשך באהלו — בשביל אהלו, ואין "אהלו" אלא אשתו. **יצרו צעדי אונו** — בתריה כתיב.

TRANSLATION AND COMMENTARY

around him, as the verse states (Job 18:6): **"The light shall be dark in his tent, and his candle over him shall be put out."** Rabbi Alexandri interprets the word בְּאָהֳלוֹ, translated here as "in his tent," to mean "on account of his tent," — a man's tent symbolizing his wife. Thus, the verse teaches that the world is dark for a man who loses his wife. [1]**Rabbi Yose bar Ḥanina said:** When a man's wife dies during his lifetime, **his steps are shortened,** [2]**as the** very next **verse states** (v. 7): **"The steps of his strength shall be straitened."** [3]**Rabbi Abbahu said:** The woman's death causes her husband's **counsel** to **fail,** [4]**as the same verse continues: "And his own counsel shall cast him down."**

אָמַר [5]The Gemara continues: **Rabbah bar Bar Ḥanah said in the name of Rabbi Yoḥanan: It is** just **as difficult to join** a man and a woman together in marriage **as** it was to **part the Red Sea,** [6]**as the verse states** (Psalms 68:7): **"God makes the solitary ones dwell in a house; he brings out prisoners into prosperity."** [7]**Do not read** the verse exactly as it is written: מוֹצִיא אֲסִירִים — **"He brings out prisoners."** [8]**But rather** read it as follows: כְּמוֹצִיא אֲסִירִים — "As He brings out prisoners," so that the verse may be understood as drawing a comparison between the two clauses. [9]And **do not read** the last word as it is written: בַּכּוֹשָׁרוֹת — **"Into prosperity,"** [10]**but rather** read it as if it were written: בְּכִי וְשִׁירוֹת — **"[with] crying and [with] songs."** Read this way, the second clause alludes to the Exodus, which culminated in the parting of the Red Sea, amidst the "cries" of the Egyptians and the "songs" of praise of the Jewish people. Thus, the verse draws an analogy between the difficulty of pairing off men and women in marriage and that of parting the Red Sea. God Himself brought the Jewish prisoners out of Egypt and parted the Red Sea for them. Divine intervention is similarly needed in order to join men and women, so that "the solitary ones may dwell together" and establish a house on the basis of a happy marriage.

אִינִי [11]The Gemara asks: **Is** matchmaking really **so** difficult? [12]**But surely Rav Yehudah said in the name of Rav: Forty days before a child is formed, a heavenly voice issues forth and says:** [13]**"The daughter of so-and-so** will be married off **to so-and-so"!** Since the choice of one's spouse is foreordained, it cannot be so difficult to bring the partners together in marriage!

לָא קַשְׁיָא [14]The Gemara answers: **There is no difficulty.** [15]**Here,** where Rav said that a person's spouse is preordained, he was dealing **with a** person's **first marriage.** [16]**There,** where Rabbi Yoḥanan said that joining a couple in marriage is as difficult as parting the Red Sea, he was dealing **with a** person's **second marriage.**

אָמַר [17]**Rabbi Shmuel bar Naḥman said: Anything** that is lost **can be replaced, except for the wife of one's**

SAGES

רַבִּי יוֹסֵי בַּר חֲנִינָא Rabbi Yose bar Ḥanina. A Palestinian Amora of the second generation, Rabbi Yose bar Ḥanina was a younger contemporary of Rabbi Yoḥanan and one of his first students. Rabbi Yoḥanan ordained him, and he grew in knowledge of Torah until he came to be regarded as Rabbi Yoḥanan's colleague. Many differences of opinion between the two are recorded (see *Bava Kamma* 39a). Rabbi Yose was also closely associated with Resh Lakish. Rabbi Yoḥanan's pupils also studied with him. Many of them, especially Rabbi Abbahu and Rabbi Ḥama bar Ukva, transmitted teachings in his name. He is known to have had sons who died during his lifetime.

רַבָּה בַּר בַּר חָנָה Rabbah bar Bar Ḥanah. An Amora of the third generation, he was a student of Rabbi Yoḥanan. He was apparently born in Babylonia, emigrated to study Torah in Eretz Israel, and wandered in many lands. He transmitted teachings in the name of Rabbi Yoḥanan, his teacher, as well as in the name of Rabbi Yehoshua ben Levi, Resh Lakish, and Rabbi Elazar. He was also a student of Rabbi Yoshiyah of Usha. One of his sons, Rabbi Yitzḥak, was a Sage. Rabbah bar Bar Ḥanah relates many stories of the wonders he saw in his travels.

רַבִּי שְׁמוּאֵל בַּר נַחְמָן Rabbi Shmuel bar Naḥman. A Palestinian Amora of the second and third generations, also known as Rabbi Shmuel bar Naḥmani. See *Sanhedrin*, Part I, p. 65.

BACKGROUND

קְרִיעַת יַם סוּף As the splitting of the Red Sea. The Aḥaronim explained the similarity between the two in various ways. Some argued that, just as the splitting of the Red Sea was a supernatural act, so, too, is matching men with women a truly miraculous achievement, joining separate essences in a manner that surpasses human understanding.

TRANSLATION AND COMMENTARY

youth who died, [1]**as the verse states** (Isaiah 54:6): **"But a wife of youth, can she be cast off?"**

מַתְנֵי לַהּ [2]**Rav Yehudah taught his son Rav Yitzḥak: A man only finds satisfaction in his first wife,** [3]**as the verse states** (Proverbs 5:18): **"Let your fountain be blessed; and rejoice with the wife** [22B] **of your youth."** [4]Rav Yitzḥak **said to his** father: **Like whom?** [5]Rav Yehudah **said to his** son: I refer to a man who is married to a woman **like your mother.**

אִינִי [6]The Gemara asks: **Is it true,** that Rav Yehudah was so satisified with his wife? [7]**But surely Rav Yehudah read** the following verse **to his son Rav Yitzḥak** (Ecclesiastes 7:26): **"And I find more bitter than death the woman whose heart is snares and nets."** [8]**And** Rav Yitzḥak **said to his** father: **Like whom?** [9]**And** Rav Yehudah **said to him:** The verse refers to a woman **like your mother.** How can Rav Yehudah apply to his wife the verse: "Rejoice with the wife of your youth," when he also said that he finds her more bitter than death?

מִיתְקַף [10]The Gemara explains that there is really no difficulty: Rav Yehudah's wife **was** indeed **a hot-tempered** woman. **But** there was also satisfaction, for she would **get over** her anger **with a** kind **word.**

אָמַר [11]**Rav Shmuel bar Unya said in the name of Rav: A woman who** has not engaged in sexual intercourse **is** like **an unfinished vessel.** [12]And she **only makes a covenant with** her first husband **who fashions her into a** finished **vessel** when they first make love. [13]This is learned from **the verse** that **states** (Isaiah 54:5): **"For your maker is your husband; the Lord of Hosts is his name."**

תָּנָא [14]**A Sage taught** the following Baraita: **"A man dies only for his wife,** she being the one who suffers most from his passing; **and a woman dies only for her husband,** he being the one who is the most distressed that she is gone." The Gemara now brings Scriptural support for what was taught in the Baraita: [15]**A man dies only for his wife, as the verse states** (Ruth 1:3): **"And Elimelech, Naomi's husband, died,"** relating Elimelech's death only to his wife Naomi, and not to his two sons. [16]**And a woman dies only for her husband, as the verse states** (Genesis 48:7): **"And as for me, when I came from Paddan, Rachel died unto me,"** relating Rachel's death only to her husband Jacob, and not to her children.

נְעוּרִים, [1]שֶׁנֶּאֱמַר: "וְאֵשֶׁת נְעוּרִים, כִּי תִמָּאֵס"?
[2]מַתְנֵי לַהּ רַב יְהוּדָה לְרַב יִצְחָק בְּרֵיהּ: אֵין אָדָם מוֹצֵא קוֹרַת רוּחַ אֶלָּא מֵאִשְׁתּוֹ רִאשׁוֹנָה, [3]שֶׁנֶּאֱמַר: "יְהִי מְקוֹרְךָ בָרוּךְ וּשְׂמַח מֵאֵשֶׁת [22B] נְעוּרֶיךָ". [4]אֲמַר לוֹ: כְּגוֹן מַאן? [5]אֲמַר לוֹ: כְּגוֹן אִמָּךְ.
[6]אִינִי? [7]וְהָא מַקְרֵי לֵיהּ רַב יְהוּדָה לְרַב יִצְחָק בְּרֵיהּ: "וּמוֹצֶא אֲנִי מַר מִמָּוֶת אֶת הָאִשָּׁה אֲשֶׁר הִיא מְצוֹדִים וַחֲרָמִים". [8]וְאָמַר לוֹ: כְּגוֹן מַאן? [9]וְאָמַר לוֹ: כְּגוֹן אִמָּךְ!
[10]מִיתְקַף תַּקִּיפָא, עִיבּוּרֵי מְעַבְּרָא בְּמִלָּה.
[11]אָמַר רַב שְׁמוּאֵל בַּר אוּנְיָא מִשְּׁמֵיהּ דְּרַב: אִשָּׁה גּוֹלֶם הִיא, [12]וְאֵינָהּ כּוֹרֶתֶת בְּרִית אֶלָּא לְמִי שֶׁעֲשָׂאָהּ כְּלִי, [13]שֶׁנֶּאֱמַר: "כִּי בֹעֲלַיִךְ עֹשַׂיִךְ ה׳ צְבָאוֹת שְׁמוֹ".
[14]תָּנָא: "אֵין אִישׁ מֵת אֶלָּא לְאִשְׁתּוֹ, וְאֵין אִשָּׁה מֵתָה אֶלָּא לְבַעְלָהּ". [15]אֵין אִישׁ מֵת אֶלָּא לְאִשְׁתּוֹ, שֶׁנֶּאֱמַר "וַיָּמָת אֱלִימֶלֶךְ אִישׁ נָעֳמִי". [16]וְאֵין אִשָּׁה מֵתָה אֶלָּא לְבַעְלָהּ, שֶׁנֶּאֱמַר: "וַאֲנִי בְּבֹאִי מִפַּדָּן מֵתָה עָלַי רָחֵל".

LITERAL TRANSLATION

of one's youth, [1]as it is stated: "But a wife of youth, can she be cast off?"

[2]Rav Yehudah taught his son Rav Yitzḥak: A man only finds satisfaction in his first wife, [3]as it is stated: "Let your fountain be blessed; and rejoice with the wife [22B] of your youth." [4]He said to him: Like whom? [5]He said to him: Like your mother.

[6]Is it so? [7]But surely Rav Yehudah read to his son Rav Yitzḥak: "And I find more bitter than death the woman whose heart is snares and nets." [8]And he said to him: Like whom? [9]And he said to him: Like your mother.

[10]She is hot-tempered, but gets over it with a word.

[11]Rav Shmuel bar Unya said in the name of Rav: A woman is an unfinished vessel, [12]and she only makes a covenant with the one who fashioned her into a vessel, [13]as it is said: "For your maker is your husband; the Lord of Hosts is his name."

[14][A Sage] taught: "A man dies only for his wife, and a woman dies only for her husband." [15]A man dies only for his wife, as it is said: "And Elimelech, Naomi's husband, died." [16]And a woman dies only for her husband, as it is said: "And as for me, when I came from Paddan, Rachel died unto me."

RASHI

עבורי מעברא במלה — מעברת על מדותיה. **גולם היא** — קודם שנבעלה. גולם = כלי שלא נגמר קרוי גולם, כדתנן: גולמי כלי עץ טמאין.

[1]״אֵין רוֹאִין אוֹתוֹ כו׳״. [2]תָּנוּ רַבָּנַן: ״מֶלֶךְ מִסְתַּפֵּר בְּכָל יוֹם. [3]כֹּהֵן גָּדוֹל מֵעֶרֶב שַׁבָּת לְעֶרֶב שַׁבָּת. כֹּהֵן הֶדְיוֹט אֶחָד לִשְׁלֹשִׁים יוֹם״.

[4]״מֶלֶךְ מִסְתַּפֵּר בְּכָל יוֹם״. [5]שֶׁנֶּאֱמַר: ״מֶלֶךְ בְּיָפְיוֹ תֶּחֱזֶינָה עֵינֶיךָ״.

[6]״כֹּהֵן גָּדוֹל מֵעֶרֶב שַׁבָּת״. [7]אָמַר רַב שְׁמוּאֵל בַּר נַחְמָן אָמַר רַבִּי יוֹחָנָן: הוֹאִיל וּמִשְׁמָרוֹת מִתְחַדְּשׁוֹת.

[8]״כֹּהֵן הֶדְיוֹט אֶחָד לִשְׁלֹשִׁים יוֹם״. [9]דִּכְתִיב: ״וְרֹאשָׁם לֹא יְגַלֵּחוּ וּפֶרַע לֹא יְשַׁלֵּחוּ כָּסוֹם יִכְסְמוּ אֶת רָאשֵׁיהֶם״. [10]וְיָלֵיף ״פֶּרַע״ ״פֶּרַע״ מִנָּזִיר. [11]כְּתִיב הָכָא: ״פֶּרַע לֹא יְשַׁלֵּחוּ״.

LITERAL TRANSLATION

[1]"They may not look at him, etc." [2]Our Rabbis taught: "The king has his hair cut every day; [3]the High Priest, from Friday to Friday; an ordinary priest, once in thirty days."

[4]"The king has his hair cut every day." [5]As it is stated: "Your eyes shall see the king in his beauty."

[6]"The High Priest, from Friday [to Friday]." [7]Rav Shmuel bar Naḥman said in the name of Rabbi Yoḥanan: Because of the changing (lit., "renewal") of the priestly watches.

[8]"An ordinary priest once in thirty days." [9]As it is written: "Nor shall they shave their heads, nor let their locks grow long; but they shall crop their heads." [10]And "locks" is learned from "locks" regarding a Nazirite. [11]It is written here: "Nor let their locks grow long."

TRANSLATION AND COMMENTARY

אֵין רוֹאִין אוֹתוֹ [1]We learned in our Mishnah: **"No one may observe** the king while his hair is being cut." [2]**Our Rabbis taught** a Baraita saying: **"The king must have his hair cut every day;** [3]**the High Priest, on Fridays; an ordinary priest, once** every **thirty days."**

מֶלֶךְ מִסְתַּפֵּר [4]The Gemara now explains the rationale underlying each of these regulations. **"The king must have his hair cut every day."** [5]This obligation is derived from **the verse** that **states** (Isaiah 33:17): **"Your eyes shall see the king in his beauty."**

כֹּהֵן גָּדוֹל [6]It was taught in the next clause of the Baraita: **"The High Priest** must have his hair cut **on Fridays."** [7]**Rav Shmuel bar Naḥman said in the name of Rabbi Yoḥanan:** This is **because the** priestly watches **changed** on Shabbat. The High Priest had to have his hair cut on Fridays, so that the members of the incoming priestly watch would see him when he was perfectly groomed.

כֹּהֵן הֶדְיוֹט [8]The Baraita concluded: **"An ordinary priest** must cut his hair at least **once** every **thirty days."** This regulation is inferred on the basis of the hermeneutical principle of *gezerah shavah,* an analogy based on the similarity between expressions in two verses. [9]Now, with respect to the priests, **the verse states** (Ezekiel 44:20): **"Nor shall they shave their heads, nor let their locks grow long; but they shall crop their heads."** [10]The meaning of the expression **"locks,"** as it is used here with respect to the priests, **is learned from** another mention of the same expression, **"locks," regarding a Nazirite,** who, among other things, must refrain from cutting his hair. [11]**Here** (Ezekiel 44:20), **the verse says** with respect to the priests: "Nor shall they shave their heads, **nor let their locks to grow long,"** from which we learn that a priest may not let

RASHI

משמרות — מתחלפות ומתחדשות בשבת, זו יוצאה וזו נכנסת, וצריך להסתפר מפני משמרת חדשה זו הנכנסת שיראוהו ביופי.

CONCEPTS

מִשְׁמָר Priestly watch. The priests who served in the Temple were divided into twenty-four groups, known as *mishmarot,* priestly watches. Each watch served for one week at a time and was replaced every Shabbat. Each watch performed the Temple service for approximately two weeks every year. During the Pilgrim Festivals, all the watches went to the Temple and performed the Temple service together. Each watch received the priestly gifts, *matanot kehunah,* which were contributed to the Temple during their week of Temple service. The watches were divided into *batei av,* families. Corresponding to each watch there was a *ma'amad* — "post" or "division" — a group of nonpriests, who accompanied the members of the watch to Jerusalem.

BACKGROUND

הוֹאִיל וּמִשְׁמָרוֹת מִתְחַדְּשׁוֹת Because of the renewal of the priestly watches. It is proper that every contingent of priests should see the High Priest with his hair cut well, for he is like a king and a general leader of the people.

NOTES

וְיָלֵיף פֶּרַע פֶּרַע מִנָּזִיר And "locks" is learned from "locks" regarding a Nazirite. *Ran* notes that, here, the Gemara does not strictly apply the hermeneutical principle of *gezerah shavah,* for there is a rule that an analogy may not be drawn by way of *gezerah shavah* between a verse from the Pentateuch and a verse from the Prophets. Rather, the verse regarding the Nazirite merely sheds light on an aspect of the verse regarding the priests. Since the analogy is not a true *gezerah shavah,* it is restricted to deriving a single matter that the two laws have in common.

HALAKHAH

מֶלֶךְ מִסְתַּפֵּר בְּכָל יוֹם The king has his hair cut every day. "The king must have his hair cut every day, and he must always keep himself properly groomed and well dressed, for the verse states: 'Your eyes shall see the king in his beauty.'" (*Rambam, Sefer Shofetim, Hilkhot Melakhim* 2:5.)

כֹּהֵן הֶדְיוֹט אֶחָד לִשְׁלֹשִׁים יוֹם An ordinary priest, once in thirty days. "A priest who let his hair grow long is forbidden to enter the Temple courtyard past the altar. An ordinary priest is only forbidden to have long hair when he enters the Temple for service. But the High Priest may never let his hair grow long, for he is always in the Temple. Long hair is hair which was not cut for thirty days. Thus, an ordinary priest serving in the Temple must have his hair cut at least once in thirty days." According to *Ra'avad,* a priest may not go with his hair uncut for more than thirty days, even if he is not serving in the Temple. (*Rambam, Sefer Avodah, Hilkhot Bi'at Mikdash* 1:8-11.)

TRANSLATION AND COMMENTARY

his hair grow long. [1]**And there** (Numbers 6:5), **the verse says** in reference to a Nazirite: "He shall be holy, **and shall let the locks of the hair of his head grow long,"** from which we learn that a Nazirite must indeed let his hair grow long. [2]**Just as there,** the Nazirite may not cut his hair for at least **thirty days,** [3]**so too here,** the priest may not let his hair go uncut for **thirty days.** Regarding the Nazirite, we know that the expression "grow long" means thirty days, [4]from what **we have learned** in the Mishnah (*Nazir* 5a): **"One who** takes the Nazirite vow but **does not specify how long he wishes to be a Nazirite** assumes Nazirite obligations **for** a period of **thirty days,** which was also the minimum period." Now, since a Nazirite must refrain from cutting his hair while he is bound by his vow, he must refrain from cutting his hair for at least thirty days. And since every Nazirite is required to grow his hair long, it follows that the Torah regards hair that was not cut for thirty days as having "grown long."

וְהָתָם [5]**And from where do we know the law there**, that Nazirites must remain bound by their vows for at least thirty days? [6]**Rav Matnah said:** This is derived from **the** very same **verse** that **states** (Numbers 6:5): **"He shall be** (יִהְיֶה) **holy."** [7]**The numerical value** of the word יהיה **is thirty** (10=י, 5=ה, 10=י, 5=ה).

אֲמַר לֵיהּ [8]The Gemara now questions its interpretation of the verse forbidding a priest to let his hair grow long. **Rav Pappa said to Abaye:** [9]But perhaps we should **say** that Scripture meant to teach us **that** priests **should not grow their hair long at all,** and must cut their hair every day!

אֲמַר לֵיהּ [10]Abaye **said to** Rav Pappa: **Had the verse been formulated:** [11]"The priests **shall not let their locks grow long** (פֶּרַע לֹא יְשַׁלֵּחוּ)" — I might have interpreted the verse **as you have suggested.** [12]But **now that the verse has been formulated: "Their long locks they shall not let to grow** (וּפֶרַע לֹא יְשַׁלֵּחוּ)," the verse must be interpreted to mean that the priests' locks **may indeed be** grown **long,** for as long as thirty days, [13]but **they may not be** allowed to **grow wild.** Thus, we learn that a priest must cut his hair at least once in thirty days.

אִי הָכִי [14]The Gemara seeks clarification: **If it is so,** that the priest's obligation to cut his hair at least once in thirty days is derived from Scripture, then **even nowadays,** when there is no Temple, priests should be obligated to have their hair cut at least once a month!

דּוּמְיָא דְּיַיִן [15]The Gemara answers: The law forbidding priests to grow their hair long is **similar to** the law forbidding priests to drink **wine.** The verse in Ezekiel (44:20) forbidding priests to grow their hair long is followed by a verse forbidding them to drink wine, implying an analogy. [16]**Just as** with respect to the

[1]וּכְתִיב הָתָם: ״גַּדֵּל פֶּרַע שְׂעַר רֹאשׁוֹ״. [2]מַה לְּהַלָּן שְׁלֹשִׁים, [3]אַף כָּאן שְׁלֹשִׁים. [4]וּתְנַן נַמִי: סְתַם נְזִירוּת שְׁלֹשִׁים יוֹם.

[5]וְהָתָם מְנָא לָן? [6]אָמַר רַב מַתְנָה: דְּאָמַר קְרָא: ״קָדֹשׁ יִהְיֶה״ [7]בְּגִימַטְרִיָּא תְּלָתִין הָווּ.

[8]אֲמַר לֵיהּ רַב פַּפָּא לְאַבַּיֵי: [9]אֵימָא לָא לִירְבּוּ כְּלָל!

[10]אֲמַר לֵיהּ: אִי כְּתִיב: [11]״לֹא יְשַׁלְּחוּ פֶּרַע״ — כִּדְקָאָמְרַתְּ, [12]הָשְׁתָּא דִּכְתִיב: ״וּפֶרַע״ — פֶּרַע לֶיהֱוֵי, [13]שַׁלּוּחֵי לָא לִישַׁלְּחוּ.

[14]אִי הָכִי, הָאִידָּנָא נַמִי!

[15]דּוּמְיָא דְּיַיִן. [16]מַה יַּיִן — בִּזְמַן

LITERAL TRANSLATION

[1]And it is written there: "And shall let the locks of the hair of his head grow long." [2]Just as there thirty [days], [3]so too here thirty [days]. [4]And we have also learned: "An unspecified period of Naziritism is thirty days."

[5]And from where do we [know the law] there? [6]Rav Matnah said: The verse states: "He shall be (יִהְיֶה) holy" — [7]its numerical value is thirty.

[8]Rav Pappa said to Abaye: [9]Say that they should not grow [their hair] at all!

[10]He said to him: Had it been written: [11]"They shall not let their locks grow long (לֹא יְשַׁלְּחוּ פֶּרַע)" — as you said. [12]Now that it is written: "Their long locks [they shall not let to grow] (וּפֶרַע לֹא יְשַׁלֵּחוּ)" — long they may be, [13]wild they may not be grown.

[14]If so, nowadays as well!

[15]Similar to wine. [16]Just as wine — at the time

RASHI

לא לירבו כלל — ואפילו עד שלשים. **אמר ליה** — "פרע" מקרי בשלשים יום. **אי הוה כתיב לא ישלחו פרע** — הוה משמע לא יגדלו פרע — עד שיעור פרע, השתא דכתיב: "ופרע לא ישלחו", דקאמר "פרע", והדר "לא ישלחו", משמע פרע דשלשים יום ליהוי, אבל שלוחי טפי לא לשלחו. **דומיא דיין** — דסמוך ליה "ויין לא ישתו בבואם וגו'" מקיש פרועי ראש לשתויי יין, וכתיב ביין בבואם.

HALAKHAH

סְתַם נְזִירוּת An unspecified period of Naziritism. "If someone takes the Nazirite vow without specifying how long he wishes to be a Nazirite, he assumes the Nazirite obligations for a period of thirty days." (*Rambam, Sefer Hafla'ah, Hilkhot Nezirut* 3:1.)

בִּיאָה הוּא דְּאָסוּר, [1] שֶׁלֹּא בִּזְמַן בִּיאָה שָׁרֵי; [2] אַף פְּרוּעֵי רֹאשׁ — [3] בִּזְמַן בִּיאָה אָסוּר, [4] שֶׁלֹּא בִּזְמַן בִּיאָה שָׁרֵי.

[5] וְיַיִן שֶׁלֹּא בִּזְמַן בִּיאָה שָׁרֵי? [6] וְהָתַנְיָא: ״רַבִּי אוֹמֵר: אוֹמֵר אֲנִי: כֹּהֲנִים אֲסוּרִין לִשְׁתּוֹת יַיִן לְעוֹלָם, [7] אֲבָל מָה אֶעֱשֶׂה שֶׁתַּקָּנָתוֹ קַלְקָלָתוֹ״. [8] וְאָמַר אַבַּיֵי: כְּמַאן שָׁתֵי כָּהֲנֵי חַמְרָא הָאִידָּנָא? [9] כְּרַבִּי. מִכְּלָל דְּרַבָּנַן אָסְרִי!

LITERAL TRANSLATION

of entry [into the temple] it is forbidden, [1] not at the time of entry it is permitted; [2] so too [regarding] long hair — [3] at the time of entry it is forbidden, [4] not at the time of entry it is permitted.

[5] But is wine not at the time of entry permitted? [6] But surely it was taught: "Rabbi says: I say: Priests are forever forbidden to drink wine, [7] but what can I do? — its remedy is its ruin." [8] And Abaye said: In accordance with whom do the priests nowadays drink wine? [9] In accordance with Rabbi. [This proves] by implication that the Rabbis forbid [this]!

TRANSLATION AND COMMENTARY

prohibition forbidding priests to drink **wine,** it is only **at a time when** the Temple stands and **entry** is possible that drinking wine **is forbidden,** [1] but if it is **not a time when entry** into the Temple is possible, drinking wine **is permitted;** [2] **so too** here with respect to the prohibition forbidding priests to let their **hair grow long,** [3] it is only **at a time when entry** into the Temple is possible that the priest **is forbidden** to let his hair grow long, [4] but if it is **not at the time when entry into** the Temple is possible, he **is permitted** to do so.

וְיַיִן [5] The Gemara raises an objection: **But is** it true about **wine,** that if it is **not a time when entry** into the Temple is possible, priests are **permitted** to drink wine as they like? [6] **But surely it was taught** in a Baraita: "**Rabbi** Yehudah HaNasi **says:** The Sages maintain that even today, when the Temple no longer stands, a priest is forbidden to drink wine at a time when it would be his turn to serve in the Temple, for the Temple might speedily be rebuilt and the priest might be called in suddenly for service. And if the priest does not know to which priestly watch he belongs or to which priestly family he belongs, he is forbidden to drink wine all year long, for any day might be his family's turn to serve in the Temple, and since the Temple might speedily be rebuilt, he must be prepared for service. This is the position of the Sages. But **I say** that if we are concerned that the Temple might suddenly be rebuilt, then all **priests should forever be forbidden to drink wine.** When the Temple is rebuilt, the entire priesthood might be called in to serve at the rededication ceremonies, or the watches might be rearranged, and so no priest should ever be allowed to become drunk. [7] **But what can I do?** The long time that the Temple remains **in ruins** works to **the priests' advantage.** We need not be concerned that the Temple will suddenly be rebuilt, and the priests will be called upon to serve there. Hence, the restrictions that were once imposed on priests regarding the drinking of wine are no longer in force." [8] **And Abaye said** regarding this matter: **In accordance with whose** view **do the priests nowadays drink wine** without restriction? [9] And he answered: **In accordance with** the view of **Rabbi** Yehudah HaNasi, who said that we are not concerned that the Temple will suddenly be rebuilt, and so the restrictions imposed on the priests regarding the drinking of wine no longer apply. Now, surely **this proves by implication that the Sages** who disagree with Rabbi Yehudah HaNasi **forbid** priests to drink wine even today, when entry into the Temple is not possible, if only by Rabbinic decree. Consequently they should maintain that the prohibition forbidding priests to grow their hair long is also still in force today.

RASHI

רבי אומר אני כהן אסור לשתות יין לעולם — רישא דברייתא קתני: כהן המכיר משמרתו ומשמרת בית אב שלו — אסור ביין כל אותו היום, אף בזמן הזה. מכיר משמרתו ואינו מכיר בית אב שלו — אסור כל אותו שבת. אינו מכיר לא משמרתו ולא משמרת בית אב שלו — אסור לשתות יין לעולם, שמא עכשיו זמנו הוא ויש לחוש שמא יבנה בית המקדש. **רבי אומר אני** — אם באנו לחוש שמא יבנה, אסור ביין לעולם, ואפילו הוא מכיר שאינו עכשיו זמן משמרתו — שמא יבנה, וכל הקודם ואיטרח, עייל ועביד. **אבל מה אעשה שתקנתן קלקלתן** — חורבן הבית שקלקלן ועירבב סדר משמרותיהן, שהיה אוסרן ביין בזמן משמרתן, ומתירן שלא בזמן משמרתן, הוא תיקנן עכשיו לשתות יין לעולם, דלא חיישו שמא יבנה פתאום. **כמאן שתו האידנא כהני חמרא כרבי** — שהרי רוב כהנים אינן בקיאין בזמן משמרותיהן ואסורין לעולם לרבנן.

BACKGROUND

כֹּהֲנִים אֲסוּרִין Priests are forbidden. If a priest can trace back his ancestry to a particular watch (records regarding the priestly watches were kept long after the destruction of the Temple) and the week during which that watch was to serve in the Temple, and similarly he knows to which priestly family he belongs and the day on which that family was to serve (each watch was divided into six families, each family serving one day in the Temple), he is forbidden to drink wine for the whole day that his family was to serve, for the Temple might speedily be rebuilt and he must be prepared to serve there. If the priest knows to which watch he belongs and the week during which that watch was to serve in the Temple, but he does not know to which family he belongs and so he cannot know the particular day of the week that his family was to serve, he is forbidden to drink wine for that whole week. Every day of that week might be the day on which the priest's family was to serve, and since the Temple might suddenly be rebuilt he must keep himself sober so that he can serve there.

תַּקָּנָתוֹ קַלְקָלָתוֹ Its remedy is its ruin. From various sources it appears that even after the destruction of the Temple, the priests knew to which *mishmar* they belonged, and they preserved the memory of the *mishmarot* and their place of residence in following generations. However, the commentators note that even priests who knew their *mishmar* did not always know to which priestly family they belonged, and some authorities hold that if a priest did know to which priestly family he belonged, he was only forbidden to drink wine on the day when that priestly family was supposed to serve in the Temple. Moreover, the order of service of *mishmarot* became confused, so that no *mishmar* knows when it is its time to perform the Temple service.

NOTES

תַּקָּנָתוֹ קַלְקָלָתוֹ Its remedy is its ruin. *Remah* explains that in our times, no priest should ever be permitted to drink wine, because after the destruction of the Temple, the priests no longer kept track of the *mishmar* to which they belong. And if the Temple is rebuilt, it might be any particular priest's turn to perform the Temple service. But that very factor which should be to the priests' disadvantage, the destruction of the Temple, actually works to their

[1]הָתָם הַיְינוּ טַעְמָא: מְהֵרָה יִבָּנֶה בֵּית הַמִּקְדָּשׁ, [2]וּבָעֵינַן כֹּהֵן הָרָאוּי לַעֲבוֹדָה, וְלֵיכָּא.
[3]הָכָא נַמִי בָּעֵינָא כֹּהֵן הָרָאוּי לַעֲבוֹדָה, וְלֵיכָּא!
[4]הָכָא אֶפְשָׁר דִּמְסַפֵּר וְעָיֵיל.
[5]הָתָם נַמִי אֶפְשָׁר דְּנָיֵים פּוּרְתָּא וְעָיֵיל, [6]דְּאָמַר רַב אַחָא: דֶּרֶךְ מִיל וְשֵׁינָה כָּל שֶׁהוּא מְפִיגִין אֶת הַיַּיִן!
[7]וְלָאו אִיתְּמַר עֲלָהּ: [8]אָמַר רַב נַחְמָן אָמַר רַבָּה בַּר אֲבוּהּ: לֹא שָׁנוּ אֶלָּא שֶׁשָּׁתָה כְּדֵי רְבִיעִית. [9]אֲבָל יוֹתֵר מִכְּדֵי רְבִיעִית, [10]כָּל שֶׁכֵּן דְּדֶרֶךְ טוֹרַדְתּוֹ וְשֵׁינָה מְשַׁכַּרְתּוֹ.

LITERAL TRANSLATION

[1]There the reason is: Speedily the Temple will be rebuilt, [2]and we will need a priest who is fit for service, and there will be none.
[3]Here, too, I will need a priest who is fit for service, and there will be none!
[4]Here it is possible that he cut his hair and go in.
[5]There, too, it is possible that he sleep a little and go in, [6]for Rav Aḥa said: A walk of a mil or some sleep mitigates [the effects] of wine!
[7]Was it not stated regarding this: [8]Rav Naḥman said in the name of Rabbah bar Avuha: They only taught [this] when he drank the amount of a *revi'it*. [9]But [if he drank] more than the amount of a *revi'it*, [10]all the more so walking makes him unsteady and sleep intoxicates him!

RASHI

התם היינו טעמא כו' — שינויא היא, ובניחותא גרסינן לה, כלומר: מדאורייתא שרי ורבנן הוא דגזור, ופרכינן: הכא נמי מהרה יבנה וכו'.

TRANSLATION AND COMMENTARY

הָתָם [1]The Gemara answers: **There, the reason** that the Sages forbade priests to drink wine, even today when the Temple is no longer standing, **is** that they were concerned that **the Temple might speedily be rebuilt,** [2]**and a priest who is fit for service would** suddenly **be needed, but there would be none,** because all the priests would be drunk. But there was no reason for the Sages to forbid priests to let their hair grow long, especially not today when there is no Temple.

הָכָא נַמִי [3]The Gemara objects: If you say that the Sages were concerned that the Temple might speedily be rebuilt, then **here, too,** they should have said that even today the priests are forbidden to let their hair grow long, because the Temple might speedily be rebuilt, and **a priest who is fit for service would** suddenly **be needed, but there would be none, for** all the priests would have overgrown hair!

הָכָא [4]The Gemara answers: **Here,** the Sages had no reason to extend the prohibition, because **it would be possible** for the priests **to cut their hair in** a very short time **and** prepare themselves to **enter** the Temple and perform the service.

הָתָם נַמִי [5]The Gemara raises another objection: But if this is so, then the prohibition forbidding priests to drink wine should also lapse. **There, too, it would be possible** for them **to sleep a little and thus** prepare themselves in a very short time to **enter** the Temple and perform the service. [6]As **Rav Aḥa said: A walk of a mil** (960 m., 1,049 yd.) **or** even **some sleep after** one has been drinking **mitigates the** intoxicating **effects of wine.**

וְלָאו אִיתְּמַר עֲלָהּ [7]The Gemara rebuts this objection: **Was it not stated regarding this** statement of Rav Aḥa: [8]**Rav Naḥman said in the name of Rabbah bar Avuha:** This regulation, that a mil-long walk or even the slightest amount of sleep mitigates the intoxicating effects of wine, **only applies where** a person **drank** wine **in the amount of a *revi'it*** (a quarter of a *log*; 86.4 c.c., 3 fl. oz.). [9]**But if** a person **drank more than the amount of a *revi'it*** of wine, [10]then **all the more so does walking** about **make him unsteady** on his feet, **and sleep intoxicates him** even more! Thus, the Sages maintain that the prohibition forbidding priests to drink wine is still in effect. But they, too, agree that the prohibition forbidding priests to let their hair grow long no longer applies, for the priests could quickly cut their hair and begin their service immediately, if the Temple were suddenly restored.

NOTES

advantage, for even if the Temple is rebuilt, a court would have to meet to re-establish the *mishmarot*. Therefore, there is no immediate worry that any particular priest would be sent into the Temple in a state of intoxication.

HALAKHAH

פְּרוּעֵי רֹאשׁ Long hair. "If a priest enters the Temple with long hair and participates in the service, he is punishable by death at the hand of Heaven, but his service is not disqualified," following the Gemara's conclusion in *Ta'anit*. (*Rambam, Sefer Avodah, Hilkhot Bi'at Mikdash* 1:8-9.)

דֶּרֶךְ מִיל וְשֵׁינָה כָּל שֶׁהוּא A walk of a mil or some sleep. "A walk of a mil or some sleep mitigates the intoxicating effects of wine, provided that only a *revi'it* or less was consumed. But if a person drank more than a *revi'it*, sleep intoxicates him even more, and walking about makes him even more unsteady." (*Shulḥan Arukh, Oraḥ Ḥayyim* 99:2.)

[1]רַב אַשִׁי אָמַר: שְׁתוּיֵי יַיִן דִּמְחַלֵּי עֲבוֹדָה, [2]גָּזְרוּ בְּהוּ רַבָּנַן. [3]פְּרוּעֵי רֹאשׁ דְּלָא מְחַלֵּי עֲבוֹדָה, [4]לָא גָּזְרוּ בְּהוּ רַבָּנַן. [5]מֵיתִיבִי: ״וְאֵלּוּ שֶׁבְּמִיתָה: פְּרוּעֵי רֹאשׁ, וּשְׁתוּיֵי יַיִן״. [6]בִּשְׁלָמָא שְׁתוּיֵי יַיִן — [7]דִּכְתִיב: ״יַיִן וְשֵׁכָר אַל תֵּשְׁתְּ אַתָּה וּבָנֶיךָ וְלֹא תָמֻתוּ״. [8]אֶלָּא פְּרוּעֵי רֹאשׁ מְנָא לָן?

LITERAL TRANSLATION

[1]Rav Ashi said: [Regarding] those drunk with wine, who disqualify [their] service, [2]the Sages decreed. [3][Regarding] those with overgrown hair who do not disqualify [their] service, [4]the Sages did not decree. [5]They raised an objection: "And these are liable to [the penalty of] death: Those with overgrown hair, and those who are drunk with wine." [6]Granted those who are drunk with wine — [7]for it is written: "Do not drink wine or strong drink, [neither] you, nor your sons [with you, when you enter the Tabernacle], lest you die." [8]But from where [do we know about] those with overgrown hair?

TRANSLATION AND COMMENTARY

רַב אַשִׁי [1]**Rav Ashi suggested** that there is another reason to distinguish between the prohibition forbidding priests to drink wine and that forbidding them to let their hair grow long: If a priest enters the Temple while he is **intoxicated with wine,** and serves, **his service is disqualified.** This is derived from the passage (Leviticus 10:9-10): "Do not drink wine or strong drink.... That you may differentiate between holy and unholy." [2]Thus, **the Sages decreed** that even nowadays priests are forbidden to drink wine. [3]But if a priest serves while his **hair is overgrown, his service is not disqualified,** for there is no Biblical verse indicating that his service is indeed disqualified. [4]Thus, **the Sages did not decree** that priests are forbidden nowadays to let their hair grow long.

מֵיתִיבִי [5]**An objection was raised** against Rav Ashi's distinction from a Baraita, which stated: **"And these are** the transgressors who are **liable to** be punished by **death** at the hand of Heaven: Priests who serve in the Temple while **their hair is overgrown, and** priests who serve while **they are drunk with wine."** The Gemara asks: From where do we know that these two transgressions are capital offenses? [6]**Granted that** priests **who** serve in the Temple while they **are drunk with wine** are liable for the death penalty, [7]**for the verse states** explicitly (Leviticus 10:9): **"Do not drink wine or strong drink,** neither **you, nor your sons with you, when you enter the Tabernacle, lest you die."** [8]**But from where do we know that those** priests who serve

RASHI

שתויי יין דמחלי עבודה — דכתיב (ויקרא י): ״יין ושכר וגו׳״ וסמיך: ״ולהבדיל בין הקדש ובין החול״ משמע בין עבודה קדושה לעבודה מחוללת גזרו בהו רבנן בזמן הזה משום ״מהרה יבנה״.

NOTES

פְּרוּעֵי רֹאשׁ Those with overgrown hair. The question has been raised: Why does the Gemara infer from the verse in Ezekiel that priests serving in the Temple with overgrown hair are liable to the penalty of death? This is stated explicitly in the Torah (Leviticus 10:6): "Let the hair of your heads not grow long, neither rend your clothes; lest you die." *Ran* and *Rabbenu Yonah* suggest that, without the verse in Ezekiel, we might have understood the verse in Leviticus as an injunction directed only at the sons of Aaron, instructing them not to grow their hair long or rend their clothes in mourning over their brothers Nadab and Abihu during the period of the dedication of the Tabernacle, an injunction that applied even when the priests were not actually engaged in the service. The verse in Ezekiel teaches that there is a perpetual prohibition for all generations against serving in the Temple with overgrown hair, and that prohibition applies only while the priests are actually involved in the service. (See also *Rambam, Sefer HaMitzvot,* Negative Commandment 163 and *Ramban.*)

HALAKHAH

שְׁתוּיֵי יַיִן דִּמְחַלֵּי עֲבוֹדָה Those drunk with wine, who disqualify their service. "If a priest drank a *revi'it* of wine, he is forbidden to enter the Temple courtyard past the altar. If he enters and participates in the Temple service, his service is disqualified, and he is punishable by death at the hand of Heaven." (*Rambam, Sefer Avodah, Hilkhot Bi'at Mikdash* 1:1.)

שְׁתוּיֵי יַיִן Those drunk with wine. "The members of the priestly watch whose week it is to serve in the Temple are permitted to drink wine during the night, but not during the day. This is so even if it is not their day to perform the service, lest they be called in to assist those whose day it is to serve. The members of the priestly family whose day it is to serve in the Temple are forbidden to drink wine even at night, lest the effects of the alcohol are still felt the next morning, while they are engaged in the service (or for the burning of the fat, which can be carried out even at night; *Ra'avad*). Today, a priest who knows to which watch he belongs, and to which priestly family he belongs, is forbidden to drink wine on the day that his family would have served in the Temple. If he only knows to which watch he belongs, he is forbidden to drink wine during the entire week that his watch would have served. If he does not even know to which watch he belongs, he should be forbidden to drink wine all the time, but the Rabbis permitted him to drink wine without any restrictions," following Rabbi Yehudah HaNasi. (*Rambam Sefer Avodah, Hilkhot Bi'at Mikdash* 1:6-7.)

TRANSLATION AND COMMENTARY

in the Temple while **their hair is overgrown** are also punishable by death at the hands of Heaven? [1]The Gemara answers: This is learned from the fact that **those** priests **who** serve in the Temple while they **are drunk are compared** in Scripture **to those who** serve there while **their hair is overgrown.** [2]**One verse states** (Ezekiel 44:20): **"Neither shall they shave their heads, nor let their locks to grow long,"** [3]**and the** very next **verse states** (v. 21): **"Neither shall any priest drink wine,** when they enter into the inner court." [4]**Just as those who** serve in the Temple while they **are drunk with wine are liable to be punished by death** at the hand of Heaven (as is learned from the verse in Leviticus), [5]**so, too, are those** who serve **with overgrown hair liable to be punished by death** at the hand of Heaven. The Gemara now comes to its objection: Since the Scripture compares these two prohibitions, it should be legitimate to extend that analogy [6]and also learn **from it: Just as those who** serve in the Temple while they **are drunk with wine disqualify their service,** [7]**so, too,** should **those** who serve **with overgrown hair disqualify their service!**

קַשְׁיָא [8]The Gemara concludes: Indeed, the analogy drawn here between the two prohibitions poses **a difficulty** for Rav Ashi.

אֲמַר לֵיהּ [9]Continuing on the same theme, **Ravina said to Rav Ashi: Before Ezekiel came** and taught that a priest is forbidden to let his hair grow long, and his serving with overgrown hair is punishable by the death penalty, **who taught these laws?** As we learned above, the prohibition is not recorded in the Torah itself, but only in Ezekiel (44:20): "Neither shall they shave their heads, nor let their locks to grow long." Surely a prophet is not authorized to issue new laws that were not mentioned in the Torah!

וְלִיטַעְמִיךְ [10]Rav Ashi said to Ravina: **According to your reasoning, there** is a similar problem with **what Rav Ḥisda said concerning** the law of an apostate or uncircumcised priest, who may not serve in the Temple. For Rav Ḥisda said: [11]**We did not learn this matter from the Torah of our master Moses,** and in fact it was not recorded anywhere in Scripture [12]**until Ezekiel came and taught** it to **us** in the following verse (Ezekiel 44:9): **"No stranger, uncircumcised in heart and uncircumcised in flesh, shall enter into my sanctuary" to serve me.** [13]**Before Ezekiel came, who said** that an apostate or an uncircumcised priest is forbidden to serve in the Temple?

אֶלָּא [14]**Rather,** until the days of Ezekiel, this matter **was learned as an** oral **tradition** going back to Sinai, just like the rest of the Oral Law. [15]**And Ezekiel came and supported** the oral tradition **with a** written **verse.**

[1]דְּאִיתְקַשׁ שְׁתוּיֵי יַיִן לִפְרוּעֵי רֹאשׁ. [2]כְּתִיב: ״וְרֹאשָׁם לֹא יְגַלֵּחוּ וּפֶרַע לֹא יְשַׁלֵּחוּ״. [3]וּכְתִיב: ״וְיַיִן לֹא יִשְׁתּוּ וגו׳״. [4]מַה שְּׁתוּיֵי יַיִן בְּמִיתָה, [5]אַף פְּרוּעֵי רֹאשׁ בְּמִיתָה. [6]וּמִינָּהּ, מַה שְּׁתוּיֵי יַיִן דִּמְחַלֵּי עֲבוֹדָה, [7]אַף פְּרוּעֵי רֹאשׁ דִּמְחַלֵּי עֲבוֹדָה!

[8]קַשְׁיָא.

[9]אֲמַר לֵיהּ רָבִינָא לְרַב אַשִׁי: הַאי, עַד דְּלָא אֲתָא יְחֶזְקֵאל מַאן אֲמָרָהּ? [10]וְלִיטַעְמִיךְ, הָא דְּאָמַר רַב חִסְדָּא: [11]דָּבָר זֶה מִתּוֹרַת מֹשֶׁה רַבֵּינוּ לֹא לָמַדְנוּ, [12]עַד שֶׁבָּא יְחֶזְקֵאל וְלִימְּדָנוּ: ״כָּל בֶּן נֵכָר עֶרֶל לֵב וְעֶרֶל בָּשָׂר לֹא יָבוֹא אֶל מִקְדָּשִׁי לְשָׁרְתֵנִי״. [13]עַד דְּלֹא בָּא יְחֶזְקֵאל, מַאן אֲמָרָהּ? [14]אֶלָּא, גְּמָרָא גְּמִירִי לָהּ, [15]וַאֲתָא יְחֶזְקֵאל וְאַסְמְכָהּ

LITERAL TRANSLATION

[1]Because those who are drunk with wine were compared to those with overgrown hair. [2]It is written: "Neither shall they shave their heads, nor let their locks to grow long." [3]And it is written: "Neither shall any priest drink wine, etc." [4]Just as those who are drunk with wine [are liable] to [the] death [penalty], [5]so too those with overgrown hair [are liable] to death. [6]And from this [say also] just as those who are drunk with wine disqualify [their] service, [7]so too those with overgrown hair disqualify [their] service!

[8]It is difficult.

[9]Ravina said to Rav Ashi: Before Ezekiel came, who said it?

[10]And according to your opinion, that which Rav Ḥisda said: [11]This matter we did not learn from the Torah of our teacher Moses, [12]until Ezekiel came and taught us: "No stranger, uncircumcised in heart and uncircumcised in flesh, shall enter into my sanctuary" to serve me. [13]Before Ezekiel came, who said it?

[14]Rather, it was learned as a tradition, [15]and Ezekiel came and supported it with

RASHI

הכי גרסינן: אף פרועי ראש מחלי עבודה קשיא. הא עד דלא אתא יחזקאל – ולקשינהו. מאן אמרה – פירוש: מהיכא נפקא לן פרועי ראש במיתה. הא דאמר רב חסדא – בזבחים בפרק שני, דבר זה דכהן ערל פסול לעבודה. כל בן נכר – כהן משומד שנתנכרו מעשיו לאביו שבשמים וערל לבו, או ערל בשר שמתו אחיו מחמת מילה.

BACKGROUND

עַד דְּלָא אֲתָא יְחֶזְקֵאל וכו׳ Before Ezekiel came, etc. One does not learn Torah law from the Prophets. Moreover, Prophets are forbidden to issue new Halakhic rulings on the basis of prophecy, and any Prophet who teaches new Halakhic rulings is by definition a false Prophet. So even if this Halakhah is recorded in the Book of Ezekiel, it must have existed beforehand.

כָּל בֶּן נֵכָר וכו׳ No stranger, uncircumcised in heart, etc. Two Halakhot are derived from this. One is that anyone who is an "alien" with respect to his acts and opinions (and is thus said to be "uncircumcised in heart"), that is, anyone who has converted to another religion, may not serve in the Temple, even if he is of priestly descent. Moreover, we learn that any uncircumcised man, even if his condition is not a matter of choice (such as when circumcision would endanger his life), is regarded as blemished, and he may not perform the Temple service.

LANGUAGE

לוּלְיָינִית Lulian. This word apparently derives from the Roman name "Julianus," referring either to a particular individual or to the emperors of that name, whose hair was combed in that distinctive manner.

SAGES

בֶּן אֶלְעָשָׂה Ben El'asa. Ben El'asa was the son-in-law of Rabbi Yehudah HaNasi. Little is known about him from the sources. He was apparently extremely wealthy and was not known to be a Torah scholar. For that reason there were conflicts between him and Rabbi's students, who would provoke him in various ways. It appears that Rabbi's words here are meant to defend Ben El'asa from possible ridicule.

BACKGROUND

תִּסְפּוֹרֶת שֶׁל כֹּהֵן גָּדוֹל Coiffure of the High Priest.

Ben El'asa's coiffure, according to the approach of *Ra'avad*.

The Talmudic description of the High Priest's coiffure is not entirely clear, and the commentators disagree about it. According to *Rambam*, whose remarks are also in need of clarification, it appears that the High Priest's hair was cut short all around, and that it was all of equal length, so that no hair curled over another one, and the phrase כָּסוֹם יִכְסְמוּ means cut short like a field that has been harvested all at once.

According to *Ra'avad*, the High Priest's coiffure consisted of row upon row of curls, between which all the hair was cut off. Thus the top of each curl touched the base of the adjacent one.

Others maintain (see *Arukh*) that the High Priest's coiffure was in the form of layers, one on top of the other.

TRANSLATION AND COMMENTARY

[1]**Here, too,** regarding the prohibition forbidding a priest to let his hair grow long, the matter **was** originally **learned as an** oral **tradition** going back to Sinai, [2]**and** then **Ezekiel came and supported** the oral tradition **with a** written **verse.** [3]And **when they learned the** transmitted **law** regarding the prohibition forbidding a priest to let his hair grow long, **it was** only **regarding the death penalty.** The oral tradition received from Sinai only taught that a priest who serves in the Temple with overgrown hair is liable to be punished by death at the hands of Heaven. [4]But **regarding the disqualification of his service, they did not have** an oral **tradition.** Therefore, Ravina provides support for Rav Ashi's original statement that the service of corrupt priests with overgrown hair is not disqualified.

מַאי [5]The Gemara above cited the verse (Ezekiel 44:20): "Neither shall they shave their heads, nor let their locks to grow long; but they shall crop their heads." **What is the meaning of** the end of that verse, "but **they shall crop their heads**"?

תָּנָא [6]A Tanna taught a Baraita that explains those words: "The verse teaches that the High Priest must cut his hair **in the Lulian style.**"

מַאי [7]**What is meant by the Lulian haircut?**

אָמַר רַב יְהוּדָה [8]**Rav Yehudah said in the name of Shmuel:** This means that the High Priest must cut his hair in **a** particularly **distinguished** style.

הֵיכִי דָּמֵי [9]The Gemara asks: **How do we visualize the case?** [10]**Rav Ashi said:** The Baraita refers to hair that is cut so that **the ends** of the hair **of one** row **touch the roots** of the hair **of the next** row.

שָׁאֲלוּ [11]It was related that **Rabbi** Yehudah HaNasi **was asked** by his disciples: **Which haircut** is appropriate for **the High Priest?** [12]**He said to them: Go out and see the haircut of** my son-in-law, **Ben El'asa,** for he cuts his hair in the manner of the High Priest.

אַקְּרָא. [1]הָכָא נַמִי, גְּמָרָא גְּמִירִי לָהּ, [2]וַאֲתָא יְחֶזְקֵאל וְאַסְמְכָהּ אַקְּרָא. [3]וְכִי גָּמְרִי הֲלָכָה — לְמִיתָה. [4]לְאַחוּלֵי עֲבוֹדָה — לָא גְּמִירִי.

[5]מַאי "כָּסוֹם יִכְסְמוּ אֶת רָאשֵׁיהֶם"?

[6]תָּנָא: "כְּמִין תִּסְפּוֹרֶת לוּלְיָינִית".

[7]מַאי תִּסְפּוֹרֶת לוּלְיָינִית?

[8]אָמַר רַב יְהוּדָה אָמַר שְׁמוּאֵל: תִּסְפּוֹרְתָּא יְחִידָאָה.

[9]הֵיכִי דָּמֵי? [10]אָמַר רַבִּי אַשִׁי: רֹאשׁוֹ שֶׁל זֶה בְּצַד עִיקָּרוֹ שֶׁל זֶה.

[11]שָׁאֲלוּ אֶת רַבִּי: אֵיזֶהוּ תִּסְפּוֹרֶת שֶׁל כֹּהֵן גָּדוֹל? [12]אָמַר לָהֶן: צְאוּ וּרְאוּ מִתִּסְפּוֹרֶת שֶׁל בֶּן אֶלְעָשָׂה.

LITERAL TRANSLATION

a verse. [1]Here too, it was learned as a tradition, [2]and Ezekiel came and supported it with a verse. [3]And when they learned [this transmitted] law, [it was] regarding the death penalty. [4]Regarding the disqualification of service, they did not learn [a tradition].

[5]What is [the meaning of] "They shall crop their heads"?

[6][A Tanna] taught: "Like the Lulian style of haircut."

[7]What is [meant by] the Lulian style of haircut?

[8]Rav Yehudah said in the name of Shmuel: A distinguished haircut.

[9]How do we visualize it (lit., "how is it like")? [10]Rav Ashi said: The tip of this [hair] next to the root of that.

[11]They asked Rabbi: What is the haircut of the High Priest? [12]He said to them: Go out and see the haircut of Ben El'asa.

RASHI

יחידאה — נאה, ואין דוגמתה.

NOTES

כָּסוֹם יִכְסְמוּ They shall crop their heads. The Rishonim seek clarification: This verse (Ezekiel 44:20) seems to refer not only to the High Priest, but also to ordinary priests. Why, then, does the Gemara interpret it as referring to the special haircut of the High Priest? *Remah* answers that the verse is referring to the Messianic period, when all the priests will cut their hair in the style of the High Priest. *Ran* argues that there are a number of verses in that section of Ezekiel which do not specifically mention the High Priest, but must be understood as referring to him and not to priests in general, such as Ezekiel 44:23, which records the prohibition against marrying a widow, which applies only to the High Priest. Our verse may also be interpreted, then, as referring to the High Priest, even though he is not explicitly mentioned.

תִּסְפּוֹרְתָּא יְחִידָאָה A distinguished haircut. Some Rishonim had the reading תִּסְפּוֹרְתָּא יְתֵירְתָּא, "an extraordinary haircut," surpassing all others in its attractiveness (*Rabbenu Yonah*).

HALAKHAH

תִּסְפּוֹרֶת שֶׁל כֹּהֵן גָּדוֹל The haircut of the High Priest. "The High Priest may not let his hair grow long (even when he does not enter the Temple), and must cut his hair every Friday. The end of one hair should reach the root of another hair. *Rambam* seems to understand that the High Priest's hair must be cut very short, so that all of his hair is of equal length (*Kesef Mishneh*). According to *Ra'avad*, the High Priest must cut his hair in the front to the roots so that all of his forehead is exposed. *Rambam* apparently understands that this regulation applies only to the High Priest." (*Rambam, Sefer Avodah, Hilkhot Kelei HaMikdash* 5:1.)

TRANSLATION AND COMMENTARY

תַּנְיָא [1]The Gemara concludes this chapter with a related Baraita, in which **it was taught: "Rabbi** Yehudah HaNasi **says: Ben El'asa did not lavish his money in vain** on haircuts, [2]**but rather** he spent a great deal of money to learn how to cut his hair in that special way, **in order** to be able **to demonstrate the haircut of the High Priest."**

[1]תַּנְיָא: "רַבִּי אוֹמֵר: לֹא עַל חִנָּם פִּיזֵּר בֶּן אֶלְעָשָׂה אֶת מָעוֹתָיו, [2]אֶלָּא כְּדֵי לְהַרְאוֹת בּוֹ תִּסְפּוֹרֶת שֶׁל כֹּהֵן גָּדוֹל".

הדרן עלך כהן גדול

LITERAL TRANSLATION

[1]It was taught: "Rabbi says: Ben El'asa did not lavish his money in vain, [2]but rather in order to demonstrate the haircut of the High Priest."

RASHI

בן אלעשה – חתנו של רבי היה, ונתן ממון, ולמדו לו אותה תספורת.

הדרן עלך כהן גדול

Conclusion to Chapter Two

This chapter dealt with some of the laws concerning the High Priest and the main laws concerning the king.

Since the functions of the High Priest are connected to the service in the Temple, especially the rites of the Day of Atonement, most of the laws concerning the High Priest belong to the Order of *Kodashim* and tractate *Yoma*. Tractate *Sanhedrin* deals mainly with the High Priest as an eminent man, with his unique legal status, and his honor compared to other Jews. It was concluded that, in terms of his legal status, the High Priest was like any other Jew. However, he was treated differently if he was accused of a capital crime, when he was tried before a court of seventy-one. Regarding his eminence above the nation, we have learned how he was honored at all times. For even when he was in mourning, he was seated above the people, and the people, as it were, took his grief upon themselves. Moreover, as was explained in the Gemara, the High Priest was not permitted to adopt the full practice of mourning, and he was not permitted to contract ritual impurity by proximity to the corpse even of his closest relatives. He was not permitted to follow the bier, and therefore the people bore his grief, as it was said of Aaron the Priest in the time of his mourning, "and your brothers, the whole House of Israel, shall weep for the the fire that the Lord burned" (Leviticus 10:6).

In this chapter prominent place is given to the law that distinguishes between a king who must observe all the laws and commandments of the Torah ("kings of the House of David") and other kings of the Jews, such as the Hasmonean dynasty during the Second Temple period. The former were different from other Jews only in that, if they were to be tried for capital crimes, it would have to be before a great tribunal of seventy-one. However, the second type of king, the type dicussed by the Mishnah, observed the main laws of the Torah, but could not be tried under any circumstances, for the power of the Sanhedrin did not extend so far. A king of this kind was freed from the obligation to stand trial (and therefore he was also not qualified to serve as a judge in any court), so as not to cause conflict between the monarchy and the judges. Elsewhere we have also found instances in which the Sages of the Sanhedrin waived some of their authority when it became merely an abstract principle with no connection to actual events.

With respect to his rights and duties, the commandments and laws applying to the king fall into two categories: some laws affect the king as private, personal commandments, which obligate him because he is a king; and others apply more or less to the governing of the country. In the first category of laws is the prohibition against marrying more than eighteen wives, a restriction that applies solely to the king, and the positive commandment to have a special Torah scroll written in his name, which he must always have with him. Further prohibitions against keeping too many horses or owning excessive amounts of silver and gold also affect his personal conduct. For, according to the Halakhah, these prohibitions do not restrict the king's right to collect silver and gold for state purposes, even if they are very costly, or to keep a large number of horses in order to wage war with them. The king was only forbidden to indulge in self-glorification; excesses were permitted for reasons of state.

The areas of rule and the privileges of the king are not stated explicitly and in full detail in this chapter. Since it was accepted as the Halakhah that the passage concerning the king in I Samuel 8:11-19, though originally formulated as a threat, nevertheless contains a list of the king's privileges, there was no need for further detail. In the laws concerning the king, the Torah states how the king is to be obeyed, especially the passage in Joshua 1:18; Joshua was, practically speaking, a king of the Jews. Hence there was no need to present these laws in great detail. This is also understandable because of the function of the king, as the head of the executive branch. By virtue of his function, there cannot be a prior definition of the things the king is required to do, since all the needs of the state must be before him. The Torah therefore gave him very extensive rights to do as he saw fit for the security and benefit of the state. He was given the authority to impose corporal punishment, even the death sentence, and to levy fines against anyone who stood in his way, especially rebels, and he could also institute laws and practices concerning the safety of the residents of the state, when Rabbinical courts were incapable of doing so (because of legal restrictions or some other reason). It is a special positive commandment to accept the rule of the king with awe and respect. Because respect for the king was tantamount to respect for the entire nation, and not only personal respect, the king himself was not permitted to renounce that respect. Therefore on all occasions, even when he is in mourning, everyone (including the High Priest) had to treat him with honor and awe.

Introduction to Chapter Three

זֶה בּוֹרֵר

In the first chapter of the tractate we learned the definition and function of the various legal tribunals, and this chapter fills in the picture in one respect by clarifying how the tribunals are constituted and describing their methods of action.

The High Courts (the Sanhedrins of twenty-three and of seventy-one) were permanent bodies, and the task of selecting the judges who sat on them was placed in the hands of the Great Sanhedrin itself. However, tribunals of three, which mainly dealt with day-to-day legal problems, were not all permanent. Often a tribunal was constituted only for a specific case.

In every instance a practical question arises: How was it determined who would be the judges? A tribunal of experts may be constituted only of experts or ordained Rabbis, but what about a tribunal of laymen? Can any Jew be a judge? Moreover, in Jewish law witnesses are the most important factor in judicial deliberations, and their testimony ultimately determines the outcome of the trial. Therefore, regulations must be established to remove false witnesses, untrustworthy witnesses, and those who are disqualified for some other reason.

The Torah states that the testimony of evil witnesses (עֵד חָמָס) is not to be accepted, but who is to be called an evil witness, and how is it to be determined that he is evil in this respect? Similarly we learn from the Bible that relatives of parties to a court case are not qualified to testify — but who is regarded as a relative in this respect? Do the same considerations apply to relatives in matters of inheritance and mourning?

A practical matter is that of judicial procedure. The Torah states explicitly that it is the duty of the judges to examine the truth of the testimony very thoroughly, by interrogating the witnesses and by exercising their faculty of judgment. But how does one do this in practice? Clearly, the court must ascertain the truth to the best of its ability, but are there time-limits to this process? Is it possible to restrict these deliberations, and what happens when a court decides that the time has come to sum up the deliberations?

The following chapter examines these issues in practical fashion.

דִּינֵי

[1]מְמוֹנוֹת בִּשְׁלֹשָׁה. [2]זֶה בּוֹרֵר לוֹ אֶחָד וְזֶה בּוֹרֵר לוֹ אֶחָד, [3]וּשְׁנֵיהֶן בּוֹרְרִין לָהֶן עוֹד אֶחָד. [4]דִּבְרֵי רַבִּי מֵאִיר. [5]וַחֲכָמִים אוֹמְרִים: שְׁנֵי דַיָּינִין בּוֹרְרִין לָהֶן עוֹד אֶחָד.

[6]זֶה פּוֹסֵל דַּיָּינוֹ שֶׁל זֶה וְזֶה פּוֹסֵל דַּיָּינוֹ שֶׁל זֶה. [7]דִּבְרֵי רַבִּי מֵאִיר. [8]וַחֲכָמִים אוֹמְרִים: אֵימָתַי? [9]בִּזְמַן שֶׁמֵּבִיא עֲלֵיהֶן רְאָיָה שֶׁהֵן קְרוֹבִין אוֹ פְּסוּלִין; [10]אֲבָל, אִם הָיוּ כְּשֵׁרִין אוֹ מוּמְחִין מִפִּי בֵית דִּין, אֵינוֹ יָכוֹל לְפוֹסְלָן.

[11]זֶה פּוֹסֵל עֵדָיו שֶׁל זֶה, וְזֶה פּוֹסֵל עֵדָיו שֶׁל זֶה. [12]דִּבְרֵי רַבִּי מֵאִיר. [13]וַחֲכָמִים אוֹמְרִים: אֵימָתַי? [14]בִּזְמַן שֶׁמֵּבִיא עֲלֵיהֶן רְאָיָה שֶׁהֵן קְרוֹבִין אוֹ פְּסוּלִין; [15]אֲבָל, אִם הָיוּ כְּשֵׁרִין, אֵינוֹ יָכוֹל לְפוֹסְלָן.

LITERAL TRANSLATION

MISHNAH [1]Monetary cases [are judged] by three. [2]This [litigant] selects for himself one and that [litigant] selects for himself one, [3]and the two of them [jointly] select for themselves another one. [4][These are] the words of Rabbi Meir. [5]But the Sages say: The two judges select for themselves another one.

[6]This [litigant] may reject that one's judge and that one may reject this one's judge. [7][These are] the words of Rabbi Meir. [8]But the Sages say: [9]When? When he brings proof about them that they are related or unfit; [10]however, if they were fit or [declared] expert by a court, he cannot reject them.

[11]This [litigant] may reject that one's witnesses and that one may reject this one's witnesses. [12][These are] the words of Rabbi Meir. [13]But the Sages say: [14]When? When he brings proof about them that they are related or unfit; [15]however, if they were fit, he cannot reject them.

TRANSLATION AND COMMENTARY

MISHNAH **דִּינֵי מָמוֹנוֹת** [1]**Monetary cases** are adjudicated **by** a court of **three** judges who need not be certifiably expert. [2]**One litigant selects for himself one** judge **and the other litigant selects for himself one** judge, [3]**and** then **the two of them jointly select for themselves another one.** [4]These are **the words of Rabbi Meir.** [5]**But the Sages say: The two judges select for themselves another one.**

זֶה פּוֹסֵל [6]**This** litigant **may reject the** other litigant's choice of **judge,** just as **that** litigant may **reject this one's** choice of **judge.** [7]**These are the words of Rabbi Meir.** [8]**But the Sages ask: When** do we say that one litigant may reject the other's choice of a judge? The reply: [9]**When** the litigant **brings proof that** the contested judges **are** either **related** to one of the litigants or to one of the other judges, **or** are **unfit** for reasons of corrupt character (see the Mishnah on 24b). [10]**However, if they were** found to be **fit or** were declared to be **expert** judges **by a court, he cannot reject them.**

זֶה פּוֹסֵל [11]**This litigant may reject the** other litigant's **witnesses,** just as **that** litigant can **reject this one's witnesses.** [12]These are **the words of Rabbi Meir.** [13]**And the Sages ask: When** do we say that one litigant may reject another litigant's witnesses? The reply: [14]**When he brings proof that** the witnesses **are** either **related** to the litigants or to one another, **or** are **unfit** because they are corrupt. [15]**However, if they** were found to be **fit, he cannot reject them.**

RASHI

משנה זה בורר לו אחד – משמע זה בורר לו בית דין אחד שהן שלשה, וזה אחד הרי ששה, ושניהם בוררין להם עוד אחד הרי תשעה, והיינו דקא מתמה מאי זה בורר כו׳ הא בתלתא סגי.

NOTES

דִּינֵי מָמוֹנוֹת בִּשְׁלֹשָׁה Monetary cases are adjudicated by three. *Ran* and others point out that our Mishnah elaborates on the very first Mishnah in the tractate, which opens with these same words. In fact, there were those who arranged the chapters in the tractate so that this one would appear between the first and second chapters, in order to emphasize this continuity (*Rabbi Yehudah Almandri*).

וְזֶה בּוֹרֵר לוֹ אֶחָד This litigant selects for himself one. *Ran* asks: Why is the tribunal selected with the cooperation of the litigants? Have we not already learned in the first

HALAKHAH

זֶה בּוֹרֵר וְזֶה בּוֹרֵר This one selects and that one selects. "Where each of the litigants chooses a judge to sit on the tribunal, the two judges then collaborate in selecting the remaining judge, without the necessary consent of the respective litigants," in accordance with the opinion of the Sages as interpreted by Rav. "This procedure ensures that the court's decision will be issued in a balanced and truthful manner, and that it will be honored by the litigants," in accordance with Rabbi Zera in our Gemara. (*Rema.*) (*Shulḥan Arukh, Ḥoshen Mishpat* 13:1.)

TRANSLATION AND COMMENTARY

GEMARA מַאי ¹The Gemara asks: **What is** the meaning of the Mishnah's **teaching** that **"this litigant selects for himself one and that litigant selects for himself one,** and then the two of them select for themselves an additional one"? The Gemara first entertains the possibility that the litigants may each choose a court. But if that were so, nine judges would be convened, ²whereas according to the first Mishnah in *Sanhedrin* (2a) **it is sufficient** to adjudicate with **three judges** alone! ³Consequently our Mishnah must be understood as **saying: When this litigant selects for himself one court** of three, **and that** litigant, rejecting the first one's choice, **selects for himself** a different **court** of three, which is rejected, in turn, by the first litigant, ⁴**the two of them** must compromise and **select for themselves another court** of three that is acceptable to both of them, and which actually hears the case.

וַאֲפִילוּ ⁵But can it be that **even a debtor** is allowed to **reject** the creditor's choice of a tribunal? ⁶**For surely Rabbi Elazar said** otherwise regarding a litigant who wants to force his opponent to bring their case before the assembly of great scholars (see below, 31b). Although some Amoraim argued that a litigant can always reject the local court, Rabbi Elazar maintained that the Sages **only taught** this right of veto **with regard to a creditor;** ⁷however, if **a debtor** wishes to go to the place of assembly, the authorities can **force him** to accept the creditor's choice of local court **and litigate in his town** (as supported by Proverbs 22:7: "The borrower is a servant to the lender")!

כְּדְאָמַר ⁸The Gemara turns to a ruling on a different matter to prove that either litigant may reject a court: **Rabbi Yoḥanan said: "The Sages taught** what they did there **in reference to the lay courts in Syria,** which were composed of judges who were not well tutored in Torah law." ⁹**Here, too,** our Mishnah was taught

LITERAL TRANSLATION

GEMARA ¹Why does [it teach] "this [litigant] selects for himself one and that [litigant] selects for himself one"? ²It is [surely] sufficient with three! ³This is what it says: When this [litigant] selects for himself one court, and that [litigant rejects it and] selects for himself one court [which was rejected] — ⁴the two [litigants] select for themselves another [court].

⁵And may even a debtor reject [the creditor's court]? ⁶For surely Rabbi Elazar said: They only taught [this regarding] a creditor; ⁷however, [regarding] a debtor, they coerce him and he litigates in [the creditor's] town!

⁸As Rabbi Yoḥanan said: They taught [there] about the lay courts in Syria. ⁹Here, too,

גמרא

¹גְּמָרָא מַאי "זֶה בּוֹרֵר לוֹ אֶחָד וְזֶה בּוֹרֵר לוֹ אֶחָד"? ²בִּתְלָתָא סַגִּי! ³הָכִי קָאָמַר: כְּשֶׁזֶּה בּוֹרֵר לוֹ בֵּית דִּין אֶחָד, וְזֶה בּוֹרֵר לוֹ בֵּית דִּין אֶחָד — ⁴שְׁנֵיהֶן בּוֹרְרִין לָהֶן עוֹד אֶחָד. ⁵וַאֲפִילוּ לוֶֹה מָצֵי מְעַכֵּב? ⁶וְהָאָמַר רַבִּי אֶלְעָזָר: לֹא שָׁנוּ אֶלָּא מַלְוֶה; ⁷אֲבָל לֹוֶה, כּוֹפִין אוֹתוֹ וְדָן בְּעִירוֹ! ⁸כְּדְאָמַר רַבִּי יוֹחָנָן: בְּעַרְכָּאוֹת שֶׁבְּסוּרְיָא שָׁנוּ. ⁹הָכָא נָמִי:

RASHI

גמרא הכי קאמר כשזה בורר לו בית דין אחד וזה בורר לו בית דין אחד — וכל אחד פוסל אותו בית דין שבירר חבירו, ואינו רוצה לדון לפניו. שניהן בוררין להם אחד — כלומר אין יכולין לכוף זה את זה, אלא בוררין בית דין שיתרצו בו שניהם. ואפילו לוה מצי מעכב — בתמיה. והאמר רבי אלעזר — לקמן בסוף פירקין (לא, ב). לא שנו — אחד אמר: נידון כאן, ואחד אמר: נלך לבית הוועד — כופין אותו והולך לבית הוועד. [אלא דקאמר מלוה נלך לבית הוועד] — דעבד לוה לאיש מלוה. כדאמר רבי יוחנן — לקמן בשמעתין. בערכאות שבסוריא — שלא היו בקיאין בדין תורה, הלכך אפילו לוה מצי מעכב.

NOTES

chapter that any three judges, even if they are not expert ones, may force litigants to appear before them? He answers: The law in the first chapter, allowing coercion, applies to a defendant who refuses to appear in court altogether; however, our Mishnah is addressing the case of a defendant who has agreed to appear in court, but wishes to appeal the composition of that court.

מַאי זֶה בּוֹרֵר לוֹ אֶחָד **Why does it teach "this litigant selects for himself one"?** Our commentary follows *Rashi's* explanation of the question in the Gemara. *Tosafot* rejects this approach and explains the question as follows: In the case addressed by the Mishnah, two litigants first rejected each other's choice of court before settling on three judges who were acceptable to both of them. The Gemara asks: Why

was it necessary for this case to be taught in the Mishnah as if it were a mandated procedure rather than an individual event? *Ran*, on the other hand, interprets the Gemara's question altogether differently: If we assume that the Mishnah is stating that in the event each litigant rejects the other's choice of a judge (not tribunal), the two litigants need only agree on a single judge to hear their case, the Mishnah would appear to say that the case would then be adjudicated by a single judge. Clearly, this is impossible, as monetary cases require three judges.

בְּעַרְכָּאוֹת שֶׁבְּסוּרְיָא **Lay courts that were in Syria.** Such courts were composed of individuals who were not Torah scholars. Nevertheless, the Gemara implies that, even according to Rabbi Meir, such individuals do indeed qualify

בְּעַרְכָּאוֹת שֶׁבְּסוּרְיָא שָׁנוּ, [1]אֲבָל מוּמְחִין לֹא.

[2]רַב פַּפָּא אָמַר: אֲפִילּוּ תֵּימָא מוּמְחִין, [3]כְּגוֹן בֵּי דִינָא דְּרַב הוּנָא וּדְרַב חִסְדָּא, [4]דְּקָאָמַר לֵיהּ: ״מִי קָא מַטְרַחְנָא לָךְ״?

[5]תְּנַן: וַחֲכָמִים אוֹמְרִים: [6]״שְׁנֵי דַּיָּינִין בּוֹרְרִין לָהֶן עוֹד אֶחָד״. [7]וְאִי סָלְקָא דַּעְתָּךְ כִּדְקָאָמְרִינַן — [8]בֵּית דִּין — [9]בֵּית דִּין, בָּתַר דְּפָסְלִי לְהוּ, [10]אָזְלוּ וּבָרְרוּ לְהוּ בֵּי דִינָא אַחֲרִינֵי? [11]וְעוֹד: מַאי ״זֶה בּוֹרֵר לוֹ אֶחָד וְזֶה בּוֹרֵר לוֹ אֶחָד״?

[12]אֶלָּא, הָכִי קָאָמַר: [13]כְּשֶׁזֶּה בּוֹרֵר לוֹ דַּיָּין אֶחָד וְזֶה בּוֹרֵר לוֹ דַּיָּין אֶחָד — [14]שְׁנֵיהֶן בּוֹרְרִין לָהֶן עוֹד אֶחָד. [15]מַאי שְׁנָא דְּעָבְדִי הָכִי? [16]אָמְרִי בְּמַעְרְבָא מִשְּׁמֵיהּ דְּרַבִּי זֵירָא: מִתּוֹךְ שֶׁזֶּה בּוֹרֵר לוֹ דַּיָּין אֶחָד וְזֶה בּוֹרֵר לוֹ דַּיָּין אֶחָד, [17]וּשְׁנֵיהֶן בּוֹרְרִין לָהֶן עוֹד אֶחָד, [18]יֵצֵא הַדִּין לַאֲמִיתּוֹ.

TRANSLATION AND COMMENTARY

with reference to cases brought before **the lay courts in Syria.** Even a debtor can demand to be heard by a more learned tribunal. [1]**However**, when the court is composed of **expert** judges, the debtor may **not** refuse to appear before them.

רַב פַּפָּא [2]**Rav Pappa**, however, **said: You may even say** that our Mishnah grants the debtor veto power over the selection of a court of **expert** judges, [3]**as with the courts of Rav Huna and of Rav Ḥisda,** which were located in the same city. [4]In such a case, **the debtor can say to** his creditor: **"Am I inconveniencing you** by requesting that we appear before this other court?"

תְּנַן [5]**We have learned** in our Mishnah: **"But the Sages say:** [6]**The two judges select for themselves another one."** [7]Now, **if it were to enter your mind** to say, **as we have said** up till now, [8]that the two litigants may each select **a court** of three judges that is rejected by the other, [9]how could the judges of such **a court, after they have been rejected,** [10]**go and select for themselves another court** before which the litigants must appear? [11]**And, furthermore: What is** the meaning of the Tanna's statement: **"This** litigant **selects for himself one and that** litigant **selects for himself one"?**

אֶלָּא [12]**Rather,** we must say that the Tanna of our Mishnah **is saying:** [13]**After this litigant selects one judge for himself, and that** litigant **selects** a second **judge for himself,** [14]**the two** litigants then **together select** a third **judge for themselves.** [15]**What is the reason** for the litigants **acting** in this manner in choosing a court? [16]**They say in Eretz Israel in the name of Rabbi Zera: As a result of this litigant selecting one judge for himself, and that** litigant **selecting** a second **judge for himself,** [17]**and the two of them** jointly **selecting** an **additional,** third, judge **for themselves,** [18]**the law will be issued in accordance with the truth.** Each judge will give the utmost consideration to the claims of the litigant who chose him, and the litigants will be fully reconciled to the verdict of the court.

LITERAL TRANSLATION

[they taught] about the lay courts in Syria, [1]but not [with reference to] expert [judges].

[2]Rav Pappa said: You may even say [with reference to] expert [judges], [3]such as the court of Rav Huna and of Rav Ḥisda, [4]for the [debtor] can say to him: "Am I inconveniencing you?"

[5]We have learned: "But the Sages say: [6]The two judges select for themselves another one." [7]And if it were to enter your mind as we have said — [8]a court — [9]could a court, after they have been rejected, [10]go and select for themselves another court? [11]And furthermore: Why does [it teach] "this [litigant] selects for himself one [court] and that [litigant] selects for himself one [court]"?

[12]Rather, this is what it says: [13]After this [litigant] selects for himself one judge, and that one selects for himself one judge — [14]the two of them [together] select for themselves an additional [judge]. [15]Why should they do so? [16]They say in Eretz Israel (lit., "the West") in the name of Rabbi Zera: As a result of this [litigant] selecting for himself one judge and that one selecting for himself one judge, [17]and the two of them selecting for themselves another [judge], [18]a true judgment will be issued.

RASHI

בי דינא דרב הונא ורב חסדא — דתרוייהו בחד מקום. ועוד מאי זה בורר — דמשמע דהכי דינא. יצא דין אמת לאמיתו — דלייתי בעלי דינין, דסבר החייב הרי אני בעצמי ביררתי האחד ואם היה יכול להפך בזכותי היה מהפך, והדיינין בעצמן נוחה דעתן להפך בזכות שניהן מפני ששניהם ביררום.

NOTES

as valid judges should the litigants accept them. *Rabbi David Bonfil* attributes this to the presumption that at least one of them is sufficiently learned. *Ran* explains that, even if none of them is sufficiently learned, each community has the power to decide who will adjudicate such cases that arise within their local jurisdiction. Similarly, we find (cited in a later Baraita) that a litigant can even accept as a judge a person who would normally be unfit according to Torah law (such as a relative or a cowherd).

מַאי שְׁנָא דְּעָבְדִי הָכִי **Why should they act thus?** Some of the Rishonim explain the question as follows: If the purpose is to guarantee a balanced court, why not require the two

[1]״וַחֲכָמִים אוֹמְרִים כו׳״. [2]נֵימָא בִּדְרַב יְהוּדָה אָמַר רַב קָמִיפַּלְגִי, [3]דְּאָמַר רַב יְהוּדָה אָמַר רַב: אֵין הָעֵדִים חוֹתְמִין עַל הַשְּׁטָר אֶלָּא אִם כֵּן יוֹדְעִין מִי חוֹתֵם עִמָּהֶן — [4]רַבִּי מֵאִיר לֵית לֵיהּ דְּרַב יְהוּדָה אָמַר רַב, [5]וְרַבָּנַן אִית לְהוּ דְּרַב יְהוּדָה אָמַר רַב? [6]לָא, דְּכוּלֵּי עָלְמָא אִית לְהוּ דְּרַב יְהוּדָה אָמַר רַב; [7]וְדַעַת הַדַּיָּינִין, כּוּלֵּי עָלְמָא לָא פְּלִיגִי דְּבָעֵינַן. [8]כִּי פְּלִיגִי? [9]דַּעַת בַּעֲלֵי דִינִין. [10]רַבִּי מֵאִיר סָבַר: דַּעַת בַּעֲלֵי דִינִין נַמִי בָּעֵינַן. [11]וְרַבָּנַן סָבְרִי: דַּעַת הַדַּיָּינִין בָּעֵינַן; דַּעַת בַּעֲלֵי דִינִין לָא בָּעֵינַן.

LITERAL TRANSLATION

[1]"And the Sages say, etc." [2]Shall we say that they are arguing about [the statement] of Rav Yehudah in the name of Rav, [3]for Rav Yehudah said in the name of Rav: The witnesses do not sign the document unless they know who is signing with them — [4][and] Rabbi Meir does not accept [the ruling] of Rav Yehudah in the name of Rav, [5]and the Rabbis do accept [the ruling] of Rav Yehudah in the name of Rav?

[6]No — for everyone accepts [the ruling] of Rav Yehudah in the name of Rav; [7]and [as far as] the consent of the judges [is concerned], everyone agrees that we need [their consent]. [8]When do they argue? [9][With regard to] the consent of the litigants. [10]Rabbi Meir maintained: We also need the consent of the litigants. [11]And the Sages maintained: We need the consent of the judges; we do not need the consent of the litigants.

TRANSLATION AND COMMENTARY

וַחֲכָמִים אוֹמְרִים [1]The Mishnah continues: **"And the Sages say**: The two judges select for themselves another one." [2]**Shall we say that** Rabbi Meir and the Sages **are arguing about** the principle implied by the statement **of Rav Yehudah in the name of Rav?** [3]**For Rav Yehudah said in the name of Rav:** It is proper that **the witnesses** to a transaction or agreement **do not sign the** attesting **document unless they know** all the witnesses **who** are **signing with them,** lest one of them subsequently be found to be an invalid witness, thereby disqualifying the document. [4]And we might say that **Rabbi Meir does not accept** the principle implied by **the ruling of Rav Yehudah in the name of Rav,** and therefore leaves the selection of the third judge to the litigants. [5]On the other hand, it would appear that **the Rabbis accept** the principle implied by the **ruling of Rav Yehudah in the name of Rav**, which is why they require the first two judges jointly to select the third. The independent choice of the second judge without the consent of the first judge does not contradict the ruling of Rav Yehudah in the name of Rav, because either of the judges could refuse to participate in the court before it is assembled. However, once the first two have agreed to sit with one another, they might be wary of breaking up the entire tribunal and embarrassing the third judge. Therefore, they should be consulted.

לָא [6]The Gemara now rejects the explanations that Rabbi Meir and the Sages disagree about whether to accept the ruling of Rav Yehudah in the name of Rav, and suggests an alternative disagreement. **No,** this is indeed not the case — **for everyone**, including Rabbi Meir, **can accept** the statement **of Rav Yehudah in the name of Rav;** [7]**and** regarding **the opinion of the judges, everyone agrees that we need** to solicit it when completing the composition of the court. [8]**When do** Rabbi Meir and the Sages **disagree?** [9]They disagree with respect to seeking **the consent of the litigants** at that point. [10]**Rabbi Meir maintains: We also need the consent of the litigants.** [11]**And the Sages maintain: We need the consent of the judges,** but **we do not need the consent of the litigants.**

RASHI

אלא אם כן יודעין מי חותם עמהן — שמא יחתמו עמהם עד אחד פסול ומבטל עדות כולם, ונמצאו אלו בושים. **ורבנן אית להו דרב יהודה** — הלכך דעת הדיינין בעינן שיבררו מי ישב עמהם אדם הגון.

NOTES

litigants to agree on the choice of all three judges? The Gemara's answer implies that when each of the disputing parties may designate his own judge, it increases his faith in the court's decision, since he assumes that the judge he chose must have defended whatever merit there was to his claim (*Rabbi Yehudah Almandri, Rabbi Yehonatan of Lunil*).

HALAKHAH

אֵין הָעֵדִים חוֹתְמִין עַל הַשְּׁטָר Witnesses do not sign on the document. "Proper witnesses do not sign on a document unless they know that the other witnesses signing with them are qualified." (*Rambam, Sefer Shoftim, Hilkhot Sanhedrin* 22:10.)

[1]גּוּפָא: [2]אָמַר רַב יְהוּדָה אָמַר רַב: אֵין הָעֵדִים חוֹתְמִין עַל הַשְּׁטָר כו׳. [3]תַּנְיָא נַמִי הָכִי: ״כָּךְ הָיוּ נְקִיֵּי הַדַּעַת שֶׁבִּירוּשָׁלַיִם עוֹשִׂין: [4]לֹא הָיוּ חוֹתְמִין עַל הַשְּׁטָר אֶלָּא אִם כֵּן יוֹדְעִין מִי חוֹתֵם עִמָּהֶן; [5]וְלֹא הָיוּ יוֹשְׁבִין בַּדִּין אֶלָּא אִם כֵּן יוֹדְעִין מִי יוֹשֵׁב עִמָּהֶן; [6]וְלֹא הָיוּ נִכְנָסִין בִּסְעוּדָה אֶלָּא אִם כֵּן יוֹדְעִין מִי מֵסֵב עִמָּהֶן״.

[7]״זֶה פּוֹסֵל דַּיָּינוֹ כו׳״. [8]כָּל כְּמִינֵּיהּ דְּפָסֵיל דַּיָּינֵי? [9]אָמַר רַבִּי יוֹחָנָן: בַּעֲרְכָּאוֹת שֶׁבְּסוּרְיָא שָׁנוּ, [10]אֲבָל מוּמְחִים לֹא.

[11]הָא מִדְּקָתָנֵי סֵיפָא: [12]״וַחֲכָמִים אוֹמְרִים: אֵימָתַי? [13]בִּזְמַן שֶׁמֵּבִיא רְאָיָה שֶׁהֵן

LITERAL TRANSLATION

[1][Returning to] the statement quoted above (lit., "the thing itself"): [2]Rav Yehudah said in the name of Rav: The witnesses do not sign the document, etc. [3]It was also taught thus: "The clear-minded [men] who were in Jerusalem would do as follows: [4]They would not sign the document unless they knew who was signing with them; [5]and they would not sit in judgment unless they knew who was sitting with them; [6]and they would not enter [to dine at] a feast unless they knew who was dining with them."

[7]"This [litigant] may reject that one's judge, etc." [8]Is it in his power to reject judges? [9]Rabbi Yoḥanan said: They taught [there] with reference to the lay courts in Syria, [10]but not [with reference to] expert judges.

[11]Surely, since the last clause teaches: [12]"But the Sages say: When? [13]When [the litigant] brings proof about them

TRANSLATION AND COMMENTARY

גּוּפָא [1]The Gemara now examines the statement of Rav Yehudah in the name of Rav and quotes a Baraita that supports his position. **Returning to the statement quoted above:** [2]**Rav Yehudah said in the name of Rav: The witnesses** who are party to a transaction or agreement **do not sign the** attesting **document unless they know** all the witnesses **who** are **signing with them.** A Baraita sheds further light on this ruling: [3]**It was also taught thus: "The clear-minded** men **who were in Jerusalem would do as follows:** [4]**They would not sign on a document unless they knew who was signing with them;** [5]**they would not sit** on a court **in judgment** of others **unless they knew who was sitting with them;** [6]**and they would not participate at a feast unless they knew who was dining with them."**

[7]The Gemara now discusses the next clause of the Mishnah: **"This litigant may reject that** litigant's choice of **judge,** just as that litigant can reject this one's choice of judge; these are the words of Rabbi Meir." [8]The Gemara asks: **Is it in** the litigant's **power to reject** a recognized **judge** by merely stating that he does not wish to appear before him? [9]It replies: We should understand the Mishnah according to **Rabbi Yoḥanan,** who **said** that the Mishnah **taught** its opinion only **with reference to** a judge of **the lay courts in Syria** whose members were not learned in Torah, but who received a mandate from their communities to serve as judges; [10]**but** if the judges chosen to hear the case were recognized **experts** in Torah law and jurisprudence, then even Rabbi Meir would agree that the litigants may **not** disqualify them.

הָא [11]**Surely,** the implication is that Rabbi Meir is also speaking of expert judges, **since the last clause of** the Mishnah **teaches:** [12]**"But the Sages say: When is** one litigant allowed to reject the other's choice of judge? [13]**When he brings proof about** the contested judges **that they are** either **related** to one of the litigants or to

RASHI

ואין נכנסין לסעודה כו׳ — שגנאי הוא לתלמידי חכמים ליסב אלא עם הארץ בסעודה. **זה פוסל דיינו של זה וזה פוסל דיינו של זה** — יכול לומר לו: לא אדון לפניו (עד כאן).

NOTES

נְקִיֵּי הַדַּעַת שֶׁבִּירוּשָׁלַיִם The clear-minded men who were in Jerusalem. The reference is to men of great prominence who could not afford to waste their time attesting to documents that might later be invalidated because improper witnesses had signed them (*Rabbi Yehonatan of Lunil*). Furthermore, it would bring such men undue humiliation to have their signatures invalidated because the other witnesses were disqualified (*Rabbi Yehudah Almandri*).

HALAKHAH

לֹא הָיוּ יוֹשְׁבִים בַּדִּין They would not sit in judgment. "A judicious man should not agree to sit on a court unless he is familiar with the other men sitting with him, lest they be exposed as corrupt and he be implicated by association." (*Shulḥan Arukh, Ḥoshen Mishpat* 3:4.)

וְלֹא הָיוּ נִכְנָסִין בִּסְעוּדָה They would not enter into a feast. "The wise and virtuous men of Jerusalem would not participate in a feast unless they knew with whom they were dining, as it is unbecoming for a scholar to mix with men ignorant in Torah." (*Shulḥan Arukh, Oraḥ Ḥayyim* 170:20.)

קְרוֹבִין אוֹ פְּסוּלִין; [1] אֲבָל, אִם הָיוּ כְּשֵׁרִין אוֹ מוּמְחִין מִפִּי בֵּית דִּין, אֵינוֹ יָכוֹל לְפוֹסְלָן״, [2] מִכְּלָל דְּרַבִּי מֵאִיר מוּמְחִין נַמִּי קָאָמַר!

[3] הָכִי קָאָמַר: אֲבָל אִם הָיוּ כְּשֵׁרִין נַעֲשׂוּ כְּמוּמְחִין מִפִּי בֵּית דִּין, וְאֵינוֹ יָכוֹל לְפוֹסְלָן.

[4] תָּא שְׁמַע: ״אָמְרוּ לוֹ לְרַבִּי מֵאִיר: [5] לֹא כָּל הֵימֶנּוּ שֶׁפּוֹסֵל דַּיָּין שֶׁמּוּמְחֶה לָרַבִּים״!

[6] אֵימָא: [7] ״לֹא כָּל הֵימֶנּוּ שֶׁפּוֹסֵל דַּיָּין שֶׁהִמְחוּהוּ רַבִּים עֲלֵיהֶם״. [8] תַּנְיָא נַמִּי הָכִי: ״לְעוֹלָם, פּוֹסֵל וְהוֹלֵךְ, עַד שֶׁיְּקַבֵּל עָלָיו בֵּית דִּין שֶׁמּוּמְחֶה לָרַבִּים. [9] דִּבְרֵי רַבִּי מֵאִיר״.

[10] וְהָא עֵדִים כְּמוּמְחִין דָּמֵי, וְאָמַר רַבִּי מֵאִיר: [11] ״זֶה פּוֹסֵל עֵדָיו שֶׁל זֶה וְזֶה פּוֹסֵל עֵדָיו שֶׁל זֶה״!

LITERAL TRANSLATION

that they are related or unfit; [1] however, if they were fit or [declared] expert by a court, he cannot reject them," [2] this implies that Rabbi Meir is also speaking of expert [judges]! [3] This is what they said: However, if they were fit, they are considered as [if they were declared] expert [judges] by a court, and he cannot reject them.

[4] Come [and] hear: "They said to Rabbi Meir: [5] It is not in [the litigant's] power to reject a publicly acknowledged expert judge"!

[6] Say: [7] "It is not in [the litigant's] power to reject a judge whom [members of] the public have declared for themselves as an expert." [8] It was also taught thus: "In fact, he may continue to reject [the other litigant's judges] until he accepts upon himself a court that is publicly acknowledged as expert. [9] [These are] the words of Rabbi Meir."

[10] But surely witnesses are considered as experts, and Rabbi Meir said: [11] "This [litigant] may reject that one's witnesses and that one may reject this one's witnesses"!

TRANSLATION AND COMMENTARY

one of the other judges, **or** are **unfit** for reasons of corrupt character; [1] **however, if they were** found to be **fit or** were **declared** to be **expert** judges **by a** recognized **court, he cannot reject them."** [2] **This** teaching of the Sages **implies that Rabbi Meir**, who argues with them and permits the litigant to reject a judge, **is also speaking of** an **expert** judge. [3] To avoid this interpretation, the Gemara proposes: Rather, **this is what** the Sages said: **However, if the** contested judges **were** found to be **fit, they are considered as** if they were **declared experts by a** recognized **court; and** thus, dissatisfied litigants **cannot reject them.** The Sages only disagree with Rabbi Meir about judges chosen to sit on the court whose qualification was based on convention rather than knowledge.

תָּא שְׁמַע [4] **Come and hear** a Baraita that contradicts this view: "The Sages **said to Rabbi Meir:** [5] **It is not in the litigant's power to reject a publicly acknowledged expert judge"!** This Baraita demonstrates that Rabbi Meir did indeed maintain that a litigant could oppose the selection of a judge, even if he is a recognized expert!

אֵימָא [6] The Gemara counters: **Say** that the above Baraita actually reads as follows: "The Sages said to Rabbi Meir: [7] It is not **in the litigant's power to reject** a lay **judge** who has been **publicly declared** to be sufficiently **expert** to adjudicate their claims." [8] **It was also taught thus** in a Baraita: **"In fact,** the litigant **may continue to reject** judges chosen by his adversary **until he** is forced to **accept a court that is publicly acknowledged as expert.** [9] These are **the words of Rabbi Meir."**

וְהָא עֵדִים [10] The Gemara now attempts once more to bring a contradiction to our understanding that Rabbi Meir does not allow a litigant to reject an expert judge. Basing itself on a later clause in the Mishnah, the Gemara states: **But surely** all **witnesses are considered** to be **like experts** with regard to the testimony they give**, and** nevertheless **Rabbi Meir said** further on in our Mishnah: [11] **"This** litigant may **reject that** litigant's **witnesses, and that** litigant may **reject this** litigant's **witnesses."** If witnesses are equivalent to qualified judges, and if Rabbi Meir grants to litigants the right to reject each other's witnesses, then they should be able to reject qualified judges.

RASHI

הכי קאמר אבל אם היו כשרין – שאינם קרובין ולא פסולין, אף על פי שהן יושבי קרנות – **נעשו כמומחין. עד שיקבל עליו בפני בית דין מומחה** – אלמא: במומחין מודה רבי מאיר. **והא עדים כמומחין דמו** – אם אינם קרובים או פסולים.

NOTES

עַד שֶׁיְּקַבֵּל עָלָיו בֵּית דִּין **Until he accepts upon himself a court which is publicly acknowledged as expert.** There are those who read the Baraita as follows: "...until he complains about it [the root קבל can also denote 'complaint'] *before* a court that is publicly acknowledged as expert." According to this reading, the Baraita tells us that a litigant cannot contest his adversary's choice of judge unless he registers his complaint before an expert court (*Rashash*).

[1]הָא אִיתְּמַר עֲלָהּ: [2]"אָמַר רֵישׁ לָקִישׁ: 'פֶּה קָדוֹשׁ יֹאמַר דָּבָר זֶה'"? [3]תְּנֵי: "עֵדוֹ".

[4]עֵדוֹ לְמַאי? [5]אִילֵימָא לְמָמוֹן, [6]רַחֲמָנָא פָּסְלֵיהּ. [7]אִי לִשְׁבוּעָה, הֵימוּנֵי מְהֵימַן כְּבֵי תְרֵי! [8]לְעוֹלָם לְמָמוֹן, [9]לָא צְרִיכָא דְּקַבְּלֵיהּ עֲלֵיהּ כְּבֵי תְרֵי.

[10]מַאי קָא מַשְׁמַע לָן — דְּמָצֵי הֲדַר בֵּיהּ? [11]תָּנֵינָא: "אָמַר לוֹ: 'נֶאֱמָן עָלַי אַבָּא', [12]'נֶאֱמָן עָלַי אָבִיךָ', [13]'נֶאֱמָנִין עָלַי שְׁלֹשָׁה רוֹעֵי בָקָר' — [14]רַבִּי מֵאִיר אוֹמֵר: יָכוֹל לַחֲזוֹר בּוֹ, [15]וַחֲכָמִים אוֹמְרִים: אֵינוֹ יָכוֹל

LITERAL TRANSLATION

[1]Surely, it was stated concerning this: [2]"Resh Lakish said: 'Can a holy mouth say such a thing?!'" [3]Teach: "His [sole] witness."

[4]His witness for what? [5]If you say for [collecting] money, [6]the Torah disqualified him; [7]if for [administering] an oath he is surely believed as two [witnesses]! [8]In fact, for [collecting] money, [9]it is needed only when he accepted [the witness] upon himself as two [witnesses].

[10]What is he telling us — that he may retract? [11]We have learned: "[If] he [one litigant] said to [the other]: 'Father is trustworthy to me,' [12]'Your father is trustworthy to me,' [13]'The three cattle herders are trustworthy to me' — [14]Rabbi Meir says: He can retract, [15]and the Sages say: He cannot

RASHI

דקבלו עליו בתרי – בתחלת דבריהם קבלוהו עליהם בשנים. **נאמן עלי וכו'** – בדיינין קמיירי, מדקתני שלשה רועי בקר.

TRANSLATION AND COMMENTARY

הָא אִיתְּמַר עֲלָהּ [1]The Gemara, however, resolves this apparent contradiction by reporting the following teaching: **Surely it was stated concerning this** latter remark by Rabbi Meir in our Mishnah: [2]**Resh Lakish said:** Can **a holy mouth**, such as that possessed by Rabbi Meir, **say such a thing?** Surely one cannot simply reject perfectly good witnessses! Rather, one must **learn** the Mishnah as follows: [3]"This litigant can invalidate that litigant's **sole witness** [in the singular]" and vice versa. Since it is generally necessary to bring at least two witnesses in support of a monetary claim, Rabbi Meir is telling us that any litigant can invalidate testimony offered by a single witness.

עֵדוֹ לְמַאי [4]Now that we have explained that Rabbi Meir permits the litigant to invalidate the testimony of a single witness, the Gemara attempts to clarify the circumstances of such a disqualification: **For what** purpose did the claimant bring **his witness** in the situation addressed above by Rabbi Meir? [5]**If you say** that he brought him to testify in support of his claim **to collect money** that the defendant owed him — [6]surely **the Torah** itself (see Deuteronomy 19:15) already **disqualified** the testimony of a sole witness to create a liability! [7]And **if** you say that he brought him **for** the purpose of forcing the court to **administer an oath** to the defendant affirming that he has no obligation — then **surely** a single witness in that situation should be **believed** to the same extent **as two** witnesses would be believed elsewhere, since the Torah itself acknowledges that the testimony of one witness is effective for that purpose (see *Ketubot* 87b)! [8]**In fact,** the claimant brought his witness **for** the purpose of collecting **money** from the defendant, in which case Rabbi Meir's statement appears to be superfluous, since the Torah has already made it clear that a single witness cannot create liability. [9]Nevertheless, his statement **would still be needed if** the defendant initially **accepted upon himself** the testimony of this single witness **as** if it were equivalent to the testimony of **two.** You might think that the litigant could not change his mind, but Rabbi Meir teaches that he retains the power to reject the witness.

מַאי קָא מַשְׁמַע לָן [10]**What is** Rabbi Meir then **telling us** — simply **that he may retract** his initial consent to accept otherwise inadequate testimony? [11]But **we learn** this from a later Mishnah (below, 24b): "If one litigant **said to** the other: 'My **father is trustworthy to me** as a judge in our case,' or: [12]**'Your father is trustworthy to me** as a judge in our case,' [13]or even: **'Three** ignorant **cattle herders are trustworthy to me** as judges in our case' — [14]**Rabbi Meir says: He can** subsequently **retract** his consent and insist that the case be submitted only before individuals who are qualified to judge according to Torah law. [15]**The Sages say:**

HALAKHAH

לְמָמוֹן, רַחֲמָנָא פָּסְלֵיהּ **For collecting money, the Torah disqualified him.** "A single witness cannot engender financial liability on the part of a defendant by virtue of his testimony." (*Rambam, Sefer Shofetim, Hilkhot Edut* 5:1.)

לִשְׁבוּעָה הֵימוּנֵי מְהֵימַן כְּבֵי תְרֵי **For an oath, he is surely believed like two.** "If one claims to be owed money or a deposit and the accused denies the debt altogether — and should the claimant have only one witness who supports his contention, the defendant is Biblically required by virtue of that testimony to take an oath affirming that he does not owe the claimant anything." (*Shulḥan Arukh, Ḥoshen Mishpat* 87:1.)

לַחֲזוֹר בּוֹ״. [23B] [1]וְאָמַר רַב דִּימִי בְּרֵיהּ דְּרַב נַחְמָן בְּרֵיהּ דְּרַב יוֹסֵף: כְּגוֹן דְּקַבְּלֵיהּ עֲלֵיהּ בְּחַד! [2]צְרִיכָא. [3]דְּאִי תְּנָא ״אַבָּא״ וְ״אָבִיךָ״, [4]בְּהָא קָאָמְרִי רַבָּנַן דְּלָא מָצֵי הָדַר בֵּיהּ — [5]מִשּׁוּם דְּ״אַבָּא״ וְ״אָבִיךָ״ חֲזוּ לְעָלְמָא. [6]אֲבָל חַד כְּבֵי תְרֵי — [7]דִּלְעָלְמָא לָא חֲזֵי — [8]אֵימָא: מוֹדוּ לֵיהּ לְרַבִּי מֵאִיר. [9]וְאִי אַשְׁמְעִינַן בְּהָא — [10]בְּהָא קָאָמַר רַבִּי מֵאִיר, [11]אֲבָל בְּהַהִיא, אֵימָא: מוֹדוּ לְהוּ לְרַבָּנַן. [12]צְרִיכָא.

LITERAL TRANSLATION

retract." [23B] [1]And Rav Dimi, son of Rav Naḥman, son of Rav Yosef, said: Such as when [the litigant] accepted him upon himself as one [of the judges]! [2]It is necessary [to state both]. [3]For had he taught "father" and "your father," [4][we might have thought that] in this [case] the Sages say that they find he may not retract — [5]for "father" and "your father" are fit [to judge] elsewhere. [6]But [as for accepting] one [witness] as two — [7]who is not fit [to testify] elsewhere — [8]say: They concede to Rabbi Meir. [9]And had he taught us in this [other case] — [10][we might have thought that] Rabbi Meir stated [his ruling] in this [case], [11]but in that [case], say: He concedes to the Rabbis. [12][Therefore] it is necessary [to say both].

TRANSLATION AND COMMENTARY

He cannot retract." [23B] [1]**And Rav Dimi, son of Rav Naḥman, son of Rav Yosef, said:** This later Mishnah refers to a situation **such as when** the litigant **accepted upon himself** his otherwise ineligible relative **as one** of the judges, the remaining positions being filled by qualified candidates. Nevertheless, we see from this Mishnah that, according to Rabbi Meir, a litigant can retract his initial consent to an improper judicial procedure. Why, then, is it necessary for our Mishnah to reiterate this ruling with regard to a litigant who consented to testimony from only one witness?

צְרִיכָא [2]The Gemara now replies: **It is** indeed **necessary** for the positions of both Rabbi Meir and the Sages to be reiterated in the context of our Mishnah, [3]**for had** they only been **taught** in the later Mishnah regarding a litigant who declared "my **father** is trustworthy" or "**your father** is trustworthy" to adjudicate this case, [4]**we might have thought** as follows: **In this** case alone **the Sages teach that** the litigant **may not** later **retract** his initial consent — [5]**for** in truth "my **father" and "your father" are fit** to serve as judges **elsewhere,** but are disqualified here because of their relationship to one of the litigants. [6]**However, in the case of** a litigant who declared himself ready **to accept** the testimony of **one** witness **as** if there were **two** witnesses [7](seeing that a single witness **is not fit** to testify **anywhere else**), [8]**say** that the Sages would **concede to Rabbi Meir** that the litigant could later revoke his consent! Consequently it was necessary for both positions to be restated in the context of our Mishnah. [9]Conversely, **had** the positions of Rabbi Meir and the Sages been **taught** to **us** only **in this** case of our Mishnah, regarding a litigant who agreed to the testimony of a sole witness, [10]**we might have thought thus: In this** case alone does **Rabbi Meir teach** that the litigant may revoke his consent, since a solitary witness is generally unacceptable; [11]**but regarding** the appointment of a relative as one of his judges, **say** that Rabbi Meir would **concede to the Sages** that he may not revoke his consent since the relative is fit to serve as a judge in other cases! [12]**Therefore, it is necessary** to have this dispute spelled out in **both** passages.

RASHI

ואמר רב דימי — הא דקתני נאמן עלי אבא — כגון דקבליה עליה כחד דיין ויש שנים כשרין עמו, ואפילו הכי כיון דפסול מדאורייתא מצי הדר ביה, הכא נמי כיון דחד לממון לא מתכשר מצי הדר ביה.

NOTES

כְּגוֹן דְּקַבְּלֵיהּ עֲלֵיהּ בְּחַד Such as when he accepted him upon himself as one. *Tosafot* points out that Rav Dimi's statement is quoted in order to strengthen the Gemara's challenge to our Mishnah from the Baraita: Had the Baraita been referring to a litigant who, in addition to accepting a relative as a judge in his case, agreed to grant that individual the equivalent weight of two judges, it would have been clear why the dispute between Rabbi Meir and the Sages had to be reiterated in the context of our Mishnah. Our Mishnah is dealing with a litigant who initially consented to accept testimony from a single witness, but with the equivalent without any additional concession. Hence, had it not been stated otherwise in our Mishnah, one might have thought that in such a case Rabbi Meir agrees with the Sages that one's initial consent may not be revoked. *Ran* elaborates on this explanation by *Tosafot*: One might think that our Mishnah could be challenged directly from the case in the Baraita of the three cattle herders, where it is clear even without Rav Dimi that only one concession was made by the litigant (acceptance of their ignorance). However, in that case, a concession was made three times, in regard to each individual cattle herder, which renders the case altogether different from that of our Mishnah. Only by appending Rav Dimi's statement to the Baraita can we present a case that is truly comparable to the case of our Mishnah, thereby allowing the Gemara to ask why the dispute between Rabbi Meir and the Sages had to be stated in both sources.

דִּלְעָלְמָא לָא חֲזֵי Who ordinarily is not fit. The question is asked: How could we have thought that the Sages agree

LITERAL TRANSLATION

[1]Surely, since the first clause teaches "his judge" and the second clause teaches "his witnesses," [2]it follows that it is teaching literally!

[3]Rabbi Elazar said: [Rabbi Meir teaches] when [the litigant] and another came to reject [the witnesses].

[4]Is this in [the litigant's] power? He is an interested party (lit., "biased in his testimony"). [5]Rav Aha, the son of Rav Ika, said: Such as when he accused him of [being generally] disqualified.

[1]הָא, מִדְּקָתָנֵי רֵישָׁא "דַּיָּינוֹ" וְסֵיפָא "עֵדָיו", [2]אַלְמָא דַּוְקָא קָתָנֵי!

[3]אָמַר רַבִּי אֶלְעָזָר: בְּבָא הוּא וְאַחֵר לְפוֹסְלָן.

[4]כָּל כְּמִינֵּיהּ? נוֹגֵעַ בְּעֵדוּתוֹ הוּא! [5]אָמַר רַב אַחָא בְּרֵיהּ דְּרַב אִיקָא: כְּגוֹן שֶׁקָּרָא עָלָיו עַרְעָר.

TRANSLATION AND COMMENTARY

הָא מִדְּקָתָנֵי רֵישָׁא [1]The Gemara now questions Resh Lakish's explanation that the right of a litigant to reject witnesses, as taught in our Mishnah by Rabbi Meir, refers to a sole witness: Can one **truly** dismiss the reading we have of our Mishnah ("his witnesses") as an inaccurate one? Since **the first clause** of the Mishnah **teaches** its law employing the singular expression, **"his judge,"** which we take to mean that one litigant may reject the judge chosen by his opponent, while **the latter clause** of the Mishnah, currently under consideration, **teaches** its law using the plural expression, **"his witnesses"** — [2]**it follows that** the Mishnah **is** literal in its **teaching** and is referring to rejecting a pair of witnesses. Moreover, if one would suggest that an error occurred in the process of transcribing the Mishnaic text, such errors would tend to replace variance with uniformity. It is not likely that a scribe would take the postulated uniform text — "his judge" and "his witness" — and corrupt it to read "his judge" and "his witnesses." How, then, can Resh Lakish suggest that an error occurred in transcribing the latter clause of the Mishnah, replacing the singular form, "witness," with the anomalous plural, "witnesses"?

אָמַר רַבִּי אֶלְעָזָר [3]We must, therefore, reject Resh Lakish's reading and revert to our original understanding of the Mishnah: The litigant is disqualifying not a sole witness but one or both of a pair of witnesses. However, we are again faced with our initial difficulty: How, according to Rabbi Meir, can a litigant disqualify perfectly legitimate witnesses? The Gemara now offers an alternative interpretation of the Mishnah. **Rabbi Elazar said:** The Mishnah refers to a case **where** the litigant **and another** individual **came** together as a pair in order **to reject** his opponent's witnesses by testifying that they are unfit. Rabbi Meir maintained that the litigant and his colleague are indeed believed, since they constitute a pair of witnesses and thus the opponent's witnesses are disqualified.

כָּל כְּמִינֵּיהּ [4]The Gemara now attempts to clarify Rabbi Elazar's interpretation of the Mishnah: **Is it** really **in the litigant's power** to testify as one of a pair of witnesses and invalidate his opponent's witnesses? How can Rabbi Meir maintain his ruling when the **litigant is an interested party** and only impartial witnesses are allowed to testify? [5]**Rav Aha the son of Rav Ika said** in response: The Mishnah is not dealing with a litigant who is merely seeking to dismiss the opposing witness in his case alone, such as his testifying that that witness is related to his opponent; rather, it is speaking of a case **where** the litigant **accused** the proposed witness **of** being generally **disqualified,** and barred from testifying in any case. The Gemara continues,

RASHI

אלמא דווקא קתני – מדשני במילתיה, דבדיינין נקט לשון יחיד ובעדים נקט לשון רבים וליתא לדריש לקיש, והדרא קושיין לדוכתא: והא עדים כמומחין דמו. **אמר רבי אלעזר** – סיפא גבי עדים בבא הוא ואחר לפוסלן, דהוו להו תרי דמסהדי אפסולה ומהימני, ודיינין בערכאות שבסוריא כדאוקימנא, ולא פסול ממש קאמר אלא בעינא בי דינא מעליא. **נוגע בעדותו הוא** – האי בעל דין, דמשום דלא ליסהוד עליה קאתי למיפסליה. **שקרא עליו ערער** – בעל דין אומר לפנינו על מה הוא פוסלו, ויש אחר עמו. **ערער** – שמץ של פסול.

NOTES

with Rabbi Meir about judges or witnesses who are generally unfit (unlike those who are only occasionally unfit, such as relatives), when the Baraita itself cites the case of three cattle herders — regarded as generally unfit — among those cases subject to dispute? Some Rishonim suggest that cattle herders do not qualify as "generally unfit," in the sense intended by the Gemara, since their ineligibility is only Rabbinic in nature (*Rabbenu Shimshon of Sens, Ran*). *Rosh* points out that when cattle herders are selected as judges, they can compensate for their ignorance by inquiring about the law.

HALAKHAH

בְּבָא הוּא וְאַחֵר לְפוֹסְלָן When he and another came to reject them. "If one of the litigants came, even with another, in order to invalidate his opponent's choice of witness or judge, we do not accept his testimony — regardless of whether it aims at direct disqualification, such as testifying to his being a robber, or indirect disqualification, such as testifying to a flaw in his family lineage." This accords with the opinion of the Sages as understood by Rabbi Elazar. (*Shulhan Arukh, Hoshen Mishpat* 13:4.)

[1]עַרְעָר דְּמַאי? [2]אִילֵימָא עַרְעָר דְּגַזְלָנוּתָא, [3]כָּל כְּמִינֵיהּ? [4]נוֹגֵעַ בְּעֵדוּתוֹ הוּא! [5]אֶלָּא, עַרְעָר דִּפְגַם מִשְׁפָּחָה. [6]רַבִּי מֵאִיר סָבַר: הָנֵי אַמִּשְׁפָּחָה קָמַסְהֲדֵי [7]וְאִידהוּ מִמֵּילָא קָפָסֵיל. [8]וְרַבָּנַן סָבְרִי: סוֹף סוֹף נוֹגֵעַ בְּעֵדוּתוֹ הוּא.

[9]כִּי אֲתָא רַב דִּימִי, אָמַר רַבִּי יוֹחָנָן: [10]מַחֲלוֹקֶת בִּשְׁתֵּי כִּיתֵּי עֵדִים. [11]דְּרַבִּי מֵאִיר סָבַר:

LITERAL TRANSLATION

[1]Which disqualification? [2]If you say a disqualification [due to] robbery, [3]is this in [the litigant's] power? [4]He is an interested party (lit., "biased in his testimony")! [5]Rather, a disqualification [due to] familial blemish. [6]Rabbi Meir maintained: These [witnesses] are testifying about [his] family [7]and he is disqualified [only] indirectly. [8]And the Sages maintained: Ultimately [the litigant] is an interested party (lit., "biased in his testimony").

[9]When Rav Dimi came, he said in the name of Rabbi Yoḥanan: [10]The dispute concerns two sets of witnesses. [11]For Rabbi Meir maintains:

TRANSLATION AND COMMENTARY

asking: [1]**Which disqualification** is referred to here? [2]**If** you wish to **say** that the **disqualification** is based on the commission of a crime such as **robbery** (see 27a) — then let the previous question return: [3]**Is it** really **in the litigant's power to** invalidate his opponent's witness? [4]**He is an interested party,** his own testimony is invalid. [5]**Rather,** it must be that the Mishnah is referring to **a disqualification due to a blemish** in **family** lineage, such as being descended from a family of slaves. [6]**Rabbi Meir maintains** that a litigant may indeed join with another to testify to the existence of such a blemish, since the witnesses **are testifying about** the witness's **family** as a whole. [7]The witness in this case **is only disqualified indirectly** because of his stigmatized family. [8]**The Sages,** however, **maintain** that the litigant is not believed even in this case, for **ultimately he is** still an **interested party.**

כִּי אֲתָא [9]**When Rav Dimi arrived** in Babylonia from Eretz Israel**, in the name of Rabbi Yoḥanan he** offered a different explanation of the dispute in our Mishnah between Rabbi Meir and the Sages concerning the disqualification of witnesses: [10]**The dispute** in fact **concerns** a case of **two sets of witnesses** summoned by one of the litigants in support of his claim. In such a case, Rabbi Meir maintains that the opposing litigant can testify with another man for the purpose of disqualifying one of these two pairs since the remaining pair of witnesses can still support his opponent's case. Moreover, the first pair of witnesses are permanently disqualified, even if the second pair should never materialize, [11]**for Rabbi Meir maintained**

RASHI

דגזלנותא — מעיד עליו הוא ואחר שגזלן הוא. **נוגע בעדותו הוא** — משום דלא נסהיד עליה קאמר. **דפגם משפחה** — עבד הוא, ממשפחת עבד שלא נשתחרר בא ופסול הוא ומשפחתו. **אמשפחה קמסהדי** — ולאו משום האי לחודיה מסהדי, הלכך סהדותא אחרינא הוא, ולאו כנוגע בעדות דמי. **מחלוקת בשתי כיתי עדים** — שאמר בעל דין בפנינו: יש לי שתי כיתי עדים בדבר זה, הביא כת ראשונה, ועמד הלוה ואחר ואמר: פסולין הן, דהשתא לאו כנוגע בעדות הוא שהרי אמר מלוה שיש לו כת אחרת, ואם ביקש ולא מצא — יפסיד, דקסבר רבי מאיר צריך בעל דין לברר ולהעמיד על האמת כל דבריו שטוען בבית דין, והני מיפסלי אף לעדיות אחרות. ואם ביקש ומצא כת אחרת כשירה, אף על פי שראשונה נפסלה הרי בירר דבריו שאמר להביאם והביא, והוא לא דק דסבור שכשרים היו.

NOTES

מַחֲלוֹקֶת בִּשְׁתֵּי כִּיתֵּי עֵדִים **The dispute concerns two sets of witnesses.** Our commentary follows the first reading and interpretation of the Gemara offered by *Rashi* and supported by *Rabbenu Tam*. *Ramah* explains the Gemara somewhat differently: If one side to a dispute brings forth a set of witnesses and claims before the court to have a second set of witnesses, Rabbi Meir and the Sages in our Mishnah argue about whether the opposing litigant can opt to reject the first pair of witnesses without any proof of their ineligibility and insist that the disputant produce his alleged second pair. According to Rabbi Meir, he has that right, since it in no way weakens his disputant's position. Should the disputant be unable to produce a second pair of witnesses as claimed, Rabbi Meir maintains that the rejection of the first pair is upheld. Because the disputant was unable to verify his original claim to having additional testimony, his opponent can accuse him of being untruthful regarding the fitness of the first set of witnesses. The Sages disagree with Rabbi Meir and deny the opponent his right to reject the first set of witnesses. According to them, one need not verify every claim made before the court, and thus the disputant cannot be faulted for failing to produce the second set of witnesses.

Rambam explains the dispute between Rabbi Meir and the Sages as follows: If the disputant brought forth two different sets of witnesses in order to support his claim, and his opponent challenged their validity, Rabbi Meir maintains that we force the disputant to prove the validity of all four witnesses. This is due to the suspicion that the disputant himself creates by bringing two sets of witnesses in order to support the same claim. Suspecting that the disputant may be aware of one pair's ineligibility, Rabbi Meir requires him to prove the validity of at least one of the sets of witnesses if he wishes to be believed. The Sages disagree and say that it is unnecessary for the disputant to prove anything with regard to his witnesses. They assume that he brought more than one set of witnesses merely in order to reinforce his claim and demonstrate the truth of his case.

TRANSLATION AND COMMENTARY

that whoever claims to have witnesses who can support his claim **must verify** that **contention** in its entirety. Hence, even if the first pair were not disqualified by the opposing litigant, their testimony would be irrelevant unless the second pair of witnesses were produced as well. [1]**The Sages,** on the other hand, maintain that a litigant may never testify to invalidate his disputant's witnesses, even if the disputant claimed to have more than one pair of witnesses to support his case. This is because the Sages **maintain** that a litigant who claims to have several sets of witnesses to support his position **does not need to verify this contention** before the court and can rely upon one pair alone. Thus, if we were to accept the other litigant's testimony and disqualify one pair of witnesses, and no other witnesses were produced, it would mean that the litigant was testifying in his own behalf, which is not allowed. [2]**However, regarding** a litigant who claims he has **one set of witnesses** in support of his position — [3]**all agree**, even Rabbi Meir, **that the opposing** litigant **cannot disqualify them** by joining with another in presenting damaging testimony, since he is an interested party.

אָמְרוּ לְפָנָיו [4]After citing Rabbi Yoḥanan's opinion, Rav Dimi added the following: **Rav Ammi and Rav Assi said before** Rabbi Yoḥanan in response to his position: [5]**What is** the law if **only one pair** of witnesses were brought by the claimant? The Rabbis in Babylonia questioned Rav Dimi: [6]Did they indeed ask what the law is if **there were only one set of witnesses?** [7]**Surely you**, Rav Dimi, have already **said** in Rabbi Yoḥanan's name: **However, regarding one set** of witnesses — [8]**all agree that** the opposing litigant **cannot disqualify them!** [9]**Rather**, say that the question posed by Rav Ammi and Rav Assi to Rabbi Yoḥanan was as follows: **What is** the law if initially there were two sets of witnesses, and after the first set were disqualified through testimony offered by the opposing litigant, **the second set were found to be** ineligible, either because they proved to be **related** to one of the parties **or** were **unfit** for reasons of character? In that case would Rabbi Meir agree with the Sages, that the initial testimony of the opposing litigant is disregarded since he is an interested party, or would Rabbi Meir uphold the opposing litigant's testimony, since at the time it was offered the second set of witnesses were still qualified? Thus his testimony at that point could not have affected his fate! [10]Rabbi Yoḥanan **said** in reply **to** Rav Ammi and Rav Assi: Rabbi Meir would indeed uphold the testimony of **the first witnesses,** the opposing litigant and his colleague, **who testified** before it was known

צָרִיךְ לְבָרֵר, [1]וְרַבָּנַן סָבְרִי: אֵינוֹ צָרִיךְ לְבָרֵר. [2]אֲבָל בְּכַת אַחַת, [3]דִּבְרֵי הַכֹּל אֵין יָכוֹל לְפוֹסְלָן. [4]אָמְרוּ לְפָנָיו רַב אַמִי וְרַב אַסִי: [5]אֵין שָׁם אֶלָּא כַּת אַחַת, מַהוּ? [6]אֵין שָׁם אֶלָּא כַּת אַחַת? [7]וְהָאָמְרַתְּ: "אֲבָל בְּכַת אַחַת — [8]דִּבְרֵי הַכֹּל אֵין יָכוֹל לְפוֹסְלָן"! [9]אֶלָּא: נִמְצֵאת כַּת שְׁנִיָּה קְרוֹבִין אוֹ פְּסוּלִין, מַהוּ? [10]אָמַר לָהֶן: כְּבָר הֵעִידוּ עֵדִים

LITERAL TRANSLATION

[the litigant] must verify [this contention], [1]and the Sages maintain: He does not need to verify [this contention]. [2]However, regarding one set [of witnesses], [3]all agree that [his opponent] cannot disqualify them.

[4]Rav Ammi and Rav Assi said before [Rabbi Yoḥanan]: [5][If] there is only one set [of witnesses], what is [the law]? [6][If] there is only one set? [7]But surely you said: "However, regarding one set [of witnesses] — [8]all agree that he cannot disqualify them!" [9]Rather [say]: [If] the second set were found to be related or unfit, what is [the law]? [10][Rabbi Yoḥanan] said to them: The first witnesses

RASHI

ורבנן סברי אין צריך לברר — ויכול לומר: אין לי עוד, ונמצא זה נוגע בעדותו הוא, ולא מיפסלי אפילו בעדות זו. **נמצאת כת שניה קרובין או פסולין** — על ידי עדים גמורים, מהו? לרבי מאיר מי אמרינן השתא ודאי נוגע בעדות הוא, דאין לחבירו כת אחרת כשרה, או דילמא מעיקרא מיהת כי אסהיד בעל דין ואחר עמו אקמאי למיפסלינהו, לאו נוגע בעדות הוא, דאכתי לא אשתכח כת שנייה פסולין. הכי גרסינן לה כמו שפירשתי. ולא נהירא. חדא: דאין זה בירור דברים לרבי מאיר, הואיל וכת האחת נפסלין ועדיין נוגע בעדות הוא. ועוד: דאי נמי הוי בירור דברים בהכי, נוגע בעדות הוא! דאם לא ימצא כת אחרת כשרה אלא כת פסולה, נמצא מפסיד בפסול של ראשונים דאי לא נפסלו ראשונים היה מוציא ממונו על פיהם, ודבריו נבררין על ידי שניה. ואף על פי שפסולין ועכשיו הוא מפסיד. הלכך אומר אני דגרסינן הכי והוא עיקר: דרבי מאיר סבר: אין צריך לברר, וזה שאמר להביא שתי כיתי עדים והביאם והאחת נפסלת, אין בכך כלום, שאין צריך לברר דבריו ודיו בכת אחת הכשרין, ואלו נפסלין לעדות אחרת על פי בעל דין ואחר דאינו נוגע בעדות. ורבנן סברי: צריך לברר, ונמצא זה נוגע בעדות ולא מפסיל. נמצאת כת שניה קרובין או פסולין, לרבי מאיר מהו? נהי דאין צריך לברר מכל מקום עכשיו אין כאן עדות והוה ליה נוגע בעדות למפרע, או דילמא כי אסהיד מיהא לאו נוגע בעדות הוה, דאכתי לא מצאו כת שנייה פסולה. **כבר העידו הראשונים** — (כת ראשונה) כשנמצאת כת שניה פסולה, כבר נתקבלה בכשרות עדותן של אלו המעידין על הפסול, ועדיין לא היה נוגע בעדות. ומאחר שנתקבלה בהכשר נאמנין לפסול את הראשונים. לשון אחר: כבר העידו העדים הראשונים, כת ראשונה שהעידו בעדותן של בעלי דינין ומהימני, דכיון דשניה פסולה תו לא מפסלי קמאי, דהוה ליה נוגע בעדות. ולשון ראשון נראה, מדנקט בהאי לישנא "כבר העידו".

TRANSLATION AND COMMENTARY

that the second set of witnesses would not be produced. [1]**There are those who say** that **Rav Ashi** was the one who **said** that **the first witnesses had already testified.**

נֵימָא בִּפְלוּגְתָּא [2]The Gemara now attempts to correlate this dispute between Rabbi Meir and the Sages with another Tannaitic dispute dealing with the proofs one must present to confirm purchase of land. In principle, if someone claims to own land occupied by someone else, the occupant must show a deed of purchase to support his claim. However, if the deed was lost, the occupant can still support his claim by virtue of possession, *ḥazakah,* such as if he can produce witnesses to testify that he worked the land for three years. The Sages reasoned that no one would allow anybody to use his land illegally for such a long period without registering a protest. The Gemara suggests: **Shall we say that Rabbi Meir and the Sages disagree about the matter in dispute between Rabbi** Yehudah HaNasi **and Rabban Shimon ben Gamliel** in another Baraita in which [3]**it was taught: "One who comes to be judged** with regard to a contested piece of land, and who claims in court that he can prove his title **with a deed of purchase** as well as **with** witnesses to his having had physical **possession** of the land for at least three years, **is** ultimately **judged** on the basis of **the deed of purchase.** Consequently, if he cannot produce the document, he loses title to the last owner of the land, even though he can prove his possession. [4]These are **the words of Rabbi** Yehudah HaNasi. [5]**Rabban Shimon ben Gamliel says: He is judged** on the basis of his **right of possession."** [6]The Sages of the Gemara **were discussing this** Baraita and expressed the following difficulty: Can it be that Rabban Shimon ben Gamliel maintained that, in such a case, one is judged purely on the basis of his **right of possession and not** on the basis of **the deed of purchase?!** But surely a deed is much stronger proof of title than possession! [7]**Rather,** one must **say** that Rabban Shimon ben Gamliel meant: One is judged **even** on the basis of physical **possession** alone.

הָרִאשׁוֹנִים. [1]אִיכָּא דְּאָמְרִי: אָמַר רַב אַשִׁי: כְּבָר הֵעִידוּ עֵדִים הָרִאשׁוֹנִים.
[2]נֵימָא בִּפְלוּגְתָּא דְּרַבִּי וְרַבָּן שִׁמְעוֹן בֶּן גַּמְלִיאֵל קָמִיפַּלְגִי? [3]דְּתַנְיָא: ״הַבָּא לִידוֹן בִּשְׁטָר וּבַחֲזָקָה, נִידּוֹן בִּשְׁטָר. [4]דִּבְרֵי רַבִּי. [5]רַבָּן שִׁמְעוֹן בֶּן גַּמְלִיאֵל אוֹמֵר: נִידּוֹן בַּחֲזָקָה״. [6]וְהָוֵינַן בָּהּ: בַּחֲזָקָה וְלֹא בִּשְׁטָר?! [7]אֶלָּא, אֵימָא: אַף בַּחֲזָקָה.

LITERAL TRANSLATION

already testified. [1]There are those who say: Rav Ashi said: The first witnesses already testified.

[2]Shall we say that [Rabbi Meir and the Sages] disagree about the [matter in] dispute between Rabbi and Rabban Shimon ben Gamliel? [3]As it was taught: "One who comes to be judged [claiming to have] a deed [of purchase] and [the right of] possession, is judged by the deed [of purchase]. [4][These are] the words of Rabbi. [5]Rabban Shimon ben Gamliel says: He is judged by [the right of] possession." [6]And we were discussing this: By [the right of] possession and not by the deed [of purchase]?! [7]Rather, say: Even by [the right of] possession.

RASHI

הבא לידון בשטר ובחזקה — מחזיק בקרקע, ואמר לו חבירו: מה לך בכאן? ואמר לו: אתה מכרתיה לי, ואכלתיה שני חזקה ועדיין שטר מכירה בידי, נידון בשטר — על כרחו צריך להביא השטר ויברר דבריו, ואם לא מצא שטר — יפסיד, דלא מהניא ליה חזקה. ואף על גב דחזקה במקום שטר קיימא כדאמרי רבנן: עד תלת שנין מזדהר איניש בשטריה טפי לא מזדהר, האי כיון דאמר: ישנו בידי — צריך לברר. נידון בחזקה — משמע על כרחו יביא עדי חזקה, ושטר לא מהני, להכי פריך: בחזקה ולא בשטר?! והא שטר עיקר ראיה הוא! וכיון דיש לו שטר, אין בחזקה אפילו משום בירור דברים, דבמקום שטר לא הוזכרה חזקה. דהיא גופא לא אתיא אלא מכח השטר, דאמר: על ידי השטר החזקתי בו ואבד ממני לאחר שלש שנים. אף בחזקה — באיזה מהן שירצה, ואם יש לו עדי חזקה אין צריך לברר דבריו על השטר. והיינו דאמר רבי מאיר כרבי, ורבנן כרבי שמעון. אפילו תימא רבנן כרבי סבירא להו, דעד כאן לא קאמר רבי התם צריך לברר, אלא משום דחזקה לאו עיקר ראיה הוא, דמכח השטר הוא דאתיא, דאי הוה טעין ברישא: החזקתי בה מעצמי שלא אמר לי אדם דבר מעולם — אין זו חזקה, וכי אמר לו: אתה מכרתיה לי דהיינו בשטר ואבדתיו לאחר שלש שנים — הויא חזקה, הלכך האי הואיל ואמר: ישנו בידי — צריך לברר. אבל אמר: יש לי שתי כתי עדים,

HALAKHAH

הַבָּא לִידוֹן בִּשְׁטָר וּבַחֲזָקָה **One who comes to be judged claiming to have a deed of purchase and the right of possession.** "If someone who is currently occupying a piece of land is challenged in court by the property's last owner, and he counters by claiming both to possess the original deed of purchase and to have witnesses who can attest to his physical possession of the land for at least three years, he must produce the deed of purchase and authenticate its signatories, even if the witnesses to possession are more readily available. However, if it is impossible for him to authenticate the document's signatories, if, for example, they died or moved far away, he may base his claim upon the witnesses to possession as long as he takes a Rabbinic oath that he indeed did purchase the property." *Rif* and *Tosafot* maintain that this is in accordance with the position of Rabbi Yehudah HaNasi, whereas *Rashi, Rashbam* and *Hagahot Maimoniyot* all maintain that it is in accordance with the position of Rabban Shimon ben Gamliel. (*Shulḥan Arukh, Ḥoshen Mishpat* 140:4.)

[1] וְקַיְימָא לָן דִּבְצָרִיךְ לְבָרֵר פְּלִיגֵי.

[2] לָא. אַלִּיבָּא דְּרַבָּן שִׁמְעוֹן בֶּן גַּמְלִיאֵל, [3] כּוּלֵּי עָלְמָא לָא פְּלִיגֵי. [4] כִּי פְּלִיגֵי אַלִּיבָּא דְּרַבִּי. [5] דְּרַבִּי מֵאִיר כְּרַבִּי, [6] וְרַבָּנַן אָמְרִי לָךְ עַד כָּאן לָא קָאָמַר רַבִּי הָתָם. אֶלָּא בַּחֲזָקָה, דְּמִכֹּחַ שְׁטָרָא קָאָתֵי. [7] אֲבָל הָכָא, דְּהָנֵי עֵדִים לָאו מִכֹּחַ עֵדִים אַחֲרִינֵי קָאָתוּ, [8] אֲפִילּוּ רַבִּי מוֹדֶה דְּאֵין צָרִיךְ לְבָרֵר.

[9] כִּי אֲתָא רָבִין, אָמַר רַבִּי יוֹחָנָן: [10] רֵישָׁא [24A] בְּעֵדִים פְּסוּלִין

LITERAL TRANSLATION

[1] And we have established that Rabbi and Rabban Shimon ben Gamliel are arguing about whether [the litigant] needs to verify [his claim].

[2] No. Regarding [the position] of Rabban Shimon ben Gamliel, [3] there is no disagreement. [4] Their disagreement is with regard to [the position] of Rabbi. [5] For Rabbi Meir is like Rabbi, [6] but the Sages [can] say to you: Until now Rabbi has not said [anything] here except about possession that comes on the strength of a deed [of purchase]. [7] However here, since these witnesses do not come on the strength of other witnesses, [8] even Rabbi agrees that he does not need to verify.

[9] When Ravin came, he said in the name of Rabbi Yoḥanan: [10] The first clause [24A] [is dealing] with [the rejection of] unfit

RASHI

והביא אחת, כיון דהני לאו מכח הני אתו אין צריך לברר דבריו ולחזר אחר כת שניה. ולישנא בתרא הכי קאמר: אפילו תימא תרווייהו אליבא דרבי פליגי, ורבי מאיר אמר לך: אנא דאמר אפילו לרבי ומשום דהלכה כרבי מחבריו — מהדרינן לפלוגתייהו אליביה.

TRANSLATION AND COMMENTARY

וְקַיְימָא לָן [1] The Gemara now continues to show how this dispute relates to the dispute in our Mishnah. **We have established** through a tradition **that Rabbi** Yehudah HaNasi and **Rabban Shimon ben Gamliel are arguing** in this Baraita **about whether** a litigant who has claimed before a court to possess evidence in support of his position **needs to verify** the existence of that evidence. Rabbi Yehudah HaNasi, who maintains that he must verify all of the alleged evidence, would rule that even if the occupant can prove physical possession, he still must produce the alleged document of sale. Rabban Shimon ben Gamliel, on the other hand, would maintain that since a litigant is not required to verify the existence of all evidence which he claimed to possess, the claimant to the land can secure his title on the basis of either a *ḥazakah* or a bill of sale. The Gemara suggests that there is an analogy between these two disputes. As interpreted by Rav Dimi in the name of Rabbi Yoḥanan, in our Mishnah, Rabbi Meir's position is similar to that of Rabbi Yehudah HaNasi's ruling: A litigant must produce all the witnesses he claimed he would produce. Conversely, the Sages, who maintain that he is not required to produce all the witnesses, take a position like that of Rabban Shimon ben Gamliel, who rules that a litigant is not required to produce all the evidence he has claimed to have.

לָא [2] However, the alleged correlation between these two disputes does not necessarily hold: **No.** Granted, **regarding the position of Rabban Shimon ben Gamliel** as stated in the Baraita, that the occupant is not required to verify in court the existence of all alleged evidence in support of land title, [3] **there** can be **no disagreement** between the Sages and Rabbi Meir that Rabban Shimon also applies his ruling to the case of our Mishnah. [4] **Their disagreement is with regard to** the position **of Rabbi** Yehudah HaNasi in the Baraita — [5] **for Rabbi Meir** would maintain that his position in the Mishnah **is** exactly **like** that of **Rabbi** Yehudah HaNasi in the Baraita, [6] **whereas the Sages can say to you: Rabbi** Yehudah HaNasi **only says** that both proofs must be verified only if the occupant first claimed that he still possessed the deed in addition to physical possession of the land. In such a case he maintains that the document must be produced, for proof of possession itself is only allowed to **come** before the court **on the basis of** there having been an original **deed of purchase.** Were a defendant to claim land title simply on the basis of physical possession, his claim would not be honored. He may claim that the deed was lost or destroyed, but if he states that it is still in his possession, he must produce it before any other proof may be recognized. [7] **However, here,** in the case of our Mishnah, where a litigant has claimed to have two independent sets of witnesses in support of his position — **since** one set of **witnesses does not come on the basis of** the **other** set of **witnesses,** [8] it is possible that **even Rabbi** Yehudah HaNasi would **agree that** the litigant **need not verify** before the court the existence of all his alleged evidence.

כִּי אֲתָא רָבִין [9] **When Ravin came** to Babylonia from Eretz Israel, **he** offered a different interpretation of our Mishnah **in the name of Rabbi Yoḥanan:** The Mishnah refers to a litigant who testifies together with another individual in regard to both his disputant's choice of witness and his choice of judge. [10] **The first clause** [24A] of our Mishnah, which cites Rabbi Meir's opinion that a litigant can invalidate his opponent's choice of judge, is dealing **with witnesses** who were found by virtue of independent testimony to be **unfit,** whereas the presumption that those sitting on the court were **qualified judges** remained unchallenged except by the

וְדַיָּינִין כְּשֵׁרִין. [1]מִיגּוֹ דְּפָסְלִי עֵדִים, פָּסְלֵי נַמִי דַּיָּינֵי. [2]סֵיפָא בְּדַיָּינִין פְּסוּלִין וְעֵדִים כְּשֵׁרִין; [3]דְּמִיגּוֹ דְּפָסְלִי דַּיָּינִין, פָּסְלֵי נַמִי עֵדִים.

[4]מַתְקִיף לַהּ רָבָא: בִּשְׁלָמָא מִיגּוֹ דְּפָסְלִי עֵדִים, פָּסְלֵי נַמִי דַּיָּינֵי — [5]אִיכָּא בֵּי דִינָא אַחֲרִינָא! [6]אֶלָּא מִיגּוֹ דְּפָסְלִי דַּיָּינֵי, פָּסְלֵי נַמִי עֵדִים?! [7]וְהָא עֵדִים תּוּ לֵיכָּא!

[8]לָא. צְרִיכָא, דְּאִיכָּא כַּת אַחֶרֶת.

[9]הָא, לֵיכָּא כַּת אַחֶרֶת, מַאי? הָכִי נַמִי — [10]דְּלָא מָצֵי פָּסְלִי? [11]הַיְינוּ דְּרַב דִּימִי! [12]אִיכָּא

LITERAL TRANSLATION

witnesses and qualified judges. [1]Since the witnesses are disqualified, the judges are also disqualified. [2]The latter clause [is dealing] with [the rejection of] unfit judges and qualified witnesses; [3]for since the judges are disqualified, the witnesses are also disqualified.

[4]Rava objected to this: Granted [that] since the witnesses are disqualified, the judges are also disqualified — [5]there is [still] another court! [6]But since the judges are disqualified, the witnesses are also disqualified?! [7]Surely there are no more witnesses!

[8]No. It is necessary, where there is another set [of witnesses].

[9]But if there were not another set [of witnesses], what [would the ruling be]? [10]Would it not be so — that the [litigant] could not disqualify them? [11]That is [the position] of Rav Dimi! [12]There is [a difference]

TRANSLATION AND COMMENTARY

litigant and his fellow witness. [1]Rabbi Meir maintains that, **since the witnesses were disqualified** in accordance with independent testimony which corroborated the litigant's testimony, **the judges** should **also** be **disqualified** by that testimony, since the litigant, despite his interest in the matter, was shown to be an honest witness. [2]**The latter clause** of the Mishnah, which cites Rabbi Meir's opinion that a litigant can invalidate his opponent's choice of witness, is dealing **with judges** who were discovered to be **unfit** by independent testimony. The **witnesses** remain otherwise unchallenged and thus are still assumed to be **qualified.** Nevertheless, Rabbi Meir maintains that the litigant is believed with regard to the witnesses as well, [3]**for since the judges were disqualified** by other witnesses, and his allegations were proven true, the rest of the litigant's testimony regarding **the witnesses** should **also** be believed, and the witnesses should **be disqualified.** However, the Sages reject this reasoning.

מַתְקִיף לַהּ [4]**Rava objected to this** interpretation: **Granted,** he says, that Ravin's explication of the Mishnah can be accepted with respect to the first clause, and **since the witnesses were disqualified, the judges should also be disqualified.** [5]For **there is** always **another court.** [6]**But** how can Ravin attribute to Rabbi Meir (in the latter clause of our Mishnah) the **statement** that, **since the judges are disqualified, the witnesses** should be **disqualified as well,** even though there is no one to support the litigant in his allegations?! [7]**Surely** the two situations are not comparable! While there are always additional judges, **there are no more witnesses** available in this case to support the disputant's claim.

לָא [8]The Gemara rebuts Rava's attack on Ravin: **No, it is necessary** to apply Ravin's argument **when** the opposing litigant claims to have **another set of witnesses,** besides those being disqualified.

הָא [9]The Gemara continues to analyze Ravin's interpretation of the latter clause in our Mishnah: **If there were not another set of witnesses** available to the disputant, **what would the ruling be?** [10]**Would it not be that the litigant could not disqualify** his opponent's witnesses without corroborative testimony? [11]But **that is** exactly the position **of Rav Dimi** in his version of Rabbi Yoḥanan cited earlier! How, then, does Ravin's understanding of Rabbi Yoḥanan differ from that of Rav Dimi? [12]**There is** a difference **between them with regard** to the use,

RASHI

בעדים פסולים ודיינין כשרין — בעל דין פוסל הדיינין והעדים, ונמצאו דבריו אמת על העדים, ומשום הכי מהימנינן ליה אפילו לגבי דיינין. **סיפא** — שנמצאו דבריו אמת על הדיינין שפסולין הם, ומשום הכי מהימנינן להו אעדים אליבא דרבי מאיר, ורבנן לית להו מיגו. **איכא בי דינא אחרינא** — ואינו נוגע בעדות.

NOTES

מִיגּוֹ דְּפָסְלִי עֵדִים **Since the witnesses are disqualified.** Our commentary follows *Rashi.* However, according to *Ramah*, the judges are disqualified by the litigant's allegations, since he can say: Since my adversary has gone to great length in order to produce invalid witnesses, I can only assume that the judge he chose is also not qualified, and thus I will not appear before him. Others explain the rationale for disqualification as follows: Once the witnesses have been proven to be invalid, the case is suspended and the court disbanded. If the disputant should desire to produce alternative witnesses, his claim is considered to be a new case which requires a new selection of judges. This explanation, however, does not account for the second clause of our Mishnah, in which the witnesses are disqualified because the judge was proven unfit.

TRANSLATION AND COMMENTARY

as a general rule of evidence, of ***miggo,*** "since," which is the principle employed above in Ravin's version of Rabbi Yoḥanan's position — "since" part of his testimony was corroborated by witnesses, the rest of his testimony is accepted as well. [1]Ravin **maintains** that **we accept** the principle of *miggo* to admit otherwise deficient evidence. Furthermore, without independent confirmation of the litigant's testimony barring the witnesses or the judges (and therefore without recourse to *miggo*), Rabbi Meir in our Mishnah would never have believed the litigant's challenge of his disputant's choice of judge or of witness. [2]Rav Dimi, on the other hand, **maintains** that **we do not accept the principle of *miggo*** under such circumstances. Thus, Rabbi Meir in our Mishnah allows the litigant to challenge an opposing witness because of his disputant's obligation (as stated earlier in 23b) to verify the existence of those additional witnesses whom he claims to have. As to the first clause of the Mishnah, in which Rabbi Meir allows the litigant to disqualify his disputant's choice of judge, Rav Dimi would also reject any explanation based upon *miggo,* "since," and resort instead to the Gemara's earlier suggestion that we are dealing with communities such as the one in Syria, where the available judges were relatively ignorant.

בֵּינַיְיהוּ מִיגּוֹ, [1]דְּמָר סָבַר: אָמְרִינַן מִיגּוֹ, [2]וּמָר סָבַר: לָא אָמְרִינַן מִיגּוֹ.

[3]גּוּפָא: [4]"אָמַר רֵישׁ לָקִישׁ: 'פֶּה קָדוֹשׁ יֹאמַר דָּבָר זֶה'"?! [5]תְּנֵי: "עֵדוֹ". [6]אִינִי? [7]וְהָאָמַר עוּלָּא: הָרוֹאֶה אֶת רֵישׁ לָקִישׁ בְּבֵית הַמִּדְרָשׁ, כְּאִילּוּ עוֹקֵר הָרִים וְטוֹחֲנָן זֶה בָּזֶה! [8]אָמַר רָבִינָא: וַהֲלֹא כָּל הָרוֹאֶה רַבִּי מֵאִיר בְּבֵית הַמִּדְרָשׁ, כְּאִילּוּ עוֹקֵר הֲרֵי הָרִים וְטוֹחֲנָן זֶה בָּזֶה?!

LITERAL TRANSLATION

between them [with regard to] *miggo* ("since"), [1]for [one] master maintains [that] we accept [the principle of] *miggo* ("since"), [2]and [the other] master maintains [that] we do not accept [the principle of] *miggo* ("since").

[3][Returning to] the statement quoted above (lit., "the thing itself"): [4]"Resh Lakish said: 'Can a holy mouth say such a thing?!'" [5]Teach: "His [one] witness." [6]Is this so? [7]But surely Ulla said: [When] one observes Resh Lakish in the study hall, it is as if he is uprooting mountains and grinding them one against the other! [8]Ravina said: But is it not so [that] whosoever observes Rabbi Meir in the study hall, it is as if he is uprooting mountains upon mountains and grinding them one against the other?!

RASHI

רבין סבר — אמרינן מיגו בעלמא, כדקיימא הכא טעמא משום מיגו הוא, ואי לאו הכי הוא, לא הוה פסיל רבי מאיר, ולרב דימי לא אמרינן מיגו בעלמא. וטוחנן זה בזה — מטיח ומקיש זה בזה, אלמא: חריפא טובא הוה, מקרי ליה לרבי מאיר דרך ענוה "פה קדוש". אמר רבינא — ומאי תמהא? והלא רבי מאיר עוקר הרי הרים הוא, כלומר: אלים וגבר טפי טובא.

גּוּפָא [3]The Gemara now returns to **the** earlier **statement** of Resh Lakish's (23a) regarding the position of Rabbi Meir quoted in the latter clause of our Mishnah. [4]**"Resh Lakish said: Can a holy mouth**, such as that possessed by Rabbi Meir, **say such a thing?!** Surely one cannot arbitrarily reject perfectly good witnessses! [5]Rather, one must **learn** the Mishnah as follows: 'This litigant can invalidate that litigant's **witness** [in the singular] and vice versa.'" Since it is generally necessary to produce at least two witnesses in support of a monetary claim, Rabbi Meir teaches that any litigant can invalidate testimony offered by a single witness. Commenting on the tone of Resh Lakish's query, the Gemara asks: [6]**Is this** really **so,** that Resh Lakish spoke with deference concerning Rabbi Meir, calling him a "holy mouth"? [7]**But surely Ulla said:** When **one observes Resh Lakish in the study hall** arguing about Torah**, it** appears **as if he is uprooting** entire **mountains and grinding them one against the other** — so fierce and deft was he at exposing difficulties in the words of even the greatest Torah scholars! [8]**Ravina said:** This is not at all difficult to understand, for **is it not** also stated that **whosoever observes Rabbi Meir** arguing about Torah **in the study hall,** compares the process to **uprooting mountains upon mountains and grinding them one against the other?!** Rabbi Meir was considered even more formidable than Resh Lakish, so it is natural that Resh Lakish would defer to him.

NOTES

אִיכָּא בֵּינַיְיהוּ מִיגּוֹ There is a difference between them with regard to *miggo*. The *miggo* described in our Gemara differs from that generally employed elsewhere in the Talmud. Ordinarily, a *miggo* argues for accepting an unsupported claim when a more advantageous claim could have been made in its stead. Our Gemara, however, uses the *miggo* principle as an argument for accepting an unsupported claim because a similar claim made by the same person was independently corroborated. With regard to this principle, there is room for dispute. *Rashi* interprets the Gemara as suggesting that Ravin and Rav Dimi argue over the general admissibility of the principle of *miggo* as a rule of evidence, not only in the cases dealt with by our Mishnah. *Ramah*, however, confines their dispute to the cases in our Mishnah.

TRANSLATION AND COMMENTARY

הָכִי קָאָמַר [1]The Gemara answers: Indeed, the Talmudic Sage who commented on the words of Resh Lakish **was** actually **saying: Come and see how highly** the Sages in Eretz Israel **value one another!** [2]For example, **Rabbi** Yehudah HaNasi **was** once **sitting** before his students and **stated** the following law: **It is forbidden on the Sabbath to insulate** a container of **cold** water by wrapping it in a blanket or other insulating materials, even though this does not violate the Sabbath law. This ruling was promulgated lest it appear to a casual observer that he was insulating hot water, which is indeed prohibited, out of concern that the act might lead the person to actually heat water on the Sabbath (see *Shabbat* 34b). Upon hearing Rabbi Yehudah HaNasi make this statement, [3]**Rabbi Yishmael, the son of Rabbi Yose, said before him:** Let it be known that my **father**, Rabbi Yose, **permitted insulating** a container of **cold** water on the Sabbath. [4]**Rabbi** Yehudah HaNasi immediately turned to his students and **said to them:** Ignore my ruling, for **an elder has already instructed** us otherwise in relation to this matter. Commenting upon this incident, [5]**Rav Pappa said: Come and see** from Rabbi Yehudah HaNasi's act of deference toward Rabbi Yose **how much** the Sages in the Eretz Israel **value one another** — [6]**for had Rabbi Yose been living, he would have bent** in submission **and sat** as a student **before Rabbi** Yehudah HaNasi! [7](This is a reasonable assumption, **for behold Rabbi Yishmael, the son of Rabbi Yose, was** referred to as **one who** more than adequately **succeeded his fathers** as a Torah scholar, [8]**and** yet **he would bend in submission and sit before Rabbi** Yehudah HaNasi as his student.) [9]**And** even so, **Rabbi** Yehudah HaNasi deferred to Rabbi Yose by **stating** that **"an elder has already instructed** us otherwise on this matter."

אָמַר רַבִּי אוֹשַׁעְיָא [10]The Gemara now proceeds to cite several Midrashic statements that highlight the difference in character between the scholars in Eretz Israel and those in Babylonia. **Rabbi Oshaya said: What is** the meaning of **what is written** in Zechariah (11:7): [11]**"And I took for myself two rods; the one I called Grace**

[1]הָכִי קָאָמַר: בֹּא וּרְאֵה כַּמָּה מְחַבְּבִין זֶה אֶת זֶה. [2]כִּי הָא דִּיתֵיב רַבִּי וְקָאָמַר: אָסוּר לְהַטְמִין אֶת הַצּוֹנֵן. [3]אָמַר לְפָנָיו רַבִּי יִשְׁמָעֵאל בְּרַבִּי יוֹסֵי: אַבָּא הִתִּיר לְהַטְמִין אֶת הַצּוֹנֵן. [4]אָמַר לָהֶם: כְּבָר הוֹרָה זָקֵן. [5]אָמַר רַב פַּפָּא: בֹּא וּרְאֵה כַּמָּה מְחַבְּבִין זֶה אֶת זֶה! [6]דְּאִילוּ רַבִּי יוֹסֵי קַיָּים, הָיָה כָּפוּף וְיוֹשֵׁב לִפְנֵי רַבִּי; [7]דְּהָא רַבִּי יִשְׁמָעֵאל בְּרַבִּי יוֹסֵי מְמַלֵּא מְקוֹם אֲבוֹתָיו הֲוָה, [8]וְהָיָה כָּפוּף וְיוֹשֵׁב לִפְנֵי רַבִּי. [9]וְקָא אָמַר "כְּבָר הוֹרָה זָקֵן".
[10]אָמַר רַבִּי אוֹשַׁעְיָא: מַאי דִּכְתִיב: [11]"וָאֶקַּח לִי (אֶת) שְׁנֵי מַקְלוֹת; לְאַחַד קָרָאתִי נוֹעַם וּלְאַחַד קָרָאתִי חוֹבְלִים".

LITERAL TRANSLATION

[1]This is what he is saying: Come and see how much they value one another. [2]As [in] that [instance] when Rabbi was sitting and stated: It is forbidden [on the Sabbath] to insulate cold [water]. [3]Rabbi Yishmael, the son of Rabbi Yose, said before him: Father permitted insulating cold [water]. [4]Rabbi said to them: An elder has already instructed [us]. [5]Rav Pappa said: Come and see how much they value one another! [6]For had Rabbi Yose been living, he would have bent [in submission] and sat before Rabbi; [7]for surely Rabbi Yishmael, the son of Rabbi Yose, the one who filled the place of his fathers, [8]would bend [in submission] and sit before Rabbi. [9]And Rabbi stated: "An elder has already instructed [us]."
[10]Rabbi Oshaya said: What is [it] that is written: [11]"And I took for myself two rods; the one I called Grace and the other I called Assaulters"?

RASHI

בא וראה כמה — כלומר: לא אתמוהי קא מתמהי, אלא הכי קאמר: בא וראה כמה בני ארץ ישראל מחבבין זה את זה. דהא ריש לקיש חריף וחכים טובא הוה, וקרי ליה לרבי מאיר "פה קדוש" דקא מחבב ליה, ומיישב את הדבר להתקיים. **להטמין את הצונן** — מים צונן, ומתיירא שלא יוחמו, אסור להטמינן בחול צונן (לצורך שבת) [בשבת]. **הורה זקן** — רבי יוסי, דאזלינן בתריה. **ממלא מקום אבותיו** — חשוב כאביו.

NOTES

אִילוּ רַבִּי יוֹסֵי קַיָּים, הָיָה כָּפוּף לִפְנֵי רַבִּי For had Rabbi Yose been living, he would have bent in submission before Rabbi Yehudah HaNasi. *Rashi* explains elsewhere (*Shabbat* 51a) that, although Rabbi Yose was recognized as a greater

HALAKHAH

לְהַטְמִין אֶת הַצּוֹנֵן To insulate cold water. "It is permissible on the Sabbath to insulate a container of cold food or liquid to keep it from warming up," in accordance with the view of Rabbi Yose accepted by Rabbi Yehudah HaNasi. (*Shulḥan Arukh, Oraḥ Ḥayyim* 257:6.)

TRANSLATION AND COMMENTARY

and the other I called Assaulters"? [1]The rod on which was written **"Grace"** alludes to those **scholars who are in Eretz Israel — scholars who are gracious to one another**, even when engaged **in** a dispute regarding **Halakhah.** [2]The rod upon which was written the word **"Assaulters"** alludes to those **scholars who are in Babylonia** — scholars **who** verbally **assault one another** with belligerent questions **in** arguing about **matters of Halakhah.**

וַיֹּאמֶר אֵלַי [3]In a similar vein, Rabbi Yitzḥak interprets an earlier verse from Zechariah (4:14): **"And he** [the angel] **said to me: These are the two anointed ones** [lit., 'children of pure oil'] **who are standing** by the Master of the entire earth." The angel is here interpreting for Zechariah the symbolism behind his vision of a golden candelabrum, which, as was **written** previously (4:3), had **"two olive trees near it,** one on the right of the orb and the other on its left." [4]Referring to the "two **anointed ones"** mentioned by the angel, **Rabbi Yitzḥak said: These** allude to **the scholars who are in Eretz Israel** — [5]scholars **who are as soothing to one another, in** their discussions of **Halakhah, as olive oil.** [6]Whereas **"two olive trees above it"** alludes to those **scholars who are in Babylonia,** [7]scholars **who are as bitter to one another in** the way they argue over matters of **Halakhah as** the taste of **an olive.**

וָאֶשָּׂא עֵינַי [8]Elsewhere in Zechariah (5:9-11), we find the following account of another prophetic vision: **"And I lifted my eyes and looked, and behold two women were going out and the wind was in their wings — for they had wings like the wings of a stork — and they lifted up the ephah** [a dry-volume measure] **between the heavens and the earth; and I said to the angel who was speaking with me: Where are they bringing the ephah? And he said to me: To build her a house in the land of Shin'ar;** and when it is prepared, they will set it there upon its base." [9]**Rabbi Yoḥanan** offered **in the name of Rabbi Shimon ben Yoḥai** an interpretation of the symbolism in this vision: The two women

[1]״נוֹעַם״ — אֵלּוּ תַּלְמִידֵי חֲכָמִים שֶׁבְּאֶרֶץ יִשְׂרָאֵל, שֶׁמַּנְעִימִין זֶה לְזֶה בַּהֲלָכָה. [2]״חוֹבְלִים״ — אֵלּוּ תַּלְמִידֵי חֲכָמִים שֶׁבְּבָבֶל, שֶׁמְּחַבְּלִים זֶה לָזֶה בַּהֲלָכָה.

[3]״וַיֹּאמֶר אֵלַי אֵלֶּה [שְׁנֵי] בְנֵי הַיִּצְהָר הָעֹמְדִים וגו׳ וּשְׁנַיִם זֵיתִים עָלֶיהָ״. [4]״יִצְהָר״ — אָמַר רַבִּי יִצְחָק: אֵלּוּ תַּלְמִידֵי חֲכָמִים שֶׁבְּאֶרֶץ יִשְׂרָאֵל, [5]שֶׁנּוֹחִין זֶה לָזֶה בַּהֲלָכָה כְּשֶׁמֶן זַיִת; [6]״וּשְׁנַיִם זֵיתִים עָלֶיהָ״ — אֵלּוּ תַּלְמִידֵי חֲכָמִים שֶׁבְּבָבֶל, [7]שֶׁמְּמָרְרִין זֶה לָזֶה בַּהֲלָכָה כְּזַיִת.

[8]״וָאֶשָּׂא עֵינַי וָאֵרֶא וְהִנֵּה שְׁתַּיִם נָשִׁים יוֹצְאוֹת וְרוּחַ בְּכַנְפֵיהֶם וְלָהֵנָּה כְנָפַיִם כְּכַנְפֵי הַחֲסִידָה וַתִּשֶּׂאנָה הָאֵיפָה בֵּין הַשָּׁמַיִם וּבֵין הָאָרֶץ וָאֹמַר אֶל הַמַּלְאָךְ הַדֹּבֵר בִּי אָנָה הֵמָּה מוֹלִכוֹת אֶת הָאֵיפָה וַיֹּאמֶר אֵלַי לִבְנוֹת לָה בַיִת בְּאֶרֶץ שִׁנְעָר״. [9]אָמַר רַבִּי יוֹחָנָן מִשּׁוּם

LITERAL TRANSLATION

[1]"Grace" — these are scholars who are in Eretz Israel, who are gracious to one another in [matters of] Jewish law. [2]"Assaulters" — these are scholars who are in Babylonia, who assault one another in [matters of] Halakhah.

[3][It is written:] "And he said to me: These are the two anointed ones [lit., 'children of pure oil who are standing,' etc.]." [And it is written:] "And two olive trees near it." [4]"Anointed ones" — Rabbi Yitzḥak said: These are the scholars who are in Eretz Israel, [5]who are as soothing to one another in [matters of] Halakhah as olive oil; [6]"and two olive trees near it" — these are the scholars who are in Babylonia, [7]who are as bitter to one another in [matters of] Halakhah as an olive.

[8][It is written]: "And I lifted my eyes and looked, and behold two women were going out and the wind was in their wings — for they had wings like the wings of a stork — and they lifted up the ephah measure between the heavens and the earth; and I said to the angel who was speaking with me: Where are they bringing the ephah? And he said to me: To build her a house in the land of Shin'ar." [9]Rabbi Yoḥanan said in the name

RASHI

מחבלים – בלשון עז וחמה מקשין זה לזה. ובני ארץ ישראל נוחין יחד, ומעיינין יחד, ומתקן זה את דברי זה, והשמועה יוצאה לאור. **משמנין** – נוחין כשמן. **איפה** – זה יצר הרע. **שתי נשים** – חנופות, וגסות הרוח. **ורוח בכנפיהם** – לשון גסות הרוח. **ככנפי החסידה** – זו חנופה, שמראין עצמם חסידים. **לבנות לה בית** – ולא כתיב להם, אלמא האחת לבדה נתישבה שם.

NOTES

scholar than Rabbi Yehudah HaNasi, he would still have deferred to him as president of the Sanhedrin. *Rabbenu Tam* differs with this explanation and suggests that, although at one time Rabbi Yehudah HaNasi was indeed a disciple of Rabbi Yose, after years of heading his own academy, he surpassed him in wisdom.

רַבִּי שִׁמְעוֹן בֶּן יוֹחַאי: זוֹ חֲנוּפָּה וְגַסּוּת הָרוּחַ שֶׁיָּרְדוּ לְבָבֶל.
[1]וְגַסּוּת הָרוּחַ לְבָבֶל נָחֵית? [2]וְהָאָמַר מָר: עֲשָׂרָה קַבִּין גַּסּוּת יָרְדוּ לָעוֹלָם — [3]תִּשְׁעָה נָטְלָה עֵילָם, וְאַחַת כָּל הָעוֹלָם כּוּלּוֹ! [4]אִין, לְבָבֶל נָחֵית, וְאִישְׁתַּרְבּוּבֵי דְּאִישְׁתַּרְבַּב לְעֵילָם. [5]דַּיְקָא נַמִי, דִּכְתִיב: "לִבְנוֹת לָה בַיִת בְּאֶרֶץ שִׁנְעָר". [6]שְׁמַע מִינָּהּ.
[7]וְהָאָמַר מָר: סִימָן לְגַסּוּת הָרוּחַ עֲנִיּוּת — וַעֲנִיּוּת לְבָבֶל נָחֵית! [8]מַאי עֲנִיּוּת? [9]עֲנִיּוּת תּוֹרָה, [10]דִּכְתִיב: "אָחוֹת לָנוּ קְטַנָּה וְשָׁדַיִם אֵין לָהּ". [11]אָמַר רַבִּי יוֹחָנָן: זוֹ עֵילָם, שֶׁזָּכְתָה לִלְמוֹד וְלֹא זָכְתָה לְלַמֵּד.
[12]מַאי בָּבֶל? [13]אָמַר רַבִּי יוֹחָנָן: [14]בְּלוּלָה בְּמִקְרָא, בְּלוּלָה בְּמִשְׁנָה, בְּלוּלָה בְּתַלְמוּד.

LITERAL TRANSLATION

of Rabbi Shimon ben Yoḥai: This is the sanctimony and arrogance (lit., "inflated spirit") that descended into Babylonia.

[1]And did arrogance descend into Babylonia? [2]Surely master said: Ten *kavs* [measures] of arrogance descended to the world — [3]Elam took nine [of them], and the rest of the world one! [4]Indeed, it descended into Babylonia, but extended to Elam. [5]It is also precise, for it is written: "To build for her a house in the land of Shin'ar." [6]Infer it from this.

[7]But surely master said: Poverty is a sign of arrogance — and poverty descended into Babylonia! [8]What is poverty? [9]Poverty of Torah, [10]for it is written: "We have a young sister and she has no breasts." [11]Rabbi Yoḥanan said: This is Elam, who merited to study but did not merit to teach.

[12]What is [the meaning of the word] *Bavel* [Babylonia]? [13]Rabbi Yoḥanan said: [14]Permeated with Scripture, permeated with the Mishnah [and] permeated with the Talmud.

TRANSLATION AND COMMENTARY

borne by wings represent the twin attributes of **sanctimony and arrogance that descended into Babylonia,** which is also known as Shin'ar. The attribute of sanctimony is hinted at by the analogy to stork's wings. The Hebrew word for stork — חֲסִידָה — is said to reflect its piety (חֲסִידוּת) when in the presence of other birds (see *Ḥullin* 63a). The attribute of arrogance, on the other hand, is alluded to by the "wind" in the women's wings.

וְגַסּוּת הָרוּחַ [1]The Gemara questions the preceding interpretation: **Did** the attribute of **arrogance** really **descend into Babylonia?** [2]**Surely** a Sage has **said: Ten *kavs*** [measures] **of arrogance descended into the world** — [3]**nine** of these measures **were taken by** those dwelling in the land of **Elam,** while the remaining **one** measure was distributed throughout **the rest of the world!** If so, it is the land of Elam, and not Babylonia, that should be singled out for its arrogance! [4]The Gemara answers: **Indeed** this is so — however, it first **descended into Babylonia and** only later **extended into** the neighboring land of **Elam.** [5]This **is also** evident from a **precise** reading of the above verse, **for it is written** there: **"To build for *her*** [in the singular] **a house in the land of Shin'ar."** [6]**Infer from** this that only one of the two women in the vision attained a permanent home in Shin'ar, and, in fact, it was only the attribute of sanctimony that remained there, while the attribute of arrogance migrated into Elam.

וְהָאָמַר מָר [7]**But surely** another Sage has **said** that **poverty is a sign of** retribution for **arrogance — and** we see clearly that **poverty** has **descended into Babylonia,** more than into Elam! [8]The Gemara answers: **What is** meant by **poverty** being a sign of conceit? Not material poverty, as evident in Babylonia, [9]but rather **poverty of Torah** scholarship. And such poverty, while absent from Babylonia, was clearly evident in Elam, [10]**for it is written** in Song of Songs (4:8): **"We have a young sister and she has no breasts,"** [11]regarding which **Rabbi Yoḥanan said: This** verse **is** alluding to the Jews of **Elam, who merited** the opportunity **to study** Torah from their sister community in Babylonia **but did not merit** having their own scholars **to teach** Torah.

מַאי בָּבֶל [12]The Gemara offers a Midrashic support for the characterization of Babylonia as a land suffused with Torah scholarship: **What is** the symbolic meaning of the word **Bavel** (Hebrew for Babylonia)? [13]**Rabbi Yoḥanan said:** The root of the word Bavel implies permeation. Thus, it can be said that the name alludes to the Talmud that evolved in Babylonia, [14]a work which was **permeated with** the wisdom of **Scripture, permeated with the** wisdom of **Mishnah,** and **permeated with the** wisdom of **Talmud.**

RASHI

עניות תורה — בעילם היא. דניאל בעילם הוה דכתיב (דניאל ח) "ואני (הייתי) בשושן הבירה אשר בעילם המדינה" ולא רבן תורה. עזרא הוה בבבל ולמד חק ומשפט בישראל.

NOTES

בְּלוּלָה בְּמִקְרָא וכו׳ **Permeated with Scripture, etc.** Our commentary follows the view of *Ramah,* who understands Rabbi Yoḥanan's statement as laudatory. *Ramah* cites one opinion that even views the following statement of Rabbi Yirmeyahu, comparing the Babylonian Talmud to having "settled me in darkness," as one of praise, extolling the

TRANSLATION AND COMMENTARY

בְּמַחֲשַׁכִּים הוֹשִׁיבַנִי [1]Other Sages viewed the status of Babylonian scholarship quite differently, as is evident from an interpretation of the following verse (Lamentations 3:6): **"He has settled me in darkness, like those forever dead."** [2]**Rabbi Yirmeyah said** in reference to this verse: **This is** alluding to **the Talmud of Babylonia,** which is often so obscure that it appears to have been conceived in an atmosphere of darkness.

MISHNAH אָמַר לוֹ [3]If **one litigant said to the other:** "My **father is trustworthy to me** as a judge in our case," or **"Your father is trustworthy to me** as a judge in our case," or even **"three** ignorant **cattle herders are trustworthy to me** as judges in our case" — [4]all of whom are normally ineligible to serve as judges, **Rabbi Meir says: He can** subsequently **retract** and insist that the case only be submitted before individuals who are qualified to judge according to Torah law; [5]**and the Sages say: He cannot retract.** Similarly, if one of the litigants **was obligated to his fellow** with regard to taking **an oath** in court, as in the case of a contested monetary claim, [6]**and** the latter **said to him:** "Instead of swearing by

[1]״בְּמַחֲשַׁכִּים הוֹשִׁיבַנִי, כְּמֵתֵי עוֹלָם״. [2]אָמַר רַבִּי יִרְמְיָה: זֶה תַּלְמוּדָהּ שֶׁל בָּבֶל.

מִשְׁנָה [3]אָמַר לוֹ: ״נֶאֱמָן עָלַי אַבָּא״, ״נֶאֱמָן עָלַי אָבִיךָ״, ״נֶאֱמָנִים עָלַי שְׁלֹשָׁה רוֹעֵי בָקָר״ — [4]רַבִּי מֵאִיר אוֹמֵר: יָכוֹל לַחֲזוֹר בּוֹ; [5]וַחֲכָמִים אוֹמְרִים: אֵינוֹ יָכוֹל לַחֲזוֹר בּוֹ. [6]הָיָה חַיָּיב לַחֲבֵירוֹ שְׁבוּעָה, וְאָמַר לוֹ:

LITERAL TRANSLATION

[1][It is written]: "He has settled me in darkness, like those dead forever." [2]Rabbi Yirmeyah said: This [refers to] the Talmud of Babylonia.

MISHNAH [3][If one litigant] said to [the other]: "Father is trustworthy to me," "Your father is trustworthy to me," "The three cattle herders are trustworthy to me" — [4]Rabbi Meir says: He can retract; [5]and the Sages say: He cannot retract. [6][If] he was obligated to his fellow [with regard to] an oath, and he said to him:

RASHI

במחשכים הושיבני – שאין נוחין זה עם זה ותלמודם ספק בידם.

משנה נאמן עלי – להיות דיין. **אבא** – פסול מן התורה לדונני, לא לזכות ולא לחיוב. דנפקא לן בפירקין (כז, ב) מ״לא יומתו אבות על בנים וגו׳״.

NOTES

profundity of the Babylonian text. *Maharsha* and *Rashash* view both statements as coming to underscore the deficiencies of Babylonian scholarship when compared with the Talmudic tradition that developed in Eretz Israel, a theme expressed by earlier Midrashic statements cited on the page. These authorities understand Rabbi Yoḥanan's use of the term בְּלוּלָה as implying not "permeation" but rather "disorder" in the system of education in Babylonia — due to the prevalent arrogance that took root there. The Babylonians ignored the wisdom of gradually progressing from instruction in elementary Scripture to Mishnah, and only then to the more complex Talmudic texts. Instead, they introduced Mishnah when a child should still have been mastering the Bible, and introduced Talmud while he should still have been mastering the Mishnah. Thus Rabbi Yoḥanan's statement should not be understood as referring to the Babylonian Talmud but rather to the Babylonian Jews themselves, who possessed some knowledge in all three areas but without proper integration. *Rashi* also explains Rabbi Yirmeyahu's statement regarding the obscurity of Talmudic discourse in Babylonia as criticism of the way scholars interacted there and their often belligerent attitude toward one another, which prevented a proper grasp of the issues being discussed.

נֶאֱמָן עָלַי אַבָּא **Father is trustworthy to me.** Some commentators choose to interpret the first two cases mentioned in the Mishnah ("my father" and "your father") as referring to a litigant who agreed to accept the father not as a judge but as a witness (*Rabbenu Ḥananel, Meiri*). In the third case, involving the three cattle herders, they are obviously proposed as judges (who come in triads while witnesses come in pairs). Regardless of how one interprets the first two examples, the law in the Mishnah does not distinguish between a judge and a witness, as a father's ineligibility to be a judge in a case involving his son is actually derived from the Biblical stricture preventing him from being a witness (see 27b).

The obvious question in relation to our Mishnah is: How can we allow litigants to breach standard judicial procedure and clearly defined Torah laws? There are those who explain that this special dispensation applies only to cases of a monetary claim, where both sides are allowed to forgo

HALAKHAH

נֶאֱמָן עָלַי אַבָּא **Father is trustworthy to me.** "If a litigant accepted either a relative, or some otherwise unfit person, as a judge or witness in his case, even if he accepted him in place of an entire court or in place of two witnesses, he cannot subsequently retract his consent, as stated by the Sages according to *Rashi.* According to *Rema,* if one attached some additional concession to the initial concession of accepting an ineligible individual as judge or witness, such as granting that individual the equivalent weight of an entire court or team of witnesses, then he may retract later on, as stated by the Sages according to *Tosafot.*

The prohibition against retraction applies regardless of whether the litigant who agreed to the concession and now wishes to revoke it is the plaintiff or the defendant. However, it only applies after the verdict has been issued,

TRANSLATION AND COMMENTARY

the name of God before an official court and while holding a sacred scroll, as prescribed by Torah law, [1]I will accept in its place your **swearing unto me** privately **'by the life of your head'** and will forgo all other formalities" — [2]**Rabbi Meir says: He can** later **retract** this concession and insist on the oath being taken in accordance with strict Torah law; [3]**and the Sages say: He cannot retract.**

GEMARA אָמַר [4]The first clause of the Mishnah, "My father is trustworthy to me," is often open to interpretation, as it is not clear whether the litigant wants him to serve as a lone judge or as part of a larger tribunal. **Rav Dimi, son of Rav Naḥman, son of Rav Yosef, said:** [5]The above Mishnah is referring to a situation **where the litigant accepted** the father **upon himself as** having no more weight on the court than **one** judge normally would have, the remaining two positions having been filled by qualified candidates. Consequently, the case in the Mishnah involves only one infringement of standard judicial procedure, the serving of an invalid judge on the court, and not the widely aberrant situation of an invalid judge sitting alone in judgment — in which case even the Sages would allow the litigant to retract.

אָמַר רַב יְהוּדָה [6]**Rav Yehudah said in the name of Shmuel: The dispute** between Rabbi Meir and the Sages **in the** first clause of **our Mishnah is** only relevant **when the claimant** initially **says:** "I agree to let this otherwise ineligible individual sit in judgment on our case, and if the court decides in your favor, then I will consider

[1]״דוֹר לִי בְּחַיֵּי רֹאשְׁךָ״ — [2]רַבִּי מֵאִיר אוֹמֵר: יָכוֹל לַחֲזוֹר בּוֹ; [3]וַחֲכָמִים אוֹמְרִים: אֵין יָכוֹל לַחֲזוֹר בּוֹ.

גמרא [4]אָמַר רַב דִּימִי בְּרֵיהּ דְּרַב נַחְמָן בְּרֵיהּ דְּרַב יוֹסֵף: [5]כְּגוֹן דְּקַבְּלֵיהּ עֲלֵיהּ בְּחַד.

[6]אָמַר רַב יְהוּדָה אָמַר שְׁמוּאֵל: מַחֲלוֹקֶת בְּ״מָחוּל לְךָ״; אֲבָל

LITERAL TRANSLATION

[1]"Swear unto me by the life of your head" — [2]Rabbi Meir says: He can retract; [3]and the Sages say: He cannot retract.

GEMARA [4]Rav Dimi, son of Rav Naḥman, son of Rav Yosef, said: [Explain the Mishnah] such as where [the litigant] accepted him upon himself [5]as one [of the judges].

[6]Rav Yehudah said in the name of Shmuel: The dispute [in the Mishnah] is where [the claimant says]: "It is pardoned you [if you win]"; however,

RASHI

דור לי — לשון שבועה. **יכול לחזור בו** — ולישאל שבועה גמורה.

גמרא דקבליה עליה בחד — דיינא. ואף על גב דאיכא תרי אחריני בהדיה אמר רבי מאיר: יכול לחזור בו. **במחול לך** — אי תובע אמר לנתבע: נאמן עלי אבא או אביך, אם יזכוך יהא מחול לך — התם קאמרי רבנן: אינו יכול לחזור בו, דהא זכה זה במה שבידו מכיון שיצא זכאי.

NOTES

legal formality and decide to relinquish the claim to money either owed or in their possession. However, in cases involving either capital or corporal punishment, no such leniencies are allowed and every detail of judicial procedure is firmly observed (*Gilyon HaShas*).

כְּגוֹן דְּקַבְּלֵיהּ עֲלֵיהּ בְּחַד **Such as when the litigant accepted him upon himself as one of the judges.** Rav Dimi's clarification of the Mishnah is only applicable to its first two cases, when the litigant agreed to accept either his father or the disputant's father as a judge in his litigation; in the case when he agreed to be judged by three cattle herders, it is clear that he wished to have all three positions on the court filled by these individuals.

According to *Rashi*'s interpretation of Rav Dimi's statement, it is aimed at highlighting the leniency inherent in Rabbi Meir's position: Even when the litigant has only agreed to this single concession, he can still subsequently retract. *Ran* points out that, according to *Rashi,* this implies that the Sages would argue with Rabbi Meir even if the litigant made more than one concession. *Tosafot* and *Ramah* reject *Rashi*'s interpretation of Rav Dimi and suggest instead that his statement was intended to illuminate the Sages' position: Only if the litigant has made a single concession, is he forbidden to recant; however, if he made more than one concession, even the Rabbis would agree that he can later change his mind — for presumably one who agreed to an excessive number of concessions could not have been serious.

HALAKHAH

as taught by Rava and Rav Naḥman bar Ya'akov. If the verdict has not yet been issued, the conceding litigant may indeed retract if he so wishes, unless he made a commitment through a formal act of acquisition at the time he agreed to the concession," as taught by Shmuel. (*Shulḥan Arukh, Ḥoshen Mishpat* 22:1.)

דּוֹר לִי בְּחַיֵּי רֹאשְׁךָ **Swear to me by the life of your head.** "If, because of a monetary claim, one became obligated to take a formal oath in court, and one's disputant agreed to accept a private, informal oath in its place, as long as the latter did not commit himself to the offer through a legal act of acquisition, he may later retract and demand that the formal oath indeed be taken. This option remains available, however, only as long as the informal oath has

[1] בְּ״אֶתֵּן לְךָ״, [1] דִּבְרֵי הַכֹּל יָכוֹל לַחֲזוֹר בּוֹ. [2] וְרַבִּי יוֹחָנָן אָמַר: בְּ״אֶתֵּן לְךָ״ מַחֲלוֹקֶת.
[3] אִיבַּעֲיָא לְהוּ: בְּ״אֶתֵּן לְךָ״ מַחֲלוֹקֶת, אֲבָל בְּ״מָחוּל לְךָ״, [4] דִּבְרֵי הַכֹּל אֵין יָכוֹל לַחֲזוֹר בּוֹ; [5] אוֹ דִּילְמָא בֵּין בְּזוֹ וּבֵין בְּזוֹ מַחֲלוֹקֶת?
[6] תָּא שְׁמַע, דְּאָמַר רָבָא: [7] מַחֲלוֹקֶת בְּ״אֶתֵּן לְךָ״, אֲבָל בְּ״מָחוּל לְךָ״, [8] דִּבְרֵי הַכֹּל אֵין יָכוֹל לַחֲזוֹר בּוֹ.
[9] אִי אָמְרַתְּ בִּשְׁלָמָא בְּ״אֶתֵּן לְךָ״ מַחֲלוֹקֶת, [10] אֲבָל בְּ״מָחוּל לְךָ״, [11] דִּבְרֵי הַכֹּל אֵין יָכוֹל לַחֲזוֹר בּוֹ — [12] רָבָא דְּאָמַר כְּרַבִּי יוֹחָנָן. [13] אֶלָּא אִי אָמְרַתְּ בֵּין בְּזוֹ

TRANSLATION AND COMMENTARY

the debt as if **it is forgiven to you.**" [1] **However, if** the defendant initially agrees to the unqualified judge, promising, "If the court decides in your favor, **I will** comply with that decision and **give you** the **money** in question," **according to everyone** the defendant **can** subsequently **retract** his initial consent and demand that the decision be rendered by a court composed entirely of qualified judges. In such a case, words (without a formal act of acquisition) are insufficient to show his full acceptance of the possibility that money might be taken from him by a judge who would normally be ineligible. However, regarding the pardoning of the debt if the court decides against him, for which words alone are usually sufficient, the Sages can maintain that he may not retract. [2] **And Rabbi Yoḥanan said: The dispute** in the first clause of our Mishnah **is** relevant **when** the defendant tells his claimant: "I agree to let this otherwise ineligible individual sit in judgment on our case, and if this court should decide in your favor, then **I will give you** the amount of **money** that you demand."

אִיבַּעֲיָא לְהוּ [3] **It was asked of** the Sages in the Academy to clarify Rabbi Yoḥanan's position: Did he mean to say that **the dispute** between Rabbi Meir and the Sages **refers** exclusively to a **defendant** who tells his claimant, **"I will** abide by this judge's decision and, if need be, **give you** the money in question"? **But** regarding a **claimant** who tells the defendant, "I will abide by this judge's decision and, if need be, consider the debt you owe me as if **it is forgiven,"** [4] **everybody agrees** that the claimant **cannot** subsequently **retract** his consent? [5] **Or perhaps** Rabbi Yoḥanan meant to say that **the dispute is** relevant **in both this** case **and that** case?

תָּא שְׁמַע [6] **Come and hear** how this uncertainty might be resolved, **for** surely **Rava said** as follows: [7] **The dispute** between Rabbi Meir and the Sages **refers** only to a **defendant** who tells his claimant, **"I will** abide by this judge's decision and, if need be, **give you the** contested **money," but if the claimant** tells the defendant, "I will abide by this judge's decision and, if need be, consider the debt you owe me as if **it is pardoned you"** — [8] **according to everybody** the claimant **cannot** subsequently **retract** his consent.

אִי אָמְרַתְּ בִּשְׁלָמָא [9] Now, **granted,** Rava's stated position is understandable **if you** assume that Rabbi Yoḥanan also meant to **say that the dispute is** only relevant **to a defendant** who says, **"I will give you** money." [10] **But if a claimant** says, "I will consider the debt as if **it is pardoned you,"** [11] **according to everybody he cannot** later **retract.** [12] **For** if such is the case, one can simply conclude that **Rava stated** his position **in accordance with** the opinion of **Rabbi Yoḥanan.** [13] **But if you** assume that Rabbi Yoḥanan meant to **say that the dispute** between Rabbi Meir and the Sages in our Mishnah **is** relevant **in both this** case **and that** case,

LITERAL TRANSLATION

where [the defendant says] "I will give you [the money if you win]," [1] he can renege according to everyone. [2] And Rabbi Yoḥanan said: The dispute is where [the defendant says]: "I will give you [the money if you win]."

[3] A question was raised (lit., "it was asked of them"): Is the dispute where [the defendant says]: "I will give you [the money if you win]," [4] but where [the claimant says]: "It is pardoned you [if you win]," he cannot renege according to everybody; [5] or perhaps the dispute is in both this [case] and that [case]?

[6] Come [and] hear, for Rava said: [7] The dispute is where [the defendant says]: "I will give you [the money if you win]," but where [the claimant says]: "It is pardoned you [if you win]," [8] he cannot renege according to everybody.

[9] Granted, if you say that the dispute is where [the defendant says]: "I will give you [the money]," [10] but where [the claimant says]: "It is pardoned you," [11] he cannot renege according to everybody — [12] for Rava said like Rabbi Yoḥanan. [13] But if you say that the dispute

RASHI

אבל באתן לך — דנתבע אמר לתובע: אם יחייבוני אבא או אבין אתן לך. דברי הכל יכול לחזור — דהואיל והממון בידו, אין בו כח לתובע להוציא אלא בדיינין כשרין.

HALAKHAH

not yet been taken, and the case has not been concluded." (*Shulḥan Arukh, Ḥoshen Mishpat* 22:3.)

וּבֵין בְּזוֹ מַחֲלוֹקֶת, [1]רָבָא דְּאָמַר כְּמַאן?
[2]רָבָא טַעְמָא דְּנַפְשֵׁיהּ קָאָמַר.
[3]אֵיתִיבֵיהּ רַב אַחָא בַּר תַּחֲלִיפָא לְרָבָא: [4]"הָיָה חַיָּיב לַחֲבֵירוֹ שְׁבוּעָה, [5]וְאָמַר לוֹ: 'דּוֹר לִי בְּחַיֵּי רֹאשְׁךָ' — [6]רַבִּי מֵאִיר אוֹמֵר: יָכוֹל לַחֲזוֹר בּוֹ, [7]וַחֲכָמִים אוֹמְרִים: אֵין יָכוֹל לַחֲזוֹר בּוֹ". [24B] [8]מַאי לָאו בְּאוֹתָן הַנִּשְׁבָּעִין וְלֹא מְשַׁלְּמִין, [9]דַּהֲוָה לֵיהּ כְּ"מָחוּל לָךְ"?
[10]לֹא! בְּאוֹתָן הַנִּשְׁבָּעִין וְנוֹטְלִין, [11]דַּהֲוָה לֵיהּ כְּ"אֶתֵּן לָךְ".
[12]וְהָא תְּנָא לֵיהּ רֵישָׁא!

LITERAL TRANSLATION

is in both this [case] and that [case], [1]in accordance with whom did Rava say [his teaching]?
[2]Rava was stating his own argument.
[3]Rav Aḥa bar Taḥlifa raised an objection against Rava [from our Mishnah]: [4]"[If] he was obligated to his fellow [to take] an oath, [5]and he said to him: 'Swear unto me by the life of your head' — [6]Rabbi Meir says: He can renege; [7]and the Sages say: He cannot renege." [24B] [8]Is it not [dealing] with those who swear and do not pay, [9]which is like "It is pardoned you"?
[10]No! [It is dealing] with those who swear and take, [11]which is like "I will give you."
[12]But surely the first clause taught it!

RASHI

טעמיה דנפשיה קאמר — ופליג אתרווייהו. **באותן הנשבעין** — לפטור עצמן שלא ישלמו, דתובע קאמר: דור לי ואני מוחל לך. **הנשבעין ונוטלין** — השכיר והנגזל וכיוצא בהן, דנתבע קאמר ליה: דור לי ואתן לך. **והא תנא לה רישא** — דאוקמת לה באתן לך, ותרתי למה לי?

TRANSLATION AND COMMENTARY

[1]then **in accordance with whom did Rava state** his position? He agrees with neither Shmuel nor Rabbi Yoḥanan! Consequently, one must assume that Rabbi Yoḥanan meant to say that the dispute is relevant only in the case of a claimant who decides to accept the decision of an unqualified judge and, if need be, waive his claim.

רָבָא [2]The Gemara rejects the preceding proof: Why must we assume that Rava was conforming with one of the previously stated positions regarding the dispute in our Mishnah? One can just as well assume that **Rava was stating** his position in accordance with **his own reasoning.** Hence, it is still unclear whether Rabbi Yoḥanan views the dispute between Rabbi Meir and the Sages in our Mishnah as extending to the case of a claimant who wishes to retract his initial consent to appear before an unqualified judge.

אֵיתִיבֵיהּ [3]**Rav Aḥa bar Taḥlifa raised an objection against** the above-stated position of **Rava's,** wherein he confined the dispute between Rabbi Meir and the Sages in the first clause of our Mishnah to the case of a defendant who wishes to retract his initial consent to abide by the decision of an unqualified judge. As the very next clause in our Mishnah states: [4]"Similarly, if one of the litigants **was obligated to his fellow** with regard to taking **an oath,** as in the case of a contested monetary claim, [5]**and** the latter **said to him:** 'Instead of swearing by the name of God before an official court, and while holding a sacred scroll, as prescribed by Torah law, I will accept your **swearing to me** privately **"by the life of your head"** and forgo all other formality' — [6]**Rabbi Meir says: He can** later **retract** this concession and insist on the oath being taken in accordance with strict Torah law; [7]**and the Sages say: He cannot retract."** [24B] [8]**Are we not** dealing **with those** defendants who are required by Torah law to **swear** that they do not owe money **and** thereby are exempt from **paying** the claim? In such cases the concession made by the claimant allowing the defendant to take an informal oath rather than an official Torah oath in court [9]**is like** the concession made by the claimant who says, "I will abide by the unqualified judge's decision and, if need be, consider the debt you owe me as if **it is forgiven you."** Thus we see from the clause dealing with **the** claimant's conceding his opponent's oath that Rabbi Meir and the Sages also disagree regarding the case where the claimant concedes the ruling of the unqualified judge and pardons the debt. How, then, can Rava suggest that all agree that the claimant cannot retract his initial consent?

לֹא [10]The Gemara rejects Rav Aḥa bar Taḥlifa's attack on Rava from the Mishnah: **No!** The Mishnah can be explained by Rava to be dealing dealing **with those** claimants who must swear that the defendant owes them money before they can **take** payment (see *Shevuot* 7:1-7); in such a case, the concession made by the defendant in allowing the claimant to take an informal oath [11]**is** in essence like the concession made by the defendant who tells his claimant that **"I will** comply with the decision of an unqualified judge and, if need be, **give you** the money that you claim." Hence, this clause in the Mishnah does not prove that Rabbi Meir and the Sages disagree about the case of a claimant who tells the defendant, "If need be, I will consider the debt as if it is forgiven you." Rava is not contradicted by the Mishnah, for he maintains that Rabbi Meir and the Sages do disagree about the right to retract.

וְהָא תְּנָא [12]**But** surely, according to Rava, **the first clause** of our Mishnah has already **taught** us that such a dispute exists! What, then, is the latter clause of the Mishnah coming to add?

[1]תְּנָא תּוֹלֶה בְּדַעַת אֲחֵרִים, [2]וְתְנָא תּוֹלֶה בְּדַעַת עַצְמוֹ. [3]וּצְרִיכָא. [4]דְּאִי תְּנָא תּוֹלֶה בְּדַעַת אֲחֵרִים — [5]בְּהָא קָאָמַר רַבִּי מֵאִיר דְּמָצֵי הָדַר בֵּיהּ, [6]מִשּׁוּם דְּלָא גָּמַר וּמַקְנֵי, [7]דְּאָמַר: מִי יֵימַר דִּמְזַכֵּי לֵיהּ? [8]אֲבָל, תּוֹלֶה בְּדַעַת עַצְמוֹ, [9]אֵימָא מוֹדֵי לְהוּ לְרַבָּנַן. [10]וְאִי אַשְׁמַעִינַן בְּהָא — [11]בְּהָא קָאָמְרִי רַבָּנַן, [12]אֲבָל בְּהַהִיא: אֵימָא מוֹדוּ לֵיהּ רַבָּנַן לְרַבִּי מֵאִיר. [13]צְרִיכָא.

[14]אָמַר רֵישׁ לָקִישׁ: מַחֲלוֹקֶת לִפְנֵי גְמַר דִּין. [15]אֲבָל, לְאַחַר גְּמַר דִּין — [16]דִּבְרֵי הַכֹּל אֵין יָכוֹל לַחֲזוֹר בּוֹ. [17]וְרַבִּי יוֹחָנָן אָמַר: לְאַחַר גְּמַר דִּין מַחֲלוֹקֶת.

LITERAL TRANSLATION

[1][The Mishnah] taught [the case of] one who renders [it] contingent upon the decision of others, [2]and it taught [the case of] one who renders [it] contingent upon his own [opponent's] decision. [3]And it is necessary [to state both]. [4]For if it had [only] taught [about] one who renders [it] contingent upon the decision of others — [5]in this [case] Rabbi Meir stated that he can retract, [6]because he has not decided to transfer possession, [7]for he said: Who is to say that he will award it to [the claimant]? [8]However, [about] one who renders [it] contingent upon his own decision, [9]say [that Rabbi Meir] admits to the Sages. [10]And if it had taught us [only] this — [11]in this the Sages stated [as they did], [12]but in that say: The Sages admit to Rabbi Meir. [13][Therefore both] are necessary.

[14]Resh Lakish said: The dispute [relates to the situation] before the verdict (lit. "conclusion of judgment"). [15]However, after the verdict — [16]the opinion of all is that he cannot retract. [17]And Rabbi Yoḥanan said: The dispute [relates to the situation] after the verdict.

TRANSLATION AND COMMENTARY

תְּנָא [1]The Gemara answers: Whereas the first clause of the Mishnah taught us about the dispute in the case of **one who renders** his payment **contingent upon the decision of others,** such as an ineligible judge, [2]the latter clause **taught** us that the same dispute applies when **one renders** his payment **contingent upon his** fellow litigant's **own decision,** whether the plaintiff takes the informal oath. [3]**And it was necessary** for the Mishnah to **state** this dispute in **both** instances. [4]**For if it** had **taught** us of this dispute **only** in the case of **one who renders** his liability **contingent upon the decision of others** — [5]one might think that only **in this** case did **Rabbi Meir state that** the defendant **can** subsequently **retract,** [6]**because he had not conclusively** decided at the time of his initial consent actually **to transfer possession** of any money to the claimant. [7]**For** we assume that **he said** to himself: **"Who is to say that** this judge **will** necessarily **award** the money to my opponent?" [8]**However,** in the case of **one who renders** his payment **contingent upon his** opponent's **own decision,** as in the case of the oath, [9]one might **say that Rabbi Meir admits to the Sages** that the defendant cannot retract his initial offer — for it must certainly have been clear to him that the plaintiff would take advantage of his concession and attempt to collect his claim. [10]**And** conversely, **if** the Mishnah **had taught us** of the dispute only **in** regard to **the** case of the oath — [11]one might say that only **in this case** did **the Sages state** that the defendant may not retract his initial offer, [12]**but in** the case of one who renders his liability contingent upon the decision of a third party, one might **say that the Sages admit to Rabbi Meir** that the defendant may recant, since one can assume that he was not fully resigned to paying the claim. [13]Hence **it was necessary** for the Mishnah to teach us that Rabbi Meir and the Sages maintain their respective positions in both cases.

אָמַר רֵישׁ לָקִישׁ [14]**Resh Lakish said: The dispute** between Rabbi Meir and the Sages in our Mishnah relates to a litigant who wished to retract his initial concession **before the verdict** had been rendered in court. [15]**However, after the verdict** has been issued, **the opinion of all** — including Rabbi Meir — [16]**is that** the conceding litigant **cannot retract** and invalidate the court's decision. [17]**And Rabbi Yoḥanan said: The dispute** cited in our Mishnah relates to a litigant who wished to renege **after the verdict** was rendered.

RASHI

תולה בדעת אחרים – אבא ואבין. **בדעת עצמו** – של חבירו בעל דין. **מי יימר דמזכי ליה** – ואי הוה ידע דמזכי ליה – לא הוה אמר, הלכך הדר. **אבל תולה בדעת עצמו** – של בעל דין, אסיק אדעתיה דודאי נדר ליה כדי להפטר, וידע ומחיל. **לפני גמר דין** – לאחר שטענו בפניהם, וקודם גמר דין בא זה לחזור.

NOTES

גְּמַר דִּין The verdict. Our commentary follows the opinion of most authorities (*Tur*, *Baḥ*, and *Shakh* as based upon *Tosafot*, *Nimmukei Yosef* and *Smag*), who equate the גְּמַר דִּין ("conclusion of judgment") with the issuing of a verdict. According to *Sma*, a true verdict must identify both the liable party as well as the one who is to receive payment. *Shakh*, however, proves from numerous sources that it is sufficient for the verdict to identify the liable party alone.

[1]אִיבַּעֲיָא לְהוּ: [2]לְאַחַר גְּמַר דִּין מַחֲלוֹקֶת — אֲבָל לִפְנֵי גְּמַר דִּין, דִּבְרֵי הַכֹּל יָכוֹל לַחֲזוֹר בּוֹ — [3]אוֹ דִּילְמָא: בֵּין בְּזוֹ וּבֵין בְּזוֹ מַחֲלוֹקֶת?

[4]תָּא שְׁמַע: דְּאָמַר רָבָא: [5]קִיבֵּל עָלָיו קָרוֹב אוֹ פָּסוּל — [6]לִפְנֵי גְּמַר דִּין, יָכוֹל לַחֲזוֹר בּוֹ; [7]לְאַחַר גְּמַר דִּין, אֵין יָכוֹל לַחֲזוֹר בּוֹ.

[8]אִי אָמְרַתְּ בִּשְׁלָמָא לְאַחַר גְּמַר דִּין מַחֲלוֹקֶת, [9]אֲבָל לִפְנֵי גְּמַר דִּין דִּבְרֵי הַכֹּל יָכוֹל לַחֲזוֹר בּוֹ — [10]רָבָא דַּאֲמַר כְּרַבִּי יוֹחָנָן, וְאַלִּיבָּא דְּרַבָּנַן. [11]אֶלָּא אִי אָמְרַתְּ בֵּין בְּזוֹ בֵּין בְּזוֹ מַחֲלוֹקֶת, [12]רָבָא דַּאֲמַר כְּמַאן?

LITERAL TRANSLATION

[1]It was asked of them: Is the difference of opinion after the verdict — [2]but before the verdict, all are of the opinion that he can retract — [3]or perhaps both in this [case] and in that [case] there is a difference of opinion?

[4]Come [and] hear: For Rava said: [5][If] he accepted upon himself a relative or someone — [6]before the verdict, he can retract; [7]after the verdict, he cannot retract.

[8]It is well if you say that the dispute is after the verdict, [9]but before the verdict the opinion of all is that he can retract — [10]Rava said like Rabbi Yoḥanan and in accordance with the Sages. [11]But if you say that the dispute is both in this [case] and that [case], [12]in accordance with whom did Rava state [his ruling]?

TRANSLATION AND COMMENTARY

אִיבַּעֲיָא לְהוּ [1]**A question was raised** before the Sages in the Academy: Was it Rabbi Yoḥanan's intention to say that **the difference of opinion** between Rabbi Meir and the Sages relates exclusively to a litigant who wishes to retract **after the verdict** has been issued, [2]**but before the verdict** has been issued? **All** — even the Rabbis — **are of the opinion that** the conceding litigant **can retract.** [3]**Or perhaps** he meant to say that **both in this** case **and in that** case **there is a difference of opinion** between Rabbi Meir and the Sages?

תָּא שְׁמַע [4]**Come and hear** how this uncertainty might be resolved: **For** surely **Rava said:** [5]If a litigant **accepted upon himself** a judge or witness **who is** either **related** to a party involved in the litigation **or** is **unfit** by virtue of his corrupt behavior — [6]**before the verdict, he can retract** his concession; however, [7]**after the verdict** has already been issued, **he cannot retract.**

אִי אָמְרַתְּ [8]Granted, **it is well if you say that** Rabbi Yoḥanan maintained that **the dispute** between Rabbi Meir and the Sages relates to a litigant who wishes to retract **after the verdict** has been issued — [9]**whereas before the verdict** has been issued, **the opinion of all is that** the conceding litigant **can retract.** [10]We can then assume that **Rava stated** his decision in accordance with **Rabbi Yoḥanan and** his understanding of the law **according to the Sages.** [11]**But if you say that** Rabbi Yoḥanan understood **the dispute** between Rabbi Meir and the Sages to be relevant **both** after **and** before the verdict, [12]then **in accordance with whom did Rava state** his decision? Neither in accordance with Rabbi Yoḥanan nor in accordance with Resh Lakish, who maintain that according to the Sages one may never retract. Moreover, it is unthinkable that Rava would rule like Rabbi Meir against the Sages that the litigant may retract before

RASHI

הכי גרסינן: אי אמרת בשלמא רבי יוחנן הכי קאמר, לאחר גמר דין מחלוקת, אבל לפני גמר דין אפילו לרבנן חוזר. רבא — דפסיק הלכתא דחוזר לפני גמר דין ולא לאחר גמר דין, דאמר כרבי יוחנן ואליבא דרבנן. אלא אי אמרת — לרבי יוחנן בין בזה ובין בזה מחלוקת. רבא דאמר כמאן — בין לריש לקיש בין לרבי יוחנן, לרבנן לפני גמר דין קאמרי דלא הדר. והא ליכא למימר דרבא כריש לקיש ואליבא דרבי מאיר אמרה לשמעתיה, דלא שביק רבנן ועביד כרבי מאיר דפסקינן לקמן הלכה כחכמים. ולא שייך למימר הכא: רבא טעמא דנפשיה קאמר, וסבירא ליה דכי פליגי רבנן לאחר גמר דין אבל לפני גמר דין מודו, אבל לרבי יוחנן בין בזו ובין בזו מחלוקת, דהא לא איירי רבא בפלוגתא כלל אלא מיפסק פסק דינא.

NOTES

The position of *Rambam* is the subject of conflicting interpretations: Some view him as agreeing with the above-mentioned consensus (*Nimmukei Yosef, Bet Yosef,* and *Baḥ*), while others interpret his words as implying that the case is not concluded until the court has actually collected money from the liable party (*Tur*, *Smag*, *Leḥem Mishneh*, and *Shakh*).

When a litigant agrees to hear testimony from an ineligible witness, the majority of authorities equate the גְּמַר דִּין — "the verdict" — with the actual delivery of the contested testimony, after which retraction is disallowed. Here again, some commentators claim that *Rambam* allows the conceding party to disqualify the testimony even after it has been delivered, as long as the court has not yet collected money from the defendant.

Regarding the second clause of the Mishnah, about a litigant who agrees to allow his opponent to take an informal private oath rather than the court-administered one, the definition of גְּמַר דִּין is subject to dispute as well. Some identify it as the time when the informal oath is actually taken (*Sma* and *Shulḥan Arukh* in line with *Rambam*), while others identify it as the earlier time when the two agree in court to arrange for an out-of-court oath (*Shakh,* in accordance with *Ramban* and other Rishonim).

TRANSLATION AND COMMENTARY

the verdict is delivered. Nor can we say that Rava was offering his own interpretation of the dispute in the Mishnah, since his statement was made in the form of a legal decision. [1]**Rather, may we not conclude from** Rava's statement **that** Rabbi Yoḥanan must have been of the opinion that **the dispute** in our Mishnah between Rabbi Meir and the Sages relates exclusively to a litigant who wishes to retract **after the verdict** has been issued? [2]One can **conclude** this to be the case **from** Rava's ruling.

שְׁלַח לֵיהּ [3]In an attempt to achieve a formal ruling on the dispute cited above between Resh Lakish and Rabbi Yoḥanan, **Rav Naḥman bar Rav Ḥisda sent** the following **query to Rav Naḥman bar Ya'akov:** [4]**Let our master teach us: Does the dispute** between Rabbi Meir and the Sages deal with the situation **before the verdict** has been issued **or** with the situation **after the verdict** has been issued? [5]**And in accordance with whose opinion is** the practical **law** decided — according to Rabbi Meir or the Sages? [6]Rav Naḥman bar Ya'akov **sent** back **to him** the following **reply: The dispute** deals with the situation **after the verdict** has been issued. [7]**And** as far as **the** actual **law** is concerned, it **is in accordance with the opinion of the Sages** who say that one may not retract at that time.

רַב אַשִׁי אָמַר [8]**Rav Ashi** had a different version of this inquiry. He **said** that, according to his tradition, Rav Naḥman bar Rav Ḥisda **sent a query to** Rav Naḥman bar Ya'akov for a formal ruling on the dispute between Rav Yehudah in the name of Shmuel and Rabbi Yoḥanan: [9]**Does the dispute** between Rabbi Meir and the Sages deal with a defendant who **says to** his claimant, **"I will** comply with the decision of this unqualified judge and, if necessary, will **give you** the money you claim," [10]**or does the dispute** deal with a claimant who says to the defendant, "If this unqualified judge decides in your favor, I will consider my claim against **you as being pardoned"?** [11]**And the** actual **law — in accordance with whose opinion** is it decided? [12]Rav Naḥman bar Ya'akov **sent** back **to him the** following **reply: The dispute** deals with the case of a defendant who says to his claimant: **"I will** comply with the decision of this unqualified judge and, if necessary, will **give you** the money you claim," [13]**and the** actual **law is** decided **in accordance with the opinion of the Sages** who maintain that the defendant may not subsequently retract his consent. However, if the claimant agrees to pardon the debt, both Rabbi Meir and the Sages agree that he may not retract. [14]The Gemara adds that it was **in** the Babylonian academy of **Sura** that the preceding inquiries were **taught** as just recorded.

בְּפוּמְבְּדִיתָא [15]**In** the Babylonian academy of **Pumbedita,** however, **they taught** yet another **inquiry as follows:** [16]**Rabbi Ḥanina bar Shelemiah said:** The scholars **from the academy of Rav sent** the following query **to Shmuel:** [17]**Let our master teach us** — in the event the conceding litigant wished to retract his concesssion **before the verdict** was issued, but after the court had already **acquired** (through a formal act of acquisition)

[1]אֶלָּא, לָאו שְׁמַע מִינָּהּ לְאַחַר גְּמַר דִּין מַחֲלוֹקֶת. [2]שְׁמַע מִינָּהּ.
[3]שְׁלַח לֵיהּ רַב נַחְמָן בַּר רַב חִסְדָּא לְרַב נַחְמָן בַּר יַעֲקֹב: [4]יְלַמְּדֵנוּ רַבֵּינוּ, לִפְנֵי גְּמַר דִּין מַחֲלוֹקֶת אוֹ לְאַחַר גְּמַר דִּין מַחֲלוֹקֶת? [5]וַהֲלָכָה כְּדִבְרֵי מִי? [6]שְׁלַח לֵיהּ: לְאַחַר גְּמַר דִּין מַחֲלוֹקֶת, [7]וַהֲלָכָה כְּדִבְרֵי חֲכָמִים.
[8]רַב אַשִׁי אָמַר: הָכִי שְׁלַח לֵיהּ: [9]בְּ״אֶתֵּן לָךְ״ מַחֲלוֹקֶת, [10]אוֹ בְּ״מָחוּל לָךְ״ מַחֲלוֹקֶת? [11]וַהֲלָכָה כְּדִבְרֵי מִי? [12]שְׁלַח לֵיהּ: בְּ״אֶתֵּן לָךְ״ מַחֲלוֹקֶת, [13]וַהֲלָכָה כְּדִבְרֵי חֲכָמִים.
[14]בְּסוּרָא מַתְנֵי הָכִי.
[15]בְּפוּמְבְּדִיתָא מַתְנֵי הָכִי: [16]אָמַר רַב חֲנִינָא בַּר שֶׁלֶמְיָה: שְׁלַחוּ לֵיהּ מִבֵּי רַב לִשְׁמוּאֵל: [17]יְלַמְּדֵנוּ רַבֵּינוּ, לִפְנֵי גְּמַר דִּין

LITERAL TRANSLATION

[1]Rather, [may we] not conclude from this that the dispute [relates to the situation] after the verdict? [2]Conclude [it] from this.

[3]Rav Naḥman bar Rav Ḥisda sent [a query] to Rav Naḥman bar Ya'akov: [4]Let our master teach us: Is the dispute before the verdict or is the dispute after the verdict? [5]And in accordance with whose opinion is the law? [6]He sent [a reply] to him: The dispute is after the verdict, [7]and the law is in accordance with the opinion of the Sages.

[8]Rav Ashi said: He sent [a query to] him thus: [9]Is the dispute about "I will give you?" [10]or is the dispute about "It is pardoned you"? [11]And in accordance with whose opinion is the law? [12]He sent [a reply] to him: The dispute [is] about "I will give you," [13]and the law is in accordance with the opinion of the Sages. [14]In Sura they taught it thus.

[15][But] in Pumbedita they taught as follows: [16]Rabbi Ḥanina bar Shelemiah said: They sent from the academy of Rav to Shmuel: [17]Let our master teach us — before the verdict and they

TRANSLATION AND COMMENTARY

a commitment **from him** to abide by the initial agreement, **what** is the law? [1]Shmuel **sent** back **to them the** following **reply: Nothing** may change the terms of an agreement **after** a formal act of **acquisition** has been executed securing compliance with its terms.

MISHNAH וְאֵלּוּ הֵן [2]**And these** individuals **are unfit to serve as judges or witnesses:** [3]**A dice-player, and one who lends** money **on interest, one who** profits from **pigeon-flying, and merchants of seventh-year** produce (produce that grew during the Sabbatical Year, which one is forbidden to sell for profit). [4]**Rabbi Shimon said: Originally, the Sages would refer to** these individuals **as "harvesters of seventh-year produce"**; however, [5]**when the** number of tax **enforcers** appointed by the government **increased, they** changed their mind and **started** calling **them "merchants of seventh-year** produce." [6]**Rabbi Yehudah said: When** do all of these individuals become unfit to serve as judges or witnesses? [7]**When they have no trade other than** the objectionable one

וְקָנוּ מִיָּדוֹ, מַאי? [1]שְׁלַח לְהוּ: אֵין לְאַחַר קִנְיָין כְּלוּם.

מִשְׁנָה [2]וְאֵלּוּ הֵן הַפְּסוּלִין: [3]הַמְשַׂחֵק בְּקוּבְיָּא וְהַמַּלְוֶה בְּרִיבִּית, וּמַפְרִיחֵי יוֹנִים, וְסוֹחֲרֵי שְׁבִיעִית. [4]אָמַר רַבִּי שִׁמְעוֹן: בַּתְּחִילָּה הָיוּ קוֹרִין אוֹתָן "אוֹסְפֵי שְׁבִיעִית", [5]מִשֶּׁרַבּוּ הָאַנָּסִין, חָזְרוּ לִקְרוֹתָן "סוֹחֲרֵי שְׁבִיעִית". [6]אָמַר רַבִּי יְהוּדָה: אֵימָתַי? [7]בִּזְמַן שֶׁאֵין

LITERAL TRANSLATION

acquired from his hand, what [is the law]? [1]He sent [a reply] to them: Nothing [may change] after acquisition.

MISHNAH [2]And these are unfit: [3]A dice-player, and one who lends on interest, and pigeon-fliers, and merchants of seventh-year [produce]. [4]Rabbi Shimon said: Originally [the Sages] used to call them "harvesters of seventh-year [produce]"; [5]when the enforcers increased, they returned to calling them "merchants of seventh-year [produce]." [6]Rabbi Yehudah said: When [are they unfit]? [7]When they have no

RASHI

וקנו מידו — מתחלה שלא יחזור.

משנה ואלו הן הפסולים — לדון ולהעיד. **המשחק בקוביא** — כולהו מפרש בגמרא. וכולן מעין גזלנין הן, והתורה אמרה (שמות כג) "אל תשת רשע עד" — וכל שכן דיין. **וסוחרי שביעית** — הואיל וחימוד ממון מעבירו על דברי תורה הוה ליה כרשע דחמס, ופסול לדון ולהעיד שנוטה אחרי הבצע. **בתחילה היו קוראין אותן [כו']** — מפרש בגמרא.

NOTES

אֵלּוּ הֵן הַפְּסוּלִים **These are unfit.** Various types of ineligibility affect the selection of judges and witnesses for a Jewish court. Our Mishnah deals with a specific type of ineligibility that derives from committing a transgression for financial gain. Such individuals are disqualified as witnesses because of the verse: "Place not your hand with the wicked, to be a thievish witness" (Exodus 23:1). The Gemara (27a) interprets this to mean that any individual who commits an act that constitutes thievery or extortion is ineligible to serve as a witness. (The same Gemara quotes an Amoraic dispute over whether any wicked person, even one whose transgressions do not involve financial gain, is also disqualified as a result of the verse.) In addition to those who commit outright thievery, the Rabbis ordained that anyone who seeks illicit financial gain is also ineligible. (The ineligibility to serve as a judge is considered a logical extension of one's being unfit to serve in the lesser capacity of a witness.)

Our Mishnah does not mention obvious offenders such as thieves and robbers, who are clearly disqualified by the above verse. Instead it limits itself to lesser offenders who are motivated by the desire for illicit profits. Most commentators maintain that the Mishnah limits itself even further to types of illicit gain that are disqualified only by Rabbinic decree. (*Tosafot*, *Rabbenu Yehonatan*, and others.) *Ramah*, however, insists that the two examples of usury and selling seventh-year produce refer to violations of Biblical injunctions, and therefore people who commit these transgressions are disqualified as judges and witnesses by Torah law. However, these cases are still cited because they do not strictly constitute theft, since their profits are obtained with the willing cooperation of the other party. The Mishnah does not include people who are guilty of offenses unrelated to financial matters, but who are still unfit by virtue of being "wicked" (according to the opinion that such individuals are implicitly referred to by the verse), because the verse's main intention is to disqualify the "thievish witness" before all others. Hence the Mishnah limits itself to those cases alone (*Meiri*).

מְשַׂחֵק בְּקוּבְיָא **A dice-player.** According to some commentators, the connection between gambling and theft lies in the assumption that anyone who gambles in order to satisfy his lust for wealth would — if he had the nerve and the opportunity — commit theft. Thus he should be treated no differently from any other thief (*Rabbenu Yehonatan*).

HALAKHAH

אֵלּוּ הֵן הַפְּסוּלִין **These are unfit.** "A wicked person is ineligible as a witness. If the law that he violated was of Rabbinic origin, then his disqualification is also Rabbinical in nature. Some say that in order to be declared unfit Rabbinically, one's violation has to have been motivated by a desire for money (*Rema*)." (*Shulḥan Arukh, Ḥoshen Mishpat* 34:1,3.)

מְשַׂחֵק בְּקוּבְיָא **A dice-player.** "One who plays with dice, or engages in similar forms of gambling, is ineligible to serve as a witness as long as he has no other productive trade,"

TRANSLATION AND COMMENTARY

cited; [1]**however, if they have** engaged in **a trade that is not** discreditable, then **they are fit** to serve as judges or witnesses.

GEMARA מְשַׂחֵק בְּקוּבְיָא [2]In the case of **a dice-player, what** exactly **is he is doing** that renders him unfit to serve as a judge or a witness? [3]**Rami bar Ḥama said:** He is unfit because gambling is taking money with a conditional obligation to pay an agreed amount if the dice fall in a particular way. [4]Since the promise to pay is compromised by the obligator's reliance on not having to honor his conditional obligation — as he is hoping that the dice will fall in his favor — it does not result in a valid **acquisition** by the party receiving the money. All gambling is essentially a form of larceny, since the one who collects the wager is taking money that was not whole-heartedly given to him. [5]**Rav Sheshet said:** The case of a gambling wager, or **any case like** it, **is not** a valid example of a **conditional obligation** because all parties fully acknowledge that forces beyond their control may lead to their losing the bet. [6]**Rather,** we must say that gamblers are ineligible to serve as judges or witnesses **because they are not engaged in productive activities** that contribute to **civilizing** the world.

מַאי בֵּינַיְיהוּ [7]**What is** the practical difference **between** the rationale given by Rami bar Ḥama for disqualifying gamblers as judges or witnesses, and that given by Rav Sheshet? [8]The difference **between them applies when** the gambler has **learned another** — more

לָהֶן אוּמָּנוּת אֶלָּא הוּא. [1]אֲבָל יֵשׁ לָהֶן אוּמָּנוּת שֶׁלֹּא הוּא, כְּשֵׁרִין.

גמרא [2]״מְשַׂחֵק בְּקוּבְיָא״ — מַאי קָא עָבֵיד? [3]אָמַר רָמִי בַּר חָמָא: מִשּׁוּם דַּהֲוָה אַסְמַכְתָּא, [4]וְאַסְמַכְתָּא לֹא קָנְיָא. [5]רַב שֵׁשֶׁת אָמַר: כָּל כִּי הַאי גַּוְונָא לָאו אַסְמַכְתָּא הִיא. [6]אֶלָּא, לְפִי שֶׁאֵין עֲסוּקִין בְּיִישׁוּבוֹ שֶׁל עוֹלָם. [7]מַאי בֵּינַיְיהוּ? [8]אִיכָּא בֵּינַיְיהוּ דְּגָמַר אוּמָּנוּתָא אַחֲרִיתִי.

LITERAL TRANSLATION

trade other than this. [1]But [if] they have a trade other than this, they are fit.

GEMARA [2]"A dice-player" — what is it that he is doing [wrong]? [3]Rami bar Ḥama said: [It is] a conditional obligation [4]and a conditional obligation does not acquire. [5]Rav Sheshet said: Anything like this is not a conditional obligation. [6]Rather, [it is] because they do not engage in settling the world.

[7]What is [the difference] between them? [8]There is between them that he learned another trade.

RASHI

שאין לו אומנות אלא הוא — דהואיל ואין עסוקין ביישובו של עולם אינן בקיאין בטיב דינין ומשא ומתן, ואינן יראי חטא.

גמרא אסמכתא — היינו דבר דאינו נותן לו מדעתו אלא סומך על דבר שאינו, דסבור שהוא יכול לנצח, ופעמים שמנצחין אותו. **לא קניא** — והוה ליה כעין גזילה בידו. **כל כי האי גוונא לאו אסמכתא הוא** — והיכי דמי אסמכתא — כגון ד״אם אוביר ולא אעביד אשלם במיטבא״ (בבא מציעא עו,א) וכגון משליש את שטרו ד״גט פשוט״ (בבא בתרא קסח,א) דסומך על לא דבר, דסבור כל זה בידי לעשות, ומרישא כי מתני — אדעתא דלא יהיב ליה לאסמכתא קא מתני, דטועה וסבור לא יבא לידי כך. אבל הכא לא סמיך אמידי, דהא לא ידע אי נצח אי לא נצח, ואפילו הכי אתני — שמע מינה מספיקא אתני גמר ואקני, ולא גזילה היא.

BACKGROUND

אַסְמַכְתָּא Conditional obligation. This term refers to an obligation known as *asmakhta,* in which a person believes that it is entirely in his power to avoid a conditional liability he took upon himself, such as a promise to perform a simple job for someone or pay a penalty.

מְשַׂחֵק בְּקוּבְיָא A dice-player.

Roman drawing of dice players

Roman dice

NOTES

שֶׁאֵין לָהֶן אוּמָּנוּת אֶלָּא הוּא Who possess no trade other than this. According to the Jerusalem Talmud, this addendum of Rabbi Yehudah's applies only to individuals trading in seventh-year produce. Consequently, there is no basis for suggesting, as our Gemara does, that Rabbi Yehudah in the Mishnah supports Rav Sheshet, who claims that the same distinction applies to a gambler.

רַב שֵׁשֶׁת אָמַר Rav Sheshet said. According to some, Rav Sheshet intended only to explain the position of Rabbi Yehudah in our Mishnah, and not to disagree with Rami bar Ḥama about the reasoning behind the position of the Rabbis (*Rabbi Yehudah Almandri*).

כָּל כִּי הַאי גַּוְונָא לָאו אַסְמַכְתָּא הִיא Any case like it is not *asmakhta.* *Tosafot* points out that a gambling wager cannot be legitimately collected unless it was initially placed on a game board belonging to the bettors. It is insufficient simply to promise to pay the wager, even when anchored by a formal act of acquisition — unless that act was performed before a court.

שֶׁאֵין עֲסוּקִין בְּיִישׁוּבוֹ שֶׁל עוֹלָם For they do not engage in productive work. Various explanations are given for the disqualification of gamblers based on their not engaging in productive work. According to *Rashi,* an individual who is not involved in business or trade cannot be knowledgeable concerning the laws that govern routine business activity, and as a result he lacks both the practical training we expect of a judge, and the "fear of sinning" that we look for in a witness. *Ramah* suggests that his disqualification

HALAKHAH

in accordance with the position of Rabbi Yehudah. Because he does not have a socially responsible means of livelihood, he is not familiar with the nature of honest business dealings, does not value the possessions of his fellow, and is therefore viewed as an individual who supports himself illicitly." (*Shulḥan Arukh, Ḥoshen Mishpat* 34:16.)

[1]וּתְנַן: ״אָמַר רַבִּי יְהוּדָה: אֵימָתַי? [2]בִּזְמַן שֶׁאֵין לָהֶן אוּמָּנוּת אֶלָּא הוּא. [3]אֲבָל יֵשׁ לָהֶן אוּמָּנוּת שֶׁלֹּא הוּא, הֲרֵי זֶה כְּשֵׁרִים״. [4]אַלְמָא טַעְמָא דְּמַתְנִיתִין — מִשּׁוּם יִישּׁוּבוֹ שֶׁל עוֹלָם הוּא.

[5]קַשְׁיָא לְרָמִי בַּר חָמָא! [6]וְכִי תֵּימָא פְּלִיגִי רַבָּנַן עֲלֵיהּ דְּרַבִּי יְהוּדָה — [7]וְהָא אָמַר רַבִּי יְהוֹשֻׁעַ בֶּן לֵוִי: [8]כָּל מָקוֹם שֶׁאָמַר רַבִּי יְהוּדָה [25A] [9]״אֵימָתַי״?, וּ״בַמֶּה״?, [10]אֵינוֹ אֶלָּא לְפָרֵשׁ דִּבְרֵי חֲכָמִים. [11]רַבִּי יוֹחָנָן אָמַר: ״אֵימָתַי״ לְפָרֵשׁ, [12]וּ״בַמֶּה״ לַחֲלוֹק. [13]וּדְכוּלֵּי עָלְמָא, [14]״אֵימָתַי״ לְפָרֵשׁ הוּא!

[15]גַּבְרָא אַגַּבְרָא קָא רָמֵית? [16]מָר סָבַר: פְּלִיגִי, [17]וּמָר סָבַר:

LITERAL TRANSLATION

[1]And we have learned this: "Rabbi Yehudah said: [2]When? When they have no trade other than that. [3]But if they have a trade other than that, behold they are fit." [4]This is the purport of our Mishnah — it is because of the settling of the world.

[5]This is a difficulty for Rami bar Ḥama! [6]And if you say that our Rabbis disagree with the words of Rabbi Yehudah — [7]but surely Rabbi Yehoshua ben Levi said: [8]Every place where Rabbi Yehudah said [25A] [9]"When?" or "In what [case]?", [10]it is only to explain the words of the Sages. [11]Rabbi Yoḥanan said: "When?" [is] to explain; [12]"In what [case]?" [is] to argue. [13]But everyone is [of the opinion] [14]that "When?" is to explain!

[15]Are you casting one man against another? [16]One Sage maintains: They argue; [17]and [the other] Sage maintains:

RASHI

אימתי ובמה — אימתי, כגון במתניתין דהכא, או: במה דברים אמורים. גברא אגברא — דרבי יהושע בן לוי אדרמי בר חמא, רמי בר חמא סבר: אימתי דרבי יהודה — לחלוק בא.

TRANSLATION AND COMMENTARY

productive — **trade.** According to Rav Sheshet, he should be allowed to serve as a judge or witness since he is productive, whereas according to Rami bar Ḥama, his character is still tainted because he gambles. [1]**And** indeed **we have learned** in our Mishnah that this distinction is relevant, as it states: **"Rabbi Yehudah said: When** are all of these individuals unfit to serve as judges or witnesses? [2]**When they have no** other **trade.** [3]**But if they** also **have a trade that is not** discreditable, then **they are fit** to serve as judges or witnesses." [4]**Hence the reason our Mishnah** disqualified individuals who engage in these unworthy activities **is because** they do not engage in work that contributes to **settling the world.**

קַשְׁיָא [5]Rabbi Yehudah's distinction between gamblers with and without another trade presents **a difficulty for Rami bar Ḥama,** who addressed the inherent evils of gambling. [6]**And if you say that the** anonymous **Rabbis** of the Mishnah, who are the source of the earlier clause, **disagree with** the view **of Rabbi Yehudah** and concur with the position taken by Rami bar Ḥama — [7]**surely** this is untenable, for **Rabbi Yehoshua ben Levi** has **said:** [8]In **every place** in the Mishnah **where** we find that **Rabbi Yehudah** prefaces his opinion by **saying,** [25A] [9]**"When** is this so?" **or "In what** case does this apply?", [10]**it is only in order to explain the words of** the Tanna or **the Sages** previously cited. [11]**Rabbi Yoḥanan said:** I agree that when Rabbi Yehudah introduces his opinion with the query, **"When** is this so?", his intention **is to explain** the earlier statement; however, [12]when his opinion is preceded by **"In what case** does this apply?", his intention is really **to argue** with the earlier Tanna, who rejects his qualification. [13]Therefore **everyone,** both Rabbi Yehoshua the son of Levi and Rabbi Yoḥanan, **is of the opinion that** when Rabbi Yehudah uses the expression, [14]**"When** is this so?", as he does in our Mishnah, it **is in order to explain** the words of the Tanna cited before him. If so, there is no disagreement in our Mishnah between Rabbi Yehudah and the Rabbis. Therefore, the Mishnah seems to refute the position of Rami bar Ḥama, who says that a dice-player is unfit because gambling is similar to stealing, and a gambler would be unfit even if he had another trade.

גַּבְרָא אַגַּבְרָא [15]The Gemara rejects this challenge to Rami bar Ḥama: **Are you are casting** the position of **one Amora,** Rami bar Ḥama, **against** that of **another** two Amoraim, Rabbi Yehoshua ben Levi and Rabbi Yoḥanan? [16]Surely Rami bar Ḥama can disagree with them! And he, in fact, **maintains** that Rabbi Yehudah **argues** with the previous Tanna, even when he uses the expression "When is this so?" Hence, in our Mishnah, he understands that the Rabbis disqualify a gambler as a judge or a witness even when he also engages in a constructive trade. Rami bar Ḥama concurs with this position, [17]whereas the other two Amoraim

NOTES

derives from his lack of appreciation of the value that working people attach to assets. It is, therefore, not appropriate to allow him to affect the disposition of another person's assets. *Meiri* offers his own explanation: Since gamblers engage in activities involving duplicity and deceit, they are likely to testify falsely in court.

TRANSLATION AND COMMENTARY

maintain that the Rabbis in our Mishnah **do not argue** with Rabbi Yehudah. In their view, the expression "When is this so?" explains the words of these Rabbis. Thus, according to their stand, the Mishnah supports Rav Sheshet's position and not Rami bar Ḥama's.

וְלָא פְּלִיגִי [1]Can it indeed be said, according to these last two Amoraim, that the Rabbis in our Mishnah **do not argue** with Rabbi Yehudah?! [2]**But surely it was taught** in a related Baraita: **"Whether** the gambler **has a trade other than** gambling **or whether he has no trade other than** gambling, [3]**he is unfit** to serve as a judge or a witness"! This opinion implicitly accords with Rami bar Ḥama's contention that gambling in itself is a thievish activity. Since the Baraita is anonymous it appears to be that of the Rabbis in our Mishnah, who are indeed arguing with Rabbi Yehudah!

הַהִיא [4]However, we need not arrive at this conclusion, for the opinion cited in the above Baraita might not be that of the Rabbis. Rather, it reflects a position that **Rabbi Yehudah** stated elsewhere in the name **Rabbi Tarfon,** [5]**for it was taught** in a Baraita: **"Rabbi Yehudah says in the name of Rabbi Tarfon:** If two people make conflicting assertions with regard to an indeterminate circumstance, and each one vows to be a Nazirite should his assertion prove to be correct, both their vows are considered ineffective. [6]**Neither of them** becomes a Nazirite once the truth of the circumstance is actually determined, [7]for the Nazirite vow **must possess a degree of absoluteness."** (This is derived by Rabbi Tarfon from the verse [Numbers 6:2]: "When either man or woman shall explicitly utter a vow of a Nazir....") Neither party could have been certain that his vow would actually obligate him to become a Nazirite, since neither knew the true state of affairs nor had the power to make it accord with his assertion. The position of Rabbi Tarfon would appear to support the Baraita cited above, for it implies that a vow made in the course of a wager is not binding, because one cannot be certain of having to honor it. Consequently, money collected from gambling is illicitly gained and those who participate are considered partners in theft. They are therefore disqualified from serving as judges or witnesses, regardless of whether they possess some other constructive vocation. The Rabbis in our Mishnah, however, could concur with Rabbi Yehudah that gambling is not theft, but rather that it disqualifies a person only if he engages in no constructive vocation.

מַלְוֶה בְּרִבִּית [8]The Gemara now considers the second category of disqualification listed in our Mishnah: **"One who lends** out money **on interest."** [9]**Rava said:** The **one who borrows on interest is** also **unfit to offer testimony**, since he too transgresses the Biblical law forbidding Jews to engage in usury (see *Bava Metzia*

לָא פְּלִיגִי.
[1]וְלָא פְּלִיגִי?! [2]וְהָתַנְיָא: ״בֵּין שֶׁיֵּשׁ לוֹ אוּמָנוּת שֶׁלֹּא הוּא, בֵּין שֶׁאֵין לוֹ אוּמָנוּת אֶלָּא הוּא, [3]הֲרֵי זֶה פָּסוּל!
[4]הַהִיא רַבִּי יְהוּדָה מִשּׁוּם רַבִּי טַרְפוֹן הִיא. [5]דְּתַנְיָא: ״רַבִּי יְהוּדָה אוֹמֵר מִשּׁוּם רַבִּי טַרְפוֹן: [6]לְעוֹלָם אֵין אֶחָד מֵהֶן נָזִיר, [7]לְפִי שֶׁלֹּא נִתְּנָה נְזִירוּת אֶלָּא לְהַפְלָאָה.
[8]״מַלְוֶה בְּרִבִּית״. [9]אָמַר רָבָא: לֹוֶה בְּרִבִּית פָּסוּל לְעֵדוּת.

LITERAL TRANSLATION

They do not argue.

[1]And do they not argue?! [2]But surely it has been taught: "Whether he has a trade other than it, or whether he has no trade other than it — [3]this one is unfit"!

[4]That is Rabbi Yehudah in the name of Rabbi Tarfon, [5]for it was taught: "Rabbi Yehudah says in the name of Rabbi Tarfon: [6]In fact, neither of them is a Nazirite, [7]for Naziritism is only produced [lit., 'given'] by an [absolute] expression [of intent]."

[8]"One who lends on interest." [9]Rava said: One who borrows on interest is unfit to [offer] testimony.

RASHI

ההיא דרבי יהודה היא משום רבי טרפון – לעולם אימתי – לפרש הוא, ורבנן דמתניתין לא פליגי עליה, ומתניתא דקתני בין שיש לו כו׳ דמשמע טעמא משום אסמכתא, רבי יהודה גופיה אמרה משמיה דרבי טרפון, ופליג אדרבנן דמתניתין דטעמייהו משום יישוב, ובמתניתין רבי יהודה מילתייהו דרבנן קא מפרש. **אין אחד מהן נזיר** – שנים יושבין ואחד עובר, זה אומר: פלוני העובר נזיר הוא, וזה אומר: אינו נזיר, ואמר אחד: הריני נזיר אם כמותו הוא שהוא נזיר, וחבירו אומר: הריני נזיר אם כמותו הוא שאינו נזיר, ושניהם מתכוונין לנזירות, ונמצא כאחד מהם, ואמר רבי טרפון: אין אחד מהן נזיר, שעל הספק אמר דבריו תחילה ואין זו הפלאה, ד״כי יפליא איש״ (ויקרא כז) יפרש משמע. אלמא לרבי טרפון דכי תלי תנאה במידי דלאו בידיה ולא ידע לה, אפילו הכי הויא אסמכתא, ולא אמרינן: מספיקא גמר ואקני. **לוה בריבית פסול לעדות** – דקיימא לן (בבא מציעא עה,ב) המלוה והלוה עוברין בלא תעשה, וכיון דחימוד ממון מעבירו על דת הוה ליה כרשע דחמס, דעובר נמי על לא תעשה מפני חימוד ממון.

HALAKHAH

מַלְוֶה בְּרִבִּית **He who lends on interest.** "Both the person who lends money on interest and the one who borrows are ineligible to serve as either judge or witness. If the loan was issued with fixed interest, the disqualification is considered

LANGUAGE

בִּינִיתוֹס **Binitos.** This word derives from the Greek name, Αβιαντος, Abiantos.

TRANSLATION AND COMMENTARY

75b). [1]The Gemara questions this contention: **But have we not learned** explicitly in our Mishnah that it is the **"one who lends** out money **on interest"** who is unfit to serve as a judge or witness? Nevertheless, Rava is right, and the Mishnah actually refers to anyone who participates in [2]**a loan that involves interest**, both the lender and the borrower.

בַּר בִּינִיתוֹס [3]It is related that **two witnesses** once **testified against** a man known as **Bar Binitos.** [4]**One** of them **said: In my presence,** Bar Binitos **lent** money **for interest;** [5]**and the** other witness **said:** It was **to me** that **he lent** for **interest.** Accepting both their testimonies, [6]**Rava disqualified Bar Binitos** from serving as a judge or witness. The Gemara asks: **But** how could Rava have accepted the testimony of the second witness, whose testimony incriminated himself? [7]Surely **Rava** himself **is the one who said** that **"a person who borrows** money **for interest is also unfit for offering testimony"!** [8]By his own admission, the second witness assumes the status of **a wicked** individual who violates Biblical prohibitions — [9]**and the Torah said** (see Exodus 23:1): **"Do not place the wicked as a witness"!**

רָבָא לְטַעְמֵיהּ [10]The Gemara answers: **Rava** decided to accept the second witness's testimony **following his own argument** stated earlier in our tractate (9b). [11]**For Rava said** there: **A person is considered** as being **a relative of himself, and** since testimony either for or against one's own kin is generally inadmissible, **no person is believed to incriminate himself** by testifying to his own indiscretions, [12]thereby **making himself out to be wicked.** Consequently, we ignore the second witness's self-incriminating statements, and the remainder of his testimony stands and may be relied upon for disqualifying Bar Binitos as a judge or witness.

[1]וְהָאֲנַן תְּנַן: ״מַלְוֶה בְּרִבִּית״? [2]מִלְוֶה הַבָּאָה בְּרִבִּית. [3]בַּר בִּינִיתוֹס אַסְהִידוּ בֵּיהּ תְּרֵי סָהֲדֵי. [4]חַד אֲמַר: קַמֵּי דִּידִי אוֹזִיף בְּרִיבִּיתָא, [5]וְחַד אֲמַר: לְדִידִי אוֹזְפִי בְּרִיבִּיתָא. [6]פַּסְלֵיהּ רָבָא לְבַר בִּינִיתוֹס. [7]וְהָא רָבָא הוּא דַּאֲמַר: לֹוֶה בְּרִבִּית פָּסוּל לְעֵדוּת! [8]וַהֲוָה לֵיהּ רָשָׁע, [9]וְהַתּוֹרָה אָמְרָה: אַל ״תָּשֶׁת רָשָׁע עֵד״! [10]רָבָא לְטַעְמֵיהּ. [11]דְּאָמַר רָבָא: אָדָם קָרוֹב אֵצֶל עַצְמוֹ, [12]וְאֵין אָדָם מֵשִׂים עַצְמוֹ רָשָׁע.

LITERAL TRANSLATION

[1]But have we not learned: "One who lends on interest"? [2]A loan that comes with interest. [3]Two witnesses testified against Bar Binitos. [4]One said: In my presence, he lent on interest, [5]and one said: To me, he lent on interest. [6]Rava disqualified Bar Binitos. [7]But surely Rava is the one who said: A person who borrows on interest is unfit for [offering] testimony! [8]He is wicked, [9]and the Torah said: "Do not place a wicked one as a witness"! [10]Rava [followed] his own reasoning. [11]For Rava said: A person [considered] a relative is of himself, [12]and [thus] a person cannot [by his own testimony] make himself out to be wicked.

RASHI

מלוה הבאה בריבית — ומשמע אתרווייהו. **בר ביניתוס** — אוזיף מלוה. **והוה ליה** — האי סהדא רשע, דהא אודי דלווה ברבית. **רבא לטעמיה** — בפרק קמא, דאין אדם משים עצמו כו׳, אינו יכול לפסול עצמו על פיו, דהא אין קרוב מעיד לא לזכות ולא לחובה, ואדם קרוב אצל עצמו.

NOTES

מִלְוֶה הַבָּאָה בְּרִבִּית **A loan that involves interest.** Rava's interpretation of the Mishnah, which suggests that someone who borrows money on interest is unfit to serve as a judge or a witness, must be understood in light of the position he takes later in our chapter (27a), that only an individual who sins in terms of illicit financial gain can be disqualified. Although the borrower does not benefit from the illicit interest, he is nevertheless considered unfit since his transgression was motivated by a desire to procure the loan. *Maharik* asks why, then, does the Mishnah not explicitly mention the borrower as it does the lender? In his answer, he suggests that the borrower is disqualified only because he acts as an accessory to the lender's illicit gain. Consequently, he need not be mentioned explicitly in the Mishnah.

There are varied opinions as to whether the additional parties to an interest-producing loan — such as the scribe who draws up the loan contract, the witnesses who sign

HALAKHAH

to be Biblical in nature; if the loan was not issued with a fixed rate of interest, thereby only constituting a Rabbinic violation, then the disqualification is also only Rabbinic in nature. Some say that in the case of a Rabbinically prohibited loan, only the lender is disqualified and not the borrower (*Rema*). As regards the other parties to an interest-producing loan (the witnesses, guarantors, and scribe), *Sma* maintains that they are unfit as well, whereas *Shakh* maintains they are not." (*Shulḥan Arukh, Ḥoshen Mishpat* 34:10.)

מֵשִׂים עַצְמוֹ רָשָׁע **One who incriminates himself.** "One cannot be disqualified as a witness by one's own admission

CHAPTER THREE

LITERAL TRANSLATION

[There was once] a certain butcher who was discovered to have let a terefah [animal] ²pass through his hands. ³Rav Naḥman ruled that he was unfit and discharged him. [The butcher] went [and] let his hair and fingernails grow long. ⁴Rav Naḥman thought to declare him fit. ⁵Rava said to him: Perhaps he is acting with cunning? ⁶But what is his remedy? ⁷In accordance with Rav Idi bar Ravin, ⁸for Rav Idi bar Ravin said: One who is suspected with regard to terefah [animals] — ⁹he has no remedy until he goes to a place where they do not know

TRANSLATION AND COMMENTARY

הַהוּא טַבָּחָא ¹It was also related that there was **a certain butcher who was discovered to have let** the meat of **a terefah animal** (one with a severe organic disease or physical defect, ²which is forbidden by Torah law to be eaten) **pass through his hands** into the market as kosher, in order not to lose money. ³As a result, **Rav Naḥman ruled that he was unfit** to ever serve **as a judge or a witness and discharged him** from his duties as a butcher. Subsequently, the man **went** and **let his hair and fingernails grow long**, as a measure of self-effacing penitence. ⁴Seeing this, **Rav Naḥman thought of declaring him** once again **fit to work** as a butcher. ⁵**Rava**, however, **said to him: Perhaps he is deceiving you** with false acts of penance in order to be reinstated in his trade?

אֶלָּא מַאי ⁶The Gemara asks: **But what**, then, **is his remedy** if he should honestly wish to prove contrition? ⁷The true prescription for such an individual is **in accordance with that** put forth by **Rav Idi bar Ravin**. ⁸For **Rav Idi bar Ravin said: One who is suspected with regard to** having sold the meat of **terefah animals** as kosher ⁹**has no remedy** for his sin and may not resume his trade **until** he genuinely demonstrates a willingness to forgo personal profit when the Torah so demands. He should, for example, **go to live in a place where**

¹הַהוּא טַבָּחָא דְּאִישְׁתַּכַּח דְּנָפְקָא טְרֵיפָתָא מִתּוּתֵי יְדֵיהּ. ²פַּסְלֵיהּ רַב נַחְמָן וְעַבְרֵיהּ. ³אֲזַל רַבֵּי מַזְיֵיהּ וְטוּפְרֵיהּ. ⁴סָבַר רַב נַחְמָן לְאַכְשׁוּרֵיהּ. ⁵אָמַר לֵיהּ רָבָא: דִּילְמָא אִיעָרוּמֵי קָא מַעָרִים? ⁶אֶלָּא מַאי תַּקַּנְתֵּיהּ? ⁷כִּדְרַב אִידִי בַּר אָבִין. ⁸דְּאָמַר רַב אִידִי בַּר אָבִין: הֶחָשׁוּד עַל הַטְּרֵיפוֹת — ⁹אֵין לוֹ תַּקָּנָה עַד שֶׁיֵּלֵךְ לְמָקוֹם שֶׁאֵין מַכִּירִין

RASHI

רבי מזייה וטופריה — הגדיל שערו וציפורניו לנוול עצמו לעשות תשובה.

שאין מכירין אותו — דתשובה דהתם לאו עירומי הוא.

NOTES

it, and the guarantor who secures it — should also be disqualified. On the one hand, all of the above parties are considered to have transgressed a Biblical injunction (Exodus 22:24); on the other hand, their actions were not motivated by a desire for illicit financial gain. *Ran* suggests that the ruling depends upon the exact reading in the Gemara: According to those texts which read מִלְוָה הַבָּאָה לוֹ בְּרִבִּית, "a loan that comes *to him* with interest," the implication is that the disqualification extends to the borrower alone; however, those texts which read (as ours does) מִלְוָה הַבָּאָה בְּרִבִּית, "a loan that involves (lit., 'comes with') interest," imply that all parties involved in an interest-producing loan are disqualified as judges or witnesses by the Mishnah.

עַד שֶׁיֵּלֵךְ לְמָקוֹם שֶׁאֵין מַכִּירִין אוֹתוֹ וכו' **Until he goes to a place where they do not know him, etc.** On the next page (25b) the Gemara specifies signs that are considered to be indications of genuine repentance on the part of the offenders mentioned in our Mishnah. In none of those cases must the offender be seen to do penance in a strange town. This leads some to suggest that even in the case of the butcher, penance is effective even in his own town, as long as it manifests itself in the behavior specified by the Gemara (forgoing a large profit in order to fulfill a commandment); only if his penance is expressed by half-hearted measures that do not involve financial loss does

HALAKHAH

of having sinned. Rather, one must be disqualified on the basis of others' testimony alone. Nevertheless, the court should refrain, if possible, from calling a witness who has incriminated himself (*Rema*)." (*Shulḥan Arukh, Ḥoshen Mishpat* 34:25.)

מַאי תַּקַּנְתֵּיהּ? **What is his remedy?** "Someone who sells forbidden products (particularly nonkosher meat) is ineligible as a witness and should be discharged from his vocation. He can only rehabilitate himself by going to a place where he is not known, donning black clothes (as a sign of self-abnegation), and performing some deed that testifies to his having fully renounced his past behavior — such as returning a valuable object that he has found or discarding an unfit animal that is expensive. If circumstances do not enable him to relocate, he can still achieve rehabilitation by submitting to measures of self-abnegation that are equal in force to those prescribed above (*Taz* in the name of *Maharshal*). All of the above-mentioned signs of penitence apply only to one who has intentionally sinned or is presumed to have done so. If his transgression was inadvertent, he need only submit to those measures that are deemed sufficient by the judge in his case (*Rema*)." (*Shulḥan Arukh, Yoreh De'ah* 119:15, *Ḥoshen Mishpat* 34:34.)

אותו, [1]וְיַחֲזִיר אֲבֵידָה בְּדָבָר חָשׁוּב, אוֹ שֶׁיּוֹצִיא טְרֵיפָה מִתַּחַת יָדוֹ בְּדָבָר חָשׁוּב מִשֶּׁלּוֹ. [2]״וּמַפְרִיחֵי יוֹנִים״. [3]מַאי ״מַפְרִיחֵי יוֹנִים״? [4]הָכָא תַּרְגּוּמָה: אִי תִּקְדְּמֵיהּ יוֹנָךְ לְיוֹן. [5]רַבִּי חָמָא בַּר אוֹשַׁעְיָא אָמַר: אָרָא. [6]מַאן דְּאָמַר אִי תִּקְדְּמֵיהּ יוֹנָךְ לְיוֹן — [7]מַאי טַעְמָא לָא אָמַר ״אָרָא״? [8]אָמַר לָךְ: אָרָא מִפְּנֵי דַּרְכֵי שָׁלוֹם בְּעָלְמָא.

LITERAL TRANSLATION

him [1]and he returns a valuable lost object, or removes a valuable terefah animal of his own. [2]"And pigeon-fliers." [3]What is [the meaning of] "pigeon-fliers"? [4]This is its explanation: If your pigeon arrives before my pigeon. [5]Rabbi Ḥama bar Oshaya said: A pigeon-trapper. [6]The [Sage] who said, "If your pigeon arrives before my pigeon" — [7]why did he not say "a pigeon-trapper"? [8]He can say to you: A pigeon-trapper [is castigated] because of peaceable relations alone.

RASHI

ויחזיר אבידה — אם ימצא אבידת חבירו, דכיון דמחזיר אבידה הוא ודאי הדר ביה מחמדת ממון. **אם תקדמיה יונך ליון** — ליוני אתן לך כך וכך. **ארא** — *אשתליו״ן, מלומד להביא יונים ממקומן לבית בעלים על כרחן, ויש בהן גזל. **מפני דרכי שלום בעלמא** — דתניא (חולין קלט,ב): יוני שובך ויוני עלייה יש בהן גזל מפני דרכי שלום. ולא גזל גמור, דלא זכה בהן בעל השובך, דממילא קאתו ורבו להתם, ובגמרא ד״השואל״ (בבא מציעא קב,א) גרס לה.

TRANSLATION AND COMMENTARY

people **do not know him** or of his sin, thus obviating the need to convince anyone of his remorse; [1]**and** he should also **return a valuable lost object, or discard a valuable terefah animal** rather than sell it as kosher, thereby suffering significant financial loss.

וּמַפְרִיחֵי יוֹנִים [2]The Gemara now considers the third category of disqualification listed in our Mishnah — **"pigeon-fliers."** [3]**What** exactly **are "pigeon-fliers"?** [4]**Here is its explanation** according to two different Amoraim: One said that it refers to those who wager on pigeon races, saying **"if your pigeon arrives** at a certain destination **before my pigeon,** I promise to pay you the agreed wager." [5]**Rabbi Ḥama bar Oshaya said:** A pigeon-flier is not a pigeon-racer, but rather **a** pigeon-**trapper** who sends out his own trained pigeons as bait in order to lure pigeons out of his neighbor's cote and into his domain, thereby commiting theft.

מַאן דְּאָמַר [6]The Gemara analyzes these two interpretations of the Mishnah: **The Sage who said** that "pigeon-fliers" are those who wager on pigeon races and say **"If your pigeon arrives before my pigeon**, I will pay you money" — [7]**why did he did not** agree with Rabbi Ḥama bar Oshaya and **say** that a pigeon-flier is actually **"a pigeon-trapper"?** [8]**He can say to you** that he agrees with the opinion (see *Ḥullin* 141b) that **a pigeon-trapper is** not a thief, because the pigeons fly into his domain on their own. Pigeon-trapping is not forbidden as theft but **only** out of concern for maintaining **peaceable relations** among neighbors. This cannot disqualify one from serving as a witness.

LANGUAGE

אָרָא Pigeon-trapper. Some authorities believe that this word derives from the Latin *area*, meaning a bird-cage, a place where birds are kept. Others believe that the source of the word is a Semitic root found in Assyrian, the meaning of which is "a trap, a pitfall," and that it is used in Syrian.

BACKGROUND

אָרָא Pigeon-trapper. The removal of animals from their owners can be successful only with half-domesticated creatures. Doves raised in cotes and the like always return to a certain nesting place, even if they are not attached to it physically. Hunters use animals trained for that purpose to catch wild animals, and this is not forbidden, though it is possible that in this fashion one might catch animals which belong to someone else.

LANGUAGE (RASHI)

אשתליו״ן* This word might come from the Old French *estalonere*, meaning "a man who tempts doves to come to him by using a dove trained for that purpose."

NOTES

the Gemara require that it be observed in a strange town in order to be effective. *Meiri*, on the other hand, maintains that the Gemara indeed requires more of the butcher than of the offenders in our Mishnah, and that his penance must be observed both in a strange town and in the more demanding form of conduct cited by the Gemara. Greater stringency in the case of the butcher makes it harder for him to succumb to the temptation of fraud, an offense which, unlike those listed in our Mishnah, is easy to commit without being caught, since kosher and nonkosher meat do not differ in appearance.

דָּבָר חָשׁוּב A valuable object. The definition of valuable depends upon the particular butcher's own standards. A poor butcher will value objects of lesser worth than those valued by a rich butcher (*Ya'avetz*).

מַפְרִיחֵי יוֹנִים Pigeon-fliers. It is possible to correlate the dispute in our Gemara regarding the definition of a pigeon-flier with the dispute cited above (24b) between Rami bar Ḥama and Rav Sheshet regarding the rationale for disqualifying a dice-player. One Amora maintains that pigeon-fliers are those who race birds for profit and suggests that the Mishnah cited two examples of gambling in order to show that both involve illicit financial gain despite their slightly different dynamics. In essence he is

HALAKHAH

מַפְרִיחֵי יוֹנִים Pigeon-fliers. "Those who fly pigeons (using them as decoys in order to lure neighboring birds into their domain — *Rema*) are ineligible to serve as witnesses if they do so in residential areas, as they are then presumed to be guilty of theft. However, if they fly their pigeons in the desert, where any birds they succeed in luring are presumed to be wild, then they are fit to offer testimony." (*Shulḥan Arukh, Ḥoshen Mishpat* 34:16.)

TRANSLATION AND COMMENTARY

וּמַאן דְּאָמַר [1]**And** Rabbi Ḥama bar Oshaya, **who said** that a pigeon-flier is **"a pigeon-trapper"** — [2]**why did he not** agree with his disputant that pigeon-fliers are those who wager on pigeon races, saying: **"If your pigeon arrives before my pigeon,** I will pay you money"? [3]**He can say to you that** such an interpretation would render the Mishnah redundant, as a pigeon-flier would then represent **the same** kind of disqualification for gambling as does **"a dice-player"!**

וְאִידָךְ [4]**And** how indeed would **the other** interpreter of the Mishnah respond to this objection? He would contend that there is no redundancy in the Mishnah, [5]for while **it taught the case** of a dice-player, **who renders** his obligation to pay out the wager **contingent upon his own skill** in beating his opponent, [6]**it** also **taught** the **case of** the pigeon-racer **who renders** his obligation **contingent upon the skill of his pigeon.** [7]**And it is necessary to state both** — [8]**for if** the Mishnah had only **taught the case of** the dice-player **who renders** his obligation to pay **contingent upon his own skill,** [9]we might have thought that **it is** only **there that** we assume the gambler **did not conclusively** decide to **transfer possession** of the wager money to his opponent — [10]**for he** presumably **said** in his heart: [25B] [11]**I am sure that I know how** to play the game **better** than my opponent and will ultimately **win.** [12]**However, in the case of** the pigeon-racer **who renders** his payment of the wager **contingent upon the skill of his pigeon** to fly faster than that of his opponent, [13]we would **say** — if the Mishnah had not indicated otherwise — that, since he was **not** certain that his pigeon would win, he did intend to pay the wager if necessary. Thus his opponent would not be guilty of illicit profit and disqualified as a judge or a witness.

וְאִי תְּנָא [14]**And** conversely, **if the Mishnah had** only **taught** us **the case** of the pigeon-racer **who renders** his obligation to pay the wager **contingent upon the skill of his pigeon** to fly faster than that of his opponent, one might have thought that only this type of gambler never expected to pay his wager. [15]**For,** presumably, **he said** to himself: **The matter** of who will win the race **is dependent upon** which of us shows greater skill

[1]וּמַאן דְּאָמַר "אָרָא" — [2]מַאי טַעְמָא לָא אָמַר "אִי תִּקְדְּמֵיהּ יוֹנָךְ לְיוֹן"? [3]אָמַר לָךְ: הַיְינוּ "מְשַׂחֵק בְּקוּבְיָא".

[4]וְאִידָךְ?: [5]תְּנָא תּוֹלֶה בְּדַעַת עַצְמוֹ, [6]וּתְנָא תּוֹלֶה בְּדַעַת יוֹנוֹ. [7]וּצְרִיכָא. [8]דְּאִי תְּנָא תּוֹלֶה בְּדַעַת עַצְמוֹ, [9]הָתָם הוּא דְּלָא גָּמַר וּמַקְנֵי, [10]דְּאָמַר [25B] [11]קִים לִי בְּנַפְשַׁאי דְּיָדַעְנָא טְפֵי. [12]אֲבָל, תּוֹלֶה בְּדַעַת יוֹנוֹ, [13]אֵימָא לָא.

[14]וְאִי תְּנָא תּוֹלֶה בְּדַעַת יוֹנוֹ — [15]דְּאָמַר: בְּנַקְשָׁא תַּלְיָא מִילְּתָא,

LITERAL TRANSLATION

[1]And the one who said "a pigeon-trapper" — [2]why did he not say, "If your pigeon arrives before my pigeon"? [3]He can say to you: That is [the same as] "a dice-player."

[4]And the other? [5][The Mishnah] taught [the case of] one who renders [it] contingent upon his own skill (lit., "mind"), [6]and it taught [the case of] one who renders [it] contingent upon the skill of his pigeon. [7]And it is necessary [to state both]. [8]For had it [only] taught [the case of] one who renders [it] contingent upon his own skill, [9]it is there that he did not conclusively [decide to] transfer possession, [10]for he said: [25B] [11]I am sure of myself that I know better [how to win]. [12]However, one who renders it contingent upon the skill of his pigeon, [13][we would] say not.

[14]And if [the Mishnah] had taught [about] one who renders it contingent upon the skill of his pigeon — [15]if he said: The matter is dependent upon knocking,

RASHI

תנא תולה בדעת עצמו — דהויא אסמכתא, והדר תנא דתולה בדעת יונו. **קים לי בנפשאי** — ולא היתה ספיקא בידו, וטעות הוא, וכי אתני אדעתא דהוא נלח אתני, ולא גמר ואקני. אבל תולה בדעת יונו ספיקא הוא בידו אי נלח ואפילו הכי אתני מספיקא, הלכך גמר ומקני. **בנקשא תליא מילתא** — שיש לו דפין של עץ מנקשין זו לזו, והיונה שומעת קולן ומכרת שבעלה מזרזה וממהרת לעוף. הכי גרסינן: אנא ידענא בנקשא טפי. **נקשא** — הכאה זו על זו.

NOTES

restating the position of Rami bar Ḥama, who sees gambling as a form of theft. Rabbi Ḥama bar Oshaya, who rejects the idea that the pigeon-fliers are gamblers — if only because it would render the Mishnah redundant, having already cited the example of dice-players — appears to be reflecting the position of Rav Sheshet, who maintained that the problem with professional gambling is not theft but rather that the gamblers do not engage in a productive occupation. Since the Mishnah gains nothing by citing two examples of parasitic behavior, he suggests instead that pigeon-fliers are not gamblers and should be regarded as "pigeon-trappers," who lure their neighbors' birds into their own domain and thus appear to be stealing them.

LANGUAGE

פִּסְפָּסִים Mosaic cubes. This word derives from the Greek πσηφος, *psiphos*, meaning "a small stone used in a mosaic or a game."

LANGUAGE (RASHI)

מרלי״ש* is apparently the Old French *marels*, meaning "pebbles or wooden chips used for gambling."

TRANSLATION AND COMMENTARY

in **knocking** together wooden paddles to make the birds fly faster, [1]**and I know** how **to knock** the paddles **better** than my opponent. [2]**However,** in the case of the dice-player, **who renders** his payment **contingent upon his own skill** to win the game, [3]we would **say** — if the Mishnah had not taught otherwise — that, since the game is also dependent upon luck, the player presumably took his obligation seriously, as he was **not** entirely certain of winning. [4]**Therefore, it is necessary** for the Mishnah **to cite both** the example of the dice-player and that of the pigeon-flier to inform us that in both instances the gambler's commitment to pay his wager lacks the requisite resolve to make it binding.

מֵיתִיבִי [5]The Gemara now raises an **objection** to the above-cited opinion, that pigeon-fliers are individuals who send out birds as bait. For it was taught in a Baraita: "Among those implied in the Mishnaic category of **'a dice-player' are those who play with mosaic cubes** [tesserae also used for gambling]; [6]**and it is not only** those who gamble with **mosaic cubes that** the Sages disqualified from serving as a witness, [7]**but even** those who gamble with such sundry items as **nut shells or pomegranate skins.** [8]**And when** can we be sure that these offenders have done true **repentance** and can be accepted as witnesses? [9]**When they smash their cubes**, or other gambling apparatus, **and completely turn away from gambling,** [10]so **that** — the Gemara adds — **even** were they to be invited to play with dice **for nothing they would not do so.** [11]The next category of disqualification in the Mishnah, **'one who lends for interest,'** implies **both the one who lends and the one who borrows** for

[1]וַאֲנָא יָדַעְנָא לְנַקּוּשֵׁי טְפֵי. [2]אֲבָל, תּוֹלֶה בְּדַעַת עַצְמוֹ, [3]אֵימָא לָא. [4]צְרִיכָא.
[5]מֵיתִיבִי: ״׳הַמְשַׂחֵק בְּקוּבְיָא׳ — אֵלּוּ הֵן הַמְשַׂחֲקִים בְּפִיסְפָּסִים; [6]וְלֹא בְּפִיסְפָּסִים בִּלְבַד אָמְרוּ, [7]אֶלָּא אֲפִילּוּ קְלִיפֵּי אֱגוֹזִים וּקְלִיפֵּי רִימּוֹנִים. [8]וְאֵימָתַי חֲזָרָתָן? [9]מִשֶּׁיִּשְׁבְּרוּ אֶת פִּיסְפְּסֵיהֶן וְיַחְזְרוּ בָּהֶן חֲזָרָה גְמוּרָה, [10]דַּאֲפִילּוּ בְּחִנָּם לָא עָבְדִי. [11]׳מַלְוֶה בְּרִיבִּית׳ — אֶחָד הַמַּלְוֶה וְאֶחָד הַלֹּוֶה.

LITERAL TRANSLATION

[1]and I know [how] to knock better. [2]However, one who renders it contingent upon his own skill, [3][we would] say not. [4][Therefore] it is necessary [to say both].

[5]They objected: "'A dice-player' — these are the ones who play with mosaic cubes; [6]and they said this not only [about] mosaic cubes, [7]but even nut shells or pomegranate skins. [8]And when is their repentance? [9]When they smash their cubes and completely turn away [from gambling], [10]so that even for nothing they would not do so. [11]'One who lends for interest' — both one who lends and one who borrows.

RASHI

פספסין — שברי עליס, והן *מרלי״ש בלעז. **אפילו קליפי אגוזים** — שאין עשוין לכך, ואקראי בעלמא הוא.

NOTES

דַּאֲפִילּוּ בְּחִנָּם לָא עָבְדִי So that even for nothing they would not do so. This clarification of the intent of the Baraita, following the words "and completely turn away from gambling so that even...," is the first of a series of statements added by the Gemara as it quotes the actual Tannaitic source. Consequently, some of these statements may appear to conform with one Amora's opinion and not another's, which would be inadmissible, were these clarifications an integral part of the Tannaitic source (Amoraim do not generally have the authority to dispute Tannaitic sources.) According to *Ran*, this first addendum of the Gemara's appears to follow the opinion of the Amora who views dice-playing as objectionable because it brings illicit gains. Were gambling a vice simply because it keeps one from gainful employment, as the other Amora contends, why would playing for nothing be considered to be less objectionable, as the Gemara here implies? To reconcile the Gemara's statement with this other Amora, *Ran* suggests that since one who plays for entertainment (not money) is presumed to earn his living from some other trade, he cannot be condemned for eschewing productive activity. Therefore, when he refrains from even recreational gambling, it shows that he has truly repented.

HALAKHAH

הַמְשַׂחֵק בְּקוּבְיָא The dice-player. "The Mishnah's disqualification applies also to those who gamble using nut shells, pomegranate skins, or any other object not usually employed in such games.

Dice-players are only considered to have done complete repentance, enabling them to once again serve as witnesses, if we see that they have smashed their dice and distanced themselves from gambling to the extent that they even refuse to play for nothing." (*Shulḥan Arukh, Ḥoshen Mishpat* 34:16,30.)

מַלְוֶה בְּרִיבִּית One who lends on interest. "Those who lend on interest are only reinstated as eligible witnesses when they tear up their promissory notes and demonstrate their repentance to the extent that they would not even lend for interest to a gentile. In addition, any interest already collected must be returned to the borrower. If the borrower cannot be identified or found, the money should be given over for communal use (*Rosh, Tur*)." (*Shulḥan Arukh, Ḥoshen Mishpat* 34:29.)

TRANSLATION AND COMMENTARY

interest. [1]**And when** can we be sure of **their repentance** and reinstate them as witnesses? [2]**When they tear up** the **promissory notes,** in which the interest is recorded, **and completely turn away from lending for interest,** [3]so **that they would not even lend** for interest **to a gentile,** which is permitted by the Torah. [4]**And** with regard to the category **'pigeon-fliers' — this** includes those **who train pigeons to fight** or to trap other pigeons; [5]**and not only did they refer to pigeons, but even** to the less common use of **domesticated animals,** wild **animals and fowl.** [6]**And when** can we be sure that pigeon-fliers have done **their repentance?** [7]**When they smash the** wooden **boards** from which they send off their birds **and completely turn away from this activity, so that even when alone in the desert,** where birds fly wild, **they would not** train birds to fight or trap wild birds. [8]The final category cited in the Mishnah — **'merchants of seventh-year** produce' — refers to those **who deal in** the sale of **seventh-year produce** for profit. [9]**And when** can we be sure of **their repentance?** [10]**When a subsequent seventh-year arrives and they refrain** from

[1]וְאֵימָתַי חֲזָרָתָן? [2]מִשֶּׁיִּקְרְעוּ אֶת שְׁטָרֵיהֶן וְיַחְזְרוּ בָּהֶן חֲזָרָה גְּמוּרָה, [3]אֲפִילּוּ לְגוֹי לֹא מוֹזְפִי. [4]'וּמַפְרִיחֵי יוֹנִים' — אֵלּוּ שֶׁמַּמְרִין אֶת הַיּוֹנִים. [5]וְלֹא יוֹנִים בִּלְבַד אָמְרוּ, אֶלָּא אֲפִילּוּ בְּהֵמָה חַיָּה וְעוֹף. [6]וְאֵימָתַי חֲזָרָתָן? [7]מִשֶּׁיְּשַׁבְּרוּ אֶת פִּגְמֵיהֶן, וְיַחְזְרוּ בָּהֶן חֲזָרָה גְּמוּרָה, דַּאֲפִילּוּ בַּמִּדְבָּר נַמִי לָא עָבְדִי. [8]'סוֹחֲרֵי שְׁבִיעִית' — אֵלּוּ שֶׁנּוֹשְׂאִין וְנוֹתְנִין בְּפֵירוֹת שְׁבִיעִית. [9]וְאֵימָתַי חֲזָרָתָן? [10]מִשֶּׁתַּגִּיעַ שְׁבִיעִית אַחֶרֶת

LITERAL TRANSLATION

[1]And when is their repentance? [2]When they tear up their bills and completely turn away [from usury], [3]so that even to a gentile they would not lend [for interest]. [4]And 'pigeon-fliers' — these [are the ones] who train pigeons [to fight]; [5]and they said this not only [about] pigeons, but even domesticated animals, wild animals, and birds. [6]And when is their repentance? [7]When they smash their [platform] boards and completely turn away [from this activity] so that even [when alone] in the desert they also would not do so. [8]'Merchants of seventh-year [produce]' — these [are the ones] who deal (lit., 'take and give') in seventh-year produce. [9]And when is their repentance? [10]When another seventh year arrives

RASHI

דאפילו לגוי — שישתכח שם ריבית מפיהם, דתו לא הדרי לקלקולייהו. שממרים את היונים — מרגיזים אותן זה על זה להלחם. אפילו בהמה וחיה — דלאו מילתא דשכיחא הוא. פגמיהן — אלו דפין שמזרזים בהן. אפילו במדבר — דלא שכיחי יונים דיישוב. והאי פירושא ללישנא דארא נקיט ליה, ולא מגופא דברייתא היא. וללישנא ד״אי תקדמה יונך ליון״ איכא לפרושי: חזרה גמורה — דהא אפילו בחנם נמי לא עבדו, כדפרישית גבי קוביא.

LANGUAGE

פִּגְמֵיהֶן **Their boards.** This word derives from the Greek πῆγμα, *pygma*, meaning "an addition to a building," or "a stage, a structure of beams to support something." By extension it came to mean the place where doves are placed for competition with each other, or the trained dove.

NOTES

מִשֶּׁיְּשַׁבְּרוּ אֶת פִּגְמֵיהֶן **After they smash their boards.** According to the Amora who identifies these individuals as pigeon-racers, the wooden boards mentioned here serve to make a noise that impels birds to fly faster. According to the opposing Amora, who understands that the Mishnah is referring to pigeon-trappers, these boards are wooden anchors that the trapper attaches to his birds to keep them from venturing too far afield (*Ramah*).

דַּאֲפִילּוּ בַּמִּדְבָּר נַמִי לָא עָבְדִי **That even in the desert, they also would not do so.** This addendum to the Baraita, inserted by the Gemara, clearly accords with the position of Rabbi Ḥama bar Oshaya, who defined pigeon-fliers as those who release their pigeons as bait. Hence, to do so in the desert, where any lured bird would be ownerless, would not be considered objectionable. The dissenting

שֶׁמַּמְרִין אֶת הַיּוֹנִים **Who train the pigeons.** As indicated in the previous note, this statement of the Baraita's should accord with both Amoraic positions cited in the Gemara regarding the definition of "pigeon-fliers." According to the Amora who defined pigeon-flying as gambling, the Baraita informs us that this activity does not necessarily involve wagering on races. Training pigeons to fight one another and then betting on the outcome would be just as objectionable. Rabbi Ḥama bar Oshaya, who defines pigeon-flying as a tactic for luring other birds into one's domain, would either explain the "training" as a reference to agitating the decoy pigeons so that they attract other birds around them, or would reinterpret the word מַמְרִין altogether so that it is a synonym of אָרָא ("to trap"), used in his initial definition (*Ramah, Rabbi Yehudah Almandri*).

HALAKHAH

מַפְרִיחֵי יוֹנִים **Pigeon-fliers.** "Included in this category of disqualified witness are pigeon-trappers and pigeon-racers, as well as those who race animals of any kind and wager on the outcome. If they have no other gainful means of employment, they are Rabbinically ineligible to serve as witnesses," following the Baraita here. "Those who trap or race pigeons are only reinstated as eligible witnesses after having smashed the apparatus used in such activities and shown a degree of repentance indicating an unwillingness to trap or race pigeons even in the desert. Some say that they must return any profits earned from the activity as well (*Rema*)." (*Shulḥan Arukh, Ḥoshen Mishpat* 34:16,31.)

סוֹחֲרֵי שְׁבִיעִית **Merchants of seventh-year produce.** "Those who profit from the sale of produce grown during the Sabbatical Year are only reinstated as eligible witnesses once we see that another Sabbatical Year has arrived and they refrain entirely from dealing with its produce. In addition to this restraint and verbally confessing their sin,

TRANSLATION AND COMMENTARY

business **dealings** connected with the harvest or sale of produce grown in that year. [1]**And Rabbi Neḥemyah said: Not only did** the Rabbis **say** that it is necessary for there to be **verbal repentance** and self-restraint, [2]**but rather** there must also be **monetary reparation.** [3]**How so?** [4]The offender should **say** something like: **'I, so-and-so, accumulated two hundred zuz** profit from **seventh-year produce,** [5]**and** I hereby proclaim as an act of atonement that these profits **now** be **given as a gift to the poor.'"**

קָתָנֵי מִיהַת [6]The **Tanna** of this Baraita **nevertheless teaches** that the objection to pigeon-fliers serving as judges or witnesses also applies to parallel activities involving **"domesticated animals."** [7]Now, **it is well** understood **according to the one who said** that pigeon-fliers are those who race birds, each one saying, [8]**"If your pigeon arrives before my pigeon,** I will pay you such and such" — [9]**that** that **is the reason** why the Baraita teaches **that you** can also **find** individuals who are banned for racing various trainable **domesticated animals;** [10]**but according to the one who said** that a pigeon-flier is **"a pigeon-trapper,"** who releases his pigeons as a lure, [11]**is** it possible that the Baraita would imply that **a domesticated animal** is capable of luring other animals back into its master's domain?

וַיִּבָּדְלוּ. [1]וְאָמַר רַבִּי נְחֶמְיָה: לֹא חֲזָרַת דְּבָרִים בִּלְבַד אָמְרוּ, [2]אֶלָּא חֲזָרַת מָמוֹן. [3]כֵּיצַד? [4]אוֹמֵר: ׳אֲנִי, פְּלוֹנִי בַּר פְּלוֹנִי, כִּינַּסְתִּי מָאתַיִם זוּז בְּפֵירוֹת שְׁבִיעִית, [5]וַהֲרֵי הֵן נְתוּנִין בְּמַתָּנָה לַעֲנִיִּים׳״.

[6]קָתָנֵי מִיהַת ״בְּהֵמָה״. [7]בִּשְׁלָמָא לְמַאן דְּאָמַר [8]״אִי תִּקְדְּמֵיהּ יוֹנָךְ לְיוֹן״ — [9]הַיְינוּ דְּמַשְׁכַּחַתְּ לָהּ בְּהֵמָה. [10]אֶלָּא לְמַאן דְּאָמַר ״אָרָא״, [11]בְּהֵמָה בַּת הָכִי הִיא?

LITERAL TRANSLATION

and they refrain [from their dealings]. [1]And Rabbi Neḥemyah said: Not only did they say this [about] verbal repentance, [2]but rather monetary repentance [as well]. [3]How so? [4]He says: 'I, so-and-so, accumulated two hundred zuz in seventh-year produce, [5]and they are now given as a gift to the poor.'"

[6][The Tanna] nevertheless teaches "domesticated animals." [7]It is well according to the one who said, [8]"If your pigeon arrives before my pigeon" — [9]that is [the reason] that you [also] find animals [mentioned]. [10]But according to the one who said "a pigeon-trapper," [11]is a domesticated animal so [capable]?

RASHI

ויבדלו — שלא ישאו ויתנו בפירותיהן, ויפקרו גנותיהן לעניים. **לא חזרת דברים** — לומר: לא נוסיף עוד. אלא חזרה הנכרת: שיפזרו פירות שביעית שבגנותיהן לעניים. **היינו דמשכחת לה בהמה** — דאפשר שמלמדה לרוץ כשתשמע קולו. **בת הכי היא** — שתביא בהמות הבר לביתה עמה? והלא ירדפוה החיות! שור הבר — דומה לחיה, ואם מגדלו בביתו — הולך למדברות ומטעה החיות לבא אחריו. ויש בהן גזל מפני דרכי שלום, שמביא אותן מן הביברין. והא דקרי ליה בהמה — כמאן דאמר מין בהמה הוא, ופלוגתייהו לענין התרת חלבו וכיסוי הדם.

NOTES

Amora, who defines pigeon-flying as a form of gambling, would identify a pigeon-racer's repentance with that of a dice-player: When he refrains from racing pigeons even for nothing (*Rashi*, *Ramah*, *Rabbi Yehonatan of Lunel*).

לֹא חֲזָרַת דְּבָרִים בִּלְבַד אָמְרוּ, אֶלָּא חֲזָרַת מָמוֹן Not only did they say this with regard to verbal repentance but rather monetary reparation as well. *Rashi* appears to explain the position of Rabbi Neḥemyah as an addition to that of the previous Tanna, who simply requires the transgressor to wait until the next Sabbatical Year and then refrain from marketing its produce. According to Rabbi Neḥemyah, he would also have to actively distribute that produce among the poor. Our commentary, however, explains the position of Rabbi Neḥemyah in accordance with other Rishonim (*Ramah*, *Ran*), who require him to transfer to the poor all profits obtained from his past sale of seventh-year produce. According to these Rishonim, Rabbi Neḥemyah disputes the previous Tanna (an interpretation that appears to be supported by the Jerusalem Talmud): Whereas the previous Tanna does not require the seller of seventh-year produce to relinquish past profits, but to refrain from any further violation of the law during the next Sabbatical Year, Rabbi Neḥemyah insists that one can only acquit himself by giving past profits to the poor. Thus the seller of seventh-year produce can secure his repentance even before the advent of the next Sabbatical Year.

These Rishonim explain the dispute in the following way: Since seventh-year produce is considered ownerless, the first Tanna does not view profits from its sale as proceeds of theft that must be returned before one can achieve atonement. Rabbi Neḥemyah, on the other hand, maintains that the Torah intended all seventh-year produce to be available for the poor. Thus any profit from its sale is at the expense of the poor and must be returned to them before the merchant can achieve atonement.

The Rishonim point out that it is implicitly understood that

HALAKHAH

they must testify verbally or in writing to having received a certain amount of money from the sale of seventh-year produce and instruct that these profits be distributed among the poor," following the Baraita here. (*Shulḥan Arukh, Ḥoshen Mishpat* 34:32.)

[1]אִין, בְּשׁוֹר הַבָּר. [2]וּכְמַאן דְּאָמַר שׁוֹר הַבָּר מִין בְּהֵמָה הוּא. [3]דִּתְנַן: ״שׁוֹר הַבָּר מִין בְּהֵמָה הוּא. [4]רַבִּי יוֹסֵי אוֹמֵר: מִין חַיָּה״.

[5]תָּנָא: ״הוֹסִיפוּ עֲלֵיהֶן: הַגַּזְלָנִין וְהַחַמְסָנִין״. [6]גַּזְלָן דְּאוֹרַיְיתָא הוּא!

[7]לָא נִצְרְכָא אֶלָּא לִמְצִיאַת חֵרֵשׁ, שׁוֹטֶה וְקָטָן. [8]מֵעִיקָּרָא סְבוּר: מְצִיאַת חֵרֵשׁ שׁוֹטֶה וְקָטָן לָא שְׁכִיחָא — [9]אִי נַמִי, מִפְּנֵי דַרְכֵי שָׁלוֹם בְּעָלְמָא.

LITERAL TRANSLATION

[1]Yes, so [is] a wild ox. [2]And like the one who said that a wild ox is a kind of domesticated animal. [3]For we have learned: "The wild ox is a kind of domesticated animal. [4]Rabbi Yose says: A kind of wild animal."

[5][A Tanna] taught: "They added to them: Robbers and extortioners." [6][But] a robber is [unfit] by Torah [law]!

[7]It is only needed [to teach us] that it [applies] even to [one who stole] an object found by a deaf-mute, an insane person or a minor. [8]At first it was thought [that the theft of] an object found by a deaf-mute, an insane person or a minor is not common — [9]or else, [it is condemned] merely [to preserve] peaceable relations.

TRANSLATION AND COMMENTARY

אִין [1]The Gemara responds: **Yes,** according to the Baraita, a domesticated animal can serve as bait — assuming that the reference **is to a wild ox.** Technically a domesticated animal, the wild ox is capable of gathering other beasts around him and leading them back to his master's domain. [2]**And** this interpretation of the Baraita can only stand **in accordance with the** Tanna **who said that a wild ox is a kind of domesticated animal.** [3]**For we have learned** elsewhere in the Mishnah (*Kilayim* 8:6): **"The wild ox is a kind of domesticated animal.** [4]**Rabbi Yose** argues and **says:** It is **a kind of** wild **animal."**

תָּנָא [5]The Tanna of the Baraita also **taught** the following regarding our Mishnah: "The Rabbis **added to** the list of unsavory characters who are ineligible to serve as witnesses **those who rob** outright **and those who extort** goods." [6]This addition appears superfluous, for **is** not **a robber** explicitly excluded from offering testimony **by** virtue of **Torah law** (Exodus 23:1): "Place not your hand with the wicked, to be a thievish witness"?

לָא נִצְרְכָא [7]Indeed, the addition of "robbers" by the Rabbis **is only needed to teach us** that **someone who stole an object** that was initially **found** and kept **by a deaf-mute, an insane person or a minor** is unfit to serve as a judge or a witness. These categories of people have no formal claim to a found object because they lack the mental competence needed to acquire it. Consequently, someone who steals such an object from them cannot be considered a "robber" in the usual sense of the word. [8]**At first** — before the Rabbis disqualified this kind of robber — **it was thought** that this kind of "theft" should not disqualify a person from serving as a witness, since the seizing of **an object found by a deaf-mute, an insane person or a minor is not** sufficiently **common** to warrant a Rabbinical injunction — [9]**or else** it was thought that such behavior was condemned not because of its similarity to theft but **merely to preserve peaceable relations** between neighbors.

BACKGROUND

שׁוֹר הַבָּר **Wild ox.**

Some authorities suggest that the wild ox mentioned here belongs to a species that is now extinct, *Bos primigenus.* This ox was very large (approximately three meters in length and almost two meters tall). It was black and known for its enormous strength. Some believe that this is the *re'em* (רְאֵם) mentioned in the Bible. The Sages disagreed about whether it was the same species as the domestic ox, but not domesticated, putting it in the Halakhic category of a domesticated animal (בְּהֵמָה), or whether it was another type of animal (buffalo, or *re'em*), putting it in the Halakhic category of a non-domesticated animal (חַיָּה).

RASHI

חמסן — יהיב דמי, אלא שאין רצון הבעלים למכור. **דאורייתא הוא** — ״אל תשת רשע עד״. ובמסכת גיטין (נט,ב) תנן: מציאת חרש שוטה וקטן — יש בהן גזל מפני דרכי שלום, שלא יתקוטט אביו או קרוביו.

NOTES

the gambler (according to the opinion that gambling is a form of theft) and the lender on interest must also return their profits before they can once again be trusted. It is only because of the dispute as to whether or not the merchant's profits need be returned to the poor that the issue of monetary reparation is explicitly raised in that case (*Ramah, Ran, Rosh*).

HALAKHAH

שׁוֹר הַבָּר **A wild ox.** "A wild ox is considered to be a type of domesticated animal, and not a true wild animal. As such, it is not necessary that its blood be covered with earth at the time of its slaughter. In addition, its fatty concretions (חֵלֶב) are forbidden to be eaten." (*Shulḥan Arukh, Yoreh De'ah* 80:3.)

הַגַּזְלָנִין וְהַחַמְסָנִין וְהָרוֹעִים **The robbers and the extortioners and the herdsmen.** "One who commits a Rabbinically proscribed act of theft is Rabbinically disqualified from serving as a witness. Included among these are those who rob a deaf-mute, an insane person, or a minor of some object that has been found and kept; those who extort property by coercing owners to sell against their will; and those who graze their herds freely, be they small or large animals, knowing full well that some of their animals may stray into others' fields and eat their crops." (*Shulḥan Arukh, Ḥoshen Mishpat* 34:13.)

"An ordinary herdsman is disqualified, even though no one has testified to having seen him lead his herd into private pastures. Those who raise small animals in Eretz Israel are disqualified, even if they keep their animals within enclosures and do not graze them freely. However,

[1]כֵּיוָן דַּחֲזוּ דְּסוֹף סוֹף מָמוֹנָא הוּא דְּקָא שָׁקְלִי, [2]פָּסְלִינְהוּ רַבָּנַן.

[3]״הַחַמְסָנִין״ — מֵעִיקָּרָא סְבוּר: דָּמֵי קָא יָהֵיב; אַקְרַאי בְּעָלְמָא הוּא. [4]כֵּיוָן דַּחֲזוּ דְּקָא חָטְפִי, גְּזַרוּ בְּהוּ רַבָּנַן.

[5]תָּנָא: ״עוֹד הוֹסִיפוּ עֲלֵיהֶן: הָרוֹעִים, הַגַּבָּאִין, וְהַמּוֹכְסִין״. [6]״רוֹעִים״ — מֵעִיקָּרָא סְבוּר: [7]אַקְרַאי בְּעָלְמָא הוּא, כֵּיוָן דַּחֲזוּ דְּקָא מִכַּוְּונִי וּשְׁדוּ לְכַתְּחִילָּה, גְּזַרוּ בְּהוּ רַבָּנַן.

[8]״הַגַּבָּאִין וְהַמּוֹכְסִין״ — [9]מֵעִיקָּרָא סְבוּר: מַאי דְּקִיץ

LITERAL TRANSLATION

[1]Since they saw that ultimately these [robbers] were taking valuables, [2]the Rabbis disqualified them.

[3]"Extortioners" — at first it was thought: He is giving [its] value; [and] it is merely chance. [4]Since they saw that they were seizing, the Rabbis decreed against them.

[5][The Tanna] taught: "They further added to them: The herdsmen, tax collectors, and customs officers." [6]"Herdsmen" — at first it was thought: It was merely chance. [7]Since they saw that they were sending [them in] deliberately from the start, the Rabbis decreed against them.

[8]"The tax collectors and customs officers" — [9]at first it was thought that they took what was assessed

TRANSLATION AND COMMENTARY

כֵּיוָן [1]However, **once** the Rabbis **saw that ultimately** people who seize such objects have an abiding desire for **valued objects** that were found, [2]they **disqualified them** from serving as witnesses, lest they succumb to bribery.

הַחַמְסָנִין [3]The Gemara now turns to the second disqualification mentioned by the Tanna — **"those who extort** goods," referring to individuals who, rather than stealing outright, coerce others into accepting money for goods that they had no desire to give up. **At first** — before the Rabbis disqualified these individuals — **it was thought** that since the extortioner **is giving** the owner **the value** of his goods, the incident should be dismissed as a **mere** chance **occurrence.** [4]However, **once** the Rabbis **saw that** these extortioners habitually **seized** goods and only afterwards left the money, they **decreed against** extortioners that they may not serve as witnesses.

תָּנָא [5]The Tanna **taught** the following Baraita as well: "The Rabbis **further added to** the list of ineligible witnesses **herdsmen** who graze their stock on the open range, **tax collectors** appointed by the local gentile ruler to exact various duties from the Jewish populace, **and the customs officers** who accost wayfarers and impose on them various tariffs." [6]Regarding **"herdsmen": At first, it was thought** that, when a herd was found grazing in private pastures, **it was** a **merely** chance **occurrence.** [7]**Once** the Rabbis **saw that** herdsmen **were sending** their livestock into other people's fields deliberately, they **decreed against them** that they may not serve as witnesses.

הַגַּבָּאִין וְהַמּוֹכְסִין [8]The Gemara now explains the reason for disqualifying **"the** tax **collectors and customs-officers."** [9]**At first it was thought** that **they were** only **taking** those duties and tariffs **that were assessed**

RASHI

סוף סוף ממונא שקלי — ועברי אתקנתא דרבנן מחמת חימוד ממון. **פסלינהו** — דחשידי למשקל אגרא ואסהודי שקרא. **כיון דחזו דחטפי** — ושקלי, כלומר דאפילו דמי קא יהבי אתי לידי גזלנות, כלומר: שהיה קשה לבעלים למכור ובעל כרחן חוטפין וזורקין המעות לפניהם. **גבאין** — ממונין שהעמידן המלך לגבות מס, ומנת המלך, וכרגא, וארנונא, מישראל חביריהם. **אקראי בעלמא** — מה שהבהמה נכנסת לשדות של אחרים ורועה — אקראי הוא, ואין הרועה מתכוין לכך.

NOTES

כֵּיוָן דַּחֲזוּ דְּקָא מְכַוְּונִי וּשְׁדוּ **Once they saw that they were sending in their livestock deliberately.** *Ramah* cites an alternative interpretation of the Gemara: Once the Rabbis saw that herdsmen were intentionally taking other people's grain and throwing it before their animals, they disqualified them.

HALAKHAH

if they raise them abroad, they are not disqualified, unless it is known that they sent them out to feed in private pastures. Those who raise large animals, even in Eretz Israel, are fit to serve as witnesses unless it is known that they sent them into private pastures." (*Rambam, Sefer Shoftim, Hilkhot Edut* 10:4.)

הַגַּבָּאִין, וְהַמּוֹכְסִין **The tax collectors and customs officers.** "Ordinary customs officers are considered unfit to serve as witnesses since it is presumed that they collect more than the amount fixed by the ruler and keep the excess duty for themselves. However, ordinary tax collectors are not disqualified unless we know that they took, even on one occassion, more tax money than was assessed by the sovereign authority. Some authorities explain that customs officers first appraise the goods they are taxing and thus can easily disguise their favoring one individual over another. However, ordinary tax collectors must exact a fixed amount from all individuals, which cannot be altered without calling attention to their impropriety (*Rema*)." (*Rambam, Sefer Shoftim, Hilkhot Edut* 10:4; *Shulḥan Arukh, Ḥoshen Mishpat* 34:14.)

לְהוּ קָא שָׁקְלִי. [1]כֵּיוָן דַּחֲזוּ דְּקָא שָׁקְלִי יְתֵירָא פַּסְלִינְהוּ.
[2]אָמַר רָבָא: רוֹעֶה שֶׁאָמְרוּ, אֶחָד רוֹעֶה בְּהֵמָה דַּקָּה [3]וְאֶחָד רוֹעֶה בְּהֵמָה גַּסָּה. [4]וּמִי אָמַר רָבָא הָכִי? [5]וְהָאָמַר רָבָא: רוֹעֶה בְּהֵמָה דַּקָּה בְּאֶרֶץ יִשְׂרָאֵל, פְּסוּלִין; [6]בְּחוּצָה לָאָרֶץ, כְּשֵׁרִין. [7]רוֹעֶה בְּהֵמָה גַּסָּה, אֲפִילּוּ בְּאֶרֶץ יִשְׂרָאֵל, כְּשֵׁרִין!
[8]הַהוּא בִּמְגַדְּלִים אִיתְּמַר.
[9]הָכִי נַמִי מִסְתַּבְּרָא, [10]מִדְּקָתָנֵי: ״נֶאֱמָנִין עָלַי שְׁלֹשָׁה רוֹעֵי בָקָר״. [11]מַאי לָאו לְעֵדוּת?!

LITERAL TRANSLATION

for them [by the rulers]. [1]Since they saw that they were taking more, they disqualified them.

[2]Rava said: The herdsman of whom they spoke is one who herds a small animal, [3]as well as one who herds a large animal. [4]But did Rava say this? [5]But surely Rava said: A herdsman of small animals — in Eretz Israel, they are unfit; [6]outside Eretz Israel, they are fit. [7]A herdsman of large animals, even in Eretz Israel, they are fit!

[8]That was stated in regard to those who raise [their own livestock].

[9]This also stands to reason, [10]since we have been taught: "The three cattle herders are trustworthy to me." [11]Is it not for testimony?!

RASHI

יתירתא — יותר מן הקצבה. **בארץ ישראל** — אמירי טפי, משום ישוב ארץ ישראל. **מגדלין איתמר** — שמגדלין אותם בבתיהם, ואפילו הכי בארץ ישראל פסולין מגדלי בהמה דקה, דעבידא דמשמטא ורהטא לתוך השדות, אבל גסה לא משתמטא ואפשר לנוטרה. אבל רועה שמרעה בחוץ באפר של ישוב — אפילו בהמה גסה פסול, שנכנסת בשדה של אחרים. **הכי נמי מסתברא** — דרועה בהמה גסה פסול. **נאמנין עלי שלשה רועי בקר** — מכלל דאי לא קבלינהו עליה לא מהימני.

TRANSLATION AND COMMENTARY

for the people by the authorities. [1]**Once** the Rabbis **saw that they were taking more** than what was assessed, **they disqualified them** from serving as witnesses.

אָמַר רָבָא [2]**Rava said: The herdsman of whom** the Rabbis spoke as being ineligible as a witness includes **one who herds a small animal**, such as a sheep or a goat, [3]**as well as one who herds a large animal,** such as an ox or a horse. The Gemara asks: [4]**But did Rava** really **say this?** [5]On the contrary — **surely Rava said** elsewhere: **A herdsman of small animals** who resides **in Eretz Israel is unfit** to testify as a witness, because his vocation threatens the settlement and cultivation of the land. [6]But if such herdsmen reside **outside Eretz Israel, they are** considered **fit** to testify, unless witnesses saw them leading their herds into private pastures. [7]**Herdsmen of large animals, even** if they reside **in Eretz Israel, are** considered **fit** to testify, if they do not graze their animals on other people's property!

ההוא [8]The Gemara replies: In fact, Rava's last ruling **was stated in regard to** herdsmen **who raise** livestock on their own fenced-in grounds or barns and do not send them out to pasture. Nevertheless, those who raise small livestock in Eretz Israel are still considered ineligible, because they cannot adequately prevent these animals from occasionally wandering into nearby fields and eating their neighbor's crops. Large animals, being easier to watch, do not disqualify their owners. However, Rava's first statement, disqualifying herdsmen of both large and small animals, was stated in regard to those who intentionally lead their animals into open pasture. Both large and small animals are likely to damage crops on their way to the open pasture.

הָכִי נַמִי [9]**So, too, does it stand to reason** that one who intentionally gets his herd to graze on the open range is ineligible to serve as a witness, even if it is a herd of large animals. [10]We infer this **from** what **we have been taught** in an earlier Mishnah (24a): "If one litigant said to the other: '...**the three** ignorant **cattle herders are trustworthy to me,**' Rabbi Meir says: He can subsequently retract his consent. The Sages say: He cannot subsequently retract his initial consent." [11]**Does it not follow that,** since the Mishnah specifically mentions cattle herders **for** the purpose of offering **testimony,** without the litigant's consent they would not be fit to do so?

NOTES

כֵּיוָן דַּחֲזוּ דְּקָא שָׁקְלִי יְתֵירָא Once they saw that they were taking more. Several commentators (*Rabbenu Ḥananel, Arukh, Ramah* and others) suggest that the Rabbis eventually disqualified the tax collectors and customs officers because they saw that they were exempting the rich from paying their due and compensating the kingdom by overcharging the poor.

בִּמְגַדְּלִים אִיתְּמַר It was stated in regard to those who raise their own livestock. According to *Rashi*, Rava only disqualified those who raise small livestock, but not large animals, because only small livestock tend to escape from their pens into neighboring fields. Large livestock can be adequately guarded and thus do not present a threat to the land's settlement and cultivation. *Tosafot* offers an alternative explanation: Although large livestock are just as difficult to guard as small livestock, the Rabbis felt that they could not penalize someone who insisted on raising large animals in Eretz Israel, since such animals often draw plows and are essential for the cultivation of the land. To ban them would constitute a burden too difficult for the

[1] לֹא! לְדִינָא. [2] דַּיְקָא נַמִי, דְּקָתָנֵי, ״שְׁלֹשָׁה רוֹעֵי בָקָר״, [3] וְאִי לְעֵדוּת, [4] שְׁלֹשָׁה לָמָּה לִי?!

[5] וְאֶלָּא מַאי — לְדִינָא? [6] מַאי אִירְיָא ״שְׁלֹשָׁה רוֹעֵי בָקָר״? [7] כָּל בֵּי תְלָתָא דְּלָא גָּמְרִי דִּינָא נַמִי!

[8] הָכִי קָאָמַר: אֲפִילּוּ הָנֵי דְּלָא שְׁכִיחִי בְּיִישּׁוּב.

[9] אָמַר רַב יְהוּדָה: סְתָם רוֹעֶה פָּסוּל; [10] סְתָם גַּבַּאי כָּשֵׁר.

[11] אֲבוּהּ דְּרַבִּי זֵירָא עֲבַד גַּבָּיוּתָא תְּלֵיסַר שְׁנִין. [12] כִּי הֲוָה אָתֵי רֵישׁ נַהֲרָא לְמָתָא, כִּי הֲוָה חָזֵי

LITERAL TRANSLATION

[1] No! [It is] for judgment. [2] It is also precise, for it teaches, "three cattle herders," [3] and if [it was] for testimony, [4] why did [it teach three]?!

[5] But what then — for judgment? [6] Why specify "three cattle herders"? [7] Any group of three who have not learned the laws [are implied] as well!

[8] He is saying the following: Even these, who are not usually in settled regions.

[9] Rav Yehudah said: An ordinary herdsman is unfit; [10] an ordinary tax collector is fit.

[11] Rabbi Zera's father performed tax collection [for] thirteen years. [12] Whenever the regional chief (lit., "chief of the river") came, if [Rabbi Zera's father] saw

RASHI

לא לדינא — דלדינא מודינא דפסולין, משום דלא גמירי דינא. **דלא שכיחי בישוב** — ולא ראו ולא שמעו עסקי דין בין אדם לחבירו, אי קבלינהו עלויה — לא מצי למיהדר. **סתם רועה** — דאכתי לא חזינן דעיילו בהמותיו בשדות אחרות. **סתם גבאי כשר** — עד דשמעינן ביה דשקיל יתירתא. **כי הוה חזי** — אבוה דרבי זירא.

TRANSLATION AND COMMENTARY

לֹא [1] **No**, this is not the intent of the Mishnah. It refers to a litigant who agreed to accept cattle herders as **judges** in his case, a position that they certainly would not have otherwise been fit to assume. [2] Such an interpretation **is also precise** with respect to the language of the Mishnah, **for it states** there that the litigant offered to accept **"three cattle herders,"** [3] **and if** they were accepted **for** the purpose of giving **testimony,** [4] **why did it teach** three, when two surely would have been sufficient for testimony?!

וְאֶלָּא מַאי [5] The Gemara questions this conclusion: **But what, then,** is being suggested — that the litigant agreed to accept three ignorant men **for** the purpose of hearing his case and rendering **judgment?** [6] If so, **why does it specify** in the Mishnah that they were **three cattle herders?** [7] **Any set of three** individuals **who have not learned the laws** would otherwise be ineligible **as well!**

הָכִי קָאָמַר [8] By specifying three cattle herders, the Tanna **is** interested in **saying** as follows: **Even** men such as **these, who are not** usually present **in settled regions** and thus are exceptionally ignorant of the principles and procedures that guide civil law, can still serve as judges if the litigants agree.

אָמַר רַב יְהוּדָה [9] The Gemara resumes discussion of the individuals disqualified by the second Baraita quoted above: **Rav Yehudah said: An ordinary herdsman**, who has not yet been identified as one who grazes his herd in other people's fields, **is** still **unfit** to serve as a witness; however, [10] **an ordinary tax collector,** about whom we have no suspicions, **is fit** to serve as a witness until we know that he has taken more than his due.

אֲבוּהּ דְּרַבִּי זֵירָא [11] Having established that not all tax collectors are immediately suspect, the Gemara relates the following story: **Rabbi Zera's father collected taxes for thirteen years.** [12] **When the regional chief came to town** to assess the community's expected taxable revenues, Rabbi Zera's father would give him a low population figure so that the town would not be assessed too heavily. Consequently, **when he saw the**

NOTES

community to bear. *Ramah* cites a somewhat similar opinion, explaining that the difference between large and small livestock relates to the ease of importing small livestock from abroad, whereas large livestock must be locally raised.

סְתָם גַּבַּאי כָּשֵׁר **An ordinary tax collector is fit to testify.** As stated in our commentary (in accordance with *Rashi*), the Tanna taught that only a tax collector who is specifically known to have collected more than his due, is Rabbinically disqualified. *Tosafot* adds that the Tanna could not have intended simply to teach that the tax collector who takes unwarranted funds was disqualified by the Rabbis. Such an individual would be disqualified as a thief, according to Torah law. Rather the Rabbis' intention was to teach that, unlike an ordinary thief, who upon repenting and returning what he stole can be reinstated as a valid witness, the tax collector (or customs officer) remains disqualified even after having atoned for his sin. This may be because he has no way of knowing to whom he should refund the surfeit monies that were collected arbitrarily, or else because of the fear that, if he continued to serve as a tax collector, he would ultimately repeat his past indiscretions.

Ramah explains why Rav Yehudah distinguishes between an ordinary herdsman and an ordinary tax collector: An ordinary herdsman, even when he does not intend to graze his animals on others' property, is aware that many of his stock will stray. He is therefore penalized by the Rabbis for his occupation. The tax collector, however, is perfectly capable of ensuring that no one incurs an unwarranted loss

TRANSLATION AND COMMENTARY

Rabbis of the town, Rabbi Zera's father **would say to them** (paraphrasing Isaiah 26:20): **"Go, my people, and enter into your chambers** and shut your doors behind you; hide yourselves for a while until the anger is past." [1]**When he saw** the other **townspeople, he would say in** a language they could understand: [2]**"The regional chief has come to town, and he will now slaughter the father in front of the son and the son in front of the father,"** intimating that he would demand huge amounts of money from the community unless the townspeople took pains to hide themselves. [26A] [3]**And** as a result **everyone would hide.** [4]**When the regional chief came** to see Rabbi Zera's father in order to assess the town, the humble tax collector **would say to him: "From whom shall we ask** taxes here? As you see, there are few people in town, and the total assessment will have to be small." [5]It is told that **when** Rabbi Zera's father **was about to die,** [6]**he said to** those who were attending him: **"Take the thirteen ma'ot which I have tied up in a sheet and return them to so-and-so,** [7]**for I took them from him** as payment for his taxes **and** in the end **did not need them**, as the authorities were satisfied with what I had already collected." From the above account we see that it is indeed possible for a tax collector to retain his virtue, thereby offering support to the ruling of Rav Yehudah that a tax collector not known to have behaved wrongly may serve as a witness.

אָמַר רַבִּי שִׁמְעוֹן [8]We learned in our Mishnah as follows: **"Rabbi Shimon said:** Originally **the Sages used to call them 'harvesters of seventh-year produce'**; however, once the tax enforcers appointed by the government multiplied in number, they began to call them 'merchants of seventh-year produce.'" [9]**What is** Rabbi Shimon **saying?** [10]**Rav Yehudah said: This is what** Rabbi Shimon **is saying:** [11]**Originally,** the Sages **used to teach** that **harvesters of seventh-year** produce who were found accumulating large crops, **were fit** to serve as witnesses, as it was assumed that they were harvesting the produce for their own consumption, as permitted by the Torah. [12]Only **merchants** who profited from the sale of such produce were considered **unfit.** [13]However, **once** it became apparent that many people were beginning to **offer money to the poor** as wages for harvesting the fields, [14]**and** that **the poor would** actually **go and harvest** large amounts of

רַבָּנַן, אָמַר לְהוּ: ״לֵךְ עַמִּי בֹּא בַּחֲדָרֶיךָ״! [1]כִּי הֲוָה חָזֵי אֱינָשֵׁי דְּמָתָא, אָמַר: [2]״רֵישׁ נַהֲרָא אֲתָא לְמָתָא, וְהָאִידָּנָא נָכֵיס אַבָּא לְפוּם בְּרָא וּבְרָא לְפוּם אַבָּא״. [26A] [3]וּמִיגַּנְזוּ כּוּלֵּי עָלְמָא. [4]כִּי אָתֵי, אָמַר לֵיהּ: מִמַּאן נִבְעֵי? [5]כִּי נָיְחָא נַפְשֵׁיהּ, [6]אֲמַר לְהוּ: שְׁקוֹלוּ תְּלֵיסַר מָעֵי דְּצַיְירִי לִי בִּסְדִינַאי וַהֲדַרוּ לֵיהּ לִפְלָנְיָא, [7]דִּשְׁקַלְתִּינְהוּ מִינֵּיהּ וְלָא אִיצְטְרִיכוּ לִי.

[8]״אָמַר רַבִּי שִׁמְעוֹן: בַּתְּחִילָּה הָיוּ קוֹרְאִין אוֹתָן ׳אוֹסְפֵי שְׁבִיעִית׳״. [9]מַאי קָאָמַר? [10]אָמַר רַב יְהוּדָה, הָכִי קָאָמַר: [11]בַּתְּחִילָּה הָיוּ אוֹמְרִים: אוֹסְפֵי שְׁבִיעִית כְּשֵׁרִין [12]סוֹחֲרִין פְּסוּלִין. [13]מִשֶּׁרַבּוּ מַמְצִיאֵי מָעוֹת לַעֲנִיִּים, [14]וְאָזְלִי עֲנִיִּים

LITERAL TRANSLATION

the Rabbis, he would say to them: "Go, my people, and enter into your chambers!" [1]If he saw townspeople, he would say: [2]"The regional chief has come to town, and will now slaughter the father in front of the son and the son in front of the father." [26A] [3]And everyone would hide themselves. [4]When [the regional chief] came, he would say to him: From whom shall we ask? [5]When [Rabbi Zera's father] was about to die (lit., "when his soul rested"), [6]he said to them: Take the thirteen ma'ot which I have tied up in my sheet and return them to so-and-so, [7]for I took them from him and did not need them.

[8]"Rabbi Shimon said: At first [the Sages] used to call them 'harvesters of seventh-year [produce].'" [9]What is he saying? [10]Rav Yehudah said: This is what he is saying: [11]At first they used to say [that] harvesters of seventh-year [produce] were fit [12][but] merchants were unfit. [13]When those offering money to the poor multiplied [in number], [14]and the poor would go

RASHI

רבנן — מיושבי העיר. **אמר לך עמי בא בחדריך** — דלא נחזינא בך ריש נהרא, שהוא שר העיר, ורואה שרבים יושבי העיר ושואל ממון הרבה לכל שנה. והוא היה מיקל עליהם המס, ומדחה את שר העיר לאמר שיושביה מועטין, ואין ממי לגבות. **נכיס אבא לפום ברא** = ישחוט את האב לפני הבן, כלומר: יגבה מהן ממון. **מיגנזו** = מתחבאין. **אוספין כשרין** — דמלי למיכלינהו קודם זמן הביעור. **ואזלי עניים אספי להו** — בשביל המעות, והוו להו סוחרי שביעית, ורחמנא אמר "לאכלה" ולא לסחורה (עבודה זרה,

NOTES

from his activity, and thus is not penalized for merely having entered into this vocation. Alternatively, one can say that, since the herdsman on the open range is not scrutinized, he can graze his animals illegally without it ever being noticed. The Rabbis therefore decided to disqualify herdsmen in general. The tax collector, however, is subject to constant scrutiny, and thus need not be disqualified unless specifically accused of impropriety.

TRANSLATION AND COMMENTARY

produce **for** these people **and bring** it to them, [1]the Sages **retracted and started to teach** that **both** the merchants who sold the produce **and** those who harvested it in large amounts **were unfit** to serve as witnesses.

קָשׁוּ בָּהּ [2]**The sons of Raḥavah** the Sage **had a difficulty with** Rav Yehudah's interpretation of Rabbi Shimon in our Mishnah: If Rabbi Shimon meant to say that the Sages revised their teaching when the poor started to collect seventh-year produce for monetary gain, why, then, does Rabbi Shimon say that the Sages revised their teaching [3]**"when the** tax **enforcers increased in number"?** [4]He **should have said "once the vendors increased in number"!** [5]**Rather,** one must interpret Rabbi Shimon's statement differently: **Initially** the Sages **used to say** that **both** the merchants of seventh-year produce **and** the harvesters **were unfit** to serve as witnesses, as it was assumed that they were both selling the produce at a profit. [6]However, **once** it became apparent that **the** number of tax **enforcers** appointed by the government **had increased** — [7]**and who are these** tax collectors? [8]Collectors of **produce-tax** who would demand from each farmer a certain quantity of produce each year, or confiscate his land. **This** is evident from **Rabbi Yannai**, who **would announce** at the start of each Sabbatical Year: [9]**"Go out and sow** your fields **in the seventh year**, as this is permitted **because of** the consequences of not handing over **the** yearly **produce-tax** to the authorities" — [10]the Sages **retracted and started saying** that **harvesters** who were seen gathering large quantities of seventh-year produce were **fit** to serve as witnessses, since it could be assumed that they were doing so in order to meet the tax assessment. [11]But those who were known to be **merchants** of such produce were still considered **unfit**.

וְאָסְפִי לְהוּ וּמַיְיתוּ, [1]חָזְרוּ לוֹמַר: אֶחָד זֶה וְאֶחָד זֶה פְּסוּלִין.
[2]קָשׁוּ בָּהּ בְּנֵי רַחֲבָה: [3]הַאי "מִשֶּׁרַבּוּ הָאַנָּסִים"? [4]"מִשֶּׁרַבּוּ הַתַּגָּרִין" מִיבָּעֵי לֵיהּ! [5]אֶלָּא: בַּתְּחִילָּה הָיוּ אוֹמְרִים: אֶחָד זֶה וְאֶחָד זֶה פְּסוּלִין. [6]מִשֶּׁרַבּוּ הָאַנָּסִין — [7]וּמַאי נִינְהוּ? [8]אַרְנוֹנָא, כִּדְמַכְרִיז רַבִּי יַנַּאי: [9]פּוּקוּ וְזִרְעוּ בַּשְּׁבִיעִית מִשּׁוּם אַרְנוֹנָא. [10]חָזְרוּ לוֹמַר: אוֹסְפִין כְּשֵׁירִין, [11]סוֹחֲרִין פְּסוּלִין.

LITERAL TRANSLATION

and harvest for them and bring, [1]they retracted and [started] saying [that] both this one and that one are unfit.

[2]The sons of Raḥavah had a difficulty with this: [3]Is that "when the enforcers increased"? [4]It should have said "when the vendors increased [in number]"! [5]Rather, at first they used to say [that] both this one and that one were unfit. [6]When the [number of] enforcers had increased — [7]and who are they? [8][Collectors of] produce-tax, as Rabbi Yannai would announce: [9]Go out and sow in the seventh year because of produce-tax — [10]they retracted and [started] saying [that] harvesters are fit [11][and] merchants unfit.

RASHI

סב,א), והכי משמע מתניתין: בתחלה, לאלו הפסולין עכשיו משום סוחרי שביעית, היו קורין אותן אוספי שביעית – וכשרין, משרבו האנסין חזרו לקרות את האוספין סוחרין – ופסולין. ארנונא – מס שגובה המלך מן התבואות, כך וכך כורין מן השדה לשנה. **פוקו זרעו בשביעית** – שביעית בזמן הזה דרבנן, דבטלה קדושת הארץ.

LANGUAGE

אַרְנוֹנָא **Produce-tax.** This term apparently derives from the Latin *annona*, meaning "taxes or special imposts imposed by the authorities, generally collected from harvests."

NOTES

פּוּקוּ וְזִרְעוּ בַּשְּׁבִיעִית **Go out and sow in the seventh year.** *Tosafot* raises the question as to how a Biblical injunction, such as that prohibiting the cultivation of one's land during the seventh year, could be waived by the Rabbis because of possible financial loss. *Tosafot* offers two solutions: The first assumes that this dispensation was applicable only when and where the Sabbatical laws ceased to possess Biblical force and were binding only by Rabbinic decree. In such an instance, we follow the general principle that if a significant financial loss is inevitable, the Rabbis did not intend their decrees to be binding. A second solution, given in the Jerusalem Talmud, posits that the allowance made in the Gemara for working one's field in order to supply the yearly produce-tax applies even when the Sabbatical laws are Biblically binding. This is because of the possible danger to one's life that can result from imprisonment or

HALAKHAH

פּוּקוּ וְזִרְעוּ בַּשְּׁבִיעִית מִשּׁוּם אַרְנוֹנָא **Go out and sow on the seventh year because of the produce-tax.** "There was once an increase in the number of agents appointed by the ruling empire to compel Jews under its rule to provide a yearly quota of produce for the imperial legions, as well as an increase in the instances where Jews were forced to raise crops in the employment of the king, and the Rabbis decided to allow those violations of Sabbatical law which were necessary to meet these obligations (in accordance with the pronouncement of Rabbi Yannai). *Radbaz* interprets *Rambam* as saying that the produce-tax implicitly referred to in our Mishnah was intended to provide subsistence for the royal legions and not a source of revenue for the ruler himself. Hence, the decision to allow the violation of Sabbatical law was made even in the event that the law was Biblically binding, as it was assumed that resisting the

TRANSLATION AND COMMENTARY

רַבִּי חִיָּיא בַּר זַרְנוֹקִי [1]Concerning the special circumstances that enable Jews to work their fields in the Sabbatical Year, the Gemara offers the following relevant account: **Rabbi Ḥiyya bar Zarnokai and Rabbi Shimon ben Yehotzadak were traveling** together, on their way **to intercalate the year in** the region of **Assia,** outside of Eretz Israel. [2]**Resh Lakish met them** and **joined them.** [3]**He said** to himself: **I will go** along **to see how they** actually **execute the procedure** of intercalation. [4]Along the way **Resh Lakish saw a certain man who was plowing** his field, even though it was the Sabbatical Year when such work is forbidden. [5]**He said to** his companions Rabbi Ḥiyya and Rabbi Shimon: I just saw **a priest and he was plowing** his field in violation of the law! [6]**They replied to him:** Why assume that he was acting wrongly? Perhaps **he can say** in his defense: **"I am an imperial servant** who has been employed to work **in this field** by the Roman authorities," a circumstance which would exonerate him from wrongdoing. In those times, observance of the seventh year was only of Rabbinic authority, and he was only working the land of a non-Jew. Further along the way, [7]**Resh Lakish again saw a certain man who was pruning in a vineyard**, which is also prohibited during the seventh year. [8]**He** turned to his companions and **said to them:** I just saw **a priest and he was pruning** grapevines in violation of the law! [9]**One of** his companions came to the man's defense and **said to** Resh Lakish: Why assume that the man is guilty? **He, too, can say: "I need**

[1]רַבִּי חִיָּיא בַּר זַרְנוֹקִי וְרַבִּי שִׁמְעוֹן בֶּן יְהוֹצָדָק הָווּ קָאָזְלִי לְעַבֵּר שָׁנָה בְּעַסְיָא. [2]פְּגַע בְּהוּ רֵישׁ לָקִישׁ, אִיטְפִּיל בַּהֲדַיְיהוּ, [3]אֲמַר: אֵיזִיל אֶיחֱזֵי הֵיכִי עָבְדִי עוּבְדָא. [4]חֲזְיֵיהּ לְהַהוּא גַּבְרָא דְּקָא כָּרֵיב. [5]אֲמַר לְהֶן: כֹּהֵן, וְחוֹרֵשׁ! [6]אָמְרוּ לוֹ: יָכוֹל לוֹמַר: "אַגִּיסְטוֹן אֲנִי בְּתוֹכוֹ". [7]תּוּ חַזְיֵיהּ לְהַהוּא גַּבְרָא דַּהֲוָה כָּסַח בְּכַרְמֵי. [8]אֲמַר לְהֶן: כֹּהֵן, וְזוֹמֵר! [9]אָמְרוּ לוֹ: יָכוֹל לוֹמַר:

LITERAL TRANSLATION

[1]Rabbi Ḥiyya bar Zarnokai and Rabbi Shimon ben Yehotzadak were traveling to intercalate the year in Assia. [2]Resh Lakish met them [and] joined them. [3]He said: I will go [and] see how they execute the procedure. [4][Resh Lakish] saw a certain man who was plowing. [5]He said to them: A priest, and he is plowing?! [6]They said to him: He may say: "I am an imperial servant (lit., 'an Augustan') in [this field]." [7]Again, he saw a certain man who was pruning in a vineyard. [8]He said to them: A priest, and he is pruning?! [9][One of them] said to him: He may say:

RASHI

כריב — חריש. אמר להו — ריש לקיש. כהן וחורש — זה כהן הוא שחורש בשביעית, דאמרינן לקמן: נחשדו כהנים על השביעית. אגיסטון — שכיר, וקרקע של גוי הוא, אי נמי: משום ארנונא שכרו בעל הבית לחרוש. כסח — זומר כרם.

BACKGROUND

עַסְיָא **Assia.** This word derives from the Greek Ασία, *asia*, referring to what is now known as Asia Minor. Part of Asia Minor was included in the Roman province of Asia. When used by the Sages, the term apparently refers to a certain region (perhaps Cilicia) within Asia Minor.

LANGUAGE

אַגִּיסְטוֹן **Imperial servant** (lit., *Augustan*). The meaning and derivation of this word are not certain. Some authorities claim it is derived from the Greek εἰχοστωης, *ekostonis*, meaning a tenant farmer, a peasant who works fields belonging to the state.

NOTES

corporal punishment for not complying with the ruler's edict. The obligation to sacrifice one's life rather than violate a Biblical commandment is only binding if one is publicly coerced to transgress for the sake of displaying that one has rejected the Torah. If one is coerced purely for reasons of a non-Jew's personal gain, as in the case of the produce-tax, one need not compromise one's own personal safety by observing the commandment. *Meiri* adds that if an individual is allowed to cultivate his crops during the seventh year for tax requirements, he must take care not to do more work than necessary to meet his minimal obligation to the authorities.

לְעַבֵּר שָׁנָה בְּעַסְיָא In order to intercalate the year in Assia. The question arises as to how the Rabbis were allowed to intercalate the year in Assia, considering that intercalation is permissible only within the boundaries of Eretz Israel (see above, 11b). Moreover, the incident took place in the seventh year, during which it was not customary to intercalate the year (see above, 12a). In response to these difficulties, *Tosafot* suggests that the Rabbis convened in Assia not in order to conduct the actual intercalation but rather to consider the factors and make the calculations necessary to determine whether the subsequent year would need to be intercalated. Alternatively, *Ramah* suggests that the Rabbis conducted themselves in accordance with the opinion recorded above (12a), that it is permitted to intercalate the year during the seventh year. There is also a commentator who reinterprets the account in the Gemara to read that the Rabbis set out from Assia in the direction of Eretz Israel for the sake of intercalating the year there (*Imrei Tzvi*).

אַגִּיסְטוֹן אֲנִי בְּתוֹכוֹ I am an imperial servant in its midst. According to *Rashi*, the implication of this statement is either that the priest was an employee of the Romans, working on land that they had acquired and which was thus exempt from the Sabbatical laws; or that the priest

HALAKHAH

king's armies would entail a risk to one's life (this, in accordance with *Tosafot* and the Talmud Yerushalmi). *Ra'avad*, on the other hand, identifies the produce-tax with duties that were demanded by special tax agents as revenue for the empire itself. Since the only threat in such an instance was to one's land and not to one's life, *Ra'avad* concluded that the special allowance to work one's field would only apply when Sabbatical law was Rabbinically, and not Biblically, binding (as apparent in *Rashi*)." (*Rambam, Sefer Zeraim, Hilkhot Shemittah* 1:11.)

BACKGROUND

עֵקֶל בֵּית הַבַּד Olive-press bale. This term refers to a basket in which olives were placed before they were pressed. The beam of the olive press would compress it until the oil oozed out of the holes in the basket. The basket itself was meant to keep the olives together, so they would not scatter during the pressing.

TRANSLATION AND COMMENTARY

the vine cuttings **for an olive-press bale** that I am weaving," which would render his activity permissible since it is not done for the purpose of facilitating the growth of the vine. [1]Unconvinced, Resh Lakish **said to** his companions — in a play on words: Only **the** man's **heart knows whether** he was truly collecting twigs **for baling** (*ekel*) **or** if he was simply saying so **for** the sake of **cunning** (*akalkalot*), in order to cover up his violation of the law.

הֵי אֲמַר לְהוּ [2]The Gemara stops at this point to consider various aspects of the above account: **Which** accusation **did** Resh Lakish **make first to** Rabbi Ḥiyya and Rabbi Shimon? [3]**If you say that he made the former** accusation (involving the man plowing his field) **to them first,** [4]**let them also say** in response to the second accusation that the man pruning grapevines could also defend himself by saying: [5]**"I am an imperial servant** who has been employed to work **in** this vineyard by the Roman authorities." That would have been a more convincing claim. [6]**Rather,** one must conclude that Resh Lakish **stated this** last accusation (involving the pruner) **to** his companions **first, and** only **subsequently related to them** his observation of the man plowing his field.

מַאי שְׁנָא כֹּהֵן [7]Further, why did Resh Lakish assert that the laborers were priests? **How is a priest different** from anyone else? [8]A priest is different **because** of a presumption that priests **are suspect** in any event **with regard to** violating the laws of **the seventh year.** [9]This contention is supported by a Baraita in which **it was taught:** [10]**"A *se'ah*** measure **of terumah** (a share of one's crop set aside exclusively for the priest and forbidden to all others) **that fell into one hundred *se'ahs* of seventh-year produce** is, as a result, **neutralized** and takes on the same status as the majority of seventh-year produce, which is permissible for all, including non-priests, until the time of *bi'ur* ('removal') when all seventh-year produce in one's possession must either be consumed or abandoned. [11]However, if the *se'ah* of terumah fell into an amount of seventh-year produce **less than** one hundred *se'ahs*, it retains its identity. Consequently, all the produce must be left to **rot,** since any bit of it may conceivably be the forbidden terumah."

״לְעֵקֶל בֵּית הַבַּד אֲנִי צָרִיךְ״. [1]אָמַר לָהֶם: הַלֵּב יוֹדֵעַ אִם לְעֵקֶל אִם לַעֲקַלְקַלּוֹת.

[2]הֵי אֲמַר לְהוּ בְּרֵישָׁא? [3]אִילֵימָא הָא קַמַּיְיתָא אֲמַר לְהוּ בְּרֵישָׁא, [4]הָא נַמִי לֵימְרוּ: [5]״אַגִיסְטוֹן אֲנִי בְּתוֹכוֹ״! [6]אֶלָּא, הָא אֲמַר לֵיהּ בְּרֵישָׁא וַהֲדַר אֲמַר לְהוּ הָךְ.

[7]מַאי שְׁנָא כֹּהֵן? [8]מִשּׁוּם דַּחֲשִׁידִי אַשְּׁבִיעִית. [9]דִּתְנַן: דְּתַנְיָא: [10]״סְאָה תְּרוּמָה שֶׁנָּפְלָה לְמֵאָה סְאִין שֶׁל שְׁבִיעִית תַּעֲלֶה, [11]פָּחוֹת מִיכָּן יֵרָקְבוּ״.

LITERAL TRANSLATION

"I need [them] for an olive-press bale." [1]He said to them: [Only] the heart knows whether [it is] for a bale or for crookedness.

[2]Which [of the two] did [Resh Lakish] say to them first? [3]If you say that he said the former one to them first, [4]let them also say [in the second instance]: [5]"I am an imperial servant in [this field]"! [6]Rather, he said this [latter] one to them first and he subsequently said to them that one.

[7]How is a priest different? [8]Because they are suspect with regard to seventh-year produce. [9]For it was taught: [10]"A *se'ah* of terumah that fell into one hundred *se'ahs* of seventh-year [produce] is neutralized; [11]less than that, let them rot."

RASHI

עקל — דורסא, וצריכא לבית הבד לקשור את תפוח הזיתים כשעוצרין אותן בקורה. הלב יודע — לבו יודע אם לעקל נתכוין או לעקלקלות. לעקלקלות — לעבור על הדת. תעלה — דתרומה בטילה באחד ומאה, והשביעית יאכל זר קודם זמן הביעור. לפחות — ממאה, דהויא ליה מדומע ואסורה לזרים.

NOTES

was working his own field, but for the permissible reason of providing the Roman authorities with his quota of produce-tax for the year. *Tosafot* rejects the first implication, because the Gemara elsewhere (*Gittin* 62a) states that one is not allowed to assist a non-Jew in working his field during the Sabbatical Year. The Geonim explain that an imperial servant is one who is forced to serve the empire or risk his life. Therefore, he cannot be held accountable for his violation of Sabbatical law.

מַאי שְׁנָא כֹּהֵן? How is a priest different? Our commentary follows the approach of *Rashi*, who explains that Resh Lakish was merely conjecturing that the transgressors he encountered along the way were priests. Hence the Gemara here is inquiring why he did so. *Ramah*, however, explains that Resh Lakish knew that these two individuals were priests. The Gemara's question then is: How is a priest different from anyone else? The Gemara answers that priests in particular were suspect with regard to violating the Sabbatical laws and thus would not have been allowed to work their fields, even under pressure from the authorities, lest they came to overstep the boundaries of the Rabbinic dispensation and cultivated more than was necessary for the tax.

TRANSLATION AND COMMENTARY

וַהֲוֵינַן בָּהּ [1]**The Sages** of the Gemara then **discussed** the last part of the Baraita, asking: **Why** should one have to **let** all the produce **rot?** [2]**Let** the owner **sell** the entire mixture **to a priest at the price of *terumah,*** which is less than that of regular produce — [3]**except for the value of the** original ***se'ah*** of *terumah,* which the priest in any case was to receive as a gift. This way the produce can all be eaten and the owner will receive partial compensation for his loss of the produce that he was intending to eat.

וְאָמַר רַב חִיָּיא [4]**Rav Ḥiyya said in the name of Ulla:** This solution was not suggested in the Baraita, which **implies** that **priests were suspect with regard to** keeping the laws dealing with the sanctity of the **seventh-year**, particularly with regard to divesting themselves of seventh-year produce at the time of *bi'ur.* Their laxity was most probably due to mistakenly equating the sanctity of terumah with that of seventh-year produce. The former is intended for the benefit of the priests alone, and has no requirement of *bi'ur.* Knowing that the Rabbis did not want seventh-year produce to be transferred to a priest, Resh Lakish assumed that those whom he saw working the fields were priests. Since priests are suspected of violating the laws of the seventh year by not destroying produce when it becomes forbidden, they are also suspected of violating those laws by working their fields.

אָמְרוּ [5]Resh Lakish's accusatory manner led Rabbi Ḥiyya and Rabbi Shimon **to say** to each other: **"This one is** indeed **a contentious fellow.** It is best that we not include him in our deliberations concerning the intercalation of the year." [6]So, **when they** finally **arrived** in Assia, Rabbi Ḥiyya and Rabbi Shimon **ascended to the roof** where the other Rabbis had already convened for the deliberations, and **pulled the ladder up from under** Resh Lakish so that he could not join them. [7]Disgruntled, **Resh Lakish came before Rabbi Yoḥanan** and **said to him:** [8]I wish to ask you whether **people** such as Rabbi Ḥiyya and Rabbi Shimon, **who are suspect with regard to** guarding the sanctity of **the seventh-year**, having excused the behavior of those who openly violated it, [9]**are fit to intercalate the year?** [10]However, before Rabbi Yoḥanan could answer him, Resh Lakish himself **said:** In truth, the question as to whether they are fit to intercalate the year **is not difficult for**

[1]וַהֲוֵינַן בָּהּ: אַמַּאי יֵרָקְבוּ? [2]יִמְכְּרֶנּוּ לַכֹּהֵן בִּדְמֵי תְרוּמָה, [3]חוּץ מִדְּמֵי אוֹתָהּ סְאָה! [4]וְאָמַר רַב חִיָּיא מִשְּׁמֵיהּ דְּעוּלָּא: זֹאת אוֹמֶרֶת נֶחְשְׁדוּ כֹּהֲנִים אַשְּׁבִיעִית.

[5]אֲמַרוּ: טָרוֹדָא הוּא דֵּין. [6]כִּי מְטוּ לְהָתָם סְלִיקוּ לְאִיגְּרָא, שְׁלָפוּהּ לְדַרְגָּא מִתּוּתֵיהּ. [7]אֲתָא לְקַמֵּיהּ דְּרַבִּי יוֹחָנָן, אֲמַר לֵיהּ: [8]בְּנֵי אָדָם הַחֲשׁוּדִין עַל הַשְּׁבִיעִית, [9]כְּשֵׁרִין לְעַבֵּר שָׁנָה? [10]הֲדַר אֲמַר: לָא קַשְׁיָא

LITERAL TRANSLATION

[1]And we were discussing this: Why let them rot? [2]Let him sell it to a priest at the price of terumah, [3]except for the value of that *se'ah*! [4]And Rav Ḥiyya said in the name of Ulla: This implies (lit., "says") [that] priests were suspect with regard to the seventh-year [produce].

[5]They said: This one [Resh Lakish] is a contentious fellow. [6]When they arrived there, they ascended to the roof [and] pulled the ladder out from under him. [7][Resh Lakish] came before Rabbi Yoḥanan [and] said to him: [8]People who are suspect with regard to the seventh-year produce, [9]are they fit to intercalate the year? [10][Resh Lakish] then said: This is not difficult

RASHI

ימכרו לכהן – דהא שרייה ליה תרומה. **בדמי תרומה** – כלומר בזול, דתרומה אין דמיה יקרים כחולין, לפי שאינה ראויה אלא לכהנים, כלומר: ימכרנה בעליהם לכהנים במה שיכול, חוץ מדמי התרומה שהוא חייב לתתם לכהן בחנם, דמותר למכור שביעית על מנת לאכול היא ודמיה קודם הביעור. **נחשדו כהנים** – להשהות שביעית אחר זמן הביעור, דמורו בה היתירא משום דאיתסרו תרומה וקדשי קדשים לגבייהו, והשביעית נמי קדושת הארץ היא. **אמרי** – רבי חייא בר זרנוקי ורבי שמעון עליה דריש לקיש. **טרודא הוא דין** – קנתרן הוא זה, ומטריח בדבריו. **כי מטי התם** – לעלייה שמעברין בה שנה כדאמרינן בפרק קמא (יא,א). **החשודין על השביעית** – שנעשו סניגורין לרשעים.

NOTES

יִמְכְּרֶנּוּ לַכֹּהֵן **Let him sell it to a priest.** According to *Rashi,* such a sale would be permissible, even though normally one is not allowed to trade seventh-year produce, since the sale was made on condition that the buyer must consume the produce by the date of *bi'ur* and that the seller must exchange the money for produce which he too must

HALAKHAH

נֶחְשְׁדוּ כֹּהֲנִים אַשְּׁבִיעִית **Priests were suspect with regard to the seventh year.** "Priests are suspect with regard to violating Sabbatical law. This is presumed to be due to a false equation made by them between *terumah* produce, which is prohibited by virtue of its special sanctity to everyone but a priest, and seventh-year produce, which is similarly prohibited under certain circumstances for reasons of sanctity. Consequently, if an amount of *terumah* too large

לִי. [1]מִידֵּי דַּהֲוָה אַשְׁלֹשָׁה רוֹעֵי בָקָר, [2]וְרַבָּנַן אַחוּשְׁבְּנַיְיהוּ סְמוּךְ. [3]וַהֲדַר אֲמַר: לָא דָּמֵי, [4]הָתָם — הֲדוּר אִימְּנוּ רַבָּנַן וְעִבְּרוּהָ לְהַהוּא שַׁתָּא, [5]הָכָא, קֶשֶׁר רְשָׁעִים הוּא, [6]וְקֶשֶׁר רְשָׁעִים אֵינוֹ מִן הַמִּנְיָן. [7]אֲמַר רַבִּי יוֹחָנָן: דָּא עָקָא. [8]כִּי אֲתוּ לְקַמֵּיהּ דְּרַבִּי יוֹחָנָן אֲמַרוּ לֵיהּ: [9]קָרֵי לָן רוֹעֵי בָקָר, וְלָא אֲמַר לֵיהּ מָר וְלָא מִידֵּי? [10]אֲמַר לְהוּ: וְאִי קָרֵי לְכוּ רוֹעֵי צֹאן, [11]מַאי אָמֵינָא לֵיהּ? [12]מַאי "קֶשֶׁר רְשָׁעִים"? [13]שֶׁבְנָא הֲוָה דָּרֵישׁ בִּתְלֵיסַר רִבְּוָותָא. [14]חִזְקִיָּה הֲוָה דָּרֵישׁ

LITERAL TRANSLATION

for me. [1]For it is something like [the case of] the three cattle herders, [2]but the Rabbis relied on their [own] calculations. [3]And then he said: It is not similar — [4]there, the Rabbis subsequently voted and intercalated that year; [5]here, it is a collaboration of wicked men, [6]and a collaboration of wicked men is not [counted as] part of a quorum. [7]Rabbi Yoḥanan said: This [statement of yours] is troubling. [8]When they came before Rabbi Yoḥanan, they said to him: [9]He called us cattle herders and master said nothing to him? [10]He said to them: And if he called you sheep herders, [11]what could I have said to him?

[12]What constitutes "a collaboration of wicked men"?

[13]Shebna would expound before [a crowd of] one hundred and thirty thousand. [14]Hezekiah would expound

TRANSLATION AND COMMENTARY

me. [1]This situation **is something like the case of the three cattle herders** (see above, 18b) who were heard by the Rabbis in the month of Adar to say that the weather was similar to what could be expected in Shevat. Consequently, the Rabbis decided to intercalate the year by adding another Adar to the calendar. [2]**But** as the Gemara there explains: **the Rabbis**, although concurring with the cattle herders' conclusion, **relied** not on them but **on their** own **calculations.** Similarly, in this instance, we can assume that if the Rabbis intercalate the year, they will do so on the basis of their own calculations, and not the opinion of Rabbi Ḥiyya and Rabbi Shimon. [3]Resh Lakish **then** retracted and **said** that the situation of the three cattle herders **was** indeed **not similar** to that of Rabbi Ḥiyya and Rabbi Shimon — [4]for **there,** in the case of the cattle herders, **the Rabbis subsequently polled themselves**, without including the herders in their quorum, **and intercalated that year** on the basis of their own calculations; [5]**here,** in our case, the Rabbis will most certainly include Rabbi Ḥiyya and Rabbi Shimon — **a collaboration of wicked men** — in their quorum, [6]**and a collaboration of wicked men is not** to be counted as **part of a quorum** for deciding such matters. [7]**Rabbi Yoḥanan said** to him: Your allowing yourself to think of your esteemed colleagues as wicked men **is** certainly **troubling**! [8]Subsequently, **when** Rabbi Ḥiyya and Rabbi Shimon **came before Rabbi Yoḥanan** and heard of the accusations made against them by Resh Lakish, **they asked him** bitterly: [9]Resh Lakish **called us cattle herders and master said nothing to him?** [10]Rabbi Yoḥanan **said to them** in reply: **And if he had called you** by the even more insulting name of **sheep herders,** [11]**what could I have said to him?**

מַאי קֶשֶׁר רְשָׁעִים [12]In response to Resh Lakish's comment regarding the invalidity of a quorum whose members include wicked men, the Gemara asks: **What constitutes "a collaboration of wicked men"?**

שֶׁבְנָא [13]As an example, the Gemara cites the following story: **Shebna**, one of King Hezekiah's ministers, was so widely esteemed among the people that at times he **would expound** the Torah **before** a crowd of **one hundred and thirty thousand;** [14]whereas when King **Hezekiah** himself **would expound** the Torah, it would

RASHI

שלשה רועי בקר — בפרק "כהן גדול" (סנהדרין יח,ב). **קשר רשעים הוא** — והיאך אנן סומכין על מנין זה לעשות כדבריהם? ואפילו אי הן עושין עבור כדין וכדת, אין השנה מתעברת על ידיהן, דבעינן בית דין נימנין וזה אינו מנין. **דא עקא** — שאתה קורא אותן רשעים. **שבנא** — ממונה על ביתו של חזקיהו מלך יהודה.

BACKGROUND

שֶׁבְנָא Shebna.

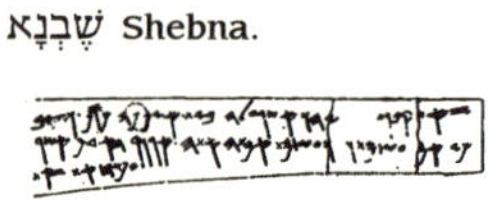

Section remaining from an inscription in a burial cave from the First Temple period.

The cave is situated in a prominent place to the east of the Kidron stream, and, based on the inscription, it dates from approximately the period of Hezekiah.

The inscription states: "This is the tomb of ...yahu who was over the house. There is no silver or gold here, but only [his bones] and the bones of his handmaiden Ata. ...Cursed be the man who opens this." Some scholars suggest reading: "Shebniyahu who was over the house," and that this was the tomb built for him, against which the Prophet was aroused.

NOTES

consume by the appointed date. *Tosafot* suggests that the sale is permissible because it was exceptional, not part of an ongoing business.

דָּא עָקָא **This is troubling.** Our commentary follows the opinion of *Rashi* and *Maharsha*, that Rabbi Yoḥanan was rebuking Resh Lakish for judging his fellow Rabbis so severely. Hence, when Rabbi Ḥiyya and Rabbi Shimon confront Rabbi Yoḥanan shortly thereafter, they do not accuse him of having silently acquiesced in Resh Lakish's charges against them. Rather, they complain because he did not protest more vigorously. *Ramah*, on the other hand, interprets Rabbi Yoḥanan's response to Resh Lakish as one

HALAKHAH

to become nullified (more than one percent) fell into a container of seventh-year produce belonging to a non-priest, the resultant mixture must be left to rot and cannot be given or sold to a priest, who might not be careful to consume the produce by the prescribed date of *bi'ur,*" in accordance with the Baraita, as explained by Ulla. (*Rambam, Sefer Zeraim, Hilkhot Shemittah* 8:18.)

בְּחַד סָר רִבְּוָותָא. [1]כִּי אֲתָא
סַנְחֵרִיב וְצַר עֲלָהּ דִּירוּשָׁלַיִם,
כְּתַב שֶׁבְנָא פִּתְקָא, שְׁדָא
בְּגִירָא: [2]״שֶׁבְנָא וְסִיעָתוֹ
הִשְׁלִימוּ; חִזְקִיָּה וְסִיעָתוֹ לֹא
הִשְׁלִימוּ״. [3]שֶׁנֶּאֱמַר: ״כִּי הִנֵּה
הָרְשָׁעִים יִדְרְכוּן קֶשֶׁת כּוֹנְנוּ
חִצָּם עַל יֶתֶר״. [4]הֲוָה קָא
מִסְתְּפֵי חִזְקִיָּה. [5]אָמַר: דִּילְמָא,
חַס וְשָׁלוֹם, נָטְיָה דַּעֲתֵיהּ
דְּקוּדְשָׁא בְּרִיךְ הוּא בָּתַר רוּבָּא,
[6]כֵּיוָן דְּרוּבָּא מִימְסְרִי, אִינְהוּ
נַמִי מִימְסְרִי. [7]בָּא נָבִיא וְאָמַר
לוֹ: ״לֹא תֹאמְרוּן קֶשֶׁר לְכֹל
אֲשֶׁר יֹאמַר הָעָם הַזֶּה קָשֶׁר״.
[8]כְּלוֹמַר: קֶשֶׁר רְשָׁעִים הוּא,
וְקֶשֶׁר רְשָׁעִים אֵינוֹ מִן הַמִּנְיָן.
[9]הָלַךְ לַחְצֹב לוֹ קֶבֶר בְּקִבְרֵי
בֵּית דָּוִד. [10]בָּא נָבִיא וְאָמַר לוֹ:
״מַה לְּךָ פֹה וּמִי לְךָ פֹה, כִּי
חָצַבְתָּ לְּךָ פֹּה קָבֶר? [11]הִנֵּה ה׳
מְטַלְטֶלְךָ טַלְטֵלָה גָּבֶר. [12]אָמַר
רַב: טִלְטוּלָא דְּגַבְרָא קָשֵׁי
מִדְּאִיתְּתָא. [13]״וְעֹטְךָ עָטֹה״.

LITERAL TRANSLATION

before [a crowd of] one hundred and ten thousand. [1]When Sennacherib came and besieged Jerusalem, Shebna wrote a note [and] sent [it] on an arrow: [2]"Shebna and his followers have made peace; Hezekiah and his followers have not made peace." [3]For it is stated: "For behold the wicked stretch the bow, they position their arrow on the string." [4]Hezekiah was fearful. [5]He said: Perhaps, God forbid, the mind of the Holy One, blessed be He, leans toward the majority; [and] since the majority have given up, [6]we (lit., "they") have also given up. [7]The Prophet [Isaiah] came and said to him: "Call not a conspiracy; all that this people will call a conspiracy." [8]That is to say: It is a collaboration of wicked men, and a collaboration of wicked men is not [counted as] part of a quorum. [9][Shebna] went to hew for himself a tomb among the tombs of the House of David. [10]The Prophet came and said to him: "What have you here and who have you here, that you have hewn for yourself here a tomb? [11]Behold God will cast you away with a mighty heave." [12]Rav said: The rootlessness of a man is harder [to bear] than that of a woman — [13]"and He will surely cover you up."

TRANSLATION AND COMMENTARY

be **before** a crowd of only **one hundred and ten thousand.** [1]It happened that **when Sennacherib**, the Assyrian king, **came and besieged Jerusalem, Shebna wrote** him the following **note** and **sent** it over the city wall **on an arrow:** [2]**"Shebna and his followers have made peace** with their fate and are prepared to surrender; however, **Hezekiah and his followers have not made peace** and are determined to resist you." (This is hinted at in Scripture, [3]**for it is stated** in Psalms 11:2 as follows: **"For behold the wicked stretch the bow, they position their arrow on the string."**) [4]After hearing of Shebna's conspiracy, **Hezekiah was fearful.** [5]**He said: Perhaps, God forbid, the mind of the Holy One, blessed be He, leans toward the majority** of the nation who identify with Shebna and his willingness to surrender. **Once the majority** of the people **have given themselves over** to the Assyrian oppressor, those who wish to resist, [6]such as myself and my followers, will in effect **also have surrendered.** [7]Seeking to relieve Hezekiah's fears, **the Prophet** Isaiah **came and said to him** (as recorded in Isaiah 8:12): "Call **not a conspiracy, all that this people will call a conspiracy."** [8]**That is to say:** Say not that God intends to accept the will of Shebna and his followers, for although their camp comprises a majority of the nation, **it is** a majority based upon **a collaboration of wicked men, and a collaboration of wicked men is not** accepted as **part of a quorum.**

הָלַךְ [9]It is further related that **Shebna**, as part of his plan to seize the kingdom from Hezekiah, **went to hew out for himself a tomb among the** royal **tombs of the House of David.** [10]**The Prophet** Isaiah **came and said to him** (Isaiah 22:16-17): **"What have you here and who have you here, that you have hewn for yourself here a tomb**....among the sepulchers of the kings? [11]**Behold God will cast you away** as a man is cast away with a mighty heave." [12]**Rav said:** From this last **expression** we learn that **rootlessness is harder for a man to bear than for a woman.** [13]Isaiah continues: **"And He will surely** cover **you up."**

RASHI

השלימו — לעובדך. **ידרכון קשת כוננו חצם וגו׳** — על שם שעל ידי החץ הוא מבקש להמית את אדוניו בלשון הרע הכתוב שם. **לא תאמרון קשר** — אל תחשוב בדעתך חזקיהו, שיהא מניינו של שבנא מנין, ליחשב רוב. **בקברי בית דוד** — שהיה מתגאה למרוד במלכות, וליקבר במותו בקבורת המלכים.

NOTES

of sympathy, implying that it was indeed troubling that the year was about to be intercalated by men who had come under suspicion of being wicked.

טִלְטוּלָא דְּגַבְרָא קָשֵׁי מִדְּאִיתְּתָא The rootlessness of a man is harder to bear than that of a woman. According to *Maharsha*, a rootless woman when passing through strange

TRANSLATION AND COMMENTARY

[1]**Rabbi Yose the son of Rabbi Ḥanina said:** This last threat of Isaiah's **teaches** us **that** Shebna **broke out with** *tzara'at* (a skin disease which renders an individual ritually impure). [2]For **it is written here** regarding Shebna, **"and He will surely cover you up,"** [3]**and it is written there,** in the Biblical verse discussing the measures adopted by one afflicted with *tzora'at* (Leviticus 13:45): **"And on** his **upper lip, he shall cover himself."**

צָנוֹף [4]The Gemara now resumes its quotation of Isaiah's prophecy to Shebna (Isaiah 22:18): **"He** (God) **will surely violently turn and toss you as a wrapped turban, exiling you into a land of vast expanses**; there you will die and there the chariots of your glory [will experience] the disgrace of your master's house." [5]A Sage **taught** in relation to this verse: Shebna **sought to disgrace the house of his master,** King Hezekiah — **therefore his** own **glory was turned into disgrace**, as is evident from the following account: [6]**When** Shebna **was leaving Jerusalem** together with his group of followers in order to deliver themselves into the hands of the Assyrians, [7]the Angel **Gabriel came** and **held the gate** shut **before his retinue** so that they could not follow him into the enemy encampment. [26B] [8]When Shebna reached the Assyrians, **they said to him: Where is your** entire **retinue** of followers? [9]**He said** to them: Apparently **they have broken** their promise to **me.** [10]**They** then **said to him: If so, you are surely making light of us!** [11]As punishment, the Assyrians **bored holes through his heels and suspended him by the tails of their horses,** and the horses **dragged him over thorns and thistles.**

אָמַר רַבִּי אֶלְעָזָר [12]In a further discussion of the character of Shebna, **Rabbi Elazar said: Shebna was a pleasure-seeker,** [13]for **it is written here** (Isaiah 22:15) that when God commanded the Prophet to approach Shebna, He said to him: **"Go, come to this attendant,** to Shebna who is over the house"; [14]**and it is written there** in I Kings 1:2 regarding Abishag: **"And let her be for him an attendant** and let her lie in your bosom so that my master the king shall be warm." Apparently Shebna was referred to as "an attendant" because, like Abishag, he offered his services to those who sought physical warmth.

[1]אָמַר רַבִּי יוֹסֵי בְּרַבִּי חֲנִינָא: מְלַמֵּד שֶׁפָּרְחָה בּוֹ צָרַעַת. [2]כְּתִיב הָכָא: ״וְעֹטְךָ עָטֹה״, [3]וּכְתִיב הָתָם: ״וְעַל שָׂפָם יַעְטֶה״.

[4]״צָנוֹף יִצְנָפְךָ צְנֵפָה כַּדּוּר אֶל אֶרֶץ רַחֲבַת יָדַיִם וגו׳״. [5]תָּנָא: הוּא בִּיקֵּשׁ קָלוֹן בֵּית אֲדֹנָיו — לְפִיכָךְ נֶהְפַּךְ כְּבוֹדוֹ לְקָלוֹן. [6]כִּי הֲוָה נָפֵיק אִיהוּ, [7]אֲתָא גַּבְרִיאֵל אַחֲדֵיהּ לְדַשָּׁא בְּאַפֵּי מַשִׁרְיָיתֵיהּ. [26B] [8]אָמְרוּ לֵיהּ: מַשִׁירְיָיתָךְ הֵיכָא? [9]אֲמַר: הֲדַרוּ בִּי. [10]אָמְרוּ לֵיהּ: אִם כֵּן, אַחוּכֵי קָא מְחַיְּיכַתְּ בָּן! [11]נְקָבוּהוּ בַּעֲקֵבָיו וּתְלָאוּהוּ בְּזַנְבֵי סוּסֵיהֶם וְהָיוּ מְגָרְרִין אוֹתוֹ עַל הַקּוֹצִים וְעַל הַבַּרְקָנִין.

[12]אָמַר רַבִּי אֶלְעָזָר: שֶׁבְנָא בַּעַל הֲנָאָה הָיָה, [13]כְּתִיב הָכָא: ״לֶךְ, בֹּא אֶל הַסֹּכֵן הַזֶּה״, [14]וּכְתִיב הָתָם: ״וּתְהִי לוֹ סֹכֶנֶת״.

LITERAL TRANSLATION

[1]Rabbi Yose the son of Rabbi Ḥanina said: It teaches that he broke out with *tzara'at.* [2]It is written here: "And He will surely cover you up," [3]and it is written there: "And on [his] upper lip, he shall cover himself."

[4]"He will surely violently turn and wind you as a wrapped turban, [exiling you] into a land of vast expanses, etc." [5]He taught: He sought to disgrace the house of his master — therefore his glory was turned into disgrace. [6]When he was leaving [Jerusalem], [7]Gabriel came [and] held the gate [shut] before his retinue. [26B] [8]They said to him: Where is your retinue? [9]He said: They have rejected [their promise to] me. [10]They said to him: If so, you are surely mocking us! [11]They bored holes through his heels and suspended him by the tails of their horses and they dragged him over the thorns and over the thistles.

[12]Rabbi Elazar said: Shebna was a pleasure-seeker (lit., "a master of pleasure"), [13][for] it is written here: "Go, come to this attendant," [14]and it is written there: "And let her [Abishag] be for him an attendant."

RASHI

צנוף יצנפך צנפה כדור — סבב יסבבוך חיילות, כדור — כשורה להגלותך אל ארץ רחבת ידים — סיפיה דקרא ״שמה תמות ושם מרכבות כבודך קלון בית אדונך״. **כי הוה** — שבנא נפיק עם סיעתו לצאת מירושלים ולהשלים עם סנחריב. **משרייתך היכא** — שכתבת לנו שבנא וסיעתו השלימו. **הדרו בי** — חזרו ממה שהבטיחוני. **בעל הנאה** — כמשמעו, ויש אומרים משכב זכור. **סוכנת** — מחממתו, וחבירו ״ובוקע עצים יסכן בם״ (קהלת י).

NOTES

environs evokes more compassion and offers of support than does a rootless man. Therefore, his rootlessness entails greater suffering.

שֶׁפָּרְחָה בּוֹ צָרַעַת That he broke out with *tzara'at.* Shebna's contracting *tzara'at* is considered particularly appropriate, because our Sages identify this disease as divine retribution for having engaged in divisive feuding, the very sin which Shebna had commited (*Iyyun Ya'akov*).

TRANSLATION AND COMMENTARY

וְאוֹמֵר [1]The Gemara now returns to the verse cited above (26a) as hinting at Shebna's conspiracy (Psalms 11:2: "For behold the wicked stretch the bow, they position their arrow on the string"): **It says** in the verse immediately following: **"When the foundations are destroyed, what has the righteous one done?"** [2]**Rav Yehudah and Rav Eina** each interpreted this verse differently. [3]**One said** that it intends to teach: **If Hezekiah and his party are destroyed** by Sennacherib, people will ask: **"What has** God, **the Righteous One, done** to reward those who served him so faithfully?" [4]**And** the other **one said** that it intends to teach: **If the Holy Temple is destroyed** as a result of Shebna's collaboration with Sennacherib, people will ask: **"What has the Righteous One done** to save the Temple from destruction?" [5]**And Ulla said** that the verse has this meaning: Let the devious thoughts of that wicked one, Shebna, be destroyed, for **if the thoughts of that wicked one are not destroyed, what has the righteous one**, Hezekiah, **accomplished** with all his prayers and good deeds?

בִּשְׁלָמָא [6]The Gemara now discusses the meaning of the word "foundations" in these interpretations of the verse. It is **consistent with** Ulla, **who said** that "foundations" refers to **"the thoughts of that wicked one."** [7]For **this is** indeed a possible implication of **what is written: "When the foundations are destroyed."** "Foundations" can signify thoughts that are established firmly in one's heart. [8]**And** it is **also** acceptable **according to the one who said** that "foundations" refers to **"the Holy Temple."** [9]**For we have learned** in a Mishnah (*Yoma* 53b) that **"there was a stone** situated **there** beneath the Holy Ark **from the days of the early prophets** that **was called** *shetiyyah* (foundation)" — for this rock was the first foundation stone that God set into the earth (see *Yoma* 54b). [10]**However, according to the one who said** that "foundations" refers to **"Hezekiah and his party,"** [11]**where do we find** elsewhere in Scripture that **righteous ones are called "foundations"?** [12]Indeed we do, **for it is written** in I Samuel 2:8: **"For the pillars of the earth are the Lord's, and He has founded the world upon them,"** the "pillars of the earth" signifying the righteous

[1]וְאוֹמֵר: ״כִּי הַשָּׁתוֹת יֵהָרֵסוּן צַדִּיק מַה פָּעָל״? [2]רַב יְהוּדָה וְרַב עֵינָא — [3]חַד אָמַר: אִילּוּ חִזְקִיָּה וְסִיעָתוֹ נֶהֱרָסִים, צַדִּיק מַה פָּעַל?; [4]וְחַד אָמַר: אִילּוּ בֵּית הַמִּקְדָּשׁ יֵהָרֵס, צַדִּיק מַה פָּעַל? [5]וְעוּלָּא אָמַר: אִילּוּ מַחְשְׁבוֹתָיו שֶׁל אוֹתוֹ רָשָׁע אֵינָן נֶהֱרָסוֹת, צַדִּיק מַה פָּעַל?
[6]בִּשְׁלָמָא לְמַאן דְּאָמַר ״אִילּוּ מַחְשְׁבוֹתָיו שֶׁל אוֹתוֹ רָשָׁע״, [7]הַיְינוּ דִּכְתִיב: ״כִּי הַשָּׁתוֹת יֵהָרֵסוּן״. [8]וּלְמַאן דַּאֲמַר ״בֵּית הַמִּקְדָּשׁ״ נַמִי, [9]דִּתְנַן: ״אֶבֶן הָיְתָה שָׁם מִימוֹת נְבִיאִים הָרִאשׁוֹנִים וּשְׁתִיָּיה הָיְתָה נִקְרֵאת. [10]אֶלָּא לְמַאן דְּאָמַר ״חִזְקִיָּה וְסִיעָתוֹ״, [11]הֵיכָא אַשְׁכְּחַן צַדִּיקֵי דְּאִיקְּרוּ ״שָׁתוֹת״? [12]דִּכְתִיב ״כִּי לַה׳ מְצֻקֵי אֶרֶץ וַיָּשֶׁת עֲלֵיהֶם תֵּבֵל״.

LITERAL TRANSLATION

[1]And it says: "When the foundations are destroyed, what has the righteous one done?" [2]Rav Yehudah and Rav Eina — [3]one said: If Hezekiah and his party are destroyed, what has the Righteous One done? [4]And one said: If the Holy Temple is destroyed, what has the Righteous One done? [5]And Ulla said: If the thoughts of that wicked one (Shebna) are not destroyed, what has the righteous one [Hezekiah] done? [6]Granted according to the one who said, "If the thoughts of that wicked one," [7]this is what is written: "When the foundations are destroyed." [8]And also according to the one who said "the Holy Temple," [9]for we have learned: "There was a stone there from the days of the first prophets, and it was called *shetiyyah* (foundation)." [10]But according to the one who said, "Hezekiah and his party," [11]where do we find righteous ones who are called "foundations"? [12]For it is written: "For the pillars of the earth are the Lord's, and He has founded the world upon them."

RASHI

(ואומר) כי השתות יהרסון וגו׳ — בתריה ד״כי הנה הרשעים ידרכון קשת״ כתיב. **צדיק מה פעל** — הקדוש ברוך הוא מה שכר שהוא משלם. ולקמן מפרש מאי משמע שתות לשון סיעת צדיקים. **אילו בית המקדש חרב** — על ידי סנחריב בעצתו של שבנא, ״צדיק מה פעל״ — איה נפלאותיו של הקדוש ברוך הוא. **אילו מחשבות של שבנא הרשע אין נהרסות** — והכי משמע קרא: ״כי השתות יהרסון״ — מחשבותיו של אותו רשע הכתוב למעלה ״כי הנה הרשעים ידרכון קשת״. ולשון ״שתות״ — מחשבות שהוא משית בקירות לבו, ״יהרסון״ — ראויות הן ליהרס, שאם לא כן ״צדיק מה פעל״ — מה פעלו של חזקיהו והיכא שכרו. ״כי השתות״ — לשון ״ולא שת לבו גם לזאת״ (שמות ז). **אבן היתה שם** — תחת הארון. **ושתייה היא נקראת** — שממנה נשתת עולם, שנאמר (תהלים נ) ״דיבר ויקרא ארץ״, ואומר ״מציון מכלל יופי וגו׳״ במסכת יומא (נד,ב) אומר: עולם מציון נברא.

HALAKHAH

אֶבֶן שְׁתִיָּיה **Foundation stone.** "There was a stone at the western end of the Holy of Holies upon which was placed the Ark of the Holy Covenant during the time of the First Temple." (*Rambam, Sefer Avodah, Hilkhot Bet HaBeḥirah* 4:1.)

TRANSLATION AND COMMENTARY

ones. [1] **And if you wish,** you can **say** that the support comes **from here** (Isaiah 28:29): "This too emerged from the Lord of Hosts, who **gave marvelous counsel and increased wisdom."** The Hebrew word used here for "wisdom" — *tushiyah* — resembles the Hebrew word *shetiyyah* ("foundation"); hence the implication that those righteous ones who embody the divine wisdom of Torah, both in thought and in practice, are the foundations of the universe.

אָמַר רַבִּי חָנָן [2] The Gemara now cites alternative opinions as to why the divine wisdom of the Torah is referred to by the term *tushiyah*: **Rabbi Ḥanan asked: Why is** the divine **wisdom** of the Torah **called by the name** ***tushiyah?*** [3] **Because** proper study and practice of the Torah **wears** (*mateshet*) **a man's strength.** [4] **Another interpretation** is: Torah wisdom is called ***tushiyah*** **for it was given in secrecy** (the word *tushiyah* being an acronym of the words *nitnah beḥashai*, "given in secrecy"), **because of the** fear that if **Satan** (the prosecuting angel) were to know of Israel's receiving the Torah, he would argue convincingly against its being taken from the angels and delivered unto man. [5] Yet **another interpretation** is: Torah wisdom is called ***tushiyah*** because it is made up of nonmaterial **words** — yet they are the substance **upon which the world is founded.** (Here also the term *tushiyah* is understood as an acronym of the terms *tohu* — emptiness — and *shetiyyah* — "foundation.")

אָמַר עוּלָּא [6] The Gemara interprets another verse in which the word *tushiyah* appears: **Ulla said:** Any **worry** over the hardships of daily life while engaged in intellectual endeavors inevitably **succeeds** in distracting one, **even** when studying the **words of Torah,** [7] **for it is written** in Job 5:12: **"He** (God) **nullifies the thoughts**

[1] וְאִיבָּעֵית אֵימָא מֵהָכָא: ״הִפְלִא עֵצָה הִגְדִּיל תּוּשִׁיָּה״. [2] אָמַר רַבִּי חָנָן: לָמָּה נִקְרָא שְׁמָהּ תּוּשִׁיָּה? [3] מִפְּנֵי שֶׁהִיא מַתֶּשֶׁת כֹּחוֹ שֶׁל אָדָם. [4] דָּבָר אַחֵר: תּוּשִׁיָּה — שֶׁנִּיתְּנָה בַּחֲשַׁאי מִפְּנֵי הַשָּׂטָן. [5] דָּבָר אַחֵר: תּוּשִׁיָּה — דְּבָרִים שֶׁל תּוֹהוּ, שֶׁהָעוֹלָם מְשׁוּתָת עֲלֵיהֶם.

[6] אָמַר עוּלָּא: מַחֲשָׁבָה מוֹעֶלֶת אֲפִילּוּ לְדִבְרֵי תוֹרָה, [7] שֶׁנֶּאֱמַר: ״מֵפֵר מַחְשְׁבוֹת עֲרוּמִים

LITERAL TRANSLATION

[1] And if you wish, say from here: "He gave marvelous counsel and increased wisdom (*tushiyah*)." [2] Rabbi Ḥanan said: Why is [wisdom] called by the name *tushiyah*? [3] Because it weakens (*mateshet*) a man's strength. [4] Another interpretation (lit., "word"): *Tushiyah* — for it was given in secrecy on account of the Satan (prosecuting angel). [5] Another interpretation: *Tushiyah* — nonmaterial words upon which the world is founded.

[6] Ulla said: Worry (lit., "thought") succeeds [in causing one to forget] even words of Torah, [7] for it is said: "He nullifies the thoughts of the crafty,

RASHI

תושיה — על שם שהעולם מושתת על התורה ולומדיה, נקראת תושיה. **מפני השטן** — שהוא מקטרג, ואמר: מסתפק לעליונים ולא ימסרו הלוחות ביד משה. **דברים של תוהו** — דיבור וקרייה בעלמא, וכל דיבור אין בו גשישה ממש כתוהו הזה, ואף על פי כן עולם מושתת עליהם. ונוטריקון הוא: תי״ו — תוהו, שיה — מושתת. **מחשבה** — דאגת הלב על מזונותיו של אדם. **מועלת** — מהניא לשכח למודו. **מפר מחשבות ערומים** — נותן להם מזונות ומבטל מחשבות מלבם, שלא היו מניחין אותן לעשות תושיה. לישנא אחרינא: מחשבה שאדם מחשב כך וכך אעשה כך וכך תעלה בידי — מועלת להשבית הדבר, שאין מחשבתו מתקיימת אפילו לדבר תורה. כגון האומר עד יום פלוני אסיים כך וכך מסכתות בגירסא. **מפר מחשבות ערומים** — שאין מחשבותיו עולה בידו ואפילו לתושיה.

NOTES

שֶׁנִּיתְּנָה בַּחֲשַׁאי For it was given in secrecy. The secrecy surrounding the giving of the Torah may be a reference to the private and hidden revelation of the Torah in all its detail — the Oral Torah and Kabbalistic secrets — accorded Moshe while alone atop Mount Sinai. *Ramah* interprets this secrecy as referring to God's giving of the Torah to Israel without consulting, as it were, His own standard of strict justice (represented here by Satan), which most certainly would have mitigated against His giving it to Israel. The nature of Satan's argument is discussed by the commentators. Our commentary follows *Rashi* and *Ramah*, who say that Satan would argue that the Torah, being eternal, should remain the sole property of the angels and not be delivered to mortal man. However, according to *Tosafot* (*Shabbat* 89a), Satan argued that the Children of Israel were unfit to receive the Torah, as they would soon decline into idolatry and worship the golden calf.

דְּבָרִים שֶׁל תּוֹהוּ Nonmaterial words. Our commentary is in accordance with *Rashi,* who explains that the words in the Torah, being abstract symbols and verbal utterances, are deemed "nonmaterial." *Ramah* cites an additional interpretation, according to which this expression refers exclusively to particular statutes in the Torah, such as the prohibition against wearing linen and wool or the ceremony of the red heifer, which appear "nonmaterial" insofar as they lack a rational basis in the material world.

מַחֲשָׁבָה מוֹעֶלֶת Thought succeeds. Our commentary accords with the first interpretation of Ulla's statement appearing in *Rashi* (attributed in *Tosafot* to Rabbi Yitzḥak the son of Asher). An alternative interpretation appearing in *Rashi* understands Ulla's statement as follows: Setting goals that are too high for a particular task (such as finishing it within an unrealistically short time) often leads to failure, even in the study of Torah. *Tosafot* cites an

TRANSLATION AND COMMENTARY

of the crafty, that their hands not practice wisdom (*tushiyah*)." This verse can be understood as saying that God — through physically providing for those who are devoted to the study of His Torah — neutralizes the "thoughts" or worries of the "crafty" scholars, which interfere with their practice of wisdom. [1]**Rabbah said: If** individuals **engage** in the study of Torah **for its own sake,** and not for some ulterior benefit, then worries concerning the hardships of life **will not succeed** in breaking one's concentration, [2]**for it is said** in Proverbs 19:21: **"Many are the thoughts in the heart of man, yet the counsel of the Lord shall prevail."** [3]This teaches us that **"counsel" that possesses within it the word of the Lord,** such as the Torah, **will prevail forever** over those other thoughts in the heart of man that vie for his attention.

אָמַר רַבִּי יְהוּדָה [4]We now return to our Mishnah: **"Rabbi Yehudah said: When** do these gamblers qualify as being unfit to serve as judges or witnesses? When they have no trade other than gambling." [5]**Rabbi Abbahu said in the name of Rabbi Elazar: The law is in accordance with Rabbi Yehudah.** [6]**And Rabbi Abbahu** further **said in the name of Rabbi Elazar: All** those declared ineligible to serve as witnessses **require a** public **proclamation in court** of their ineligibility before their testimony can be disqualified.

רוֹעֶה [7]As for **a herdsman,** who was decreed by the Rabbis to be ineligible as a witness by virtue of his vocation (above, 25b), **Rav Aḥa and Ravina disagree about** whether each individual herdsman must be publicly proclaimed ineligible: [8]**One** of them **said** that **he requires a** public **proclamation,** since his ineligibility may not be known to all; [9]**and** the other **one said** that **he does not require a** public **proclamation,** because of the nature of his job. Everyone knows this is an objectionable vocation.

וְלֹא תַעֲשֶׂינָה יְדֵיהֶם תּוּשִׁיָּה". [1]אָמַר רַבָּה: אִם עֲסוּקִין לִשְׁמָהּ אֵינָהּ מוֹעֶלֶת, [2]שֶׁנֶּאֱמַר: "רַבּוֹת מַחֲשָׁבוֹת בְּלֶב אִישׁ וַעֲצַת ה׳ הִיא תָקוּם" — [3]עֵצָה שֶׁיֵּשׁ בָּהּ דְּבַר ה׳, הִיא תָּקוּם לְעוֹלָם.

[4]"אָמַר רַבִּי יְהוּדָה: אֵימָתַי". [5]אָמַר רַבִּי אַבָּהוּ אָמַר רַבִּי אֶלְעָזָר: הֲלָכָה כְּרַבִּי יְהוּדָה. [6]וְאָמַר רַבִּי אַבָּהוּ אָמַר רַבִּי אֶלְעָזָר: כּוּלָּן צְרִיכִין הַכְרָזָה בְּבֵית דִּין.

[7]רוֹעֶה — פְּלִיגִי בָּהּ רַב אַחָא וְרָבִינָא: [8]חַד אָמַר: בָּעֵי הַכְרָזָה, [9]וְחַד אָמַר: לָא בָּעֵי הַכְרָזָה.

LITERAL TRANSLATION

that their hands not practice wisdom (*tushiyah*)." [1]Rabbah said: If they engage [in study] for its own sake, it will not succeed [in causing them to forget their Torah], [2]for it is said: "Many are the thoughts in the heart of man, yet the counsel of the Lord shall prevail" — [3]counsel that possesses within it the word of the Lord will prevail forever.

[4]"Rabbi Yehudah said: When?" [5]Rabbi Abbahu said in the name of Rabbi Elazar: The law accords with Rabbi Yehudah. [6]And Rabbi Abbahu said in the name of Rabbi Elazar: They all require a proclamation in court.

[7]A herdsman — Rav Aḥa and Ravina disagree about it: [8]One says: He requires a proclamation, [9]and one says: He does not require a proclamation.

RASHI

הכרזה בבית דין — ולאין נפסלין לעדות עד שיכריזו בבית דין להודיע פסולן. **לא בעי הכרזה** — שעבירה שלו מפורסמת לכל.

NOTES

additional interpretation, which understands the verb מוֹעֶלֶת in the sense of "misleads" or "perverts" rather than "succeeds." Ulterior thoughts or motives for engaging in a particular activity (such as a desire to become wealthy) pervert the activity, dooming one to failure. This is so even with Torah study, which must be pursued for its own sake. Others understand Ulla as referring to obstructions erected by others, which can even thwart successful Torah study (*Iyyun Ya'akov*). *Maharsha* adds an altogether different interpretation of Ulla: Engaging in thought alone, without the attendant verbalization and vocalization of one's ideas, renders one's study ineffective, even in the study of Torah, though it appears to depend mainly upon silent contemplation.

הֲלָכָה כְּרַבִּי יְהוּדָה **The law accords with Rabbi Yehudah.** We saw above (25a) that the Amoraim disagree as to whether Rabbi Yehudah in our Mishnah is merely elaborating on the anonymous first Tanna or disagrees with him. Hence, Rabbi Elazar's statement that the law accords with Rabbi Yehudah appears to reflect the position of those Amoraim who maintain that Rabbi Yehudah is arguing against the earlier Tanna who, according to this view, considers gambling a form of theft, because the wagerer does not truly intend to part with his money. By concluding that the Halakhah is in accordance with Rabbi Yehudah, our Gemara establishes that gambling is not considered theft, yet it is objectionable nonetheless. Gamblers, who have no other source of livelihood, do not "engage in

HALAKHAH

כּוּלָּן צְרִיכִין הַכְרָזָה בְּבֵית דִּין **They all require proclamation in a court.** "Should one who is Biblically disqualified from offering testimony nevertheless give evidence, his testimony is annulled, even if his status was not known prior to giving testimony or his ineligibility was not formally proclaimed in court. However, someone whose ineligibility is Rabbinic in

[1]בִּשְׁלָמָא, לְמַאן דְּאָמַר לָא בָּעֵי הַכְרָזָה, [2]הַיְינוּ דְּאָמַר רַב יְהוּדָה אָמַר רַב: סְתָם רוֹעֶה פָּסוּל. [3]אֶלָּא לְמַאן דְּאָמַר בָּעֵי הַכְרָזָה — [4]מַאי ״סְתָם רוֹעֶה פָּסוּל״? [5]דִּבְסְתָמָא מַכְרְזִינַן עֲלֵיהּ. [6]הַהִיא מַתָּנָה דַּהֲווּ חֲתִימֵי עֲלַהּ תְּרֵין גַּזְלָנִין. [7]סְבַר רַב פַּפָּא בַּר שְׁמוּאֵל לְאַכְשׁוּרַהּ, [8]דְּהָא לָא אַכְרְזִינַן עֲלַיְיהוּ. [9]אֲמַר לֵיהּ רָבָא: נְהִי דְּבָעֵינַן הַכְרָזָה [10]בְּגַזְלָן דְּרַבָּנַן, בְּגַזְלָן דְּאוֹרַיְיתָא — מִי בָּעֵינַן הַכְרָזָה?! [11]סִימָן: דָּבָ״ר וַעֲרָיו״ת גַּנָּ״ב. [12]אָמַר רַב נַחְמָן: אוֹכְלֵי דָּבָר

TRANSLATION AND COMMENTARY

בִּשְׁלָמָא [1]The Gemara proceeds to consider these two positions: **Granted** that, **according to the one who said** that a herdsman **does not require** prior **proclamation** in court before his testimony can be disqualified, [2]**this is** essentially **what Rav Yehudah** meant when he **said in the name of Rav:** Even **an ordinary herdsman,** who has not been officially accused of trespassing, **is unfit** to serve as a witness. [3]**However, according to the one who said** that a herdsman **does require** a prior **proclamation,** [4]**what is** the meaning of Rav's statement that "even **an ordinary herdsman is unfit** to testify"?

דִּבְסְתָמָא [5]According to that Amora, Rav's intention clearly was to inform us that **we must always proclaim** a professional herdsman ineligible as a witness, due to the compromising nature of his vocation.

הַהִיא [6]Once, **a certain** deed of **gift on which the names of two robbers appeared** as witnesses was brought to court for ratification. [7]**Rav Pappa bar Shmuel thought of validating** the deed of gift in spite of its witnesses, [8]**because** the court **had not proclaimed them to be unfit.** [9]**Rava said to him: Granted that we require** prior **proclamation regarding** someone who is only classified as **a robber by Rabbinic standards;** his thievery is not obvious. [10]However, **regarding** one who is **a robber by Biblical standards**, having blatantly seized another's property, **do we** indeed **require** prior **proclamation** before he can be disqualified? No.

סִימָן [11]The following is **a** useful **mnemonic** for remembering the order of topics related to other kinds of wrongdoers and their eligibility to offer testimony, to be dealt with below: **"Something, and illicit sexual relations, a thief."**

אָמַר רַב נַחְמָן [12]**Rav Nahman said: Those who enjoy the charity of gentiles** (the Gemara here uses the

LITERAL TRANSLATION

[1]Granted, according to the one who says [that] he does not require a proclamation, [2]this is what Rav Yehudah said in the name of Rav: An ordinary herdsman is unfit. [3]But according to the one who says [that] he requires a proclamation — [4]what is [the meaning of] "an ordinary herdsman is unfit"?

[5]That we [must] ordinarily proclaim him [to be unfit].

[6][There was] a certain [deed of] gift on which were signed [the names of] two robbers. [7]Rav Pappa bar Shmuel thought of validating it, [8]because [the court] had not proclaimed them [to be unfit]. [9]Rava said to him: Granted that we require proclamation for a robber by Rabbinic [standards], [10]as regards a robber by Biblical [standards] — do we require proclamation?!

[11]A mnemonic: Something, and illicit sexual relations, a thief.

[12]Rav Nahman said: Those who enjoy the charity of gentiles (lit., "consume something

RASHI

דבסתמא מכרזינן עליה — אף על פי שלא באו עדים שהכניס עדרו לשדה אחר. גזלן דרבנן — הנך דמתניתין. גזלן דאורייתא — החוטף ממש, כגון בניהו בן יהוידע דכתיב (שמואל ב׳ כג) ״ויגזול את החנית מיד המצרי״, הכי מפרש ב״מרובה״ (בבא קמא עט,ב). אוכלי דבר אחר — מקבלי צדקה מן הנכרים דהוי חילול

NOTES

productive work" that benefits society. However, gambling is not considered theft only when two gamblers place their respective wagers on the gameboard, thereby effectively depositing the money in the domain of the eventual winner. Should no money be placed on the board — even if the two parties formally obligate themselves through some other means to pay their debts — the obligation lacks sufficient intention, and any money collected by the winner is an illicit gain (*Tosafot*).

אוֹכְלֵי דָּבָר אַחֵר **Those who consume "something other."** Our commentary accords with the explanation of *Rashi,* who identifies the implicit offense in accepting charity from

HALAKHAH

nature can only have his testimony annulled if he was previously proclaimed in court to be unfit," in accordance with Rava's distinction. If such an individual was publicly punished for his offense, it is the equivalent of his having been proclaimed unfit (*Rema*). (*Shulhan Arukh, Hoshen Mishpat* 34:23.)

אוֹכְלֵי דָּבָר אַחֵר **Those who consume "something other."** "Those who take charity in public from a non-Jew, when

TRANSLATION AND COMMENTARY

euphemistic expression "those who consume something other") **are unfit to** offer **testimony,** because they desecrate the name of Heaven for the sake of financial gain. [1]The Gemara elaborates: **This** ruling of Rav Naḥman's **applies** exclusively to an individual who accepted such charity **in public; but** if he did so **in private** — then he is **not** disqualified from serving as a witness. [2]**And even** in the case of one who accepted such charity **in public, we only apply** Rav Naḥman's ruling **when it was possible for** this man **to provide for himself** by soliciting charity from the gentile **in private,** [3]**but** nevertheless **he** chose to **demean himself** by doing it **in public.** [4]**But,** if **it was not possible for him** to arrange to get the charity in private, then he is not held accountable for taking it in public — for the charity **is** necessary in order to guarantee **his existence**, and this is not one of those situations that requires one to sacrifice his life in order to avoid desecrating God's Name.

אָמַר רַב נַחְמָן [5]**Rav Naḥman said: One who is suspected of** engaging in **illicit sexual relations is** still **fit to** offer **testimony.** [6]**Rav Sheshet said** to Rav Naḥman in protest: **Answer me** this, **my master** — [7]can it be that an individual who is subject to **forty** lashes **on his shoulder** for having conducted himself immorally can be **fit** to serve as a witness? One who is subject to lashes is referred to in the Torah (Deuteronomy 25:2) as a "wicked person," and we have learned that a wicked person is ineligible to serve as a witness (see 9b and 27a)!

אַחֵר פְּסוּלִין לְעֵדוּת. [1]הָנֵי מִילֵּי בְּפַרְהֶסְיָא, אֲבָל בְּצִינְעָה — לֹא. [2]וּבְפַרְהֶסְיָא נַמִי, לָא אֲמָרָן אֶלָּא דְּאֶפְשָׁר לֵיהּ לְאִיתְזוּנֵי בְּצִינְעָה [3]וְקָא מְבַזֵּי נַפְשֵׁיהּ בְּפַרְהֶסְיָא; [4]אֲבָל לֹא אֶפְשָׁר לֵיהּ, חַיּוּתֵיהּ הוּא.

[5]אָמַר רַב נַחְמָן: הֶחָשׁוּד עַל הָעֲרָיוֹת כָּשֵׁר לְעֵדוּת. [6]אָמַר רַב שֵׁשֶׁת: עָנֵי מָרִי — [7]אַרְבְּעִין בְּכִתְפֵּיהּ, וְכָשֵׁר?

LITERAL TRANSLATION

other") are unfit to [offer] testimony. [1]This applies (lit., "these words are") in public; but in private — not. [2]And even in public, we only say [this] when it was possible for him to provide for himself in private [3]and he humiliates himself in public; [4]but [if] it was not possible for him [to do so], it is his existence.

[5]Rav Naḥman said: One who is suspected of illicit sexual relations is fit to [offer] testimony. [6]Rav Sheshet said: Answer me, my master — [7]forty [lashes] on his shoulder, and he is fit?

RASHI

השם מחמת ממון, הוה ליה כרשע דחמס. **כשר לעדות** — דבעינן רשע דחמס, כדכתיב (שמות כג) אל תשת וגו' עד חמס. **עני מרי** — ענני אדוני. **ארבעין בכתפיה** — חייב מלקות הוא, אף על פי שאין שם התראה, דאמר מר (קדושין פא, א): מלקין על לא טובה השמועה, שנאמר אל בני כי לא טובה השמועה. **וכשר** — בתמיה.

LANGUAGE

פַּרְהֶסְיָא **Public.** This word derives from the Greek παρρησια, *parresia*, the original meaning of which was "freedom of speech"; it was also used to described a free political regime. As used by the Sages, the word means "in public," something visible to everyone.

NOTES

a non-Jew as the desecration of God's Name for the sake of obtaining financial gain — thereby disqualifying one as a witness according to all interpretations of the relevant verse in Exodus (see 27a). Others explain that the desecration lies in the impression one creates that Jews do not care for their own brethren in distress (*Rabbi Yehonatan of Lunel*). *Meiri* suggests that the disqualification referred to in Rav Naḥman's ruling stems not from a particular offense associated with taking charity from a gentile, but rather from the character deficiency that it implies — for it is apparent from other rulings that someone who disgraces himself in public (such as by snatching food from the street and devouring it there, or walking about in a state of undress) cannot serve as a witness, since he does not possess the basic self-respect that presumably deters one from perjury and the risk of humiliation.

הֶחָשׁוּד עַל הָעֲרָיוֹת **One who is suspected of engaging in illicit sexual relations.** The commentators differ as to the degree to which an individual may be suspected of improper sexual relations and still be considered fit as a witness. According to *Tosafot*, and apparently *Rashi* as well, the person referred to by Rav Naḥman is merely suspected of engaging in such relations, either because of rumors to that effect or because he was seen secluding himself with a woman who is forbidden to him. But if witnesses testified to his engaging in such relations, he would clearly be ineligible to serve as a witness — just as is someone who was caught eating forbidden carrion or submitting to sodomy (see 9b). Since these individuals could not withstand temptation and violated clear Torah laws, it is suspected that they would testify falsely if tempted with a bribe. According to another opinion cited in *Tosafot* (and supported by *Rif* and *Ran*), Rav Naḥman's permission applies even to someone who was known to have engaged in illicit relations and is still regarded as liable to do so in the future. Nevertheless, such an individual is fit to serve as a witness, because of the difference in the intensity of the drive for illicit sex and that for eating carrion or giving false testimony. Because the sex drive is extremely powerful, we cannot assume that, because someone has succumbed to sexual temptation, it means that he is also liable to perjure himself for the lesser enticement of a bribe.

אַרְבְּעִין בְּכִתְפֵּיהּ **Forty on his shoulder.** According to the position given in the previous note that the person

HALAKHAH

they could just as easily arrange to receive it in private, are Rabbinically disqualified from serving as witnesses." (*Shulḥan Arukh, Ḥoshen Mishpat* 34:18.)

הֶחָשׁוּד עַל הָעֲרָיוֹת **One who is suspected of engaging in illicit sexual relations.** "One who is suspected of having violated Torah law, even to the extent of being subject to

26B SANHEDRIN כו ע"ב

TRANSLATION AND COMMENTARY

אָמַר רָבָא ¹**Rava said: Rav Naḥman,** however, **admits that** in **testifying** about the marital status of **a particular woman,** a man who is suspected of engaging in illicit sexual relations **is** indeed **unfit** to serve as a witness, since the testimony touches on issues which are related to his vice. ²**Ravina said (and some say** it was **Rav Pappa): We only say** that he is unfit to testify **when** his testimony is intended **to release her** from her marriage (either by reporting that her husband died or divorced her), thereby rendering her available to himself. ³**But if** his testimony was intended **for** the purpose **of restricting her** freedom to marry (by reporting, for example, that someone betrothed her) — ⁴**we have no** problem accepting **it.**

פְּשִׁיטָא ⁵The Gemara comments: Surely **it is obvious** that his testimony that prohibits the woman to himself need not be rejected!

מַהוּ דְּתֵימָא ⁶In truth, this is not obvious — for **you might have said that** a forbidden woman is **preferred** by him, ⁷**for it is written** in Proverbs 9:17: **"Stolen waters are sweet,** and bread eaten in secret is pleasant." Hence his testimony should be disqualified in either case. ⁸Ravina thus **teaches us that, as** long as the **woman has** her present unmarried status, **she is** more likely to make herself **available to him.** Thus it is certainly not in his interest to testify that she is married; and if he does, we believe him.

וְאָמַר רַב נַחְמָן ⁹**And** finally, **Rav Naḥman said: A Nisan-thief or a Tishrei-thief,** someone who steals produce during the month of reaping (Nisan) or the month of harvesting (Tishrei), **is not called a thief** and thus is still eligible to serve as a witness. ¹⁰The Gemara comments: This teaching of Rabbi Naḥman's **applies to a**

¹אָמַר רָבָא: וּמוֹדֶה רַב נַחְמָן לְעִנְיַן עֵדוּת אִשָּׁה, שֶׁהוּא פָּסוּל. ²אָמַר רָבִינָא — וְאִיתֵּימָא רַב פַּפָּא: ³לָא אָמְרָן אֶלָּא לְאַפּוּקָהּ. אֲבָל לְעַיּוּלַהּ — ⁴לֵית לָן בָּהּ.
⁵פְּשִׁיטָא!
⁶מַהוּ דְּתֵימָא: הָא עֲדִיפָא לֵיהּ, ⁷דִּכְתִיב: "מַיִם גְּנוּבִים יִמְתָּקוּ וגו'". ⁸קָא מַשְׁמַע לָן: דְּכַמָּה דְּקַיְימָא הָכִי, שְׁכִיחָא לֵיהּ.
⁹וְאָמַר רַב נַחְמָן: גַּנָּב נִיסָן וְגַנָּב תִּשְׁרֵי, לָא שְׁמֵיהּ גַּנָּב. ¹⁰הָנֵי

LITERAL TRANSLATION

¹Rava said: And Rav Naḥman admits with regard to the matter of testifying about [the marital status of] a woman, that he is unfit. ²Ravina said — (and some say Rav Pappa [said]): We only say [this] when [the testimony] is to release her. ³But [if it is] to restrict her (lit., "bring her up") — ⁴we have no [problem] about it.

⁵It is obvious!

⁶You might have said: That [a forbidden woman] is preferable for him, ⁷for it is written: "Stolen waters are sweet, etc." ⁸[Therefore] it tells us that as she is [now], she is [more] available to him.

⁹And Rav Naḥman said: A Nisan-thief or a Tishrei-thief is not called a thief. ¹⁰This

RASHI

לאפוקה — לומר מת בעלה או גירשה, דניחא ליה לשווייה פנויה. דמיהוי שכיחא ליה. לעיולה — לומר פלוני קידשה. הא עדיפא ליה — דמיהוי אסורה עליה ולא מיהוי שכיחא ליה. דכתיב מים גנובים ימתקו — ושקורי משקר. ניסן — זמן קציר, תשרי זמן בציר ואסיף. לא שמיה גנב — כדמפרש ואזיל.

NOTES

accepted as a witness is merely suspected of having engaged in illicit relations, either because of rumors or having been seen secluding himself with a woman forbidden to him, it follows that his punishment should consist of lashes administered by Rabbinical decree (see *Kiddushin* 81a). However, according to those who maintain that we are dealing here with someone who is known to have engaged in such relations, one would have to say that a technicality (such as a failure to forewarn him) prevents the court from issuing a formal conviction and meting out a more severe punishment. Hence, the offender can only be declared "wicked," even according to this position, by virtue of the lashes that he receives for conducting himself immorally.

עֵדוּת אִשָּׁה **Testimony about a woman.** Many of the early Geonim contend that the reference here is not to testimony concerning a woman's marital status, for even a non-Jew's testimony is accepted for this purpose, but rather to the formal witnessing of the nuptial ceremony — a condition for a valid marriage ceremony. The Rabbis decided that a man who is suspect of engaging in illicit sexual relations should not be trusted to serve in such an important capacity, one that affects the status of the marriage with implications in the event of a divorce.

HALAKHAH

incessant rumors to that effect, is still legally fit to testify unless witnesses are produced to corroborate the rumors. However, one who is suspected of engaging in illicit sexual relations (or even one who simply acts frivolously in the company of a woman who is forbidden to him) is disqualified from offering testimony about a woman's marital status or from serving as a witness at her marriage ceremony, even if witnesses cannot corroborate the suspicion," in accordance with Rav Naḥman's position as reported by Rava. Nevertheless, he is still fit to testify in regard to the death of a woman's husband, as are all other ineligible witnesses. (*Shulḥan Arukh, Even HaEezer* 42:2; *Ḥoshen Mishpat* 34:25, *Rema*.)

מִילֵּי — בַּאֲרִיסָא, וְדָבָר מוּעָט, וּבְדָבָר שֶׁנִּגְמְרָה מְלַאכְתּוֹ. [1]אִיכָּרֵיהּ דְּרַב זְבִיד, חַד גְּנַב קַבָּא דְּשַׂעֲרֵי וּפַסְלֵיהּ; [2]וְחַד גְּנַב קִיבּוּרָא דְּאַהִינֵי, וּפַסְלֵיהּ. [3]הָנְהוּ קַבּוּרָאֵי דְּקַבוּר נַפְשָׁא בְּיוֹם טוֹב רִאשׁוֹן שֶׁל עֲצֶרֶת — [4]שַׁמְתִּינְהוּ רַב פַּפָּא וּפַסְלִינְהוּ לְעֵדוּת. [5]וְאַכְשְׁרִינְהוּ רַב הוּנָא בְּרֵיהּ דְּרַב יְהוֹשֻׁעַ. [6]אֲמַר לֵיהּ רַב פַּפָּא: וְהָא רְשָׁעִים נִינְהוּ?! [7]סָבְרִי מִצְוָה קָא עָבְדִי. [8]וְהָא קָא מְשַׁמְּתִינָא לְהוּ! [9]סָבְרִי: כַּפָּרָה קָא עָבְדִי לָן רַבָּנַן.

LITERAL TRANSLATION

applies to (lit., "these words are") a tenant farmer and a small amount and ripe produce (lit., "something whose labor was completed").

[1]The farmers of Rav Zevid — one [of them] stole a *kav* measure of barley, and he disqualified him; [2]and [the other] one stole a cluster of unripe dates, and he disqualified him.

[3]There were gravediggers who buried a person on the first day of the Shavuot Festival — [4]Rav Pappa excommunicated them and disqualified them from testimony. [5]And Rav Huna, the son of Rav Yehoshua, declared them fit. [6]Rav Pappa said to him: But are they not wicked?! [7][He replied:] They think they are are doing a mitzvah. [8][Rav Pappa again queried:] But we excommunicated them! [9][Rav Huna replied:] They think [that] the Rabbis are performing an atonement for us.

TRANSLATION AND COMMENTARY

tenant farmer who takes **a small amount** of **ripe produce** beyond his allotted share. The Torah allows small amounts of ripe produce to be eaten by a hired laborer in the course of his work in the field (see Deuteronomy 23:25-26). The tenant farmer might think that he deserves the same privilege. Therefore the "Nisan-thief" or the "Tishrei-thief" can hardly be treated as an ordinary robber.

אִיכָּרֵיהּ [1]Once two **farmers** were employed as ordinary laborers by **Rav Zevid. One stole a** *kav* **measure of barley** from his field **and** as a result Rav Zevid **disqualified him** from serving as a witness. [2]The other **one stole a cluster of unripe dates and** Rav Zevid **disqualified him** as well. In both instances, the laborers were disqualified because they took produce that the Torah did not allow them to take, and, they had no rationale — not even a mistaken one — for assuming that their action was permitted.

הָנְהוּ קַבּוּרָאֵי [3]Once **gravediggers buried a person on the first day of the Shavuot Festival**, in contravention of Torah law, which forbids digging on the Sabbath or holidays. [4]Consequently, **Rav Pappa excommunicated them and disqualified them from** offering **testimony** since he assumed that they had committed the offense for the sake of financial gain. [5]Nevertheless, **Rav Huna, the son of Rav Yehoshua, declared them fit.** [6]**Rav Pappa said to him: But are they not wicked?** [7]Rav Huna replied: But **they think they are are doing a mitzvah** by burying the dead. Hence, they are no different from the tenant farmer who thinks he is allowed to take extra produce during the busy work season, and he is not disqualified! [8]Rav Pappa again sought clarification: **But** the two cases are not the same, for in this case **we excommunicated them,** and they continued to perform burials on festival days! [9]Rav Huna replied: The reason they continue to conduct burials is because **they** mistakenly **think,** "By excommunicating us, **the Rabbis are performing a** rite of **atonement for us,** allowing us to continue performing the mitzvah of burying the dead even though we are forced to desecrate the holiday."

RASHI

באריסא — דטרח בה, ומורה היתירא ליטול דבר מועט יותר על חלקו מפני טרחו. **ודבר שנגמרה מלאכתו** — דמשויה נפשיה כפועל, ומורי בה היתירא וסבר לא קפיד. **איכר** — לאו היינו אריס ואינו חולק בפירות. **קיבורא דאהיני** — כמין אשכול, יש תמרים הרבה בענף אחד. **קבוראי** = קוברי מתים. **ופסלינהו לעדות** — דמשום שכר ממון עוברים על דת, והוו להו כרשע דחמס. **והא משמתינן להו** — על הראשונה, וחוזרין ועוברין ושונין בעבירה. **סברי** — האי דשמתינן משום כפרה הוא על שעברנו, ולא משום דנהדר בן, אלא מותר לחלל יום טוב בשביל המלוה, ונשב בנידוי משום כפרה.

NOTES

חַד גְּנַב קַבָּא דְּשַׂעֲרֵי **One stole a** ***kav*** **of barley.** A *kav* is more than the amount allotted by the Torah to an ordinary worker in the course of his labors (*Rabbi Yehonatan*). *Ramah* has a variant reading of the Gemara which states that the farmer stole a small sheaf of barley.

HALAKHAH

אֲרִיסָא שֶׁגָּנַב **A tenant farmer who stole.** "A tenant farmer who takes a small amount of additional produce without the owner's knowledge during either the month of Tishrei or Nisan, provided that the produce has not yet fully ripened (as maintained by *Rambam* and *Rif*; in contrast to *Rema* and *Sma* who, on the basis of our Gemara, require the produce to be fully ripe), is not considered a robber (as it is assumed the owner would not object). Thus he is not disqualified from serving as a witness." (*Shulḥan Arukh, Ḥoshen Mishpat* 34:15; and see *Rambam, Sefer Shoftim, Hilkhot Edut* 10:5.)

הָנְהוּ קַבּוּרָאֵי **Those gravediggers.** "Gravediggers who, in violation of Biblical law, buried someone on the first day of a Festival — and continued to do so even after they were excommunicated — are nevertheless still fit to serve as witnesses, for we assume that they thought they were

[1]אִיתְּמַר [27A] עֵד זוֹמֵם — [2]אַבַּיֵי אָמַר: לְמַפְרֵעַ הוּא נִפְסָל; [3]וְרָבָא אָמַר: מִיכָּן וּלְהַבָּא הוּא נִפְסָל. [4]אַבַּיֵי אָמַר: לְמַפְרֵעַ הוּא נִפְסָל: [5]מֵעִידָּנָא דְּאַסְהֵיד, רָשָׁע הוּא, [6]וְהַתּוֹרָה אָמְרָה: ״אַל תָּשֶׁת יָדְךָ עִם רָשָׁע״ — [7]אַל תָּשֶׁת רָשָׁע עֵד. [8]רָבָא אָמַר: מִיכָּן וּלְהַבָּא הוּא נִפְסָל. [9]עֵד זוֹמֵם חִידּוּשׁ הוּא. [10]מַאי חָזֵית דְּסָמְכַתְּ אַהָנֵי? [11]סְמוֹךְ אַהָנֵי! [12]אֵין לָךְ בּוֹ אֶלָּא מִשְּׁעַת חִידּוּשׁוֹ וְאֵילָךְ.

TRANSLATION AND COMMENTARY

אִיתְּמַר [1]Concerning other categories of ineligible witnesses: **It was stated** that the Amoraim argued regarding someone [27A] who was declared **a conspiring witness** (a witness whose testimony was overthrown by other witnesses who testified that he was with them elsewhere at the time he claimed to have seen what he did). [2]**Abaye said: He is disqualified retroactively.** Testimony he may have given from the time of his original testimony becomes null and void as well. [3]**Rava said: He is** only **disqualified from now on** — that is, from the moment he is declared a conspiring witness.

אַבַּיֵי אָמַר [4]The Gemara proceeds to elaborate on these two positions: **Abaye said** that **he is disqualified retroactively** because, once discredited in court, [5]it becomes clear that **at the time he** originally **testified, he** already acted in **a wicked** manner — [6]**and the Torah states** (Exodus 23:1): **"Place not your hand with the wicked,** that he be a thievish witness," which we interpret to mean: [7]**Place not a wicked man as a witness.** As a result, any testimony offered by him subsequent to the testimony now discredited in court is null and void. [8]**Rava**, on the other hand, **said** that **he is** only **disqualified from now on** because, although it is Torah law, [9]the procedure of disqualifying one set of witnesses as **conspiring witnesses** on the basis of testimony by another set is a **novel precept.** [10]For it can be asked: **Why do you rely on those** who appear now in order to discredit their predecessors? [11]In principle, you may just as well **rely on** the first pair of witnesses. [12]Consequently, **you have no** claims of disqualification **against them except from the time that this novel precept** takes effect (from when they are discredited in court) **and onward.** They are only regarded as "wicked" from the moment the court finds them "wicked."

LITERAL TRANSLATION

[1]It was stated: [27A] A conspiring witness — [2]Abaye said: He is disqualified retroactively; [3]and Rava said: He is disqualified from now on.

[4]Abaye said: He is disqualified retroactively: [5]From the time that he testified, he is wicked, [6]and the Torah states: "Place not your hand with the wicked" — [7]do not place a wicked man as a witness. [8]Rava said: He is disqualified from now on. [9][The law of] a conspiring witness is a novel precept. [10]Why (lit., "what did you see that you") rely on these [witnesses]? [11]Rely on these! [12]You [therefore] have nothing against him except from the time that this novel precept [takes effect] and onwards.

RASHI

עד זומם — העיד בניסן והוזם בתשרי על עדות זו. **למפרע** — כל עדויות שהעיד מניסן ואילך פסולין, שהרי משהעיד עדות זו הוא רשע. **מיכן ולהבא** — משהוזם. **חידוש הוא** — שנפסלין שנים בשביל שנים שאומרים עמנו הייתם, דמאי חזית דסמכת אהני, סמוך אהני. אלא גזירת הכתוב הוא, הלכך אין לך בו אלא משעת חידוש ואילך, משעה שהוזם.

NOTES

עֵד זוֹמֵם חִידּוּשׁ הוּא **A conspiring witness is a novel precept.** The Gemara seems to imply that had the Torah not taught us that we believe the latter witnesses in their claim against the earlier ones, we would have thought that the earlier witnesses' testimony would stand (*Rashi, Tosafot* and *Ramah*). *Tosafot*, however, cites an alternative interpretation,

HALAKHAH

doing a meritorious deed and that the excommunication was intended to afford them atonement for the unavoidable desecration of the holiday. Similarly, anyone who violates Torah law, if we can assume he was misled by ignorance or erroneous thinking, need not be disqualfied as a witness. (Certain later authorities argue as to whether we can merely assume the offender's innocence or whether we must hear him voice the mistaken claim in his defense; *Pithei Teshuvah.*) However, someone who violates Torah law in a manner that is obviously known to be forbidden becomes disqualified from serving as a witness even if he was not duly warned of the illegality of his act prior to committing the offense." (*Shulhan Arukh, Hoshen Mishpat* 34:4; *Rambam, Sefer Shoftim, Hilkhot Edut* 11:1.)

עֵד זוֹמֵם **A conspiring witness.** "One who is found to have been a conspiring witness, even if only in regard to a civil case, is Biblically unfit to offer testimony concerning any matter related to Torah law. If he is discredited for testimony rendered in the past, any and all intervening testimony of his is considered to be retroactively null and void." This ruling follows the position of Abaye, with whom the law accords in the six cases of יע״ל קג״ם. (*Shulhan Arukh, Hoshen Mishpat* 34:8.)

אַל תָּשֶׁת רָשָׁע עֵד **Do not place a wicked man as a witness.** "Who qualifies as 'wicked' and unfit to testify? Anyone who (intentionally) violates a law of the Torah carrying the

TRANSLATION AND COMMENTARY

אִיכָּא דְּאָמְרִי [1]**There are those**, however, **who say** that **Rava also agrees with Abaye,** that a conspiring witness is considered "wicked" from the time of his discredited testimony. [2]If so, **why did he say** the witness's testimony is only disqualified **from now on?** [3]Rava's reason is based on the potential **loss to** innocent **land purchasers** who may have used him as a witness on their deeds of purchase when it was still not known that he had testified falsely. Were we retroactively to invalidate all those contracts, these purchasers would stand to lose their property should the sales be contested in court.

מַאי בֵּינַיְיהוּ [4]**What is** the practical difference **between** the two explanations of Rava's position? [5]**There is** indeed a difference **between them** that is related to the manner in which the first witnesses are disqualified. **When two** people **testified against one** of the witnesses and discredited his earlier testimony, according to the first explanation, Rava would have to agree that they succeeded in retroactively establishing his wickedness and invalidating any intervening testimony. For it is not a novel precept that two witnesses (the second pair) are believed over one (from the first pair). However, according to the second explanation, Rava would still maintain that the disqualification should not be applied retroactively, out of concern for the potential loss to land purchasers. [6]**Or else** there is a difference **when** the later witnesses **disqualify** the earlier ones **because** they saw them commit **robbery** prior to their giving testimony. According to the first explanation, Rava would conclude that the first set of witnesses must be disqualified retroactively on grounds of wickedness, because believing these later witnesses is not a novel precept. Their testimony does not bear on the testimony of the first witnesses, but only on their character. However, according to the second explanation, Rava's concern over the potential loss to others still remains. Consequently, the first set of witnesses should only be disqualified from now on.

[1]אִיכָּא דְּאָמְרִי: רָבָא נַמִי כְּאַבַּיֵי סְבִירָא לֵיהּ. [2]וּמַאי טַעַם קָאָמַר מִכָּאן וּלְהַבָּא? [3]מִשּׁוּם פְּסֵידָא דְּלָקוֹחוֹת.

[4]מַאי בֵּינַיְיהוּ? [5]אִיכָּא בֵּינַיְיהוּ דְּאַסְהִידוּ בֵּי תְּרֵי בְּחַד, [6]אִי נַמִי דְּפָסְלִינְהוּ בְּגַזְלָנוּתָא.

LITERAL TRANSLATION

[1]There are [some] who say: Rava also agrees with Abaye. [2]But what is the reason that he said [he is disqualified] from now on? [3]Because of the [possible] loss to [land] purchasers.

[4]What is [the difference] between them? [5]There is [a difference] between them when two people testify against one, [6]or else when they disqualify [the witnesses] for robbery.

RASHI

פסידא דלקוחות – שלקחו שדות על פיו וחתם בשטרא מניסן עד תשרי, ועדיין לא היה ידוע שהוא פסול. **מאי בינייהו** – בין הני תרי טעמי דרבא. **תרי בחד** – תרי כיתות שהעידו בכת זו, שנים אמרו לכל אחד "עמנו הייתם במקום פלוני". **חידוש** – ליכא, **פסידא דלקוחות** – איכא. **אי נמי דפסלינהו** – להני תרי. **בגזלנותא** – שהעידו שגזלנין הם על גזילה שגזלו בניסן. **חידוש** – ליכא, דהא מילתא אחריני קמסהדי, אבל פסידא דלקוחות איכא.

NOTES

which understands that the Gemara implies that the novelty of the law lies not in the invalidation of the first set of witnesses, but rather in the validity of the latter set of witnesses. For reason would dictate that where two sets of witnesses contradict one another, both should be disqualified.

דְּאַסְהִידוּ בֵּי תְּרֵי בְּחַד **Where two people testified against one.** Our commentary follows the approach of *Rabbenu Tam* and *Ramah*, who explain the Gemara in accordance with its explicit reading, suggesting that two witnesses testified against one. An alternative reading of the Gemara, appearing in tractate *Bava Kamma* (73a) and suggested by *Baḥ* as an amendation here as well, states as follows: דְּאַסְהִידוּ בֵּי תְּרֵי לְחַד וּתְרֵי לְחַד — "Where they testified against him, two against one and two against the other." This reading, which is adopted by *Rashi* in our Gemara and *Tosafot* in *Bava Kamma,* suggests the following explanation: If two witnesses challenge an earlier witness by claiming that he was with them elsewhere at the time, and then another two witnesses challenge his colleague, testifying that he was with them at the time, this is not a novel precept. We believe the latter two pairs and will discredit the two individuals against whom they testified from the time of their original testimony. *Tosafot,* however, poses a question on this interpretation: We have a principle that any two witnesses testifying together have the same status as if they were a hundred. Why, then, should the latter four witnesses discredit the former ones retroactively, just because they are four against two? The answer suggested by *Tosafot* in *Bava Kamma* (and alluded to in *Ramah* as well) is that, in this particular case, the two original witnesses offered independent testimony, each having seen the crime from a different vantage point, and they were unaware of each other's presence. Consequently, they do not have the same status as a pair of witnesses observing and then testifying together. Their being discredited by the testimony of two other pairs is not a novelty and would discredit them retroactively.

דְּפָסְלִינְהוּ בְּגַזְלָנוּתָא **When they disqualify them for robbery.** This reading implies that both earlier witnesses were

HALAKHAH

minimum punishment of lashes, regardless of whether he violates the law because of temptation or for the sake of rebellion." (*Shulḥan Arukh, Ḥoshen Mishpat* 34:2.)

[1] וְאָמַר רַבִּי יִרְמְיָה מִדִּיפְתִּי: עֲבַד רַב פַּפִּי עוּבְדָּא כְּוָותֵיהּ דְּרָבָא. [2] מָר בַּר רַב אַשִׁי אָמַר: הִלְכְתָא כְּוָותֵיהּ דְּאַבַּיֵי. [3] וְהִלְכְתָא כְּוָותֵיהּ דְּאַבַּיֵי ביע״ל קג״ם.

[4] מוּמָר אוֹכֵל נְבֵילוֹת לְתֵיאָבוֹן — [5] דִּבְרֵי הַכֹּל פָּסוּל; [6] לְהַכְעִיס — [7] אַבַּיֵי אָמַר: פָּסוּל, רָבָא אָמַר: כָּשֵׁר. [8] אַבַּיֵי אָמַר: פָּסוּל, דַּהֲוָה לֵיהּ רָשָׁע, [9] וְרַחֲמָנָא אָמַר "אַל תָּשֶׁת רָשָׁע עֵד". [10] וְרָבָא אָמַר: כָּשֵׁר, [11] רָשָׁע דְּחָמָס בָּעֵינַן.

LITERAL TRANSLATION

[1] And Rabbi Yirmeyah of Difti said: Rav Pappi acted in accordance with Rava. [2] Mar bar Rav Ashi said: The law is in accordance with Abaye. [3] And the law is in accordance with Abaye in יע״ל קג״ם

[4] [Regarding] an apostate who eats carrion in order to [satisfy his] appetite — [5] all say [that] he is unfit; [6] [but if he eats] in order to show contempt [for the law] — [7] Abaye said: He is unfit. Rava said: He is fit. [8] Abaye said: He is unfit, for he is wicked, [9] and the Torah states: "Place not [your hand] with the wicked [as] a witness." [10] And Rava said: He is fit, [11] as we require a wicked man [who engages] in thievery.

TRANSLATION AND COMMENTARY

וְאָמַר [1] The Gemara now turns to determining the opinion accepted as law in the above dispute between Abaye and Rava: **Rabbi Yirmeyah from Difti said** that **Rav Pappi acted in accordance with** the position **of Rava** and only disqualified a conspiring witness from the time he was declared to be such in court. [2] In contrast, **Mar the son of Rav Ashi said** that **the law is in accordance with** the position **of Abaye,** who retroactively disqualified all testimony given by conspiring witnesses. [3] **Moreover,** although the law is usually in accordance with the viewpoint of Rava in his differences of opinion with Abaye, nevertheless **the law** in the case of a conspiring witness (עֵד זוֹמֵם) **is in accordance with** the position **of Abaye.** This is one of the six cases represented by the mnemonic יע״ל קג״ם.

מוּמָר [4] The Gemara now presents another dispute between Abaye and Rava that also deals with the issue of ineligible witnesses: As regards **an apostate who eats** forbidden **carrion** (the meat of an unslaughtered, or improperly slaughtered, animal) simply **in order to** satisfy his **appetite** (such meat also being cheaper and easier to obtain than the properly slaughtered variety) — [5] **all say** that **he is unfit** to serve as a witness. His behavior proves that he is willing to violate the Torah when sufficiently tempted. [6] However, if he eats the forbidden meat purposely, **in defiance** of the laws of the Torah, the Amoraim disagree as to his status: [7] **Abaye said: He is unfit. Rava said: He is fit.** [8] **Abaye said: He is unfit** to serve as a witness, **for** as one obligated to receive lashes, **he is** referred to in the Torah as **"wicked"** (see Deuteronomy 25:2); [9] **and the Torah states** (Exodus 23:1): "Place not your hand with the wicked, that he be a thievish witness," which we interpret to mean: **Place not a wicked man** as **a witness.** [10] **And Rava said: He is** indeed **fit** to serve as a witness, as — in order to invalidate him — [11] **we require a wicked man** who engages **in thievery** — and there is no thievery here, only impiety.

RASHI

יע״ל קג״ם — יאוש שלא מדעת ב״אלו מציאות״ (בבא מציעא כא,ב), עד זומם הכא, לחי העומד מאליו בפרק קמא דעירובין (טו,א), קידושין שלא נמסרו לביאה ב״האיש מקדש״ (קדושין נא,א) גילוי דעת בגיטין ב״השולח גט״ (גיטין לד,א), מומר אוכל נבלות להכעיס לקמן. הכי גרסינן: **מומר אוכל נבילות לתיאבון דברי הכל פסול** — דכיון דמשום ממון קעביד, דהא שכיחא בזול טפי מדהיתירא, הוה ליה כרשע דחמס ופסול לעדות.

NOTES

disqualified for committing robbery. *Rabbenu Tam* (cited in *Tosafot* as well as in *Ran*) has the following problem: If both were disqualified for robbery, what is the relevance to the dispute under discussion — the invalidation of conspiring witnesses? Consequently, *Rabbenu Tam* suggests emending the text so that it reads דְּפַסְלוּהוּ בִּגְזַלְנוּתָא, "when they disqualified *him* on account of robbery." With this reading, only one of the original witnesses was disqualified as a robber, and his colleague was indeed discredited as a conspiring witness on the basis of testimony that he was elsewhere at the time. Since in this case only his testimony is being directly contradicted by the two later witnesses, there is no novelty in stating that we believe the latter two.

יע״ל קג״ם The mnemonic יע״ל קג״ם. Except for the dispute alluded to by the letter *lamed,* there is a general consensus among the commentators as to the disputes alluded to in this mnemonic. *Rashi* identifies as the *lamed* the dispute in *Eruvin* 27a concerning *leḥi*; *Rabbenu Tam* cites the dispute in *Niddah* 37a concerning *ledah*; and the scholars of Navonne cite the dispute in *Pesaḥim* 25b regarding *lo efshar velo mekhaven*.

אוֹכֵל נְבֵילוֹת לְתֵיאָבוֹן One who eats carrion in order to satisfy his appetite. Even Rava, who requires that there be an element of thievery or avarice in one's actions before one can be disqualified as a witness, agrees that someone who consumes carrion in order to satiate his appetite is unfit. This is either because he chooses nonkosher over kosher meat in order to save money (*Rashi*) or because it is assumed that someone so easily tempted to sin will similarly fall prey to a bribe (*Ramah*).

TRANSLATION AND COMMENTARY

מֵיתִיבִי [1]The Sages **objected** to Rava's position on the basis of the following Baraita: "The verse in Exodus (23:1) reads: 'Place not your hand with the wicked one, that he be a thievish witness.' Explain this to mean: **'Place not a wicked man** as **a witness,'** [2]and: **'Place not** one guilty of **thievery** as **a witness.'** [3]Among **those** implicated **are robbers and those who violate oaths."** [4]The Sages elaborate: **What** is the Baraita referring to when it mentions "oaths" in the plural? **Is it not** referring to **both an oath taken in vain and a false oath** involving **money** matters (such as that required by bailees)? If the verse disqualifies someone who takes an oath in vain, then the impious are invalid witnesses. This Baraita thus seems to contradict Rava!

לֹא [5]The Gemara rejects this refutation of Rava: **No** This is not a successful refutation, for the use of the plural of "oaths" in the Baraita does not necessarily include taking an oath in vain. Rather, **both this oath and that oath** involve **money** matters and are disqualified by the verse. [6]But **what,** then, **is** the purpose of the Baraita's stating **"oaths"** in the plural? [7]That usage hints that, **in general,** one can be rejected as a witness by the abuse of various **oaths** that involve money — such as partial denial of a monetary claim, and the denial of negligence in regard to an object deposited with one for safekeeping.

מֵיתִיבִי [8]The Sages now **object** to Abaye's position on the basis of a different Baraita: "The verse in Exodus (23:1) should be interpreted as implying these principles: **'Place not a wicked man** as **a witness,'** [9]and **'Place not** one guilty of **thievery** as **a witness.'** [10]Among those implicated **are robbers and those who lend** out money **on interest."** [11]This Baraita limits its examples to crimes that involve an element of thievery, which implies **a refutation of Abaye.** [12]The Gemara concludes that this Baraita is indeed **a refutation** of Abaye.

נֵימָא כְּתַנָּאֵי [13]The Gemara asks: **Shall we say** that the above dispute between Abaye and Rava is in essence **like** the following dispute between **Tannaim:** [14]"One who is discredited as **a conspiring witness is**

[1]מֵיתִיבִי: ״׳אַל תָּשֶׁת רָשָׁע עֵד׳; [2]׳אַל תָּשֶׁת חָמָס עֵד׳ [3]אֵלּוּ גַּזְלָנִין וּמוֹעֲלִין בִּשְׁבוּעוֹת״. [4]מַאי לָאו אֶחָד שְׁבוּעַת שָׁוְא וְאֶחָד שְׁבוּעַת מָמוֹן?

[5]לֹא. אִידִי וְאִידִי שְׁבוּעַת מָמוֹן. [6]וּמַאי ״שְׁבוּעוֹת״? [7]שְׁבוּעוֹת דְּעָלְמָא.

[8]מֵיתִיבִי: ״אַל תָּשֶׁת רָשָׁע עֵד, [9]׳אַל תָּשֶׁת חָמָס עֵד׳ — [10]אֵלּוּ גַּזְלָנִין וּמַלְוֵי רִבִּיּוֹת״. [11]תְּיוּבְתָּא דְּאַבַּיֵּי! [12]תְּיוּבְתָּא.

[13]נֵימָא כְּתַנָּאֵי: [14]״עֵד זוֹמֵם

LITERAL TRANSLATION

[1]They objected: "'Place not a wicked one [as] a witness'; [2]'Place not a thief [as] a witness.' [3]These are robbers and those who violate oaths." [4]Is it not [referring to] both an oath taken in vain and a [false] oath [involving] money [matters]?

[5]No. Both this [oath] and that oath [involve] money [matters]. [6]And what is [the meaning of] "oaths"? [7]Oaths in general.

[8]They objected: "'Place not the wicked [as] a witness; [9]place not a thief [as] a witness.' [10]These are robbers and those who lend for interest." [11][This is] a refutation of Abaye! [12][It is] a refutation.

[13]Shall we say [that this dispute is] like [the following dispute between] Tannaim: [14]"A conspiring witness

RASHI

שבועת שוא — על העמוד של אבן שהוא של אבן. שבועת שקר — על העמוד של אבן שהוא של זהב. אף על גב דלאו רשע דחמס הוא. ומלוי רבית — הני — אין, אבל אוכל נבילות להכעיס — לא. ומיהו לתיאבון כגזלנין ומלוי ריבית דמו, דמשום ממון קעביד, הלכך חשוד למישקל שוחדא ולאסהודי שקרא.

NOTES

אַל תָּשֶׁת רָשָׁע עֵד; אַל תָּשֶׁת חָמָס עֵד **Do not place a wicked man as a witness; do not place one guilty of thievery as a witness.** This Tannaitic interpretation of the verse in Exodus (23:1) would be explained by Abaye as follows: The Baraita could be implying that, for the sake of interpretation, the verse should be divided into two independent clauses: "Place not your hand with the wicked" (excluding any wicked person from giving testimony), and "that he be a thievish witness" (excluding, in particular, a thief). Alternatively, it could be interpreted as stating that one may not accept the testimony of a wicked man for fear that he may turn out to be a "thievish witness," one willing to perjure himself for money. Rava, on the other hand, interprets the verse as referring exclusively to one guilty of thievery, and thus would simply explain the second exhortation of this Baraita as an explanation of the first (*Ramah*).

שְׁבוּעַת שָׁוְא **An oath taken in vain.** A vain oath may attest to an obvious fact or to an obvious falsehood, according to *Rashi* here and the opinion of *Rambam* (*Hilkhot Shevuot* 1:4-5), which (as pointed out in *Arukh Laner*) agrees with the Jerusalem Talmud. A vain oath is distinct from a false oath, one attests to some untrue fact that is not known to

HALAKHAH

מוֹעֲלִין בִּשְׁבוּעוֹת **Those who abuse oaths.** "Someone who takes an oath in vain or swears falsely regarding to money or violates an oath of expression is unfit to serve as a witness by Torah law." (*Shulḥan Arukh, Ḥoshen Mishpat* 34:5.)

TRANSLATION AND COMMENTARY

unfit to testify **in regard to** any matter dealt with in **the entire Torah.** [1]These are **the words of Rabbi Meir.** [2]**Rabbi Yose says: In what** circumstances **are these things** applicable? [3]They are applicable **when** the conspiring witness **was discredited** for testimony that he gave **in a capital case.** We assume that someone willing to lie about a capital crime would certainly be willing to lie about more lenient cases, such as those involving ritual or civil law. [4]**However,** if **he was discredited** for testimony that he gave **in a civil case,** then **he is** still **fit** to testify **in capital cases."**

נֵימָא אַבַּיֵי [5]The Gemara now restates its question in greater detail: **Shall we say** that **Abaye is like Rabbi Meir and Rava is like Rabbi Yose?** [6]That is to say: **Abaye** — who maintained, above, that someone who eats carrion (sinning against Heaven but not against his fellow man) can also be suspected of perjuring himself (which involves sinning against both Heaven and one's fellow man) — **is like Rabbi Meir,** [7]**who** implicitly **stated** in the above Baraita that **we generalize from** a **situation** of relative **leniency** (testifying falsely in a civil case) **to** one of greater **stringency** (doing so in a capital case). [8]**And Rava,** who does not suspect the one who ate carrion (if he did so in order to rebel) of perjuring himself, **agrees with Rabbi Yose,** [9]**who** implicitly **stated** in that Baraita that **we generalize from a** situation of relative **stringency** (testifying falsely in a capital case) **to** one of greater **leniency** (doing so in a civil or ritual case); [10]but **from** a situation of relative **leniency to** one of greater **stringency, we do not** generalize.

לָא [11]The Gemara answers: **No!** We cannot assume the preceding correlation. For **according to Rabbi Yose,** [12]**all** would **agree** that when someone eats carrion in order to rebel, he is fit to serve as a witness — as says Rava. **When** then **do** Abaye and Rava **disagree?** [13]They would disagree about the law in this case **according to Rabbi Meir:** [14]**Abaye** would claim that his position alone **accords with Rabbi Meir,** and that they both invalidate the testimony of any conspiring witness in all matters dealt with in the Torah. [15]Whereas **Rava** would say: Rabbi Yose and Rabbi Meir, I am compatible with both for **until now** we **only** find **Rabbi Meir stating** his opinion **as regards a conspiring witness** who testified falsely in matters **of money.** In such cases, generalizing from a relatively lenient situation to a more stringent one is reasonable.

פָּסוּל לְכָל הַתּוֹרָה כּוּלָּהּ. [1]דִּבְרֵי רַבִּי מֵאִיר. [2]רַבִּי יוֹסֵי אוֹמֵר: בַּמֶּה דְּבָרִים אֲמוּרִים? [3]שֶׁהוּזָם בְּדִינֵי נְפָשׁוֹת, [4]אֲבָל, הוּזָם בְּדִינֵי מָמוֹנוֹת, כָּשֵׁר לְדִינֵי נְפָשׁוֹת״.

[5]נֵימָא אַבַּיֵי כְּרַבִּי מֵאִיר וְרָבָא כְּרַבִּי יוֹסֵי? [6]אַבַּיֵי כְּרַבִּי מֵאִיר דְּאָמַר: [7]אָמְרִינַן מִקּוּלָּא לְחוּמְרָא. [8]וְרָבָא דְּאָמַר כְּרַבִּי יוֹסֵי, [9]דְּאָמַר: מֵחוּמְרָא לְקוּלָּא, אָמְרִינַן, [10]מִקּוּלָּא לְחוּמְרָא לָא אָמְרִינַן.

[11]לָא! אַלִּיבָּא דְּרַבִּי יוֹסֵי, [12]כּוּלֵּי עָלְמָא לָא פְּלִיגִי. [13]כִּי פְּלִיגִי אַלִּיבָּא דְּרַבִּי מֵאִיר. [14]אַבַּיֵי כְּרַבִּי מֵאִיר. [15]וְרָבָא: עַד כָּאן לָא קָאָמַר רַבִּי מֵאִיר הָתָם אֶלָּא גַּבֵּי עֵד זוֹמֵם דְּמָמוֹן,

LITERAL TRANSLATION

is unfit [to testify] in regard to the entire Torah. [1][These are] the words of Rabbi Meir. [2]Rabbi Yose says: In what [case] are these things said? [3]When he was discredited [as a witness] in a capital case; [4]however, [when] he was discredited [as a witness] in a civil case, he is fit [to testify] in capital cases."

[5]Shall we say [that] Abaye is like Rabbi Meir and Rava is like Rabbi Yose? [6]Abaye is like Rabbi Meir, [7]who stated: We generalize (lit., "say") from a lenient [situation] to a stringent [situation]. [8]And [it is] Rava who said like Rabbi Yose, [9]who stated: From a stringent [situation] to a lenient [situation], we say; [10]from a lenient [situation] to a stringent [situation], we do not say.

[11]No! With regard to Rabbi Yose, [12]all agree (lit., "the whole world does not disagree"). [13]When they disagree [it] is with regard to Rabbi Meir. [14]Abaye is like Rabbi Meir, [15]and Rava [says]: Rabbi Meir only stated [his position] there regarding a conspiring witness [in matters] of money,

RASHI

בדיני נפשות — שכיון שהוחשד לחמור הוחשד לקל. **אביי כרבי מאיר** — דהיינו נמי מקולא לחומרא, דאוכל נבילות רע לשמים ואינו רע לבריות, אבל מעיד שקר בממון רע לשמים ורע לבריות, שהרי מפסידן בעדותו, וקא פסיל ליה אביי משום נבילות לעדות ממון. **אליבא דרבי יוסי דכולי עלמא לא פליגי** — כלומר, אביי ודאי לאו כרבי יוסי מצי לאוקומא למילתיה, דכיון דאמר רבי יוסי ממון לנפשות לא מיפסל, ואף על גב דממון הוי רע לשמים ורע לבריות, וכל שכן דמנבלה לממון לא אפסיל. ולאביי על כרחיה תנאי היא. **כי פליגי אליבא דרבי מאיר** — כלומר: לרבא לא תוקמא כתנאי, דרבא אפילו אליבא דרבי מאיר אמר למילתיה.

NOTES

all. Other commentators (*Ramah* and *Rashi* on the *Rif*), define a vain oath to include only swearing to an obvious falsehood; this is in accordance with tractate *Shevuot* (29a).

[1]דְּרַע לַשָּׁמַיִם וְרַע לַבְּרִיּוֹת. [2]אֲבָל הָכָא, דְּרַע לַשָּׁמַיִם וְאֵין רַע לַבְּרִיּוֹת, לָא. [3]וְהִלְכְתָא כְּוָותֵיהּ דְּאַבַּיֵי. [4]וְהָא אִיתּוֹתַב?! [5]הַהִיא רַבִּי יוֹסֵי הִיא. [6]וְתֶיהֱוֵי נַמִי רַבִּי יוֹסֵי. [7]רַבִּי מֵאִיר וְרַבִּי יוֹסֵי, הֲלָכָה כְּרַבִּי יוֹסֵי! [8]שָׁאנֵי הָתָם, [9]דִּסְתַם לָן תַּנָּא כְּרַבִּי מֵאִיר. [10]וְהֵיכָא סְתָם לָן? [11]כִּי הָא דְּבַר חָמָא קְטַל נַפְשָׁא. [12]אֲמַר לֵיהּ רֵישׁ גָּלוּתָא לְרַב אַבָּא בַּר יַעֲקֹב: [13]פּוֹק עַיֵּין בָּהּ, [14]אִי וַדַּאי קְטַל, לִיכְהֲיוּהוּ לְעֵינֵיהּ. [15]אֲתוּ תְּרֵי סָהֲדֵי אַסְהִידוּ בֵּיהּ

LITERAL TRANSLATION

[1]for [he is] evil toward Heaven and evil toward people. [2]However here, where he is evil toward Heaven but not evil toward people, not. [3]And the law is in accordance with Abaye. [4]But was he not refuted?! [5]That [refutation] is [in accordance with] Rabbi Yose. [6]Let it also be like Rabbi Yose. [7][In a dispute between] Rabbi Meir and Rabbi Yose, the law is like Rabbi Yose! [8]It is different there, [9]for a Tanna has anonymously taught us like Rabbi Meir. [10]And where are we anonymously taught [this]? [11]When Bar Ḥama killed a person. [12]The Exilarch said to Rav Abba bar Ya'akov: [13]Go out [and] examine [the case]. [14]If it is certain [that] he killed, let them gouge out his eyes! [15]Two witnesses came [and] testified against him

TRANSLATION AND COMMENTARY

[1]**For** perjury in monetary cases is **evil toward Heaven and evil toward** his **people,** in attempting to cause them financial loss. [2]**However, here,** in the case of someone who ate carrion in order to show contempt for the law, **where he is evil toward Heaven but not evil toward** his fellow man, Rabbi Meir would **not** necessarily generalize in the same way by suspecting him of testifying falsely, too.

וְהִלְכְתָא [3]The Gemara concludes: **And** as far as **the law** is concerned, it **is in accordance with** the position of **Abaye,** who interprets the Biblical verse as disqualifying any wicked person from serving as a witness, even if his sin does not entail an element of thievery.

וְהָא אִיתּוֹתַב [4]**But was not** Abaye **refuted** by that Baraita cited above, which mentions only examples of thievery (robbers and usurers) when explaining the verse prohibiting "evil men" to serve as witnesses?! To support its above ruling in favor of Abaye, [5]the Gemara explains **that** this "refuting" Baraita **is** taught in accordance with the position of **Rabbi Yose,** who, as we have just seen, refuses to generalize from a lesser offense to a greater one; thereby implying that one who was merely wicked in his relationship with God is not suspected of sinning against both God and man.

וְתֶיהֱוֵי נַמִי [6]The Gemara persists in challenging the above Halakhic conclusion: **Let it be** the case, **as well,** that the Baraita refuting Abaye is **in accordance with Rabbi Yose.** This only strengthens the question as to why the law accords with Abaye, [7]for we are taught that in a dispute between **Rabbi Meir and Rabbi Yose, the law is in accordance with Rabbi Yose!**

שָׁאנֵי הָתָם [8]The Gemara resolves its problem: Although normally the law does accord with Rabbi Yose when he is in dispute with Rabbi Meir, the situation **is different** in our case, [9]**for the Tanna,** Rabbi Yehudah HaNasi, **has anonymously taught us** a Mishnah elsewhere that appears to be **in accordance with Rabbi Meir**'s position regarding a conspiring witness. And the generally accepted principle is that the law always accords with the ruling of an anonymous Mishnah.

וְהֵיכָא [10]**And where are we anonymously taught** a Mishnah in support of Rabbi Meir's position? [11]The source of this anonymous Mishnah can be found in an account of **the incident** in which **Bar Ḥama** was accused of having **killed someone.** [12]Upon hearing the allegations, **the Exilarch** (leader of the Diaspora community) **said to Rav Abba bar Ya'akov:** [13]**Go out** and **examine** the case against Bar Ḥama. [14]**If it is certain** that **he killed** someone, **let them gouge out his eyes!** [15]In response to Rav Abba bar Ya'akov's inquiry, **two witnesses came**

RASHI

האי — דקתני: אלו הגזלנין ומלוי ריבית, דמשמע אבל אוכלי נבילות כשרין. **רבי יוסי היא** — דאמר: מקולתא לחמירתא — לא, ויחידאה הוא. **לכהיוהו לעיניה** = ינקרו את עיניו. דבטלו מיתות בית דין, והאי קנסא קא עבדינן ביה, דבית דין מכין ועונשין שלא מן התורה. ויש אומרים: יטלו ממונו ויתנו ליורשין.

NOTES

כִּי הָא דְּבַר חָמָא **As in this case of Bar Ḥama.** Some commentators say that the Gemara chose to relate the entire account, rather than just cite its relevant conclusion, in accordance with the principle that one should always quote a Torah ruling or insight in the name of the individual who initially proposed it. Others suggest that the account was related in its entirety in order to show us the importance of seeking ways to vindicate those accused of capital crimes (*Ḥamra Veḥaye*).

לִיכְהֲיוּהוּ לְעֵינֵיהּ **Let them gouge out his eyes.** *Rashi* explains that, although capital punishment was no longer allowed at the time, the courts still retained the right to

TRANSLATION AND COMMENTARY

forth and **testified against** Bar Ḥama **that he definitely killed.** [1]Subsequently, **Bar Ḥama went** and **brought two** other **witnesses** who **testified against one of those** who had incriminated him, stating that he was a thief and ineligible to testify. [2]**One** of Bar Ḥama's witnesses **said:** While **in my presence** and in full view, **he stole a** ***kav*** **of peeled barley.** [3]**And** the other **one said:** While **in my presence, he stole** [27B] **the shaft of a spear.** After considering their testimony, [4]Rav Abba bar Ya'akov **said to Bar Ḥama: What is your intention** in bringing these witnesses? [5]Do you suppose that the law is **in accordance with Rabbi Meir,** who suspected that those guilty of testifying falsely in civil crimes will testify falsely in capital cases such as yours? If so, then you are mistaken, [6]for in disputes between **Rabbi Meir and Rabbi Yose, the law is in accordance with Rabbi Yose;** [7]**and did not Rabbi Yose say** that if a witness was **discredited in regard to** testimony which he gave in a **civil case,** [8]**he is** still **fit to** testify in **capital cases?** Consequently, we may not disqualify the witness in your case simply because you have shown him to be a thief. [9]**Rav Pappi**, who was present at the time, turned to Rav Abba bar Ya'akov and **said to him:** Your conclusion is mistaken, [10]for **the rule** you offer in support of accepting Rabbi Yose's position **applies** only if **the Tanna**, Rabbi Yehudah HaNasi, **has not anonymously taught us** a Mishnah **in accordance with Rabbi Meir**'s position. [11]**Here,** in this dispute, however, **the Tanna** has **anonymously taught us** a Mishnah **in accordance with Rabbi Meir**'s position. Hence Bar Ḥama indeed has succeeded in invalidating the testimony brought against him.

מִמַּאי [12]The Gemara asks: **From what** anonymous Mishnah did Rav Pappi know that the law here is in accordance with Rabbi Meir? [13]**If** you wish, we may **say** that he knew it **from** the Mishnah **that we have learned** in *Niddah* (49b): [14]**"Whoever is fit to judge capital cases is fit to judge civil cases."** [15]For **who** may we assume **is** the source of this Mishnah? As we learned earlier, the laws of ineligibility that apply to judges apply also

דְּוַדַּאי קְטַל. [1]אֲזַל אִיהוּ אַיְיתֵי תְּרֵי סָהֲדֵי, אַסְהִידוּ בֵּיהּ בְּחַד מֵהָנָךְ. [2]חַד אֲמַר: קַמַּאי דִּידִי גְּנַב קַבָּא דְחוּשְׁלָא. [3]וְחַד אֲמַר: קַמַּאי דִּידִי גְּנַב [27B] קַתָּא דְבוֹרְטִיָּא. [4]אֲמַר לֵיהּ: מַאי דַּעְתֵּיךְ — [5]כְּרַבִּי מֵאִיר? [6]רַבִּי מֵאִיר וְרַבִּי יוֹסֵי, הֲלָכָה כְּרַבִּי יוֹסֵי; [7]וְרַבִּי יוֹסֵי — הָאָמַר: הוּזַם בְּדִינֵי מָמוֹנוֹת, [8]כָּשֵׁר לְדִינֵי נְפָשׁוֹת?! [9]אֲמַר לֵיהּ רַב פַּפִּי: [10]הָנֵי מִילֵּי הֵיכָא דְּלָא סְתַם לָן תַּנָּא כְּרַבִּי מֵאִיר. [11]הָכָא, סְתַם לָן תַּנָּא כְּרַבִּי מֵאִיר.

[12]מִמַּאי? [13]אִילֵימָא מֵהָא דִּתְנַן: [14]״כָּל הָרָאוּי לָדוּן דִּינֵי נְפָשׁוֹת, רָאוּי לָדוּן דִּינֵי מָמוֹנוֹת״. [15]מַנִּי?

LITERAL TRANSLATION

that he definitely killed. [1]He [Bar Ḥama] went [and] brought two witnesses [who] testified against one of those [two]. [2]One said: In my presence he stole a *kav* of peeled barley. [3]And one said: In my presence he stole [27B] the shaft of a spear. [4]He said to him: What is your intention [in bringing these witnesses] — [5]like Rabbi Meir? [6][In disputes between] Rabbi Meir and Rabbi Yose, the law is like Rabbi Yose; [7]and Rabbi Yose — did he not say: [If] he was discredited in regard to civil cases, [8]he is [still] fit for capital cases?! [9]Rav Pappi said to him: [10]This applies (lit., "these words") where the Tanna has not anonymously taught us in accordance with Rabbi Meir. [11]Here, the Tanna did anonymously teach us in accordance with Rabbi Meir.

[12]From where [do we know this]? [13]If you say from what we have learned: [14]"Whoever is fit to judge capital cases, is fit to judge civil cases." [15][According to] whom is it?

RASHI

ויש אומרים: שמתא, וראשון עיקר. חושלא = שעורין קלופין. קתא דבורטיא — בית יד של רומח. כרבי מאיר — דכיון דחשידי אממון חשידי אעדות נפשות. כל הראוי לדון כו׳ — ומוקמא לה בחשודין.

LANGUAGE

בּוֹרְטִיָּא Spear. This word apparently derives from βηρύττα, *birytta,* the Greek form of the Latin *verutum,* meaning "a spear."

NOTES

mete out other forms of physical punishment, in accordance with the Biblical dictum (Deuteronomy 13:6): "And you shall root out the evil from within your midst." *Rabbi David Bonfil* (cited in *Ran*), maintaining that a Babylonian court would not have had the authority to mete out so severe a punishment, suggests instead that the Exilarch was here wielding the special powers granted him by virtue of his being the surrogate king of Israel in the Diaspora.

In either case, the form of punishment chosen to discipline the people need not conform with any other prescribed in the Torah. Indeed, numerous opinions exist as to what form of punishment the Exilarch was referring to: *Rashi* understands him literally to mean that Bar Ḥama's eyes must be gouged out. Others suggest that he meant to have Bar Ḥama reduced by punishment to the point of extreme feebleness, as an old man whose eyes are dimmed. Such punishment is described as either taking his money and distributing it among the victim's heirs (*Geonim*) or excommunicating him from society (*Rabbi Yehudah Almandri*). Some Geonim suggest that he was to be administered an indeterminate number of lashes, while *Meiri* goes as far as to suggest that, as surrogate king, the Exilarch intended to kill Bar Ḥama in accordance with his royal prerogative.

TRANSLATION AND COMMENTARY

to witnesses. [1]**If** you **say** that **Rabbi Yose** is the source of the Mishnah in *Niddah*, [2]**there is** the problem of reconciling it with the law regarding **a conspiring witness** who falsely testified in a case involving **money:** [3]According to Rabbi Yose, such a person **is fit to** testify in **capital cases and** yet **unfit to** testify in **civil cases.** [4]**Rather,** since it explicitly contradicts a ruling of Rabbi Yose's, **is it not** so that this anonymous Mishnah must reflect the view of **Rabbi Meir,** who does not distinguish between capital and civil cases when disqualifying a conspiring witness.

מִמַּאי [5]The Gemara now rejects this explanation by Rav Pappi: **From what** in this Mishnah in *Niddah* do we deduce that it is talking about a suspected perjurer? [6]**Perhaps it is referring there to those who are unfit because of** a problem about their **family descent.** We have learned elsewhere (36b) that the judge in a capital case must be free of any taint in his family descent (such as being a *mamzer* — born of an adulterous relationship). [7]This interpretation of the Mishnah seems unavoidable, **for if you do not say** this, [8]you must face the following question regarding **the** Mishnah's **latter clause that teaches: "There are some who are fit to judge civil cases but** are **not fit to judge capital cases."** [9]**Why** would a suspected perjurer be fit to judge a civil case and yet **not** be **fit** to judge a capital one? [10]If you say **that** he is unfit because **he was discredited in regard to a capital case,** [11]then **is he** indeed **fit to judge civil cases** as the Mishnah implies? [12]Surely not, for **according to everyone** — both Rabbi Meir and Rabbi Yose — **he would be unfit!** [13]**Rather,** we must conclude that this latter clause of the Mishnah **is referring to one who is unfit** to judge a capital case because of a flaw in his **family descent,** and he indeed may judge civil cases. [14]**Here, too,** in the Mishnah's opening clause, we must conclude that **it is referring to** a judge **who is unfit** because of a flaw in his **family descent** and not to one who is suspected of perjury. Thus we are left without an anonymous Mishnaic source definitively supporting Rabbi Meir, and Bar Ḥama's legal defense is in deep trouble.

אֶלָּא [15]**Rather,** say that it is **here** that **the Tanna**, Rabbi Yehudah HaNasi, **has anonymously taught us** a Mishnah based upon Rabbi Meir. [16]**For we have learned: "These are unfit** to testify to having seen the New Moon: [17]A dice-player, **and one who lends on interest, and** pigeon-fliers, **and merchants of seventh-year**

[1]אִילֵימָא רַבִּי יוֹסֵי הִיא, [2]הָא אִיכָּא עֵד זוֹמֵם דְּמָמוֹן, [3]דְּכָשֵׁר לְדִינֵי נְפָשׁוֹת וּפָסוּל לְדִינֵי מָמוֹנוֹת. [4]אֶלָּא, לָאו רַבִּי מֵאִיר הִיא?

[5]מִמַּאי? [6]דִּילְמָא בִּפְסוּלֵי יוֹחָסִין קָאֵי. [7]דְּאִי לָא תֵּימָא הָכִי, [8]סֵיפָא דְּקָתָנֵי: "יֵשׁ רָאוּי לָדוּן דִּינֵי מָמוֹנוֹת וְאֵין רָאוּי לָדוּן דִּינֵי נְפָשׁוֹת". [9]אַמַּאי אֵינוֹ רָאוּי? [10]דְּאִיתַּזַּם בְּדִינֵי נְפָשׁוֹת, [11]רָאוּי לָדוּן דִּינֵי מָמוֹנוֹת?! [12]וְהָא דִּבְרֵי הַכֹּל פָּסוּל הוּא! [13]אֶלָּא, בִּפְסוּל יוֹחָסִין קָאֵי. [14]הָכָא נַמִי בִּפְסוּל יוֹחָסִין קָאֵי. [15]אֶלָּא, הָכָא קָא סְתַם לָן תַּנָּא, [16]דִּתְנַן: "אֵלּוּ הֵן הַפְּסוּלִים: [17]הַמְשַׂחֵק בְּקוּבְיָא, וּמַלְוֵי בְּרִבִּית, וּמַפְרִיחֵי יוֹנִים, וְסוֹחֲרֵי

LITERAL TRANSLATION

[1]If you say it is Rabbi Yose, [2]there is [the case of] a conspiring witness [in a matter] of money, [3]who is fit for capital cases and unfit for civil cases. [4]Rather, is it not Rabbi Meir?!

[5]From where [do we know this]? [6]Perhaps [it refers here] to those who are unfit because of family descent. [7]For if you do not say this, [8][say] the latter clause that teaches: "There are some who are fit to judge civil cases but not fit to judge capital cases." [9]Why is he not fit? [10][If you say] that he was discredited in regard to capital cases, [11]is he fit to judge civil cases?! [12]But, according to everyone, he is unfit! [13]Rather, [it refers] to someone who is unfit because of family descent. [14]Here, too, [it refers] to someone who is unfit due to family descent.

[15]Rather, [it is] here [that] the Tanna has anonymously taught us. [16]For we have learned: [17]"These are unfit [to testify regarding the new moon]: A dice-player, and one who lends on interest, and pigeon-fliers, and merchants

RASHI

אלא לאו רבי מאיר — דאמר: כיון שהוחשד לממון פסול לעדות נפשות, הלכך לא משכחת לה כשר לנפשות דליהוי פסול לממון. **בפסול יוחסין** — דלנפשות בית דין מיוחסין בעינן, כדתני רב יוסף (סנהדרין לו,ב): כשם שבית דין מנוקים בצדק, שנאמר "בצדק תשפוט", כך בית דין מנוקין מכל מום, שנאמר "כולך יפה רעיתי ומום אין בך". **דאי לא תימא הכי** — דגבי יוחסין קאי, אלא בחשודין אוקמת ליה. **ראוי לדון דיני ממונות** — בתמיה, והא דברי הכל פסול הוא! **אלא בפסול יוחסין קאי** — כגון גר וממזר, דכשרין לדון דיני ממונות, ופסולין לדון דיני נפשות.

HALAKHAH

פְּסוּלֵי יוֹחָסִין **Those who are unfit due to family descent.** "Only those whose family descent allows them to marry their daughters off to a priest (being neither converts nor the issue of an adulterous relationship) are accepted as

LANGUAGE

כַּרְגְּיָה **Poll tax.** This word apparently stems from the ancient Persian *charak,* meaning "land tax."

TRANSLATION AND COMMENTARY

produce, **and** Canaanite **slaves.** [1]**This is the rule: Any testimony that a woman is not fit** to render (almost all testimony), these others **are also not fit** to render." [2]Now **who** may we assume **is** the source of this Mishnah? [3]**If we say** it is **Rabbi Yose,** we have a difficulty — [4]for **is there not** a problem regarding **testimony in capital cases,** [5]**for which a woman is not fit** but for which, according to him, these others would be **fit,** as their ineligibility stems only from civil offenses?! [6]**Rather, is it not** that this anonymous Mishnah agrees with **Rabbi Meir,** who indeed maintains that those guilty of civil offenses are unfit to testify in capital cases as well?! Hence, this was the Mishnah alluded to by Rav Pappi in his defense of Bar Ḥama's challenge to the testimony leveled against him.

קָם בַּר חָמָא [7]Upon hearing Rav Pappi defend him before Rav Abba bar Ya'akov, **Bar Ḥama stood** and **kissed** Rav Pappi's foot, [8]**and** obligated **himself to** pay **his poll tax for the rest of his life.**

MISHNAH וְאֵלּוּ הֵן הַקְּרוֹבִין [9]**And these are unfit** to serve either as witnesses or as judges in a court case because they are **relatives** of one of the principals: His **brother, and his father's brother, and his mother's**

שְׁבִיעִית וְהָעֲבָדִים. [1]זֶה הַכְּלָל: כָּל עֵדוּת שֶׁאֵין הָאִשָּׁה כְּשֵׁירָה לָהּ, אַף הֵן אֵין כְּשֵׁירִין לָהּ". [2]מַנִּי? [3]אִילֵימָא רַבִּי יוֹסֵי — [4]וְהָאִיכָּא עֵדוּת בְּדִינֵי נְפָשׁוֹת, [5]שֶׁאֵין הָאִשָּׁה כְּשֵׁרָה לָהּ וְהֵן כְּשֵׁרִין לָהּ?! [6]אֶלָּא, לָאו רַבִּי מֵאִיר הִיא?!

[7]קָם בַּר חָמָא נַשְׁקֵיהּ אַכַּרְעֵיהּ, [8]וְקַבְּלֵיהּ לְכַרְגְּיָה דְּכוּלֵּי שְׁנֵיהּ.

משנה [9]וְאֵלּוּ הֵן הַקְּרוֹבִין: אָחִיו, וַאֲחִי אָבִיו, וַאֲחִי אִמּוֹ,

LITERAL TRANSLATION

of seventh-year [produce], and slaves. [1]This is the rule: Any testimony for which a woman is not fit, they also are not fit." [2][According to] whom? [3]If you say Rabbi Yose — [4]is there not testimony in capital cases, [5]for which a woman is not fit and for [which] they are fit?! [6]Rather, is it not Rabbi Meir?!

[7]Bar Ḥama stood [and] kissed [Rav Pappi's] foot, and he accepted upon himself to [pay] his poll tax for the rest of his life (lit., "all his years").

MISHNAH [8]And these are the [unfit] relatives: His brother, [9]and his father's brother, and his mother's brother,

RASHI

ונשקיה לכרעיה דרב פפי — שהיפך בזכותו. **וקבליה לכרגיה דכוליה שניה** — להעלו כל ימיו ממנת המלך.

משנה אחיו ואחי אביו ואחי אמו — הן ובניהן ילפינן מקראי בגמרא.

NOTES

וְקַבְּלֵיהּ לְכַרְגְּיָה **And obligated himself to pay his poll tax.** How could Rav Pappi have accepted Bar Ḥama's favor without having it look as if he were accepting a prearranged bribe, thereby disqualifying himself from the panel of judges? One must therefore say that Rav Pappi argued as he did, not as a judge, but rather as a scholar who had simply come to observe the proceedings (*Ramah*).

וְאֵלּוּ הֵן הַקְּרוֹבִין **And these are the [unfit] relatives.** The list of relatives presented in this Mishnah is both incomplete and redundant. The Rishonim point out that the most obvious relation — one's father — is missing from the list (although some versions of the Mishnah do indeed include "his father"). Some authorities (*Rambam* and *Ran*) explain that the mutual ineligibility of father and son is explicitly stated in the Torah (see ensuing Gemara), and thus did not have to be taught in the Mishnah. *Rashi* points out that many of the relatives listed here can be deduced from other disqualifying relationships which are alluded to — either through logical deduction, by the rule of reciprocity (as each ineligibility works in both directions) or by virtue of being a son or a son-in-law of an already disqualified relative. *Tosafot* suggests that these cases do not constitute true redundancies, for there is a practical consequence to stating their ineligibility outright as opposed to leaving it implicit: The ineligibility of their sons and sons-in-law extends only to those relations explicitly cited in the Mishnah.

Ramah, in noting that many of the relatives cited in our Mishnah could be inferred from those listed previously, concludes that the Mishnah progressed from simpler to more complex situations (or as expressed in Talmudic terms: לא זו אף זו — "not only this, but also this"). The first relationship mentioned, that of one's brother, represents the most obvious category of ineligibility after that of one's father. One's father's brother follows as the next logical choice for ineligibility by virtue of his being the closest paternal relative after one's own brother. One's mother's brother, though seemingly on a par with one's father's brother, represents a lesser degree of relationship, as only paternal kin are invested by the Torah with rights of inheritance. The next three relationships mentioned in the Mishnah (his sister's husband, his father's sister's husband,

HALAKHAH

judges in a capital case." (*Rambam, Sefer Shoftim, Hilkhot Sanhedrin* 11:11.)

הָעֲבָדִים **The Canaanite slaves.** "A Canaanite slave is ineligible to serve as a witness by Torah law, for he is not a full partner to the Covenant of Israel." (*Ramban, Sefer Shoftim, Hilkhot Edut* 9:4; *Shulḥan Arukh, Ḥoshen Mishpat* 34:19.)

אֵלּוּ הֵן הַקְּרוֹבִין **These are the [unfit] relatives.** "Those who are related — be it from the father's side, the mother's side, or even by marriage — are unfit to serve as witnesses," as detailed in the Gemara. (*Shulḥan Arukh, Ḥoshen Mishpat* 33:2.)

TRANSLATION AND COMMENTARY

brother, and his sister's husband, and his father's sister's husband, [1]**and his mother's sister's husband, and his mother's husband** (his stepfather), **and his father-in-law, and his brother-in-law** (his wife's sister's husband). Not only are **they** themselves unfit, [2]but **their sons and their sons-in-law** are unfit also.

וְחוֹרְגוֹ, לְבַדּוֹ [3]However, in the case of **one's stepson, he alone** is unfit but not his sons or sons-in-law.

אָמַר רַבִּי יוֹסֵי [4]**Rabbi Yose said: This** list just mentioned **is** in accordance with **the** later **Mishnah of Rabbi Akiva. However, the early Mishnah**, preceding that of Rabbi Akiva, contained an alternative listing of relatives: [5]**His uncle** (his father's brother), **and his cousin** (the son of his father's brother), **and anyone** else from his father's family **who is fit to inherit** from **him.**

וּבַעַל אֲחוֹתוֹ, וּבַעַל אֲחוֹת אָבִיו, [1]וּבַעַל אֲחוֹת אִמּוֹ, וּבַעַל אִמּוֹ, וְחָמִיו, וְגִיסוֹ — [2]הֵן וּבְנֵיהֶן וְחַתְנֵיהֶן. [3]וְחוֹרְגוֹ, לְבַדּוֹ. [4]אָמַר רַבִּי יוֹסֵי: זוֹ מִשְׁנַת רַבִּי עֲקִיבָא. אֲבָל מִשְׁנָה רִאשׁוֹנָה: [5]דּוֹדוֹ, וּבֶן דּוֹדוֹ, וְכָל הָרָאוּי לְיוֹרְשׁוֹ.

LITERAL TRANSLATION

and his sister's husband, and his father's sister's husband, [1]and his mother's sister's husband, and his mother's husband, and his father-in-law, and his brother-in-law — [2]they and their sons and their sons-in-law.

[3]And one's stepson, he alone.

[4]Rabbi Yose said: This is the Mishnah of Rabbi Akiva. However, the early Mishnah [reads]: [5]One's uncle, and his cousin, and anyone who is fit to inherit from him.

RASHI

בעל אחותו — כאחיו הוא, דילפינן בעל כאשתו, ובנו דהוה ליה בן אחותו כבן אחיו, וילפינן בגמרא — קרובי האם כקרובי האב. **בעל אחות אביו** — כאחי אביו. **בעל אחות אמו** — כאחי אמו. ובעל אמו גרסינן בהדייהו. **וגיסו** — בעל אחות אשתו. **וחורגו** — בן אשתו. **לבדו** — ולא בנו וחתנו. ואי קשיא לך: כיון דתנא בעל אמו פסול לו, ממילא ידענא דהוא נמי פסול לבעל אמו, למה לי למיתני חורגו אי משום דאתא לאשמעינן לבדו — לישתוק מיניה, וכל כמה דלא תני ליה, מכללא דבעל אמו לא משתמע אלא הוא לבדו לא תיקשי, דכל הנך דמשתמע מכללא — מיתני במתניתין בהדיא, כגון אחי פסול לי ואני לו דאנא נמי אחיו, ובנו פסול לי ואני לו דאנא אחי אביו, ובמתניתין תני לה: אחי אבי פסול לי ואני לו שאני בן אחיו, והא תנא ליה אחיו ובנו בן אחי אבי פסול לי ואני לו שאני בן אחי אביו, אחי אמי פסול לי ואני לו שאני בן אחותו, ותנן במתניתין: בעל אחותו הוא ובנו, דהיינו בן אחותו. (בן) [אחי] אחות אמי פסול לי ואני לו שאני בן אחות (אמו) [אביו], ותנן במתניתין: בעל אחות אביו ובנו, דהיינו בן אחות אביו. בעל אחותי פסול לי ואני לו שאני בן חמיו ותנן במתניתין: חמיו ובנו, וכן כולהו כי מעיינת להו משכחת להו בהדיא, בר מבן אחי אשתו — דמפיק מכלל בעל אחות אביו, וחתנו — דמפיק מכלל דחמיו, דלא מיתניא בהדיא. **וכל הראוי ליורשו** — דהיינו קרובי האב, אבל קרובי האם כגון אחי אמו — כשר לו, שהרי אינו ראוי ליורשו דתנן (בבא בתרא קח,א): אחי האם מנחילין ולא נוחלין, אבל הוא פסול לאחי אמו שהרי מעיד זה ראוי ליורשו, וגיסו נמי כשר להעיד לו — שאינו ראוי ליורשו.

NOTES

and his mother's sister's husband) actually parallel the first three relationships in the Mishnah as follows: His sister's husband, having become one flesh with her through marriage, is considered like his own brother; similarly, his father's sister's husband becomes like his father's brother, and his mother's sister's husband is parallel to his mother's brother. The same equivalency principle can be used to explain the ineligibility attached to the remaining relationships cited in the Mishnah: His step-father and father-in-law are both likened to his own father; the first by virtue of his mother's marriage, the second by virtue of his own. Finally, his wife's sister's husband is likened to his own brother, but only after applying this principle twice — through his own marriage, his wife's sister becomes like his own sister; and through her marriage, her husband becomes like his own brother.

גִּיסוֹ His brother-in-law. As pointed out in our commentary, the brother-in-law relationship alluded to by the term גיס in our Mishnah (as well as in the ensuing Gemara) is that which exists between men married to two sisters. The relationships more usually referred to in English as brothers-in-law have already been alluded to in the Mishnah, either explicitly (one's sister's husband) or indirectly (such as one's father-in-law's son, who is the same as one's wife's brother or half-brother).

וְכָל הָרָאוּי לְיוֹרְשׁוֹ And anyone who is fit to inherit from him. Our commentary follows those Rishonim (*Rashi, Ramah, Ran* and others) who attribute this statement to the early Mishnah cited by Rabbi Yose. *Rashi* interprets it as an inclusionary statement teaching us that, in addition to one's paternal uncle and cousin, anyone who can theoretically inherit the estate of the defendant is ineligible to testify in his case — thereby limiting ineligibility to paternal relatives (who alone are granted powers of inheritance; see *Bava Batra* 108b). This early Mishnah also contradicts the rule of reciprocity that holds true in Rabbi Akiva's Mishnah (for one does not necessarily have the right to inherit from every individual who may inherit from one). *Ramah* offers three possible explanations of the role of inheritance in invalidating witnesses: (1) Someone who stands to benefit from the defendant's estate cannot be trusted to testify on matters that will affect the size and status of that estate; (2) The Tanna understands that the term "family" as used by the Torah in inheritance (Numbers 27:11) and other matters applies only to paternal relatives and not maternal ones. (3) The Biblical verse from which the whole principle of familial ineligibility derives speaks only of paternal relationships.

Other Rishonim (*Rabbenu Zerahyiah HaLevi, Ran*) interpret the early Mishnah as disqualifying any relative who is tied

[1] וְכָל הַקָּרוֹב לוֹ בְּאוֹתָהּ שָׁעָה. [2] הָיָה קָרוֹב וְנִתְרַחֵק הֲרֵי זֶה כָּשֵׁר. [3] רַבִּי יְהוּדָה אוֹמֵר: אֲפִילּוּ מֵתָה בִּתּוֹ וְיֵשׁ לוֹ בָּנִים מִמֶּנָּה — [4] הֲרֵי זֶה קָרוֹב. [5] הָאוֹהֵב וְהַשּׂוֹנֵא. [6] אוֹהֵב — זֶה שׁוֹשְׁבִינוֹ, [7] שׂוֹנֵא — כָּל שֶׁלֹּא דִּבֵּר עִמּוֹ שְׁלֹשָׁה יָמִים בְּאֵיבָה. [8] אָמְרוּ לוֹ: לֹא נֶחְשְׁדוּ יִשְׂרָאֵל עַל כָּךְ.

גמרא [9] מְנָהָנֵי מִילֵּי? [10] דְּתָנוּ רַבָּנַן: ״לֹא יוּמְתוּ אָבוֹת

LITERAL TRANSLATION

[1] And anyone who was related to him at the time. [2] [If] he was a relative and [then] became unrelated (lit. "distanced"), he is fit. [3] Rabbi Yehudah says: Even [if] his daughter died, but [the son-in-law] has children from her — [4] he is a relative.

[5] His friend and his enemy [are unfit]: [6] His friend — this is his groomsman; [7] his enemy — anyone who has not spoken with him for three days out of animosity. [8] [The Sages] said to him: [The people of] Israel are not suspected of this.

GEMARA [9] From where [do we derive] these things? [10] For the Rabbis taught: "Fathers shall not be put to death

TRANSLATION AND COMMENTARY

וְכָל הַקָּרוֹב לוֹ [1] Rabbi Akiva's Mishnah also states that only **one who was related to** the litigant **at the time** of the trial or at the time of the witnessed event is unfit. [2] However, if **he was** once **a relative** of the litigant **but** then **became unrelated** prior to witnessing the event, as in a relationship that was dissolved through divorce or death, **he is** then **fit** to serve as a judge or a witness. [3] **Rabbi Yehudah says:** This rule does not always hold, for in the case of a son-in-law, [4] **he is** still **a relative even** if **his** wife, the litigant's **daughter, died,** if **he has** children **from her.**

הָאוֹהֵב וְהַשּׂוֹנֵא [5] Rabbi Yehudah continues: There are two more individuals who are considered unfit to serve as either judge or witness: **His friend and his enemy.** [6] **His friend — this** refers to **his best man** (the principal groomsman at his wedding). [7] **His enemy** — this refers to **anyone who has not spoken with him for** at least **three days out of animosity.** [8] The Sages **said to** Rabbi Yehudah: The people of **Israel are not suspected of** testifying falsely out of love or hate for their fellow man.

GEMARA מְנָהָנֵי מִילֵּי [9] **From where** do we derive **the ruling** that relatives may not serve as witnesses in one's trial? The Gemara brings proof from a Baraita. [10] **Our Rabbis taught:** It states in Deuteronomy (24:16): **"Fathers shall not be put to death because of sons** and sons shall not be put to death because of

RASHI

באותה שעה — שהוא בא להעיד או שראה העדות. **היה קרוב** — כגון חתנו שראוי ליורשו. **ונתרחק** — שמתה אשתו קודם שראה עדות זו. **שושבינו** — פסול לו בימי חופתו. **לא נחשדו ישראל על כך** — להעיד שקר משום איבה ואהבה, ודווקא בעדות פליגי, אבל בדין מודו רבנן דפסול לו לדון, דכיון דסני ליה ולא מצי להפוכי בזכותיה.

גמרא לא יומתו — שני אבות בעדות בניהם, ועל כרחיך הני שני אבות באחין קא מישתעי שהן קרובין מן הכל, דבאב ובנו לא

NOTES

to the defendant through the laws of inheritance, regardless of whether it is the witness or the defendant who is the potential heir. *Ran* justifies this interpretation for the following reason: If the Mishnah intended to disqualify the potential heir for reasons of partiality, then it should have limited his ineligibility only where this testimony would benefit the defendant. However, the potential heir is disqualified even from testifying to his detriment.

Ran further states that the early Mishnah singled out the uncle and first cousin before specifying the general rule of ineligibility to inform us that no one may be disqualified who is further removed in relationship than a first cousin. According to *Ramban,* however (as cited in *Ran*), the examples of uncle and first cousin were presented to emphasize that the rule of ineligibility applies only to someone who is related to the defendant directly rather than through marriage, since a relative by marriage only has the right to inherit if the marriage is still intact at the time of the defendant's death.

In contrast to those mentioned above, who attribute the statement כָּל הָרָאוּי לְיוֹרְשׁוֹ to the early Mishnah, the opinion of *Rambam* (in his *Commentary to the Mishnah*), *Rav* and others is that this statement actually is meant to qualify Rabbi Akiva's Mishnah. Consequently, the various categories of ineligibility listed there apply only if the witness could possibly inherit from the litigant, but not vice versa. For instance, in the case of "his mother's brother," testimony is only disqualified when the nephew (who is a rightful heir of his mother's brother) testifies for his uncle; the mother's brother, however, could testify about his nephew, since he does not inherit from him.

שֶׁלֹּא דִּבֵּר עִמּוֹ שְׁלֹשָׁה יָמִים בְּאֵיבָה **Anyone who has not spoken with him for three days out of animosity.** The *Sifri* derives this formula from the Biblical verse (Deuteronomy 19:4) which equates lack of malice with "not hating one from yesterday and the day before." (*Ramah.*)

HALAKHAH

הָיָה קָרוֹב וְנִתְרַחֵק **If he was a relative and then became unrelated.** "One who was unfit to testify because he was related by marriage to the subject of his testimony, becomes fit once the marital relationship is dissolved through death (or divorce), even if there are children from the marriage," in accordance with the anonymous Tanna of our Mishnah. (*Shulḥan Arukh, Ḥoshen Mishpat* 33:12.)

הָאוֹהֵב וְהַשּׂוֹנֵא **His friend and his enemy.** "Neither friends nor enemies are considered ineligible to testify in one's case, for Jews are not suspect of perjuring themselves

TRANSLATION AND COMMENTARY

fathers" — [1]**what does the verse** teach? [2]**If** you suggest that **it teaches** us **that fathers shall not be put to death for** their **sons' iniquity** nor **sons for** their **fathers' iniquity,** this would be redundant. [3]**It was already stated** in the same verse that **"every man shall be put to death for his own sin"!** [4]**Rather,** conclude that the first part of the verse, **"fathers shall not be put to death because of sons,"** teaches us that **fathers** shall not be convicted and punished **because** of their **sons' testimony.** [5]Similarly, as the verse continues, **"and sons shall not be put to death because of fathers,"** conclude that sons shall not be convicted and punished **because** of their **fathers' testimony.**

וּבָנִים [6]The Gemara reconsiders one of the premises in the above Baraita: **And** is it indeed so, that **sons** are **not** killed **because of** their **fathers' iniquity?** [7]Is **it not written** explicitly in Exodus (20:5): "For I, the Lord your God, am an exacting God, **visiting the fathers' iniquity upon** their **sons** and upon their children to the third and fourth generation"? [8]Rather, we must say that the intention **there,** in Exodus, is to teach us that children may indeed be punished for their fathers' sins, but only **when they continue practicing their fathers'** evil **deeds.** [9]**This** is confirmed by what **was taught** in a Baraita: "The verse in Leviticus (26:39) states: 'And those left among you shall waste away because of their iniquity, in the lands of their enemies; **and also in the iniquities of their fathers' shall they waste away with them.'"** [10]From here we see that sons are punished for their fathers' iniquity only **when they continue practicing their fathers'** evil **deeds.**

אַתָּה אוֹמֵר כְּשֶׁאוֹחֲזִין [11]The Baraita now subjects this conclusion to closer inspection: **Should you** indeed **say** that this verse is speaking only of cases **where** sons **retain** their fathers' evil ways, [12]**or** does **it** also teach us that sons are punished for their fathers' deeds **when they do not retain** and continue their evil

עַל בָּנִים״, [1]מַה תַּלְמוּד לוֹמַר? [2]אִם לְלַמֵּד שֶׁלֹּא יוּמְתוּ אָבוֹת בַּעֲוֹן בָּנִים וּבָנִים בַּעֲוֹן אָבוֹת, [3]הֲרֵי כְּבָר נֶאֱמַר: ״אִישׁ בְּחֶטְאוֹ יוּמָתוּ״! [4]אֶלָּא, ״לֹא יוּמְתוּ אָבוֹת עַל בָּנִים״ — בְּעֵדוּת בָּנִים; [5]״וּבָנִים לֹא יוּמְתוּ עַל אָבוֹת״ — בְּעֵדוּת אָבוֹת.
[6]וּבָנִים בַּעֲוֹן אָבוֹת לֹא? [7]וְהָכְתִיב: ״פֹּקֵד עֲוֹן אָבוֹת עַל בָּנִים״? [8]הָתָם, כְּשֶׁאוֹחֲזִין מַעֲשֵׂה אֲבוֹתֵיהֶן בִּידֵיהֶן, [9]כִּדְתַנְיָא: ״וְאַף בַּעֲוֹנֹת אֲבֹתָם אִתָּם יִמָּקוּ״ — [10]כְּשֶׁאוֹחֲזִין מַעֲשֵׂה אֲבוֹתֵיהֶם בִּידֵיהֶם. [11]אַתָּה אוֹמֵר כְּשֶׁאוֹחֲזִין, [12]אוֹ אֵינוֹ אֶלָּא כְּשֶׁאֵין אוֹחֲזִין?

LITERAL TRANSLATION

because of sons," [1]what does the verse say? [2]If it is to teach that fathers shall not be put to death for [their] sons' iniquity and sons [shall not be put to death] for [their] fathers' iniquity, [3]this has already been stated: "Every man shall be put to death for his own sin"! [4]Rather, "Fathers shall not be put to death because of sons" — because of [their] sons' testimony; [5]"and sons shall not be put to death because of fathers" — because of [their] fathers' testimony.

[6]And sons are not [killed] because of [their] fathers' iniquity? [7]Is it not written: "Visiting the fathers' iniquity upon [their] sons"? [8]There, [it is] when they retain (lit., "hold in their hands") their fathers' [evil] deeds; [9]as it is taught: "And also in the iniquities of their fathers shall they waste away with them" — [10]when they retain their fathers' [evil] deeds.

[11]Should you say [only] when they retain, [12]or perhaps it is even when they do not retain?

RASHI

מלי למימר דאם כן לא הוה קרי להו אבות, דחד אב וחד בן סגי, ולקמן מפרש כוליה מיניה. כשאוחזין מעשה אבותיהם בידיהם — ונפרעין מהן עונותיהן ועון אבותיהם.

NOTES

לֹא יוּמְתוּ אָבוֹת בְּעֵדוּת בָּנִים **Fathers shall not be put to death because of their sons' testimony.** *Rashi* and *Ramah* elaborate on this teaching and demonstrate how the Baraita proves not only the mutual ineligibility of father and son, but that of uncle and nephew as well. They explain that the verse's use of the plural "fathers" and "sons" implies more than one father and son relationship disqualifies testimony. Hence, they extend the disqualification to testimony by nephews against their paternal uncles and vice versa.

כְּשֶׁאוֹחֲזִין מַעֲשֵׂה אֲבוֹתֵיהֶן בִּידֵיהֶן **When they retain their fathers' deeds in their hands.** According to *Rashi,* the son who repeats his father's sinful behavior is punished for his own sin as well as for that of his father. *Ramban* (in his Commentary on the Torah) and *Meiri,* on the other hand, insist that no one's punishment is ever augmented because of another's sin, even if guilty of the same wrongdoing. However, if one does not have the merit of a righteous father, God is less prone to suppress His anger and suspend punishment.

HALAKHAH

simply because of love or hate for their fellowman. However, if there is sufficient cause to suspect that a particular enemy might perjure himself to exact revenge from the defendant, then that individual should be disqualified (*Maharshal*)." (*Shulḥan Arukh, Ḥoshen Mishpat* 33:1.)

TRANSLATION AND COMMENTARY

behavior? [1]It would appear that this latter proposition is untenable, for **when** the Torah **states** elsewhere (Deuteronomy 24:16) that **"every man shall be put to death for his own sin,"** it becomes clear that people are only punished for their own deeds. [2]**Here,** it must **be** that the verse, "in the iniquities of their fathers they shall waste away," indeed means only **when** sons **repeat their fathers'** evil **deeds.**

וְלֹא [3]The Gemara continues to challenge the above premise: **But** it is **not** so, that sons are not punished for their fathers' sins! [4]**Is it not written** in Leviticus (26:37) that when God punishes Israel for its iniquities, **"every man shall stumble over his brother"**? [5]This is interpreted as meaning: **Every man will stumble** and suffer **because of his brother's iniquity,** [6]thereby **teaching** us **that all of** Israel **are "guarantors"** (i.e., responsible) **for one another.** Consequently, sons will be punished for their fathers' iniquity!

הָתָם [7]The Gemara answers: **There,** the verse means that **when** Jews suffer, it is not because of ancestral sins, but rather because **it was in their power to protest** against the sinful deeds of others **and they did not protest.**

[28A] אַשְׁכַּחַן [8]As evident from the Baraita cited above, **we have found** a verse supporting the ruling that **fathers** who are brothers may not testify **about** each other's **sons**; conversely, **sons** who are paternal first cousins may not testify **about** each other's **fathers.** [9]**And** it logically follows that if uncles and nephews cannot testify about one another, **certainly** the **fathers** themselves, being brothers, cannot testify **about each other.** [10]But **from where do we know** (as indicated in our Mishnah) that **sons** may not testify **about sons** who are first cousins?

אִם כֵּן [11]This law is derived by reasoning as follows: **If** it is **so,** that first cousins may indeed testify about one another, **let the verse write:** [12]**"Fathers shall not be put to death because of a son,"** still implying that a man may not testify about his father or his uncle. [13]**Why,** then, does the verse state "because of **sons,"** in the plural? [14]It then teaches us **that even** the **sons**, when first cousins, may not testify **about one another.**

אַשְׁכַּחַן [15]**We have** now **found** support for the ruling in our Mishnah that **sons** who are first cousins cannot testify **about one another;** [16]but **from where do we know** that they, or any other pair of close relatives, may not testify together **about outsiders** who are not related to them?

אָמַר רָמִי בַּר חָמָא [17]**Rami bar Ḥama said: It is** a matter of **logic,** [18]**as it was taught** in the following Baraita: "Two **witnesses** who jointly testify against another **are not declared** to be **'conspiring** witnesses' **until**

[1]כְּשֶׁהוּא אוֹמֵר ״אִישׁ בְּחֶטְאוֹ יוּמָתוּ״. [2]הֲרֵי כְּשֶׁאוֹחֲזִין מַעֲשֵׂה אֲבוֹתֵיהֶן בִּידֵיהֶן.

[3]וְלֹא? [4]וְהָכְתִיב: ״וְכָשְׁלוּ אִישׁ בְּאָחִיו״ — [5]אִישׁ בַּעֲוֹן אָחִיו, [6]מְלַמֵּד שֶׁכּוּלָּן עֲרֵבִים זֶה בָּזֶה!

[7]הָתָם שֶׁהָיָה בְּיָדָם לִמְחוֹת וְלֹא מִיחוּ.

[28A] [8]אַשְׁכַּחַן אָבוֹת לְבָנִים וּבָנִים לְאָבוֹת, [9]וְכָל שֶׁכֵּן אָבוֹת לַהֲדָדֵי. [10]בָּנִים לְבָנִים מְנָלַן? [11]אִם כֵּן לִיכְתּוֹב קְרָא: [12]״לֹא יוּמְתוּ אָבוֹת עַל בֵּן״. [13]מַאי ״בָּנִים״? [14]דַּאֲפִילּוּ בָּנִים לַהֲדָדֵי. [15]אַשְׁכַּחַן בָּנִים לַהֲדָדֵי; [16]בָּנִים לְעָלְמָא, מְנָלַן?

[17]אָמַר רָמִי בַּר חָמָא: סְבָרָא הוּא, [18]כִּדְתַנְיָא: ״אֵין הָעֵדִים

LITERAL TRANSLATION

[1][The latter applies] when it states, "Every man shall be put to death for his own sin." [2]Here [sons are punished] when they retain their fathers' [evil] deeds.

[3]But [say] no! [4]For it is written: "And every man shall stumble over his brother" — [5]every man for his brother's iniquity, [6]teaching [us] that they are all guarantors for one another!

[7]There, [it is] when it was in their power to protest and they did not protest.

[28A] [8]We have found [that] fathers [cannot testify] about sons and sons about fathers, [9]and certainly fathers about one another. [10][That] sons [cannot testify] about sons, from where do we know [it]?

[11]If so, let the verse write: [12]"Fathers shall not be put to death because of a son." [13]Why [write] "sons"? [14]That even sons [cannot testify] about one another.

[15]We have found sons [cannot testify] about one another; [16][that] sons [cannot testify together] about others (lit., "the world"), from where do we know [it]?

[17]Rami bar Ḥama said: It is logical, [18]as it was taught: "Witnesses are not

RASHI

איש באחיו — איש בשביל אחיו. **אשכחן אבות לבנים** — ראובן לבן שמעון, דהיינו אחי אביו. **ובנים לאבות** — בן שמעון לראובן, דהיינו בן אחיו, וכל שכן אבות להדדי, דהא בנים מכח דידהו קא אתו, ואימעיטו להו מהאי קרא אחיו ובנו ואחי אביו. **בנים להדדי מנלן** — דקתני במתניתין, בן אחי אביו פסול לו. **ליכתוב לא יומתו אבות על הבן** — דכיון דכתיב ״אבות״ שני אחים משמע, ועל הבן — הוי משמע בנו של כל אחד ואחד הוי פסול לשניהם. **לעלמא** — שיהו שני קרובים פסולין להעיד על אדם מן השוק.

TRANSLATION AND COMMENTARY

they are both discredited." This occurs when other witnesses prove that the first ones were elsewhere at the time they claim to have seen what they did. [1]Now, **if it should** enter **your mind** to say **that** close relatives **are fit** to testify jointly **about** people to whom they are not related, [2]**it would turn out that** if their testimony led to a capital conviction and then they were discredited as **conspiring witnesses**, each **would** stand to **be killed because of his brother's** discredited **testimony.** Conspiring witnesses receive the penalty their false testimony would have imposed on another (see Deuteronomy 19:19). Had either brother not testified falsely, the other would have been spared punishment! Since our verse invalidates testimony that results in the conviction of a relative, we must conclude that close relatives are not allowed jointly to testify even about an unrelated third party.

אָמַר לֵיהּ רָבָא [3]The Gemara now suggests: **Rava said to** Rami bar Ḥama: Your logic is faulty, for, **according to your reasoning,** [4]it is difficult to understand **what we have learned** in a Mishnah (*Bava Batra* 56b) dealing with the testimony of brothers aimed at establishing ownership of a field based upon three consecutive years of uncontested physical possession by a single individual: [5]"If each of **three brothers** witnessed a single year's possession of the field; **and** each of them was **joined** separately **in testimony** by **one** unrelated party who witnessed all three years of possession, [6]**these are** considered as **three** separate and valid **testimonies.** The man's ownership is established in spite of the brothers' kinship. [7]Nevertheless, the separate testimonies **are** still considered as **one testimony for** purposes of **discreditation** (that is, all four witnesses must be discredited before they can be declared 'conspiring witnesses' and required to pay the penalty of discreditation to the original owner)." [8]Now, according to this Mishnah, **it turns out that a conspiring witness** is obligated to **pay out money because of his brother's testimony,** an eventuality that should have invalidated their testimony according to the logic

נַעֲשִׂין זוֹמְמִין עַד שֶׁיּוּזַּמּוּ שְׁנֵיהֶן". [1]וְאִי סָלְקָא דַּעְתָּךְ בָּנִים לְעָלְמָא כְּשֵׁרִין, [2]נִמְצָא עֵד זוֹמֵם נֶהֱרָג בְּעֵדוּת אָחִיו! [3]אָמַר לֵיהּ רָבָא: וְלִיטַעְמִיךְ, [4]הָא דִּתְנַן: [5]"שְׁלֹשָׁה אַחִין וְאֶחָד מִצְטָרֵף עִמָּהֶן, [6]הֲרֵי אֵלּוּ שָׁלֹשׁ עֵדֻיּוֹת; [7]וְהֵן עֵדוּת אַחַת לַהֲזָמָּה". [8]נִמְצָא עֵד זוֹמֵם מְשַׁלֵּם מָמוֹן בְּעֵדוּת אָחִיו!

LITERAL TRANSLATION

declared 'conspiring' until they are both discredited." [1]And if it entered your mind that sons are fit [to testify together] about others (lit., "the world"), [2]it would turn out that a conspiring witness could be killed because of his brother's testimony!

[3]Rava said to him: And according to your reasoning, [4]that which we have learned: [5]"[If] three brothers [testify separately] and one joins [each of] them, [6]these are three [separate] testimonies; [7]nevertheless they are [as] one testimony for [purposes of] discreditation." [8]It turns out that a conspiring witness pays out money because of his brother's testimony!

RASHI

בעדות אחיו — דאי לאו דאסהיד האי קרובו בהדיה, לא הוה מיקטל. נמלא בנים מתים זה על זה. **שלשה אחים ואחד** — מן השוק, עם כל אחד ואחד מעידים על אכילת שני חזקה של קרקע של אדם מן השוק, ומעיד אחד מן האחין והבא מן השוק על שנה ראשונה, ואחד מן האחין והבא מן השוק על שנה שניה. והשלישי על השלישית, והרי אלו שלש עדיות והחזקה קיימת, ולא אמרינן עדות אחת היא והרי העדים קרובים, אלא שלש עדיות נינהו, דאשתא דקא מסהיד האי לא מסהיד האי. **והן עדות אחת להזמה** — **דעד דמתזמי כולהו** לא משלמי ממונא, דהא לא הוה מתוקמא בידא דלוקח אלא בסהדותא דכולהו.

NOTES

נֶהֱרָג בְּעֵדוּת אָחִיו He could be killed because of his brother's testimony. In truth, Rami bar Ḥama did not need to rely on the Baraita in order to prove this point, for even if one witness could be declared conspiring without his partner being discredited as well, one brother would nevertheless be punished because of the other brother's testimony. Had the innocent brother not testified at all, the guilty one's testimony by itself would not have been accepted in court. Nevertheless, the Baraita does strengthen Rami bar Ḥama's argument by showing the strong connection between the two witnesses (*Rosh*).

HALAKHAH

עַד שֶׁיּוּזַּמּוּ שְׁנֵיהֶן Until they are both discredited. "Conspiring witnesses are not killed or flogged or obligated to pay out money until they have both been discredited subsequent to the verdict. If only one of them is discredited, neither is penalized or punished — even though the discredited witness is no longer considered eligible to testify about any Torah matter." (*Rambam, Sefer Shofetim, Hilkhot Edut* 20:1.)

הֲרֵי אֵלּוּ שָׁלֹשׁ עֵדֻיּוֹת וְהֵן עֵדוּת אַחַת לַהֲזָמָּה These are three separate testimonies, but they are as one testimony for purposes of discreditation. "Two witnesses who testify that a particular person occupied another's field for a period of at least three years, and are later found to have testified falsely, must pay the owner of the field its full value. If one pair of witnesses testified in regard to the first

TRANSLATION AND COMMENTARY

of Rami bar Ḥama. [1]One must say, **rather,** that since the actual **discreditation** leading to the brothers' liability **comes from** testimony leveled against them by **outsiders,** they are not penalized because of one another. [2]**Here, too,** in your scenario, when two brothers jointly testify against someone in a capital case and are then discredited, one can also say that the **discreditation** leading to their liability **comes from outsiders,** they are not punished by their relative's testimony. Why, then, are two close relatives disqualified from jointly testifying about an outside party?

אֶלָּא [3]**Rather,** say as follows: **If** it were **so,** that close relatives could jointly testify about an outside party, **let the verse write: "And a son** (in the singular) shall not be put to death **because of fathers"; or else** let it write: "and **they** shall not be put to death **because of fathers."** [4]**Why,** then, does the verse repeat the plural noun, **"and sons"?** We must surely infer from it that the prohibition applies **even** to **sons,** or other close relatives, who seek jointly to testify **about outsiders.**

אַשְׁכְּחַן [5]The Gemara now seeks Scriptural support for additional details found in our Mishnah: Granted **we have found** support in the above verse for disqualifying **the father's relatives** from testifying about one another; [6]but **from where do we know** that **the mother's relatives** are ineligible as well? We learn it from a Scriptural redundancy, [7]for **the** same **verse states "fathers" twice,** when it could have omitted the second reference and replaced it with the appropriate pronoun. [8]**If** this additional instruction **has no relevance to the father's relatives,** their ineligibility having already been sufficiently established, [9]then **teach** that **it** is **relevant to the mother's** relatives. They are also included in the prohibition.

אַשְׁכְּחַן לְחוֹבָה [10]**We have found** support in the above verse **for** disqualifying a relative's testimony when it is directed at **condemnation** (as it is written there, "they shall not be put to death"); [11]but **from where do we know** that such testimony is equally invalid when rendered for the acquittal of the defendant? This, too, is derived from a Scriptural redundancy, [12]for **the verse states "they shall** (not) **be put to death" twice,** when

[1]אֶלָּא, הַזָּמָה מֵעָלְמָא קָאָתֵי. [2]הָכָא נַמִּי, הַזָּמָה מֵעָלְמָא קָאָתֵי.

[3]אֶלָּא, אִם כֵּן, לִיכְתּוֹב קְרָא: "וּבֵן עַל אָבוֹת", אִי נַמִּי "הֵם עַל אָבוֹת". [4]מַאי "וּבָנִים"? אֲפִילּוּ בָּנִים לְעָלְמָא.

[5]אַשְׁכְּחַן קְרוֹבֵי הָאָב; [6]קְרוֹבֵי הָאֵם, מְנָלַן? [7]אָמַר קְרָא: "אָבוֹת" "אָבוֹת" תְּרֵי זִימְנֵי, [8]אִם אֵינוֹ עִנְיָן לִקְרוֹבֵי הָאָב, [9]תְּנֵיהוּ עִנְיָן לִקְרוֹבֵי הָאֵם.

[10]אַשְׁכְּחַן לְחוֹבָה; לִזְכוּת, [11]מְנָא לַן? [12]אָמַר קְרָא:

LITERAL TRANSLATION

[1]Rather, [say the penalty of] discreditation comes from [testimony] of the others (lit., "the world"). [2]Here, too, [the penalty of] discreditation comes from the [testimony] of the others (lit., "the world").

[3]Rather — if so, let the verse write: "And a son because of fathers," or else "they because of fathers." [4]Why [write] "and sons"? Even sons [cannot testify together] about others (lit., "the world").

[5]We have found the father's relatives [are unfit]; [6]the mother's relatives, from where do we know [it]? [7]The verse states "fathers" "fathers" twice. [8]If it has no relevance to the father's relatives, [9]teach it as having relevance to the mother's relatives.

[10]We have found [relatives are unfit] for condemnation; for acquittal, [11]from where do we [know it]? [12]The verse states:

RASHI

אלא הזמה מעלמא קא אתי להו — על ידי המזימין אותן הן משלמים, ולא זה על ידי זה.

NOTES

לִזְכוּת, מְנָא לַן **From where do we know for acquittal?** One might think that the inadmissibility of beneficial testimony from a close relative is self-evident, for the Torah has already established the less obvious rule that forbids

HALAKHAH

year, while a different pair testified in regard to the second, and yet another pair in regard to the third — and they were all discredited — the law is that they all share equally in paying the value of the field to its owner. Although the three testimonies are legally independent (each one dealing with a different year), they are considered as one for purposes of discreditation. Therefore, when three brothers, together with one who is unrelated to them, testify independently with regard to the three successive years, they are considered to have rendered three separate testimonies and the possession is duly established. However, for purposes of discreditation, they are considered as having rendered one unit of testimony; hence they are only penalized as conspiring witnesses if all four are discredited jointly — the three brothers being obligated to pay half the value of the field and the unrelated witness the other half." (*Rambam, Sefer Shoftim, Hilkhot Edut* 21:7.)

אַשְׁכְּחַן לְחוֹבָה, לִזְכוּת מְנָא לַן? **We have found regarding condemnation; from where do we know regarding acquittal?** "The Biblical prohibition against having any relatives

TRANSLATION AND COMMENTARY

it could have deleted the second reference altogether. [1]If the additional instruction implied by this redundancy **has no relevance** pertaining **to condemnation,** [2]then **teach** that **it** is **relevant to acquittal.**

אַשְׁכְּחַן בְּדִינֵי נְפָשׁוֹת [3]Since the above verse speaks about capital punishment, **we have found** support for disqualifying the testimony of relatives **in** regard to **capital cases;** [4]but **from where do we know** that such testimony is invalid when offered **in** regard to **civil cases?** [5]This is derived from **the verse** in Leviticus (24:22) which **states: "One law shall be for you."** [6]This implies that **the law** dictating judicial procedure **is** meant **for you** to apply **uniformly** in both capital and civil cases.

אָמַר רַב [7]The Gemara now considers various statements dealing with the testimony of relatives: **Rav said: Father's brother** may **not testify in regard to me,** neither **he nor his son nor his son-in-law.** [8]**Also, I** may **not testify in regard to him,** neither **I nor my son nor my son-in-law.**

וְאַמַּאי [9]The Gemara questions the latter part of Rav's statement: Granted that, according to our Mishnah, Rav (as a nephew) would be ineligible to testify about his father's brother; **but why** would his son and son-in-law be ineligible to testify about him as well? [10]After all, such testimony **constitutes** a case of **a third-degree** relative (a grandnephew or grandnephew-in-law) testifying **about a first-degree** relative (their great uncle); [11]**and** while **we have learned** in our Mishnah that **a second-degree** relative (a son) may not testify **about** another **second-degree** relative (his first cousin), [12]nor **a second-degree** relative **about a first-degree** relative (his uncle), [13]**we have not learned** in the Mishnah that **a third-degree** relative may not testify **about a first-degree** relative, as Rav indeed states! (See note for the definition of the degrees of relationships.)

״יוּמְתוּ״ ״יוּמְתוּ״ תְּרֵי זִימְנֵי. [1]אִם אֵינוֹ עִנְיָן לְחוֹבָה, [2]תְּנֵהוּ עִנְיָן לִזְכוּת.
[3]אַשְׁכְּחַן בְּדִינֵי נְפָשׁוֹת; [4]בְּדִינֵי מָמוֹנוֹת, מְנָלַן? [5]אָמַר קְרָא: ״מִשְׁפַּט אֶחָד יִהְיֶה לָכֶם״ — [6]מִשְׁפָּט הַשָּׁוֶה לָכֶם.
[7]אָמַר רַב: אֲחִי אַבָּא לֹא יָעִיד לִי, הוּא וּבְנוֹ וַחֲתָנוֹ. [8]אַף אֲנִי לֹא אָעִיד לוֹ, אֲנִי וּבְנִי וַחֲתָנִי. [9]וְאַמַּאי? [10]הֲוָה לֵיהּ שְׁלִישִׁי בְּרִאשׁוֹן. [11]וַאֲנַן שֵׁנִי בְּשֵׁנִי [12]תְּנַן, שֵׁנִי בְּרִאשׁוֹן תְּנַן, [13]שְׁלִישִׁי בְּרִאשׁוֹן לָא תְּנַן!

LITERAL TRANSLATION

"They shall (not) be put to death" "they shall (not) be put to death" twice. [1]If has no relevance to condemnation, [2]teach it as having relevance to acquittal.

[3]We have found [relatives are unfit] in capital cases; [4]in monetary cases, from where do we know [it]? [5]The verse states: "One law shall be for you" — [6]a law which is uniform for you.

[7]Rav said: Father's brother may not testify about me, [neither] he nor his son nor his son-in-law. [8]Also I may not testify about him, [neither] I nor my son nor my son-in-law. [9]But why? [10]This is [a case of] a third-degree [relative testifying] about a first-degree [relative]. [11]And [while] we have learned [that] a second-degree [relative is unfit] for a second-degree [relative], [12]and we have learned a second-degree [relative is unfit] for a first-degree [relative], [13]we have not learned [that] a third-degree [relative is unfit] for a first-degree [relative]!

RASHI

הוה ליה שלישי בראשון — בני שלישי הוא, ואחי אבא ראשון, דאבא ואחיו ראשונים, ואני שני, ובני שלישי, ואמר רב דשלישי לא יעיד בראשון. **ואנן** — במתניתין שני בשני ושני בראשון תנן, אבל כולי האי לא פסיל מתניתין. **שני בשני** — כגון אחי אביו ובנו, אחי אבא לי ואני לו הרי ראשון בשני ושני בראשון, בן אחי אבא לי ואני לו הרי שני בשני, אבל בני לאחי אבא לא תנן.

NOTES

detrimental testimony. Since the Gemara seeks Scriptural support for this law, we infer that Jews would be no more prone to perjure themselves in the one case than in the other (*Rabbi Yeshayahu Pik*). Others suggest that the Gemara's question is not essentially concerned with one relative testifying about another (its inadmissibility being self-evident, as noted), but rather with the joint testimony of two relatives to acquit an unrelated outside party (*Ran*).

רִאשׁוֹן שֵׁנִי וּשְׁלִישִׁי First-, second-, and third-degree relatives. The ordinal system used in the Gemara for assigning degrees of kin should be viewed in context of the Biblical verse in Deuteronomy (24:16) which, as interpreted

HALAKHAH

testify in a case does not derive from suspicion of partiality, for their testimony is equally unacceptable when condemning or acquitting their kin; rather, the prohibition is based solely upon a Scriptural decree." (*Shulḥan Arukh, Ḥoshen Mishpat* 33:10.)

שְׁלִישִׁי בְּרִאשׁוֹן A third-degree relative about a first-degree relative. "Brothers, be they from a common father or a common mother, are considered first-degree relatives (as are a father and son); their sons (each others' first cousins) are considered second-degree relatives; and their son's sons

TRANSLATION AND COMMENTARY

מַאי [1]The Gemara suggests that Rav could rationalize his position as follows: **What is** the essential meaning of **"son-in-law" that is stated in our Mishnah** ("they and their sons and their sons-in-law")? It is not, as appears at first glance, that the individual's own son-in-law is ineligible (this being implicitly understood for reasons stated later), [2]but rather that **his son's son-in-law** is ineligible (the pronoun "their" modifying son-in-law refers to "sons," not to "they"). Hence we find explicit reference in our Mishnah to the ineligibility of a third-degree relative.

וְלִיתְנֵי [3]**And** if you should object, "**let** the Mishnah, if it wishes to include another generation within the scope of ineligibility, **teach** us this by reference to **his son's son** rather than his son's son-in-law!" [4]I can answer that the Tanna thereby **teaches us something incidentally:** [5]**That a husband is like his wife** with respect to her relatives. Therefore, a son's son-in-law has the same status of ineligibility as a son's son.

וְאֶלָּא [6]The Gemara now questions the preceding resolution of Rav's statement: **But** according to this approach, how can we explain **what Rabbi Ḥiyya taught** in relation to our Mishnah: [7]"The list of ineligible relatives in the Mishnah consists of **eight principal relatives who**, when counted together with their respective sons and sons-in-law, [8]constitute a group of **twenty-four**"? According to Rav, who interprets the Mishnah as invalidating the testimony of third-degree relatives as well, the number of relatives directly alluded to in the Mishnah amounts to **thirty-two!** [9]**Rather,** one must say that the son-in-law referred to in our Mishnah **is** the principal's **actual son-in-law** and not his son's son-in-law.

[1]מַאי "חֲתָנוֹ" דְּקָתָנֵי בְּמַתְנִיתִין? [2]חֲתַן בְּנוֹ.

[3]וְלִיתְנֵי "בֶּן בְּנוֹ"! [4]מִילְּתָא אַגַּב אוֹרְחֵיהּ קָא מַשְׁמַע לָן: [5]דְּבַעַל כְּאִשְׁתּוֹ.

[6]וְאֶלָּא הָא דְּתָנֵי רַבִּי חִיָּיא: [7]"שְׁמוֹנָה אָבוֹת שֶׁהֵן עֶשְׂרִים וְאַרְבָּעָה" — [8]הָנֵי תְּלָתִין וְתַרְתֵּין הָוֵי! [9]אֶלָּא, לְעוֹלָם חֲתָנוֹ מַמָּשׁ.

LITERAL TRANSLATION

[1]What is the "son-in-law" that is stated in our Mishnah? [2]His son's son-in-law.

[3]But let him teach "his son's son"! [4]He teaches us something incidentally: [5]That a husband is like his wife.

[6]But [about] that which Rabbi Ḥiyya taught: [7]"Eight principal [relatives] who are twenty-four" — [8]there would be thirty-two! [9]Rather, it is his actual son-in-law.

RASHI

מאי חתנו דקתני מתניתין — אחי אביו ובנו וחתנו, האי חתנו דמתניתין אבנו קאי דהוה שלישי האי חתן, ולקמן פריך: אם כן הוה שלישי בשני. **אגב אורחיה** — דבעי לאשמועינן שלישי פסול — נקט חתן בנו דאשמועינן נמי בעל כאשתו. **שמנה אבות** — עם בניהם וחתניהם הוו עשרים וארבעה, אף על גב דבמתניתין תשעה תנן בר מחורגו שאין בן וחתן עמו, לקמן פריך להו. **תלתין ותרתין** — שמנה אבות ושמנה בנים ושמנה חתנים ושמנה בני בנים, ואף על גב דאיכא תו שמנה חתנים שם חתנות חד קרי ליה.

NOTES

in our Gemara, begins with a reference to two fathers (who are brothers) who each have sons and grandsons. These "fathers" (brothers) of the verse represent the first degree of kinship; their "sons" represent the second degree; and their sons' sons, the third degree. The Gemara assumes that any kinship to a first-degree relative is stronger than that to a second-degree relative. Thus a grandnephew's relationship to his great-uncle (third to first) is considered stronger than his relationship to his uncle (third to second). One exception to this generational hierarchy is the relationship between father and son, which is considered to be that of first degree to first degree despite the difference in generations.

תְּלָתִין וְתַרְתֵּין הָוֵי It is thirty-two. The Rishonim ask why only eight additional categories of relatives result from factoring in third-degree relatives? When both grandsons and grandsons-in-law are included, this adds sixteen types of relatives, bringing the total to forty! *Tosafot* suggests that the grandsons are not included in the tally, because they are not specified in the Mishnah. *Rashi* explains that it is the grandsons-in-law who are excluded from the count, as they are subsumed under the general category of sons-in-law.

HALAKHAH

(each others' second cousins) are considered third-degree relatives. A third-degree relative is always considered eligible to testify, even in regard to a first-degree relative; a second-degree relative is ineligible to testify about a first-degree relative or another second-degree relative; and a first-degree relative is ineligible to testify about another first-degree relative or a second-degree relative. The above system of degrees of kinship also applies to female relatives (with the practical implications being relevant to their husbands, who, as we learned in the Gemara, are considered to have the identical kinship status as their wives). Hence, two sisters or a brother and sister, be they from a common father or a common mother, are first-degree relatives; their children, whether boys or girls, are each other's second-degree relatives; and their grandsons and granddaughters are each other's third-degree relations. And some say (*Rabbenu Tam* in accordance with Rav in our Gemara) that third-degree and first-degree relatives are ineligible to testify about each other as well. According to *Rema,* this opinion should be adopted in practice." (*Shulḥan Arukh, Ḥoshen Mishpat* 33:2.)

[1]וְאַמַּאי קָרֵי לֵיהּ חֲתַן בְּנוֹ? [2]כֵּיוָן דְּמֵעָלְמָא קָאָתֵי, [3]כְּדוֹר אַחֵר דָּמֵי.

[4]אִי הָכִי, הֲוָה לֵיהּ שְׁלִישִׁי בְּשֵׁנִי — [5]וְרַב אַכְשַׁר שְׁלִישִׁי בְּשֵׁנִי!

[6]אֶלָּא, רַב דְּאָמַר כְּרַבִּי אֶלְעָזָר, [7]דְּתַנְיָא: ״רַבִּי אֶלְעָזָר אוֹמֵר: [8]כְּשֵׁם שֶׁאֲחִי אַבָּא לֹא יָעִיד לִי — הוּא וּבְנוֹ וַחֲתָנוֹ; [9]כָּךְ בֶּן אֲחִי אַבָּא לֹא יָעִיד לִי — הוּא וּבְנוֹ וַחֲתָנוֹ״.

LITERAL TRANSLATION

[1]But why would [Rav] refer to him as his son's son-in-law? [2]Since he comes from the [outside] world, [3]he is considered as another generation.

[4]If so, it is [a case of] a third-degree [relative testifying] about a second-degree [relative] — [5]and Rav sanctioned [the testimony of] a third-degree [relative] about a second-degree [relative]!

[6]Rather, what Rav said is in accordance with Rabbi Elazar, [7]for it is taught: "Rabbi Elazar says: [8]Just as father's brother may not testify about me — [neither] he nor his son nor his son-in-law; [9]so, too, the son of [my] father's brother shall not testify about me — [neither] he nor his son nor his son-in-law."

TRANSLATION AND COMMENTARY

וְאַמַּאי [1]**But why,** then, **would** Rav not allow his own son or son-in-law to testify against his uncle — a third-degree relative against a first-degree relative — thereby implying that Rav explains that "his son-in-law" in our Mishnah **refers** to **his son's son-in-law?** Rav's reasoning was as follows: [2]**Since** a son-in-law, unlike other relatives, **comes from the outside** and is not related to the defendant by blood, [3]**he is considered as** if removed from him by **another generation.** Hence, the son-in-law identified in our Mishnah (who truly is the principal's own) is nonetheless considered to be the equivalent of a third-degree relative. By implication, a third-degree relative by blood — such as his son — is ineligible to testify as well.

אִי הָכִי [4]But there is also a difficulty with this reasoning: **If** it is indeed **so,** that the son-in-law referred to in our Mishnah must be considered as a third-degree relative, **it** would mean that the Mishnah **is** disqualifying **a third-degree** relative (the son-in-law) from testifying **about a second-degree** relative (his wife's first cousin) — [5]**and** yet we find that **Rav** himself **sanctioned** the testimony of **a third-degree** relative **about a second-degree** relative. As Rav said: "Neither I nor my son" may testify against him (the uncle), implying that Rav's son (a third-degree relative) could testify against Rav's uncle's son (a second-degree relative).

אֶלָּא [6]**Rather,** we must say as follows: **What Rav said** above, regarding the invalidation of a third-degree relative, is not based on a reinterpretation of our Mishnah (the principal's son-in-law is indeed a second-degree relative); but rather it **is in accordance with** the position of the Tanna **Rabbi Elazar,** [7]**for it is taught** in a Baraita as follows: **"Rabbi Elazar says:** [8]**Just as my father's brother may not testify** about **me** — neither **he nor his son nor his son-in-law** may do so; [9]**also, the son of** my **father's brother shall not testify about me** — neither **he nor his son nor his son-in-law** may do so." It is evident from Rabbi Elazar's statement that even a third-degree relative (such as his first cousin's son or his son-in-law) may not testify about him.

RASHI

ואמאי קרי ליה — רב לחתנו דמתניתין חתן בנו כיון דחתן לא הוי מזרעו ומעלמא אתי, כדור שלישי חשיב ליה רב, והלכך בני נמי לאחי אבא דהוי שלישי בראשון פסול, ואיכא לאקשויי לרב: כיון דאמר חתן כדור אחד דמי, אמאי פסול חתנו לאחי אבא? הוה ליה רביעי בראשון! אלא מילתא אחריתי אקשי ליה, עד דאפקיה מהאי טעמא לגמרי. **אי הכי** דחתן נמי כדור אחר דמי, וקתני מתניתין: חתן אחי אבא פסול לי הוה ליה שלישי פסול להעיד בשני, ורב אכשר שלישי בשני דקאמר אף אני לא אעיד לו אני ובני, אבל בני לבנו — יעיד. הכי גרסינן: **אלא רב דאמר כרבי אלעזר** — ולעולם חתן לאו כדור אחר דמי, ורב דפסיל שלישי בראשון כרבי אלעזר דאמר שלישי בשני פסול. וכל שכן שלישי בראשון. ומיהו לית הלכתא כוותיה, דאמרינן ב״יש נוחלין״ (בבא בתרא קכח,א): דשלישי (בראשון) כשר, והלכתא כוותיה דרב מדבתראי הוא. **בן בנו של אחי אבא** — לדידי הוי שלישי בשני, ורב שלישי בראשון נפקא ליה מדכתיב ״בנים״ הוו שנים.

NOTES

וְרַב אַכְשַׁר שְׁלִישִׁי בְּשֵׁנִי **Rav sanctioned the testimony of a third-degree [relative] about a second-degree [relative].** According to *Rashi*, the Gemara concludes this because Rav only forbade his son (a third-degree relative) from testifying about his son's great-uncle (first degree), while not mentioning any ineligibility of his son in regard to the son's uncle (second degree). Other commentators maintain that the Gemara's contention is not based upon an inference from Rav's earlier statement, but rather that this statement of Rav's sanctioning the testimony of third-degree relatives about second-degree relatives is an independent report of a decision made by Rav (*Rabbenu Yonah*).

TRANSLATION AND COMMENTARY

וְאַכַּתִּי [1]The Gemara continues to seek clarification: **But it is still** difficult, for Rabbi Elazar says that **a third-degree** relative is ineligible to testify **about a second**-degree relative (Rabbi Elazar himself), [2]**and** yet we learned above that **Rav sanctioned** the testimony of **a third**-degree relative **about a second**-degree relative!

רַב סָבַר לֵיהּ [3]Rather, we must say that **Rav** ruled similarly to Rabbi Elazar **in one** regard (concerning a third-degree relative's ineligibility to testify about a first-degree relative), [4]**but argued against him in** the other regard (concerning the same individual's eligibility to testify about a second-degree relative). [5]**What is Rav's reason** for distinguishing between these two cases? It stems from an alternative interpretation of our verse from Exodus — [6]**for the verse states: "Fathers shall not be put to death because of sons and sons."** Because of the seemingly extra "and," the verse should be understood **to** mean "Fathers shall not be put to death because of sons and their sons," [7]and **to include another generation** of sons (one's son's sons) among those considered ineligible to testify. However, since even according to this reading the verse limits itself to grandfathers and grandsons (a first-degree/third-degree relationship), there is no basis for extending the ineligibility to second-degree/third-degree relationships.

וְרַבִּי אֶלְעָזָר [8]**And Rabbi Elazar**, who indeed did generalize in this way, bases himself upon an additional inference in the verse: [9]**The Torah states** that "fathers shall not be put to death **because of sons** (עַל בָּנִים)." The literal meaning of the words עַל בָּנִים — "upon sons" — suggests the following to Rabbi Elazar: In determining who is ineligible to testify about sons, [10]simply **extend those** categories of **unfit** relationships relevant to **"fathers"** (first-, second-, and third-degree relations) **to the "sons"** as well. Consequently, a third-degree relation (such as a grandson or grandnephew) is also ineligible to testify about his uncle (a second-degree relation).

אָמַר רַב נַחְמָן [11]The Gemara cites a new statement relevant to our Mishnah: **Rav Naḥman said: My mother-in-law's brother** may **not testify in regard to me;** [12]**the son of my mother-in-law's brother** may **not testify in regard to me;** [13]and **the son of my mother-in-law's sister** may **not testify in regard to me.** [14]**And** it can be said that **our Tanna** in the Mishnah also **taught** all these relationships, for it is stated there:

[1]וְאַכַּתִּי הָוָה לֵיהּ שְׁלִישִׁי בְּשֵׁנִי,
[2]וְרַב אַכְשַׁר שְׁלִישִׁי בְּשֵׁנִי!
[3]רַב סָבַר לֵיהּ כְּוָותֵיהּ בַּחֲדָא,
[4]וּפָלֵיג עֲלֵיהּ בַּחֲדָא. [5]מַאי טַעְמָא דְּרַב? [6]דְּאָמַר קְרָא: "לֹא יוּמְתוּ אָבוֹת עַל בָּנִים וּבָנִים" — [7]לְרַבּוֹת דּוֹר אַחֵר.
[8]וְרַבִּי אֶלְעָזָר? [9]"עַל בָּנִים" אָמַר רַחֲמָנָא — [10]פְּסוּלֵי דְּאָבוֹת שְׁדֵי אַבָּנִים.
[11]אָמַר רַב נַחְמָן: אֲחִי חֲמוֹתִי לֹא יָעִיד לִי; [12]בֶּן אֲחִי חֲמוֹתִי לֹא יָעִיד לִי; [13]בֶּן אֲחוֹת חֲמוֹתִי לֹא יָעִיד לִי. [14]וְתָנָא תּוּנָא:

LITERAL TRANSLATION

[1]But it is still [a case of] a third-degree [relative testifying] about a second-degree [relative], [2]and Rav sanctioned [the testimony of] a third-degree [relative] about a second-degree [relative]!

[3]Rav had an opinion like his in one [regard], [4]but argued with him in another [regard]. [5]What is Rav's reason? [6]For the verse states: "Fathers shall not be put to death because of sons; and sons" — [7]in order to include another generation [as unfit].

[8]And Rabbi Elazar? [9]"Because of (lit., 'upon') sons," the Torah stated — [10]throw those unfit for fathers onto the sons.

[11]Rav Naḥman said: My mother-in-law's brother may not testify about me; [12]the son of my mother-in-law's brother may not testify about me; [13][and] the son of my mother-in-law's sister may not testify about me. [14]And our Tanna taught [as well]:

RASHI

וי״ו לרבות בני בנים — דפסולין לאבות, דהוה שלישי בראשון. **רבי אלעזר** — כרב סבירא ליה דוי״ו לרבות אתא, ודריש "על בנים" למימר דכל דפסילי לאבות פסול לבנים. הלכך כי היכי דשלישי בראשון פסול, שלישי בשני נמי פסול. **ותנא תונא** — תנא דידן, כמו אבונא, אחונא. חתן בעל אחותי, פסול לי ואני לו, שאני אחי חמותו. ואני לחתן בעל אחות אבי — בן אחי חמותו אני, ולחתן

NOTES

לֹא יוּמְתוּ אָבוֹת עַל בָּנִים וּבָנִים **Fathers shall not be put to death because of sons and sons.** *Rashi* and *Ramah* indicate that Rav's interpretation of the verse is facilitated by the seemingly superfluous attachment of the letter *vav* (the conjunction "and") to the word בָּנִים ("sons") in its second appearance in the verse. The rules of hermeneutics allow Rav to infer an additional detail from the appearance of that one letter. *Rashash*, on the other hand, as given in our commentary, understands Rav's interpretation as based upon a straightforward reading of the verse — albeit with different punctuation. When a comma is placed after the second appearance of "sons," the verse implies that a father may not be put to death "because of [either his] sons or [their] sons."

[1]״בַּעַל אֲחוֹתוֹ, וּבַעַל אֲחוֹת אָבִיו, וּבַעַל אֲחוֹת אִמּוֹ — [2]הֵן וּבְנֵיהֶן וַחֲתָנֵיהֶן״.
[3]אָמַר רַב אַשִׁי: כִּי הָוֵינַן בֵּי עוּלָּא, [4]אִיבָּעֵי לָן: [5]אֲחִי חָמִיו מַהוּ? [6]בֶּן אֲחִי חָמִיו מַהוּ? [7]בֶּן אֲחוֹת חָמִיו מַהוּ? [8]אָמַר לָן: ״תְּנִיתוּהָ: [9]אָחִיו, וְאָחִי אָבִיו, וְאָחִי אִמּוֹ — [10]הֵן וּבְנֵיהֶן וַחֲתָנֵיהֶן״.
[11]רַב אִיקְלַע לְמִזְבַּן [28B] גְּוִילֵי. [12]בָּעוּ מִינֵּיהּ: מַהוּ שֶׁיָּעִיד אָדָם בְּאֵשֶׁת חוֹרְגוֹ? [13]בְּסוּרָא אָמְרִי: בַּעַל כְּאִשְׁתּוֹ. [14]בְּפוּמְבְּדִיתָא אָמְרִי: אִשָּׁה כְּבַעְלָהּ.

LITERAL TRANSLATION

[1]"His sister's husband, and his father's sister's husband, and his mother's sister's husband — [2]they and their sons and their sons-in-law."

[3]Rav Ashi said: When we were in Ulla's house, [4]we asked: [5]What is [the law concerning] one's father-in-law's brother? [6]What is [the law concerning] the son of one's father-in-law's brother? [7]What is [the law concerning] the son of one's father-in-law's sister? [8]He said to us: You have learned it: [9]"His brother and his father's brother and his mother's brother — [10]they and their sons and their sons-in-law."

[11]Rav happened to be buying [28B] parchments. [12]They asked of him: What is [the law regarding] a man testifying about his stepson's wife? [13][Rav answered:] In Sura they said: A husband is like his wife. [14]In Pumbedita they said: A wife is like her husband.

TRANSLATION AND COMMENTARY

[1]**"His sister's husband, and his father's sister's husband, and his mother's sister's husband** — [2]**they and their sons and their sons-in-law** [are ineligible to testify about him and he about them]." To his mother-in-law's brother, Rav Naḥman is the sister's son-in-law; to the son of his mother-in-law's brother, he is the father's sister's son-in-law; and to the son of his mother-in-law's sister, he is the mother's sister's son-in-law. Thus Rav Naḥman's pronouncement in regard to these relatives reflects the categories already alluded to in the Mishnah's reference to sons-in-law.

אָמַר רַב אַשִׁי [3]**Rav Ashi said: When we were** reviewing these laws **in Ulla's house** of study, [4]**we asked** the following questions: [5]**What is** the law concerning the eligibility of **one's father-in-law's brother?** [6]**What is** the law concerning **the son of one's father-in-law's brother?** [7]And **what is** the law concerning **the son of one's father-in-law's sister?** [8]Ulla **said to us: You have** already **learned** the answer to these questions in the Mishnah, for it is stated there: [9]**"His brother and his father's brother and his mother's brother** — [10]**they and their sons and their sons-in-law** [are all ineligible to testify about him and he about them]." To one's father-in-law's brother, one is the brother's son-in-law; to one's father-in-law's brother's son, one is the father's brother's son-in-law; and to one's father-in-law's sister's son, one is the mother's brother's son-in-law. Thus all the relatives you inquired about are disqualified by the Mishnah.

רַב אִיקְלַע [11]It is told that once, when **Rav happened to be buying** [28B] **parchments,** [12]some people **asked him: What is** the law about **a man testifying about his stepson's wife** in a civil case brought against her? Since — unlike all principal relatives — the Mishnah specifically allows a person to testify about his stepson's son, is it possible that the man's wife, too, may be testified about? Rav answered: **In Sura they said** that **a husband is like his wife.** [13]Consequently, the stepfather becomes, as it were, his stepson's father. Since a biological father is ineligible to testify about his daughter-in-law, so, too, is the stepfather ineligible to testify about his stepson's wife. [14]**In Pumbedita they put it** slightly differently, but with the same consequence, that **a wife is like her husband.** Since a stepfather cannot testify about his stepson, so, too, is he ineligible to testify about his stepson's wife.

RASHI

בעל אחות אמי — בן אחות חמותו אני, מילתיה דרב נחמן מחתניהן דקתני מתניתין יליף. וכן מילתיה דרב אשי מחתניהן, דאחיו ואחי אביו ואח אמו שפסולין לו והוא להם, הוי איהו לגבייהו אחי חמיו, ובן אחי חמיו, ובן אחות חמיו. **גוילי** — קלפים. **באשת חורגו** — על נכסי מלוג שלה בהשפטה עם אדם מן השוק. ובנשי שאר קרובים לא איבעי להו, דכיון דבניהם פסולין לו והוא להם — פסול אף לנשים, לפי שהבנים ראויין לירש את אמן. אבל חורגו דבנו כשר מיבעיא לן באשתו. **בעל באשתו** — ואשה כבעלה, והרי הוא כאילו חמיה ותנן (כז,ב): חמיו פסול, קרוב הוא.

NOTES

בַּעַל כְּאִשְׁתּוֹ...וְאִשָּׁה כְּבַעְלָהּ **A husband is like his wife...and a wife is like her husband.** Our commentary follows *Rashi*, who views Rav as citing both principles in order to address the single issue posed to him — that of a man testifying about his stepson's wife. Several other Rishonim (*Ramah, Rabbi Yehonatan of Lunel* and others) suggest that, whereas

HALAKHAH

בַּעַל כְּאִשְׁתּוֹ...וְאִשָּׁה כְּבַעְלָהּ **A husband is like his wife...and a wife is like her husband.** "If a man is ineligible to testify about a woman because of kinship, he is equally ineligible to testify about her husband, for a husband is like his wife

[1] דְּאָמַר רַב הוּנָא אָמַר רַב נַחְמָן: [2] מִנַּיִין שֶׁהָאִשָּׁה כְּבַעְלָהּ? [3] דִּכְתִיב: "עֶרְוַת אֲחִי אָבִיךָ לֹא תְגַלֵּה; אֶל אִשְׁתּוֹ לֹא תִקְרָב, דֹּדָתְךָ הִיא". [4] וַהֲלֹא אֵשֶׁת דּוֹדוֹ הִיא? [5] מִכְּלָל דְּאִשָּׁה כְּבַעְלָהּ.

[6] "וּבַעַל אִמּוֹ, הוּא וּבְנוֹ וַחֲתָנוֹ". [7] "בְּנוֹ" — [8] הַיְינוּ אָחִיו? [9] אָמַר רַבִּי יִרְמְיָה: לֹא נִצְרְכָה אֶלָּא לַאֲחִי הָאָח.

[10] רַב חִסְדָּא אַכְשַׁר בְּאַחֵי הָאָח. [11] אָמְרוּ לֵיהּ: לָא שְׁמִיעַ לָךְ הָא דְּרַבִּי יִרְמְיָה? [12] אֲמַר לְהוּ: לָא שְׁמִיעַ לִי, כְּלוֹמַר, [13] לָא סְבִירָא לִי. [14] אִי הָכִי הַיְינוּ "אָחִיו"?

LITERAL TRANSLATION

[1] For Rav Huna said in the name of Rav Naḥman: [2] From where [do we know] that a wife is like her husband? [3] For it is written: "You shall not uncover the nakedness of your father's brother; you shall not approach his wife, she is your aunt." [4] But is she not his uncle's wife? [5] [This proves] by implication that a wife is like her husband.

[6] "And his mother's husband (his stepfather), he and his son and his son-in-law." [7] "His son" — [8] is this [not] "one's brother"? [9] Rabbi Yirmeyah said: It is only needed [to teach us] the [case of his] brother's brother.

[10] Rav Ḥisda sanctioned [testimony] about [his] brother's brother. [11] They said to him: Did you not hear that [teaching] of Rabbi Yirmeyah? [12] He said to them: I did not hear it, meaning, [13] I do not accept it. [14] If so — is this [not] "one's brother"?

RASHI

אחי האח — בן שיש לבעל אמו מאשה אחרת, פסול לו, מפני שהוא אחי אחיו.

TRANSLATION AND COMMENTARY

דְּאָמַר רַב הוּנָא [1] The above principle is well established, **for Rav Huna said in the name of Rav Naḥman:** [2] **From where** in Scripture do we know **that a wife is like her husband?** We know it from the verse in Leviticus (18:14), [3] **for it is written** there: **"You shall not uncover the nakedness of your father's brother; you shall not approach his wife, she is your aunt."** [4] **But is not** this woman, in essence, **his uncle's wife** and not a blood relation? [5] Hence this verse proves **by implication that a wife is like her husband.**

וּבַעַל אִמּוֹ [6] We have learned in our Mishnah that among those ineligible to testify are: **"His mother's husband** [his stepfather] — **he and his son and his son-in-law."** [7] The Gemara asks: Why restate the ineligibility of **"his** stepfather's **son"?** [8] **Is this not** already known from the Mishnah's earlier reference to **"one's brother"** [which also implies a half-brother]? [9] **Rabbi Yirmeyah said:** In our Mishnah, "his stepfather's son" **is only required** to add the case of his half-**brother's** half-**brother**, meaning his stepfather's son from another marriage. Even though there is no blood relationship between them whatsoever, the Mishnah informs us that if they share a common half-brother (related to one of them through the father and to the other through the mother), the two are ineligible to testify about one another.

רַב חִסְדָּא [10] **Rav Ḥisda** once **sanctioned** testimony offered **about** one's half-**brother's** half-**brother**. [11] Those present **said to him: Did you not hear that** teaching **of Rabbi Yirmeyah,** which interprets the Mishnah as invalidating such testimony? [12] Rav Ḥisda **said to them: I did not hear it — meaning:** [13] I heard it but **I do not accept it.** This ruling brings us back to the prior interpretation of the Mishnah. [14] Therefore, the Gemara asks: **If** it is indeed **so,** according to Rav Ḥisda, that the Mishnah simply means a half-brother, then we return to our original question: **Is this not** already known from the Mishnah's earlier reference to **"one's brother"?**

NOTES

Rav indeed does use the principle of Pumbedita (that a wife is like her husband) in order to resolve the question posed to him, he cites the reciprocal principle of Sura (that a husband is like his wife) for the sake of addressing another, related issue — that of testifying about one's stepdaughter's husband. The latter citation implies that a stepdaughter's husband is no different from the stepdaughter herself in regard to the stepfather's eligibility to testify about him.

מִכְּלָל דְּאִשָּׁה כְּבַעְלָהּ It follows by implication that a wife is like her husband. There are those who maintain that the implication of the verse effectively erases any legal distinction between man and wife, rendering them, as it were, one "corporate entity." However, many of the Rishonim maintain otherwise: The verse, in referring to one's uncle's wife as his aunt, intends only to imply that a woman takes on the identity of her husband, an idea that is also reflected in the legal conception of marriage as the bride's entry into her husband's domain. However, the reverse principle — that a husband takes on his wife's identity — is by no means suggested in the verse, and thus is only adopted in specific instances.

HALAKHAH

in this regard. Conversely, if a man is ineligible to testify about a certain man because of kinship, he is also ineligible to testify about the man's wife, for a woman, too, is like her husband in these matters." These two rulings are based on the dicta of Sura and Pumbedita. (*Shulḥan Arukh, Ḥoshen Mishpat* 33:3.)

אֲחִי הָאָח One's half-brother's half-brother. "Two individuals whose only family connection is that they have a

TRANSLATION AND COMMENTARY

Hence, Rav Ḥisda would have to explain the Mishnah as follows: [1]The Tanna first **taught** us of the ineligibility associated with **one's paternal brother, and** now — in the reference to his stepfather's son — [2]**he is teaching** us about the ineligibility associated with **one's maternal brother.**

אָמַר רַב חִסְדָּא [3]The Gemara now goes on to discuss other relationships not covered in our Mishnah. **Rav Ḥisda said:** Although marriage creates new bonds of kinship with implications invalidating testimony, **the groom's father and the bride's father** are not affected by that bond and **may** continue to **testify about one another** in all matters; [4]for **their** relationship **to one another is nothing more than** that of **a lid to a barrel.**

אָמַר [5]**Rabbah bar Bar Ḥanah said: A man may testify about his betrothed wife,** for until the marriage is completed, they are not considered to be relatives. [6]**Ravina said: We only said** this **regarding** testimony aimed at **removing** money or property **from** his betrothed; [7]**however, he is not believed in regard to** testimony aimed at **crediting her** with money or property she is claiming as hers, for his own future interest in her estate renders him a biased witness.

וְלָא הִיא [8]The Gemara rejects the preceding opinion: In truth, **this is not so,** [9]**because there is no difference between** testimony aimed at **removing** money or property from her **and** testimony aimed at **crediting** her. [10]In either case her betrothed **is not believed.** [11]**For what was your intention** in suggesting that under certain circumstances a person may testify about his betrothed? [12]Perhaps you have inferred a lack of kinship **in accordance with what Rabbi Ḥiyya bar Ammi stated in the name of Ulla:** [13]"If **one's betrothed wife** should

[1]תָּנָא אָחִיו מִן הָאָב, [2]וְקָתָנֵי אָחִיו מִן הָאֵם.

[3]אָמַר רַב חִסְדָּא: אֲבִי חָתָן וַאֲבִי כַלָּה מְעִידִין זֶה עַל זֶה, [4]וְלֹא דָּמוּ לַהֲדָדֵי אֶלָּא כִּי אַכְלָא לְדַנָּא.

[5]אָמַר רַבָּה בַּר בַּר חָנָה: מֵעִיד אָדָם לְאִשְׁתּוֹ אֲרוּסָה. [6]אָמַר רָבִינָא: לָא אֲמָרַן אֶלָּא לְאַפּוֹקֵי מִינָּהּ; [7]אֲבָל לְעַיּוֹלֵי לָהּ, לָא מְהֵימַן.

[8]וְלָא הִיא. [9]לָא שְׁנָא לְאַפּוֹקֵי וְלָא שְׁנָא לְעַיּוֹלֵי — [10]לָא מְהֵימַן. [11]מַאי דַּעְתֵּיךְ? [12]כְּדַאֲמַר רַבִּי חִיָּיא בַּר אַמִי מִשְּׁמֵיהּ דְּעוּלָּא: [13]״אִשְׁתּוֹ אֲרוּסָה

LITERAL TRANSLATION

[1]He taught [us about] his paternal brother, [2]and [now] he is teaching [us about] his maternal brother.

[3]Rav Ḥisda said: The groom's father and the bride's father may testify about one another, [4]and their [relationship] to one another is nothing more than that of a lid to a barrel.

[5]Rabbah bar Bar Ḥanah said: A man may testify about his betrothed wife. [6]Ravina said: We only said [this] regarding removing [property] from her; [7]but for crediting her, he is not believed.

[8]But this is not so. [9]There is no difference between removing and crediting — [10][for in either case] he is not believed. [11]What was your intention [in permitting him to testify]? [12][That the law is] in accordance with what Rabbi Ḥiyya bar Ammi said in the name of Ulla: [13]"His betrothed wife

BACKGROUND

אַכְלָא לְדַנָּא Lid to a barrel. According to *Rashi's* commentary, the אַכְלָא or lid is not a permanent part of the keg which belonged to it from the moment it was made. Rather the אַכְלָא is a temporary cover of the keg that is not similar to it, and sometimes it is not even made of the same kind of material at all.

RASHI

אבי חתן ואבי כלה — בן ראובן שנשא בת שמעון לא נתקרבו ראובן ושמעון בכך — וכשרין להעיד זה לזה בכל עדיות, ולא אמרינן בשביל בנו שנתקרב ראובן לשמעון נפסל ראובן לשמעון. **ולא דמו** — ראובן ושמעון להדדי. **אלא כי אבלא לדנא** — כמגופה שאינה דומה לחבית. **לאפוקי מינה** — לחוב לה ולזכות לבעל דינה, דקרוב לא הוי כל זמן שלא נשאה, ומיהו לעיולי לה לא מהימן, דאדעתא דידיה קעביד. **מאי דעתיך** — דלא חשבת ליה קרוב.

NOTES

כִּי אַכְלָא לְדַנָּא As the lid to the barrel. The Geonim translate the expression, "as the pestle to the mortar," to imply that, aside from not being related, the fathers of the bride and the groom are often in opposition, like a pestle grinding against a mortar.

HALAKHAH

common half-brother, but who themselves are born of different parents, may testify about one another, for theirs is not considered to be a blood relationship." This ruling is in accordance with the position of Rav Ḥisda in our Gemara. (*Shulḥan Arukh, Ḥoshen Mishpat* 33:7.)

אֲבִי חָתָן וַאֲבִי כַלָּה The father of the groom and the father of the bride. "The fathers of the bride and groom may testify about one another, for they are not relatives; in accordance with Rav Ḥisda. Nevertheless, neither one may judge a case concerning the other, for it is assumed that their feelings toward each other will unduly influence their judgment. If, however, one of them did serve as a judge in the other's case, the judgment stands (*Rema*). Regarding their serving together on the same court in someone else's case, there is no problem whatsoever (*Netivot HaMishpat*)." (*Shulḥan Arukh, Ḥoshen Mishpat* 33:6.)

אִשְׁתּוֹ אֲרוּסָה His betrothed wife. "A bridegroom may not testify about his betrothed even before their marriage is finalized, as their close feelings for each other render them equivalent to actual relatives (in accordance with the

TRANSLATION AND COMMENTARY

die, **he does not mourn** for her in the ritual manner (see *Yevamot*, 73-4); **or** if he is a priest, **he may not defile himself for her** through contact with her corpse. [1]**And similarly,** if he died, **she does not mourn** for him in the ritual manner **nor defile herself for him** if there are others to attend to his burial. [2]If **she died, he does not inherit from her;** [3]**but** if **he died, she collects her ketubah** settlement, should he have voluntarily written her a marriage contract during their betrothal (see *Bava Metzia* 18a)." If this indeed is the source of your ruling, then it is based upon a misplaced inference — [4]for **there,** in the case of a person whose betrothed died, **the Torah made** the obligation of mourning, as well as the rights of inheritance, [5]**contingent upon** the deceased's being **"his flesh"** (see Leviticus 21:2 and Numbers 27:11); and a betrothed spouse **is still not** completely **"his flesh,"** since the couple have not yet consummated their union and become "one flesh" (Genesis 2:24). [6]**Here,** however, in the case of one who wishes to testify about his betrothed, we declare him ineligible **because of** his **feelings** of closeness toward her; [7]**and** we must assume that **he** already **possesses feelings** of closeness **toward her** even before their marriage.

— לֹא אוֹנֵן וְלֹא מִטַּמֵּא לָהּ. [1]וְכֵן הִיא, לֹא אוֹנֶנֶת וְלֹא מִטַּמְּאָה לוֹ. [2]מֵתָה, אֵינוֹ יוֹרְשָׁהּ; [3]מֵת הוּא, גּוֹבָה כְּתוּבָּתָהּ". [4]הָתָם, בִּ"שְׁאֵרוֹ" תָּלָה רַחֲמָנָא, [5]אַכַּתִּי לָאו "שְׁאֵרוֹ" הִיא. [6]הָכָא, מִשּׁוּם אִיקְרוּבֵי דַּעְתָּא הוּא, [7]וְהָא אִיקַּרְבָא דַּעֲתֵיהּ לְגַבָּהּ.

LITERAL TRANSLATION

— he does not mourn or defile himself for her. [1]And similarly, she does not mourn or defile herself for him. [2][If] she dies, he does not inherit from her; [3]but [if] he dies, she collects her ketubah." [4][But] there, the Torah made it contingent upon her [being] "his flesh," [5][and] she is still not "his flesh." [6]Here, it is because of feelings of closeness, [7]and he [already] possesses feelings of closeness toward her.

RASHI

לא אונן — אם מתה אינו נאסר בקדשים מחמת אנינות. **ואין מטמא לה** — אם כהן הוא. ואית דלא גרסי: אינה מטמאה, וכן היא אינה נאסרת באנינות מיתתו בקדשים ואינה מטמאה — אינה מצווה להתעסק בו, ואיידי דתנא לא אוננת תנא ולא מיטמאת, ולאו דווקא — דנשים דכהונה לא הוזהרו על הטומאה. **גובה כתובתה** — בדכתב לה מן האירוסין מוקמינן לה ב"שנים אוחזין" (בבא מציעא יח, א), והא דקתני לא מטמא לה קא סמכת ואמרת לאו קרוב הוא? **התם** — גבי טומאה וירושה. **בשארו תלה רחמנא** — כדכתיב (ויקרא כא): "כי אם לשארו הקרוב", ואמר מר (יבמות כב,ב): שארו — זו אשתו, וכן בירושת הבעל לשארו הקרוב אליו ממשפחתו וירש אותה — מיכן שהבעל יורש את אשתו ב"יש נוחלין" (בבא בתרא קט,ב).

NOTES

וְלֹא מִטַּמְּאָה לוֹ And she does not defile herself for him. *Rashi* asks of the Baraita: As females of the priestly class are permitted to come into contact with impurity, why would this woman be forbidden to defile herself for her betrothed? In response, he suggests: Although normally one is obligated to defile oneself for close relatives who have died (see *Sotah* 3a), a betrothed woman need not do so for her husband, unless she so wishes. Elsewhere (*Yevamot* 29b), *Rashi* and *Tosafot* offer an alternative explanation: During the Festival days, when all Jews must refrain from defiling themselves unnecessarily, a betrothed woman must also abstain from defiling herself for her deceased bridegroom.

מִשּׁוּם אִיקְרוּבֵי דַּעְתָּא Because of feelings of closeness. Various commentators ask (see *Minḥat Ḥinukh*, Commandment 589): Why does the Gemara state here that the ineligibility of relatives to testify about one another logically derives from their close feelings for each other, when it has already been established that it is based on a Scriptural decree (see above, 27b)? Some suggest that the Gemara intended to inform us that the special feelings of a betrothed couple renders them equivalent to relatives, thereby implying that they are also disqualified by this Scriptural source. However, unlike other relatives included in the verse, they may testify about each other's close

HALAKHAH

conclusion of the Gemara). Further, the bridegroom may not testify about his betrothed bride's relatives; however, if he does, his testimony is valid. The above ruling only applies to a couple who are formally betrothed through *kiddushin* — an act forbidding the bride to marry anyone else — and not to a couple who are merely engaged to marry. Nevertheless, it may be that even in this latter case a man would be prohibited from testifying in his fiancée's favor regarding a monetary issue (*Rema*)." (*Shulḥan Arukh, Ḥoshen Mishpat* 33:9; also see *Rambam, Sefer Shofetim, Hilkhot Edut* 13:14.)

לֹא אוֹנֵן וְלֹא מִטַּמֵּא לָהּ He does not mourn or defile himself for her. "One whose betrothed wife dies, does not mourn for her as he would for other relatives, nor does he inherit from her; and if he is a priest, he does not defile himself for her. Similarly, a betrothed woman does not mourn her deceased bridegroom, nor is she obligated to defile herself for him, although she may do so if she so wishes" (*Shakh*). (*Shulḥan Arukh, Yoreh De'ah* 373:4, 374:4; *Even HaEzer* 55:5.)

מֵת הוּא, גּוֹבָה כְּתוּבָּתָהּ If he dies, she collects her ketubah settlement. "A betrothed woman whose husband wrote her a marriage contract at the time of their betrothal, collects the base sum of her settlement (either two hundred or one hundred zuz, depending on the circumstances) should her bridegroom die before the marriage is finalized. Any

TRANSLATION AND COMMENTARY

חוֹרְגוֹ לְבַדּוֹ [1]The Gemara now returns to the Mishnah: **"One's stepson, he alone** is considered unfit to testify, but not the stepson's sons or sons-in-law." [2]**Our Rabbis taught** in a related Baraita: "Regarding **his stepson, he alone** is considered unfit to testify. [3]**Rabbi Yose says:** In the case of **his brother-in-law** (his wife's sister's husband), he alone is unfit to testify." [4]**And** in **another** Baraita, it **is taught:** "Regarding **his brother-in-law, he alone** is unfit to testify. [5]**Rabbi Yehudah says:** In the case of **his stepson**, he alone is unfit to testify." These two Baraitot present a number of diverse opinions that puzzle the Gemara. [6]**What is** each of the Tannaim in these two Baraitot **saying?** [7]**If you wish, say** that Rabbi Yehudah (the anonymous author of the first Baraita and the respondent in the second) **is stating the following:** [8]Regarding **one's stepson, he alone** is unfit to testify; [9]**and the law is the same in regard to his brother-in-law** (implying that Rabbi Yehudah in the second Baraita extends Rabbi Yose's position rather than arguing about it). [10]**And Rabbi Yose** (the respondent in the first Baraita and anonymous author of the second) repeated the same teaching: Regarding **his brother-in-law, he alone** is unfit to testify; [11]**and the law is the same in regard to his stepson** (implying that Rabbi Yose in the first Baraita also intends to extend the ruling rather than contradict it). [12]**But** if this is

[1]״חוֹרְגוֹ לְבַדּוֹ״. [2]תָּנוּ רַבָּנַן: ״חוֹרְגוֹ לְבַדּוֹ. [3]רַבִּי יוֹסֵי אוֹמֵר: גִּיסוֹ״. [4]וְתַנְיָא אִידָךְ: ״גִּיסוֹ לְבַדּוֹ. [5]רַבִּי יְהוּדָה אוֹמֵר: חוֹרְגוֹ״. [6]מַאי קָאָמַר? [7]אִילֵימָא הָכִי קָאָמַר: [8]חוֹרְגוֹ לְבַדּוֹ; [9]וְהוּא הַדִּין לְגִיסוֹ. [10]וַאֲתָא רַבִּי יוֹסֵי לְמֵימַר: גִּיסוֹ לְבַדּוֹ, [11]וְהוּא הַדִּין לְחוֹרְגוֹ. [12]אֶלָּא

LITERAL TRANSLATION

[1]"One's stepson, he alone [is unfit]." [2]Our Rabbis taught: "His stepson, he alone. [3]Rabbi Yose says: His brother-in-law." [4]And another [Baraita] was taught: "His brother-in-law, he alone. [5]Rabbi Yehudah says: His stepson." [6]What is he saying? [7]If you [wish] say [that] he is stating thus: [8]His stepson, he alone; [9]and the law is the same in regard to his brother-in-law. [10]And Rabbi Yose came to say: His brother-in-law, he alone; [11]and the law is the same in regard to his stepson. [12]But [then]

RASHI

גיסו – לבדו, אבל בנו וחתנו כשרים לגיסו. ורבי יוסי פליג אמתניתין בתרתי, חדא, דקתני מתניתין בגיסו בן וחתן. ופליג נמי אבעל אחות אמו, דקתני מתניתין דהוה קרוב וכן גם הוא קרוב לו, דהוי לו בן גיסו פסול הוא לו משום דאיהו לדידיה בעל אחות אמו. אבל משום קורבה דבן גיסו לא מיפסיל. ונפקא מינה דחתן גיסו כשר להעיד לו, (והוא הדין לגיסו, והיינו דקתני בברייתא בתרייתא: רבי יהודה אומר: חורגו – אף חורגו, דמודה נמי בגיסו. ואתא רבי יוסי למימר גיסו – לבדו, והוא הדין לחורגו), זהו נוסח אחר בפירוש, ונראה: גיסו לבדו ורבי יוסי פליג אמתניתין בחדא – דקתני מתניתין גיסו ובנו וחתנו (כשרים לגיסו), דאבעל אחות אמו דקתני מתניתין דהוי קרוב וכן גם הוא קרוב לו. דהוי ליה בן גיסו, לא פליג רבי יוסי עלה ומודה הוא דבן גיסו פסול לו, משום דאיהו לדידיה בעל אחות אמו, אבל משום קורבה דבן גיסו לא מפסיל, ונפקא מינה דחתן גיסו כשר וכו׳. מאי גיסו דקאמר רבי יוסי אף גיסו – ומר אמר חדא, ומר אמר חדא ולא פליגי.

NOTES

relatives, until the marriage is finalized. Others suggest that the Gemara's contention is based on Rav Naḥman's earlier interpretation of the verse in Leviticus (18:14), in which he taught that a woman takes on the identity of her husband, making him ineligible to testify against her. Since that verse also refers to an uncle's betrothed wife, it implies that the feelings created by betrothal are sufficient to disqualify one's testimony (*Rabbi Yehudah Bakhrakh*).

Ramah circumvents the difficulty altogether, as his reading of the Gemara replaces the term "close feelings" (אִיקְרוּבֵי דַּעְתָּא) with the term "relationship" (קוּרְבָא). Hence, the Gemara is suggesting that the relevant distinction here is between the special physical relationship of שְׁאֵר ("one's flesh"), necessary in order to permit defilement or inheritance by a spouse, and the ordinary status of קָרוֹב ("relation"), which is sufficient for disqualifying one's testimony and applies to a betrothed.

גִּיסוֹ לְבַדּוֹ, וְהוּא הַדִּין לְחוֹרְגוֹ His brother-in-law, he alone; and all the more so, his stepson. As pointed out by both *Rashi* and *Tosafot*, Rabbi Yose must distinguish between the two cases: Whereas in the case of his stepson, both the son and the son-in-law of someone's stepson are allowed

HALAKHAH

supplemental sum, however, is only collectable if her husband dies after the completion of their marriage." (*Shulḥan Arukh, Even HaEzer* 55:6.)

חוֹרְגוֹ לְבַדּוֹ One's stepson, he alone. "Because spouses are considered first-degree relatives, a husband may not testify about his wife's son or daughter from another marriage or about their respective spouses; nor may he testify about her parents or step-parents. However, he may testify about the children of her children by another marriage, for they are already third-degree relatives in relation to him" (*Sma*). Similarly, his stepson may not testify about him; but his stepson's son would indeed be eligible to do so (*Smag*). (*Shulḥan Arukh, Ḥoshen Mishpat* 33:8.)

גִּיסוֹ His brother-in-law. "The husbands of first-degree relatives (such as two sisters or a mother and a daughter) may not testify about one another; for by assuming their wives' legal identity, they become the equivalent of each other's brother-in-law. However, if their wives were only

TRANSLATION AND COMMENTARY

the explanation of these Baraitot, **who is** the author of **our Mishnah which teaches** that, "regarding **his brother-in-law** — [1]**he and his son and his son-in-law** are all ineligible to testify"? [2]It is **neither like Rabbi Yehudah nor Rabbi Yose** — for both say that the brother-in-law alone is ineligible to testify, but his son may do so!

וְאֶלָּא הָכִי קָאָמַר [3]**Rather** one must explain the Baraitot as follows: Rabbi Yehudah **states thus:** Regarding **his stepson, he alone** is unfit to testify; [4]**but** in the case of **his brother-in-law** — **he and his son and his son-in-law** are all ineligible to testify (implying that Rabbi Yehudah in the second Baraita argues against Rabbi Yose). [5]**And Rabbi Yose** says as follows: Regarding **his brother-in-law, he alone** is unfit to testify; [6]**but** in the case of **his stepson — he and his son and his son-in-law** are all ineligible to testify (implying that Rabbi Yose in the first Baraita intends to argue against Rabbi Yehudah). According to this interpretation, we can attribute our Mishnah to Rabbi Yehudah.

וְאֶלָּא הָא דְּתָנֵי [7]**But** if we interpret the Baraitot as just suggested, **in accordance with whom** is the following Baraita **that** was **taught by Rabbi Ḥiyya:** [8]"Among the ten relatives identified in our Mishnah, there are **eight principal** relatives **who** convey their ineligibility both to their sons and sons-in-law, thereby producing **twenty-four** categories of ineligibility altogether"? [9]It is **neither in accordance with Rabbi Yose nor in accordance with Rabbi Yehudah** — for according to Rabbi Yose, the stepson must be added to the list of principals; and according to Rabbi Yehudah, the son-in-law must be added to that list. In both cases, we now have nine principals and twenty-seven categories of ineligibility!

אֶלָּא, הָכִי קָאָמַר [10]**Rather,** one must say as follows: Rabbi Yehudah, as suggested in the previous interpretation, **states thus:** Regarding **his stepson, he alone** is unfit to testify; [11]**but** in the case of **his brother-in-law — he and his son and his son-in-law** are all ineligible to testify. [12]**And Rabbi Yose teaches**

מַתְנִיתִין דְּקָתָנֵי: ״גִּיסוֹ, [1]הוּא וּבְנוֹ וַחֲתָנוֹ, מַנִּי? [2]לֹא רַבִּי יְהוּדָה וְלֹא רַבִּי יוֹסֵי!

[3]וְאֶלָּא הָכִי קָאָמַר: חוֹרְגוֹ לְבַדּוֹ; [4]אֲבָל גִּיסוֹ — הוּא וּבְנוֹ וַחֲתָנוֹ. [5]וַאֲתָא רַבִּי יוֹסֵי לְמֵימַר: גִּיסוֹ לְבַדּוֹ, [6]אֲבָל חוֹרְגוֹ — הוּא וּבְנוֹ וַחֲתָנוֹ.

[7]וְאֶלָּא הָא דְּתָנֵי רַבִּי חִיָּיא: [8]שְׁמוֹנָה אָבוֹת שֶׁהֵן עֶשְׂרִים וְאַרְבָּעָה, כְּמַאן? [9]לֹא כְּרַבִּי יוֹסֵי וְלֹא כְּרַבִּי יְהוּדָה!

[10]אֶלָּא, הָכִי קָאָמַר: חוֹרְגוֹ לְבַדּוֹ, [11]אֲבָל גִּיסוֹ — הוּא וּבְנוֹ וַחֲתָנוֹ. [12]וַאֲתָא רַבִּי יוֹסֵי

LITERAL TRANSLATION

our Mishnah, which teaches: "His brother-in-law, [1]he and his son and his son-in-law," who is it [like]? [2]Not Rabbi Yehudah and not Rabbi Yose!

[3]Rather, [Rabbi Yehudah] is stating thus: His stepson, he alone; [4]but his brother-in-law — he and his son and his son-in-law. [5]And Rabbi Yose came to say: His brother-in-law, he alone; [6]but his stepson — he and his son and his son-in-law.

[7]But that which Rabbi Ḥiyya taught: [8]Eight principals who are twenty-four, in accordance with whom [is it]? [9][It is] not like Rabbi Yose and not like Rabbi Yehudah!

[10]Rather, [Rabbi Yehudah] states thus: His stepson, he alone; [11]but his brother-in-law — he and his son and his son-in-law. [12]And Rabbi Yose came

RASHI

הכי גרסינן: אלא הכי קאמר: חורגו לבדו, אבל גיסו הוא ובנו וחתנו, ואתא רבי יוסי למימר, גיסו לבדו, אבל חורגו — הוא ובנו וחתנו, אלא הא דתני רבי חייא כו׳ לא רבי יהודה ולא רבי יוסי — דלרבי יהודה תשעה אבות הויין במתניתין בר מחורגו, וכן לרבי יוסי תשעה הוין. אלא חורגו לבדו, אבל גיסו הוא ובנו וחתנו ואתא רבי יוסי למימר גיסו לבדו, וכל שכן חורגו.

NOTES

to testify about him, in the case of his brother-in-law (his wife's sister's husband), only the brother-in-law's son-in-law is eligible. The brother-in-law's son must perforce be ineligible even according to Rabbi Yose; for in agreeing that one's mother's sister's husband (one of the eight principal relatives alluded to by Rabbi Ḥiyya) is ineligible, he automatically disqualifies a brother-in-law's son (that individual being the son's mother's sister's husband).

HALAKHAH

second-degree relatives (such as first cousins), then they may testify about one another, for we do not say that a man is like his wife in regard to testifying about second-degree relatives. For the same reason, the two husbands may testify about each other's children, even if their wives are first-degree relatives. (It should be noted that, as brothers-in-law, they are allowed to testify about each other's children, but if they are also uncles to the child (if the child's mother was his wife's sister) they may not testify about him" — *Rosh*.) The above is in accordance with Rabbi Yose of our Gemara. (*Shulḥan Arukh, Ḥoshen Mishpat* 33:4.)

לְמֵימַר: גִּיסוֹ לְבַדּוֹ, [1]וְכָל שֶׁכֵּן חוֹרְגוֹ. [2]וּמַתְנִיתִין רַבִּי יְהוּדָה. [3]בָּרַיְיתָא רַבִּי יוֹסֵי.
[4]אָמַר רַב יְהוּדָה אָמַר שְׁמוּאֵל: הֲלָכָה כְּרַבִּי יוֹסֵי.
[5]הַהִיא מַתַּנְתָּא דַּהֲוֵי חֲתִימֵי עֲלַהּ תְּרֵי גִּיסֵי. [6]סָבַר רַב יוֹסֵף לְאַכְשׁוּרַהּ, דְּאָמַר רַב יְהוּדָה אָמַר שְׁמוּאֵל: הֲלָכָה כְּרַבִּי יוֹסֵי. [7]אֲמַר לֵיהּ אַבַּיֵי: מִמַּאי דְּרַבִּי יוֹסֵי דְּמַתְנִיתִין, [8]דְּמַכְשַׁר בְּגִיסוֹ? [9]דִּילְמָא רַבִּי יוֹסֵי דִּבְרַיְיתָא, דְּפָסֵיל בְּגִיסוֹ?
[10]לָא סָלְקָא דַּעְתָּךְ, דַּאֲמַר שְׁמוּאֵל: [11]"כְּגוֹן אֲנָא וּפִנְחָס", [12]דַּהֲוֵינַן אַחֵי וְגִיסֵי. [13]אֲבָל גִּיסֵי דְעָלְמָא — שַׁפִּיר דָּמֵי. [14]וְדִילְמָא "כְּגוֹן אֲנָא וּפִנְחָס" [15]מִשּׁוּם דְּגִיסוֹ קָאָמַר!

LITERAL TRANSLATION

to say: His brother-in-law, he alone; [1]and all the more so, his stepson. [2]And our Mishnah [is in accordance with] Rabbi Yehudah. [3]The Baraita [of Rabbi Ḥiyya is in accordance with] Rabbi Yose.

[4]Rav Yehudah said in the name of Shmuel: The law is in accordance with Rabbi Yose.

[5][There was] a certain [deed of] gift which two brothers-in-law had signed. [6]Rav Yosef thought to validate it, for Rav Yehudah said in the name of Shmuel: The law is like Rabbi Yose. [7]Abaye said to him: From what [have you inferred] that it is Rabbi Yose of our Mishnah, [8]who sanctions [testimony] about one's brother-in-law? [9]Perhaps [it is] Rabbi Yose of the Baraita, who disqualifies [testimony] about one's brother-in-law!

[10]This cannot enter your mind, for Shmuel said: [11]"Such as I and Pineḥas," [12]who were [both] brothers and brothers-in-law; [13]however, [regarding] ordinary brothers-in-law — it is fine.

[14]But perhaps he stated "such as I and Pineḥas" [only] [15]because of [being] his brother-in-law!

TRANSLATION AND COMMENTARY

as follows: Regarding **his brother-in-law, he alone** is unfit to testify; [1]**and all the more so** in the case of **his stepson.** [2]According to this interpretation of the Baraitot, **our Mishnah** agrees with the position of **Rabbi Yehudah**, [3]while **the Baraita** of Rabbi Ḥiyya agrees with **Rabbi Yose**, who maintains that only eight of the relatives listed in our Mishnah convey their ineligibility to their sons and sons-in-law.

אָמַר רַב יְהוּדָה [4]**Rav Yehudah said in the name of Shmuel: The law is in accordance with Rabbi Yose.** (The Gemara at this point assumes that Shmuel is referring to Rabbi Yose in our Mishnah, who cited an earlier Mishnaic source limiting ineligibility to those relatives who can be heirs to the party about whom they are testifying. Hence brothers-in-law, who do not inherit from one another, may indeed testify about each other.)

הַהִיא [5]The Gemara relates the following case in regard to Rav Yehudah's ruling: **There was** once **a certain** deed of **gift which two brothers-in-law** (men married to two sisters) had **signed** as witnesses. [6]**Rav Yosef thought of validating** the certificate in spite of the witnesses' kinship, **for Rav Yehudah said in the name of Shmuel** that **the law is in accordance with Rabbi Yose.** Since Rabbi Yose says that brothers-in-law may testify about one another, they may by extension also act jointly as witnesses. [7]**Abaye said to** Rav Yosef: **What** leads you to conclude **that** Shmuel **is** referring to **Rabbi Yose of our Mishnah, who** cites a source **sanctioning** testimony offered **about,** [8]or in conjunction with, **one's brother-in-law?** [9]**Perhaps** he is referring to **Rabbi Yose of the Baraita, who** personally **disqualifies** testimony rendered about, or in conjunction with, **one's brother-in-law!**

לָא סָלְקָא דַּעְתָּךְ [10]Rav Yosef retorted: **This** possibility **cannot enter your mind, for Shmuel** once **said** that the only brothers-in-law who are ineligible to testify are [11]those **"such as I and Pineḥas,"** [12]**who were** both **brothers and brothers-in-law** (having married two sisters). [13]**However,** when it comes to **ordinary brothers-in-law**, **it is** perfectly **proper** for them to testify together about an outsider or about one another — in accordance with Rabbi Yose of our Mishnah.

וְדִילְמָא [14]Abaye persisted: **But perhaps** Shmuel **stated "such as I and Pineḥas"** in all seriousness, with the intention of informing us that even sisters' husbands may be disqualified [15]as a result **of** being each other's **brother-in-law**, and he was not dealing with their other family relationship — thus teaching in accordance with Rabbi Yose of the Baraita!

RASHI

ומתניתין רבי יהודה — דקתני בן וחתן בגיסו. **ברייתא רבי יוסי** — אפיק גיסו וחורגו הוי שמנה אבות ובנים וחתנים, ואית דמוקמי להאי בן גיסו דקא מכשר רבי יוסי בבן שיש לו לגיסו מאשה אחרת, כי היכי דלא לפלוג רבי יוסי אבעל אחות אמו, ולא מיתוקמא שפיר, דכל בניהם דמתניתין מאותה אשה קאמר. ועוד: אי מאשה אחרת מכשיר רבי יוסי, מכלל דתנא דידן מאשה אחרת נמי פסול משום קרוב מחמת קרוב. — תיקשי לרב חסדא דאכשר באחי האב, דהשתא בן גיסו פסול משום אחי בן אחות אשתו, אחי (האת) [האם] מיבעיא. **הלכה כרבי יוסי** — קסלקא דעתך כרבי יוסי דמתניתין דלא פסול אלא קרוב הראוי לירש, וגיסו אינו ראוי ליורשו. **דפסיל בגיסו** — דקתני גיסו לבדו. **לא סלקא דעתך** — דהא בהדיא פריש שמואל לפסולא דגיסו, כגון אנא ופנחס שהיה אחיו וגיסו, מכלל דגיסו דעלמא כשרין. **משום גיסו** — ושמואל פירושא דגיסו אתא לאשמעינן.

[1] אֲמַר לֵיהּ: זִיל קְנְיָהּ בְּעֵדֵי מְסִירָה, [2] כְּרַבִּי אֶלְעָזָר.
[3] וְהָאָמַר רַבִּי אַבָּא: מוֹדֶה רַבִּי אֶלְעָזָר בִּמְזוּיָּף מִתּוֹכוֹ שֶׁהוּא פָּסוּל?!
[4] אֲמַר לֵיהּ: זִיל, [5] לָא שָׁבְקִי לִי דְּאוֹתְבִינֵיהּ לָךְ.
[6] "רַבִּי יְהוּדָה אוֹמֵר כו׳". [7] אָמַר רַבִּי תַּנְחוּם אָמַר רַבִּי טַבְלָא אָמַר רַבִּי בְּרוּנָא אָמַר רַב: הֲלָכָה כְּרַבִּי יְהוּדָה. [8] רָבָא אָמַר רַב נַחְמָן: אֵין הֲלָכָה כְּרַבִּי יְהוּדָה. [9] וְכֵן אָמַר רַבָּה בַּר בַּר חָנָה אָמַר רַבִּי יוֹחָנָן: אֵין הֲלָכָה כְּרַבִּי יְהוּדָה.
[10] אִיכָּא דְּמַתְנֵי לָהּ לְהָא דְּרַבָּה בַּר בַּר חָנָה אַהָא: [11] "אֶת זוֹ דָּרַשׁ רַבִּי יוֹסֵי הַגְּלִילִי: 'וּבָאתָ

LITERAL TRANSLATION

[1] [Rav Yosef] said to him: Go, acquire it with witnesses of delivery, [2] in accordance with Rabbi Elazar.

[3] But did not Rabbi Abba say: Rabbi Elazar agrees that [a document] testifying to its own deception (lit., "forged from within") is invalid?!

[4] [Rav Yosef] said to him: Go. [5] They did not allow me to assign [the gift] to you.

[6] "Rabbi Yehudah says, etc." [7] Rabbi Tanḥum said in the name of Rabbi Tavla, who said in the name of Rabbi Beruna, who said in the name of Rav: The law is in accordance with Rabbi Yehudah. [8] Rava said in the name of Rabbi Naḥman: The law is not in accordance with Rabbi Yehudah. [9] And so said Rabbah bar Bar Ḥannah in the name of Rabbi Yoḥanan: The law is not in accordance with Rabbi Yehudah.

[10] There are those who learn this [ruling] of Rabbah bar Bar Ḥanah with reference to this: [11] "This [verse was] interpreted [by] Rabbi Yose the Galilean: 'And you shall come

TRANSLATION AND COMMENTARY

אֲמַר לֵיהּ [1] Deferring to Abaye, Rav Yosef turned to the bearer of the deed and **said to him: Go** and **acquire** your gift **by** virtue of those **witnesses** who observed the actual **delivery** of the deed of gift to you; [2] and **in accordance with** the position of **Rabbi Elazar** (*Gittin* 3b), who maintains that the essential witnesses who validate a divorce or an act of acquisition (*kinyan*) involving a deed are those who observe its delivery and not those who signed it.

וְהָאָמַר רַבִּי אַבָּא [3] Abaye challenged Rav Yosef once again: **But did not Rabbi Abba say** (there, in *Gittin*) that **Rabbi Elazar agrees** regarding a document **that testifies to its own deception,** being signed by ineligible witnesses, that it **is** indeed **invalid?** The witnesses to delivery are sufficient when there is no signature at all on the document, but not when the signatures are invalid or forged! So, how can you instruct the bearer of this certificate to collect his gift if the document he holds is invalid?

אֲמַר לֵיהּ [4] Rav Yosef finally turned to the bearer and **said to him: Go** — [5] **they did not allow me** any option by which **I could assign** the gift to you.

רַבִּי יְהוּדָה [6] We learned in our Mishnah: "Only someone who was related to the litigant at the time of the trial or at the time of the witnessed event is unfit. However, if he was once a relative to the litigant by marriage, but then became unrelated prior to witnessing the event, when the marriage in question was dissolved through divorce or death, he is then fit to serve as a judge or a witness. **Rabbi Yehudah says:** This rule does not always apply, for a son-in-law is still considered to be a relative even if his wife, the litigant's daughter, died, if he has children from her who perpetuate the kinship." [7] **Rabbi Tanḥum said in the name of Rabbi Tavla, who said in the name of Rabbi Beruna, who said in the name of Rav: The law** here **is in accordance with Rabbi Yehudah.** [8] However, **Rava said in the name of Rabbi Naḥman** that **the law** here **is not in accordance with Rabbi Yehudah.** A man may not testify about his widowed son-in-law, regardless of whether he has grandchildren by him. [9] **And so said Rabbah bar Bar Ḥanah in the name of Rabbi Yoḥanan: The law is not in accordance with Rabbi Yehudah** in our Mishnah.

אִיכָּא דְּמַתְנֵי לָהּ [10] **There are those who learn** that **this** ruling **of Rabbah bar Bar Ḥanah** was stated **with reference to** the following Baraita: [11] **"This** verse from Deuteronomy (17:9) was **interpreted** by **Rabbi Yose the**

RASHI

אמר ליה – למקבל מתנה. זיל קנייה בעדי מסירה – אם יש לך עדים אחרים שמסר לך שטר זה בפניהם, הביאם ויעידו ותהיה שלך. דסבר כרבי אלעזר דאמרינן במסכת גיטין (ג,ב): אפילו לא חתמו בו עדים אלא שנתנו לה בפני עדים – כשר וגובה מנכסים משועבדים, שאין העדים חותמים על הגט אלא מפני תקון העולם. במזויף מתוכו – שחתמו בו עדים פסולים שהוא פסול, דבמאי קני ליה, בהאי שטרא? האי שטרא חספא בעלמא הוא.

HALAKHAH

בִּמְזוּיָּף מִתּוֹכוֹ **A document testifying to its own deception.** "A bill of divorce that is signed by an invalid witness is null and void, even if it was delivered to the woman in the presence of qualified witnesses." (*Shulḥan Arukh, Even HaEzer* 130:17.)

אֶל הַכֹּהֲנִים הַלְוִיִּם וְאֶל הַשּׁוֹפֵט אֲשֶׁר יִהְיֶה בַּיָּמִים הָהֵם׳. [1]וְכִי תַּעֲלֶה עַל דַּעְתְּךָ שֶׁאָדָם הוֹלֵךְ אֵצֶל שׁוֹפֵט שֶׁלֹּא הָיָה בְּיָמָיו? [2]אֶלָּא, זֶה שֶׁהָיָה קָרוֹב וְנִתְרַחֵק״. [3]אָמַר רַבָּה בַּר בַּר חָנָה אָמַר רַבִּי יוֹחָנָן: הֲלָכָה כְּרַבִּי יוֹסֵי הַגְּלִילִי.

[4]בְּנֵי חֲמוּהּ דְּמָר עוּקְבָא [29A] קְרוֹבִים וְנִתְרַחֲקוּ הָווּ. [5]אָתוּ לְקַמֵּיהּ לְדִינָא. [6]אֲמַר לְהוּ: פְּסִילְנָא לְכוּ לְדִינָא. [7]אֲמַרוּ לֵיהּ: מַאי דַּעְתֵּיךְ, [8]כְּרַבִּי יְהוּדָה? [9]אֲנַן מַיְיתִינַן אִיגַּרְתָּא מִמַּעַרְבָא דְּאֵין הֲלָכָה כְּרַבִּי יְהוּדָה! [10]אֲמַר לְהוּ: אַטּוּ בְּקַבָּא דְּקִירָא אִידַּבַּקְנָא בְּכוּ?! [11]דְּלָא קָאָמִינָא פְּסִילְנָא לְכוּ לְדִינָא אֶלָּא מִשּׁוּם דְּלָא צַיְיתִיתוּ דִּינָא.

[12]״אוֹהֵב זֶה שׁוֹשְׁבִינוֹ וכו׳״. [13]וְכַמָּה? [14]אָמַר רַבִּי אַבָּא אָמַר

LITERAL TRANSLATION

to the priests, the Levites, and to the judge who shall be in those days.' [1]But would it enter your mind that a man would go to a judge who was not in his days? [2]Rather, this [is referring to] one who was related and [then] became unrelated." [3]Rabbah bar Bar Ḥanah said in the name of Rabbi Yoḥanan: The law is in accordance with Rabbi Yose the Galilean.

[4]The sons of Mar Ukva's father-in-law [29A] were related [to him] and [then] became unrelated. [5]They came before him for adjudication. [6]He said to them: I am unfit for you as a judge. [7]They said to him: What was your intention [in so teaching]? [8][That the law is] in accordance with Rabbi Yehudah? [9]We are bringing a letter from Eretz Israel (lit., "the West") that the law is not in accordance with Rabbi Yehudah! [10]He said to them: Am I stuck to you with a *kav* of wax?! [11]For I have not said that I am unfit for you as a judge [for any reason] other than that you do not heed judgment.

[12]"His friend, this is his best-man, etc." [13]And [for] how [long]? [14]Rabbi Abba said in the name of

TRANSLATION AND COMMENTARY

Galilean: 'And you shall come to the priests, the Levites, and to the judge who shall be in those days and you shall inquire; and they shall tell you the matter of judgment.' [1]Rabbi Yose queried: **Would it enter your mind** to say **that a man would go to a judge who is not 'in his days,'** i.e., currently eligible to hear the case? [2]**Rather,** one must say that **this** verse hints that **if** the judge **was** once **related** by marriage to the litigant **and** then **became unrelated** (if the marriage was dissolved by death or divorce), the litigant may appear before him 'in those days' that he is permitted to hear his case, after the dissolution of their kinship." [3]And **Rabbah bar Bar Ḥanah said in the name of Rabbi Yoḥanan: The law is in accordance with Rabbi Yose the Galilean.** (Since this Baraita reflects the opinion of the Tanna in our Mishnah who argues against Rabbi Yehudah, this ruling of Rabbah bar Bar Ḥanah's essentially implies, as stated above, that the law is not in accordance with Rabbi Yehudah in our Mishnah.)

בְּנֵי חֲמוּהּ [4]**The sons of Mar Ukva's father-in-law** are an example of relatives [29A] who once **were related** to Mar Ukva, their brother-in-law, **but** who then **became unrelated** when their sister (Mar Ukva's wife) died. [5]It is told that **they** once **came before him for adjudication,** [6]and **he said to them:** Seek someone else, for **I am unfit** to serve **for you as a judge.** [7]**They said to him: Why are you** disqualifying yourself? [8]Do you think that the law is **in accordance with Rabbi Yehudah,** who forbade former in-laws to judge or testify about one another if the deceased left behind children? [9]If so, you should be aware that **we are bringing a letter from Eretz Israel** in which it is written **that the law is not in accordance with Rabbi Yehudah,** and hence you may in fact judge our case! [10]Mar Ukva **said to them** in response: **Am I stuck to you with a *kav* of wax?!** Certainly I realize that our past kinship no longer prevents me from judging your case. Nevertheless, my decision stands, [11]**for I have not said that I am unfit to judge you** for any reason **other than that** I know **you do not heed judgment**; and I am not willing to render a decision that I know will not be honored.

אוֹהֵב זֶה [12]We also learned in our Mishnah, according to Rabbi Yehudah, that "other men who may not serve as judge or witness include a litigant's friend and his enemy. **His friend — this** refers to **his best man** (the principal groomsman at his wedding). His enemy — this refers to anyone who has not spoken with him for at least three days out of animosity." [13]For **how many** days does the best man's ineligibility last? [14]**Rabbi**

RASHI

קרובים ונתרחקו הוו — שמתה אחותם אשת מר עוקבא. בקבא דקירא אידבקי בכו — בקב של שעוה נדבקתי בכם? בתמיה, כלומר: איני דבוק בכם כלל, אלא אתון לא צייתיתון דינא.

LANGUAGE

קִירָא **Wax.** This word derives from the Greek χήρος, *kiros*, meaning "wax."

BACKGROUND

שׁוֹשְׁבִין **Groomsman.** The best man spoken of here is the groom's closest friend, who accompanies him during the time of the festivities and the wedding ceremony. The best man also gives a present to the groom and holds a banquet for him. It was a moral, even a legal, obligation to reciprocate the honor of being a best man by serving as best man to one's own best man when he married, or by having one's son serve as best man to the best man. Nowadays the best man accompanies the bride and groom beneath the bridal canopy, but he does not have the same degree of closeness and importance as in Talmudic times.

HALAKHAH

דַּיָּין אוֹהֵב אוֹ שׂוֹנֵא **A judge who loves or hates.** "One may not act as a judge for any person whom one likes or dislikes. Rather, both litigants must have equal standing in the judge's eyes and heart; in accordance with the opinion of the Sages (*Kesef Mishneh*). Some state that one need not disqualify oneself as a judge if the degree of friendship or

רַבִּי יִרְמְיָה אָמַר רַב: כָּל שִׁבְעַת יְמֵי הַמִּשְׁתֶּה. [1]וְרַבָּנַן מִשְּׁמֵיהּ דְּרָבָא אָמְרִי: אֲפִילּוּ מִיּוֹם רִאשׁוֹן וְאֵילָךְ.

[2]"הַשּׂוֹנֵא כָּל שֶׁלֹּא דִּבֵּר כו'".

[3]תָּנוּ רַבָּנַן: "'וְהוּא לֹא אוֹיֵב לוֹ' — יְעִידֶנּוּ." [4]'וְלֹא מְבַקֵּשׁ רָעָתוֹ' — יְדִינֶנּוּ.

[5]אַשְׁכַּחַן שׂוֹנֵא, אוֹהֵב מְנָלַן? [6]קְרֵי בֵּיהּ הָכִי: [7]"וְהוּא לֹא אוֹיֵב לוֹ וְלֹא אוֹהֵב לוֹ" — יְעִידֶנּוּ. [8]"וְלֹא מְבַקֵּשׁ רָעָתוֹ וְלֹא טוֹבָתוֹ" — יְדִינֶנּוּ.

[9]מִידֵי "אוֹהֵב" כְּתִיב? [10]אֶלָּא,

LITERAL TRANSLATION

Rabbi Yirmeyah [who] said in the name of Rav: All seven days of the feasting. [1]And the Rabbis in the name of Rava said: Even from the first day onward [he is fit].

[2]"His enemy, — [this is] anyone who has not spoken, etc." [3]The Rabbis taught: "'And he was neither his enemy' — [then] he may testify about him. [4]'Nor one seeking his misfortune' — [then] he may judge him."

[5]We have found [support for] an enemy; from where do we know [about] a friend? [6]Read it as follows: [7]"And he was neither his enemy nor his friend" — [then] he may testify about him. [8]"Nor one seeking his misfortune or his good" — [then] he may judge him.

[9]Is [the word] "friend" written? [10]Rather,

TRANSLATION AND COMMENTARY

Abba said in the name of Rabbi Yirmeyah, who **said in the name of Rav:** It lasts for **all seven days of** the customary post-nuptial **feasting**, when the two are particularly close. [1]However, **the Rabbis in the name of Rava** disagreed and **said:** It lasts only for the day of the wedding. Subsequently, **even from the first day** after the wedding, it is assumed that the groom and his best man can be objective about each other.

הַשּׂוֹנֵא [2]The Gemara now considers the other case of ineligibility cited by Rabbi Yehudah: **"His enemy** — this refers to **anyone who has not spoken** to him for at least three days due to animosity." The Gemara now quotes a Baraita that provides Scriptural support for this ruling. "In dealing with a person who kills unintentionally, the Torah (Numbers 35:22-4), states: 'If suddenly, and without enmity, he pushed him . . . and he died; and he was neither his enemy nor one seeking his misfortune; then the congregation shall judge between the killer and the avenger of blood.' Now, since the Torah informs us elsewhere of the need to verify the killer's lack of malice (see Deuteronomy 4:42), it appears that the repetition of this idea in our verse is not required in order to teach us this. [3]The **Rabbis** therefore **taught** in a Baraita: The Torah teaches, **'And he was neither his enemy'** — this refers to a witness to the killing, who **may testify about** the killer only if he bears no enmity toward him. Similarly, when the verse states, [4]**'nor one seeking his misfortune'** — it refers to the court members, who **may judge** the killer only if they are free of animosity toward him."

אַשְׁכַּחַן שׂוֹנֵא [5]The Gemara seeks clarification: **We have found** support in the verse for disqualifying **an enemy** of the litigant. But **from where do we know** that **a friend** is also ineligible? [6]**Read** the verse as if it was written **this way:** [7]**"And he was neither his enemy nor his friend"** — only then **may he testify about him.** [8]**"Nor one seeking his misfortune or his good"** — only then **may he judge him.**

מִידֵי "אוֹהֵב" כְּתִיב [9]The Gemara challenges this reading of the verse: But **is** the word **"friend"** actually **written** there? How can we arbitrarily insert it into the verse? [10]**Rather,** one must say that **it is logic** that

RASHI

מיום ראשון ואילך — בטלה שושבינות וכשר להעיד. **והוא לא אויב לו — יעידנו** — דהאי "והוא" אעד קאי, דמעיד שהוא חייב גלות והעד לא אויב לו לרוצח. דאי ברוצח הא כתיב (דברים ד) "והוא לא שונא לו" וקראי אחריני טובא. **ולא מבקש רעתו — ידיננו** — דסמיך ליה "ושפטו העדה", וקאמר רבי יהודה דהאי "לא מבקש רעתו" אשופטים קאי, ולשון זה מצאתי בברייתא דסיפרי ולא בספרי שלנו, "והוא לא אויב לו" — העד "ולא מבקש רעתו" — השופט.

NOTES

אֲפִילּוּ מִיּוֹם רִאשׁוֹן Even from the first day onward. Our commentary is in accordance with *Rashi*, who appears to understand the Gemara's question as follows: According to Rabbi Yehudah in our Mishnah, for how long is a best man disqualified? *Ramah*, however, understands the Gemara's question differently: How many days must one rejoice with the groom in order to qualify as a best man? According to Rav, he must participate in all seven days of feasting; according to Rava, he is considered a best man even if he only rejoiced with the groom on the first day.

"וְלֹא מְבַקֵּשׁ רָעָתוֹ" — יְדִינֶנּוּ "Nor one seeking his misfortune" — he may judge him. *Rashi* suggests that the Baraita applied this clause to judges because of the words that follow it in the verse: "And the congregation shall judge."

HALAKHAH

enmity is not great. However, as a matter of piety, it is best to refrain from judging even in such cases (*Rema*)." (*Rambam, Sefer Shofetim, Hilkhot Sanhedrin* 23:6; *Shulḥan Arukh, Ḥoshen Mishpat* 7:7.)

סְבָרָא הוּא: [1]אוֹיֵב מַאי טַעְמָא? [2]מִשּׁוּם דִּמְרַחֲקָא דַּעֲתֵיהּ. [3]אוֹהֵב נַמִּי מְקָרְבָא דַּעֲתֵיהּ. [4]וְרַבָּנַן, הַאי "לֹא אוֹיֵב לוֹ וְלֹא מְבַקֵּשׁ רָעָתוֹ" מַאי דָּרְשֵׁי בֵּיהּ? [5]חַד, לְדַיָּין; [6]אִידָךְ, כִּדְתַנְיָא: [7]"אָמַר רַבִּי יוֹסֵי בְּרַבִּי יְהוּדָה: 'וְהוּא לֹא אוֹיֵב לוֹ וְלֹא מְבַקֵּשׁ רָעָתוֹ' — [8]מִכָּאן לִשְׁנֵי תַלְמִידֵי חֲכָמִים שֶׁשּׂוֹנְאִין זֶה אֶת זֶה שֶׁאֵין יוֹשְׁבִין בַּדִּין כְּאֶחָד".

משנה [9]כֵּיצַד בּוֹדְקִים אֶת הָעֵדִים? [10]הָיוּ מַכְנִיסִין אוֹתָן לְחֶדֶר וּמְאַיְּימִין עֲלֵיהֶן; [11]וּמוֹצִיאִין אֶת כָּל הָאָדָם לַחוּץ

LITERAL TRANSLATION

it is [a matter of] logic: [1]What is the reason [we disqualify] an enemy? [2]Because he has estranged feelings. [3]A friend, too, [he] has close feelings. [4]And the Sages, how do they interpret this [verse:] "And he was neither his enemy nor one seeking his misfortune"? [5]One, for the judge; [6][and] the other, as was taught: [7]"Rabbi Yose the son of Rabbi Yehudah said: 'And he was neither his enemy nor one seeking his misfortune' — [8]from here [we learn] that two scholars who hate each other may not sit together in judgment."

MISHNAH [9]How do they examine the witnesses? [10]They bring them into the room and intimidate them; [11]and [then] they send everyone outside

TRANSLATION AND COMMENTARY

dictates the above interpretation. [1]For **what is the reason** we disqualify **an enemy** from testifying or judging? [2]It is **because he has estranged feelings** toward the litigant, which may affect his judgment. [3]If so, **a friend** should **also** be disqualified, for he **has close feelings** for the litigant, which may also impair his objectivity.

וְרַבָּנַן [4]**And the Sages** of our Mishnah, who disagree with Rabbi Yehudah and claim that "the people of Israel are not suspected of testifying falsely simply out of love or hate of their fellow man" — **how do they interpret this** seemingly repetitive verse: **"And he was neither his enemy nor one seeking his misfortune"?** [5]They maintain as follows: **One** of the clauses is required **in order** to teach us that the restriction applies only to a **judge.** [6]**The other** clause in the verse also applies to judges, **in accordance with what was taught** in the following Baraita: [7]**"Rabbi Yose the son of Rabbi Yehudah said:** The verse in Numbers (35:23) states: **'And he was neither his enemy nor one seeking his misfortune.'** [8]**From here** — that is, from the seemingly repetitive latter clause — we learn **that two scholars who hate each other may not sit together** on the same court **in judgment**, lest their personal differences impair their objectivity."

MISHNAH כֵּיצַד בּוֹדְקִים [9]**How do** the judges **examine the witnesses** in a civil case? [10]First, **they bring them into the** courtroom **and intimidate them.** [11]Then **they send everyone outside and** leave only **the** most

RASHI

חד לדיין — דבדיין מודו רבנן דשונא לא ידון, דלא מלי חזי ליה זכותא. **ואידך** — לפסול בדין אחד שני דיינין ששונאין זה את זה.

משנה מאיימין עליהם — מפרש בגמרא.

NOTES

וּמוֹצִיאִין אֶת כָּל הָאָדָם לַחוּץ They send everyone outside. Our reading of the Mishnah implies that spectators are sent out of the courtroom as well, so that the court can examine the witness in private. (The litigants, of course, must remain in the room, as the law requires that testimony be given in the presence of the parties involved.) *Arukh Laner* suggests that the spectators are removed so that the witnesses will not be ashamed to admit that their testimony was false.

Rif and *Rosh* have an alternative reading of the Mishnah (וּמוֹצִיאִין אוֹתָן לַחוּץ), which implies that the court sends out only the additional witness, to prevent them from coordinating their responses to the court's interrogation.

HALAKHAH

שְׁנֵי תַלְמִידֵי חֲכָמִים שֶׁשּׂוֹנְאִין זֶה אֶת זֶה Two scholars who hate each other. "Two scholars who dislike each other should not sit together in judgment, for their mutual animosity may impel them to unjustly attack each other's arguments during the judicial deliberations," following the opinion of Rabbi Yose the son of Rabbi Yehudah. Nevertheless, should such individuals sit together on a court, we do not invalidate their verdict unless they are known to be outright enemies (*Baḥ*). (*Shulḥan Arukh, Ḥoshen Mishpat* 7:8.)

מְאַיְּימִין עֲלֵיהֶן They intimidate them. "Before accepting testimony, the court intimidates the witnesses into testifying truthfully by describing the severe consequences of perjury (famine and pestilence; *Sma*), and the humiliation that they can expect, even from those who bribed them to lie." (*Shulḥan Arukh, Ḥoshen Mishpat* 28:7.)

כֵּיצַד בּוֹדְקִים אֶת הָעֵדִים How do they examine the witnesses? "After intimidating the witnesses and warning them of the consequences of testifying falsely, the court sends everyone outside except for the most prominent of the witnesses. It then interrogates him about what he actually observed, for anything that he did not see with his own eyes is unacceptable as testimony. Afterwards, they send him out and bring in the other witness for a similar interrogation. If their testimony is consistent, the court proceeds to deliberate the matter," as explained in the Mishnah. (*Shulḥan Arukh, Ḥoshen Mishpat* 8:8-9; 81:8.)

TRANSLATION AND COMMENTARY

prominent of the witnesses standing before them. [1]**They say to** him: **Tell** us exactly **how you know that** the defendant **owes this** claimant money. [2]**If he says: The defendant told me** outright: **'I owe** the claimant money'; [3]or if the witness says: **So-and-so,** whom I trust implicitly, **told me that the defendant owes** him money — **he** has **said nothing.** [4]Indeed, the witness is not believed **until he states** as follows: **In front of us,** and with the obvious intention that we serve as witnesses, the defendant **admitted to** the claimant **that he owes him two hundred zuz.** [5]**Afterwards,** the judges **bring in the second** witness, **and examine him** the same way. [6]If their **statements are found** to **correspond,** then the judges **deliberate the matter** on the basis of their testimony.

שְׁנַיִם אוֹמְרִים זַכַּאי [7]After deliberation, the three judges render their opinions. If **two** of them **say** that the defendant is **free of liability and one says** that he is **liable,** the defendant is **free of liability.** [8]If **two say** that he is **liable and one says** that he is **free of liability,** then he is **liable.** [9]However, if **one** of the judges **says** that the defendant is **liable and one says** that he is **free of liability** — [10]or **even** if **two** of the judges **free** him **of liability or two find** him **liable** — **and** the remaining **one says "I do not know,"** [11]then the court **must add** additional **judges** so that a decision can be rendered by a majority consisting of at least three.

גָּמְרוּ אֶת הַדָּבָר [12]Once **they** have **finished** deliberating **the matter** and arrived at a majority verdict, **they reconvene** the court and announce their decision. (The Mishnah here is ambiguous as to whether it is the witnesses or the litigants who are returned to court.) [13]**The** most **prominent of the judges says** to the defendant: **'So-and-so, you are exempt'**; [14]or: **'so-and-so, you are liable.'** And with that, the trial comes to an end.

וּמְשַׁיְּירִין אֶת הַגָּדוֹל שֶׁבָּהֶן, [1]וְאוֹמְרִים לוֹ: אֱמוֹר הֵיאַךְ אַתָּה יוֹדֵעַ שֶׁזֶּה חַיָּיב לָזֶה. [2]אִם אָמַר: ״הוּא אָמַר לִי ׳שֶׁאֲנִי חַיָּיב לוֹ׳, [3]אִישׁ פְּלוֹנִי אָמַר לִי ׳שֶׁהוּא חַיָּיב לוֹ׳ — לֹא אָמַר כְּלוּם, [4]עַד שֶׁיֹּאמַר: ׳בְּפָנֵינוּ הוֹדָה לוֹ שֶׁהוּא חַיָּיב לוֹ מָאתַיִם זוּז׳״. [5]וְאַחַר כָּךְ, מַכְנִיסִין אֶת הַשֵּׁנִי, וּבוֹדְקִין אוֹתוֹ. [6]אִם נִמְצְאוּ דִּבְרֵיהֶן מְכוּוָּנִין, נוֹשְׂאִין וְנוֹתְנִין בַּדָּבָר. [7]שְׁנַיִם אוֹמְרִים זַכַּאי וְאֶחָד אוֹמֵר חַיָּיב — זַכַּאי. [8]שְׁנַיִם אוֹמְרִים חַיָּיב וְאֶחָד אוֹמֵר זַכַּאי — חַיָּיב. [9]אֶחָד אוֹמֵר חַיָּיב, וְאֶחָד אוֹמֵר זַכַּאי, [10]אֲפִילּוּ שְׁנַיִם מְזַכִּין אוֹ שְׁנַיִם מְחַיְּיבִין וְאֶחָד אוֹמֵר ״אֵינִי יוֹדֵעַ״ — [11]יוֹסִיפוּ הַדַּיָּינִין. [12]גָּמְרוּ אֶת הַדָּבָר, הָיוּ מַכְנִיסִין אוֹתָן. [13]הַגָּדוֹל שֶׁבַּדַּיָּינִין אוֹמֵר: אִישׁ פְּלוֹנִי אַתָּה זַכַּאי, [14]אִישׁ פְּלוֹנִי אַתָּה חַיָּיב.

LITERAL TRANSLATION

and leave the [most] prominent of them, [1]and they say to him: Tell [us] how you know that this one owes this one. [2]If he says: He told me, 'I owe him'; [3][or] so-and-so told me that he owes him — [the witness] said nothing, [4]until he states: In front of us, he admitted to him that he owes him two hundred zuz. [5]And afterwards, they bring in the second one, and examine him. [6]If their statements are found [to] correspond, [the judges] deliberate the matter.

[7][If] two say [he is] free of liability and one says [he is] liable, [he is] free of liability. [8][If] two say [he is] liable and one says [he is] free of liability, [he is] liable. [9][If] one says [he is] liable and one says [he is] free of liability — [10][or] even [if] two free [him] of liability or two find [him] liable — [11]and one says "I do not know," they must add judges.

[12][Once] they finished [deliberating] the matter, they would bring them in. [13]The [most] prominent of the judges said: So-and-so, you are free of liability; [14][or] so-and-so, you are liable.

RASHI

הוא אמר לי — הלוה אמר לי. **לא אמר כלום** — דעביד איניש דאמר ״פלוני נושה בי״ כדי שלא יחזיקוהו עשיר. **הודה לו** — שהיו שניהם בפנינו להודות נתכוון להיות לו עדים בדבר. **שנים אומרים זכאי ואחד אומר חייב זכאי** — דכתיב (שמות כג) ״אחרי רבים להטות״. **אפילו שנים מחייבין או מזכין והשלישי אומר איני יודע** — **יוסיפו הדיינין** — ואף על גב דאי הוה פליג עלייהו הוי בטל במיעוטא, כי אמר ״איני יודע״ הוי כמי שלא ישב בדין ונמצא הדין בשנים, ואנן תלתא בעינן. **מכניסין אותן** — לבעלי דינין, ובגמרא פריך: הא לא אפקינהו!

HALAKHAH

הַכְרָעַת הַפְּסָק **Determination of the verdict.** "If there is no unanimity among the judges after having concluded their deliberations, the verdict is decided on the basis of the majority opinion. If one of the judges remains undecided, even if there is a majority that agree, two more judges are added to the panel and the matter is reopened for discussion. If after the second vote there is no majority, another two judges are added and the matter is considered once again. This procedure continues until a majority opinion is achieved. That majority opinion is accepted even if there is one judge remaining undecided," all as explained in the Mishnah. (*Shulḥan Arukh, Ḥoshen Mishpat* 18:1.)

קְרִיאַת הַפְּסָק **Pronouncement of the verdict.** "After the verdict is determined, the litigants are ushered back into

TRANSLATION AND COMMENTARY

וּמִנַּיִן [1] **From where** do we know **that when** a judge **exits** the courtroom, **he should not say:** [2] "I wanted to **free** the defendant **from liability, but my colleagues found** him **liable; yet there was nothing I could do, for my colleagues outnumbered me**"? [3] **Concerning this** kind of behavior, **it is stated** in Leviticus (19:16): **"You shall not go about as a talebearer among your people"**; [4] **and it** also **states** in Proverbs (11:13) that **"a talebearer reveals secrets,"** but he of trustworthy spirit conceals the matter."

GEMARA הֵיכִי אָמְרִינַן לְהוּ [5] The Mishnah states that we must intimidate the witnesses as part of their interrogation. **How,** exactly, **do we speak to them?** [6] **Rav Yehudah said: We say to them thus:** The verse in Proverbs (25:14) states: [7] **"Clouds and wind, but no rain;** (so for) **the man who prides himself over a false gift."** (Rav Yehudah means that someone who prides himself for accepting a bribe to offer false testimony brings drought and famine to the world — from which he and his family will also suffer.)

אֲמַר לֵיהּ רָבָא [8] **Rava said to** Rav Yehudah: Such a threat will not necessarily be effective, for **they can** counter it by **saying** to themselves: [9] **"Seven years was there famine, but it did not pass through the craftsman's gate** (a popular adage implying that a craftsman's livelihood is not dependent on rain)." [10] **Rather, Rava said: We** intimidate witnesses by **saying to them:** The verse in Proverbs (25:18) states: [11] **"A mallet, a sword, and a sharpened arrow,** (so for) **the man who testifies falsely against his fellow."** (Rava implies that giving false testimony condemns one to an early death.)

אֲמַר לֵיהּ רַב אַשִׁי [12] **Rav Ashi said to** Rava: Your suggestion is equally problematic, for **the** witnesses **can** counter it by **saying** to themselves: [13] **"Seven years was there pestilence, but no man died without** completing **his years** (an adage reflecting on the predestination of a man's death)." [14] **Rather, Rav Ashi said: Natan bar Mar Zutra said to me:** If we truly wish to intimidate the witnesses, [15] **we** should **say to them** that, by testifying

[1] וּמִנַּיִן לִכְשֶׁיֵּצֵא לֹא יֹאמַר: [2] "אֲנִי מְזַכֶּה וַחֲבֵירַיי מְחַיְּיבִים, אֲבָל מָה אֶעֱשֶׂה שֶׁחֲבֵירַיי רַבּוּ עָלַי" — [3] עַל זֶה נֶאֱמַר: "לֹא תֵלֵךְ רָכִיל בְּעַמֶּיךָ" [4] וְאוֹמֵר: "הוֹלֵךְ רָכִיל מְגַלֶּה סּוֹד".

גמרא [5] הֵיכִי אָמְרִינַן לְהוּ? [6] אָמַר רַב יְהוּדָה: הָכִי אָמְרִינַן לְהוּ: [7] "נְשִׂיאִים וְרוּחַ וְגֶשֶׁם אַיִן אִישׁ מִתְהַלֵּל בְּמַתַּת שָׁקֶר". [8] אֲמַר לֵיהּ רָבָא: יָכְלִי לְמֵימַר: [9] "שַׁב שְׁנֵי הֲוָה כַּפְנָא, וְאַבָּבָא אוּמָּנָא לָא חֲלֵיף". [10] אֶלָּא אָמַר רָבָא: אָמְרִינַן לְהוּ: [11] "מֵפִיץ וְחֶרֶב וְחֵץ שָׁנוּן אִישׁ עֹנֶה בְרֵעֵהוּ עֵד שָׁקֶר". [12] אֲמַר לֵיהּ רַב אַשִׁי: יָכְלִי לְמֵימַר: [13] "שַׁב שְׁנֵי הֲוָה מוֹתָנָא, וְאִינִישׁ בְּלָא שְׁנֵיהּ לָא שְׁכִיב". [14] אֶלָּא, אָמַר רַב אַשִׁי: אָמַר לִי נָתָן בַּר מָר זוּטְרָא: [15] אָמְרִינַן

LITERAL TRANSLATION

[1] And from where [do we know] that when [a judge] exits, he should not say: [2] "I freed [him] from liability but my colleagues found [him] liable; yet what could I do, for my colleagues outnumbered me"? [3] Concerning this, it is stated: "You shall not go about as a talebearer among your people"; [4] and it states: "A talebearer reveals secrets."

GEMARA [5] How do we intimidate (lit., "speak to") them? [6] Rav Yehudah said: We say to them thus: [7] "Clouds and wind, but no rain; [so for] the man who prides himself for a false gift."

[8] Rava said to him: They can say: [9] "Seven years was there famine, but it did not pass through the craftsman's gate." [10] Rather, Rava said: We say to them: [11] "A mallet, a sword, and a sharpened arrow, [so for] the man who testifies falsely against his fellow."

[12] Rav Ashi said to him: They can say: [13] "Seven years was there pestilence, but no man died without [completing] his years." [14] Rather, Rav Ashi said: Natan bar Mar Zutra said to me: [15] We say

RASHI

גמרא היכי אמרינן להו — לעדים כשמאיימין עליהם. **נשיאים ורוח וגשם וגו'** — בשביל "מתהלל במתת שקר" דהיינו מעידי שקר גשמים נעצרים, ואפילו כשהשמים מתקשרים בעבים ורוח להוריד גשמים, אין הגשם בא. **אמר רבא** — מאי איכפת להו אם לא ירדו גשמים? אמרי בלבם משל הדיוט שב שני הוה כפנא ואבבא אומנא לא חליף, על פתח מי שיודע אומנות ובעל מלאכה לא עבר הרעב. **מפיץ וחרב וגו' איש עונה וגו'** — בעון עדות שקר דבר בא, ויתייראו שלא ימותו.

NOTES

וְאוֹמֵר: הוֹלֵךְ רָכִיל מְגַלֶּה סּוֹד **And it states: "A talebearer reveals secrets."** The first verse cited by the Mishnah ("You shall not go about as a talebearer among your people") can be construed as implying that talebearing is only forbidden

HALAKHAH

the courtroom and the chief justice announces that the defendant is either liable or free of liability. No judge may reveal how he or any other judge voted in the deliberations, since by doing so he qualifies as 'one who goes forth talebearing, revealing secrets.'" (*Shulḥan Arukh, Ḥoshen Mishpat* 19:1.)

TRANSLATION AND COMMENTARY

falsely, they risk public contempt — for **false witnesses are despised** even **by those who hire them** to lie. [1]This is derived from Scripture, **for it is written** in I Kings (21:9-10) that, in plotting the murder of Nabot, the wicked Queen Jezebel forged an order in the name of King Ahab and sent it to the elders of the town where Nabot lived, saying: "Call a fast and seat Nabot at the head of the people. [2]**And seat two men, base men, opposite him; so that they may testify against him, saying, 'You cursed God and the king.'** And then take him out and stone him, that he may die." Jezebel, who herself called for the false witnesses to be recruited, referred to them as "base men."

אִם אָמַר [3]We learned in our Mishnah: "They say to the witness: Tell us exactly how you know that the defendant owes this claimant money. **If he says:** The defendant **told me** outright: 'I owe the claimant money'; or if the witness says: So-and-so, whom I implicitly trust, told me that the defendant owes him money — he has in effect said nothing. Indeed, the witness is not believed **until he states** as follows: **In front of us,** and with the obvious intention that we serve as witnesses, the defendant **admitted to** the claimant **that he owes him two hundred zuz."** [4]The Gemara comments: This statement of the Mishnah **is a support for Rav Yehudah, for Rav Yehudah said in the name of Rav:** For witnesses to testify that they heard someone admitting to a loan, [5]**it is necessary that** the debtor expressly **say** to them, **"You are my witnesses."**

אִיתְּמַר נַמִי [6]This principle **was also stated: "Rabbi Ḥiyya bar Abba said in the name of Rabbi Yoḥanan:** If a man approached his friend in the presence of two witnesses and said, [7]**'A maneh** (one hundred zuz) **of mine is in your possession'** — [8]and the respondent **said to him, 'Yes,** that is so.' [9]And **the next day,** the claimant **said to** him, 'Now **give me** my money,' [10]to which the respondent **said: 'I was** only **joking with you** yesterday.' [11]In such a case, he **is free of liability** should the case come to court, because he did not formally designate the witnesses as such."

לְהוּ: "סָהֲדֵי שִׁקְרֵי אַאוֹגְרַיְיהוּ זִילֵי", [1]דִּכְתִיב: [2]"וְהוֹשִׁיבוּ שְׁנַיִם אֲנָשִׁים בְּנֵי בְלִיַּעַל נֶגְדּוֹ וִיעִדֻהוּ לֵאמֹר בֵּרַכְתָּ אֱלֹהִים וָמֶלֶךְ".

[3]"אִם אָמַר הוּא אָמַר לִי כו׳ עַד שֶׁיֹּאמְרוּ: בְּפָנֵינוּ הוֹדָה לוֹ שֶׁהוּא חַיָּיב לוֹ מָאתַיִם זוּז". [4]מְסַיֵּיעַ לֵיהּ לְרַב יְהוּדָה, דְּאָמַר רַב יְהוּדָה אָמַר רַב: [5]צָרִיךְ שֶׁיֹּאמַר "אַתֶּם עֵדַיי".

[6]אִיתְּמַר נַמִי: "אָמַר רַבִּי חִיָּיא בַּר אַבָּא אָמַר רַבִּי יוֹחָנָן: [7]'מָנֶה לִי בְּיָדְךָ'. [8]אָמַר לוֹ: 'הֵן'. [9]לְמָחָר אָמַר לוֹ: 'תְּנֵהוּ לִי'! [10]אָמַר: 'מְשַׁטֶּה אֲנִי בָּךְ' — [11]פָּטוּר".

LITERAL TRANSLATION

to them: "False witnesses are despised [even] by those who hire them," [1]for it is written: [2]"And seat two men, base men, opposite him; so that they may testify against him, saying, 'You cursed God and the king.'"

[3]"If he says: He told me, etc.; until they state: In front of us, he admitted to him that he owes him two hundred zuz." [4]This supports Rav Yehudah, for Rav Yehudah said in the name of Rav: [5]It is necessary that he say, "You are my witnesses."

[6]It was also stated: "Rabbi Ḥiyya bar Abba said in the name of Rabbi Yoḥanan: [7][A claimant said:] 'A maneh of mine is in your possession.' [8][The respondent] said to him: 'Yes.' [9]The next day, [the claimant] said to him: 'Give it to me!' [10]He said: 'I was joking with you.' [11][In such a case] he is free of liability."

RASHI

אאוגרייהו זילי — השוכרים אותם מבזים אותם וקלים הם בעיניו. **והושיבו שנים אנשים בני בליעל** — גבי נבות היזרעאלי כתיב, שיועלי המלך היו יועצים לשוכרם והיו קורין אותם בני בליעל. **בפנינו** — משמע שעשאונו עדים. **פטור** — ואף על פי ששמעו עדים אתמול שהודה לו, הואיל ולא אמר "אתם עדיי". **משטה אני בך** — שוחק הייתי בך בשביל שהיית שואלני מה שלא היה.

NOTES

when it involves direct slander, which is not the situation here, as the judge is simply telling what transpired in court. Hence it is necessary to cite this second verse, from which it is evident that divulging confidential information is also considered as talebearing (*Ḥamra Veḥaye, Tosafot Yom Tov*).

צָרִיךְ שֶׁיֹּאמַר: "אַתֶּם עֵדַיי" **It is necessary that he say: "You are my witnesses."** Rav did not mean to say that the debtor must explicitly designate witnesses using this language, for our Mishnah makes no mention of such a formulation. Rather, we must say that both Rav and the

HALAKHAH

מְשַׁטֶּה אֲנִי בָּךְ **I was only joking with you.** "If a claimant, in the presence of witnesses, asked his friend to confirm an outstanding debt, and the friend did so — the admission may later be discounted in court if the debtor claims that

[1]תַּנְיָא נַמִי הָכִי: ״׳מָנֶה לִי בְּיָדְךָ׳. [2]אָמַר לוֹ: ׳הֵן׳. [3]לְמָחָר אָמַר לוֹ: ׳תְּנֵהוּ לִי׳! [4]אָמַר לוֹ: ׳מְשַׂטֶּה אֲנִי בְּךָ׳ — פָּטוּר. [5]וְלֹא עוֹד אֶלָּא אֲפִילּוּ הִכְמִין לוֹ עֵדִים אֲחוֹרֵי גָּדֵר, [6]וְאָמַר לוֹ: ׳מָנֶה לִי בְּיָדְךָ׳. [7]אָמַר לוֹ: ׳הֵן׳. [8]׳רְצוֹנְךָ שֶׁתּוֹדֶה בִּפְנֵי פְלוֹנִי וּפְלוֹנִי׳? [9]אָמַר לוֹ: ׳מִתְיָירֵא אֲנִי שֶׁמָּא תַּכְפֵּינִי לַדִּין׳. [10]לְמָחָר, אָמַר לוֹ: ׳תְּנֵיהוּ לִי׳, [11]אָמַר לוֹ: ׳מְשַׂטֶּה אֲנִי בְּךָ׳, [12]פָּטוּר. [13]וְאֵין טוֹעֲנִין לַמֵּסִית.

[14]מֵסִית, מַאן דְּכַר שְׁמֵיהּ? [15]חַסּוּרֵי מִיחַסְּרָא, [16]וְהָכִי קָתָנֵי: [17]״אִם לֹא טָעַן, [18]אֵין טוֹעֲנִין לוֹ.

TRANSLATION AND COMMENTARY

תַּנְיָא נַמִי הָכִי [1]**This** principle **was also taught** in a Baraita **thus:** "If a man approached someone in the presence of two witnesses and said, **'A maneh of mine is in your possession'** — [2]and the other man **said to him, 'Yes,** that is so.' [3]And **the next day,** the claimant **said to** him: 'Now **give me** my money,' [4]to which the other man **said to him: 'I was** only **joking with you** yesterday,' he **is free of liability** should the case come to court. [5]**And not only that, but even** if the claimant **concealed** two **witnesses behind a fence and,** in their proximity, [6]**said to** someone: **'A maneh of mine is in your possession.'** [7]And the other man **said to him 'Yes,** that is so.' [8]And the claimant then retorted: **'Are you willing to admit** this **before so-and-so and so-and-so?'** (the two witnesses he had concealed). [9]And the other man then **said to him: 'I am afraid** to do so, **lest you force me** on the basis of my admission **to** abide by the **judgment** of a court and give you the money.' [10]And **the next day,** when the claimant **said to** him: 'Now **give me** my money,' [11]the other man answered **him: 'I was** only **joking with you** yesterday.' [12]Even in such a case, the other man **is free of liability** should the case come to court. The initial admission was not made with knowledge of the presence of witnesses. [13]In addition, judges **do not enter a** favorable **plea on behalf of an 'inciter'** (one who provokes others into idol worship)."

מֵסִית [14]The Gemara immediately addresses this last, seemingly unconnected, statement: **"An inciter** to idolatry"? **Who** in the Baraita **mentioned** anything about an inciter?! [15]The version of the Baraita we have **must be incomplete**. [16]**And this is how it should be taught:** [17]**"If** the defendant **did not claim** before the court that he was only joking when he admitted to having the maneh in his possession, [18]then the judges considering his case **do not enter** this **claim for him** and he must

LITERAL TRANSLATION

[1]It was also taught thus: "'[A claimant said:] A maneh of mine is in your possession.' [2][The respondent] said to him: 'Yes.' [3]The next day, he said to him: 'Give it to me!' [4]He said to him: 'I was joking with you.' [5][In such a case,] he is exempt. And not only that, but even [if the claimant] concealed witnesses for himself behind a fence, [6]and [the claimant] said to him: 'A maneh of mine is in your possession.' [7][And] he said to him: 'Yes.' [8][And the claimant then retorted]: 'Are you willing to admit [it] before so-and-so and so-and-so?' [9][And] he said to him: 'I am afraid, lest you force me to trial.' [10][And] the next day, he said to him: 'Give it to me,' [11][and] he said to him: 'I was joking with you.' [12][In such a case,] he is exempt. [13]And they do not make a plea on behalf of an inciter."

[14]An inciter [to idolatry] — who mentioned this (lit., "his name")? [15][The Baraita] is incomplete, [16]and this is how it should be taught: [17]"If [the defendant] did not enter a plea, [18]they do not enter for him.

RASHI

הכמין — החביא, כמו וארב לו (דברים יט), ויכמון ליה. **ואין טוענין למסית** — המסית חבירו לעבודת כוכבים אין טוענין אותו בית דין בשבילו טענת זכות, אלא אם כן טוענה הוא. **ואם לא טען** — משטה הייתי בכך כשהודיתי, אלא אמר לא אתן לך, הבא עדים שהלוית לי, אין טוענין בשבילו אלא אומרין לו: אחרי שהודיתה לך שלם.

NOTES

Mishnah simply require the debtor unequivocally to confess to the fact that he owes money in the presence of witnesses. Any element of ambiguity, such as the possibility of his jesting or intentionally attempting to feign poverty, can serve later as a basis for invalidating the testimony of those who witnessed the admission (*Ramah*).

אֵין טוֹעֲנִין לַמֵּסִית **They do not plead on behalf of an inciter.** The commentators ask: Why did the Baraita see fit to teach this law, since it is already obvious from Deuteronomy (13:9): "Have no compassion and protect him

HALAKHAH

he was only joking at the time. However, he must take an oath of inducement (שְׁבוּעַת הֶיסֵּת) to support his denial of liability." (*Shulḥan Arukh, Ḥoshen Mishpat* 81:1.)

הִכְמִין לוֹ עֵדִים **He concealed witnesses for him.** "If one concealed witnesses and then, in their proximity, elicited an admission of debt from someone who then refused to repeat the admission in front of witnesses — the confessed debtor may later deny in court that his admission was meant seriously. One can only be held accountable for an admission that was intentionally made in front of witnesses." (*Shulḥan Arukh, Ḥoshen Mishpat* 81:11.)

אִם לֹא טָעַן, אֵין טוֹעֲנִין לוֹ **If he did not claim, they do not claim for him.** "Even when a claim of jest would theoretically be acceptable, the court does not make it on

TRANSLATION AND COMMENTARY

pay the maneh if witnesses to his admission are produced. [1]**In capital cases,** however, this is not so — for **even if** the defendant **did not enter a plea** in his own favor, [2]the judges **enter** the **plea for him.** [3]Nevertheless, **they do not enter** a favorable **plea on behalf of an inciter** who is charged by witnesses with having provoked someone into idol worship, even though his is also a capital case."

מַאי שְׁנָא מֵסִית [4]**What is the difference** between **an inciter** and any other capital offender? [5]**Rabbi Ḥama bar Ḥanina said: From the lectures of Rabbi Ḥiyya bar Abba,** [6]**I have learned** that **an inciter is** indeed **different** from other offenders, [7]**for the Torah** (in Deuteronomy 13:9) **stated** about him: **"Have no compassion and protect him not."**

אָמַר [8]**Rabbi Shmuel bar Naḥman said in the name of Rabbi Yonatan:** [9]**From where** do we know **that** the judges in his case **do not** make a favorable **plea for an inciter?** [10]We know it **from the** story of the **primordial serpent** that provoked Eve into eating from the tree of knowledge. [11]**For Rabbi Simlai said: The serpent could have made many pleas** in its defense, **but it did not make** them. [12]**And why did the Holy One, blessed is He, not plead for it?** [13]**Because** the serpent itself **did not** enter such **pleas,** the heavenly Judge did not do so in its stead. A judge may not plead in favor of someone who incites to rebel against God.

מַאי הֲוָה לֵיהּ [14]**What,** indeed, **was there** for the serpent **to say** in its defense? It could have quoted the famous Talmudic dictum: [15]"If **the words of the Master and the words of** His **disciple** conflict — [16]**whose words do we heed?** [17]Certainly **we heed the words of the Master!"** It could then have asked: "Why should I be held responsible if Adam and Eve chose to disobey Your commandment and heed my counsel instead?"

[1]וּבְדִינֵי נְפָשׁוֹת, אַף עַל גַּב דְּלָא טָעַן, [2]טוֹעֲנִין לוֹ. [3]וְאֵין טוֹעֲנִין לַמֵּסִית.

[4]מַאי שְׁנָא מֵסִית? [5]אָמַר רַבִּי חָמָא בַּר חֲנִינָא: מִפִּירְקֵיהּ דְּרַבִּי חִיָּיא בַּר אַבָּא שְׁמִיעַ לִי: [6]שָׁאנֵי מֵסִית, [7]דְּרַחֲמָנָא אָמַר: "לֹא תַחְמֹל וְלֹא תְכַסֶּה עָלָיו". [8]אָמַר רַבִּי שְׁמוּאֵל בַּר נַחְמָן אָמַר רַבִּי יוֹנָתָן: [9]מִנַּיִין שֶׁאֵין טוֹעֲנִין לַמֵּסִית? [10]מִנָּחָשׁ הַקַּדְמוֹנִי. [11]דְּאָמַר רַבִּי שִׂמְלַאי: הַרְבֵּה טְעָנוֹת הָיָה לוֹ לַנָּחָשׁ לִטְעוֹן וְלֹא טָעַן. [12]וּמִפְּנֵי מָה לֹא טָעַן לוֹ הַקָּדוֹשׁ בָּרוּךְ הוּא? [13]לְפִי שֶׁלֹּא טָעַן הוּא. [14]מַאי הֲוָה לֵיהּ לְמֵימַר? [15]"דִּבְרֵי הָרַב וְדִבְרֵי תַלְמִיד — [16]דִּבְרֵי מִי שׁוֹמְעִין? [17]דִּבְרֵי הָרַב שׁוֹמְעִין"!

LITERAL TRANSLATION

[1]But in capital cases, even though [the defendant] did not enter a plea, [2]they plea for him. [3]But they do not enter a plea on behalf of an inciter [to idolatry].

[4]What is the difference [in the case of] an inciter? [5]Rabbi Ḥama bar Ḥanina said: From the lectures of Rabbi Ḥiyya bar Abba, [6]I have learned [that] an inciter is different, [7]for the Torah [lit., "the Merciful One"] stated: "Have no compassion and protect him not."

[8]Rabbi Shmuel bar Naḥman said in the name of Rabbi Yonatan: [9]From where [do we know] that they do not [enter a] plea for an inciter? [10]From the primordial serpent. [11]For Rabbi Simlai said: The serpent could have entered many pleas, but he did not plea. [12]And why did the Holy One, blessed be He, not plea for him? [13]Because [the serpent himself] did not plea.

[14]What was there for [the serpent] to say? [15]"The words of the Master and the words of a disciple — [16]whose words do we heed? [17]We heed the words of the Master!"

RASHI

ובדיני נפשות — אם יש טענת זכות והוא אינו יודע לטעון, טוענין לו. **לפי שלא טען** — הנחש לא טען הקדוש ברוך הוא בשבילו.

NOTES

not"? *Imrei Zvi* suggests that, without this Baraita, one might have interpreted that verse as addressing only witnesses to incitement (forbidding them from withholding testimony), but not judges. Once the Baraita states this rule, and the Gemara supports it from the story of the serpent, it becomes evident that judges are also forbidden to have mercy on an alleged inciter. *Ramah* resolves the problem by suggesting that the Baraita is directed at those judging a case of incitement against any Torah observance, whereas the prohibition mentioned in the verse applies strictly to incitement to idol worship.

דִּבְרֵי הָרַב וְדִבְרֵי תַלְמִיד **The words of the Master and the words of the disciple.** The Rishonim ask: Since the Gemara implies that this argument would have been valid had the serpent introduced it in his defense, why is it not valid as a defense for all inciters? *Tosafot* answers as

HALAKHAH

the defendant's behalf if he did not raise it himself. Some rule that if the defendant contests the allegations against him for some other reason, the court may then also introduce this claim, even if he did not introduce it himself (*Shakh*)." (*Shulḥan Arukh, Ḥoshen Mishpat* 81:3.)

[1]אָמַר חִזְקִיָּה: מִנַּיִין שֶׁכָּל הַמּוֹסִיף, גּוֹרֵעַ? [2]שֶׁנֶּאֱמַר: [3]"אָמַר אֱלֹהִים לֹא תֹאכְלוּ מִמֶּנּוּ וְלֹא תִגְּעוּ בּוֹ". [4]רַב מְשָׁרְשִׁיָּא אָמַר: מֵהָכָא: [5]"אַמָּתַיִם וָחֵצִי אָרְכּוֹ". [6]רַב אַשִׁי אָמַר: "עַשְׁתֵּי עֶשְׂרֵה יְרִיעֹת". [7]אָמַר אַבַּיֵי: לֹא שָׁנוּ אֶלָּא דְּאָמַר: [8]"מְשַׁטֶּה אֲנִי בְּךָ", [9]אֲבָל

LITERAL TRANSLATION

[1]Hizkiyah said: From where [do we know] that whoever adds, detracts? [2]For it is stated: [3][And Eve said...] "God said: Do not eat from it and do not touch it."

[4]Rav Mesharshiya said: From here: [5]"Two cubits and a half shall be its length."

[6]Rav Ashi said: [From here:] "Eleven curtains."

[7]Abaye said: They taught it only if he said: [8]"I was joking with you"; [9]however,

TRANSLATION AND COMMENTARY

אָמַר חִזְקִיָּה [1]Regarding Eve's sin, **Ḥizkiyah said: From where** do we know **that whoever adds** words to the Torah that are not stated there, **detracts** from it? [2]We know this from Eve's sin, **for it is stated** in Genesis (3:3) that, when asked by the serpent if God forbade her to eat from the trees of the garden, Eve replied: "We may eat from the fruit of the trees of the garden. But of the fruit of the tree which is in the midst of the garden, [3]**God said: Do not eat from it and do not touch it."** God only forbade her to eat from the tree (see Genesis 2:17); she herself added the prohibition against touching it. Once the serpent succeeded in demonstrating to her that no harm came from touching it, it became much easier for her to ignore the actual prohibition against eating its fruit. Adding a prohibition led to violating the initial prohibition.

רַב מְשָׁרְשִׁיָּא אָמַר [4]**Rav Mesharshiya said:** Another proof that addition to the Torah can lead to detraction **from** it is found in Exodus (25:10), where it states: "And they shall make an ark of acacia wood: [5]**Two cubits and a half shall be its length."** If the first letter of the word אַמָּתַיִם ("two cubits") were missing, we would have the word מָתַיִים, which means "two hundred." Thus the addition of a single letter drastically reduces the meaning of the word to which it is attached.

רַב אַשִׁי אָמַר [6]**Rav Ashi said:** I learn the very same thing from a later verse (Exodus 26:7): "And you shall make curtains of goats' hair for a covering over the tabernacle; **eleven curtains** shall you make." Removing the first letter of עַשְׁתֵּי עֶשְׂרֵה ("eleven") leaves us with the words שְׁתֵּי עֶשְׂרֵה, which mean "twelve." Thus, again we see that adding a single letter to a word results in reducing its meaning.

אָמַר אַבַּיֵי [7]The Gemara now resumes its consideration of the Baraita dealing with an admission made before hidden witnesses: **Abaye said:** The Sages of the Baraita **taught** their ruling as **only** applicable if the defendant **said** to the claimant: [8]**"I was** only **joking with you** yesterday"; [9]**however,** if **he** denied ever having

RASHI

ולא תגעו בו – הקדוש ברוך הוא לא הזהירם על הנגיעה, ומתוך תוספת – גירעו. שדחף הנחש את חוה על האילן עד שנגעה בו, אמר לה: ראי שאין מיתה על הנגיעה, אף על האכילה לא תמותי. **אמתים** – דל אל״ף מהכא – קרי ביה (מתים) הוי שתי מאות אמה. כל אותיות שבתורה הדרשם ככתיבתם, כמו "ועשית ואמרת" – כאלו כתובה בה״א, וכן אתה חסר כמו אותה מלא. **עשתי עשרה** – דל עיי״ן מהכא, הוו להו שתים עשרה.

NOTES

follows: Since the serpent was never commanded to refrain from incitement, it was only held accountable for having indirectly caused others to sin. Had it made the above argument, shifting responsibility to the sinners themselves, it would have been exonerated altogether. The situation is different, however, when we are explicitly forbidden by the Torah to incite: Now, one is held accountable for incitement, even if it did not lead others to sin. Hence, the above argument would in no way mitigate the inciter's responsibility.

Ramah offers a different distinction: Incitement to idolatry is the only crime regarding which the court does not allow the above plea to affect its judgment, for the Torah explicitly states that we are not to exercise any compassion concerning that offense. However, if someone who incited against any other aspect of Torah observance were to raise this argument, the court would be allowed to consider it — as is implied by the case of the serpent (which did not incite to idol worship) as well as by the language of the Baraita.

The Gemara's recognition of the validity of the above argument leads the *Ramah* to conclude that the legal principle absolving one of responsibility for transgressions committed by an agent (hiring someone to murder, for example) applies only if the one who commissioned the transgression argues in his own defense that the agent should have obeyed the Master rather than His disciple.

לֹא תֹאכְלוּ מִמֶּנּוּ וְלֹא תִגְּעוּ בּוֹ Do not eat from it and do not touch it. According to *Rosh,* Eve's addition to God's original command included not only the introduction of a prohibition against touching the fruit, but also the implication that they would die immediately after touching it. Although the Gemara and its commentaries imply that Eve invented these additional restrictions, *Avot of Rabbi Natan* (1:5) states that Adam did so when communicating God's words to Eve. He told her not to touch it, thereby providing a "fence" around the Torah, which is acceptable Rabbinic practice. But Eve invented the punishment for touching the fruit and then fell prey to the serpent's apparent demonstration of divine fallibility.

אַמָּתַיִם וָחֵצִי Two cubits and a half. Some say that the addition to the verse referred to here is not the *aleph* of אַמָּתַיִם but rather the *vav* of וָחֵצִי. Without that *vav,* the verse would read as follows: "Two cubits [is] half its length,"

אָמַר [29B] [1]"לֹא הָיוּ דְּבָרִים מֵעוֹלָם" — הוּחְזַק כַּפְרָן. [2]אָמַר רַב פַּפָּא בְּרֵיהּ דְּרַב אַחָא בַּר אַדָּא: [3]הָכִי אָמְרִינַן מִשְּׁמֵיהּ דְּרָבָא: כָּל מִילֵּי דִּכְדִי לָא דְּכִירִי אֱינָשֵׁי.

[4]הַהוּא דְּאַכְמִין לֵיהּ עֵדִים לְחַבְרֵיהּ בְּכִילְתֵּיהּ. [5]אֲמַר לֵיהּ: "מָנֶה לִי בְּיָדְךָ". [6]אֲמַר לֵיהּ: "הֵין". [7]אֲמַר: "עֵירֵי וְשָׁכְבֵי לֶיהֱווּ — עֲלָךְ סָהֲדֵי"! [8]אֲמַר לֵיהּ: "לָא". [9]אֲמַר רַב כָּהֲנָא: הָא אֲמַר לֵיהּ "לָא".

[10]הַהוּא דְּאַכְמִין עֵדִים בְּקִיבְרָא לְחַבְרֵיהּ. [11]אֲמַר לֵיהּ: "מָנֶה לִי בְּיָדְךָ". [12]אֲמַר לֵיהּ: "הֵין". [13]"חַיֵּי וּמֵיתֵי לֶיהֱווּ — עֲלָךְ סָהֲדֵי"! [14]אֲמַר לֵיהּ: "לָא". [15]אֲמַר רַבִּי שִׁמְעוֹן: [16]הָא אֲמַר לֵיהּ "לָא".

LITERAL TRANSLATION

[if] he said: [29B] [1]"This [admission] never took place (lit., 'there were never such things')" — he is presumed [to be] a liar. [2]Rav Pappa the son of Rav Aḥa bar Adda said: [3]We say as follows in the name of Rava: People do not remember [their] frivolous words.

[4][There was] a man who concealed witnesses against his friend behind the curtain of his bed. [5]He said to him: "A maneh of mine is in your possession." [6]He said to him: "Yes." [7]He said: "Those who are awake and those who are asleep — let them be witnesses for you!" [8]He said to him: "No." [9]Rav Kahana said: Surely, he said "No" to him.

[10][There was] a man who concealed witnesses against his friend in a grave. [11]He said to him: "A maneh of mine is in your possession." [12]He said to him: [13]"Yes." "The living and the dead — let them be witnesses for you!" [14]He said to him: "No." Rabbi [15]Shimon said: [16]Surely, he said "No" to him.

TRANSLATION AND COMMENTARY

made the admission and **said** to the claimant: [29B] [1]**"This never took place** — I never admitted to owing you money" — **he is presumed** to be **a liar**, for there are witnesses who testify to the contrary. Once he has made a patently false claim, he cannot change his story and admit that he indeed did make the admission, albeit only in jest. [2]**Rav Pappa the son of Rav Aḥa bar Adda** argued with Abaye and **said** that, under the circumstances, he is not presumed to be a liar, [3]for **we say in the name of Rava: People do not** necessarily **remember frivolous words** that they say in jest. He might have forgotten his facetious admission.

הַהוּא [4]**A man once concealed** two **witnesses** behind the **curtain** around his bed as part of a plan to acquire testimony **against his friend.** [5]He then invited his friend in and **said to him: "A maneh of mine is in your possession,"** [6]to which his friend **said to him** in return: **"Yes**, it is so." Realizing that his friend would refuse to repeat this admission in front of witnesses, [7]**he said** to him: **"Let those who are awake and those who are asleep** — whoever may hear us now — **be witnesses to** what **you** have just said!" [8]His friend **said to him: "No**, I am not willing to admit this before witnesses." [9]The alleged creditor presented his case before **Rav Kahana,** who **said: Surely** the friend **said to him "No**, I am not willing to designate witnesses"; hence, there is no basis for obligating him to pay.

הַהוּא [10]Similarly, **a man concealed witnesses in a grave** as part of a plan to acquire testimony **against his friend.** [11]**He** then brought his friend to the cemetery and **said to him: "A maneh of mine is in your possession,"** [12]to which his friend **said to him: "Yes**, it is so." He then said to his friend: [13]**"Let the living and the dead be witnesses in regard to** what **you** have just said!" [14]His friend **replied: "No**, I am not willing to admit this before witnesses." [15]When this case was presented before **Rabbi Shimon**, he also **said:** [16]**Surely** the friend **said to him "No"**; hence, there is no basis for obligating him to pay.

RASHI

לא היו דברים — לא הודיתי לך, והרי עדים ששמעו. **הוחזק כפרן** — ואינו נאמן עליו בשבועה. **כל מילי דכדי לא דכירי אינשי** — דברים של חנם, כלומר: הואיל ואותה הודאה דברי רוח היו, ששטה בו, לא דכירי אינשי ושכח אותה הודאה. **כילתא** — יריעה הפרוסה סביבות המטה. **עירי ושכבי ליהוו עלך סהדי** — רואה אתה שיהו כל השומעין מעידין בין ניעורין בין ישינים, שהיה מכיר זה בו שלא יודה בפני עדים, אמר בלבו: שמא יהא סבור שכולם ישינים ויאמר הן.

NOTES

thereby implying that the full length of the ark would be four cubits. Adding the *vav* thus reduces the length of the ark by one-and-a-half cubits (*Ya'avetz*).

HALAKHAH

אָמַר לֹא הָיוּ דְּבָרִים מֵעוֹלָם If he said: "This never happened." "If the alleged debtor claims in court that the admission never took place, even though witnesses testify that it did, he is free from liability after being administered an oath of inducement — for it is assumed that his admission was meant in jest and thus, being of no consequence to him, was subsequently forgotten," in accordance with the opinion of Rav Pappa, the son of Rav Aḥa bar Adda. If he neither denies the admission nor claims that it was made in jest, he must pay back the contested loan even if he

[1]אֲמַר רָבִינָא וְאִיתֵּימָא רַב פַּפָּא: [2]שְׁמַע מִינָּהּ מֵהָא, הָא דְּאָמַר רַב יְהוּדָה אָמַר רַב: [3]צָרִיךְ שֶׁיֹּאמַר ״אַתֶּם עֵדַיי״, [4]לָא שְׁנָא כִּי אֲמַר לֹוֶה, [5]וְלָא שְׁנָא כִּי אֲמַר מַלְוֶה וְשָׁתֵיק לֹוֶה. [6]טַעְמָא דַּאֲמַר לֹוֶה ״לָא״; [7]אֲבָל, אִי שָׁתֵיק — הָכִי נַמִי. [8]הַהוּא דַּהֲוָה קָרוּ לֵיהּ ״קַב רְשׁוּ״, [9]אֲמַר: ״מַאן מַסִּיק בִּי אֶלָּא פְּלוֹנִי וּפְלוֹנִי״? [10]אָתוּ תְּבָעוּהוּ לְדִינָא קַמֵּיהּ דְּרַב נַחְמָן. [11]אָמַר רַב נַחְמָן: ״אָדָם עָשׂוּי שֶׁלֹּא לְהַשְׂבִּיעַ אֶת עַצְמוֹ.

LITERAL TRANSLATION

[1]Ravina and some say Rav Pappa said: [2]Infer from this [about] what Rav Yehudah said in the name of Rav: [3]it is necessary that he say, "You are my witnesses," [4][it makes] no difference if the debtor says [it] [5]and [it makes] no difference if the creditor says [it] and the debtor is silent. [6]The reason [for the disqualification of the witnesses] is that the debtor said "No"; [7]however, if he was silent — it would have been so.

[8]A certain man, whom they called "a *kav* — of debt," said [in public]: [9]"Who has a claim against me besides so-and-so and so-and-so?" [10]They came [and] summoned him to judgment before Rav Naḥman. [11]Rav Naḥman said: "A person is likely not to make himself [appear] wealthy (lit., 'sated')."

TRANSLATION AND COMMENTARY

אֲמַר רָבִינָא [1]**Ravina, and some say Rav Pappa, said:** [2]It is possible to **infer from** these accounts an important principle relevant to the statement of **Rav Yehudah** (above, 29a) **in the name of Rav.** For witnesses to testify that they heard someone admitting a loan, [3]**it is necessary that** the debtor designate them by **saying: "You are my witnesses."** [4]From these cases we see that it makes **no difference whether the debtor says:** "You are my witnesses," [5]**or the creditor says** it and **the debtor** remains **silent.** In both instances, the designation is valid. [6]**The reason** for this **is** evident. The creditor's designation of witnesses was invalidated by Rav Kahana and Rabbi Shimon **because the debtor said "No."** [7]This implies that **if** the debtor **had been silent,** the designation **would have been** valid and the testimony allowed in court.

הַהוּא דַּהֲוָה [8]**A man, who** was **referred to as "a** ***kav*****-full of debts,"** once **said** publicly: [9]**"Who** actually **has a** monetary **claim against me besides so-and-so and so-and-so?"** [10]Hearing of his admission, the two men **came** and **summoned him to** appear for **judgment before Rav Naḥman**. [11]After hearing their claims, **Rav Naḥman said: A person is likely** falsely to admit to owing money so as **not to make himself appear wealthy,** thereby arousing envy. Therefore, we cannot obligate him to pay until he explicitly designates witnesses in your presence and specifies before them how much he owes you.

RASHI

קב רשו — מלא קב שטרות יש עליו. מאן מסיק בי — למי אני חייב כלום. אדם עשוי — לומר לבריות חייב אני מעות לפלוני, להתרחק מעין הרע. שלא להשביע — שלא ליראות שבע ממון.

NOTES

אָדָם עָשׂוּי שֶׁלֹּא לְהַשְׂבִּיעַ אֶת עַצְמוֹ **A person is likely not to make himself appear wealthy.** Although we said earlier (29a) that judges do not plead in defense of someone denying an admission of debt, unless the defendant himself initiated the plea, this case is different. Here the admission of debt was not made in the presence of the creditors or in response to their claim. Hence, the court entertains the possibility that the self-professed debtor never intended his words to have a legal effect. In the earlier case, however, when the admission of debt was made in response to a claim by the creditor, the court does not initiate a defense on behalf of the professed debtor, for it is assumed that he understood the import of his confession.

It is further evident from this incident that the earlier defense ("I was only joking with you") is inappropriate here, as the claimant was not present at the time of admission. Similarly, the defense that Rav Naḥman employs here would also be inappropriate when someone allegedly admitted debt in response to his creditor's claim.

There is, however, one problem with Rav Naḥman's defense of the professed debtor in this case: How could he claim that the man was intentionally trying to make himself

HALAKHAH

insists that he never borrowed the money (*Sma, Shakh*). (*Shulḥan Arukh, Ḥoshen Mishpat* 81:1.)

צָרִיךְ שֶׁיֹּאמַר, אַתֶּם עֵדַיי **It is necessary that he say: "You are my witnesses."** "If someone admitted in the presence of his own designated witnesses to owing money, he cannot later retract his words. Similarly, if one admitted before witnesses designated by his claimant and did not reject them, he may not retract his words," in accordance with the opinion cited by Rav Yehudah in the name of Rav. (*Shulḥan Arukh, Ḥoshen Mishpat* 81:6.)

אָדָם עָשׂוּי שֶׁלֹּא לְהַשְׂבִּיעַ אֶת עַצְמוֹ **A man is likely not to make himself appear wealthy.** "If a man willingly admitted a debt in the presence of witnesses without having been asked to do so by the creditor, and then later denied the debt in court, claiming to have fabricated his admission in order to create the appearance of poverty — he is believed (regardless of whether he truly is wealthy or poor; *Rema*). The court may make this plea on his behalf if he himself did not do so (*Rema*). If the creditor was present at the time that the self-confessed debtor made his original

TRANSLATION AND COMMENTARY

הַהוּא דְּהָווּ [1]**There was** once **a** wealthy **man** who was called **"the mouse who lies upon the dinarim,"** [2]because of his miserly ways. **When he was dying, he said:** [3]**"So-and-so and so-and-so** both **have** valid **monetary claims against me** in regard **to the zuzim** that I owe them." [4]**After he died,** the two men **came** and **claimed** their money **from the heirs.** The heirs responded that their father's confession was contrived to make it look as if he had no money. [5]**They** all **came before Rabbi Yishmael the son of Rabbi Yose** and presented their case. In rendering his decision, [6]**he said to them: When do we say that a person is likely** falsely to acknowledge debt so as **not to make himself appear wealthy?** [7]**We say this** only **when** the alleged debtor **is alive** and can benefit from avoiding envy; [8]**however, after death,** the logic of this presumption does not apply. Thus we must assume his confession was **not** contrived. [9]Consequently, the heirs **paid back half** the sum that was demanded of them. [10]When the claimants **summoned** the heirs **to court** for **the other half,** [11]the litigants **came** before **Rabbi Ḥiyya.** After hearing their conflicting claims, [12]**he said to them: Just as a person is likely** falsely to acknowledge debt so as **not to make himself appear to be wealthy,** [13]**so,** too, **is a person likely** to do the same in order **not to make his children,** who stand to inherit from him, **appear to be wealthy** and subject to envy. On, the basis of this ruling, [14]the heirs **said to** Rabbi Ḥiyya: **May we** now **go and retrieve** the

LITERAL TRANSLATION

[1][There was] a certain man [who] was called "the mouse who lies upon the dinarim." [2]As he was dying, he said: [3]"So-and-so and so-and-so have a monetary claim against me." [4]After he died, they came [and] claimed [their money] from the heirs. [5]They came before Rabbi Yishmael the son of Rabbi Yose. [6]He said to them: When we say that a person is likely not to make himself [appear] wealthy, [7]these words apply [when he is] alive; [8]however, after death — not. [9]The [heirs] paid back half. [10]They summoned them to court for the other half. [11]They came before Rabbi Ḥiyya. [12]He said to them: Just as a person is likely not to make himself [appear] wealthy, [13]so is a person likely not to make his children [appear] wealthy. [14]The [heirs] said to him: May we go and retrieve [the earlier payment]?

[1]הַהוּא דְּהָווּ קָרוּ לֵיהּ "עַכְבְּרָא דִּשְׁכֵיב אַדִּינָרֵי", [2]כִּי קָא שָׁכֵיב, אֲמַר: [3]"פְּלָנְיָא וּפְלָנְיָא מַסְקוּ בִּי זוּזֵי". [4]בָּתַר דִּשָׁכֵיב, אָתוּ תַּבְעִינְהוּ לְיוֹרְשִׁין. [5]אָתוּ לְקַמֵּיהּ דְּרַבִּי יִשְׁמָעֵאל בְּרַבִּי יוֹסֵי. [6]אֲמַר לְהוּ: כִּי אָמְרִינַן: אָדָם עָשׂוּי שֶׁלֹּא לְהַשְׂבִּיעַ אֶת עַצְמוֹ, [7]הָנֵי מִילֵּי מֵחַיִּים; [8]אֲבָל לְאַחַר מִיתָה — לֹא. [9]פָּרְעוּ פַּלְגָא. [10]תַּבְעִינְהוּ לְדִינָא לְאִידָךְ פַּלְגָא. [11]אָתוּ לְקַמֵּיהּ דְּרַבִּי חִיָּיא. [12]אֲמַר לְהוּ: כְּשֵׁם שֶׁאָדָם עָשׂוּי שֶׁלֹּא לְהַשְׂבִּיעַ אֶת עַצְמוֹ, [13]כָּךְ אָדָם עָשׂוּי שֶׁלֹּא לְהַשְׂבִּיעַ אֶת בָּנָיו. [14]אָמְרוּ לֵיהּ: נֵיזִיל וְנִיהְדַּר!

RASHI

עכברא דשכיב אדינרי – עשיר שלא נהנה ממונו כעכבר זה ששוכב על דינרי זהב ואינו נהנה מהן. ניזול וניהדר – נשלם החצי שקיבלנו.

NOTES

appear ridden with debt when his apparent motive was just the opposite — to minimize his appearance of debt?! We must say that he had both motives in mind. On the one hand, he wished to deny that he had any debts; on the other hand, he was afraid that, by doing so, he would arouse envy. Hence, he admitted a moderate amount of debt, and thereby satisfied both of these goals (*Ramah*).

עַכְבְּרָא דִּשְׁכֵיב אַדִּינָרֵי The mouse who lies upon the dinarim. The explanation of this metaphor given in our commentary is according to *Rashi*. *Ramah* offers his own interpretation: Just as a mouse will hide coins without having any use for them, so did this man have no need for all the money he had accumulated. For this reason it is suggested that perhaps he fabricated an admission of debt, so as to make it appear that his idle wealth was borrowed money (*Rabbi Yehonatan of Lunel*).

אָתוּ לְקַמֵּיהּ דְּרַבִּי חִיָּיא They came before Rabbi Ḥiyya. Even though Rabbi Yishmael the son of Rabbi Yose had rendered a judgment on the case, Rabbi Ḥiyya was not afraid to contradict him. This could be for one of three reasons: One, Rabbi Yishmael had died; two, Rabbi Ḥiyya was living elsewhere; or, three, perhaps he maintained that Sages can contradict each other in deciding civil cases (*Meiri*).

נֵיזִיל וְנִיהְדַּר? May we go and retrieve? Our commentary accords with the opinion of *Ramah,* who attributes this

HALAKHAH

admission, then the debtor may no longer claim that his admission was fabricated (*Rambam*). Others state that, as long as the admission was not provoked by a previous claim of the creditor, the debtor may indeed identify it as a fabrication (*Tur*)." (*Shulḥan Arukh, Ḥoshen Mishpat* 81:14.)

כָּךְ אָדָם עָשׂוּי שֶׁלֹּא לְהַשְׂבִּיעַ אֶת בָּנָיו Similarly, a man is likely to make his sons appear not to be wealthy. "Someone who, on the verge of death, freely admits to owing money, can be presumed to have done so in order to make his heirs appear needy; thus the alleged creditor cannot pursue a claim against the heirs based upon the admission of the deceased," in accordance with the opinion of both Rabbi Ḥiyya and Rav Naḥman. (*Shulḥan Arukh, Ḥoshen Mishpat* 81:14.)

TRANSLATION AND COMMENTARY

money we paid as a result of the earlier judgment? [1]**He said to them:** You may not, for **the elder** whose judgment you solicited (Rabbi Yishmael the son of Rabbi Yose) **has already ruled** in regard to that money.

הוֹדָה בִּפְנֵי שְׁנַיִם [2]Regarding the admission of debt, if someone **admitted before two** witnesses that he owed money, **and** the witnesses **acquired from him** a confirmation of that through a formal act of acquisition (*kinyan*), **they may write** and sign a document of admission without consulting the debtor. (A document of admission, which is deposited with the creditor, is much like a promissory note in that it creates a lien on the debtor's property. Moreover, if held by the creditor, it is considered proof that repayment never took place.) [3]**If** the debtor, however, did **not** agree to perform an act of acquisition, the witnesses **may not write** out a document of admission.

בִּפְנֵי שְׁלֹשָׁה [4]If a person admitted **before three** witnesses that he owed someone money, **and** the witnesses **did not acquire from him** a formal confirmation to that effect (*kinyan*), there is a disagreement among Amoraim as to how the witnesses may proceed: [5]**Rav Ammi said: They may write** out a document of admission attesting to the loan and sign upon it; for as an assembly of three, they can act as a court and order that the loan be recorded in writing, even though the debtor did not instruct them to do so. [6]**Rav Assi said: They may not** act as a court and **write** out a document of admission, for it is assumed that the debtor intended them only to serve as witnesses. [7]**There was** once **an incident** in which someone admitted owing money before three witnesses without formally committing himself; **and Rav**, who was asked to decide the matter, **considered** as binding **the** view **of Rav Assi,** who forbade the witnesses to write out a document of admission.

[1]אֲמַר לְהוּ: כְּבָר הוֹרָה זָקֵן. [2]הוֹדָה בִּפְנֵי שְׁנַיִם וְקָנוּ מִיָּדוֹ, כּוֹתְבִין; [3]וְאִם לָאו, אֵין כּוֹתְבִין. [4]בִּפְנֵי שְׁלֹשָׁה, וְלֹא קָנוּ מִיָּדוֹ — [5]רַב אַמִי אָמַר: כּוֹתְבִין; [6]וְרַב אַסִי אָמַר: אֵין כּוֹתְבִין. [7]הֲוָה עוּבְדָּא וְחָשׁ לָהּ רַב לְהָא דְּרַב אַסִי.

LITERAL TRANSLATION

[1]He said to them: The elder has already ruled.

[2][If] he admitted before two and they acquired from his hand, they may write [it]; [3]and if not, they may not write [it].

[4]Before three, and they did not acquire from his hand — [5]Rav Ammi said: They may write [it]; [6]and Rav Assi said: They may not write [it]. [7]There was an incident and Rav considered this [position] of Rav Assi [as binding].

RASHI

כבר הורה זקן – רבי ישמעאל שקיבלתם על פיו, ולא אחלוק על מה שעשה. וקנו מידו – כותבין שטר הודאה, ואף על פי שלא אמר כתבו, דסתם קנין לכתיבה עומד. ואם לאו אין כותבין – ואף על גב דאמר להו אתם עדיי, וחייב לשלם לו, אפילו הכי ניחא ליה מלוה על פה ממלוה בשטר. שלשה – עשאן בית דין והפקירן הפקר, ויכולין לשנותו לעשות מלוה בשטר, ולהיות במקום הלוה לעשות שליח לכותבה.

NOTES

question to the heirs. *Rashi*, however, attributes it to the claimants, interpreting it as follows: "Shall we go and return the portion of the claim that we have already received?" There is an obvious problem with *Rashi*'s interpretation, for it appears from their question that the claimants were not sure of the truth behind their original claim. According to one commentator, it is possible that, following the dying father's declaration of his debt, they assumed that he did owe them money, though they had no record of it (*Ḥayyim Shenayyim Yeshalem*).

כְּבָר הוֹרָה זָקֵן **The elder has already ruled.** Rabbi Yishmael's ruling was not rejected because of an oversight on his part, or even an error in judgment. Rather, Rabbi Ḥiyya simply differed with him as to whether we assume a man falsely admits to debt in order to spare his children the appearance of having inherited wealth (*Rosh*).

וְקָנוּ מִיָּדוֹ **And they acquired from his hand.** The form of acquisition alluded to in this reference is one that confirms one's acceptance of a financial obligation. The act, known as *kinyan sudar,* is generally performed by symbolically taking a handkerchief (or some other small article) from the person to whom one is obligating himself and then returning it.

HALAKHAH

הוֹדָה בִּפְנֵי שְׁנַיִם וְקָנוּ מִיָּדוֹ **If he admitted before two, and they acquired a commitment from him.** "If someone admitted debt in the presence of two witnesses, who then acquired a formal confirmation from him to that effect (via a *kinyan sudar*), the witnesses may draw up a document attesting to the debt and deposit it with the creditor." (*Shulḥan Arukh, Ḥoshen Mishpat* 39:3.)

הוֹדָה בִּפְנֵי שְׁלֹשָׁה **If he admitted before three.** "If someone assembled three men, as if he were convening a court, and admitted before them to owing money, they may not take it upon themselves to record the admission and deposit the document of admission with the creditor unless they acquired an explicit commitment from the debtor. However, a formal court convening in its usual quarters may record such an admission even if it did not explicitly acquire a commitment from the debtor," in accordance with the opinion of Mar the son of Rav Ashi. (*Shulḥan Arukh, Ḥoshen Mishpat* 39:7.)

TRANSLATION AND COMMENTARY

אָמַר [1]**Rav Adda bar Ahavah said:** In regard to **this document of admission — sometimes we** allow the witnesses to **write** it out **and sometimes we do not** allow them to **write** it out. How so? [2]If the three people before whom the admission was made happened to **be assembled and sitting** together before the debtor approached them, then **we do not** allow them to **write** a document of admission, for there is no indication that the debtor actively sought out a quorum of three. [3]However, if the debtor himself **assembled** three witnesses for the purpose of hearing his admission, we must assume that he intended them to act as a court (for two witnesses would have sufficed); hence, **we** allow them to **write** a document of admission without the debtor's instructions. [4]**Rava**, however, **said: Even** if the debtor himself **assembled** these three witnesses before making his admission, **we** still **do not** allow them to **write** a document of admission **until he says to them** explicitly: **"Be my judges** in this regard." [5]**Mar bar Rav Ashi** was even stricter in this matter and **said: Even if** the debtor **said** to the three whom he assembled, **"Be my judges,"** [6]**we do not** allow them to **write** a document of admission **until they** actually function as a court. [7]They must **establish a venue** for sitting in judgment **and send** a bailiff in order to **summon** the debtor **to court** to make his admission in their presence.

הוֹדָה בְּמִטַּלְטְלֵי [8]The Gemara now cites additional statements of the Amoraim dealing with a witnessed admission. If a person **admitted** in the presence of two witnesses that he had borrowed **movable property** (anything other than real estate) from someone else, **and** the witnesses **got from him** a formal confirmation to this effect (*kinyan*), [9]then **they** may **write** a document of admission attesting to this fact. [10]**If** the borrower, however, did **not** commit himself to perform an act of acquisition, then the witnesses **do not** have the power to **write** such a document without his permission.

בְּמְקַרְקְעֵי [11]The Gemara asks: **If someone admitted** in the presence of two witnesses to occupying another's **land, and** the witnesses **did not acquire from him** a formal confirmation to that effect — **what is** the law? [12]**Amemar said:** it is comparable to movable property; hence, the witnesses **do not** have the power to **write**

[1]אֲמַר רַב אַדָּא בַּר אַהֲבָה: הָא אוֹדִיתָא — זִימְנִין כָּתְבִינַן וְזִימְנִין לָא כָּתְבִינַן. [2]כְּנִיפֵי וְיָתְבֵי, לָא כָּתְבִינַן; [3]כַּנְפִינְהוּ אִיהוּ, כָּתְבִינַן. [4]רָבָא אָמַר: אֲפִילּוּ כַּנְפִינְהוּ אִיהוּ, לָא כָּתְבִינַן — עַד דְּאָמַר לְהוּ: "הֱווּ עֲלַי דַּיָּינַי". [5]מָר בַּר רַב אַשִׁי אָמַר: אֲפִילּוּ אָמַר "הֱווּ עֲלַי דַּיָּינַי", [6]לָא כָּתְבִינַן — [7]עַד דְּקָבְעִי דוּכְתָּא וְשָׁלְחִי וּמְזַמְּנִי לֵיהּ לְבֵי דִינָא.

[8]הוֹדָה בְּמִטַּלְטְלֵי וְקָנוּ מִיָּדוֹ, כּוֹתְבִין; [9]וְאִם לָאו, [10]אֵין כּוֹתְבִין.

[11]בִּמְקַרְקְעֵי, וְלֹא קָנוּ מִיָּדוֹ, מַאי? [12]אַמֵימָר אָמַר: אֵין

LITERAL TRANSLATION

[1]Rav Adda bar Ahavah said: This document of admission — sometimes we write [it] and sometimes we do not write [it]. [2][If] they were assembled and sitting, we do not write [it]; [3][if] he assembled them, we write [it]. [4]Rava said: Even [if] he assembled them, we do not write [it] — until he says to them: "Be my judges." [5]Mar bar Rav Ashi said: Even if he said, "Be my judges," [6]we do not write [it] — [7]until they establish a venue [for the court] and send [a bailiff] to summon him to the court.

[8][If] he admitted in [regard to] movable property and they acquired from his hand, [9]they write [it]; [10]and if not, they do not write [it].

[11][If someone admitted] in [regard to] land, and they did not acquire from his hand, what is [the law]? [12]Amemar said: They do not

RASHI

אודיתא – שטר הודאה בפני שלשה שלא קנו מידו. כניפי ויתבי – שלשה שהיו יושבין ובא והודה לו בפניהם, הואיל ולא זימנום וקיבצום לכך לא נעשו בית דין אלא עדים, דדילמא אי לא הוו אלא תרי הוה מודי ליה קמייהו ולא הוה מהדר אחר בית דין. כנפינהו איהו כתבינן – דמדכניף תלתא דעתא אבי דינא. דקבעי דוכתא – כדרך הדיינין. ושלחו – שליח בשמייהו ללוה למיתי קמייהו לדינא ולאודויי, והואיל ועומד בדין נעשית כמלוה בשטר שגלויה לכל הלכך כתבינן. במקרקעי – קרקע שהיה ראובן מוחזק בה והודה לשמעון שהיא שלו.

NOTES

בְּמְקַרְקְעֵי, אַמֵימָר אָמַר: אֵין כּוֹתְבִין **In regard to land, Amemar said: They may not write it.** The Rishonim ask the following question about Amemar's position: If land immediately reverts to its true owner upon the admission of the present occupier, what additional damage would there be to that occupier if the witnesses recorded his admission

HALAKHAH

הוֹדָה בְּמְקַרְקְעֵי **If he admitted in regard to land.** "The law that prevents witnesses to an admission from recording what they heard applies only to an admission involving money or movable property, when there was no formal acquisition of responsibility on the part of the debtor. If the admission was in regard to land, the witnesses may draw

כּוֹתְבִין. [1]מָר זוּטְרָא אָמַר: כּוֹתְבִין. וְהִלְכְתָא: כּוֹתְבִין.
[2]רָבִינָא אִיקְלַע לְדַמְהַרְיָא. אֲמַר לֵיהּ רַב דִּימִי בַּר רַב הוּנָא מִדַּמְהַרְיָא לְרָבִינָא: [3]מִטַּלְטְלֵי, וְאִיתְנְהוּ בְּעֵינַיְיהוּ, מַאי? [4]אֲמַר לֵיהּ: כִּמְקַרְקְעֵי דָּמוּ. [5]רַב אַשִׁי אָמַר: כֵּיוָן דִּמְחַסְּרִי גּוּבַיְינָא — לָא.
[6]הַהִיא אוֹדִיתָא דְּלָא הֲוָה כָּתוּב בָּהּ: [7]"אֲמַר לַנָא: כִּתְבוּ וְחִתְמוּ וַהֲבוּ לֵיהּ". [8]אַבַּיֵי וְרָבָא

LITERAL TRANSLATION

write [it]. [1]Mar Zutra said: They write [it]. And the law [is that] they write [it].

[2]Ravina happened to come to Damharya. Rav Dimi bar Rav Huna from Damharya said to Ravina: [3][If someone admits in regard to] movable property, and it exists as it was, what is [the law]? [4]He said to him: It is like land. [5]Rav Ashi said: Since [movable property] lacks collection — [it is] not.

[6][There was] a certain document of admission in which it was not written: [7]"He said to us: Write [it] and sign [it] and give [it] to him." [8]Abaye and Rava

RASHI

כותבין – דהא כיון דאודי ליה, דידיה הוא, ולא מיחסרא גוביינא, דבשלמא מטלטלי – מלוה להוצאה ניתנה וחוב בעלמא הוא, ומלוה על פה ריעא ממלוה בשטר ולא ניחא ליה לאלומה. אבל הכא – גלויי מילתא בעלמא הוא. לדימהריא – שם מקום. איתנהו בעינייהו – בשעת הודאה. מאי – מי אמרינן: כיון דצבורין ומונחין ואודי ליה – כל היכא דאיתנהו דידיה הוו, או דילמא: כיון דמלוה להוצאה ניתנה – שמא יוציאה, ולא ניחא ליה למיהוי שטרא עילויה, ובהודאה בפני שני עדים קאמר. ההיא אודיתא – שנים חתומים עליה.

TRANSLATION AND COMMENTARY

a document of admission unless they were instructed to do so. [1]**Mar Zutra said:** The cases are not comparable; when a tenant admits that property belongs to its original owner, that property immediately reverts to the owner's possession, rendering any written record a mere formality. However, even after someone has admitted that movable property is not his own, it still requires physical transfer to its correct owner. The witnesses may **write** a document of admission even without the consent of the party who makes the admission, since it does not make his case any weaker. **And the law** is in accordance with Mar Zutra, who maintains that the witnesses may **write** a document of admission in the case of landed property.

רָבִינָא אִיקְלַע [2]Once, when **Ravina happened** to pass through the town of **Damharya, Rav Dimi bar Rav Huna from Damharya said to** him: [3]If someone admits before witnesses to having borrowed **movable property** belonging to another, **and it exists as it was** at the time of his admission — **what is** the law? [4]Ravina **said to him:** The property **is like land,** as it immediately reverts to its original owner, and the witnesses' writing a document of admission does not make his case weaker. [5]**Rav Ashi said: Since** the movable property still **requires** the physical act of **collection** by its rightful owner, it is **not** like land but rather like money. Hence, there is a disadvantage to the borrower in having a written record of his admission. The witnesses may not write a document without his instructions.

הַהִיא אוֹדִיתָא [6]It is told that there was once **a certain** document of **admission in which** the following **was not written** by the witnesses: [7]**"He** (the debtor) **said to us: Write** out a document of admission, **sign** it **and give** it **to** my creditor." [8]**Abaye and Rava both said:** Such a case **is** comparable to that implied in a statement

NOTES

without his consent? *Rabbenu Yonah* suggests that the written record could be problematical, should the present occupier subsequently decide to buy the land from its rightful owner. In such an event, he would have to preserve his bill of sale indefinitely to protect himself, should the seller later attempt to contest his ownership on the basis of the earlier document of admission. *Ran* contends that Amemar simply maintained that we never write out a legal document without being instructed to do so by the one who becomes obligated through it. *Ḥamra Veḥaye* explains Amemar's position as follows: One who admits to not owning a particular piece of real estate may prefer not have his admission recorded, for if he has many outstanding promissory notes, he is interested in appearing to hold as much land as possible. If people think that he is in danger of bankruptcy, the value of all his land will drop. Mar Zutra dismissses this concern, for in our case the document simply indicates that he recognizes another as the owner of real estate in his possession — and outsiders would assume from his admission that he is wealthy enough to have given the land away as a gift, were it his.

HALAKHAH

up the record even without first procuring a formal commitment from the one making the admission." (*Shulḥan Arukh, Ḥoshen Mishpat* 39:8.)

הַהִיא אוֹדִיתָא דְּלָא הֲוָה כָּתוּב בָּהּ: "אֲמַר לַנָא: כִּתְבוּ" **A document of admission in which was not written "He said to us: Write."** "A document of admission in which the witnesses did not write that they were instructed by the debtor to draw up the document and deposit it with the creditor is nonetheless valid, for it is presumed that the witnesses would not have drawn up and signed such a

TRANSLATION AND COMMENTARY

by Resh Lakish, [1]**for Resh Lakish** once **said:** There is **a presumption** that **witnesses do not sign a document** of land sale **unless** they know that the seller is **legally of age** to effect the transaction. Similarly, we must assume that witnesses would not write and sign a document of admission unless they were certain of its validity, guided either by the debtor's express instruction or implicit assent (as when he confirms the admission through a formal act of acquisition). The absence of any such reference within the document itself is no more problematic than the seller's age not appearing on a bill of sale.

מַתְקִיף לָהּ [2]**Rav Pappi, and some say Rav Huna the son of Rabbi Yehoshua, attacks** the preceding conclusion: [3]**Is there anything which we** judges **do not** all **know** (i.e., the law forbidding witnesses to record an admission without the debtor's consent), [4]**and** yet **the scribes of the court** are assumed to **know** without exception? Certainly, if some Rabbis are unfamiliar with this law, then some scribes must be unfamiliar with it, too. Consequently, a document of admission is suspect unless it explicitly states that the debtor commissioned its writing.

שְׁאֵילִינְהוּ [5]In response to Rav Pappi's attack, the Rabbis **asked the scribes of Abaye**'s court whether they knew of the above condition for writing documents of admission; **and they knew** of it. Similarly, [6]they asked **the scribes of Rava**'s court; **and they,** too, **knew** of it.

הַהִיא אוֹדִיתָא [7]It is told that there was once **a certain** document of **admission** signed by two witnesses **on which was written:** [8]"Behold this is **a memorandum of** certain **affairs** brought to our attention," [30A] [9]and the document included **all the terminology** usually associated with the proceedings **of a court.** However, the report had only two signatures on it, and the statement normally placed on a court record was signed by only two judges — [10]**"we were** originally **a panel of three, but** today **one** of us **is absent"** — **was not written there.** It thus appears that the document of admission may have been drafted by two ordinary witnesses, who had no judicial authority to do so. [11]**Ravina thought of explaining** that **this was** one of the cases included in the ruling of **Resh Lakish,** who established that people do not sign an official document unless they are certain of

LITERAL TRANSLATION

both said: That is [the case] of Resh Lakish, [1]for Resh Lakish said: [There is] a presumption [that] witnesses do not sign a document unless [the seller] has reached adulthood.

[2]Rav Pappi attacks it, and some say Rav Huna the son of Rabbi Yehoshua: [3]Is there anything that we do not know, [4]and the scribes of the court do know?

[5]They asked the scribes of Abaye and they knew; [6]the scribes of Rava and they knew.

[7][There was] a certain [document of] admission in which was written [8]"a memorandum of affairs" [30A] [9]and all the terminology [was that] of a court, [10]but "we were a panel of three and one is absent" was not written in it. [11]Ravina thought to say: This is [the case] of Resh

דְּאָמְרִי תַּרְוַיְיהוּ: הַיְינוּ דְּרֵישׁ לָקִישׁ, [1]דַּאֲמַר רֵישׁ לָקִישׁ: חֲזָקָה אֵין הָעֵדִים חוֹתְמִין עַל הַשְּׁטָר אֶלָּא אִם כֵּן נַעֲשָׂה גָּדוֹל.

[2]מַתְקִיף לָהּ רַב פַּפִּי, וְאִיתֵּימָא רַב הוּנָא בְּרֵיהּ דְּרַב יְהוֹשֻׁעַ: [3]מִי אִיכָּא מִידֵּי דַּאֲנַן לָא יָדְעִינַן, [4]וְסָפְרֵי דְּבֵי דִינָא יָדְעִי? [5]שְׁאֵילִינְהוּ לְסָפְרֵי דְּאַבַּיֵּי וְיָדְעִי; [6]לְסָפְרֵי דְּרָבָא וְיָדְעִי.

[7]הַהִיא אוֹדִיתָא דַּהֲוָה כָּתַב בֵּיהּ [8]"דּוּכְרַן פִּיתְגָּמֵי" [30A] [9]וְכָל לִישָּׁנֵי דְּבֵי דִינָא, [10]וְלָא הֲוָה כָּתַב בָּהּ "בְּמוֹתַב תְּלָתָא הֲוֵינָא, וְחַד לֵיתוֹהִי". [11]סָבַר רָבִינָא לְמֵימַר: הַיְינוּ דְּרֵישׁ

RASHI

נעשה גדול — המוכר, דקיימא לן (בבא בתרא קנו, א): ולמכור בנכסי אביו — עד שיהא בן עשרים. הכא נמי, כיון דשנים לא מלי כתבי אלא ברשותו — ודאי איהו אמר להו. דאנן לא ידעינן — כלומר: יש דיינין הרבה שאין בקיאין בהלכה זו שאמרנו, דשנים שלא קנו מידו אין כותבין. דוכרן פיתגמי — לא היה כתוב בה זכרון עדות בלשון עדים, אלא בלשון זכרון דברים, והוא לשון דיינין. וכל לישני דבי דינא — כל דבריהם היו כתובין בלשון בית דין, ולא היו חתומין אלא שנים. ולא הוה כתיב ביה במותב תלתא הוינא וחד ליתוהי — כדמפרשינן בכתובות (כב, א) בשלשה שישבו לקיים את השטר ומת אחד מהם. היינו דריש לקיש — דאמר: חזקה אין בית דין

HALAKHAH

document unless they had a proper mandate to do so. However, some authorities suggest that a debt cannot be collected on the basis of such a document." (*Shulḥan Arukh, Ḥoshen Mishpat* 39:11.)

חֲזָקָה אֵין הָעֵדִים חוֹתְמִין עַל הַשְּׁטָר אֶלָּא אִם כֵּן נַעֲשָׂה גָּדוֹל **There is a presumption that witnesses do not sign on a document unless its subject has achieved adulthood.** "A bill of sale (or gift) which was challenged in court on the basis of a claim that the seller (or benefactor) was a minor at the time of the transaction, is valid even if the witnesses themselves support the claim. This is because of the presumption that witnesses do not sign a document unless they know for a fact that the transaction attested to therein was conducted legally. The witnesses themselves are not believed should they contradict this presumption." (*Shulḥan Arukh, Ḥoshen Mishpat* 46:38; 235:13.)

לָקִישׁ. [1]אֲמַר לֵיהּ רַב נָתָן בַּר אַמִי: [2]הָכִי אָמְרִינַן מִשְּׁמֵיהּ דְּרָבָא: כָּל כִּי הַאי גַּוְונָא, [3]חָיְישִׁינַן לְבֵית דִּין טוֹעִין.
[4]אָמַר רַב נַחְמָן בַּר יִצְחָק: אִי כָּתַב בָּהּ ״בֵּי דִינָא״, [5]תוּ לָא צְרִיךְ.
[6]וְדִילְמָא בֵּית דִּין חָצוּף הוּא, [7]דְּאָמַר שְׁמוּאֵל: שְׁנַיִם שֶׁדָּנוּ — דִּינֵיהֶן דִּין, [8]אֶלָּא שֶׁנִּקְרְאוּ בֵּית דִּין חָצוּף!
[9]דְּכָתַב בֵּיהּ: ״בֵּי דִינָא דְּרַבָּנָא אַשִׁי״.
[10]וְדִילְמָא רַבָּנַן דְּבֵי רַב אַשִׁי כִּשְׁמוּאֵל סְבִירָא לְהוּ!
[11]דִּכְתִיב בּוֹ: ״וַאֲמַרְנָא לֵיהּ לְרַבָּנָא אַשִׁי...[12]וַאֲמַר לָן רַבָּנָא אַשִׁי...״.

LITERAL TRANSLATION

Lakish. [1]Rav Natan bar Ammi said to him: [2]We say as follows in the name of Rava: [In] any case like this, [3]we fear a court [that] erred.

[4]Rav Naḥman bar Yitzḥak said: If "a court" was written in it, [5]no more is required.

[6]But perhaps it was an "impudent court," [7]for Shmuel said: Two who judged — their decision is a [valid] judgment, [8]but they are called an impudent court!

[9]When [it was] written in it: "The court of Rabbana Ashi."

[10]But perhaps the Rabbis of Rav Ashi's academy maintained like Shmuel!

[11]For written in it [was]: "And we said to him, to Rabbana Ashi...[12]and Rabbana Ashi said to us...."

TRANSLATION AND COMMENTARY

the document's legality. We can therefore accept the document. [1]**Rav Natan bar Ammi**, however, **said to** Ravina: [2]**We say as follows in the name of Rava:** In **any case like this,** when only two signatures are found on an official court record, [3]we must **fear** that the document was drawn up by **a court that erred,** thinking that two judges are sufficient to adjudicate such cases. Hence, this document of admission must be dismissed.

אָמַר [4]**Rav Naḥman bar Yitzḥak said:** If a direct reference to themselves as **"a court" was written** anywhere **on the document,** [5]**no more is required** — for the term "court" can only refer to a tribunal of at least three judges.

וְדִילְמָא [6]The Gemara challenges Rav Naḥman bar Yitzḥak's statement: **But perhaps** the court that drew up the record **was an "impudent court"** — one which, although composed of only two judges, called itself a court. [7]**As Shmuel said:** If **two** laymen **judged** a monetary case, **their judgment is binding** on the litigants (as Biblical law recognizes even one judge in a civil case); [8]but the two judges **are called an impudent court** for having defied the Rabbinic decree calling for no fewer than three judges. If so, the document drafted by such a court should be dismissed, as Shmuel's validation of a two-member court is not accepted as law!

דְּכָתַב בֵּיהּ [9]Rather, we must say that the document is only validated **if** the reference **written on** it was **"the court of Rabbana Ashi"** (or any other court of comparable stature); such a tribunal would not term itself a court unless it consisted of at least three judges.

וְדִילְמָא [10]**But perhaps the Rabbis of Rav Ashi's academy ruled as Shmuel** did, that two judges are also called a court, albeit an impudent one.

דִּכְתִיב בּוֹ [11]Rather, one must say that the following was **written on** the document: **"And we said to Rabbana Ashi** that we heard the preceding admission; [12]**and Rabbana Ashi said to us**: Record it." Certainly, Rav Ashi would not have authorized them to record the admission unless three judges had presided at the original proceedings.

RASHI

כותבין שטר אלא כדת וכהלכה. והני וודאי תלתא הוו. לבית דין טועין — סבורין שיהו שנים כשרים לדון. בי דינא — הכל יודעין שאין שנים קרויס בית דין. בי דינא דרבנא אשי — דאינהו ודאי ידעי שאין בית דין קרויין בשנים. ואמר לן רבנא אשי — לכתוב כך, דכיון דהוא היה שם מסתמא לא נוח לפחות משלשה לכתוב, והאי דנקט רב אשי — לפי שבית דינו היה ראש בימי רבינא ושניהם סידרו גמרא של תלמוד בבלי כדאמרינן התם ב״השוכר את הפועלים״ (פו,א) רב אשי ורבינא סוף הוראה, ובימיו

NOTES

בֵּי דִינָא דְּרַבָּנָא אַשִׁי **The court of Rabbana Ashi.** According to some commentators, Rabbi Ashi's court was cited as an example because it served at the end of the Amoraic era when legal conclusions, such as the decision to discount Shmuel's validation of a two-man court, were already fixed as law (*Rabbi Yehonatan of Lunel*).

אֲמַר לָן רַבָּנָא אַשִׁי **Rabbana Ashi said to us.** According to *Ramah*, the evidence of the legality of the document stems not from Rabbi Ashi's apparent familiarity with its contents (as explained by *Rashi*), but rather from his own implied participation as the third judge who was responsible for producing the document.

HALAKHAH

חָיְישִׁינַן לְבֵית דִּין טוֹעִין **We fear a court that erred.** "A document of admission that was written in the terminology of the court, but on which appeared only two signatories (with no indication of a third having been present at the

[1] תָּנוּ רַבָּנַן: ״אָמַר לָהֶן אֶחָד: אֲנִי רָאִיתִי אֲבִיכֶם שֶׁהִטְמִין מָעוֹת בְּשִׁידָּה, תֵּיבָה, וּמִגְדָּל; [2] וְאָמַר: ׳שֶׁל פְּלוֹנִי הֵן׳, [3] ׳שֶׁל מַעֲשֵׂר שֵׁנִי הֵן׳ — [4] בַּבַּיִת, [5] לֹא אָמַר כְּלוּם; [6] בַּשָּׂדֶה, דְּבָרָיו קַיָּימִין. [7] כְּלָלוֹ שֶׁל דָּבָר: כָּל שֶׁבְּיָדוֹ לִיטְּלָן, דְּבָרָיו קַיָּימִין; [8] אֵין בְּיָדוֹ לִיטְּלָן, [9] לֹא אָמַר כְּלוּם.

[10] הֲרֵי שֶׁרָאוּ אֶת אֲבִיהֶן שֶׁהִטְמִין מָעוֹת בְּשִׁידָּה, תֵּיבָה, וּמִגְדָּל; [11] וְאָמַר: ׳שֶׁל פְּלוֹנִי הֵן׳, [12] ׳שֶׁל מַעֲשֵׂר שֵׁנִי הֵן׳ — [13] אִם כְּמוֹסֵר, [14] דְּבָרָיו קַיָּימִין; [15] אִם כִּמְעַרְעֵרִים, [16] לֹא אָמַר כְּלוּם.

LITERAL TRANSLATION

[1] Our Rabbis taught: "[If] someone said to them: I saw your father hiding money in a chest, a box, or a closet; [2] and he said [to me]: 'They are so-and-so's' [3] [or] 'they are second tithe' — [4] [if it was hidden] in the house, [5] [the witness] has said nothing; [6] in a field, his words stand. [7] The general rule in this matter [is]: Anything that is in his hands to take [for himself], his words stand; [8] [if] it is not in his hands to take them [for himself], [9] he said nothing.

[10] [If heirs] saw their father hide money in a chest, a box, or a closet; [11] and he said [to them]: 'They are so-and-so's' [12] [or] 'they are second tithe' — [13] if in the manner of one who is informing, [14] his words stand; [15] if in the manner of one who is deceiving, [16] he said nothing.

TRANSLATION AND COMMENTARY

תָּנוּ רַבָּנַן [1] The Gemara now returns to the earlier discussion of a confession of liability: **Our Rabbis taught** in a Baraita: "If **someone said to** the heirs of a deceased man: I once **saw your father hiding money in a chest** (or in **a box** or **a closet**), [2] **and he said** to me at the time: **'This money belongs** to **so-and-so,'** [3] or 'this money is invested with the sanctity **of the second tithe** (thus necessitating its being taken to Jerusalem should one wish to derive benefit from it)' — if the money is indeed found in this enclosure, [4] and it was located **in the** deceased's **house,** [5] then it is considered as if the witness had **said nothing.** [6] However, if the hiding place was **in a field, his words stand** and the heirs must distribute the money in accordance with the sole witness's testimony. [7] **The general rule** governing such a **matter** is as follows: Should someone make a statement about **something that was in his hands to** freely **take** for himself, **his words stand** regarding the ownership of the money. For if his intention was to lie and dispossess the heirs, he could have simply taken the money. [8] If, however, **it was not in his hands to** freely **take** the object (as when it is hidden in the deceased's home), then there is a possibility that he may be lying in order to dispossess the heirs. [9] Since he was a single witness, the Rabbis rejected his statement and considered it as if **he** had **said nothing."**

הֲרֵי שֶׁרָאוּ [10] The Baraita continues: "If the heirs themselves **saw their father hide money in a chest** (or in a **box** or a **closet**); [11] **and he said to them:** 'This money **is so-and-so's,'** [12] or 'this money **is** invested with sanctity **of the second tithe'** — [13] **if** it was apparent from the father's demeanor that he was speaking **in the manner of one who** is **informing** them of the status of the money, [14] **his words stand** and we accept his admission. [15] **If** it seems, however, that he was speaking harshly, **in the manner of one who is deceiving** his children, to keep them from taking the money, [16] then we discount his admission and it is considered as if **he** had **said nothing."**

RASHI

נאמרו דברים הללו והוקבעו בגמרא. **בבית לא אמר כלום** — אינו נאמן, לפי שאין בידו ליטלן. **בשדה דבריו קיימין** — דמה לו לשקר? — אם רוצה נוטלן ונותנן לאותו שהוא מעיד עליו. **אם כמוסר** — אם נראה להם כמוסר דבריו לבניו באמת בלשון צוואה. **במערים** — שהוא מתירא שלא יטלם בחייו, או שלא יחזיקוהו כעשיר להוסיף על יציאותיו.

NOTES

בַּבַּיִת, לֹא אָמַר כְּלוּם **In the house, he said nothing.** The Rishonim ask: Why do we dismiss the man's claim that the money was used to redeem second-tithe produce? After all, in matters of ritual law (such as the redemption of tithes or the kashrut of the food), the testimony of a single witness is taken as true! *Ran* points out that this applies only to matters that are exclusively ritual in nature; when there is a financial aspect, testimony must be offered by two witnesses in order to be acceptable. *Meiri* suggests that in our case we do not accept the single witness because

HALAKHAH

time of the admission), is suspected of having been drawn up by two judges who mistakenly thought that they comprised a valid court," in accordance with the opinion of Rava. (*Shulḥan Arukh, Ḥoshen Mishpat* 39:12.)

אֲנִי רָאִיתִי אֲבִיכֶם שֶׁהִטְמִין מָעוֹת **I saw your father hiding money.** "If someone said to his friend: I saw your father hiding money, which he told me belonged to so-and-so (or was invested with sanctity of the second tithe) — if the money was subsequently found in a place to which the witness himself had access, he is believed; otherwise he is not believed." (*Shulḥan Arukh, Ḥoshen Mishpat* 255:8.)

רָאוּ אֶת אֲבִיהֶן שֶׁהִטְמִין מָעוֹת **If they saw their father hiding money.** "In the case of a son who saw his father hiding money and claims that his father told him that the

[1]הֲרֵי שֶׁהָיָה מִצְטַעֵר עַל מָעוֹת שֶׁהִנִּיחַ לוֹ אָבִיו? [2]וּבָא בַּעַל הַחֲלוֹם וְאָמַר לוֹ: [3]'כָּךְ וְכָךְ הֵן, בְּמָקוֹם פְּלוֹנִי הֵן, [4]שֶׁל מַעֲשֵׂר שֵׁנִי הֵן'. [5]זֶה הָיָה מַעֲשֶׂה, וְאָמְרוּ: [6]דִּבְרֵי חֲלוֹמוֹת לֹא מַעֲלִין וְלֹא מוֹרִידִין".

[7]"שְׁנַיִם אוֹמְרִים זַכַּאי כו'". [8]מִיכְתַּב הֵיכִי כָּתְבִי? [9]רַבִּי יוֹחָנָן אָמַר: זַכַּאי. [10]רֵישׁ לָקִישׁ אָמַר: פְּלוֹנִי וּפְלוֹנִי מְזַכִּין [11]וּפְלוֹנִי וּפְלוֹנִי מְחַיְּיבִין. [12]רַבִּי אֱלִיעֶזֶר אָמַר: מִדִּבְרֵיהֶן נִזְדַּכָּה פְּלוֹנִי.

LITERAL TRANSLATION

[1]If [a person] was troubled over [not finding] money that his father left him, [2]and the master of dreams came and said to him: [3]'They [amount to] such-and-such, they are in such-and-such a place, [4][but] they are second tithe.' [5]This was an incident [that came to the Rabbis], and they said: [6]Words of dreams do not raise and do not lower [in law]."

[7]"Two say he is free of liability, etc." [8]How is it recorded? [9]Rabbi Yohanan said: [He is] free of liability. [10]Resh Lakish said: So-and-so and so-and-so free [him of liability] [11]or so-and-so and so-and-so find [him] liable. [12]Rabbi Elazar said: As a result of their [concurring] words, so-and-so was freed of liability.

TRANSLATION AND COMMENTARY

הֲרֵי שֶׁהָיָה מִצְטַעֵר [1]The Baraita concludes as follows: "It once happened **that** a person **was troubled about** inherited **money that his father left him** in an undisclosed location. [2]While sleeping, **the** Angel appointed as **master** over men's **dreams came and said to him:** [3]'The money you are seeking is **such-and-such** an amount and **is in such-and-such a place;** [4]however, **it is** invested with the sanctity **of the second tithe** and you can use it only in Jerusalem.' Upon awakening, the man went to the place and found the money there. [5]**This was an** actual **incident** that came before the Sages**, and they said:** [6]When it comes to deciding law, **words of dreams have no weight.**"

שְׁנַיִם אוֹמְרִים [7]We learned earlier in our Mishnah: "If **two** of the judges **say** that the defendant **is free of liability** and one says that he is liable, the defendant is free of liability." [8]The Gemara asks: When the judges disagree, **how is** the verdict **recorded?** [9]**Rabbi Yoḥanan said:** It is written simply that the defendant was found to be **free of liability.** [10]**Resh Lakish said:** It must be written that Judges **so-and-so and so-and-so free** the defendant **of liability,** or, in the case of conviction, [11]that Judges so**-and-so and so-and-so find** him **liable.** [12]**Rabbi Elazar said:** The positions of individual judges need not be spelled out in the record. But it should be stated that, **as a result of the words** of those judges who supported his innocence, **so-and-so was freed of liability** in court — thereby indicating that there was a dissenting opinion.

RASHI

שהניח לו אביו — ולא אמר להו היכן הם. **בעל החלום** — שר המראה חלומות בלילה. **כך וכך הם** — מגיד לו כמה יש. **לא מעלין כו'** — ויכול להוציאם במקומן. **מיכתב היכי כתבינן** — פסק דין, במקום שיש מחלוקת ונטו אחרי הרבים. **זכאי** — פלוני. **מדבריהם נזדכה** — משמע שהיה מחלוקת ביניהם ומתוך דבריהם נזדכה.

NOTES

it creates a prohibition, preventing the heirs from using the money except in Jerusalem. Normally, the testimony of a single witness is only accepted in ritual cases for the sake of leniency — permitting something that otherwise might have been forbidden due to doubt.

בָּא בַּעַל הַחֲלוֹם וְאָמַר לוֹ The master of dreams came and said to him. *Ran* asks: Why did the Baraita, after having already established that a human witness would not be believed in this case, feel it necessary to teach us that testimony conveyed through a dream is unacceptable as well? He answers: Since our Rabbis have taught us that dreams constitute one sixtieth of prophecy, and in this case the verifiable elements of the dream (the amount and the location of the money) were actually borne out, it could enter one's mind that the remaining element of the dream (concerning the second tithe) would be believed as well.

לֹא מַעֲלִין וְלֹא מוֹרִידִין They have no weight in law. The reason dreams are considered to be unworthy of the court's attention is the inclusion within them of meaningless and confusing details. For our Rabbis have taught: Just as there can be no grain without straw, so can there be no dream without idle elements. Consequently, our Baraita fears that perhaps the claim voiced in the man's dream, that the money had the sanctity of the second tithe, was an idle and unreliable detail (*Meiri*). Others suggest that we do not entertain this claim because it is introduced by a single individual, the heir who had the dream, and thus is no different from the testimony of a single witness, which, as we have already seen, is ineffective in this case (*Rabbi Yehonatan of Lunel*).

מִיכְתַּב הֵיכִי כָּתְבִי How is it recorded? Normally, a court verdict is issued orally without indicating whether it was a

HALAKHAH

money belonged to so-and-so (or was invested with the sanctity of the second tithe), if it was apparent that the father was speaking seriously, the money must be distributed accordingly; however, if it appears that the father was engaging in a ruse, the heirs need not honor his claim." (*Shulḥan Arukh, Ḥoshen Mishpat* 255:7.)

בָּא בַּעַל הַחֲלוֹם The master of dreams came. "If someone dreamt that his father hid a certain sum of money somewhere, but that the money belonged to someone else (or was invested with sanctity) — should the money actually be discovered in that place, the heir may do with it as he wishes; for dreams do not determine an object's legal status." (*Shulḥan Arukh, Ḥoshen Mishpat* 255:9.)

הֵיכִי כָּתְבִי How is the verdict recorded? "If one of the

TRANSLATION AND COMMENTARY

מַאי בֵּינַיְיהוּ [1]The Gemara now asks: **What** practical difference **is** there **between** the above positions? [2]**There is** a legal difference **between them** with regard **to** an erroneous verdict (as determined by a more expert court), in which case the members of the first court had to pay compensation to the wronged litigant. [3]There is disagreement about whether the dissenting judge must **pay, together with** the other judges, **a share** of this compensation. [4]**For according to** Rabbi Yoḥanan, **who said** that we simply write in the document that the defendant was found to be **free of liability,** [5]he implicates the dissenting judge in the verdict and that judge should **pay** his share of the compensation. [6]**But according to** Resh Lakish, **who said** that we record: [7]**"So-and-so and so-and-so free** the defendant from liability **or so-and-so and so-and-so find** him **liable,"** [8]the dissenting judge **would not pay** any compensation in the event that such an error is found.

וּלְמַאן דַּאֲמַר [9]Can we really say that, **according to** Rabbi Yoḥanan, **who said** that the document merely states that the defendant was found to be **"free of liability,"** [10]the dissenting judge must **pay** a portion of any future compensation? [11]Should the situation arise, **let that judge say to** his colleagues: **If you had listened to me** and decided otherwise, [12]**you would not be paying** any compensation to the plaintiff!

[1]מַאי בֵּינַיְיהוּ? [2]אִיכָּא בֵּינַיְיהוּ [3]לְשַׁלּוּמֵי אִיהוּ מְנָתָא בַּהֲדַיְיהוּ. [4]דִּלְמַאן דַּאֲמַר: ״זַכַּאי״, [5]מְשַׁלֵּם; [6]וּלְמַאן דַּאֲמַר: [7]״פְּלוֹנִי וּפְלוֹנִי מְזַכִּין וּפְלוֹנִי וּפְלוֹנִי מְחַיְּיבִין״, [8]לֹא מְשַׁלֵּם. [9]וּלְמַאן דַּאֲמַר: ״זַכַּאי״, [10]מְשַׁלֵּם? [11]לֵימָא לְהוּ: אִי לְדִידִי צַיְיתִיתוּן, [12]אַתּוּן נַמִי לָא שַׁלְּמִיתוּן!

LITERAL TRANSLATION

[1]What is [the difference] between them? [2]There is [a difference] between them [with regard] [3]to [the dissenting judge's] paying a share [of compensation] together with them. [4]For according to the one who said "[He is] free of liability," [5]he pays; [6]and according to the one who said: [7]"So-and-so and so-and-so free [him] from liability, or so-and-so and so-and-so find [him] liable," [8]he does not pay. [9]According to the one who said: "[He is] free of liability," [10]he pays? [11]Let him say to them: If you had listened to me, [12]you would also not be paying!

RASHI

לשלומי איהו מנתא בהדייהו – אם טעו השנים וחייבין לשלם מביתם, פליגי הנך רבנן בדיין השלישי אם ישלם חלקו עמהם. **מאן דאמר זכאי** – כתבינן ולא כתבינן פלוגתייהו דקסבר כולם שוין ואף השלישי ישלם עמהם, דאי לא הוה איהו בהדייהו בתרי לא הוה מיפסיק דינא.

NOTES

unanimous or majority opinion or how the individual judges decided (see the Mishnah). Occasionally a written document is requested by a vindicated litigant to verify the verdict if it is ever challenged before another court. Such is the case discussed in our Gemara (*Meiri*).

אִיכָּא בֵּינַיְיהוּ לְשַׁלּוּמֵי אִיהוּ מְנָתָא בַּהֲדַיְיהוּ There is a difference between them in regard to his paying a share [of compensation] together with them. In this interpretation of the Baraita, Rabbi Elazar would agree with Rabbi Yoḥanan that the dissenting judge is responsible for his share of the compensation, even though Rabbi Elazar requires that the language of the document indicate that the verdict was not unanimous (*Ramah*).

HALAKHAH

litigants requests a written record of the verdict, the judges must provide him with one — while deleting from it any mention of the contributing arguments or of how individual judges voted. Rather, they write as follows: So-and-so came before a court and, as a result of their words, was either found free of liability or found liable." (This formula is in accordance with the opinion of Rabbi Elazar, who combined elements of both Rabbi Yoḥanan's and Resh Lakish's opposing opinions.) If the verdict was unanimous, the record need not state that it was arrived at "as a result of their words," for that clause implies that there were conflicting arguments in the court (*Kesef Mishneh*). (*Shulḥan Arukh, Ḥoshen Mishpat* 19:2.)

אִיכָּא בֵּינַיְיהוּ לְשַׁלּוּמֵי There is a difference between them in regard to paying compensation. "If a court consisting of three lay judges erred in its verdict and unjustifiably obligated the defendant to pay the claim brought against him, they must compensate him out of their own pockets (unless the litigants expressly stipulated before the trial that they would accept the verdict unconditionally). If all three judges concurred in the erroneous verdict, they divide the payment of compensation equally between them. If any of them had voted to free him of liability, that judge need not pay his portion of the compensation, and the defendant only receives two-thirds in restitution from the remaining judges. If the court was made up of five judges, three of whom concurred in an erroneous verdict, then those three judges — constituting a court unto themselves — must pay full compensation (not just three-fifths). If the judges were compelled by their community to serve in a judicial capacity, by threat of excommunication (or under threat of financial penalty; *Ir Shushan, Tumim, Netivot*), they need not compensate any defendant who is mistakenly obligated to pay as a result of their verdict (*Rema*). However, judges who receive a salary for their services (in accordance with the proper guidelines) are always held accountable for their mistakes, since they should be more exacting in the execution of their duties." (*Ketzot HaḤoshen*.) (*Shulḥan Arukh, Ḥoshen Mishpat* 25:3.)

TRANSLATION AND COMMENTARY

אֶלָּא [1] **Rather,** say: It now suggests another difference. If **there is** a practical difference **between** Rabbi Yoḥanan and Resh Lakish, it relates **to** whether the mistaken judges must **pay** their vindicated colleague's **portion** of the compensation. [2] **According to** Rabbi Yoḥanan, **who said** the document simply states that the defendant was found to be **"free of liability,"** these words indicate that the court accepts full responsibility for the verdict. [3] Therefore, the mistaken judges must **pay** full compensation, including their colleague's portion. [4] However, **according to** Resh Lakish, **who said** we record explicitly that **"So-and-so and so-and-so free** the defendant **from liability, or so-and-so and so-and-so find** him **liable,"** it is understood that, as a named individual, each judge is responsible only for his own opinion. [5] Consequently the mistaken judges **do not pay** their colleague's share of the compensation (nor need the colleague pay it himself), and the litigant receives only two-thirds in compensation.

וּלְמַאן דְּאָמַר [6] Can we really say that, **according to** Rabbi Yoḥanan, **who said** that the document simply states that the defendant was found to be **"free of liability,"** [7] the mistaken judges must **pay** their colleague's portion as well? [8] **Let them say to him** as follows: **If you had not been** sitting **with us** in court, [9] **the judgment would not have been valid at all** — for two judges alone cannot render an acceptable judgment (see above, 2a)! Hence, we should not have to shoulder your portion of the responsibility.

אֶלָּא [10] **Rather,** say: **There is** a practical difference **between** Rabbi Yoḥanan and Resh Lakish **in relation to** the verse in Leviticus (19:16) that states: [11] **"You shall not go about as a talebearer among your people."** [12] **Rabbi Yoḥanan** — who **said** that we do not record the identity of the dissenting judge, but simply write that the defendant was found to be **"free of liability"** — took this stand **because of** the verse: **"You shall not go about as a talebearer** among your people." His teaching parallels the ruling in our Mishnah (above, 29a) prohibiting a judge from exiting the courtroom and saying, "I wanted to free the defendent from liability...yet what could I do, for my colleagues outnumbered me?" [13] **Resh Lakish**, who **said** that we must write explicitly that **"So-and-so and so-and-so exempt** the defendant, or **so-and-so and so-and-so find him liable,"** differed with Rabbi Yoḥanan [14] **because of** his concern that hiding the split verdict would make the court **appear dishonest.** That concern takes precedence over the possible appearance of talebearing.

[1] אֶלָּא, אִיכָּא בֵּינַיְיהוּ לְשַׁלּוּמֵי אִינְהוּ מְנָתָא דִּידֵיהּ. [2] לְמַאן דְּאָמַר: "זַכַּאי", [3] מְשַׁלְּמֵי; [4] לְמַאן דְּאָמַר: "פְּלוֹנִי וּפְלוֹנִי מְזַכִּין וּפְלוֹנִי וּפְלוֹנִי מְחַיְּיבִין", [5] לָא מְשַׁלְּמֵי.

[6] וּלְמַאן דְּאָמַר: "זַכַּאי", [7] מְשַׁלְּמֵי? [8] וְלֵימְרוּ לֵיהּ: אִי לָאו אַתְּ בַּהֲדַן, [9] לָא הֲוָה סָלֵיק דִּינָא מִידֵּי!

[10] אֶלָּא, אִיכָּא בֵּינַיְיהוּ מִשּׁוּם [11] "לֹא תֵלֵךְ רָכִיל בְּעַמֶּיךָ". [12] רַבִּי יוֹחָנָן אָמַר: "זַכַּאי" — מִשּׁוּם: "לֹא תֵלֵךְ רָכִיל". [13] רֵישׁ לָקִישׁ אָמַר: "פְּלוֹנִי וּפְלוֹנִי מְזַכִּין וּפְלוֹנִי פְּלוֹנִי מְחַיְּיבִין" — [14] מִשּׁוּם דְּמִיחֲזֵי כְּשִׁיקְרָא.

LITERAL TRANSLATION

[1] Rather, there is [a difference] between them [with regard] to their paying his share. [2] According to the one who said: "[He is] free of liability," [3] they pay; [4] and according to the one who said: "So-and-so and so-and-so free [him] from liability, or so-and-so and so-and-so find [him] liable," [5] they do not pay.

[6] According to the one who said: "[He is] free of liability," [7] they pay? [8] Let them say to him: If you had not been [sitting] with us, [9] the judgment would not have been valid (lit., "go up") at all!

[10] Rather, there is [a difference] between them concerning [the verse]: [11] "You shall not go about as a talebearer among your people." [12] Rabbi Yoḥanan said: "[He is] free of liability" — because of [the verse]: "You shall not go about as a talebearer." [13] Resh Lakish said: "So-and-so and so-and-so free [him] from liability, or so-and-so and so-and-so find [him] liable" — [14] because [hiding the split verdict] appears [to be] a falsehood.

RASHI

לשלומי אינהו — לבעל הדין חלקו של דיין שלישי. למאן דאמר פלוני ופלוני מזכין כו׳ לא משלמי — דלהכי כתבינן פלוגתא בהדיא, לאודועי דבתרי נגמר דינא ולא קיבלו עלייהו כולי דינא.

NOTES

מִשּׁוּם דְּמִיחֲזֵי כְּשִׁיקְרָא **Because it appears dishonest.** The Rishonim ask how Resh Lakish can ignore the clear injunction cited in our Mishnah forbidding any member of the court from revealing how individual judges ruled in the case. *Ramah* and *Ran* both explain that the Mishnah's injunction applies only when a judge personally approaches a litigant with the intention of ingratiating himself by showing that he supported his position in court. In the case of an official court record, Resh Lakish does not consider the delineation of judicial opinions to be a violation of the prohibition against talebearing. *Rabbenu Yonah* offers an alternative explanation: The injunction in the Mishnah

TRANSLATION AND COMMENTARY

[1]**And** as far as **Rabbi Elazar** is concerned — **he accepts** both the position **of** Rabbi Yoḥanan (that we must avoid talebearing), as well as that of Resh Lakish (that we must avoid the appearance of a falsehood). [2]**Consequently,** he maintains that the judges **write as follows: "As a result of** the **words** of those judges who supported his innocence, [3]**so-and-so was freed of liability."** In this way, the court makes it clear that there was a dissenting opinion, but without naming the judge who rendered it.

גָּמְרוּ אֶת הַדָּבָר [4]We learned further in our Mishnah: "Once the judges have **finished** deliberating **the matter** and arrived at a majority verdict, **they bring them** back **into** court." [5]The Gemara asks: **Whom** exactly do the judges bring in at this point? [6]**If you say** they bring in **the litigants, the** Mishnah seems to indicate that **they are** still **standing there,** for there is no indication that they were ever sent out! [7]**Rather,** we must say that it is **the witnesses** whom the judges bring in. After making their statements separately when being examined by the court, they must now give their formal testimony together.

כְּמַאן [8]The Gemara challenges this conclusion: **In accordance with whom** does the Mishnah teach that the two witnesses must appear before the court again in order to testify together? [9]It is certainly **not in accordance with** the accepted opinion of **Rabbi Natan,** [10]**as it was taught** in the following Baraita: "The individual **testimonies** of two witnesses who observe a particular event related to a civil claim **may never be combined** as joint testimony **unless the two of them observe** the event **simultaneously.** [11]**Rabbi Yehoshua ben Korḥah** differs with the first Tanna and **says:** [12]Two witnesses in such a case may have their testimonies combined **even when one** witness observed one incident **after the other** one observed a similar incident, such as one witness seeing the litigant borrow a maneh on Sunday and the other seeing him borrow a maneh from the same lender on Monday. The first Tanna states further: [13]The joint **testimony** of two witnesses **is not accepted in court unless they both testify** before the court **simultaneously.** [14]**Rabbi Natan says:** This is not so, for the judges **may hear the words of one** witness **today;** [15]**and when his colleague comes tomorrow,** they **may hear his words** separately." Since Rabbi Natan's opinion is accepted as law, why does our Mishnah require that the two witnesses be ushered back into court for the sake of restating their testimony together?

[1]וְרַבִּי אֶלְעָזָר — אִית לֵיהּ דְּמָר, וְאִית לֵיהּ דְּמָר. [2]הִלְכָּךְ, כָּתְבִי הָכִי: מִדִּבְרֵיהֶם, [3]נִזְדַּכָּה פְּלוֹנִי.

[4]"גָּמְרוּ אֶת הַדָּבָר הָיוּ מַכְנִיסִין כו׳". [5]לְמַאן? [6]אִילֵימָא לְבַעֲלֵי דִינִין, הָתָם קַיְימִי! [7]אֶלָּא, לְעֵדִים.

[8]כְּמַאן? [9]דְּלָא כְּרַבִּי נָתָן, דְּתַנְיָא: [10]"לְעוֹלָם אֵין עֵדוּתָן מִצְטָרֶפֶת, עַד שֶׁיִּרְאוּ שְׁנֵיהֶן כְּאֶחָד. [11]רַבִּי יְהוֹשֻׁעַ בֶּן קָרְחָה אוֹמֵר: [12]אֲפִילּוּ בְּזֶה אַחַר זֶה. [13]וְאֵין עֵדוּתָן מִתְקַיֶּימֶת בְּבֵית דִּין, עַד שֶׁיָּעִידוּ שְׁנֵיהֶן כְּאֶחָד. [14]רַבִּי נָתָן אוֹמֵר: שׁוֹמְעִין דְּבָרָיו שֶׁל זֶה הַיּוֹם; [15]וּכְשֶׁיָּבֹא חֲבֵירוֹ לְמָחָר, שׁוֹמְעִין אֶת דְּבָרָיו".

LITERAL TRANSLATION

[1]And Rabbi Elazar — he accepts [the position] of [one] master and he accepts [the position] of [the other] master. [2]Consequently, they write as follows: As a result of their [concurring] words, [3]so-and-so was freed of liability.

[4]"[Once] they finished [deliberating] the matter, they would bring in etc." [5]Whom? [6]If you say the litigants, they are standing there [already]! [7]Rather, [say] the witnesses.

[8]In accordance with whom? [9][It is] not in accordance with Rabbi Natan, [10]for it was taught: "The testimonies [of witnesses] may never be combined unless the two of them observe simultaneously. [11]Rabbi Yehoshua ben Korḥah says: [12]Even when one [observes] after the other. [13]And their testimony is not accepted in court unless both testify simultaneously. [14]Rabbi Natan says: We may hear the words of this [witness] today; [15]and when his friend comes tomorrow, we may hear his words."

RASHI

התם קיימי — דהא לא קתני מתניתין שיוציאום לאחר ששמעו דבריהם. **עד שיראו שניהם באחת** — את העדות, ולקמן יליף טעמא. **אין עדותן מתקיימת בבית דין** — לפסוק הדין על פיהם. **עד שיעידו שניהם באחת** — וסתמא היא, ולא רבי יהושע בן קרחה קאמר לה. **לימא דלא כרבי נתן** — דהא מתניתין קתני דלעיילינהו לסהדי, משום דמתחילה כשבדקום שמעו דבריו של זה בלא זה.

NOTES

prohibits such information from being shared with the party whose claim was rejected, lest he bear a grudge against those who decided against him. The written document, however, is made available to the party whose claim was vindicated, and it is unlikely that he will hold any resentment against the dissenting judge.

הָתָם קַיְימִי **They are standing there already.** The presence of the litigants in the courtroom during the court's

TRANSLATION AND COMMENTARY

לֹא [1]The Gemara revises its understanding of the Mishnah: **No**, we can explain that the Mishnah does not argue with Rabbi Natan. The people brought back to court are **actually the litigants.** [2]**And** our Mishnah **is** in accordance with the view of **Rabbi Neḥemyah, for it was taught** in a Baraita: [3]**"Rabbi Neḥemyah says: This was the custom of the clear-minded** judges **who were in Jerusalem:** [4]**They would** first **bring in the litigants and hear their words;** [5]**and** then, in the litigants' presence, **they would bring in the witnesses and hear their testimony.** [6]Afterwards, **they** would **send** both the litigants and the witnesses **outside and deliberate the matter.** [7]Once **they** had **finished** deliberating **the matter, they** would **bring** the litigants back **into** the court **to** announce their verdict."

וְהָתַנְיָא [8]The Gemara asks: **But has it not been** explicitly **taught** otherwise in another Baraita: [9]"Once **they finished** deliberating **the matter, they** would **bring in the witnesses** so that they may testify together"?

הַהִיא [10]The Gemara responds: You may not cite that Baraita to refute an understanding of the Mishnah that the witnesses need not be brought back. For **that** Baraita **is not in accordance with** the accepted opinion of **Rabbi Natan** cited above, and we have explained our Mishnah according to Rabbi Natan.

גּוּפָא [11]The Gemara now **returns to the statement** of the Baraita **quoted above:** [12]"The individual **testimonies** of two witnesses who observe a particular event related to a civil claim **may never be combined** as joint testimony **unless the two of them observe** the event **simultaneously.** [13]**Rabbi Yehoshua ben Korḥah** differs with the first Tanna and **says:** Two witnesses in such a case may have their testimonies combined **even if one** witness observed one incident after the **other one** observed a similar incident (such as a loan)." [14]The Gemara asks: **About what do they disagree?** [15]**If you wish,** you may **say** the Tannaim are arguing about **a verse;** [16]**and if you wish,** you may **say** the Tannaim are arguing about a matter of **logic.**

[1]לֹא. לְעוֹלָם לְבַעֲלֵי דִינִין, [2]וְרַבִּי נְחֶמְיָה הִיא. דְּתַנְיָא: [3]"רַבִּי נְחֶמְיָה אוֹמֵר: כָּךְ הָיָה מִנְהָגָן שֶׁל נְקִיֵּי הַדַּעַת שֶׁבִּירוּשָׁלַיִם: [4]מַכְנִיסִין לְבַעֲלֵי דִינִין וְשׁוֹמְעִין דִּבְרֵיהֶן, [5]וּמַכְנִיסִין אֶת הָעֵדִים וְשׁוֹמְעִין דִּבְרֵיהֶם, [6]וּמוֹצִיאִין אוֹתָן לַחוּץ וְנוֹשְׂאִין וְנוֹתְנִין בַּדָּבָר. [7]גָּמְרוּ אֶת הַדָּבָר, מַכְנִיסִין אוֹתָן כו'".
[8]וְהָתַנְיָא: [9]"גָּמְרוּ אֶת הַדָּבָר, מַכְנִיסִין אֶת הָעֵדִים"?
[10]הַהִיא דְּלָא כְּרַבִּי נָתָן.
[11]גּוּפָא: [12]"לְעוֹלָם אֵין עֵדוּתָן מִצְטָרֶפֶת עַד שֶׁיִּרְאוּ שְׁנֵיהֶם כְּאֶחָד. [13]רַבִּי יְהוֹשֻׁעַ בֶּן קָרְחָה אוֹמֵר: אֲפִילּוּ בְּזֶה אַחַר זֶה". [14]בְּמַאי קָמִיפַּלְגִי? [15]אִיבָּעֵית אֵימָא קְרָא, [16]וְאִיבָּעֵית אֵימָא סְבָרָא.

LITERAL TRANSLATION

[1]No. [It is] actually [referring] to the litigants, [2]and it is [in accordance with] Rabbi Neḥemyah. For it was taught: [3]"Rabbi Neḥemyah says: This was the custom of the clear-minded [judges] who were in Jerusalem: [4]They bring in the litigants and hear their arguments, [5]and [then] they bring in the witnesses and hear their words, [6]and [then] they send them outside and deliberate the matter. [7][Once] they have finished the matter, they bring them in, etc."

[8]But has it not been taught: [9]"[Once] they have finished the matter, they bring in the witnesses"?

[10]That [Baraita] is not in accordance with Rabbi Natan.

[11]Returning to the statement quoted above (lit., "the thing itself"): [12]"The testimonies [of witnesses] may never be combined unless the two of them observe simultaneously. [13]Rabbi Yehoshua ben Korḥah says: Even when one [observes] after the other." [14]About what do they disagree? [15]If you wish, say [regarding] a verse; [16]and if you wish, say [regarding a matter of] logic.

RASHI

ורבי נחמיה היא – דאמר: בשעת משא ומתן הוו מפקי להו לבעלי דינים. **במאי קמיפלגי** – תנא קמא ורבי יהושע.

NOTES

deliberations does not necessarily mean that they were privy to their discussions, for the deliberations are conducted quietly in a far corner of the room (*Ran*).

אִיבָּעֵית אֵימָא קְרָא, וְאִיבָּעֵית אֵימָא סְבָרָא **If you wish, say it is logic; if you wish, say it is a verse.** Although generally the Gemara does not offer the alternative support of a verse where a clear-cut argument of logic is available, in this case the logic of the argument is not unassailable and the verse — by implication — strengthens this argument (*Tosafot* in *Shevuot* 22b).

HALAKHAH

כָּךְ הָיָה מִנְהָגָן שֶׁל נְקִיֵּי הַדַּעַת שֶׁבִּירוּשָׁלַיִם **Such was the custom of the clear-minded judges in Jerusalem.** "The following was customary procedure in Jerusalem, deemed worthy of emulation in other courts as well: The judges would usher in the litigants and hear their respective claims. Afterwards, they would bring in the witnesses and

TRANSLATION AND COMMENTARY

אִיבָּעֵית אֵימָא [1]**If you wish,** you may **say** they are arguing in regard to a matter of **logic:** The anonymous first Tanna, who requires that the two witnesses observe the event simultaneously, reasons as follows: If two witnesses testify that they both observed a certain loan transaction between two parties at different times, [2]then **the** borrowed **maneh about which this** witness **is testifying is not the** same borrowed maneh **about which that one is testifying;** [3]**and the** borrowed **maneh about which that** witness **is testifying is not the same** borrowed **maneh about which this one is testifying.** Hence, they are considered to be separate witnesses testifying about different events, and their testimonies cannot be joined. [4]**And the other** Tanna, Rabbi Yehoshua ben Korḥah, counters with his own reasoning: [5]Since **both** witnesses **are merely testifying about** the liability created by the borrowing of a **maneh,** what difference does it make whether they observe the same coins passing between the borrower and the lender?

וְאִיבָּעֵית אֵימָא [6]**And if you wish,** you may **say** they are arguing in regard to **a verse:** [7]**For it is written** in Leviticus (5:1), with respect to witnesses who deny under oath having any relevant testimony to offer: [8]**"And he** (who) **is a witness, either having observed or known,** if he does not tell, he shall bear his iniquity." The first Tanna maintained that, although the verse writes "witness" in the singular, it is clear from the context that it is actually referring to a pair of witnesses — for a single witness would not have been able to provide decisive testimony for him. [9]This accords with what **was taught** in the following Baraita: "The verse in Deuteronomy (19:15) states: 'One witness shall not rise up against a man, for any iniquity or for any sin.' [10]Now, **from the literal meaning of 'a witness shall not rise up** against a man,' [11]**would I not know that it is 'one** witness' that the verse is talking about? [12]**Why,** then, **does the verse state: 'One** witness,' adding the seemingly extraneous word 'one'? [13]It must be that **this** verse **creates a prototype** to be used in understanding the language of Scripture: It teaches that **wherever** the singular noun '**witness' is stated** in the Torah, [14]it implies **two** witnesses, **unless Scripture specifies for you** that it is referring to **'one** witness.'" [15]One must say that **the Torah** in Leviticus (5:1) chose to **express** its message **in singular terminology,** even though it is dealing with a plural subject, in order **to** teach us the following: [16]**Unless both** witnesses **simultaneously observe** the event to which they

[1]אִיבָּעֵית אֵימָא סְבָרָא: [2]אַמָּנֶה דְּקָא מְסַהֵיד הַאי לָא קָא מְסַהֵיד הַאי; [3]וּמָנֶה דְּקָא מְסַהֵיד הַאי לָא קָמַסְהֵיד הַאי. [4]וְאִידָךְ: [5]אַמָּנֶה בְּעָלְמָא תַּרְוַיְיהוּ קָמְסָהֲדֵי.

[6]וְאִיבָּעֵית אֵימָא קְרָא: [7]דִּכְתִיב: [8]"וְהוּא עֵד, אוֹ רָאָה אוֹ יָדָע". [9]וְתַנְיָא: [10]"מִמַּשְׁמַע שֶׁנֶּאֱמַר: 'לֹא יָקוּם עֵד', [11]אֵינִי יוֹדֵעַ שֶׁהוּא אֶחָד?! [12]מַה תַּלְמוּד לוֹמַר: 'אֶחָד'? [13]זֶה בָּנָה אָב: כָּל מָקוֹם שֶׁנֶּאֱמַר 'עֵד', [14]הֲרֵי כָּאן שְׁנַיִם, עַד שֶׁיִּפְרֵט לְךָ הַכָּתוּב 'אֶחָד'. [15]וְאַפְּקֵיהּ רַחֲמָנָא בִּלְשׁוֹן חַד לְמֵימַר: [16]עַד דְּחָזוּ תַּרְוַיְיהוּ

LITERAL TRANSLATION

[1]If you wish, say [a matter of] logic: [2][The anonymous Tanna reasons that] the maneh about which this one is testifying is not [the maneh] about which that one is testifying; [3]and the maneh about which that one is testifying is not [the maneh] about which this one is testifying. [4]And the other [Tanna reasons]: [5]Both are merely testifying about a [debt of a] maneh.

[6]And if you wish, say [regarding] a verse: [7]For it is written: [8]"And he is a witness, either having observed or known." [9]And it was taught: [10]"From the literal meaning of: 'A witness shall not rise up,' [11]would I not know that it is 'one [witness]'?! [12]Why does the verse state: 'One [witness]'? [13]This created a prototype [lit., 'constructed a father']: Wherever 'a witness' is stated, [14][it implies that] there are two unless Scripture specifies for you 'one [witness].' [15]And the Torah expressed it in singular terminology [so as] to say: [16][They are not a pair] unless they both observe

RASHI

אמנה דקא מסהיד האי — זה אומר: בפני הלוהו מנה, וזה אומר: בפני הלוהו מנה, זה לא ראה של זה — נמצא שאין כאן עדות שלם במנה אחד. **ואידך** — מכל מקום תרווייהו מסהדי דמנה קא רשי ביה. **והוא עד** — והאי קרא בשני עדים משתעי, לגבי קרבן שבועת העדות, דאילו השביע עד אחד ולא העידו — פטור. **דתניא ממשמע שנאמר כו'** — עד אחד משמע. **ואפקיה רחמנא בלשון חד** — דכתיב "והוא עד".

HALAKHAH

hear their testimony. Then they would send everyone out of the courtroom and commence their deliberations, arriving at a verdict between them. Finally, they would bring the litigants back in and the chief justice would pronounce the verdict." (*Shulḥan Arukh, Ḥoshen Mishpat* 19:1.)

כְּחַד״. [1]וְאִידָךְ: ״וְהוּא עֵד אוֹ רָאָה אוֹ יָדָע״ — [2]מִכָּל מָקוֹם.
[3]״וְאֵין עֵדוּתָן מִתְקַיֶּימֶת בְּבֵית דִּין עַד שֶׁיָּעִידוּ שְׁנֵיהֶן כְּאֶחָד. [4]רַבִּי נָתָן אוֹמֵר: שׁוֹמְעִין דְּבָרָיו שֶׁל זֶה הַיּוֹם; [5]וּכְשֶׁיָּבֹא חֲבֵירוֹ לְמָחָר, שׁוֹמְעִין דְּבָרָיו״. [6]בְּמַאי קָמִיפַּלְגִי? [7]אִיבָּעֵית אֵימָא, סְבָרָא; [8]אִיבָּעֵית אֵימָא, קְרָא.
[9]אִיבָּעֵית אֵימָא, סְבָרָא: [10]מָר סָבַר: עֵד אֶחָד — [11]כִּי אָתֵי, לִשְׁבוּעָה אָתֵי, [12]לְמָמוֹנָא לָא אָתֵי. [13]וְאִידָךְ: אַטּוּ כִּי אָתוּ בַּהֲדֵי הֲדָדֵי, [14]בְּחַד פּוּמָא קָא מְסַהֲדֵי?! [15]אֶלָּא מְצָרְפִינַן לְהוּ. [16]הָכָא נַמִי, לִיצָרְפִינְהוּ.
[17]וְאִיבָּעֵית אֵימָא, קְרָא: [18]״אִם

LITERAL TRANSLATION

simultaneously." [1]And the other: "And he is a witness, either having observed or known" — [2]in all cases.

[3]"And their testimony is not accepted in court unless both testify simultaneously. [4]Rabbi Natan says: We may hear the words of this [witness] today; [5]and when his friend comes tomorrow, we may hear his words." [6]About what do they disagree? [7]If you wish, say [regarding a matter of] logic; [8]and if you wish, say [regarding] a verse.

[9]If you wish, say [regarding a matter of] logic: [10][One] master maintained: A single witness — [11]when he comes, he comes for [extracting] an oath, [12][but] he does not come for [extracting] money. [13]And the other: If they come together, [14]do they testify with one mouth?! [15]Rather we combine them. [16]Here, too, let us combine them!

[17]And if you wish, say a verse: [18]"If

TRANSLATION AND COMMENTARY

are testifying — as if they were one — their statements may not be joined together." [1]However, **the other** Tanna, Rabbi Yehoshua ben Korḥah, maintained otherwise: When the verse states: **"And he** (who) **is a witness, either having observed or known"** — [2]**the** intention of the seemingly self-evident "having observed or known" teaches us that two witnesses may join together in offering testimony **in all cases,** whether or not they observed the event together.

וְאֵין עֵדוּתָן מִתְקַיֶּימֶת [3]The Gemara now cites the remainder of the Baraita: **"The** joint **testimony** of two witnesses **does not stand up in court unless they both testify** before the court **simultaneously.** [4]**Rabbi Natan says:** This is not so, for the judges **may hear the words of one** witness **today;** [5]**and when his colleague comes tomorrow,** they may **hear his words** separately." [6]The Gemara asks: **About what do they disagree?** [7]**If you wish,** you may **say** the Tannaim are arguing in regard to a matter of **logic;** [8]**and if you wish,** you **may say** they are arguing in regard to **a verse.**

אִיבָּעֵית אֵימָא [9]**If you wish,** you may **say** they are arguing in regard to a matter of **logic:** [10]The anonymous first Tanna, who requires that they testify simultaneously, **maintained** as follows: **When a single witness comes** alone to court in order to testify about a monetary matter, [11]**he comes** exclusively **for** the purpose of obligating the defendant to take **an oath** confirming his claim (as mandated by Torah law). [12]However, **he does not come for** the purpose of obligating the defendant to pay the plaintiff **money**, as only two witnesses have that power. Hence, if two witnesses testified separately, their testimonies cannot be combined in order to take from the defendant, for neither testimony had the power to accomplish this. [13]**The other** Tanna, Rabbi Natan, argued otherwise: **If** two witnesses **come together to** testify at the same time, [14]**do they** actually **testify with one mouth** simultaneously?! [15]**Rather** they testify one after the other, and the judges then **combine** their statements into a single unit of testimony. [16]**Here, too,** where the witnesses come and testify on consecutive days; **let** the judges **combine** their statements into a single unit of testimony.

וְאִיבָּעֵית אֵימָא [17]**And if you wish,** you may **say** they are arguing in regard to **a verse** — the one cited above from Leviticus (5:1): [18]"And he (who) is a witness, either having observed or known, **if he does not**

RASHI

לשבועה אתי – עד אחד אינו מחייבו ממון אלא שבועה, הלכך כשהעיד זה יחידי וזה יחידי לא שייכא תורת ממון בעדותן ולא מצרפינן להו, דהא לאו לחיוביה ממונא אתו.

HALAKHAH

שׁוֹמְעִין דְּבָרָיו שֶׁל זֶה הַיּוֹם וּכְשֶׁיָּבֹא חֲבֵירוֹ לְמָחָר We may hear this one's words today and his friend's tomorrow. "There is no need for witnesses in a civil case to testify together; rather, the judges may hear their individual testimony on different days and then consider them as having been presented jointly." This is in accordance with the opinion of Rabbi Natan, which was concurred with by Rabbi Yehoshua ben Korḥah. (*Shulḥan Arukh, Ḥoshen Mishpat* 30:9.)

לוֹא יַגִּיד וְנָשָׂא עֲוֹנוֹ״; [30B] [1] וְדִכוּלֵּי עָלְמָא כְּרַבָּנַן דִּפְלִיגִי עֲלֵיהּ דְּרַבִּי יְהוֹשֻׁעַ בֶּן קָרְחָה; [2] וְהָכָא, בְּאַקּוֹשֵׁי הַגָּדָה לִרְאִיָּה קָא מִיפַּלְגִי. [3] מָר סָבַר: מַקְּשִׁינַן הַגָּדָה לִרְאִיָּה; [4] וּמָר סָבַר: לָא מַקְשִׁינַן.

[5] רַבִּי שִׁמְעוֹן בֶּן אֶלְיָקִים הֲוָה מִשְׁתַּקֵּיד עֲלֵיהּ דְּרַבִּי יוֹסֵי בְּרַבִּי חֲנִינָא לְמִסְמְכֵיהּ, [6] וְלָא קָא מִיסְתַּיַּיע מִילְּתָא. [7] יוֹמָא חַד הֲוָה יָתֵיב קַמֵּיהּ דְּרַבִּי יוֹחָנָן. [8] אֲמַר לְהוּ: [9] מִי אִיכָּא דְּיָדַע הֲלָכָה כְּרַבִּי יְהוֹשֻׁעַ בֶּן קָרְחָה אוֹ לֹא? [10] אֲמַר לֵיהּ רַבִּי שִׁמְעוֹן בֶּן אֶלְיָקִים: דֵּין יָדַע. [11] אֲמַר לֵיהּ: לֵימָא אִיזוֹ! [12] אֲמַר לֵיהּ: לִיסְמְכֵיהּ מָר בְּרֵישָׁא. [13] סְמַכֵיהּ. [14] אֲמַר לֵיהּ: בְּנִי, אֱמוֹר לִי כֵּיצַד שָׁמַעְתָּ. [15] אֲמַר לֵיהּ: כָּךְ שָׁמַעְתִּי שֶׁמּוֹדֶה רַבִּי יְהוֹשֻׁעַ בֶּן קָרְחָה לְרַבִּי נָתָן.

[16] אָמַר: לָזֶה הוּצְרַכְתִּי? [17] הָשְׁתָּא, וּמָה עִיקַּר רְאִיָּה

LITERAL TRANSLATION

he does not tell, he bears his iniquity"; [30B] [1] and all (lit., "all the world") [maintain] like the Rabbis who argue against [the position] of Rabbi Yehoshua ben Korḥah; [2] and here, they argue about comparing [the act of] testifying to [the act of] witnessing. [3] [One] master maintains: We compare testifying to witnessing; [4] and [the other] master maintains: We do not compare [them].

[5] Rabbi Shimon ben Elyakim was anxious to ordain Rabbi Yose, the son of Rabbi Ḥanina; [6] however, the opportunity did not arise. [7] One day, [Rabbi Shimon ben Elyakim] was sitting before Rabbi Yoḥanan. [8] He said to them: [9] Who is here that knows [if] the law is in accordance with Rabbi Yehoshua ben Korḥah, or not? [10] Rabbi Shimon ben Elyakim said to him: This one knows. [11] [Rabbi Yoḥanan] said to him: Let him then say! [12] He said to him: Let [our] master first ordain him. [13] [Rabbi Yoḥanan] ordained him. [14] He said to him: My son, tell me what you have heard. [15] He said to him: Thus I heard, that Rabbi Yehoshua ben Korḥah agrees with Rabbi Natan.

[16] [Rabbi Yoḥanan] said: I needed this [information]? [17] Now, since [about] the main observation [taking place]

TRANSLATION AND COMMENTARY

tell, he bears his iniquity." [30B] [1] With regard to the use of "witness" in the singular in the above verse, both the anonymous first Tanna and Rabbi Natan maintain, **as do the Rabbis who argue** earlier in the Baraita, against the position **of Rabbi Yehoshua ben Korḥah**, and interpret the anomalous language as teaching us that the witnesses must observe the event simultaneously. [2] **Here,** however, **they disagree about** whether the verse implies that we may draw **a comparison between** the act of **testifying and** the act of **witnessing**. [3] **One master,** the first Tanna of this Baraita, **maintains** that the joint appearance in the verse of the words "observed" and "tell" implies that **we** may **draw a comparison between** the act of **testifying** (telling) **and** the act of **witnessing** (observing). Just as witnesses must observe simultaneously, they must also relate their testimony together. [4] **And the other master,** Rabbi Natan, **maintains** that the juxtaposition of these words in the verse is insignificant and **we may not draw a comparison** between testifying and witnessing. Consequently, he maintains that the court may hear the witnesses separately and combine their testimony.

רַבִּי שִׁמְעוֹן בֶּן אֶלְיָקִים [5] It is told that **Rabbi Shimon ben Elyakim was anxious to ordain Rabbi Yose the son of Rabbi Ḥanina;** [6] **however, the opportunity did not arise.** [7] **One day** Rabbi Shimon ben Elyakim **was sitting**, together with other scholars, **before Rabbi Yoḥanan,** [8] when the latter **said to** his students as follows: [9] **Who is here** among you **that knows** if **the law** regarding simultaneous witnessing **is in accordance with Rabbi Yehoshua ben Korḥah or not?** [10] **Rabbi Shimon ben Elyakim said to him: This one knows** — referring to Rabbi Yose the son of Rabbi Ḥanina. [11] Rabbi Yoḥanan **said to him: Let him then say** what he knows! [12] Rabbi Shimon ben Elyakim **said** in reply **to** Rabbi Yoḥanan: Before he speaks, **let** [our] **master first ordain him.** [13] Rabbi Yoḥanan **ordained** Rabbi Yose the son of Rabbi Ḥanina. [14] Then Rabbi Yoḥanan **said to him: My son, tell me** now **what you have heard** in regard to Rabbi Yehoshua ben Korḥah. [15] Rabbi Yose **said to him: I heard that Rabbi Yehoshua ben Korḥah agrees with Rabbi Natan** that witnesses need not testify together before the court, implying that since the law accords with Rabbi Natan, it accords with Rabbi Yehoshua as well.

אָמַר [16] Upon hearing Rabbi Yose's statement, Rabbi Yoḥanan **asked** disappointedly: **Did I need this** information? [17] **Now, since Rabbi Yehoshua ben Korḥah** has already **stated** that **we do not need the actual**

RASHI

ודכולי עלמא — תנא קמא ורבי נתן. **כרבנן דפליגי אדרבי יהושע בן קרחה** — סבירא להו, דאמרי בעינן שיראו שניהם כאחד, וילפינן טעמא מ"והוא עד" דליחזי כחד. וגבי הגדה פליגי תנאי דסיפא באקושיה הגדה לראיה, כדכתיב (ויקרא ה) "או ראה" "אם לא יגיד" בחד קרא. **משתקיד** — מצפה ומחזר, ושוקד לסומכו. **דין ידע** — זה יודע, ורבי יוסי ברבי חנינא היה. **שמודה רבי יהושע לרבי נתן** — דכי היכי דלא בעי רבי יהושע ראיה כי

בְּהֲדֵי הֲדָדֵי אָמַר רַבִּי יְהוֹשֻׁעַ בֶּן קָרְחָה לָא בָּעֵינַן, [1]הַגָּדָה מִיבַּעְיָא?

[2]אָמַר לֵיהּ: הוֹאִיל וְעָלִיתָ, לֹא תֵּרֵד. [3]אָמַר רַבִּי זֵירָא: שְׁמַע מִינָּהּ: גַּבְרָא רַבָּה — [4]כֵּיוָן דִּסְמִיךְ, סָמִיךְ.

[5]אָמַר רַבִּי חִיָּיא בַּר אָבִין אָמַר רַב: הֲלָכָה כְּרַבִּי יְהוֹשֻׁעַ בֶּן קָרְחָה בֵּין בְּקַרְקָעוֹת בֵּין בְּמִטַּלְטְלִין. [6]עוּלָּא אָמַר: הֲלָכָה כְּרַבִּי יְהוֹשֻׁעַ בֶּן קָרְחָה בְּקַרְקָעוֹת, [7]אֲבָל לֹא בְּמִטַּלְטְלִין.

[8]אָמַר לֵיהּ אַבָּיֵי: ״הֲלָכָה״ מִכְּלָל דִּפְלִיגִי! [9]וְהָאָמַר רַבִּי אַבָּא אָמַר רַב הוּנָא אָמַר רַב: [10]מוֹדִים חֲכָמִים לְרַבִּי יְהוֹשֻׁעַ בֶּן קָרְחָה בְּעֵדוּת קַרְקַע! [11]וְתָנֵי רַב אִידִי בַּר אָבִין בִּנְזִיקִין דְּבֵי

LITERAL TRANSLATION

while they are together, Rabbi Yehoshua ben Korḥah stated [that] we do not need it, [1]do we need [to be told that he says the same regarding] testifying?

[2][Rabbi Yoḥanan] said to him: Since you have [already] risen, you shall not descend. [3]Rabbi Zera said: Conclude from this: A great man — [4]once he has been ordained, he is ordained.

[5]Rabbi Ḥiyya bar Avin said in the name of Rav: The law is in accordance with Rabbi Yehoshua ben Korḥah both about land and about movable property. [6]Ulla said: The law is in accordance with Rabbi Yehoshua ben Korḥah about land, [7]but not in regard to movable property.

[8]Abaye said to [Ulla]: [You said:] "The law" — implying (lit., "from the rule") that they are arguing! [9]But did not Rabbi Abba say in the name of Rav Huna, who said in the name of Rav: [10]The Sages agree with Rabbi Yehoshua ben Korḥah in regard to testimony [about] land! [11]And Rav Idi bar Avin taught [the following Baraita] regarding torts [that was taught] at

TRANSLATION AND COMMENTARY

witnessing of the incident to take place **while** the witnesses **are together,** [1]**is it necessary** to tell me that he also says the same regarding the act of **testifying?** Certainly this is obvious and in no way indicates that Rabbi Yehoshua ben Korḥah's statement is based on that of Rabbi Natan; nor does it prove that the law follows him in his dispute with the Sages!

אָמַר לֵיהּ [2]Despite the disappointment with Rabbi Yose's ordination, Rabbi Yoḥanan **said to him: Since you have** already **risen** to the level of ordination, **you shall not descend.** [3]**Rabbi Zera said: Conclude from this** that, **once a great man,** worthy of ordination, [4]**has been ordained, he** remains **ordained.**

אָמַר [5]The Gemara now turns to the actual law in this matter: **Rabbi Ḥiyya bar Avin said in the name of Rav: The law is in accordance with Rabbi Yehoshua ben Korḥah — both in regard to** testimony about **land and** testimony about **movable property.** The witnesses need not have observed simultaneously the admission of debt about which they are testifying. [6]**Ulla said: The law is in accordance with Rabbi Yehoshua ben Korḥah in regard to** testimony about **land,** for the location of the land would have to be described in the admission, and both witnesses would therefore know they are referring to the same piece of property; [7]**however,** the law is **not** in accordance with Rabbi Yehoshua ben Korḥah **in regard to** testimony about **movable property** (particularly money). For unless the two witnesses heard the admission simultaneously, neither can know whether the loan admitted to in his presence was the same loan that was admitted to before the other witness.

אָמַר לֵיהּ אַבָּיֵי [8]**Abaye said to** Ulla: By stating that **the law** is in accordance with Rabbi Yehoshua regarding land, you **implied that** Rabbi Yehoshua and the Sages **are arguing** on this point! [9]**But did not Rabbi Abba say** the following **in the name of Rav Huna, who said it in the name of Rav:** [10]**The Sages agree with Rabbi Yehoshua ben Korḥah in regard to testimony** about **land!** [11]**And** similarly we find that **Rav Idi bar Avin taught**

RASHI

הדדי, הגדה נמי כי הדדי לא בעי. **בין בקרקעות** — זה אומר: בפני הודה לו שקרקע זה שלו, וזה אומר: אף בפני הודה לו. **בין במטלטלין** — זה אומר: בפני הלווהו מנה, וזה אומר: בפני הלווהו מנה, ואף על פי דאמנה דקמסהיד האי, לא מסהיד האי, מכל מקום תרווייהו מסהדי שחייב לו מנה. **הלכה כמותו בקרקעות** — שמוטל הקרקע בפנינו ושניהם מעידין עליה. **אבל לא במטלטלין** — דאין עדות שלימה לא על זה ולא על זה. **מכלל דפליגי** — עליה רבנן בקרקעות.

NOTES

מוֹדִים חֲכָמִים לְרַבִּי יְהוֹשֻׁעַ בֶּן קָרְחָה בְּעֵדוּת קַרְקַע **The Sages agree with Rabbi Yehoshua ben Korḥah on testimony about land.** The question is asked: Granted that the Sages are at liberty to accept Rabbi Yehoshua's logic selectively, should logic be the sole basis of their argument? However, since the Gemara has already pointed out (above, p.30a) that there is a textual basis as well for their disagreement (the verse in Leviticus 5:1), how can the Sages ignore the verse as they explain it and concede, even selectively, to Rabbi Yehoshua's position? Consequently we must say, according to Rav, that the difference in interpretation of the verse cited in the above Gemara serves merely as an

קַרְנָא: [1]מוֹדִין חֲכָמִים לְרַבִּי יְהוֹשֻׁעַ בֶּן קָרְחָה בְּעֵדוּת בְּכוֹר, [2]וּבְעֵדוּת קַרְקַע, וּבְעֵדוּת חֲזָקָה, [3]וְכֵן שֶׁבַּבֵּן וְשֶׁבַּבַּת!

[4]גַּבְרָא אַגַּבְרָא קָא רָמֵית? [5]מָר סָבַר פְּלִיגִי, [6]וּמָר סָבַר לָא פְּלִיגִי.

[7]מַאי "וְכֵן שֶׁבַּבֵּן וְשֶׁבַּבַּת"? [8]אִילֵימָא אֶחָד אוֹמֵר "אַחַת בְּגַבָּהּ" [9]וְאֶחָד אוֹמֵר "אַחַת בִּכְרֵיסָהּ" — [10]הַאי חֲצִי דָבָר וַחֲצִי עֵדוּת הוּא! [11]אֶלָּא, אֶחָד

TRANSLATION AND COMMENTARY

the following Baraita **regarding torts** as taught at **Karna's academy:** [1]**The Sages agree with Rabbi Yehoshua ben Korḥah concerning testimony** about **a** blemish that appeared in a **firstborn** animal, [2]**testimony** about a transaction involving **landed property, and testimony** about three years of uncontested **possession** and presumed ownership of a field. [3]**And similarly** they agree with him concerning testimony about the physical signs of maturity **that are** found **on** the body of **a boy or a girl!**

גַּבְרָא אַגַּבְרָא [4]The Gemara dismisses Abaye's objection to Ulla: **You are raising** a contradiction between **one** Amora (Ulla) **and another** (Rav or Rav Idi bar Avin), but it is perfectly permissible for two Amoraim to differ with each other! [5]One Amora **maintained** that Rabbi Yehoshua and the Sages disagree about land, [6]**and** one Amora **maintained** that **they do not** disagree about land.

מַאי [7]Parenthetically, the Gemara attempts to clarify the last part of Rav Idi's teaching cited above by Abaye: **What is** the meaning of Rav Idi's statement: **"And similarly**, the Sages agree with Rabbi Yehoshua ben Korḥah concerning testimony about the signs of maturity **that are** found **on** the body of **a boy or a girl"?** [8]**If you say** it means that we may combine the testimony of two witnesses, **one** who **says:** "I saw **one** hair **on her posterior** pubic area," [9]**and one** who **says:** "I saw **one** hair **on her abdominal** pubic area" — then the statement is certainly problematic. [10]For in such a case, each witness is only testifying about **half of the matter** (two pubic hairs being necessary in order to establish legal majority) as well as representing only **half** the **testimony** (as there were not two witnesses testifying to the existence of the same hair)! [11]**Rather,** we must say that **one** witness **says:**

LITERAL TRANSLATION

Karna's academy: [1]The Sages agree with Rabbi Yehoshua ben Korḥah in testimony [about] a firstborn, [2]and in testimony [about] land, and in testimony [about uncontested] possession — [3]and similarly [in testimony about signs of physical maturity] on a boy or on a girl!

[4]Are you casting one man against another man?! [5][One] Sage maintains [that] they argue, [6]and [one] Sage maintains [that] they do not argue.

[7]What [is the meaning of:] "And similarly [in testimony about the signs of physical maturity] that are [found] on a boy or on a girl"? [8]If you say [that it means] one [witness] says "one [hair] on her posterior" [9]and one [witness] says "one [hair] on her abdomen" — [10]that is half of the matter and half of the testimony! [11]Rather, one

RASHI

בעדות בכור — תנן בבכורות (לה,א): כל מומין הראויין לבא בידי אדם, רועים כהנים אין נאמנין לומר מאליו נפל בו מום זה, לפי שנחשדו כהנים להטיל מומין בבכורות בזמן הזה כדי להתירן בשחיטה. ואם הביא בכור להראותו לחכם, צריך שני עדים עמו שמאליו נפל בו מום זה. אם הביא עד אחד על מום זה ועד אחד על מום אחר בבכור זה — מצטרפין. ואית דאמרי בעדות בכור — להעיד שהתירו חכם. ולאו מילתא היא, דהא חד נאמן! דעד אחד נאמן באיסורין, ואפילו כהן שהוא בעליו — נאמן דתנן (בכורות לו,א): נאמן הכהן לומר הראיתי בכור זה ובעל מום הוא, דמילתא דעבידא לאיגלויי לא משקר. **ובעדות חזקה** — זה אומר: בפני אכלה שלש שנים ראשונות של שמיטה, וזה אומר: בפני אכלה שלש שנים אחרונות — מצטרפי, דאחד קרקע מסהדי חזקה מעלייתא. **וכן** — לענין שתי שערות שבבן ושבבת, וכי פליגי — בהלואת מנה פליגי, משום דלאו אחד מנה קמסהדי. **גברא אגברא** — רבי אבא ורבי אידא אדעולא. **בגבה** — בין קישרי אצבעותיה. **חצי דבר וחצי עדות** — עד אחד הוא חצי עדות, שיער אחת הוא חצי דבר. **אלא אחד אומר שתים בגבה** — דתרווייהו מסהדי דגדולה היא.

NOTES

adjunct to the disagreement in logic that is the true basis of the argument between Rabbi Yehoshua and the Sages. Once logic dictates that the Sages agree with Rabbi Yehoshua on a certain point, the verse is no longer considered an obstacle and is reinterpreted accordingly (*Arukh Laner*).

גַּבְרָא אַגַּבְרָא קָא רָמֵית **You are casting one man against another.** The Gemara's response appears difficult, as the opinion cited by Rav Idi bar Avin was derived from a Tannaitic source — the Baraita of Karna's academy — and should therefore constitute a challenge to the Amora Ulla! However, all Baraitot do not have equal authority. Since this Baraita was not taught in the academy of Rabbi Ḥiyya and Rabbi Oshaya, it is not considered authoritative. Hence, it derives its weight only from Rav Idi himself, who was an Amora (*Ḥamra Veḥaye*).

HALAKHAH

עֵדוּת בַּחֲצִי דָּבָר **Testimony about half of the matter.** "Each of the witnesses has to testify about a relevant legal entity — be it an event, an object, or an action. For instance, if they came to testify about a sign of physical maturity (the appearance of pubic hairs), they must each claim to have seen two hairs (the minimum for establishing a person's

TRANSLATION AND COMMENTARY

"I saw **two hairs on her posterior** pubic area," [1]**and one** witness **says:** "I saw **two** hairs **on her abdominal** pubic area." Since each witness identifies the required sign of maturity, the Rabbis agree with Rabbi Yehoshua that the witnesses need not have observed the same two hairs in order for their testimony to be combined and rendered effective.

אָמַר רַב יוֹסֵף [2]The Gemara now returns to the issue of simultaneous witnessing: **Rav Yosef said: I say in the name of Ulla** as follows (in contrast to the version of Ulla's statement cited above): [3]**The law is in accordance with Rabbi Yehoshua ben Korḥah both in** testimony about **land and in** testimony about **movable property.** [4]**But the Rabbis who came from Meḥoza** thought differently: [5]**Rabbi Zera said in the name of Rav** as follows: **In regard to** testimony about **land** — **yes**, the law is in accordance with Rabbi Yehoshua; [6]**however,** it is **not** in accordance with him **in regard to** testimony about **movable property.**

רַב לְטַעְמֵיהּ [7]The position of **Rav** just cited, regarding testimony about movable property, follows **his** own **opinion** given elsewhere, [8]**for Rav** has **said:** If one witness observed the **admission** to a loan **subsequent to** another witness's observation of an identical **admission** (involving the same people and the same amount of money); [9]**or** if one witness observed the **admission** to a loan **subsequent to** another witness's observation of the **loan** itself — the testimonies of the two **may be combined** in court, since they are both testifying about the same obligation. [10]However, if one witness observed **a loan** take place **subsequent to** another witness's observation of an identical **loan;** [11]or if one witness observed **a loan** take place **subsequent to** another witness's observation of an **admission** involving the same people and the same amount of money — [12]the testimonies of the two witnesses **may not be combined** by the court, since they are not testifying about the same obligation.

אוֹמֵר "שְׁתַּיִם בְּגַבָּהּ", [1]וְאֶחָד אוֹמֵר "שְׁתַּיִם בִּכְרֵיסָהּ".
[2]אָמַר רַב יוֹסֵף: אֲנָא אָמֵינָא מִשְּׁמֵיהּ דְּעוּלָּא: [3]הֲלָכָה כְּרַבִּי יְהוֹשֻׁעַ בֶּן קָרְחָה בֵּין בְּקַרְקָעוֹת בֵּין בְּמִטַּלְטְלִין. [4]וְרַבָּנַן דְּאָתוּ מִמְּחוֹזָא אָמְרִי: [5]אָמַר רַבִּי זֵירָא מִשְּׁמֵיהּ דְּרַב: בְּקַרְקָעוֹת, אִין; [6]אֲבָל לֹא בְּמִטַּלְטְלִין.
[7]רַב לְטַעְמֵיהּ, [8]דְּאָמַר רַב: הוֹדָאָה אַחַר הוֹדָאָה, [9]הוֹדָאָה אַחַר הַלְוָאָה — מִצְטָרְפִי. [10]הַלְוָאָה אַחַר הַלְוָאָה, [11]הַלְוָאָה אַחַר הוֹדָאָה — [12]לָא מִצְטָרְפִי.

LITERAL TRANSLATION

says "two [hairs] on her posterior," [1]and one says "two [hairs] on her abdomen."

[2]Rav Yosef said: I say in the name of Ulla: [3]The law is in accordance with Rabbi Yehoshua ben Korḥah, both about land and about movable property. [4]But the Rabbis who came from Meḥoza said: [5]Rabbi Zera said in the name of Rav: In regard to land, yes; [6]but not in regard to movable property.

[7]Rav [follows] his [own] opinion, [8]for Rav said: An admission [before one witness] subsequent to an admission [before another, [9]or] an admission [before one] subsequent to a loan [before another] — the [testimonies] may be combined. [10]A loan subsequent to a loan, [11][or] a loan subsequent to an admission — [12]they may not be combined.

RASHI

בקרקעות אבל לא במטלטלין — הלכה כמותו, דלא בעינן דחזו תרווייהו כחד בקרקעות, משום דכי מסהדי בני דינא תרווייהו ידעי דאחדא מילתא מסהדי, וקרינא ביה "והוא עד", ואף על גב דבשעתא דחזי לא ידע [חד] בחבריה. אבל לא במטלטלין, דכי מסהדי קמן לאו אחד מנה מסהדי. רב — דאמר אבל לא במטלטלין, משום דלאו בחד מנה מסהדי. לטעמיה דאמר רב הודאה אחר הודאה — זה אומר: בפני הודה לו על מנה באחד בשבת, וזה אומר: בפני הודה לו עליו בשני בשבת. הודאה אחר הלואה — זה אומר: בפני הלוהו מנה באחד בשבת, וזה אומר: בפני הודה לו מנה בשני בשבת. מצטרפי — דאיכא למימר בחד מנה קמסהדי, וכדמוקי לקמן. הלואה אחר הודאה — מנה אחרינא הוא ולא מצטרפי, אף על גב דתרווייהו אמרי שחייב לו מנה.

HALAKHAH

legal status as an adult). If each witness claims to have seen only one hair, their testimony is insufficient even if it is clear that they are testifying about different hairs. If they both claim to have seen two hairs, but not in the same place, their testimonies are considered complete and may be joined for the purpose of establishing the individual's adulthood." This is in accordance with both Rabbi Yehoshua ben Korḥah and the Sages. (*Shulḥan Arukh, Ḥoshen Mishpat* 30:13.)

עֵדוּתָן מִצְטָרֶפֶת אֲפִילּוּ בָּזֶה אַחַר זֶה **Their testimonies may be combined even when one saw subsequent to the other.** "The testimony of two witnesses who independently observed someone incur an identical financial obligation on two different occasions may be combined in order to obligate him to fulfill that obligation. This is true regardless of whether one of them witnessed the debtor borrowing the money while the other merely witnessed him admitting to having borrowed it (in whatever order), or whether they both witnessed an identical loan or an identical admission." This is in accordance with the opinion of Rabbi Yehoshua ben Korḥah, as elaborated by the Neharde'an Sages. (*Shulḥan Arukh, Ḥoshen Mishpat* 30:6.)

[1]אַשְׁכַּחֵיהּ רַב נַחְמָן בַּר יִצְחָק לְרַב הוּנָא בְּרֵיהּ דְּרַב יְהוֹשֻׁעַ, [2]אֲמַר לֵיהּ: מַאי שְׁנָא הַלְוָאָה אַחַר הַלְוָאָה דְּלֹא? [3]דְּמָנֶה דְּקָא חָזֵי הַאי לָא קָא חָזֵי הַאי. [4]הוֹדָאָה אַחַר הוֹדָאָה נַמִי, [5]אַמָּנֶה דְּקָא מוֹדֶה קַמֵּי הַאי, [6]לָא מוֹדֵי קַמֵּי הַאי! [7]דַּאֲמַר לֵיהּ לְהַאי בַּתְרָא: בְּהַאי מָנֶה דְּאוֹדֵיי לֵיהּ קַמָּךְ, [8]אוֹדֵיי לֵיהּ נַמִי קַמֵּי פְּלוֹנִי. [9]אַכַּתִּי, בַּתְרָא יָדַע, [10]קַמָּא לָא יָדַע! [11]דַּהֲדַר אָזֵיל אֲמַר לֵיהּ לְקַמָּא: [12]הַאי מָנֶה דְּאוֹדֵיי לֵיהּ קַמָּךְ, [13]אוֹדֵיי לֵיהּ נַמִי קַמֵּי פְּלוֹנִי. [14]אֲמַר לֵיהּ: תָּנוּחַ דַּעְתְּךָ, [15]שֶׁהִתְנַחְתָּ אֶת דַּעְתִּי. [16]אֲמַר לֵיהּ: מַאי נִיחוּתָא? [17]דְּרָבָא, וְאִיתֵּימָא רַב שֵׁשֶׁת, [18]שְׁדָא בָּהּ נַרְגָּא: [19]לָאו הַיְינוּ

LITERAL TRANSLATION

[1]Rav Naḥman bar Yitzḥak found Rav Huna, the son of Rav Yehoshua, [2][and] said to him: What is different about a loan subsequent to a loan that [the testimonies] may not [be combined]? [3]For the maneh that this one sees, that one does not see. [4][But] an admission, subsequent to an admission too — [5]the maneh to which he admits before this one, [6]he does not admit to before that one!

[7]When he said to that latter one: That maneh to which I admit before you, [8]I also admitted to before so-and-so.

[9]Still, the latter one knew, [10][and] the former one did not know!

[11]When he went back [and] said to the former one: [12]That maneh to which I admitted before you, [13]I also admitted to before so-and-so.

[14][Rav Naḥman bar Yitzḥak] said to [Rav Huna the son of Rav Yehoshua]: May your mind be at ease, [15]for you have put my mind at ease.

[16]He said to him: What ease? [17]For Rava, and some say Rav Sheshet, [18]threw an axe into it: [19]Is this not

TRANSLATION AND COMMENTARY

אַשְׁכַּחֵיהּ [1]**Rav Naḥman bar Yitzḥak met Rav Huna the son of Rav Yehoshua,** [2]and **said to him: What is** different about someone's witnessing **a loan subsequent to** another person's witnessing an identical **loan** — in **which** event Rav states that the testimonies may **not be** combined by the court? [3]In the case of two loans, **the maneh** that **one** witness **sees** being borrowed is **not seen** by the other witness to have been borrowed, and vice versa. [4]But certainly this is true **as well** in the case where someone witnessed an **admission subsequent to** the witnessing of an **admission** by someone else. [5]**The maneh to which** the debtor **admits before one** witness, [6]**he does not** necessarily **admit to before** the other witness!

דַּאֲמַר לֵיהּ [7]Rav Huna explained to Rav Naḥman bar Yitzḥak that, in the case of one admission after another, the debtor **said to the latter** witness: **That maneh to which** I just **admitted** before **you,** [8]**I also admitted** before **so-and-so,** specifically admitting to the same loan before each of the witnesses.

אַכַּתִּי Rav Naḥman persisted in seeking clarification: Even with that construction, there is [9]**still** a problem — for although **the latter** witness **knew** that his testimony was identical with his colleague's testimony, [10]**the former** witness could **not** have **known** that he was testifying about the same loan as his co-witness. Without this knowledge, how can they be seen as testifying as "one" to the debtor's admission?

דַּהֲדַר אָזֵיל [11]Rav Huna modified his explanation to take into account Rav Naḥman's objection: After the debtor notified the latter witness, **he went back** and **told the former one** as well: [12]**That maneh to which I admitted before you,** [13]**I also admitted to before so-and-so.** Since both witnesses knew that they were testifying about the same obligation, it is clear that their testimonies may be combined. It now becomes apparent that Rav's reasoning in this teaching, requiring both witnesses to testify about the same financial obligation, is in accordance with his rejection, above, of Rabbi Yehoshua ben Korḥah's position regarding testifying about money.

אֲמַר לֵיהּ [14]Having had all his difficulties with Rav's teaching resolved, Rav Naḥman bar Yitzḥak **said to** Rav Huna the son of Rav Yehoshua: **May your mind be at ease,** [15]**for you have put my mind at ease.**

אֲמַר לֵיהּ [16]Rav Huna **said to** Rav Naḥman in reply: **What ease** of mind can we enjoy, [17]**for Rava, and some say** it was **Rav Sheshet,** [18]**threw an axe into** my entire explanation with the following observation: Once we have established that Rav only allows the testimony of witnesses to be combined if they both know that they are testifying about the same obligation, why was it necessary for Rav to provide us with two different cases — an admission following an admission, and an admission following the loan itself? [19]**Is not**

RASHI

הודאה אחר הודאה נמי — דילמא מנא דאודי ליה קמי האי, לאו היינו מנה דאודי ליה קמי האי. **ואכתי בתרא ידע** — דאמנה דקא מסהיד איהו, מסהיד אידך. אבל קמא לא ידע דאחד מנה קמסהדי, הלכך לא קרינא ביה "והוא עד" דמשמע תרוייהו כחד. **לאו היינו הודאה אחר הלואה** — כיון דבעינן דידע סהדא בחבריה, על כרחיך הודאה אחר הלואה נמי הכי מוקמת לה.

TRANSLATION AND COMMENTARY

the first case, regarding two admissions, essentially the same as the case of an **admission** observed **subsequent to a loan?!**

אֲמַר לֵיהּ [1]Rav Naḥman **said to** Rav Huna: **This is** exactly **what I heard about you** scholars of Meḥoza — [2]**that you uproot palm-trees and** then proceed to **put them back up.**

נְהַרְדְּעֵי אָמְרִי [3]**The Neharde'an** Sages disagree with Rav's teaching, above, and **say: Be it** the case of one witness observing **an admission subsequent to** another witness observing the identical **admission;** [4]or the case of one witness observing **an admission subsequent to** another witness observing the **loan;** [5]or the case of one witness observing **a loan subsequent to** another witness observing an identical **loan;** [6]or the case of one witness observing **a loan subsequent to** another witness observing the **admission** to an identical loan — [7]in all these cases, the witnesses' testimonies **may be combined** in court so as to obligate the debtor. [8]The Gemara asks: **In accordance with whom** is this position? [9]The Gemara answers: It is **in accordance with Rabbi Yehoshua ben Korḥah,** who maintained that witnesses need not have observed the same thing as long as their testimonies point to a common liability.

אָמַר רַב יְהוּדָה [10]When examining witnesses, the court first conducts an "investigation" (חֲקִירָה) consisting of seven questions which determine the exact time and place of the observation. It then begins the "examination" (בְּדִיקָה), asking questions relating to the physical details observed at the scene. **Rav Yehudah said:** Joint **testimony, when one** witness **contradicts the other during** the court's **examinations, is valid in**

הוֹדָאָה אַחַר הַלְוָאָה?! [1]אֲמַר לֵיהּ: הַיְינוּ דִּשְׁמִיעַ לִי עֲלַיְיכוּ — [2]דִּרְמִיתוּ דִּיקְלֵי וְזָקְפִיתוּ לְהוּ.

[3]נְהַרְדְּעֵי אָמְרִי: בֵּין הוֹדָאָה אַחַר הוֹדָאָה; [4]בֵּין הוֹדָאָה אַחַר הַלְוָאָה; [5]בֵּין הַלְוָאָה אַחַר הַלְוָאָה; [6]בֵּין הַלְוָאָה אַחַר הוֹדָאָה — [7]מִצְטָרְפוֹת. [8]כְּמַאן? [9]כְּרַבִּי יְהוֹשֻׁעַ בֶּן קָרְחָה.

[10]אָמַר רַב יְהוּדָה: עֵדוּת הַמַּכְחֶשֶׁת זוֹ אֶת זוֹ בִּבְדִיקוֹת

LITERAL TRANSLATION

[the case of] admission subsequent to a loan?!

[1][Rav Naḥman bar Yitzḥak] said to him: This is what I heard about you — [2]that you uproot palm-trees and [then] put them back up.

[3]The Neharde'ans say: Be it an admission subsequent to an admission; [4]be it an admission subsequent to a loan; [5]be it a loan subsequent to a loan; [6][or] be it a loan subsequent to an admission — [7]they may be combined. [8]In accordance with whom?

[9]Rav Yehudah said: Testimony when one [witness] contradicts the other during [court] examinations

RASHI

דאמר ליה לבתרא מנה דמודינא קמך — יזיפי קמי פלניא. והדר אמר ליה לקמא: מנה דיזיפי קמך אודאי ליה קמי פלניא, ותרתי למה לי לרב למימר? **היינו דשמיע לי** — על בני עירך. **דרמיתו דיקלי וזקפיתו ליה** — שאתם משונים, קוצצין דקלים וחוזרין ונוטעין אותן. כלומר: בונים וסותרים, שפירשתם לי קושיא וחזרתם וסתרתם. **מצטרפין** — דמכל מקום הן מעידין שחייב לו מנה. **בבדיקות** — שאינה משבע חקירות "באיזו יום" "באיזו שעה" שהזמה תלויה בהן, אבל ב"כליו שחורין" ו"כליו לבנים", שאין דין הזמה תלויה בהן.

NOTES

נְהַרְדְּעֵי אָמְרִי: בֵּין הוֹדָאָה אַחַר הוֹדָאָה וכו׳ מִצְטָרְפוֹת **The Neharde'ans say: Be it an admission subsequent to an admission, etc. — they may be combined.** The majority of Rishonim, in explaining this ruling, state that in the latter two scenarios (a loan after a loan or a loan after an admission) the creditor supports the testimony of the witnesses by claiming to have made two separate loans of a *maneh* to the debtor. Since the two witnesses do not contradict the creditor, and they both agree that he is owed at least one *maneh*, their testimonies can be combined in obligating the debtor to repay that one *maneh*. However, if the creditor in these cases claimed to have made only a single loan, then we cannot combine their testimonies. For it appears that one of the witnesses is lying, unless the time discrepancy was so small that we can assume one of the witnesses simply forgot the exact date (*Ramah, Ramban, Rabbenu Yonah, Ran,* and *Meiri*). *Meiri* cites another opinion which interprets these last two cases as dealing with a creditor who claims to have only lent money to the debtor on one occasion; the rationale is that in monetary cases we relate only to the core testimony (the obligation of a *maneh*) while disregarding discrepancies of detail (such as conflicting dates). However, if the creditor claims to have made two separate loans, we do not combine the testimonies — for it appears that the witnesses did indeed observe two separate events. This opinion, however, enjoys less support from the actual text of the Gemara and is rejected by *Meiri.*

Insofar as the first two scenarios dealt with in the above ruling (an admission after an admission or an admission after a loan), all Rishonim agree that the creditor in these cases need not have made claim to two separate loans in order for the testimonies to be combined. Even when he claims to have lent the debtor a single *maneh*, it is possible that the debtor admitted to it on two separate occasions.

HALAKHAH

עֵדוּת הַמַּכְחֶשֶׁת זוֹ אֶת זוֹ **Testimony when one contradicts the other.** "Even though questioning of the witnesses is unnecessary in civil cases, if they nonetheless were investigated and contradicted each other about the time or

LANGUAGE

אַרְנְקִי **Purse.** This word derives from the Greek αρναχις, *arnakis*, meaning "a box or purse in which coins are placed."

אָרִירָן **Sword.** The origin of this word is doubtful. Some authorities believe it comes from the Greek άορ, *a'or*, meaning "sword." According to the Geonim, an אָרִירָן is a twisted sword or knife.

TRANSLATION AND COMMENTARY

civil cases but not in capital ones. [1] **Rava said: Rav Yehudah's words are reasonable** if **one** witness **said** that the money was **"in a black purse,"** [2] **and one** witness **said** that the money was **"in a white purse,"** these being relatively inconsequential details that a witness could have forgotten. [3] **However, if one** witness **says** that the money given was **"a grimy black maneh,"** [4] **and one says** that it was **"a shiny white maneh,"** details that relate to the essence of the testimony, then we must suspect them of lying. [5] Hence their respective statements **may not be combined.**

וְאַרְנְקִי שְׁחוֹרָה [6] Challenging Rav Yehudah the Gemara asks: Is it indeed so, that **in capital cases** a discrepancy between witnesses in regard to some minor detail, such as whether it was **a black purse** or a white purse, renders their testimony unacceptable? [7] **But did not Rav Ḥisda say:** If **one** witness **says** that **"he killed him with a sword,"** and one witness **says** that **"he killed him with a dagger,"** [8] then the testimony **is not acceptable,** as required by the verse in Deuteronomy (13:15) — "and behold the matter is true and correct." [9] However, if **one** witness **says** that **"his clothing was black,"** and **the other** witness **says** that **"his clothing was white,"** a relatively minor inconsistency — [10] the testimony **is acceptable** and the testimony stands. [31A] [11] The Gemara answers: **You are raising** a contradiction between **one** Amora (Rava) **and another** (Rav Ḥisda). That is no way to prove a point, because Amoraim may disagree about issues that had not yet been clarified by earlier Sages.

נְהַרְדְּעֵי אָמְרִי [12] The Gemara now resumes its consideration of the law: Regarding contradictory testimony in monetary cases, **the Neharde'an** Sages **say** as follows: [13] **Even if one** witness **said** that the loan involved **"a black maneh"** and the other **said** it involved **"a white maneh"** — [14] the two testimonies **may be combined** to oblige the debtor to repay a maneh.

LITERAL TRANSLATION

is valid in monetary cases. [1] **Rava said: Rav Yehudah's words are reasonable** when one said "in a black purse" [2] and one said "in a white purse"; [3] but [if] one said "a black maneh" [4] and one said "a white maneh," [5] they may not be combined.

[6] And is [the discrepancy of] "a black purse" in capital cases not [acceptable]? [7] But did not Rav Ḥisda say: [If] one says "he killed him with a sword" and the other says "he killed him with a dagger" — [8] this is not acceptable (lit., "correct"). [9] [If] one says "his clothing was black" and the other says "his clothing was white" — [10] this is acceptable! [31A] [11] Are you casting one man against another man?!

[12] The Neharde'ans say: [13] Even [if] one said "a black maneh" and one said "a white maneh" — [14] they may be combined.

כְּשֵׁרָה בְּדִינֵי מָמוֹנוֹת. [1] אָמַר רָבָא: מִסְתַּבְּרָא מִילְתֵיהּ דְּרַב יְהוּדָה בְּאֶחָד אוֹמֵר "בְּאַרְנְקִי שְׁחוֹרָה" [2] וְאֶחָד אוֹמֵר "בְּאַרְנְקִי לְבָנָה"; [3] אֲבָל אֶחָד אוֹמֵר "מָנֶה שָׁחוֹר" [4] וְאֶחָד אוֹמֵר "מָנֶה לָבָן", [5] אֵין מִצְטָרְפִין.

[6] וְ"אַרְנְקִי שְׁחוֹרָה" בְּדִינֵי נְפָשׁוֹת לֹא? [7] וְהָאָמַר רַב חִסְדָּא: אֶחָד אוֹמֵר "בְּסַיִיף הֲרָגוֹ" וְאֶחָד אוֹמֵר "בְּאָרִירָן הֲרָגוֹ" — [8] אֵין זֶה נָכוֹן. [9] אֶחָד אוֹמֵר "כֵּלָיו שְׁחוֹרִים" וְאֶחָד אוֹמֵר "כֵּלָיו לְבָנִים" — [10] הֲרֵי זֶה נָכוֹן! [31A] [11] גַּבְרָא אַגַּבְרָא קָא רָמֵית?!

[12] נְהַרְדְּעֵי אָמְרִי: [13] אֲפִילּוּ אֶחָד אוֹמֵר "מָנֶה שָׁחוֹר" וְאֶחָד אוֹמֵר "מָנֶה לָבָן" — [14] מִצְטָרְפִים.

RASHI

מנה שחור — סלע ישנה. אין מצטרפין — הואיל ובעיקר גוף העדות מתכחשי. וארנקי שחורה — דלאו בעיקר גוף העדות מתכחשי. דכוותיה בדיני נפשות לא? בתמיה. באָרִירָן — יושרמ"א* בלעז אין זה נכון — אין עדות זו מכוונת, ולישנא דקרא נקט "והנה אמת נכון הדבר" (דברים יג) דמהאי קרא נפקא לן בדיקות (סנהדרין מ,ג). גברא אגברא — דרב חסדא אדרב יהודה.

NOTES

מָנֶה שָׁחוֹר, מָנֶה לָבָן **A black maneh; a white maneh.** Some interpret this to mean a maneh coin of impure silver (black) and one of pure silver (white) (*Rabbi Yehonatan of Lunel*).

בְּסַיִיף הֲרָגוֹ בְּאָרִירָן הֲרָגוֹ **He killed him with a sword; he killed him with a dagger.** The type of weapon is considered to be an essential aspect of the testimony because the Torah attaches great significance to the lethal character of the murder instrument in establishing the killer's responsibility (*Ramah*).

HALAKHAH

place of their witnessing — their testimony is invalidated. But if they contradicted each other in regard to some other aspect or detail of the incident, then both their testimonies remain valid." (*Shulḥan Arukh, Ḥoshen Mishpat* 30:2.)

In capital cases, any contradiction whatsoever between the witnesses serves to invalidate their testimony. (*Rambam, Sefer Shofetim, Hilkhot Edut* 2:2.)

מָנֶה שָׁחוֹר וּמָנֶה לָבָן **A black maneh and a white maneh.** "If one witness said that he saw the debtor borrow a grimy black (old) maneh while the other said it was a shiny white (new) maneh, and the creditor claimed to be owed both,

TRANSLATION AND COMMENTARY

כְּמַאן [1]The Gemara attempts to clarify this ruling: In accordance **with whose views** is this decision of the Neharde'ans? [2]Is it in accordance **with Rabbi Yehoshua ben Korḥah**, who maintained, above, that we may combine two incongruous testimonies as long as they both refer to an identical financial obligation? [3]**Granted that you heard Rabbi Yehoshua ben Korḥah** express his opinion **when** the witnesses indicated that they had observed two independent loans [4]and thus **did not** actually **contradict one another**. [5]But does he indeed **maintain** the same ruling **when they** directly **contradict one another** about the same event, as in the Neharde'an's case?

אֶלָּא [6]**Rather,** the Neharde'ans must have **ruled in accordance with** the **Tanna who taught** the following Baraita: [7]**"Rabbi Shimon ben Elazar said: Bet Shammai and Bet Hillel did not argue about** the law concerning **two sets of witnesses,** [8]**when one** pair **says** that the loan involved **"two hundred** dinarim" while the other pair **says** it only involved **"one hundred** dinarim." [9]Since the sum of **one hundred is subsumed within** the sum of **two hundred**, the debtor can be obligated to pay back one hundred dinarim, as this verdict is not contradicted by either pair of witnesses. [10]**About what** law **did they argue?** [11]**About** the law in the case of **one set** of witnesses, when one witness said that the loan involved two hundred dinarim, while the other said it involved only one hundred dinarim. [12]In such a case **Bet Shammai says: Their testimony is split.** Any contradiction between two witnesses who appear jointly undermines the credibility of both. [13]**Bet Hillel says** otherwise: Since the sum of **one hundred** dinarim seen by the one witness **is subsumed within** the **two hundred** dinarim seen by the other, it is permissible to combine their testimonies for the sake of obligating the debtor to pay the one hundred dinarim about which they agree." Hence we see that the Neharde'ans had support for their ruling from the opinion attributed to Bet Hillel by Rabbi Shimon ben Elazar.

אֶחָד אוֹמֵר [14]Once **a case came before Rabbi Ammi** concerning a pair of witnesses, [15]**one** who **said** that the loan involved **"a barrel of wine,"** while the other **said** it involved **"a barrel of oil."**

[1]כְּמַאן? [2]כְּרַבִּי יְהוֹשֻׁעַ בֶּן קָרְחָה? [3]אֵימַר דְּשָׁמְעַתְּ לֵיהּ לְרַבִּי יְהוֹשֻׁעַ בֶּן קָרְחָה. [4]הֵיכָא דְּלָא מְכַחֲשׁוּ אַהֲדָדֵי, [5]הֵיכָא דִּמְכַחֲשֵׁי אַהֲדָדֵי מִי אֲמַר?!
[6]אֶלָּא, הוּא דַּאֲמַר כִּי הַאי תַּנָּא דְּתַנְיָא: [7]אָמַר רַבִּי שִׁמְעוֹן בֶּן אֶלְעָזָר: לֹא נֶחְלְקוּ בֵּית שַׁמַּאי וּבֵית הִלֵּל עַל שְׁתֵּי כִיתֵּי עֵדִים, [8]שֶׁאַחַת אוֹמֶרֶת: "מָאתַיִם", וְאַחַת אוֹמֶרֶת: [9]"מָנֶה" — שֶׁיֵּשׁ בִּכְלַל מָאתַיִם מָנֶה. [10]עַל מָה נֶחְלְקוּ? [11]עַל כַּת אַחַת, [12]שֶׁבֵּית שַׁמַּאי אוֹמְרִים: נֶחְלְקָה עֵדוּתָן, [13]וּבֵית הִלֵּל אוֹמְרִים: יֵשׁ בִּכְלַל מָאתַיִם מָנֶה.
[14]אֶחָד אוֹמֵר: "חָבִית שֶׁל יַיִן", [15]וְאֶחָד אוֹמֵר: "חָבִית שֶׁל שֶׁמֶן" הֲוָה עוּבְדָא וְאָתֵי לְקַמֵּיהּ

LITERAL TRANSLATION

[1]Like whom? [2]Like Rabbi Yehoshua ben Korḥah? [3]Say that you heard Rabbi Yehoshua ben Korḥah regarding where they do not contradict one another. [4]Regarding where they contradict one another, [5]does he [indeed] say [it]?! [6]Rather, he said [as he did] in accordance with that Tanna who taught: [7]Rabbi Shimon ben Elazar said: Bet Shammai and Bet Hillel did not disagree about [the case of] two sets of witnesses, [8]where one [set] says: "Two hundred," and one says: [9]"One hundred" — for one hundred is subsumed within two hundred. [10]About what did they disagree? [11]About [the case of] one set, [12]where Bet Shammai says: Their testimony is split, [13]and Bet Hillel says: One hundred is subsumed within two hundred. [14][The case of] one [who] says: "A barrel of wine," [15]and one [who] says: "A barrel of oil" was a case that came before

RASHI

כרבי יהושע בן קרחה – דמכל מקום שניהם מעידים שחייב לו מנה. **היכא דלא מכחשו אהדדי** – כגון זה מעיד על מנה שביום שני, וזה מעיד על מנה שביום ראשון, ושניהן מודין שזה לא ראה בשל זה, אבל היכא דשניהם מעידין על מנה אחד ומכחישין זה את זה מי אמר? **הוא דאמר כי האי תנא** – נהרדעי אמרו כי האי תנא דאמר, זה אומר: מנה, וזה אומר: מאתים, דמכחישין זה את זה, – מצטרפין למנה, שיש בכלל מאתים מנה. ולא אמרינן שתיהן שקרו, אלא הלך אחר הפחות שבהם. **נחלקה עדותן** – שכיון שהאחד שקרן שוב אין כאן עדות. **יש בבלל מאתים מנה** – שניהם מעידין על מנה, ובאותו מנה אין מכחישין זה את זה.

HALAKHAH

the two testimonies are combined for the sake of obligating the debtor to repay one maneh." This, in accordance with the ruling of the Neharde'an Sages as based upon the opinion of Rabbi Shimon the son of Elazar. (*Shulḥan Arukh, Ḥoshen Mishpat* 30:2.)

אַחַת אוֹמֶרֶת: "מָאתַיִם", וְאַחַת אוֹמֶרֶת: "מָנֶה" **One says a maneh and one says two maneh.** "If one witness said that the debtor borrowed one maneh while the other said he borrowed two maneh, the debtor is obligated to pay back one maneh — for the sum of one maneh is subsumed within the sum of two maneh," in accordance with Bet Hillel. (*Shulḥan Arukh, Ḥoshen Mishpat* 30:2.)

חָבִית שֶׁל יַיִן וְחָבִית שֶׁל שֶׁמֶן **A barrel of wine and a barrel of oil.** "If one witness said that he borrowed a barrel of

TRANSLATION AND COMMENTARY

[1]**Rabbi Ammi obligated** the borrower **to pay** the lender the value of **a barrel of wine,** the cheaper of the two commodities. It is regarded as a part of the value of a **barrel of oil,** for both witnesses testify that the borrower owed him at least the value of a barrel of wine.

כְּמַאן [2]**In accordance with whom** did Rabbi Ammi decide thus? [3]Was it **in accordance with Rabbi Shimon ben Elazar**, who cited Bet Hillel as maintaining that contradictions are disregarded when there is at least partial agreement between the witnesses over the sum of the debt? [4]One can **say** in refutation **that Rabbi Shimon** ben Elazar only **spoke** thus in regard to a monetary loan, **where** the **one hundred** dinarim reported by one witness **is** literally **subsumed within** the **two hundred** dinar reported by the other. [5]In **a case such as this,** where the witnesses were referring to two different commodities altogether, **does** Rabbi Shimon still **give** the same ruling?

לָא [6]**No,** says the Gemara. Nevertheless, **it was necessary for** Rabbi Ammi to decide as he did, for the witnesses were actually referring to the monetary **value** of the commodities rather than the commodities themselves.

אֶחָד אוֹמֵר [7]What do you do when there are two witnesses, and **one** of them **says** that the loan took place **"in the upper story"** of a building, [8]while the other **says** it took place **"in the lower story"**? [9]**Rabbi Ḥanina said:** Such a **case came before Rabbi** Yehudah HaNasi **and he combined** the witnesses' **testimony**, as did Rav Yehudah (above, 30b), who disregarded minor discrepancies when there was agreement on the essentials.

וּמִנַּיִין [10]Returning to our Mishnah, the Gemara asks: **"And from where** do we know **that when** a judge **leaves** the courtroom, he should not say: 'I sought to free the defendant from liability but my colleagues found him liable; what could I do, for my colleagues outnumbered me?'?" [11]**The Rabbis taught** similarly in a Baraita: **"From where** do we know **that when** a judge **leaves** the courtroom, [12]**he should not say: 'Behold**

דְּרַבִּי אַמִי. [1]חַיְּיבֵיהּ רַבִּי אַמִי לְשַׁלּוּמֵי לֵיהּ חָבִיתָא דְּחַמְרָא מִיגּוֹ חָבִיתָא דְּמִשְׁחָא.

[2]כְּמַאן? [3]כְּרַבִּי שִׁמְעוֹן בֶּן אֶלְעָזָר? [4]אֵימַר דַּאֲמַר רַבִּי שִׁמְעוֹן בֶּן אֶלְעָזָר הֵיכָא דְּיֵשׁ בִּכְלַל מָאתַיִם מָנֶה. [5]כִּי הַאי גַּוְונָא, מִי אֲמַר?

[6]לָא! צְרִיכָא לִדְמֵי.

[7]אֶחָד אוֹמֵר: ״בַּדְּיוֹטָא הָעֶלְיוֹנָה״, [8]וְאֶחָד אוֹמֵר: ״בַּדְּיוֹטָא הַתַּחְתּוֹנָה״, [9]אָמַר רַבִּי חֲנִינָא: מַעֲשֶׂה בָּא לִפְנֵי רַבִּי, וְצֵירֵף עֵדוּתָן.

[10]״וּמִנַּיִין לִכְשֶׁיֵּצֵא כו׳״. [11]תָּנוּ רַבָּנַן: ״מִנַּיִין לִכְשֶׁיֵּצֵא, [12]לֹא

LITERAL TRANSLATION

Rabbi Ammi. [1]Rabbi Ammi obligated him to pay him [the value of] a barrel of wine out of [that of] a barrel of oil.

[2]Like whom? [3]Like Rabbi Shimon ben Elazar? [4]Say that Rabbi Shimon [ben Elazar] said that where one hundred is subsumed within two hundred. [5]Regarding something like this, does he [still] say [it]?

[6]No! [But Rabbi Ammi's ruling] was necessary for [the case of] value.

[7]One witness says: "In the upper story," [8]and one says: "In the lower story," [9]Rabbi Ḥanina said: The case came before Rabbi and he combined their testimonies.

[10]"And from where [do we know] that when [a judge] exits, etc." [11]The Rabbis taught: "From where [do we know] that when he exits, [12]he should not

RASHI

כי האי גוונא – דתרי מיני נינהו, וכולי האי מיכחשי הדדי מי אמר? **לדמי** – זה אומר: בפני הודה לו דמי חבית של יין, וזה אומר: בפני הודה דמי חבית של שמן, דתרווייהו מסהדי אדמי חבית יין. **בדיוטא עליונה** – הלוהו מנה. **דיוטא** – עלייה הבולטת לרשות הרבים על פני רוחב הבית, ובני רשות הרבים עוברים תחתיה. **וצירוף עדותן** – כרבי יהושע בן קרחה, דתרווייהו מנה מחייבי. ואף על גב דמתכחשי בבדיקות כדרב יהודה.

NOTES

אֶחָד אוֹמֵר: בַּדְּיוֹטָא הָעֶלְיוֹנָה וכו׳ **One says: "on the upper floor," etc.** The question is posed by some Rishonim: How can the Gemara imply that the exact location where the loan was contracted is an inconsequential detail, when we have already established that the seven investigative questions relating to time and place must be answered identically by both witnesses? They answer by noting that in the "investigation" phase of questioning, a discrepancy

HALAKHAH

wine while the other said he borrowed a barrel of oil, their testimony is considered contradictory and hence invalid. However, if one said that the creditor borrowed the value of a barrel of wine while the other said he borrowed the value of a barrel of oil, their testimonies are not invalidated and the creditor must pay back the lesser of the two sums," in accordance with the words of Rabbi Ammi. (*Shulḥan Arukh, Ḥoshen Mishpat* 30:2.)

דְּיוֹטָא עֶלְיוֹנָה וּדְיוֹטָא תַּחְתּוֹנָה **The upper story and the lower story.** "If one witness said that the loan took place on an upper story while the other said it took place on a lower story, their testimonies may still be combined," in accordance with Rabbi Ḥanina. (*Shulḥan Arukh, Ḥoshen Mishpat* 30:2.)

יֹאמַר: ׳הֲרֵינִי מְזַכֶּה וַחֲבֵירַי מְחַיְּיבִין; [1]אֲבָל מָה אֶעֱשֶׂה, שֶׁחֲבֵירַי רַבּוּ עָלַי׳? [2]תַּלְמוּד לוֹמַר: ׳לֹא תֵלֵךְ רָכִיל בְּעַמֶּיךָ׳, [3]וְאוֹמֵר: ׳הוֹלֵךְ רָכִיל מְגַלֶּה סוֹד׳״.

[4]הַהוּא תַּלְמִידָא דְּנָפֵיק עֲלֵיהּ קָלָא דְּגַלֵּי מִילְּתָא דְּאִיתְּמַר בֵּי מִדְרְשָׁא. [5]בָּתַר עֶשְׂרִין וְתַרְתֵּין שְׁנִין, אַפְּקֵיהּ רַב אַמִי מִבֵּי מִדְרְשָׁא, [6]אֲמַר: ״דֵּין גַּלֵּי רַזְיָא״.

מִשְׁנָה [7]כָּל זְמַן שֶׁמֵּבִיא רְאָיָה — [8]סוֹתֵר אֶת הַדִּין. [9]אָמַר לוֹ: כָּל רְאָיוֹת שֶׁיֵּשׁ לְךָ, הָבֵא מִיכָּן עַד שְׁלֹשִׁים יוֹם — [10]מָצָא בְּתוֹךְ שְׁלֹשִׁים יוֹם, סוֹתֵר; [11]לְאַחַר שְׁלֹשִׁים יוֹם, אֵינוֹ סוֹתֵר. [12]אָמַר רַבָּן שִׁמְעוֹן בֶּן גַּמְלִיאֵל: מַה יַּעֲשֶׂה זֶה

TRANSLATION AND COMMENTARY

I sought to free the defendant **from liability and my colleagues found him liable;** [1]**yet, I could not do anything, for my colleagues outnumbered me!'?** [2]We know it from what **the Torah states** in Leviticus (19:16): **'You shall not go about as a talebearer among your people';** [3]**and** similarly **it states** in Proverbs (11:13): **'A talebearer reveals secrets,** but he of trustworthy spirit conceals the matter.'"

הַהוּא תַּלְמִידָא [4]Relating to the topic of divulging secrets, it was told that there was once **a certain disciple about whom a rumor spread that he had revealed a** confidential **matter that was spoken about in the study hall.** [5]**Twenty-two years later,** when the rumor was finally confirmed, **Rav Ammi ejected him from the study hall** as a punishment for his past indiscretion and **said** about him as follows: **"This one is a revealer of secrets** [6]and unworthy of our trust."

MISHNAH כָּל זְמַן [7]If a litigant should, at **any time** subsequent to a verdict rendered against him, **bring a** new **proof** to court in support of his claim, [8]**he undoes the** earlier **verdict** and forces the court to retry the case. [9]However, if the court **said to him** after issuing its verdict: **"Whatever** additional **proofs you** may **have** which challenge our decision, **bring** them within the next **thirty days,'** then it is indeed as the court says. [10]If **he found** a proof **within thirty days,** he can **reverse** the verdict and force a retrial; [11]however, if he only produced the new evidence **after thirty days,** we suspect fraud and consequently **he cannot reverse** the earlier verdict. [12]**Rabban Shimon ben Gamliel** challenged this ruling and **asked: What should this** litigant **have done?**

LITERAL TRANSLATION

say: 'I freed [him] from liability and my colleagues found [him] liable; [1]yet what could I do, for my colleagues outnumbered me'? [2]The Torah states: 'You shall not go about as a talebearer among your people'; [3]and it states: 'A talebearer reveals secrets.'"

[4][There was] a certain disciple about whom a rumor emerged that he had revealed a [confidential] matter that was spoken about in the study hall. [5]After twenty-two years, Rav Ammi ejected him from the study hall [6][and] said: "This one is a revealer of secrets."

MISHNAH [7]Whenever he brings a proof — [8]he undoes the verdict. [9]It said to him: "Whatever proofs you have, bring [them] between now and thirty days" — [10][if] he found [the proof] within thirty days, he undoes [the verdict]; [11]after thirty days, he does not undo [the verdict]. [12]Rabban Shimon ben Gamliel said: What should this one do?

RASHI

בתר עשרין ותרתין שנין — דאיתמר בי מדרשא, אפקיה ההוא תלמידא, ודבר לשון הרע היה.

משנה כל זמן שמביא ראיה — הבא לבית דין ולא היה שטר זכותו בידו. ויצא מבית דין חייב, ולאחר זמן מצא שטר זכותו והביאו. סותר את הדין — בית דינו סותרין לו דינו שפסקו, ומחייבין את שכנגדו.

NOTES

in location is only significant when it indicates that the witnesses themselves were in two different places. Determining the precise location is necessary so that the witnesses themselves can be challenged by others, who may have seen them elsewhere at the time of their alleged observation. Since in this particular case the witnesses were not far from each other, it is not considered consequential (*Ramah, Rosh*).

דְּאִיתְּמַר בֵּי מִדְרְשָׁא **That was spoken about in the study hall.** The purpose of this anecdote is to demonstrate that one must be careful not to spread confidential information even if a number of people are already privy to it, as in the case of information shared between scholars in the study hall or between judges in the courtroom (*Torat Ḥayyim*).

HALAKHAH

סוֹתֵר אֶת הַדִּין **He may reverse the verdict.** "Even if someone was obligated by the court to pay the claim made against him or had actually paid it, he may still introduce new evidence in his defense and force a retrial. This is so even when new evidence was introduced after the deadline set by the court to bring any new evidence," in accordance with Rabban Shimon the son of Gamliel. "If the evidence, however, was introduced after the defendant had denied having further proof, then it is no longer admissible and the verdict stands," in accordance with the first Tanna. (*Shulḥan Arukh, Ḥoshen Mishpat* 20:1.)

שֶׁלֹּא מָצָא בְּתוֹךְ שְׁלֹשִׁים, [1]וּמָצָא לְאַחַר שְׁלֹשִׁים?! [2]אָמַר לוֹ: "הָבֵא עֵדִים", [3]וְאָמַר: "אֵין לִי עֵדִים"; [4]אָמַר: "הָבֵא רְאָיָה", [5]וְאָמַר: "אֵין לִי רְאָיָה"; [6]וּלְאַחַר זְמַן הֵבִיא רְאָיָה, וּמָצָא עֵדִים — [7]הֲרֵי זֶה אֵינוֹ כְּלוּם. [8]אָמַר רַבָּן שִׁמְעוֹן בֶּן גַּמְלִיאֵל: מַה יַּעֲשֶׂה זֶה — [9]שֶׁלֹּא הָיָה יוֹדֵעַ שֶׁיֵּשׁ לוֹ עֵדִים, וּמָצָא עֵדִים; [10]לֹא הָיָה יוֹדֵעַ שֶׁיֵּשׁ לוֹ רְאָיָה, וּמָצָא רְאָיָה?! [11]רָאָה שֶׁמִּתְחַיֵּיב בַּדִּין, וְאָמַר: [12]קִרְבוּ פְּלוֹנִי וּפְלוֹנִי וִיעִידוּנִי; [13]אוֹ שֶׁהוֹצִיא רְאָיָה מִתַּחַת פּוּנְדָּתוֹ — [14]הֲרֵי זֶה אֵינוֹ כְּלוּם.

גמרא [15]אָמַר רַבָּה בַּר רַב הוּנָא: הֲלָכָה כְּרַבָּן שִׁמְעוֹן בֶּן גַּמְלִיאֵל. [16]וְאָמַר רַבָּה בַּר רַב הוּנָא: אֵין הֲלָכָה כְּדִבְרֵי חֲכָמִים. [17]פְּשִׁיטָא, כֵּיוָן דְּאָמַר הֲלָכָה כְּרַבָּן שִׁמְעוֹן בֶּן גַּמְלִיאֵל, [18]מִמֵּילָא יָדְעִנָא דְּאֵין הֲלָכָה כַּחֲכָמִים!

LITERAL TRANSLATION

He did not find [the proof] within thirty days, [1]but found [it] after thirty days?!

[2]It said to him: "Bring witnesses," [3]and he said: "I have no witnesses"; [4][or] it said: "Bring a proof," [5]and he said: "I have no proof"; [6]and after a while he brought a proof or found witnesses — [7]this is of no value. [8]Rabban Shimon ben Gamliel said: What should this one have done — [9]for he did not know that he had witnesses, and [then] found witnesses; [10]he did not know that he had proof, and [then] discovered proof?!

[11][If] he saw that he would be found liable in the case, and he said: [12]Let so-and-so and so-and-so approach and testify for me; [13]or if he withdrew [documentary] evidence from underneath his belt — [14]this is of no value.

GEMARA [15]Rabbah bar Rav Huna said: The law is in accordance with Rabban Shimon ben Gamliel. [16]And Rabbah bar Rav Huna said: The law is not like the words of the Sages.

[17]It is obvious! Once [Rabbah bar Rav Huna] said that the law is in accordance with Rabban Shimon ben Gamliel, [18]in any event we know that the law is not like the Sages!

TRANSLATION AND COMMENTARY

Is it his fault that **he did not find** the proof **within thirty days?!** [1]Rather, in such a case he may force a retrial even if he **found** the proof **after thirty days.**

אָמַר לוֹ [2]Similarly, if the court **said to** the litigant before issuing its verdict: **"Bring** additional **witnesses** in your defense," [3]**and he said: "I have no** more **witnesses"**; [4]or if the court **said: "Bring** additional **proof** in your defense," [5]**and he said: "I have no** more **proof"**; [6]**and** then **he subsequently** (after the court had already decided against him) **brought** additional **proof or found** more **witnesses** — [7]**this** new evidence **is of no value.** Since he denied having additional proofs, we suspect now that the new proofs were fabricated. [8]**Rabban Shimon ben Gamliel** challenged this ruling as well and **said: What should this** litigant **have done?** [9]Is it his fault that **he did not know** that **he had** more **witnesses,** and only **discovered them** later on; [10]or that **he did not know** that **he had** additional **proof,** and he only **discovered it** later on?!

רָאָה שֶׁמִּתְחַיֵּיב בַּדִּין [11]And finally: If after denying the existence of any additional evidence, the litigant **saw that he** would be found **liable in the case and said** in desperation: [12]**Let so-and-so and so-and-so** (witnesses who happened to be in the court at the time) **approach and testify for me;** [13]**or if he** suddenly **withdrew evidence from beneath his belt,** [14]**behold** even Rabban Shimon ben Gamliel would agree that **this** new evidence **is** probably fabricated and **of no value.** The obvious question is: Why did he wait till the last minute?

GEMARA אָמַר [15]**Rabbah bar Rav Huna said: The law** about a defendant who was asked by the court to produce proof within thirty days **is in accordance with** the opinion of **Rabban Shimon ben Gamliel**, who said that he may submit evidence after that deadline. [16]**Rabbah bar Rav Huna** also **said** that **the law** in that case **is not like the** opinion of **the Sages.**

פְּשִׁיטָא [17]The Gemara comments: **This is obvious! Once Rabbah bar Rav Huna said that the law is in accordance with Rabban Shimon ben Gamliel,** [18]we in any case **know that the law is not like the opinion of the Sages!**

RASHI

הבא ראיה — שטר זכותך. **הרי זה אין כלום** — שהרי אמר "אין לי", וחיישינן שמא זייף או שכר עדים. **קרבו פלוני ופלוני כו'** — אפילו רבן שמעון בן גמליאל מודה שכיון שהיה יודע בהן ואמר אין לי — ודאי שקרנים הן. **פונדתו** — חגורתו.

גמרא הלכה כרבן שמעון — אקמייתא קאי, כיון דלא אמר אין לי אף על גב דלא מצא בתוך שלשים יום.

NOTES

הֲרֵי זֶה אֵינוֹ כְּלוּם **This is of no value.** To explain the difference between this expression and the one used earlier in the Mishnah, "It cannot reverse the verdict" (אֵינוֹ סוֹתֵר), we can say that אֵינוֹ סוֹתֵר implies that the evidence is

HALAKHAH

רָאָה שֶׁמִּתְחַיֵּיב בַּדִּין **If he saw that he would be found liable in the case.** "If a litigant sensed the case turning against him and, after having denied possession of additional evidence, called forth new witnesses or introduced

TRANSLATION AND COMMENTARY

מַהוּ דְּתֵימָא [1]The Gemara replies: Had Rabbah bar Rav Huna not explicitly rejected the opinion of the Sages, **you might have said** that his **ruling**, expressing agreement with Rabban Shimon, **applies** to how the court conducts itself initially, should new evidence appear after the verdict has been announced but before it has been carried out. [2]**But** if the court **has** already **acted** in accordance with the Sages, and enforced the verdict in spite of new evidence, one might say that **it is considered** a **valid** decision, not to be reversed. By emphasizing that the opinion of the Sages is to be rejected, [3]Rabbah bar Rav Huna **is informing us that** even **if** the court **has** already **acted** in accordance with the Sages, **we reverse** the judgment and reconsider the case.

אָמַר לוֹ [4]Our Mishnah states: "If the court **said to** the litigant before issuing its verdict: '**Bring** additional **witnesses** in your defense,' and he said: 'I have no more witnesses'; or if the court said: 'Bring an additional proof in your defense,' and he said: 'I have no more proof'; and then after the court had decided against him, he brought additional proof or discovered more witnesses, this new evidence is of no value. [5]**Rabban Shimon ben Gamliel** challenged this ruling and **said:** He may force the court to reconsider his case if he produced new evidence, even after having denied its existence!" In this case, **Rabbah bar Rav Huna said in the name of Rabbi Yoḥanan: The law is like the words of the Sages** who disagree with Rabban Shimon ben Gamliel. [6]**And Rabbah bar Rav Huna** also **said in the name of Rabbi Yoḥanan** that **the law** in this case **is not in accordance with Rabban Shimon ben Gamliel.**

פְּשִׁיטָא [7]The Gemara protests again: **This is obvious!** [8]**Once** Rabbi Yoḥanan **said that the law is like the words of the Sages,** [9]**we know** in any event **that the law is not in accordance with Rabban Shimon ben Gamliel!**

הָא קָא מַשְׁמַע לָן [10]The Gemara replies: Rabbi Yoḥanan's second statement **tells us the following:** [11]**That** among all the cases in the Mishnah, it is only **in this** case that **the law is not in accordance with Rabban Shimon ben Gamliel;** [12]**in all** other cases, when Rabban Shimon ben Gamliel disagrees with another Tanna,

[1]מַהוּ דְּתֵימָא: הָנֵי מִילֵּי לְכַתְּחִילָּה; [2]אֲבָל, דִּיעֲבַד, שַׁפִּיר דָּמֵי. [3]קָא מַשְׁמַע לָן: דְּאִי עָבֵיד, מְהַדְּרִינַן לֵיהּ.
[4]״אָמַר לוֹ הָבֵא עֵדִים כו׳. אָמַר רַבָּן שִׁמְעוֹן בֶּן גַּמְלִיאֵל כו׳״. [5]אָמַר רַבָּה בַּר רַב הוּנָא אָמַר רַבִּי יוֹחָנָן: הֲלָכָה כְּדִבְרֵי חֲכָמִים. [6]וְאָמַר רַבָּה בַּר רַב הוּנָא אָמַר רַבִּי יוֹחָנָן: אֵין הֲלָכָה כְּרַבָּן שִׁמְעוֹן בֶּן גַּמְלִיאֵל.
[7]פְּשִׁיטָא! [8]כֵּיוָן דְּאָמַר הֲלָכָה כְּדִבְרֵי חֲכָמִים, [9]מִמֵּילָא יָדַעְנָא דְּאֵין הֲלָכָה כְּרַבָּן שִׁמְעוֹן בֶּן גַּמְלִיאֵל!
[10]הָא קָא מַשְׁמַע לָן: [11]דִּבְהַהִיא אֵין הֲלָכָה כְּרַבָּן שִׁמְעוֹן בֶּן גַּמְלִיאֵל; [12]הָא בְּכוּלְּהוּ, הֲלָכָה כְּרַבָּן שִׁמְעוֹן בֶּן גַּמְלִיאֵל.

LITERAL TRANSLATION

[1]You might have said: These words [apply] initially; [2]however, if [the court] has [already] acted, that is fine. [3][The ruling] informs us that [even] if [the court] has [already] acted, we undo it.

[4]"[If] he said to him: 'Bring witnesses,' etc. Rabban Shimon ben Gamliel said, etc." [5]Rabbah bar Rav Huna said in the name of Rabbi Yoḥanan: The law is like the words of the Sages. [6]And Rabbah bar Rav Huna said in the name of Rabbi Yoḥanan: The law is not in accordance with Rabban Shimon ben Gamliel.

[7]It is obvious! [8]Once [Rabbi Yoḥanan] said that the law is like the words of the Sages, [9]in any event we know that the law is not in accordance with Rabban Shimon ben Gamliel!

[10]It tells us this: [11]That in this [case] the law is not in accordance with Rabban Shimon ben Gamliel; [12]but in all [the rest] of them, the law is in accordance with Rabban Shimon ben Gamliel.

RASHI

דאי עבד – כרבנן ומהדר עובדא. ממילא ידעינן אין הלכה כרבן שמעון – והכא ליכא למימר כדלעיל מיניה "דאי עבד כו'" – דבשלמא התם אי לאו דהדר ואמר "אין הלכה כחכמים" הוה אמינא – אי עביד לא מהדרינן, דאלים כח דברי המרובין. אבל הכא כיון דאמר "הלכה כחכמים" פשיטא דאי עביד כיחיד מהדרינן להו. הא קא משמע לן דבהא – לחודא הוא דאין הלכה כרבן שמעון, הא בכל מקום הלכה כמותו אפילו בערב וצידן.

NOTES

ineffective after the verdict has been rendered, but it would have been worthy of consideration had it been submitted prior to the verdict. However, הֲרֵי זֶה אֵינוֹ כְּלוּם implies that the evidence is worthless regardless of when it is produced (*Rabbi Yehonatan of Lunel*).

HALAKHAH

another proof, the evidence is assumed to be fabricated and hence is ignored. If, however, he had not denied having additional evidence, he may produce new witnesses (*Rema*)." (*Shulḥan Arukh, Ḥoshen Mishpat* 20:1.)

TRANSLATION AND COMMENTARY

the law is in accordance with him. [1]The reason it was necessary for Rabbah to make this point in the name of Rabbi Yoḥanan was **to exclude** the following opinion **which Rabbah bar Bar Ḥannah reported in the name of Rabbi Yoḥanan:** [2]**Whenever Rabban Shimon ben Gamliel taught** an opinion **in our Mishnah, the law is in accordance with him** — [3]**except for** his opinions regarding the liability of **a guarantor** (*Bava Batra* 173b), the incident at **Tzidon** (*Gittin* 74a), **and the last** argument in our Mishnah between him and the Sages regarding new **proof** brought by a litigant. Rabbah's ruling contradicts that statement, declaring that only in the last of these three cases do we not rule in accordance with Rabban Shimon ben Gamliel.

הַהוּא יָנוֹקָא [4]Nevertheless, as an exception, new proof produced by a litigant can be accepted. It happened once that **a child was summoned to trial before Rav Naḥman** by his deceased father's creditors. [5]The court **said to** the young boy: **Do you have witnesses** who can testify that your father repaid these loans? [6]The boy **said to them: No.** He was then asked: **Do you have evidence** that your father repaid the loans? [7]The boy **said to him: No.** [8]Consequently, **Rav Naḥman obligated** the boy to repay the loans out of his inheritance. [9]The boy **cried and cried.** [10]A group of **men heard him** and **said to him:** [11]**We are** familiar with **your father's affairs** and can testify that he indeed did pay back those debts. [12]When the boy brought the men before **Rav Naḥman**, Rav Naḥman **said: In** a case such as **this,** [13]**even the Sages agree that** new witnesses may be introduced and the verdict overturned. Since **a child is** generally **not familiar with his father's affairs**, it is always possible that he will discover new evidence of which he was unaware.

[1]לְאַפּוּקֵי מֵהָא דְּאָמַר רַבָּה בַּר בַּר חָנָה, אָמַר רַבִּי יוֹחָנָן: [2]כָּל מָקוֹם שֶׁשָּׁנָה רַבָּן שִׁמְעוֹן בֶּן גַּמְלִיאֵל בְּמִשְׁנָתֵנוּ, הֲלָכָה כְּמוֹתוֹ — [3]חוּץ מֵעָרֵב, וְצַיְדָּן וּרְאָיָה אַחֲרוֹנָה.

[4]הַהוּא יָנוֹקָא דְּתְבָעוּהוּ לְדִינָא קַמֵּיהּ דְּרַב נַחְמָן. [5]אֲמַרוּ לֵיהּ: אִית לָךְ סָהֲדֵי? [6]אֲמַר לְהוּ: לָא. אִית לָךְ רְאָיָה? [7]אֲמַר לְהוּ: לָא. [8]חַיְּיבֵיהּ רַב נַחְמָן. [9]הֲוָה קָא בָּכֵי וְאָזֵיל. [10]שְׁמָעוּהוּ הָנָךְ אֱינָשֵׁי, אֲמַרוּ לֵיהּ: [11]אֲנַן יָדְעִינַן בְּמִילֵּי דַּאֲבוּךְ. [12]אָמַר רַב נַחְמָן: בְּהָא, [13]אֲפִילּוּ רַבָּנַן מוֹדוּ דְּיָנוֹקָא בְּמִילֵּי דַּאֲבוּהּ לָא יָדַע.

LITERAL TRANSLATION

[1][This is in order] to exclude what Rabbah bar Bar Ḥannah said in the name of Rabbi Yoḥanan: [2]Wherever Rabban Shimon ben Gamliel taught [an opinion] in our Mishnah, the law is in accordance with him — [3]except for [his opinions regarding] a guarantor, Tzidon, and the last [case of bringing] proof.

[4]A child was summoned to trial before Rav Naḥman. [5]He said to him: Do you have witnesses? [6]He said to him: No. Do you have proof? [7]He said to him: No. [8]Rav Naḥman found him liable. [9]The child cried and went. [10][When] these men heard him, they said to him: [11]We know [about] your father's affairs. [12]Rav Naḥman said: In this [case], [13]even the Rabbis agree that a child does not know [about] his father's affairs.

RASHI

ערב — ב״גט פשוט״ (בבא בתרא קעג,ב). צידן — במסכת גיטין ״במי שאחזו קורדייקוס״ (עד,א). ראיה אחרונה — הך בתרייתא דמתניתין. דאילו בקמייתא — הילכתא כוותיה.

NOTES

כָּל מָקוֹם שֶׁשָּׁנָה רַבָּן שִׁמְעוֹן בֶּן גַּמְלִיאֵל בְּמִשְׁנָתֵנוּ **Wherever Rabban Shimon ben Gamliel taught in our Mishnah.** The Rishonim disagree about the applicability of this rule. Some maintain that it is adopted fully, necessitating us to accept every opinion Rabban Shimon ben Gamliel stated in the Mishnah, aside from the three exceptions. Others maintain that only the clause citing the exceptions is accepted without qualification. However, Rabbah bar Bar Ḥannah's general opening statement was only meant to be followed when no other rule of Halakhic determination mitigates against accepting Rabban Shimon's opinion (see *Rabbenu Yonah*).

הַהוּא יָנוֹקָא **A certain child.** Rav Naḥman appears to be acting here in accordance with his position in tractate *Arakhin* (22a), where he rules that the court is empowered to collect from an orphan's estate even while he is still a minor. Some Rishonim suggest that this case is in accordance even with the position that orphans are generally exempt from litigation until they reach adulthood. They explain that we are dealing here with exceptions to that rule, such as the case of a non-Jewish creditor whose interest-bearing loan will devour the orphan's estate should its payment be delayed until the orphan reaches adulthood; or a case of the deceased's widow seeking payment of her ketubah settlement (*Rabbenu Yonah, Ran*). Another way of resolving the problem presented by Rav Naḥman's apparent authorization to make payment from an orphan's estate would be to interpret the term יָנוֹקָא as applying to an adult orphan who, because of his ignorance regarding his father's affairs, is termed a child by the Gemara (*Ran*).

יָנוֹקָא בְּמִילֵּי דַּאֲבוּהּ לָא יָדַע **A child is not familiar with his father's affairs.** The Geonim and later authorities are in

HALAKHAH

יָנוֹקָא בְּמִילֵּי דַּאֲבוּהּ לָא יָדַע **A child is not familiar with his father's affairs.** "If someone who was orphaned as a minor

[1]הַהִיא אִיתְּתָא דִּנְפַק שְׁטָרָא מִתּוּתֵי יְדָהּ. [2]אֲמַרָה לֵיהּ: יָדַעְנָא בְּהַאי שְׁטָרָא דִּפְרִיעַ הֲוָה. [3]הֵימְנָהּ רַב נַחְמָן. [4]אֲמַר לֵיהּ רָבָא לְרַב נַחְמָן: כְּמַאן? [5]כְּרַבִּי, דְּאָמַר: אוֹתִיּוֹת נִקְנוֹת בִּמְסִירָה? [6]אֲמַר לֵיהּ: שָׁאנֵי הָכָא, [7]דְּאִי בָּעֲיָא, קְלַתֵּיהּ. [8]אִיכָּא דְּאָמְרִי לֹא הֵימְנָהּ רַב נַחְמָן. [9]אֲמַר לֵיהּ רָבָא לְרַב נַחְמָן: וְהָא, אִי בָּעֲיָא, [31B] קְלַתֵּיהּ! [10]כֵּיוָן דְּאִיתַּחְזַק בְּבֵי דִינָא, [11]״אִיבַּעֲיָא קְלַתֵּיהּ״ לָא אָמְרִינַן.

LITERAL TRANSLATION

[1]A woman released a [promissory] note from her hand. [2]She said to him: I know that this bill has [already] been paid. [3]Rav Nahman believed her. [4]Rava said to Rav Nahman: In accordance with whom? [5]In accordance with Rabbi, who said [that bills containing] letters are acquired through handing over? [6]He said to him: It is different here, [7]for if she wished, she [could have] burned it.

[8]There are those who say [that] Rav Nahman did not believe her. [9]Rava said to Rav Nahman: But, if she had wished, [31B] she [could have] burned it! [10]Since its [veracity] has been established in court, [11]we do not say "if she had wished, she [could have] burned it."

TRANSLATION AND COMMENTARY

הַהִיא [1]In another incident involving Rav Naḥman, **a woman produced a** promissory **note**, which had been entrusted **to her** for safekeeping. [2]Presenting herself before the judge, she **said to him**: Having being appointed its trustee, **I know that this** note **has** already **been paid.** [3]**Rav Naḥman believed her** and declared the document nonnegotiable. [4]Hearing of his decision, **Rava said to Rav Naḥman: In accordance with whom** did you decide this case? [5]Was it **in accordance with Rabbi** Yehudah HaNasi, **who said** that the **letters** found in a document (the recorded entitlement to a debt) **may be acquired** by a third party **by** means of the original creditor simply **handing** the document **over** to him? And has the woman, by simply accepting the document, thereby acquired rights to the loan, so she is able to dictate its status? [6]Rav Naḥman **said to him**: My reasoning **here is** actually **different.** I would accept the woman's statement even were I to reject the opinion of Rabbi Yehudah HaNasi. Here, if the woman wished to spare the debtor repayment of his debt, she would not have to present the bill and claim that it was paid; [7]**for if she wished, she** could have simply **burned** the document. Hence we believe her when she testifies that the loan was actually repaid.

אִיכָּא דְּאָמְרִי [8]**There are those who**, in relating this incident, **say** that **Rav Naḥman did not believe** the woman, [9]and that **Rava said to Rav Naḥman** as follows: But **if** the woman merely **wished** to absolve the debtor of his obligation to repay the loan, [31B] **she** could have **burned** the bill of indebtedness while it was still in her possession! Why, then, should the woman not be believed? [10]Rav Naḥman answered him: **Since** the document in question **was validated in** a previous **court** and appended with the court's verification of the witnesses' signatures, [11]**we do not say** that the woman is believed and that we nullify it simply because **"if she had wished, she** could have **burned it** earlier."

RASHI

דנפק שטרא מתותי ידה — שהאמינוה הלוה והמלוה לשומרו. **אותיות ניקנות במסירה** — המוכר שטר חוב לחבירו — קנה החוב במסירת אותיות. ומילתיה דרבי ב״המוכר את הספינה״ (בבא בתרא עו, א) והכא נמי קנאתו, והוי כדידה, ונאמנת לומר פרוע. **קלתיה** — שרפתו, הלכך מה לה לשקר. **דאיתחזק בבי דינא** — שכתוב בו הנפק, לא אלימא איהי לאפקועי מעשה בית דין.

NOTES

disagreement as to whether this principle applies only to young orphans or to any legitimate heir of the father (*Rav Hai Gaon*). Others question whether this principle is applied only to an orphan who appears before the court while still a minor or even to litigation initiated after he has reached adulthood (see *Rabbenu Yonah* and others).

דְּאִיתַּחְזַק בְּבֵי דִינָא **That was validated in court.** Our commentary follows *Rashi*, who understands this validation as referring to a written authentication of the witnesses' signatures issued by a previous court and written on the document itself. *Tosafot* challenges *Rashi*'s explanation, not understanding why the existence of such an addendum

HALAKHAH

is obligated by the court to pay out a claim made against his deceased father's estate, he may subsequently introduce evidence in his favor and force a retrial even if he had earlier denied having such evidence. This is due to a presumption that children are ignorant of their father's affairs and thus cannot be held accountable for denying the existence of evidence that eventually came to their attention." (*Shulḥan Arukh, Ḥoshen Mishpat* 20:1.)

נְפַק שְׁטָרָא מִתּוּתֵי יְדָהּ דְּשָׁלִישׁ **A document that was produced by a third party.** "If a bill of indebtedness held by a third-party trustee was produced in court, and the trustee claims it has been paid, he is believed because, had he intended merely to excuse the debtor, he could have destroyed the document rather that making it available to the court. This is even true for a document that was certified as authentic by a previous court," in accordance

LANGUAGE

סִימְפוֹן Receipt. This word apparently derives from the Greek σύμφωνον, *symphonon*, meaning (among other things) "an agreement, a written contract."

[1] אֵיתִיבֵיהּ רָבָא לְרַב נַחְמָן: [2] סִימְפּוֹן שֶׁיֵּשׁ עָלָיו עֵדִים — יִתְקַיֵּים בְּחוֹתְמָיו. [3] אֵין עָלָיו עֵדִים, [4] וְיָצָא מִתַּחַת יְדֵי שָׁלִישׁ; [5] אוֹ שֶׁיָּצָא אַחַר חִיתּוּם שְׁטָרוֹת — כָּשֵׁר. [6] אַלְמָא: שָׁלִישׁ מְהֵימַן!

[7] תְּיוּבְתָּא דְּרַב נַחְמָן, תְּיוּבְתָּא.

[8] כִּי אֲתָא רַב דִּימִי, אֲמַר רַבִּי יוֹחָנָן: [9] לְעוֹלָם מֵבִיא רְאָיָה וְסוֹתֵר, עַד שֶׁיִּסְתַּתֵּם טַעֲנוֹתָיו, [10] וְיֹאמַר: קִרְבוּ פְּלוֹנִי וּפְלוֹנִי וְהָעִידוּנִי.

[11] הָא גּוּפָא קַשְׁיָא. [12] אָמְרַתְּ ״יִסְתַּתֵּם טַעֲנוֹתָיו״ — [13] אֲתָאן

LITERAL TRANSLATION

[1] Rava raised an objection against Rav Naḥman: [2] A receipt that has upon it [the signatures of] witnesses is validated by its signatories. [3] [If] it has no [signatures of] witnesses upon it, [4] but was produced by a third party; [5] or if it was issued beneath the signatures of the document, it is valid. [6] Hence, a third party is believed!

[7] [This is] a refutation of Rav Naḥman! [It is] a refutation.

[8] When Rav Dimi came he said in the name of Rabbi Yoḥanan: [9] One may always bring a proof and undo [a judgment] until [the litigant] closes off his argument, [10] and he says: Let so-and-so and so-and-so approach and testify for me.

[11] This itself is difficult. [12] You stated "[until] he closes off his argument" — [13] [apparently] we have come to [the position of]

TRANSLATION AND COMMENTARY

אֵיתִיבֵיהּ [1] **Rava raised a** strong **objection against Rav Naḥman** from the following Baraita: [2] **"A receipt that** was produced in court by a debtor as proof of his having repaid a loan — if **witnesses** signed **it**, it **may be validated by its signatories'** atttesting to the authenticity of their signatures. [3] Moreover, even if **no witnesses** signed **it,** [4] **but it was produced by a third party** trustee who affirms its authenticity; [5] **or if the** receipt **was written** as an addendum **beneath the** original witnesses' **signatures on the document** itself — then the receipt **is** also considered **valid."** [6] **Hence,** we see from this Baraita that **a third party** trustee **is believed,** and we nullify a debt on the basis of his affidavit, even though the original loan document itself was certified in court!

תְּיוּבְתָּא [7] The Gemara concludes: Indeed, the Baraita raised by Rava is **a refutation of Rav Naḥman.**

כִּי אֲתָא [8] The Gemara returns to the issue of new evidence raised in our Mishnah: **When Rav Dimi came** to Babylonia from Eretz Israel, **he said in the name of Rabbi Yoḥanan:** [9] A litigant **may always bring** additional **proof** of his claim **and** thereby **undo** a judgement already rendered against him, **until** the litigant **concludes his argument** [10] **and says** in desperation: **Let so-and-so and so-and-so,** the witnesses standing over there, **approach** the court **and testify for me.**

הָא גּוּפָא קַשְׁיָא [11] Concluding Rav Dimi's report, the Gemara notes: **This** statement of Rabbi Yoḥanan's **is difficult** in **itself,** because it seems to be self-contradictory! [12] On the one hand, **you stated** that the litigant can continue bringing evidence "until **he concludes his argument."** [13] Here **we are apparently dealing with** the position of **the Rabbis** in our

RASHI

סימפון — שובר. ויצא מתחת יד לוה כמשפטו. **יתקיים** — השטר בחותמיו, — יעידו עדים על חתימות ידיהן, וכשר. **אין עליו עדים** — והרי הוא יוצא מתחת יד שליש ולא מתחת יד הלוה. הואיל ושניהם מודים שזה מינהו להיות שליש ביניהם, כשר. **או שיצא אחר חיתום שטרות** — בתוך שטר המלוה נכתב השובר תחת העדים — כשר, שהרי המלוה עצמו מוחזק בשטרו, ואי לאו דפרעיה לא הוה שביק למיכתב תברא בגוויה. **עד שיסתתם טענותיו** — משמע שאמר בבית דין: אין לי לא עדים ולא ראיה, וחזר ואמר: קרבו פלוני ופלוני שהיו מזומנין שם, ומתחילה סותר טענותיו לומר אין לי. **הא גופא קשיא** — יסתתם טענותיו, משמע מכיון שיסתמו שוב אין מביא ראיה, ואפילו מצאם לאחר זמן. כרבנן, והדר קתני קרבו, דמשמע דהאי הוא דלא מייתי, דאפילו רבן שמעון בן גמליאל מודה בו, אבל מצאם לאחר זמן — מייתי, כרבן שמעון.

NOTES

would prevent the woman from still burning the document should she have wished to do so. Alternatively, they interpret the validation referred to in the Gemara as the present court's verification of the document's existence, which would preclude any possibility of the woman's destroying the document (see also *Ramah*).

HALAKHAH

with the Gemara's first version of the incident involving Rav Naḥman, which is supported by other Baraitot. (*Shulḥan Arukh, Ḥoshen Mishpat* 56:1.)

סִימְפוֹן שֶׁיֵּשׁ עָלָיו עֵדִים A receipt that has on it [the signatures of] witnesses. "A receipt signed by witnesses which is in the possession of the creditor is validated by asking the signatories to verify that the loan was indeed repaid. If the witnesses cannot be found or do not remember, then the receipt is considered worthless." (*Shulḥan Arukh, Ḥoshen Mishpat* 65:18.)

סִימְפוֹן שֶׁיָּצָא מִתַּחַת יְדֵי שָׁלִישׁ A receipt that was produced by a third party. "A third party who holds the receipt to a loan repayment is believed in court to validate that receipt, even if no witnesses have signed it and the court has seen the original loan document in his possession." (*Shulḥan Arukh, Ḥoshen Mishpat* 65:19.)

סִימְפוֹן שֶׁיָּצָא אַחַר חִיתּוּם שְׁטָרוֹת A receipt that was issued beneath the signatures of the document. "A receipt that was issued by writing it on the loan document itself, either on one side or the other, or in any of its margins (*Shakh*),

TRANSLATION AND COMMENTARY

Mishnah, who prevent any further evidence from being adduced once a litigant has rested his case. [1]On the other hand **you say** that he may continue bringing evidence until he says out of desperation: **"Let so-and-so and so-and-so approach and testify for me."** [2]Now **we** seem to be dealing **with** the position of **Rabban Shimon ben Gamliel,** who said that evidence can be brought even after a litigant has rested his case, as long as he does not start acting out of desperation!

וְכִי תֵּימָא [3]The Gemara entertains a possible answer: Perhaps **you** may want to **say** that Rabbi Yoḥanan's **entire** statement **is** in accordance with **Rabban Shimon ben Gamliel,** [4]**and** that Rabbi Yoḥanan **is explaining** his own words by asking, **what is** the meaning of my statement: **"Until he concludes his argument"?** [5]**Until he says: "Let so-and-so and so-and-so approach** the court **and testify for me."** Before then he may bring new evidence, even if he has already rested his case.

וְהָא אָמַר [6]The Gemara rejects this: **But did not Rabbah bar Bar Ḥannah say in the name of Rabbi Yoḥanan** as follows: [7]**Wherever Rabban Shimon ben Gamliel taught** a contradictory opinion which was recorded **in our Mishnah, the law is in accordance with him** — [8]**except for** his opinions regarding the liability of **a guarantor** (*Bava Batra* 173b), the incident at **Tzidon** (*Gittin* 74a), **and the last** argument recorded between him and the Sages about a litigant bringing new **proof** (our Mishnah, here)! Hence, we see that Rabbi Yoḥanan rejects Rabban Shimon ben Gamliel's opinion regarding testimony brought after one has rested his case!

אֶלָּא [9]**Rather,** we must conclude that Rav Dimi misquoted Rabbi Yoḥanan. Indeed, **when Rav Shmuel bar Yehudah came** to Babylonia from Eretz Israel, **he reported in the name of Rabbi Yoḥanan** a ruling which is consistent with the opinion of the Sages: [10]A litigant **may always bring** additional **proof** of his claim **and** thereby **undo** a judgment rendered against him, **until he concludes his argument,** [11]when the judges **say to him: "Bring witnesses,"** [12]**and he says: "I have no witnesses";** [13]or they say to him: **'Bring a proof,'** [14]**and he says: "I have no proof."** [15]**However,** if **witnesses come from a country overseas** and testify after the litigant

לְרַבָּנַן; [1]וַהֲדַר אָמְרַתְּ: "קִרְבוּ אִישׁ פְּלוֹנִי וּפְלוֹנִי וְהָעִידוּנִי" — [2]אֲתָאן לְרַבָּן שִׁמְעוֹן בֶּן גַּמְלִיאֵל!

[3]וְכִי תֵּימָא כּוּלָּהּ רַבָּן שִׁמְעוֹן בֶּן גַּמְלִיאֵל, [4]וּפָרוּשֵׁי קָא מְפָרֵשׁ: מַאי "עַד שֶׁיִּסְתַּתֵּם טַעֲנוֹתָיו"? [5]עַד שֶׁיֹּאמַר: "קִרְבוּ פְּלוֹנִי וּפְלוֹנִי וְהָעִידוּנִי".

[6]וְהָא אָמַר רַבָּה בַּר בַּר חָנָה אָמַר רַבִּי יוֹחָנָן: [7]כָּל מָקוֹם שֶׁשָּׁנָה רַבָּן שִׁמְעוֹן בֶּן גַּמְלִיאֵל בְּמִשְׁנָתֵינוּ, הֲלָכָה כְּמוֹתוֹ — [8]חוּץ מֵעָרֵב, וְצַיְדָּן, וּרְאָיָה אַחֲרוֹנָה!

[9]אֶלָּא, כִּי אֲתָא רַב שְׁמוּאֵל בַּר יְהוּדָה אָמַר רַבִּי יוֹחָנָן: [10]לְעוֹלָם מֵבִיא רְאָיָה וְסוֹתֵר, עַד שֶׁיִּסְתַּתֵּם טַעֲנוֹתָיו, [11]וְיֹאמְרוּ לוֹ: "הָבֵא עֵדִים", [12]וְאוֹמֵר: "אֵין לִי עֵדִים"! [13]"הָבֵא רְאָיָה", [14]וְאוֹמֵר: "אֵין לִי רְאָיָה". [15]אֲבָל, בָּאוּ עֵדִים מִמְּדִינַת

LITERAL TRANSLATION

the Sages; [1]and then you said [that he may say:] "Let so-and-so and so-and-so approach and testify for me" — [2][apparently] we have come to [the position of] Rabban Shimon ben Gamliel!

[3]And if you say [that Rabbi Yoḥanan's] entire [statement follows] Rabban Shimon ben Gamliel, [4]and he is explaining: What is [the meaning of] "until he closes off his argument"? [5]Until he says: "Let so-and-so and so-and-so approach and testify for me."

[6]But did not Rabbah bar Bar Ḥannah say in the name of Rabbi Yoḥanan: [7]Wherever Rabban Shimon ben Gamliel taught [an opinion] in our Mishnah, the law is in accordance with him — [8]except [concerning] a guarantor, [the incident at] Tzidon, and the last [case of bringing] proof!

[9]Rather, when Rav Shmuel bar Yehudah came he said in the name of Rabbi Yoḥanan: [10]One may always bring a proof and undo [the judgment] until he closes off his argument, [11]and they say to him: "Bring witnesses," [12]and he says: "I have no witnesses"; [13][they say]: "Bring a proof," [14]and he says: "I have no proof." [15]However, [if] witnesses came from a country

RASHI

ואמר אין לי עדים — ואפילו מכאן לאחר זמן אינו סותר, כרבנן.

HALAKHAH

is valid proof that the loan (or any part of it) has been repaid, even if the document was still in the possession of the creditor." (*Shulḥan Arukh, Ḥoshen Mishpat* 65:2.)

בָּאוּ עֵדִים מִמְּדִינַת הַיָּם If witnesses came from a country overseas. "If someone was obligated by the court to pay a claim after denying that he had further evidence in his favor, and then subsequently witnesses arrive from a distant land, or an unknown packet of documents belonging to his father

LANGUAGE

דִּיסַקְיָא **Pouch.** This word derives from the Greek δισάχχιον, *disakkion,* a double sack in which various objects were placed.

TRANSLATION AND COMMENTARY

has rested his case, [1]**or if his father's pouch** of documents **was deposited in another's possession** and only surfaced after the litigant rested his case — [2]**he may bring** the new evidence as **a proof** of his claim **and undo** the judgment rendered against him.

כִּי אֲתָא [3]Concerning the choice of venue for litigation: **When Rav Dimi came** to Babylonia from Eretz Israel, **he said** the following **in the name of** Rabbi Yoḥanan: [4]If **one intimidates his friend in** a matter of **litigation** before a court, [5]and he **says: "Let us be judged here** in our own town," where the aggressive litigant feels he will make a stronger impression in court, [6]and the defendant **says: "Let us go to the site of the** scholarly **assembly** where judges with better qualifications can be found," [7]**we force** the plaintiff to comply with the defendant's wish **and go to the site of the assembly**, where we assume the aggressive litigant will be less likely to have his own way.

אָמַר לְפָנָיו [8]**Rabbi Elazar said before** Rabbi Yoḥanan: **My teacher, may one who has a claim** of debt **against his friend for one maneh,** [9]be forced to **spend a maneh** in travel expenses **for** the sake of pursuing the **maneh** which he hopes to collect? Certainly this is unfair! [10]**Rather,** let us say that **we force** the defendant to comply with the plaintiff's wish **and be judged in his** own **city.**

אִיתְּמַר נַמִי [11]**It was likewise stated** as follows: **Rav Safra said in the name of Rabbi Yoḥanan:** If **two** individuals **are embroiled in litigation,** [12]and **one says: "Let us be judged here** in our own town," [13]**and the other says: "Let us go to the site of the assembly,"** [14]**we force** the one seeking a distant venue to be **judged in his** own **town.** [15]**And if a** particular **matter** which is unclear to the local judges **must be referred** to a more

הַיָּם, [1]אוֹ שֶׁהָיְתָה דִּיסַקַיָּא שֶׁל אָבִיו מוּפְקֶדֶת בְּיַד אַחֵר — [2]הֲרֵי זֶה מֵבִיא רְאָיָה וְסוֹתֵר.
[3]כִּי אֲתָא רַב דִּימִי אָמַר רַבִּי יוֹחָנָן: [4]הַתּוֹקֵף אֶת חֲבֵירוֹ בַּדִּין, [5]אֶחָד אוֹמֵר: "נָדוֹן כָּאן", [6]וְאֶחָד אוֹמֵר: "נֵלֵךְ לִמְקוֹם הַוַּועַד" — [7]כּוֹפִין אוֹתוֹ וְיֵלֵךְ לִמְקוֹם הַוַּועַד.
[8]אָמַר לְפָנָיו רַבִּי אֶלְעָזָר: רַבִּי, מִי שֶׁנּוֹשֶׁה בַּחֲבֵירוֹ מָנֶה, [9]יוֹצִיא מָנֶה עַל מָנֶה?! [10]אֶלָּא, כּוֹפִין אוֹתוֹ וְדָן בְּעִירוֹ.
[11]אִיתְּמַר נַמִי: אָמַר רַב סָפְרָא אָמַר רַבִּי יוֹחָנָן: שְׁנַיִם שֶׁנִּתְעַצְּמוּ בַּדִּין, [12]אֶחָד אוֹמֵר: "נָדוֹן כָּאן" [13]וְאֶחָד אוֹמֵר: "נֵלֵךְ לִמְקוֹם הַוַּועַד" — [14]כּוֹפִין אוֹתוֹ וְדָן בְּעִירוֹ. [15]וְאִם הוּצְרַךְ

LITERAL TRANSLATION

overseas, [1]or if his father's pouch was [found to be] deposited in another's possession — [2]he may bring a proof and undo [the judgment].

[3]When Rav Dimi came he said in the name of Rabbi Yoḥanan: [4][If] someone is overbearing with his friend in [a matter of] litigation, [5][and the aggressive litigant] says: "Let us be judged here," [6]and the other says: "Let us go to the site of the assembly" — [7]they force him and he goes to the site of the assembly.

[8]Rabbi Elazar said before him: My teacher, may one who has a claim against his friend for one maneh, [9][be forced to] spend a maneh for a maneh?! [10]Rather, we force him and he is judged in his city.

[11]It was also stated: Rav Safra said in the name of Rabbi Yoḥanan: [When] two are embroiled in a litigation — [12][if] one says: "Let us be judged here," [13]and one says: "Let us go to the site of the assembly" — [14]we force him and he is judged in his town. [15]And if it was necessary

RASHI

דסקיא — שק של עור שהיו שטרותיו של אביו מונחין בו. התוקף את חבירו בדין — בעל דין קשה ומטריח את חבירו, ואין רוצה חבירו לדון כאן אלא למקום וועד תלמידי חכמים הרבה, שיהא זה בוש מהם. נתעצמו — שנעשו קשין זה לזה.

NOTES

מְקוֹם הַוַּועַד **The site of assembly.** Some interpret the "site of assembly" as any place where the judges are appointed by community consensus, as opposed to a town where the judges assumed authority on their own. Judges appointed by the community are generally granted greater power to collect money by force from the liable party (*Meiri*).

HALAKHAH

is uncovered, we accept the new evidence, and the case is retried," in accordance with Rabbi Yoḥanan. "If the litigant, however, had explicitly denied the existence of such evidence as well, then its appearance does not affect the present verdict." (*Shulḥan Arukh, Ḥoshen Mishpat* 20:1.)

נֵלֵךְ לִמְקוֹם הַוַּועַד **Let us go to the site of the assembly.** "Should two individuals be embroiled in litigation (other than that involving a loan), and one of them desires the case to be heard before an assemblage of superior scholars located elsewhere, we force him to accept local adjudication. Nevertheless, he has the right to demand that the local court present him with a written record of the reasons for its decision, lest it erred and he wishes to seek redress," in accordance with the opinion of Rabbi Yoḥanan as cited by Rav Safra. (*Shulḥan Arukh, Ḥoshen Mishpat* 14:1.)

דָּבָר לִשְׁאוֹל כּוֹתְבִין וְשׁוֹלְחִין.
[1] וְאִם אָמַר: כִּתְבוּ וּתְנוּ לִי מֵאֵיזֶה טַעַם דַּנְתּוּנִי — [2] כּוֹתְבִין וְנוֹתְנִין לוֹ.
[3] וְהַיְּבָמָה הוֹלֶכֶת אַחַר הַיָּבָם לְהַתִּירָהּ.
[4] עַד כַּמָּה? [5] אָמַר רַבִּי אַמִי: אֲפִילּוּ מִטִּבֶּרְיָא לְצִפּוֹרִי. [6] אָמַר רַב כָּהֲנָא: מַאי קְרָא? [7] ״וְקָרְאוּ לוֹ זִקְנֵי עִירוֹ״ — [8] וְלֹא ״זִקְנֵי עִירָהּ״.
[9] אָמַר אַמֵימָר, הִילְכְתָא: [10] כּוֹפִין אוֹתוֹ וְיֵילֵךְ לִמְקוֹם הַוַּועַד.
[11] אָמַר לֵיהּ רַב אַשִׁי לְאַמֵימָר: [12] וְהָא אָמַר רַבִּי אֶלְעָזָר: כּוֹפִין אוֹתוֹ וְדָן בְּעִירוֹ?!

LITERAL TRANSLATION

to clarify a matter, they write [the question] and send [it]. [1] And if [the litigant] said: Write and give me the reason for which you have judged me [as you did] — [2] they write [it] and give [it] to him.

[3] And a woman subject to levirate marriage goes after the deceased husband's brother so he may release her.

[4] How far? [5] Rabbi Ammi said: Even from Tiberias to Sepphoris. [6] Rav Kahana said: What [is its] verse? [7] "And the elders of his city shall call him" — [8] and not the elders of "her city."

[9] Amemar said: The law [is that] [10] we force him and he goes to the site of the assembly.

[11] Rav Ashi said to Amemar: [12] But did not Rabbi Elazar state: We force him and he is judged in his city?!

TRANSLATION AND COMMENTARY

competent court, then **they** write the question **and send** it there by messenger. [1] **And if** either litigant — feeling that the judges may have erred in their verdict — **said** to the court: "I ask that you write down **and give me the reason why you have judged me** in this manner," [2] the court must indeed **record** its reasoning **and give it to him.**

וְהַיְּבָמָה [3] Rav Safra further stated as follows: A *yevamah* (a woman who is required to contract a levirate marriage) must **go after the** *yavam* (her brother-in-law), so he will **release her** from the levirate bond before the elders in his town and thus enable her to marry freely.

עַד כַּמָּה [4] The Gemara asks: **How far** must the *yevamah* travel to obtain her release to the *yavam*? [5] **Rabbi Ammi said:** She must **even** travel **from Tiberias**, whose scholars and court were renowned, **to Sepphoris**, with its less prestigious community of elders. [6] **Rav Kahana said: What is the verse** from which we learn that the *yevamah* must travel to the *yavam?* It is the verse in Deuteronomy (25:8) that states: [7] **"And the elders of his city shall call him** (the *yavam*) and speak to him, and he shall stand and say: 'I do not wish to take her'" — [8] the emphasis being on "the elders of his city" **and not** "the elders of **her city.**"

אָמַר אַמֵימָר [9] **Amemar said** that **the law** regarding choice of venue, when disputed by the litigants, is as follows: [10] **We force** the one demanding a hearing in his local court to comply with his opponent's wish **and go to the site of the assembly** in order to be judged by more competent scholars.

אָמַר לֵיהּ [11] **Rav Ashi** challenged **Amemar: But did not Rabbi Elazar state** as follows: [12] **We force** the defendant to comply with the plaintiff's wish **and be judged in his** own **city?!**

RASHI

אפילו מטבריא לציפורי – אף על פי שישיבת טבריא גדולה משל ציפורי, הלך אחריו לציפורי. **והאמר רבי אלעזר** – והא חזינן דפליג עלה רבי אלעזר לעיל, ויהיב טעמא למילתיה, דמסתבר טעמא.

NOTES

כִּתְבוּ וּתְנוּ לִי **Write and give to me.** *Tosafot* points out that the litigant is only allowed to demand a written record when he is forced by his opponent to face litigation in a local court. In such a case, the record allows him to appeal to a higher court located elsewhere should he so wish. If he accepted the local court of his own volition, he cannot demand a written record of the reasons for its verdict.

אֲפִילּוּ מִטִּבֶּרְיָא לְצִפּוֹרִי **Even from Tiberias to Sepphoris.** Our commentary follows *Rashi,* who explains that the novelty of this proposition is that, despite the superior scholarship of Tiberias's community of elders, the widow must still travel to Sepphoris to receive her freedom. Others view its novelty in terms of the relatively short distance (some 30 km) between the two towns, which might have led one to think that, since the inconvenience is minimal, the brother-in-law should be the one to make the journey (*Rabbi Yehudah Almandri*).

הִילְכְתָא: כּוֹפִין אוֹתוֹ וְיֵילֵךְ לִמְקוֹם הַוַּועַד **The law is that we force him to go to the site of the assembly.** *Ramah* maintains that Amemar's conclusion applies exclusively to

HALAKHAH

הַיְּבָמָה הוֹלֶכֶת אַחַר הַיָּבָם **The widow follows the brother-in-law.** "A widow in need of court intervention with regard to either the consummation or dissolution of the levirate bond, must travel to the court presiding in the town of the brother-in-law," in accordance with the opinion of Rabbi Yoḥanan as cited by Rav Safra.

"If the brother-in-law, however, is temporarily not residing in his home town, or if the court in his home town is not considered qualified, he must travel to the court presiding in the town of the widow. Should a qualified court be found close to his home town, the law is in doubt as to which court should be approached (*Mishneh LeMelekh*)." (*Shulḥan Arukh, Even HaEzer* 166:1.)

[1]הָנֵי מִילֵּי הֵיכָא דְּקָאָמַר לֵיהּ לֹוֶה לַמַּלְוֶה; [2]אֲבָל מַלְוֶה — ״עֶבֶד לֹוֶה לְאִישׁ מַלְוֶה״.
[3]שְׁלַחוּ לֵיהּ לְמָר עוּקְבָא: [4]לִדְזִיו לֵיהּ כְּבַר בִּתְיָה, שְׁלָם! [5]עוּקְבָן הַבַּבְלִי קְבַל קֳדָמָנָא: [6]יִרְמְיָה, אָחִי, הֶעֱבִיר עָלַי אֶת הַדֶּרֶךְ. [7]וְאִמְרוּ לוֹ; הַשִּׂיאוּהוּ וְיֵרָאֶה פָּנֵינוּ בְּטִבֶּרְיָא.
[8]הָא גּוּפָא קַשְׁיָא! [9]אָמְרַתְּ ״אִמְרוּ לוֹ״ — [10]אַלְמָא דָּיְינוּהּ אַתּוּן; [11]״הַשִּׂיאוּהוּ וְיֵרָאֶה פָּנֵינוּ בְּטִבֶּרְיָא״ — [12]אַלְמָא שַׁדְּרוּהוּ הָכָא!

LITERAL TRANSLATION

[1]These words apply where the borrower said to the lender; [2]but [if] the lender [said to the borrower] — [we say:] "And the borrower is a servant to the lender."

[3]They sent to Mar Ukva: [4]To him who possesses a radiance like the son of Bithiah, peace [be with you]! [5]Ukvan, the Babylonian, complained before us: [6]Yirmeyah, my brother, has done me a great injustice (lit., "shifted the way from before me"). [7]Speak to him; [and] force him to appear before us (lit., "see our face") in Tiberias. [8]This itself is difficult! [9]You stated "Speak to him" — [10]thus, you yourselves will judge it; [11][you also stated] "force him to appear before us in Tiberias" — [12]thus, send him here!

TRANSLATION AND COMMENTARY

הָנֵי מִילֵּי [1]Amemar replied to Rav Ashi: **This statement** of Rabbi Elazar's, that we listen to the litigant's wish to be judged in his own city, applies exclusively **when** it is **the borrower** who **said to the lender** that he wished to be judged elsewhere; [2]**however,** when **the lender** himself wishes to undertake additional expense in order to pursue his claim elsewhere, Rabbi Elazar would agree that since **"the borrower is a servant to the lender"** (Proverbs 22:7), he must comply with the lender's wish to appear before a more competent court.

שְׁלַחוּ לֵיהּ [3]It is said that the Tiberian judges once **sent** a letter **to Mar Ukva**, the Babylonian Exilarch and Chief Justice, which read as follows: [4]**"To him who possesses a radiance like** Moses, **the son of Bithiah — peace** be with you! [5]It has happened that **Ukvan, the Babylonian,** appeared here in our court and **complained before us**, saying: [6]**'Yirmeyah my brother,** who remains in Babylonia, **has done me a great injustice** and therefore I wish to summon him for litigation.' [7]Hence, we ask that you **speak to** Yirmeyah and arbitrate the claim. **Force him to appear before us in Tiberias** for judgment."

הָא גּוּפָא קַשְׁיָא [8]The Gemara seeks clarification: **The** text of the letter **is difficult** in **itself**, because it seems to be self-contradictory! On the one hand, [9]**you stated** that the letter requested of Mar Ukva that he **"speak to** Yirmeyah" about the claim, [10]**thus** implying that **"you yourselves** (Mar Ukva and his court) **will judge** the case"; on the other hand, [11]the letter asked that Mar Ukva **"force** Yirmeyah **to appear before us in Tiberias,"** [12]**thus** implying that Mar Ukva **was** not to arbitrate the case but rather **"to send him here** to Tiberias" for judgment.

RASHI

היכא דקאמר לוה — "נלך למקום הוועד" כופין אותו וידון כאן, ולא יוציא זה מנה על מנה. **מר עוקבא** — אב בית דין הוה, במסכת שבת, "במה בהמה יוצאה" (נה,א). **לדזיו ליה כבר בתיה** — כמשה שהוא בן בתיה, למי שמקרין עור פניו כמשה רבינו שגידלתו בתיה בת פרעה. לשון אחר: כבר ביתיה כמשה, שהוא בן בית, דכתיב (במדבר יב) "בכל ביתי נאמן הוא", **לדזיו ליה** — על שם שהיה חכם, וכתיב (קהלת ח) "חכמת אדם תאיר פניו". ומצאתי בספר הגדה שהיה מר עוקבא בעל תשובה, שנתן עיניו באשה אחת והעלה לבו טינא ונפל בחולי, ואשת איש היתה, לימים נצרכה ללות ממנו ומתוך דוחקה נתרצית לו, וכבש יצרו ופטרה לשלום ונתרפא. וכשהיה יוצא לשוק היה נר דולק בראשו מן השמים ועל שם כך קרי ליה רבי נתן "צוציתא" במסכת שבת (נו,ב), הכא נמי להכי כתבו ליה הכי על שם האור שהיה זורח עליו. **עוקבן הבבלי קבל קדמנא** — צעק לפנינו ואמר: ירמיה אחי העביר עלי את הדרך, איבד ממני דרך בני אדם, שסירסו, כך שמעתי. ויש אומרים: העביר עלי את הדרך — לא נהג עמי כשורה, ועל עסקי ממון היה צועק.

SAGES

מָר עוּקְבָא **Mar Ukva**. He was the Exilarch during the first and second generations of Amoraim in Babylonia. He was famous not only for occupying this elevated position but also for his learning and piety. Mar Ukva was very close to the circles of the Amora Shmuel, who respected him greatly. Mar Ukva was also renowned for his generosity in giving charity and for his great modesty. Mar Ukva was called "Natan Dezuzita," and he was a famous penitent in his generation (see *Rashi*). He apparently had two sons who were also Sages.

NOTES

loans, as evident from the ensuing exchange in the Gemara where Amemar limits his ruling to a creditor who demands that they relocate. In other monetary cases, the defendant is not subservient to the plaintiff and therefore cannot be forced by him to travel elsewhere for the hearing, as long as the local judges are qualified to adjudicate.

אָחִי, הֶעֱבִיר עָלַי אֶת הַדֶּרֶךְ **My brother has done me an injustice.** The literal translation of this phrase is, "my brother shifted the way from before me." *Rashi* suggests two possible meanings: Either his brother castrated him (deprived him of a man's way), or acted dishonestly in some financial matter. *Rah* interprets it as meaning that his brother beat him and thus strayed from the path of civility. *Maharsha* explains the phrase literally, understanding that it refers to two brothers who divided a field inherited from their father. One brother rerouted an existing path so that it no longer passed through his part of the field, but rather through his brother's.

HALAKHAH

עֶבֶד לֹוֶה לְאִישׁ מַלְוֶה **The borrower is a servant to the lender.** "If a borrower and a lender are embroiled in litigation, and the lender insists on having the case adjudicated before a superior court located in another

[1]אֶלָּא, הָכִי קָאָמְרִי: [2]״אִמְרוּ לֵיהּ״ — דָּיְינוּ אַתּוּן. [3]אִי צָיֵית, צָיֵית; [4]וְאִי לָא — ״הַשִּׁיאוּהוּ וְיִרְאֶה פָּנֵינוּ בְּטִבֶרְיָא״.
[5]רַב אַשִׁי אָמַר: דִּינֵי קְנָסוֹת הֲוָה, [6]וּבְבָבֶל לֹא דָּיְינוּ דִּינֵי קְנָסוֹת. [7]וְהָא דְּשָׁלְחוּ לֵיהּ הָכִי, כְּדֵי לַחֲלוֹק כָּבוֹד לְמָר עוּקְבָא.

הדרן עלך זה בורר

TRANSLATION AND COMMENTARY

אֶלָּא, הָכִי קָאָמְרִי [1]**Rather,** one must understand the Tiberian judges as **saying the following** in their letter: [2]**"Speak to** Yirmeyah" — that is: **"You yourselves will judge** the case. [3]**If he obeys** your ruling, **he has obeyed** it and it is acceptable to us; [4]**but if not, force him to appear before us in Tiberias."**

רַב אַשִׁי אָמַר [5]Alternatively, **Rav Ashi said:** In truth, the case dealt with in that letter **was** one involving **the laws of fines,** [6]**and in Babylonia,** where the Rabbis do not possess formal ordination, **they** are **not** qualified to **adjudicate** cases involving **the laws of fines.** Hence, the Tiberian judges really meant that Mar Ukva should exempt himself from the case and send Yirmeyah to them. [7]The reason **that they sent him** a message proposing that he arbitrate the case himself was simply **in order to accord Mar Ukva** the **honor** he deserved as Exilarch of Babylonia.

LITERAL TRANSLATION

[1]Rather, they said thus: [2]"Speak to him" — [and] you yourselves will judge it. [3]If he obeys, he has obeyed; [4]but if not, "force him to appear before us in Tiberias."

[5]Rav Ashi said: [This] involved the laws of fines, [6]and in Babylonia they do not adjudicate [cases involving] the laws of fines. [7]And that which they sent him thus [was] in order to accord honor to Mar Ukva.

RASHI

אמרו לו — לירמיה להתפייס עמו. **השיאוהו ויראה פנינו בטבריא** — הכריחוהו והזקיקוהו לבוא כאן לדון עמו. **דיני קנסות** — ״אלהים״ כתיב בהן (שמות כב), ובעינן סמוכין, ובבבל אין סמיכה כדאמרינן בפרק קמא (יד,א).

הדרן עלך זה בורר

HALAKHAH

town, we may force the borrower to accept his demand, for the borrower is subservient to the lender in such matters," in accordance with the ruling of Amemar. (*Shulḥan Arukh, Ḥoshen Mishpat* 14:1.)

דִּינֵי קְנָסוֹת בְּבָבֶל Laws of fines in Babylonia. "Any case involving the possible imposition of a fine, be it of Biblical origin (such as double compensation in the case of theft) or the result of a Rabbinic decree (such as the fine for shouting suddenly into one's friend's ear), can only be adjudicated by a judge who has obtained proper Rabbinic ordination in Eretz Israel through an unbroken chain of tradition stretching back to Moses himself, a qualification that was unattainable in Babylonia of Talmudic times and, all the more so, in the lands of subsequent dispersion." (*Shulḥan Arukh, Ḥoshen Mishpat* 1:1.)

Conclusion to Chapter Three

This chapter discusses and sums up basic problems concerning the structure and constitution of courts.

The law was settled that litigants in monetary disputes may choose a court of three judges to try their case. If the judges do not reach agreement, they are permitted to constitute a court to the satisfaction of both parties. Each litigant chooses a judge, and the two judges choose the third one to decide between them. The right to choose a court does not detract from the authority of that court to adjudicate the dispute, for once it has been chosen, the parties are not permitted to change their minds, and they must accept the decision.

Three types of people are disqualified from serving as witnesses or judges. Some are disqualified because of their personal status; some because they have committed a transgression; and some because of family relationships. The first category includes slaves, women, and, of course, non-Jews. The disqualification of non-Jews is written in the Torah, for only members of the House of Israel may be witnesses or judges. The disqualification for committing a crime ("עֵדֵי חָמָס") can be divided into two categories. The first includes those who have disobeyed a widely known Torah law; until they have fully repented, they are disqualified from serving as witnesses or judges because of their transgression. The second category includes those who have violated Rabbinical law or a Torah law that is not widely known; they must be warned against committing the transgression before they are disqualified from testifying or judging. Family relationships that disqualify one from testifying or judging are blood relations (either paternal or maternal) and relations by marriage (according to the rule, "a husband is like his wife"). It was generally agreed that the degree of relationship that disqualifies someone from testifying is from the second to the second and above (that is, when there is a gap of two generations between the parties and between the person who is related to both of them). Another kind of disqualifaction is mentioned but not fully discussed in this chapter — that of people who are interested parties, whether because of personal relations of amity or hatred, or because of some benefit or financial interest.

Regarding legal procedure and the interrogation of the witnesses, there is a primary limitation on testimony: Only direct eye-witnesses are heard. Circumstantial evidence is not acceptable in Jewish courts (though it may be considered by the judges). The witness must testify that he himself saw or heard the event about which he is testifying. However, in monetary disputes, the principle was accepted that witnesses do not themselves testify about an event or an act that took place in one way or another. Rather, they attest to the existence of a certain legal situation. Therefore, if the testimony of two witnesses may be combined into a single judicial construct, it is considered as providing corroborative testimony, although the witnesses may not have testified about exactly the same factual event.

Another principle of judicial procedure concerns the limitation placed on the time that a trial may last. According to law, the trial is not concluded so long as one of the parties can produce evidence that is significant for the matter. When one of the parties admits that he has no further proof to bring, no new evidence is admitted unless it can be proven that it could not have been known previously.

List of Sources

Aḥaronim, lit., "the last," meaning Rabbinic authorities from the time of the publication of Rabbi Yosef Caro's code of Halakhah, *Shulḥan Arukh* (1555).

Arba'ah Turim, code of Halakhah by Rabbi Ya'akov ben Asher, b. Germany, active in Spain (c. 1270-1343).

Arukh, Talmudic dictionary, by Rabbi Natan of Rome, 11th century.

Baḥ (Bayit Ḥadash), commentary on *Arba'ah Turim*, by Rabbi Yoel Sirkes, Poland (1561-1640).

Bet Yosef, Halakhic commentary on *Arba'ah Turim* by Rabbi Yosef Caro (1488-1575), which is the basis of his authoritative Halakhic code, *Shulḥan Arukh*.

Even HaEzer, section of *Shulḥan Arukh* dealing with marriage, divorce, and related topics.

Geonim, heads of the academies of Sura and Pumbedita in Babylonia from the late 6th century to the mid-11th century.

Hagahot Maimoniyot, commentary on *Mishneh Torah*, by Rabbi Meir HaKohen, Germany, 14th century.

Halakhot Gedolot, a code of Halakhic decisions written in the Geonic period. This work has been ascribed to Sherira Gaon, Rav Hai Gaon, Rav Yehudah Gaon and Rabbi Shimon Kayyara.

Ḥamra Veḥaye, novellae on tractate *Sanhedrin*, by Rabbi Ḥayyim Benevisti, Turkey, 17th century.

Ḥayyim Shenayim Yeshalem, novellae on *Sanhedrin*, by Rabbi Shmuel Vital.

Ḥokhmat Manoaḥ, commentary on the Talmud by Rabbi Manoaḥ ben Shemaryah, Poland, 16th century.

Ḥoshen Mishpat, section of *Shulḥan Arukh* dealing with civil and criminal law.

Imrei Tzvi, novellae of the Talmud by Rabbi Tzvi Kohen, Vilna, 19th century.

Iyyun Ya'akov, commentary on *Ein Ya'akov*, by Rabbi Ya'akov bar Yosef Riesher, Prague, Poland, and France (d. 1733).

Kesef Mishneh, commentary on *Mishneh Torah*, by Rabbi Yosef Caro, author of *Shulḥan Arukh*.

Leḥem Mishneh, commentary on the *Mishneh Torah*, by Rabbi Avraham di Boton, Salonica (1560-1609).

Maggid Mishneh, commentary on *Mishneh Torah*, by Rabbi Vidal de Tolosa, Spain, 14th century.

Maharam Schiff, novellae on the Talmud by Rabbi Meir ben Ya'akov HaKohen Schiff (1605-1641), Frankfurt, Germany.

Maharik, Rabbi Yosef Kolon, France and Italy (c. 1420-1480). Responsa literature.

Maharsha, Rabbi Shmuel Eliezer ben Yehudah HaLevi Edels, Poland (1555-1631). Novellae on the Talmud.

Maharshal, Rabbi Shlomo ben Yeḥiel Luria, Poland (1510-1573). Novellae on the Talmud.

Margoliyot HaYam, novellae on tractate *Sanhedrin* by Rabbi Reuben Margoliyot, Poland, 20th century.

Meiri, commentary on the Talmud (called *Bet HaBeḥirah*), by Rabbi Menaḥem ben Shlomo, Provence (1249-1316).

Mekhilta, Halakhic Midrash on the Book of Exodus.

Mishnah Berurah, commentary on *Shulḥan Arukh, Oraḥ Ḥayyim*, by Rabbi Yisrael Meir HaKohen, Poland (1837-1933).

Nimmukei Yosef, commentary on *Hilkhot HaRif*, by Rabbi Yosef Haviva, Spain, early 15th century.

Oraḥ Ḥayyim, section of *Shulḥan Arukh* dealing with daily religious observances, prayers, and the laws of the Sabbath and Festivals.

Pitḥei Teshuvah, compilation of responsa literature on *Shulḥan Arukh* by Rabbi Avraham Tzvi Eisenstadt, Russia (1812-1868).

Ra'avad, Rabbi Avraham ben David, commentator and Halakhic authority. Wrote comments on *Mishneh Torah*. Provence (c. 1125-1198?).

Rabbenu Ḥananel (ben Ḥushiel), commentator on the Talmud, North Africa (990-1055).

Rabbenu Meshulam, French Tosafist, 12th century.

Rabbenu Shimshon of Sens, Tosafist, France and Eretz Israel (c.1100-1171).

Rabbenu Tam, commentator on the Talmud, Tosafist, France (1100-1171).

Rabbenu Yehonatan of Lunel, Yehonatan ben David HaKohen of Lunel, Provence, Talmudic scholar (c.1135-after 1210).

Rabbenu Yonah, see *Talmidei Rabbenu Yonah*.

Rabbi David Bonfil (Bonfied), commentary on tractate *Sanhedrin* by Rabbi David Bonfil (Bonfied), France, 11th century.

Rabbi David Pardo, novellae on the Talmud, Italy, 18th century.

Rabbi Issac Ḥaver, novellae on the Talmud by Rabbi Issac Ḥaver,